VW
RABBIT & SCIROCCO
1975-1979 INCLUDES DIESEL
SHOP MANUAL

By
ERIC JORGENSEN

JEFF ROBINSON
Editor and Publisher

CLYMER PUBLICATIONS

World's largest publisher of books
devoted exclusively to automobiles and motorcycles

12860 MUSCATINE STREET · P.O. BOX 20 · ARLETA, CALIFORNIA 91331

FIRST EDITION
First Printing September, 1975
Second Printing October, 1975
Third Printing January, 1976

SECOND EDITION
Revised by Jim Combs to include 1976-1977 models
First Printing April, 1977
Second Printing July, 1977
Third Printing January, 1978

THIRD EDITION
Revised by Jim Combs to include 1978 models
First Printing January, 1979

FOURTH EDITION
Revised by Jim Combs to cover 1979 models
First Printing March, 1980

Printed in U.S.A.

ISBN: 0-89287-157-1

Mary Anne Holcomb, production coordinator.

•

Photographed by Mike Brown/Visual Imagery, Los Angeles, California
Assisted by Chris Ryfle
Scirocco and Rabbit courtesy Volkswagen of America

QUICK REFERENCE DATA

TIMING MARK ALIGNMENT

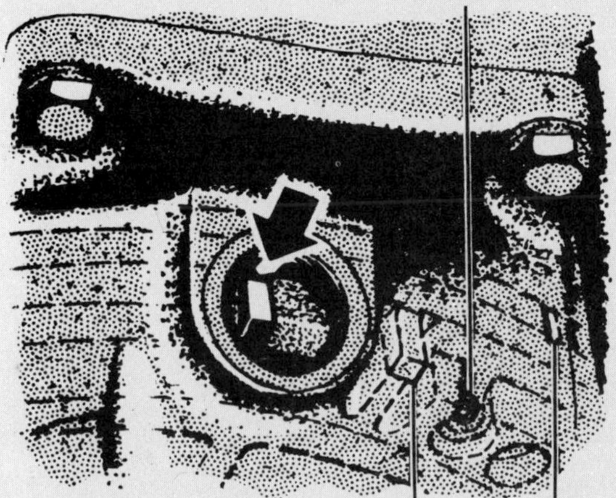

POINT REPLACEMENT

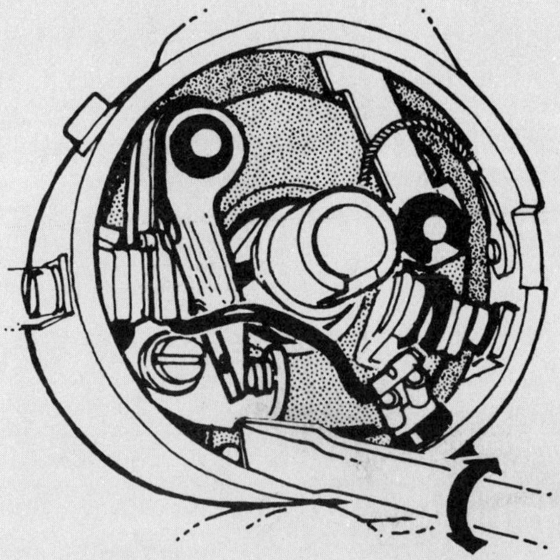

Remove distributor cap and rotor. Remove screw securing points. Replace points. Turn crankshaft until a distributor cam lobe opens the contacts fully. Loosen retaining screw, insert 0.016 in. (0.4mm) feeler gauge. Move fixed contact base with screwdriver to set point gap. More accurate measurement of breaker point gap is possible by measuring dwell angle. See Chapter Two.

TUNE-UP SPECIFICATIONS

Valve clearance ①	
Intake	0.008-0.012 in. (0.20-0.30mm)
Exhaust	0.016-0.020 in. (0.40-0.50mm)
Ignition timing ②	3° ATDC @ 925 ± 75 rpm with vacuum advance disconnected ③
Spark plug type ②	
Carburetted engine	Bosch W200T30; Beru 200/14/3A1
Fuel injected engine	Bosch W175T30; 175/14/3A
Spark plug gap ②	0.024-0.028 in. (0.6-0.7mm)
Breaker point gap ②	0.016 in. (0.4mm)
Dwell angle ②	47 ± 3°
Firing order	1 - 3 - 4 - 2
Idle speed	
Gas	925 ± 75 rpm
Diesel	820 ± 50 rpm

① Checked with engine warm. Subtract 0.0012 in. (0.05mm) for cold engine.

② Does not apply to diesel engines.

③ Set timing on special FX carburetted engine to 7.5° BTDC with vacuum hoses connected.

RECOMMENDED LUBRICANTS AND FUEL

	Temperature Range	Recommended Type	Capacity
Engine oil (gasoline engines)[1]			
Single grade oil	Above +68°F	SAE 40	3.2 quarts[2]
	+32° to +78°F	SAE 30	
	+15° to +50°F	SAE 20W-20	
	−5° to +25°F	SAE 10W	
Multi-grade oil	+15° to +80°F	SAE 20W-40; SAE 20W-50	
	−5° to +50°F	SAE 10W-30; SAE 10W-40	
	+15°F and below	SAE 5W-20	
Engine oil (diesel engines)[3]			
Single grade oil	+68°F and over	SAE 40	3.2 quarts[2]
	+32° to +78°F	SAE 30	
	+5° to +50°F	SAE 20W-20	
	Below +25°F	SAE 10	
Multi-grade oil	+15 to +80°F	SAE 20W-50; SAE 20W-40	
	Below +50°F	SAE 10W-40; SAE 10W-30	
Manual transaxle	All temperatures	SAE 80 (MIL-L-2105)	1.3 quarts
Automatic final drive	All temperatures	SAE 90 (MIL-L-2105B)	0.8 quarts
Automatic transaxle	All temperatures	ATF (DEXRON)	6.4 quarts (dry) 3.2 quarts (refill)
Fuel	All temperatures	91 octane, unleaded	9.5 gal.

1. Use only engine oil designated "Service API/SE" in gasoline engines.
2. Add 1 pint if filter is changed.
3. Use only engine oil designated "Service API/CC" in diesel engines.

EXHAUST EMISSION LEVELS (GASOLINE ENGINES)

	Carbon Monoxide (CO)	Idle RPM	Ignition Timing
1975	2.0 ± 0.5%[1] by volume	925 ± 75	3°ATDC
1976	1.5 ± 0.7%[1] by volume[2]	925 ± 75	3°ATDC
1977 and later	1.5% maximum[3 4 5]	925 ± 75	3°ATDC

1. Air pump disconnected, transmission in neutral, measured ahead of catalytic converter.
2. 1.0 ± 0.7% by volume for cars equipped with automatic transmission.
3. 0.3% maximum for all cars first sold in California, measured at tailpipe.
4. 1.0% maximum for 49 states models with automatic transmission.
5. 0.5-0.9% for 1979 Scirocco first sold in California.

COOLING SYSTEM

System pressure	17-19 psi (1.2-1.35 atm)
Capacity	6.8 U.S. qts. (6.5 liters)*
Coolant	50/50 ethylene glycol
Thermostat	
Opening begins	176°F (80°C)
Opening stroke	0.27 in. (7mm) @ 194°F (90°C)
Electric fan	
On	194°F (90°C)
Off	185°F (85°C)
Drive belt deflection	⅜-9/16 in. (10-15mm)

*4.9 U.S. qts. (4.6 liters) on cars without expansion tanks.

TIRE PRESSURES

	145-13, 155-13 155 SR 13		175/70 SR 13	
	Front	Rear	Front	Rear
Partial load	27	27	27	27
Full load	27	27	27	27

NOTE: Add 3 psi front and rear for sustained high-speed driving.

DIESEL ENGINE OIL RECOMMENDATIONS

Capacity: 3.2 U.S. qt. + 1 U.S. pint with filter change

Brand	Type*	Viscosity
B.P.	B.P. Vanellus Multigrade	SAE 20W-40 All year around
Castrol	Castrol SAE 20W-20 or Castrol SAE 30	Winter — SAE 20W-20 Summer — SAE 30
Exxon	"Exxon plus" Mono Grade HDX plus ①	Winter — SAE 20W-20 Summer — SAE 30
Mobil	Mobil Oil Super	SAE 10W-40 All year around
Shell	Shell "Rotella" "Rotella" Mono ①	Winter — SAE 20W-20 Summer — SAE 30
Texaco	Texaco Oil ED	Winter — SAE 20W-20 Summer — SAE 30
American Oil	Permalube Motor Oil Amoco 200 ①	Mono Grade 10W-20, 20W-30, 30W-40, etc.
Chevron	Chevron Special Chevron Delo, 100, 200, 400 ①	Mono Grade 10W-20, 20W-30, 30W-40, etc. Multi Grade
Gulf	Gulf Super Duty, Gulf Lube XHD, Gulf Lube Multi Viscosity Gulf Super duty ①	10W-20, 20W-30, 30W-40, etc. Mono Grade
Sunco	Sun Fleet XL, Super Fleet Special Sun Fleet Super ①	10W-40 Multi Duty 10W-20, 30, 40 Mono Grade

* Use only oil marked "Service API/CC."
① May be sold under this label at truck stops.

—NOTES—

VW
RABBIT & SCIROCCO
1975-1979 INCLUDES DIESEL
SHOP MANUAL

INTRODUCTION

This detailed, comprehensive manual covers 1975-1979 VW Rabbits and Sciroccos (including the Diesel). The expert text gives complete information on maintenance, tune-up, repair, and overhaul. Hundreds of photos and drawings guide you through every step. The book includes all you need to know to keep your VWrunning right.

Where repairs are practical for the owner/mechanic, complete procedures are given. Equally important, difficult jobs are pointed out. Such operations are usually more economically performed by a dealer or independent garage.

A shop manual is a reference. You want to be able to find information fast. As in all Clymer books, this one is designed with this in mind. All chapters are thumb tabbed. Important items are extensively indexed at the rear of the book. Finally, all the most frequently used specifications and capacities are summarized on the blue *Quick Reference* pages at the front of the book.

Keep the book handy. Carry it in your glove box. It will help you to better understand your VW, lower repair and maintenance costs, and generally improve your satisfaction with your vehicle.

CHAPTER ONE

GENERAL INFORMATION

The troubleshooting, tune-up, maintenance, and step-by-step repair procedures in this book are written for the owner and home mechanic. The text is accompanied by useful photos and diagrams to make the job as clear and correct as possible.

Troubleshooting, tune-up, maintenance, and repair are not difficult if you know what tools and equipment to use and what to do. Anyone not afraid to get their hands dirty, of average intelligence, and with some mechanical ability can perform most of the procedures in this book.

In some cases, a repair job may require tools or skills not reasonably expected of the home mechanic. These procedures are noted in each chapter and it is recommended that you take the job to your dealer, a competent mechanic, or machine shop.

MANUAL ORGANIZATION

This chapter provides general information and safety and service hints. Also included are lists of recommended shop and emergency tools as well as a brief description of troubleshooting and tune-up equipment.

Chapter Two provides methods and suggestions for quick and accurate diagnosis and repair of problems. Troubleshooting procedures discuss typical symptoms and logical methods to pinpoint the trouble.

Chapter Three explains all periodic lubrication and routine maintenance necessary to keep your vehicle running well. Chapter Three also includes recommended tune-up procedures, eliminating the need to constantly consult chapters on the various subassemblies.

Subsequent chapters cover specific systems such as the engine, transmission, and electrical systems. Each of these chapters provides disassembly, repair, and assembly procedures in a simple step-by-step format. If a repair requires special skills or tools, or is otherwise impractical for the home mechanic, it is so indicated. In these cases it is usually faster and less expensive to have the repairs made by a dealer or competent repair shop. Necessary specifications concerning a particular system are included at the end of the appropriate chapter.

When special tools are required to perform a procedure included in this manual, the tool is illustrated either in actual use or alone. It may be possible to rent or borrow these tools. The inventive mechanic may also be able to find a suitable substitute in his tool box, or to fabricate one.

The terms NOTE, CAUTION, and WARNING have specific meanings in this manual. A NOTE provides additional or explanatory information. A CAUTION is used to emphasize areas where equipment damage could result if proper precautions are not taken. A WARNING is used to stress those areas where personal injury or death could result from negligence, in addition to possible mechanical damage.

SERVICE HINTS

Observing the following practices will save time, effort, and frustration, as well as prevent possible injury.

Throughout this manual keep in mind two conventions. "Front" refers to the front of the vehicle. The front of any component, such as the transmission, is that end which faces toward the front of the vehicle. The "left" and "right" sides of the vehicle refer to the orientation of a person sitting in the vehicle facing forward. For example, the steering wheel is on the left side. These rules are simple, but even experienced mechanics occasionally become disoriented.

Most of the service procedures covered are straightforward and can be performed by anyone reasonably handy with tools. It is suggested, however, that you consider your own capabilities carefully before attempting any operation involving major disassembly of the engine.

Some operations, for example, require the use of a press. It would be wiser to have these performed by a shop equipped for such work, rather than to try to do the job yourself with makeshift equipment. Other procedures require precision measurements. Unless you have the skills and equipment required, it would be better to have a qualified repair shop make the measurements for you.

Repairs go much faster and easier if the parts that will be worked on are clean before you begin. There are special cleaners for washing the engine and related parts. Brush or spray on the cleaning solution, let it stand, then rinse it away with a garden hose. Clean all oily or greasy parts with cleaning solvent as you remove them.

WARNING

Never use gasoline as a cleaning agent. It presents an extreme fire hazard. Be sure to work in a well-ventilated area when using cleaning solvent. Keep a fire extinguisher, rated for gasoline fires, handy in any case.

Much of the labor charge for repairs made by dealers is for the removal and disassembly of other parts to reach the defective unit. It is frequently possible to perform the preliminary operations yourself and then take the defective unit in to the dealer for repair, at considerable savings.

Once you have decided to tackle the job yourself, make sure you locate the appropriate section in this manual, and read it entirely. Study the illustrations and text until you have a good idea of what is involved in completing the job satisfactorily. If special tools are required, make arrangements to get them before you start. Also, purchase any known defective parts prior to starting on the procedure. It is frustrating and time-consuming to get partially into a job and then be unable to complete it.

Simple wiring checks can be easily made at home, but knowledge of electronics is almost a necessity for performing tests with complicated electronic testing gear.

During disassembly of parts keep a few general cautions in mind. Force is rarely needed to get things apart. If parts are a tight fit, like a bearing in a case, there is usually a tool designed to separate them. Never use a screwdriver to pry apart parts with machined surfaces such as cylinder head and valve cover. You will mar the surfaces and end up with leaks.

Make diagrams wherever similar-appearing parts are found. You may think you can remember where everything came from — but mistakes are costly. There is also the possibility you may get sidetracked and not return to work for days or even weeks — in which interval, carefully laid out parts may have become disturbed.

Tag all similar internal parts for location, and mark all mating parts for position. Record number and thickness of any shims as they are removed. Small parts such as bolts can be identified by placing them in plastic sandwich bags that are sealed and labeled with masking tape.

Wiring should be tagged with masking tape and marked as each wire is removed. Again, do not rely on memory alone.

When working under the vehicle, do not trust a hydraulic or mechanical jack to hold the vehicle up by itself. Always use jackstands. See **Figure 1**.

Disconnect battery ground cable before working near electrical connections and before disconnecting wires. Never run the engine with the battery disconnected; the alternator could be seriously damaged.

Protect finished surfaces from physical damage or corrosion. Keep gasoline and brake fluid off painted surfaces.

Frozen or very tight bolts and screws can often be loosened by soaking with penetrating oil like Liquid Wrench or WD-40, then sharply striking the bolt head a few times with a hammer and punch (or screwdriver for screws). Avoid heat unless absolutely necessary, since it may melt, warp, or remove the temper from many parts.

Avoid flames or sparks when working near a charging battery or flammable liquids, such as brake fluid or gasoline.

No parts, except those assembled with a press fit, require unusual force during assembly. If a part is hard to remove or install, find out why before proceeding.

Cover all openings after removing parts to keep dirt, small tools, etc., from falling in.

When assembling two parts, start all fasteners, then tighten evenly.

The clutch plate, wiring connections, brake shoes, drums, pads, and discs should be kept clean and free of grease and oil.

When assembling parts, be sure all shims and washers are replaced exactly as they came out.

Whenever a rotating part butts against a stationary part, look for a shim or washer. Use new gaskets if there is any doubt about the condition of old ones. Generally, you should apply gasket cement to one mating surface only, so the parts may be easily disassembled in the future. A thin coat of oil on gaskets helps them seal effectively.

Heavy grease can be used to hold small parts in place if they tend to fall out during assembly. However, keep grease and oil away from electrical, clutch, and brake components.

High spots may be sanded off a piston with sandpaper, but emery cloth and oil do a much more professional job.

Carburetors are best cleaned by disassembling them and soaking the parts in a commercial carburetor cleaner. Never soak gaskets and rubber parts in these cleaners. Never use wire to clean out jets and air passages; they are easily damaged. Use compressed air to blow out the carburetor, but only if the float has been removed first.

Take your time and do the job right. Do not forget that a newly rebuilt engine must be broken in the same as a new one. Refer to your owner's manual for the proper break-in procedures.

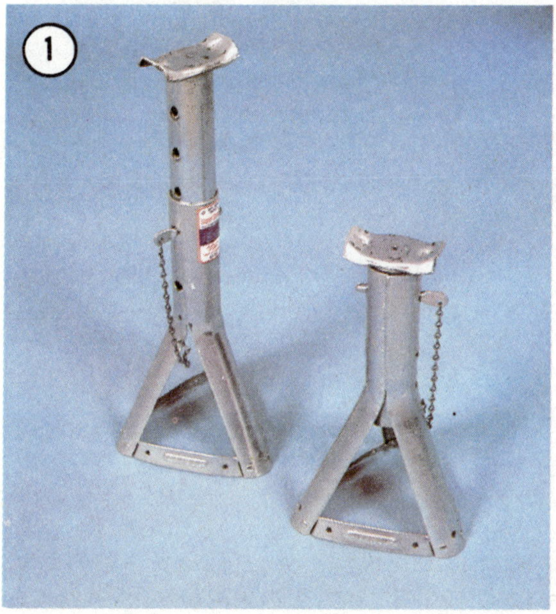

SAFETY FIRST

Professional mechanics can work for years and never sustain a serious injury. If you observe a few rules of common sense and safety, you can enjoy many safe hours servicing your vehicle. You could hurt yourself or damage the vehicle if you ignore these rules.

1. Never use gasoline as a cleaning solvent.

2. Never smoke or use a torch in the vicinity of flammable liquids such as cleaning solvent in open containers.

3. Never smoke or use a torch in an area where batteries are being charged. Highly explosive hydrogen gas is formed during the charging process.

4. Use the proper sized wrenches to avoid damage to nuts and injury to yourself.

5. When loosening a tight or stuck nut, be guided by what would happen if the wrench should slip. Protect yourself accordingly.

6. Keep your work area clean and uncluttered.

7. Wear safety goggles during all operations involving drilling, grinding, or use of a cold chisel.

8. Never use worn tools.

9. Keep a fire extinguisher handy and be sure it is rated for gasoline (Class B) and electrical (Class C) fires.

EXPENDABLE SUPPLIES

Certain expendable supplies are necessary. These include grease, oil, gasket cement, wiping rags, cleaning solvent, and distilled water. Also, special locking compounds, silicone lubricants, and engine cleaners may be useful. Cleaning solvent is available at most service stations and distilled water for the battery is available at most supermarkets.

SHOP TOOLS

For proper servicing, you will need an assortment of ordinary hand tools (**Figure 2**).

As a minimum, these include:

a. Combination wrenches
b. Sockets
c. Plastic mallet
d. Small hammer
e. Snap ring pliers
f. Gas pliers
g. Phillips screwdrivers
h. Slot (common) screwdrivers
i. Feeler gauges
j. Spark plug gauge
k. Spark plug wrench

Special tools necessary are shown in the chapters covering the particular repair in which they are used.

2

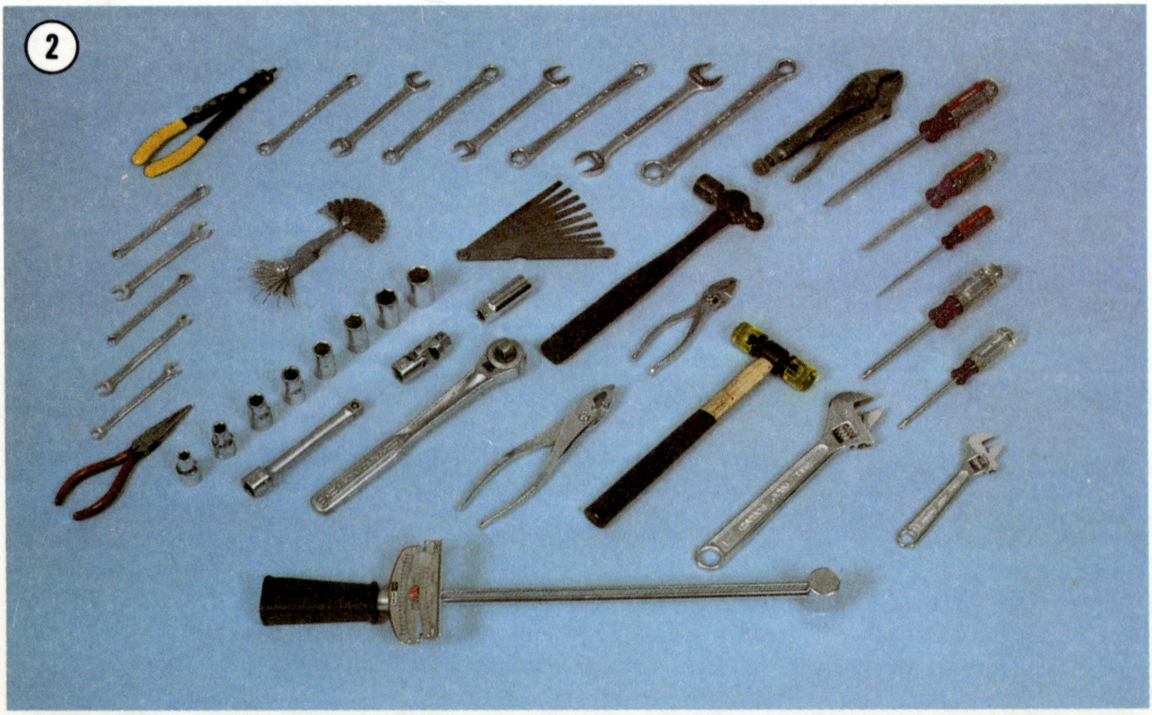

Engine tune-up and troubleshooting procedures require other special tools and equipment. These are described in detail in the following sections.

EMERGENCY TOOL KIT

A small emergency tool kit kept in the trunk is handy for road emergencies which otherwise could leave you stranded. The tools listed below and shown in **Figure 3** will let you handle most roadside repairs.

a. Combination wrenches
b. Crescent (adjustable) wrench
c. Screwdrivers — common and Phillips
d. Pliers — conventional (gas) and needle nose
e. Vise Grips
f. Hammer — plastic and metal
g. Small container of waterless hand cleaner
h. Rags for clean up
i. Silver waterproof sealing tape (duct tape)
j. Flashlight
k. Emergency road flares — at least four
l. Spare drive belts (water pump, alternator, etc.)

TROUBLESHOOTING AND TUNE-UP EQUIPMENT

Voltmeter, Ohmmeter, and Ammeter

For testing the ignition or electrical system, a good voltmeter is required. For automotive use, an instrument covering 0-20 volts is satisfac-

3

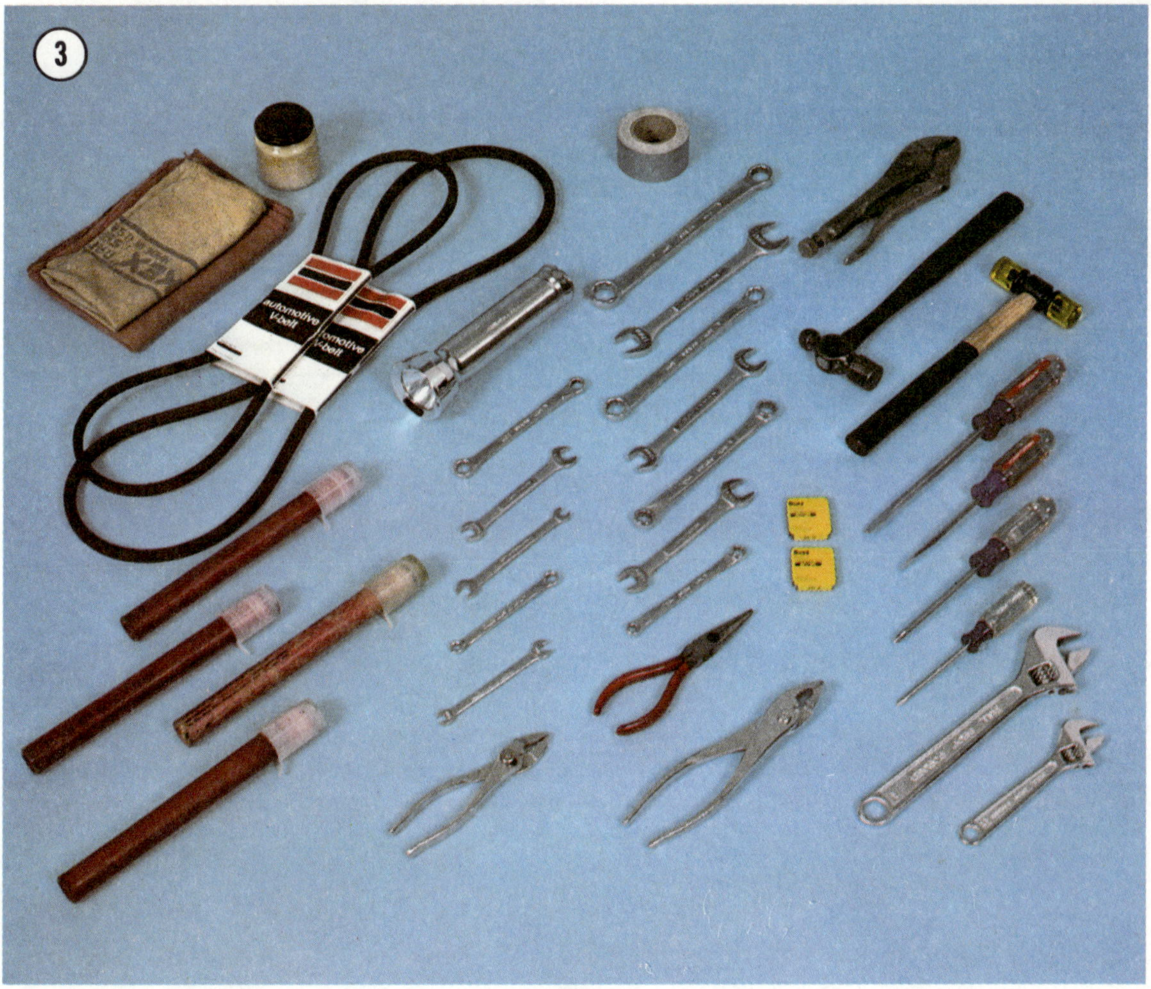

tory. One which also has a 0-2 volt scale is necessary for testing relays, points, or individual contacts where voltage drops are much smaller. Accuracy should be ± ½ volt.

An ohmmeter measures electrical resistance. This instrument is useful for checking continuity (open and short circuits), and testing fuses and lights.

The ammeter measures electrical current. Ammeters for automotive use should cover 0-50 amperes and 0-250 amperes. These are useful for checking battery charging and starting current.

Several inexpensive VOM's (volt-ohm-milliammeter) combine all three instruments into one which fits easily in any tool box. See **Figure 4**. However, the ammeter ranges are usually too small for automotive work.

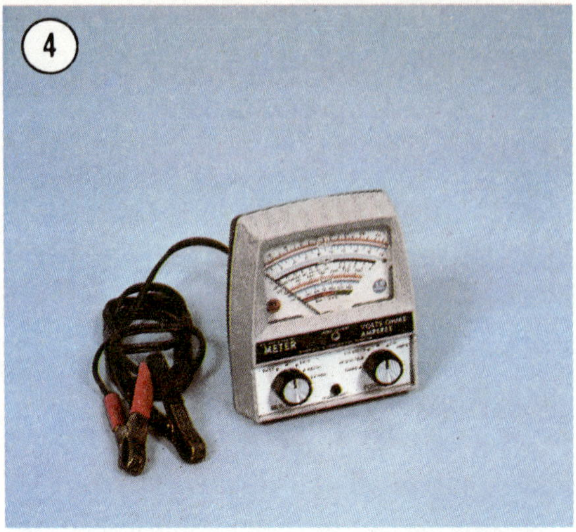
4

Hydrometer

The hydrometer gives a useful indication of battery condition and charge by measuring the specific gravity of the electrolyte in each cell. See **Figure 5**. Complete details on use and interpretation of readings are provided in the electrical chapter.

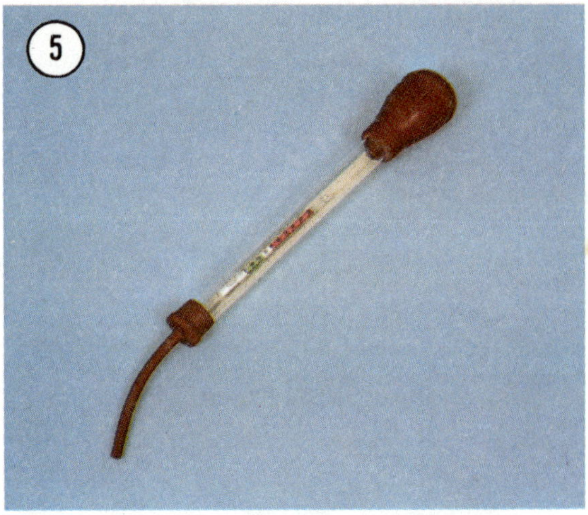
5

Compression Tester

The compression tester measures the compression pressure built up in each cylinder. The results, when properly interpreted, can indicate general cylinder and valve condition. See **Figure 6**.

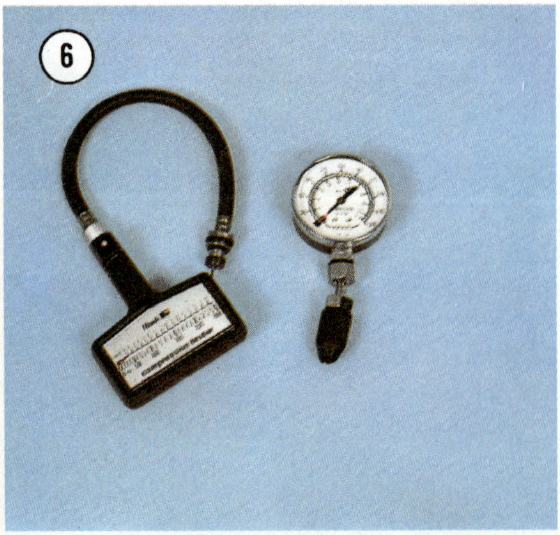
6

Vacuum Gauge

The vacuum gauge **(Figure 7)** is one of the easiest instruments to use, but one of the most difficult for the inexperienced mechanic to interpret. The results, when interpreted with other findings, can provide valuable clues to possible trouble.

To use the vacuum gauge, connect it to a vacuum hose that goes to the intake manifold. Attach it either directly to the hose or to a T-fitting installed into the hose.

NOTE: *Subtract one inch from the reading for every 1,000 ft. elevation.*

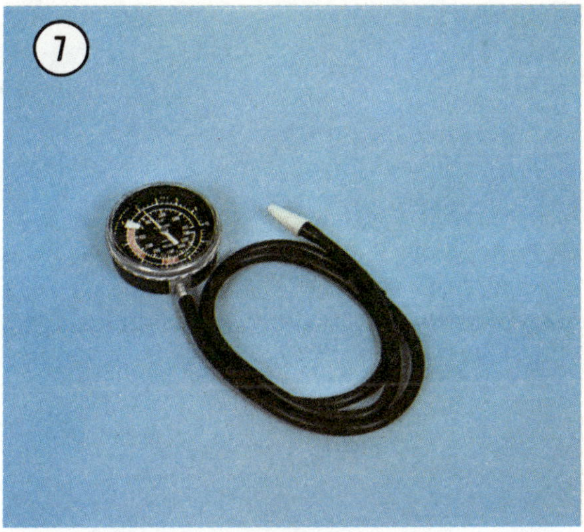

7

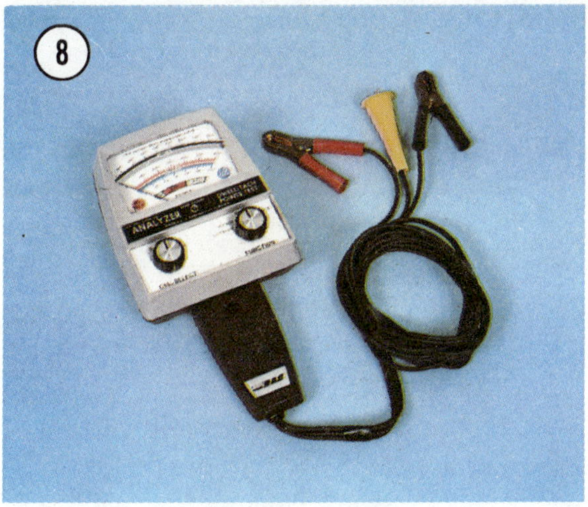

8

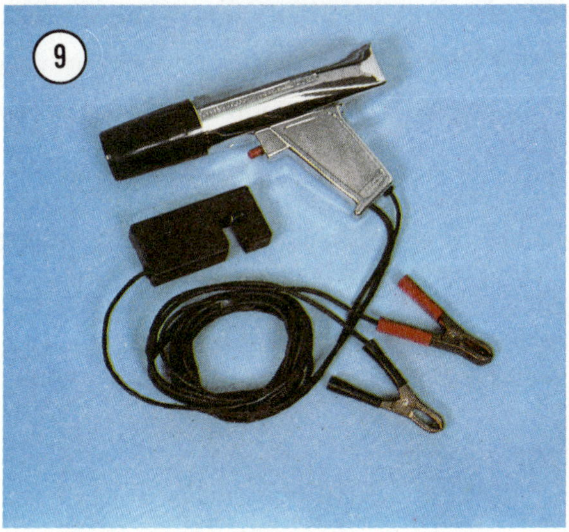

9

Fuel Pressure Gauge

This instrument is invaluable for evaluating fuel pump performance. Fuel system troubleshooting procedures in this manual use a fuel pressure gauge. Usually a vacuum gauge and fuel pressure gauge are combined.

Dwell Meter (Contact Breaker Point Ignition Only)

A dwell meter measures the distance in degrees of cam rotation that the breaker points remain closed while the engine is running. Since this angle is determined by breaker point gap, dwell angle is an accurate indication of breaker point gap.

Many tachometers intended for tuning and testing incorporate a dwell meter as well. See **Figure 8**. Follow the manufacturer's instructions to measure dwell.

Tachometer

A tachometer is necessary for tuning. See **Figure 8**. Ignition timing and carburetor adjustments must be performed at the specified idle speed. The best instrument for this purpose is one with a low range of 0-1,000 or 0-2,000 rpm for setting idle, and a high range of 0-4,000 or more for setting ignition timing at 3,000 rpm. Extended range (0-6,000 or 0-8,000 rpm) instruments lack accuracy at lower speeds. The instrument should be capable of detecting changes of 25 rpm on the low range.

Strobe Timing Light

This instrument is necessary for tuning, as it permits very accurate ignition timing. The light flashes at precisely the same instant that No. 1 cylinder fires, at which time the timing marks on the engine should align. Refer to Chapter Three for exact location of the timing marks for your engine.

Suitable lights range from inexpensive neon bulb types ($2-3) to powerful xenon strobe lights ($20-40). See **Figure 9**. Neon timing lights are difficult to see and must be used in dimly lit areas. Xenon strobe timing lights can be used outside in bright sunlight. Both types work on this vehicle; use according to the manufacturer's instructions.

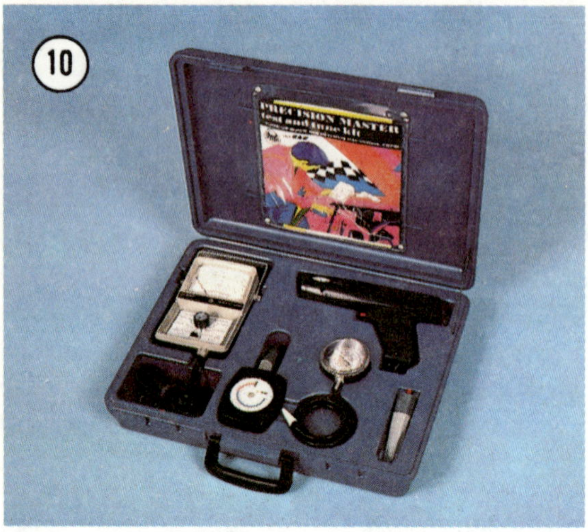

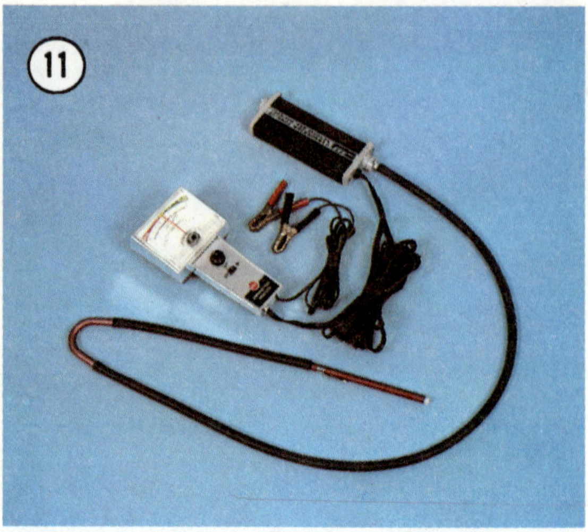

Tune-up Kits

Many manufacturers offer kits that combine several useful instruments. Some come in a convenient carry case and are usually less expensive than purchasing one instrument at a time. **Figure 10** shows one of the kits that is available. The prices vary with the number of instruments included in the kit.

Exhaust Gas Analyzer

Of all instruments described here, this is the least likely to be owned by a home mechanic. This instrument samples the exhaust gases from the tailpipe and measures the thermal conductivity of the exhaust gas. Since different gases conduct heat at varying rates, thermal conductivity of the exhaust is a good indication of gases present.

An exhaust gas analyzer is vital for accurately checking the effectiveness of exhaust emission control adjustments. They are relatively expensive to buy ($70 and up), but must be considered essential for the owner/mechanic to comply with today's emission laws. See **Figure 11**.

Fire Extinguisher

A fire extinguisher is a necessity when working on a vehicle. It should be rated for both *Class B* (flammable liquids — gasoline, oil, paint, etc.) and *Class C* (electrical — wiring, etc.) type fires. It should always be kept within reach. See **Figure 12**.

CHAPTER TWO

TROUBLESHOOTING

Troubleshooting can be a relatively simple matter if it is done logically. The first step in any troubleshooting procedure must be defining the symptoms as closely as possible. Subsequent steps involve testing and analyzing areas which could cause the symptoms. A haphazard approach may eventually find the trouble, but in terms of wasted time and unnecessary parts replacement, it can be very costly.

The troubleshooting procedures in this chapter analyze typical symptoms and show logical methods of isolation. These are not the only methods. There may be several approaches to a problem, but all methods must have one thing in common — a logical, systematic approach.

STARTING SYSTEM

The starting system consists of the starter motor and the starter solenoid. The ignition key controls the starter solenoid, which mechanically engages the starter with the engine flywheel, and supplies electrical current to turn the starter motor.

Starting system troubles are relatively easy to find. In most cases, the trouble is a loose or dirty electrical connection. **Figures 1 and 2** provide routines for finding the trouble.

CHARGING SYSTEM

The charging system consists of the alternator (or generator on older vehicles), voltage regulator, and battery. A drive belt driven by the engine crankshaft turns the alternator which produces electrical energy to charge the battery. As engine speed varies, the voltage from the alternator varies. A voltage regulator controls the charging current to the battery and maintains the voltage to the vehicle's electrical system at safe levels. A warning light or gauge on the instrument panel signals the driver when charging is not taking place. Refer to **Figure 3** for a typical charging system.

Complete troubleshooting of the charging system requires test equipment and skills which the average home mechanic does not possess. However, there are a few tests which can be done to pinpoint most troubles.

Charging system trouble may stem from a defective alternator (or generator), voltage regulator, battery, or drive belt. It may also be caused by something as simple as incorrect drive belt tension. The following are symptoms of typical problems you may encounter.

1. ***Battery dies frequently, even though the warning lamp indicates no discharge*** — This can be caused by a drive belt that is slightly too

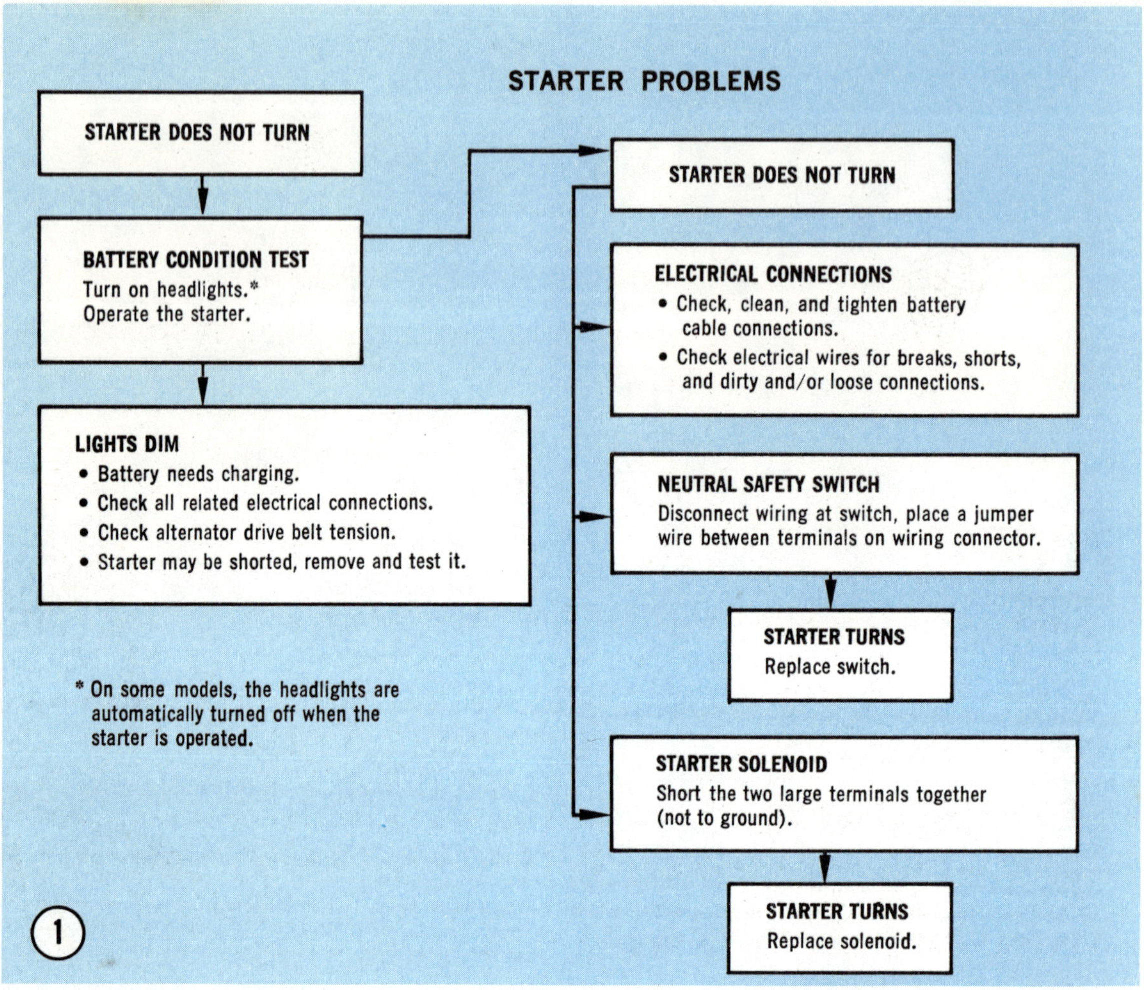
STARTER PROBLEMS
STARTER DOES NOT TURN
BATTERY CONDITION TEST
Turn on headlights.*
Operate the starter.
LIGHTS DIM
• Battery needs charging.
• Check all related electrical connections.
• Check alternator drive belt tension.
• Starter may be shorted, remove and test it.
* On some models, the headlights are automatically turned off when the starter is operated.
STARTER DOES NOT TURN
ELECTRICAL CONNECTIONS
• Check, clean, and tighten battery cable connections.
• Check electrical wires for breaks, shorts, and dirty and/or loose connections.
NEUTRAL SAFETY SWITCH
Disconnect wiring at switch, place a jumper wire between terminals on wiring connector.
STARTER TURNS
Replace switch.
STARTER SOLENOID
Short the two large terminals together (not to ground).
STARTER TURNS
Replace solenoid.
1

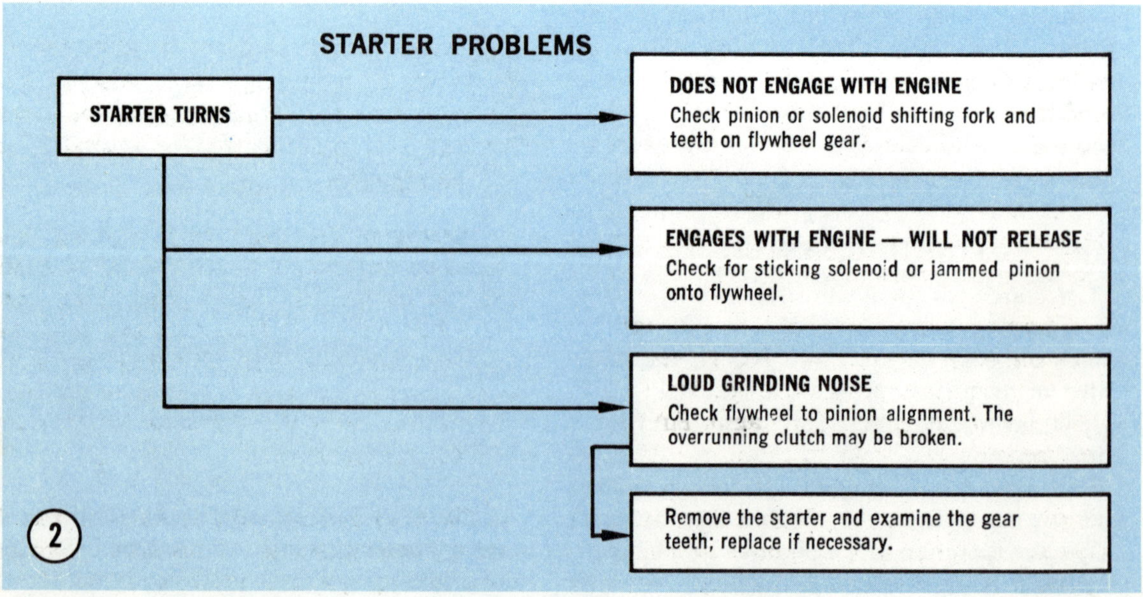
STARTER PROBLEMS
STARTER TURNS
DOES NOT ENGAGE WITH ENGINE
Check pinion or solenoid shifting fork and teeth on flywheel gear.
ENGAGES WITH ENGINE — WILL NOT RELEASE
Check for sticking solenoid or jammed pinion onto flywheel.
LOUD GRINDING NOISE
Check flywheel to pinion alignment. The overrunning clutch may be broken.
Remove the starter and examine the gear teeth; replace if necessary.
2

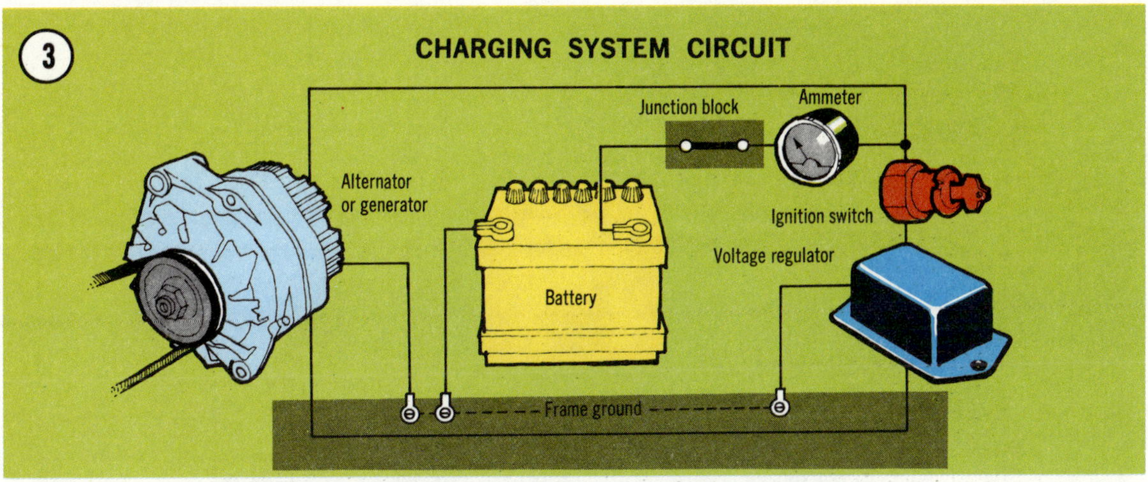

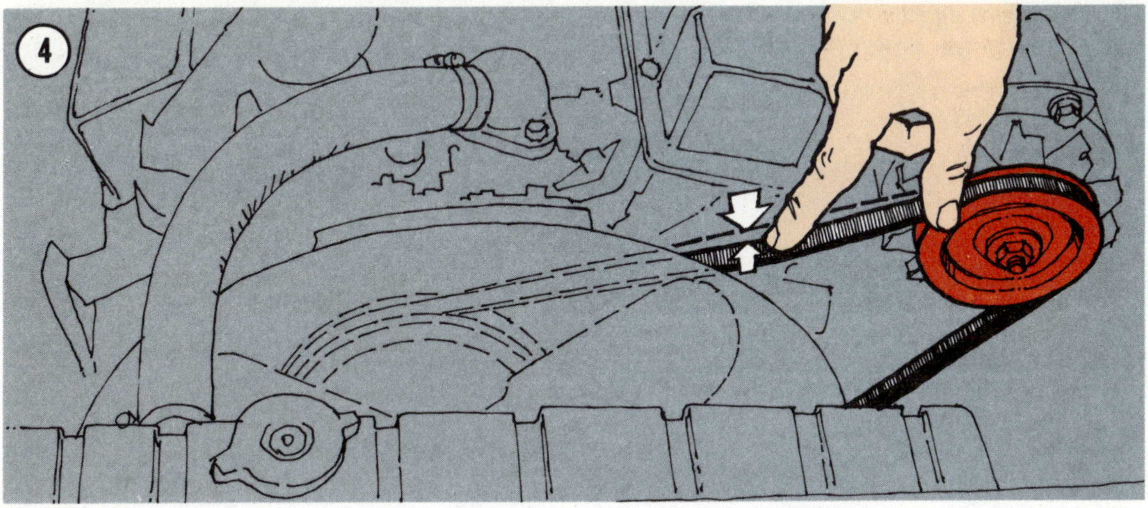

loose. Grasp the alternator (or generator) pulley and try to turn it. If the pulley can be turned without moving the belt, the drive belt is too loose. As a rule, keep the belt tight enough that it can be deflected about ½ in. under moderate thumb pressure between the pulleys (**Figure 4**). The battery may also be at fault; test the battery condition.

2. ***Charging system warning lamp does not come on when ignition switch is turned on*** — This may indicate a defective ignition switch, battery, voltage regulator, or lamp. First try to start the vehicle. If it doesn't start, check the ignition switch and battery. If the car starts, remove the warning lamp; test it for continuity with an ohmmeter or substitute a new lamp. If the lamp is good, locate the voltage regulator and make sure it is properly grounded (try tightening the mounting screws). Also the alternator (or generator) brushes may not be making contact. Test the alternator (or generator) and voltage regulator.

3. ***Alternator (or generator) warning lamp comes on and stays on*** — This usually indicates that no charging is taking place. First check drive belt tension (**Figure 4**). Then check battery condition, and check all wiring connections in the charging system. If this does not locate the trouble, check the alternator (or generator) and voltage regulator.

4. ***Charging system warning lamp flashes on and off intermittently*** — This usually indicates the charging system is working intermittently.

Check the drive belt tension (**Figure 4**), and check all electrical connections in the charging system. Check the alternator (or generator). *On generators only*, check the condition of the commutator.

5. ***Battery requires frequent additions of water, or lamps require frequent replacement*** — The alternator (or generator) is probably overcharging the battery. The voltage regulator is probably at fault.

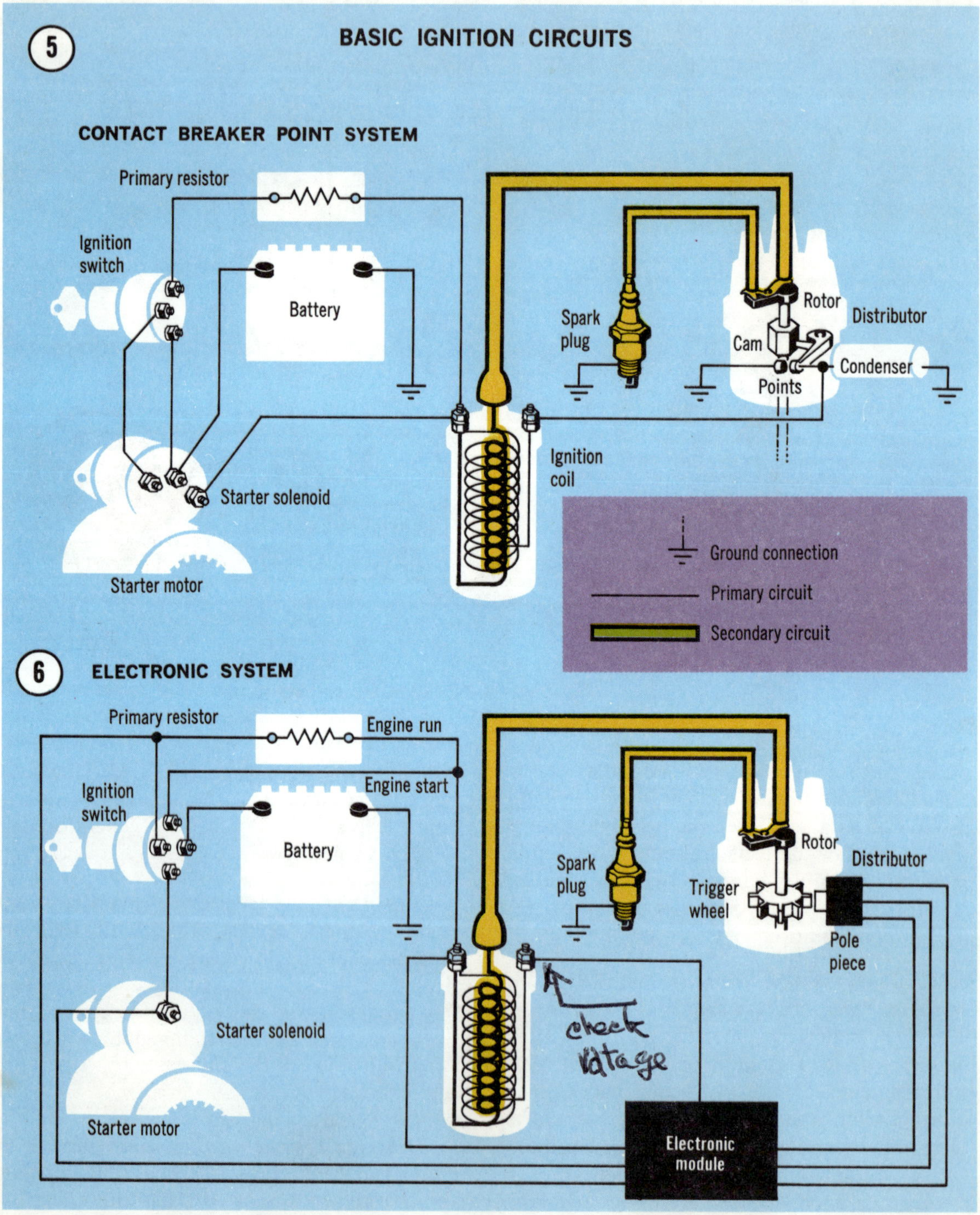

6. ***Excessive noise from the alternator (or generator)*** — Check for loose mounting brackets and bolts. The problem may also be worn bearings or the need of lubrication in some cases. If an alternator whines, a shorted diode may be indicated.

IGNITION SYSTEM

The ignition system may be either a conventional contact breaker type or an electronic ignition. See electrical chapter to determine which type you have. **Figures 5 and 6** show simplified diagrams of each type.

Most problems involving failure to start, poor performance, or rough running stem from trouble in the ignition system, particularly in contact breaker systems. Many novice troubleshooters get into trouble when they assume that these symptoms point to the fuel system instead of the ignition system.

Ignition system troubles may be roughly divided between those affecting only one cylinder and those affecting all cylinders. If the trouble affects only one cylinder, it can only be in the spark plug, spark plug wire, or portion of the distributor associated with that cylinder. If the trouble affects all cylinders (weak spark or no spark), then the trouble is in the ignition coil, rotor, distributor, or associated wiring.

The troubleshooting procedures outlined in **Figure 7** (breaker point ignition) or **Figure 8**

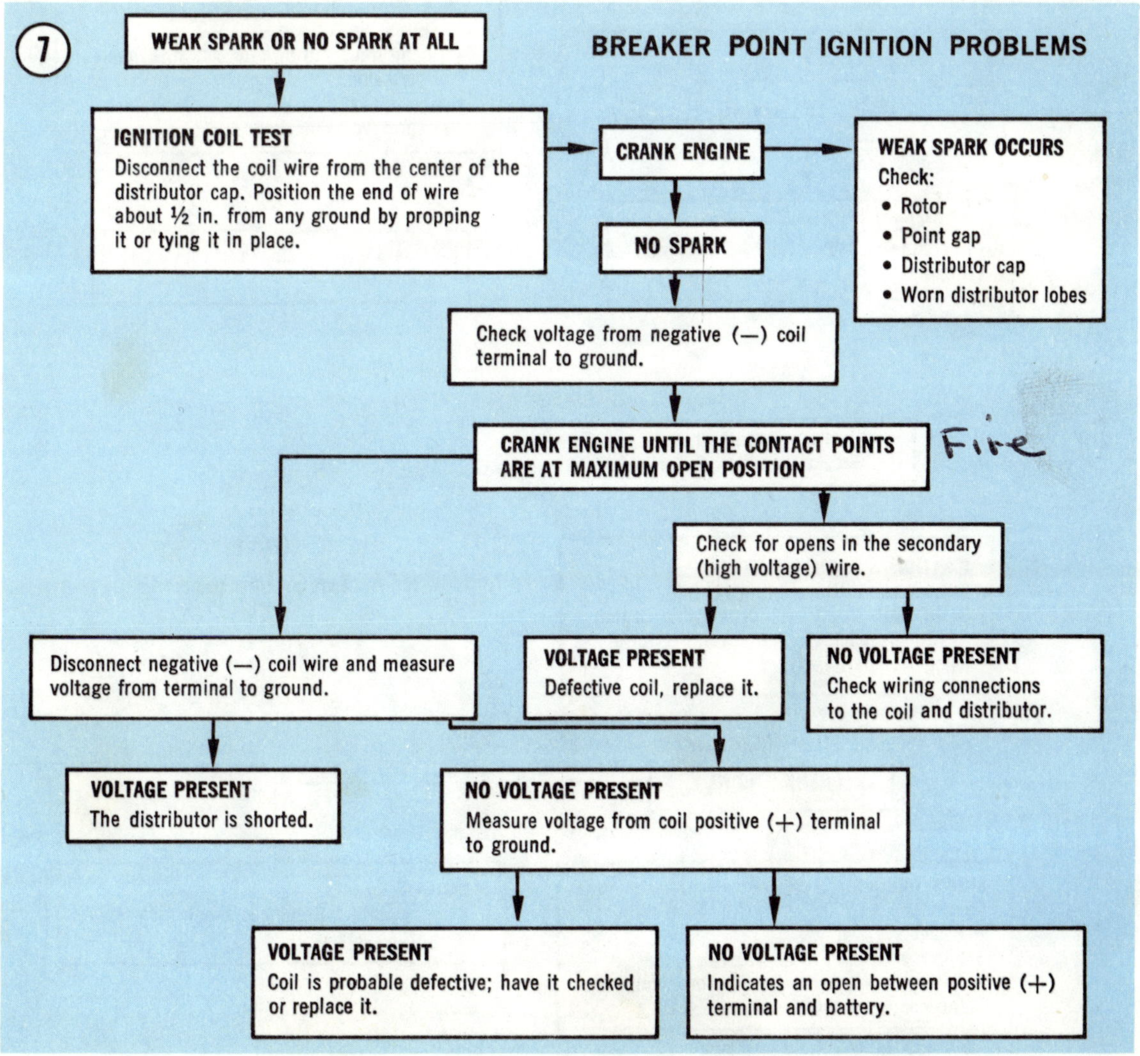

(electronic ignition) will help you isolate ignition problems fast. Of course, they assume that the battery is in good enough condition to crank the engine over at its normal rate.

ENGINE PERFORMANCE

A number of factors can make the engine difficult or impossible to start, or cause rough running, poor performance and so on. The majority of novice troubleshooters immediately suspect the carburetor or fuel injection system. In the majority of cases, though, the trouble exists in the ignition system.

The troubleshooting procedures outlined in **Figures 9 through 14** will help you solve the majority of engine starting troubles in a systematic manner.

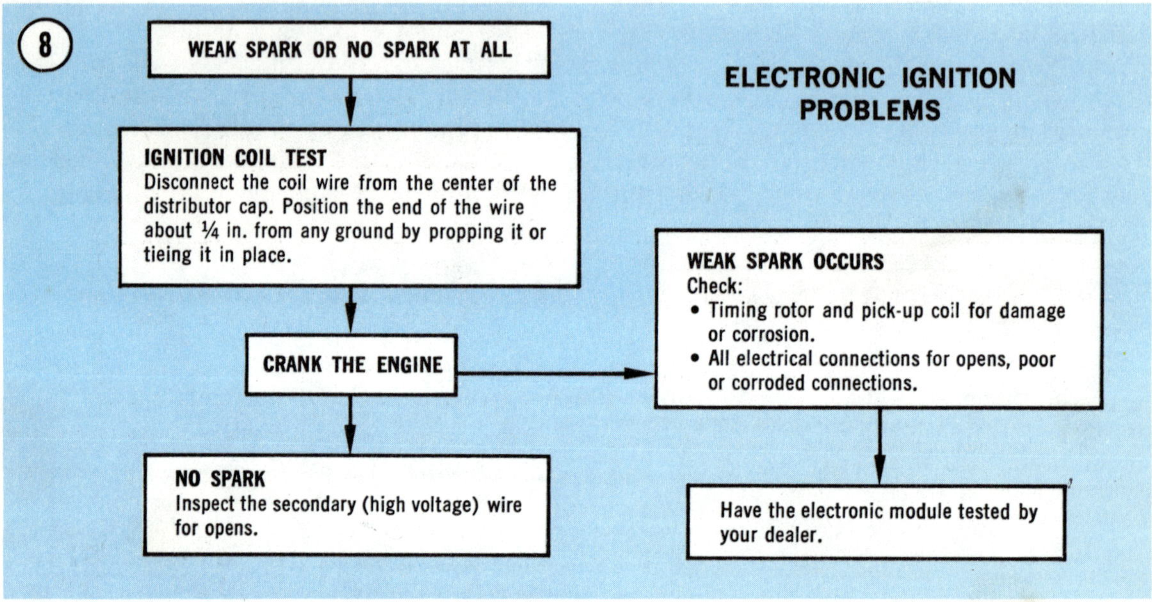

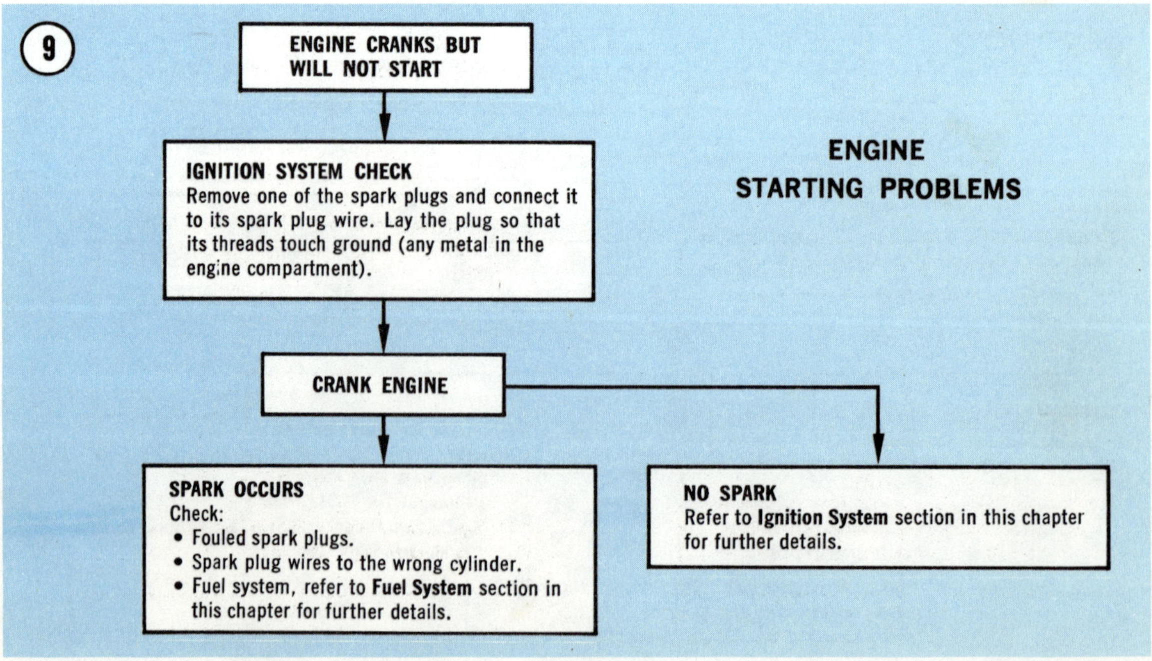

(10)

STEADY ENGINE MISS

ENGINE MISSES STEADILY

↓

DISCONNECT ONE SPARK PLUG WIRE AT A TIME

↓

START ENGINE AND LET IT IDLE

↓

MISS INCREASES
That cylinder is operating correctly—continue to next cylinder.

→

MISS REMAINS THE SAME
That cylinder is not operating correctly.

↓

Check:
- Spark plug condition and gap.
- Spark plug wires for opens or cracks in the insulation.
- Distributor cap.

(11)

ENGINE MISS AT IDLE

ENGINE MISSES — IDLE ONLY

↓

Check ignition system, refer to **Ignition System** section in this chapter for further details.

↓

Check:
- Carburetor idle adjustment.
- Vacuum lines and intake manifold for leaks. Run a compression test; one cylinder may have a defective valve or broken ring(s).

(12)

ENGINE MISS AT HIGH SPEED

ENGINE MISSES — HIGH SPEED ONLY

↓

Check the ignition system; refer to **Ignition System** section in this chapter for further details.

↓

Check:
- All vacuum lines and intake manifold for leaks.
- Fuel system, refer to **Fuel System** section in this chapter for further details.

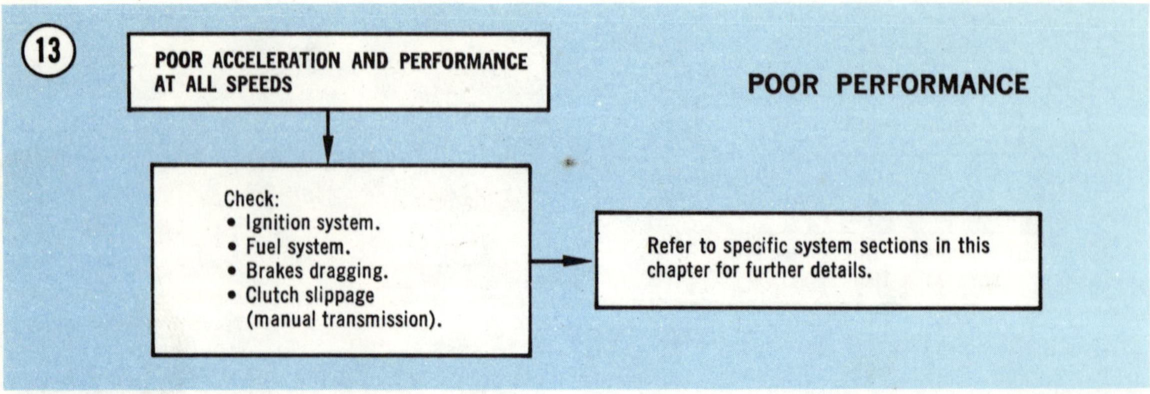

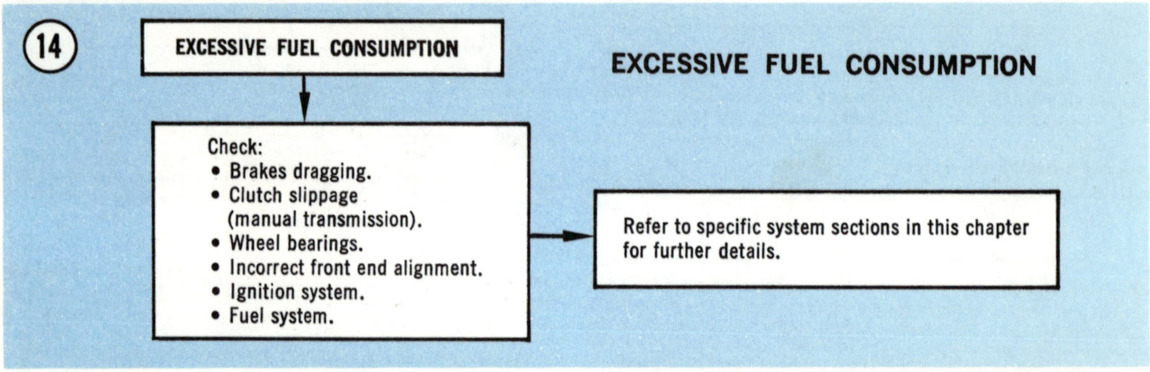

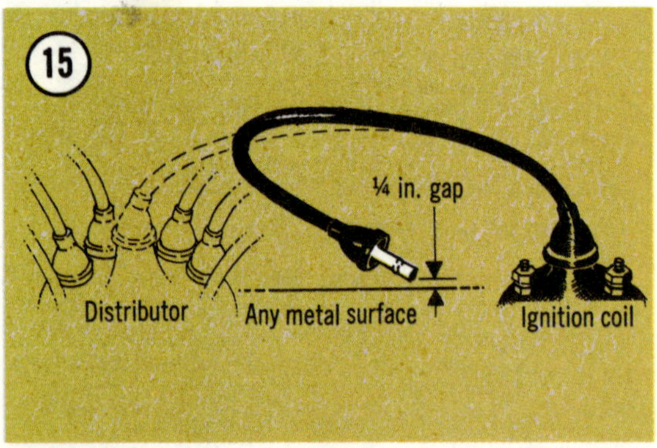

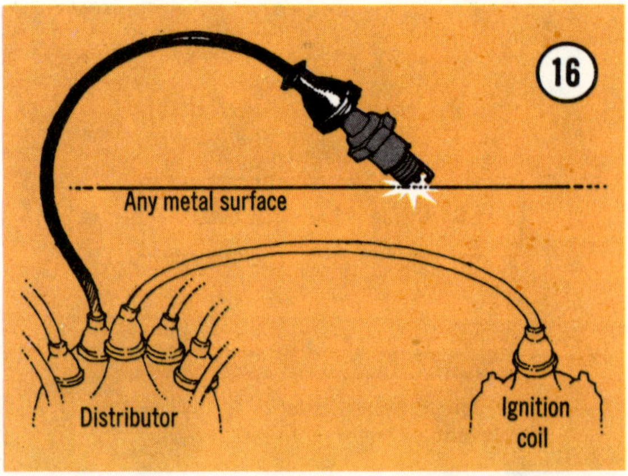

Some tests of the ignition system require running the engine with a spark plug or ignition coil wire disconnected. The safest way to do this is to disconnect the wire with the engine stopped, then prop the end of the wire next to a metal surface as shown in **Figures 15 and 16**.

WARNING

Never disconnect a spark plug or ignition coil wire while the engine is running. The high voltage in an ignition system, particularly the newer high-energy electronic ignition systems could cause serious injury or even death.

Spark plug condition is an important indication of engine performance. Spark plugs in a properly operating engine will have slightly pitted electrodes, and a light tan insulator tip. **Figure 17** shows a normal plug, and a number of others which indicate trouble in their respective cylinders.

(17)

NORMAL

- Appearance—Firing tip has deposits of light gray to light tan.
- Can be cleaned, regapped and reused.

CARBON FOULED

- Appearance—Dull, dry black with fluffy carbon deposits on the insulator tip, electrode and exposed shell.
- Caused by—Fuel/air mixture too rich, plug heat range too cold, weak ignition system, dirty air cleaner, faulty automatic choke or excessive idling.
- Can be cleaned, regapped and reused.

OIL FOULED

- Appearance—Wet black deposits on insulator and exposed shell.
- Caused by—Excessive oil entering the combustion chamber through worn rings, pistons, valve guides or bearings.
- Replace with new plugs (use a hotter plug if engine is not repaired).

LEAD FOULED

- Appearance — Yellow insulator deposits (may sometimes be dark gray, black or tan in color) on the insulator tip.
- Caused by—Highly leaded gasoline.
- Replace with new plugs.

LEAD FOULED

- Appearance—Yellow glazed deposits indicating melted lead deposits due to hard acceleration.
- Caused by—Highly leaded gasoline.
- Replace with new plugs.

OIL AND LEAD FOULED

- Appearance—Glazed yellow deposits with a slight brownish tint on the insulator tip and ground electrode.
- Replace with new plugs.

FUEL ADDITIVE RESIDUE

- Appearance — Brown colored hardened ash deposits on the insulator tip and ground electrode.
- Caused by—Fuel and/or oil additives.
- Replace with new plugs.

WORN

- Appearance — Severely worn or eroded electrodes.
- Caused by—Normal wear or unusual oil and/or fuel additives.
- Replace with new plugs.

PREIGNITION

- Appearance — Melted ground electrode.
- Caused by—Overadvanced ignition timing, inoperative ignition advance mechanism, too low of a fuel octane rating, lean fuel/air mixture or carbon deposits in combustion chamber.

PREIGNITION

- Appearance—Melted center electrode.
- Caused by—Abnormal combustion due to overadvanced ignition timing or incorrect advance, too low of a fuel octane rating, lean fuel/air mixture, or carbon deposits in combustion chamber.
- Correct engine problem and replace with new plugs.

INCORRECT HEAT RANGE

- Appearance—Melted center electrode and white blistered insulator tip.
- Caused by—Incorrect plug heat range selection.
- Replace with new plugs.

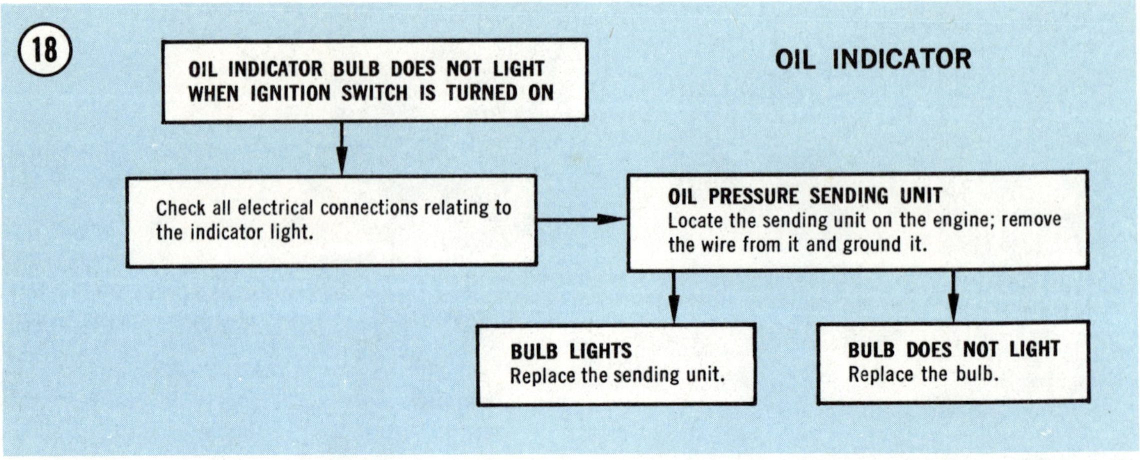

ENGINE OIL PRESSURE LIGHT

Proper oil pressure to the engine is vital. If oil pressure is insufficient, the engine can destroy itself in a comparatively short time.

The oil pressure warning circuit monitors oil pressure constantly. If pressure drops below a predetermined level, the light comes on.

Obviously, it is vital for the warning circuit to be working to signal low oil pressure. Each time you turn on the ignition, but before you start the car, the warning light should come on. If it doesn't, there is trouble in the warning circuit, not the oil pressure system. See **Figure 18** to troubleshoot the warning circuit.

Once the engine is running, the warning light should stay off. If the warning light comes on or acts erratically while the engine is running there is trouble with the engine oil pressure system. *Stop the engine immediately*. Refer to **Figure 19** for possible causes of the problem.

FUEL SYSTEM (CARBURETTED)

Fuel system problems must be isolated to the fuel pump (mechanical or electric), fuel lines, fuel filter, or carburetor. These procedures assume the ignition system is working properly and is correctly adjusted.

1. ***Engine will not start*** — First make sure that fuel is being delivered to the carburetor. Remove the air cleaner, look into the carburetor throat, and operate the accelerator

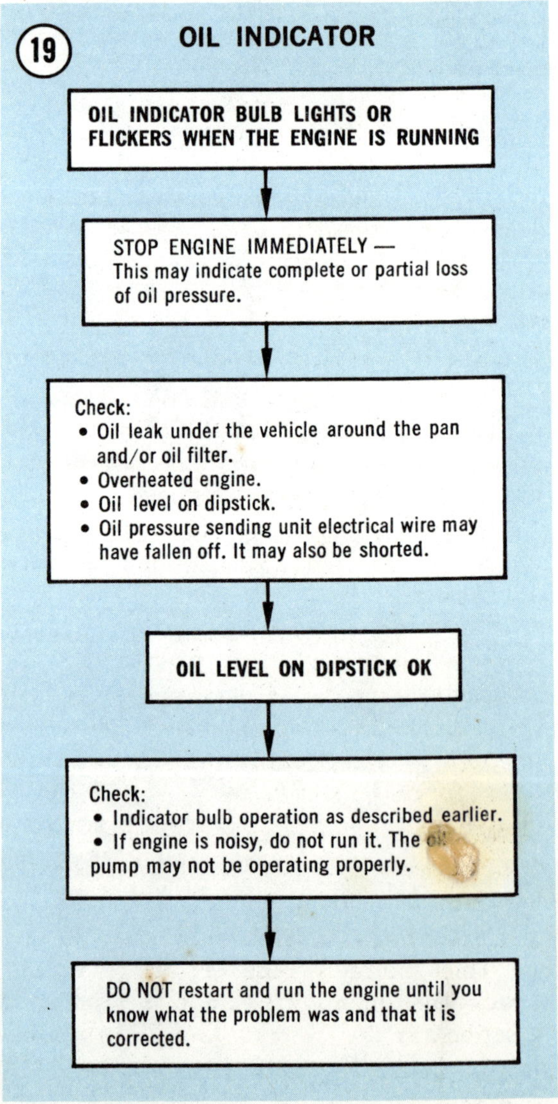

linkage several times. There should be a stream of fuel from the accelerator pump discharge tube each time the accelerator linkage is depressed (**Figure 20**). If not, check fuel pump delivery (described later), float valve, and float adjustment. If the engine will not start, check the automatic choke parts for sticking or damage. If necessary, rebuild or replace the carburetor.

2. ***Engine runs at fast idle*** — Check the choke setting. Check the idle speed, idle mixture, and decel valve (if equipped) adjustment.

3. ***Rough idle or engine miss with frequent stalling*** — Check idle mixture and idle speed adjustments.

4. ***Engine "diesels" (continues to run) when ignition is switched off*** — Check idle mixture (probably too rich), ignition timing, and idle speed (probably too fast). Check the throttle solenoid (if equipped) for proper operation. Check for overheated engine.

5. ***Stumbling when accelerating from idle*** — Check the idle speed and mixture adjustments. Check the accelerator pump.

6. ***Engine misses at high speed or lacks power*** — This indicates possible fuel starvation. Check fuel pump pressure and capacity as described in this chapter. Check float needle valves. Check for a clogged fuel filter or air cleaner.

7. ***Black exhaust smoke*** — This indicates a badly overrich mixture. Check idle mixture and idle speed adjustment. Check choke setting. Check for excessive fuel pump pressure, leaky floats, or worn needle valves.

8. ***Excessive fuel consumption*** — Check for overrich mixture. Make sure choke mechanism works properly. Check idle mixture and idle speed. Check for excessive fuel pump pressure, leaky floats, or worn float needle valves.

FUEL SYSTEM (FUEL INJECTED)

Troubleshooting a fuel injection system requires more thought, experience, and know-how than any other part of the vehicle. A logical approach and proper test equipment are essential in order to successfully find and fix these troubles.

It is best to leave fuel injection troubles to your dealer. In order to isolate a problem to the injection system make sure that the fuel pump is operating properly. Check its performance as described later in this section. Also make sure that fuel filter and air cleaner are not clogged.

FUEL PUMP TEST (MECHANICAL AND ELECTRIC)

1. Disconnect the fuel inlet line where it enters the carburetor or fuel injection system.

2. Fit a rubber hose over the fuel line so fuel can be directed into a graduated container with about one quart capacity. See **Figure 21**.

3. To avoid accidental starting of the engine, disconnect the secondary coil wire from the coil.

4. Crank the engine for about 30 seconds.

5. If the fuel pump supplies the specified amount (refer to the fuel chapter later in this book), the trouble may be in the carburetor or fuel injection system. The fuel injection system should be tested by your dealer.

6. If there is no fuel present or the pump cannot supply the specified amount, either the fuel pump is defective or there is an obstruction in the fuel line. Replace the fuel pump and/or inspect the fuel lines for air leaks or obstructions.

7. Also pressure test the fuel pump by installing a T-fitting in the fuel line between the fuel pump and the carburetor. Connect a fuel pressure gauge to the fitting with a short tube **(Figure 22)**.

8. Reconnect the primary coil wire, start the engine, and record the pressure. Refer to the fuel chapter later in this book for the correct pressure. If the pressure varies from that specified, the pump should be replaced.

9. Stop the engine. The pressure should drop off very slowly. If it drops off rapidly, the outlet valve in the pump is leaking and the pump should be replaced.

EMISSION CONTROL SYSTEMS

Major emission control systems used on nearly all U.S. models include the following:

a. Positive crankcase ventilation (PCV)
b. Thermostatic air cleaner
c. Air injection reaction (AIR)
d. Fuel evaporation control
e. Exhaust gas recirculation (EGR)

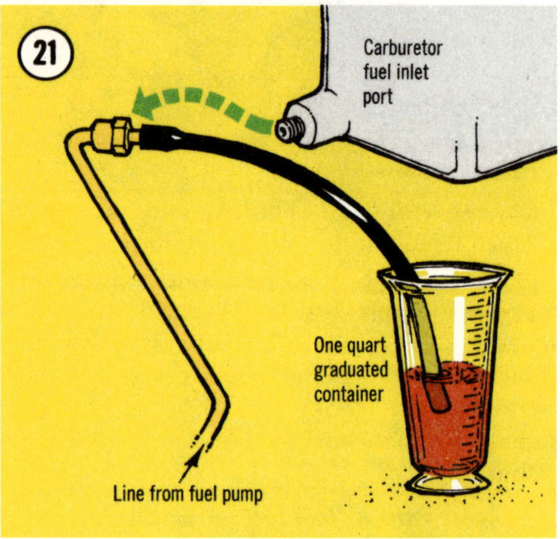

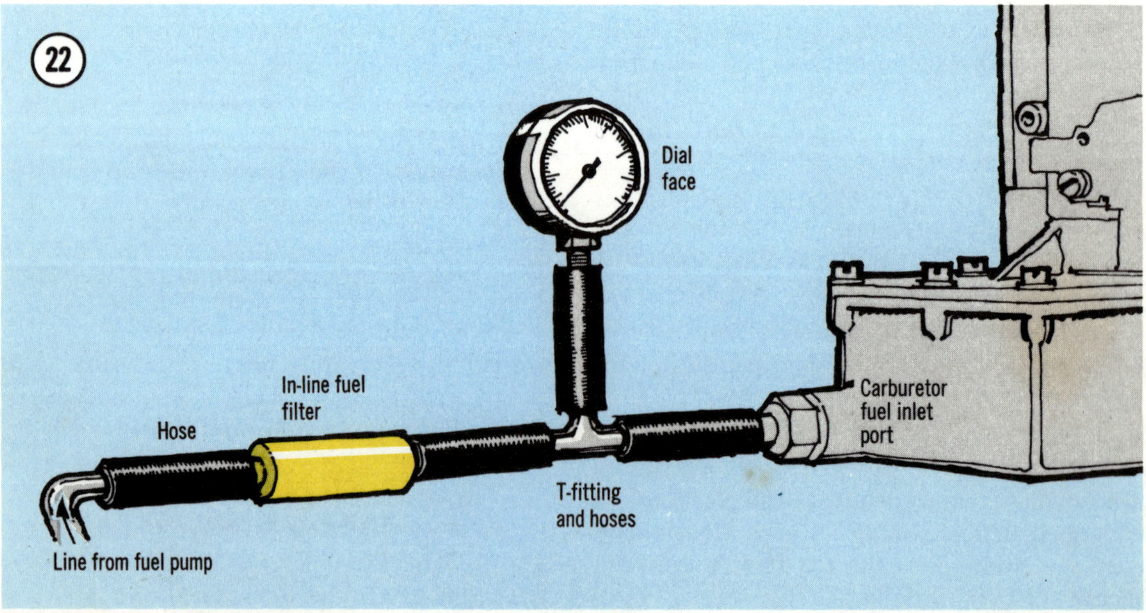

Emission control systems vary considerably from model to model. Individual models contain variations of the four systems described here. In addition, they may include other special systems. Use the index to find specific emission control components in other chapters.

Many of the systems and components are factory set and sealed. Without special expensive test equipment, it is impossible to adjust the systems to meet state and federal requirements.

Troubleshooting can also be difficult without special equipment. The procedures described below will help you find emission control parts which have failed, but repairs may have to be entrusted to a dealer or other properly equipped repair shop.

With the proper equipment, you can test the carbon monoxide and hydrocarbon levels. **Figure 23** provides some sources of trouble if the readings are not correct.

Positive Crankcase Ventilation

Fresh air drawn from the air cleaner housing scavenges emissions (e.g., piston blow-by) from the crankcase, then the intake manifold vacuum draws emissions into the intake manifold. They can then be reburned in the normal combustion process. **Figure 24** shows a typical system. **Figure 25** provides a testing procedure.

Thermostatic Air Cleaner

The thermostatically controlled air cleaner maintains incoming air to the engine at a predetermined level, usually about 100°F or higher. It mixes cold air with heated air from the exhaust manifold region. The air cleaner in-

(23) EXHAUST EMISSION PROBLEMS

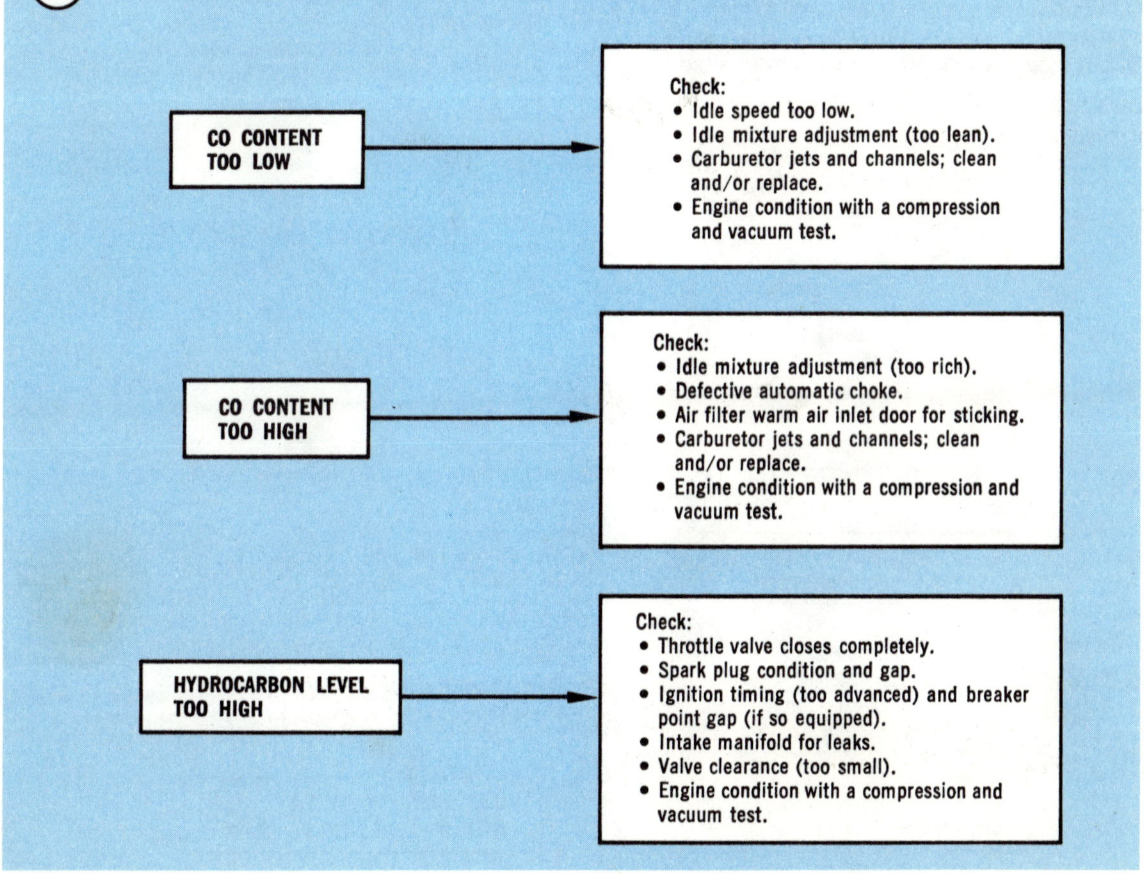

cludes a temperature sensor, vacuum motor, and a hinged door. See **Figure 26**.

The system is comparatively easy to test. See **Figure 27** for the procedure.

Air Injection Reaction System

The air injection reaction system reduces air pollution by oxidizing hydrocarbons and carbon monoxide as they leave the combustion chamber. See **Figure 28**.

The air injection pump, driven by the engine, compresses filtered air and injects it at the exhaust port of each cylinder. The fresh air mixes with the unburned gases in the exhaust and promotes further burning. A check valve prevents exhaust gases from entering and damaging the air pump if the pump becomes inoperative, e.g., from a fan belt failure.

Figure 29 explains the testing procedure for this system.

Fuel Evaporation Control

Fuel vapor from the fuel tank passes through the liquid/vapor separator to the carbon canister. See **Figure 30**. The carbon absorbs and

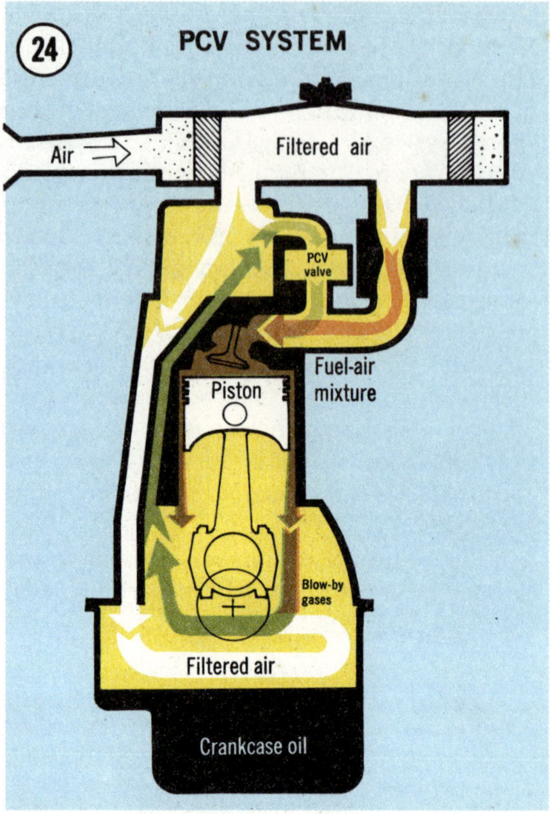

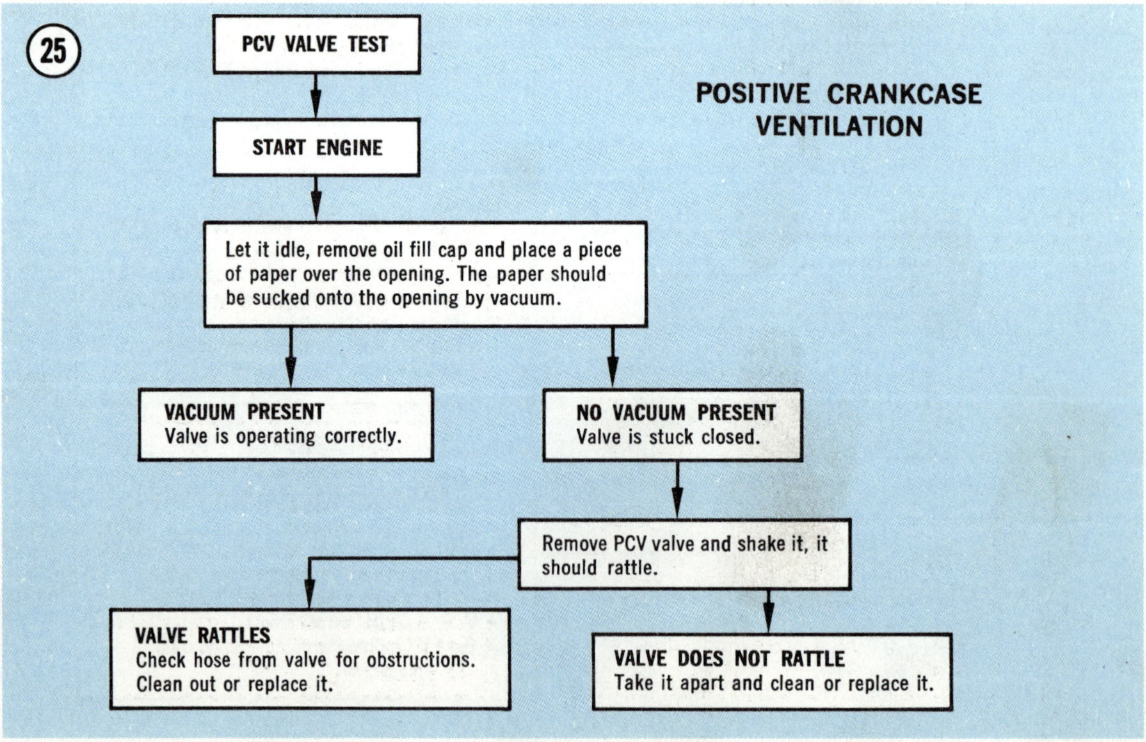

(26)

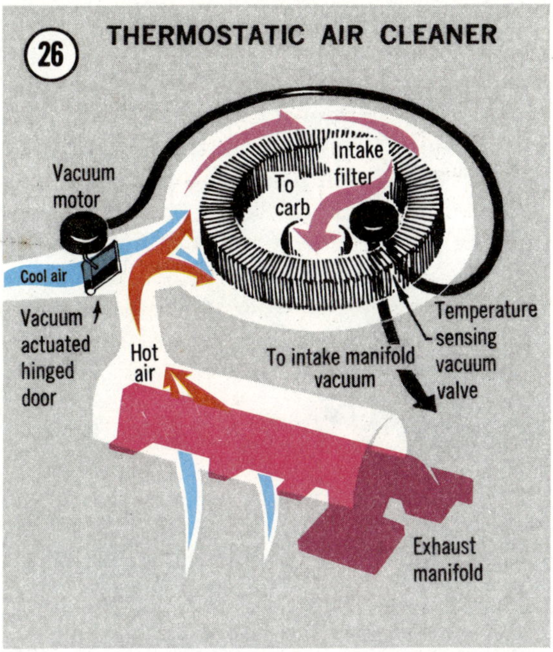

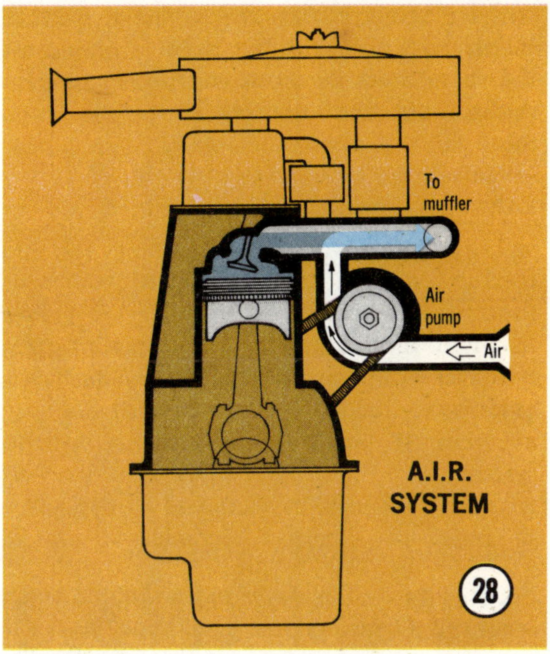

(28)

(27)

THERMOSTATIC AIR CLEANER

THERMOSTATIC AIR CLEANER

Normal operation — Closed for cold engine.
— Open for warm engine.

OPENS AND CLOSES
Is operating correctly.

DOES NOT OPEN OR CLOSE
Check for binding linkage or a leak in the vacuum line.

(29)

AIR INJECTION REACTOR

AIR INJECTION REACTOR

PUMP NOT RUNNING AT PROPER SPEED

Check:
- Drive belt tension.
- Oil the bearings (if there are provisions to do so).
- Air filter (some models have their own small air filter).

PUMP NOT PRODUCING AIR PRESSURE
(Approximately 1 psi)

REMOVE THE AIR FILTER
(if so equipped)

Let the engine idle, place a burning match or cigarette at the inlet. The pump should draw in the smoke. If not, have it serviced by your dealer.

stores the vapor when the engine is stopped. When the engine runs, manifold vacuum draws the vapor from the canister. Instead of being released into the atmosphere, the fuel vapor takes part in the normal combustion process.

Exhaust Gas Recirculation

The exhaust gas recirculation (EGR) system is used to reduce the emission of nitrogen oxides (NOx). Relatively inert exhaust gases are introduced into the combustion process to slightly reduce peak temperatures. This reduction in temperature reduces the formation of NOx.

Figure 31 provides a simple test of this system.

ENGINE NOISES

Often the first evidence of an internal engine trouble is a strange noise. That knocking, clicking, or tapping which you never heard before may be warning you of impending trouble.

While engine noises can indicate problems, they are sometimes difficult to interpret correctly; inexperienced mechanics can be seriously misled by them.

Professional mechanics often use a special stethoscope which looks similar to a doctor's stethoscope for isolating engine noises. You can do nearly as well with a "sounding stick" which can be an ordinary piece of doweling or a section of small hose. By placing one end in contact with the area to which you want to listen and the other end near your ear, you can hear

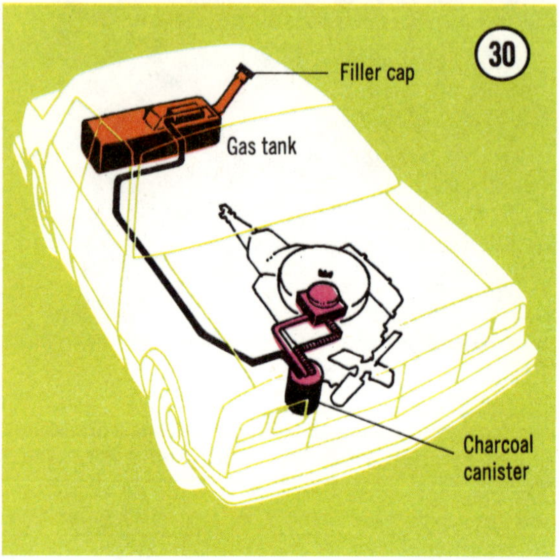

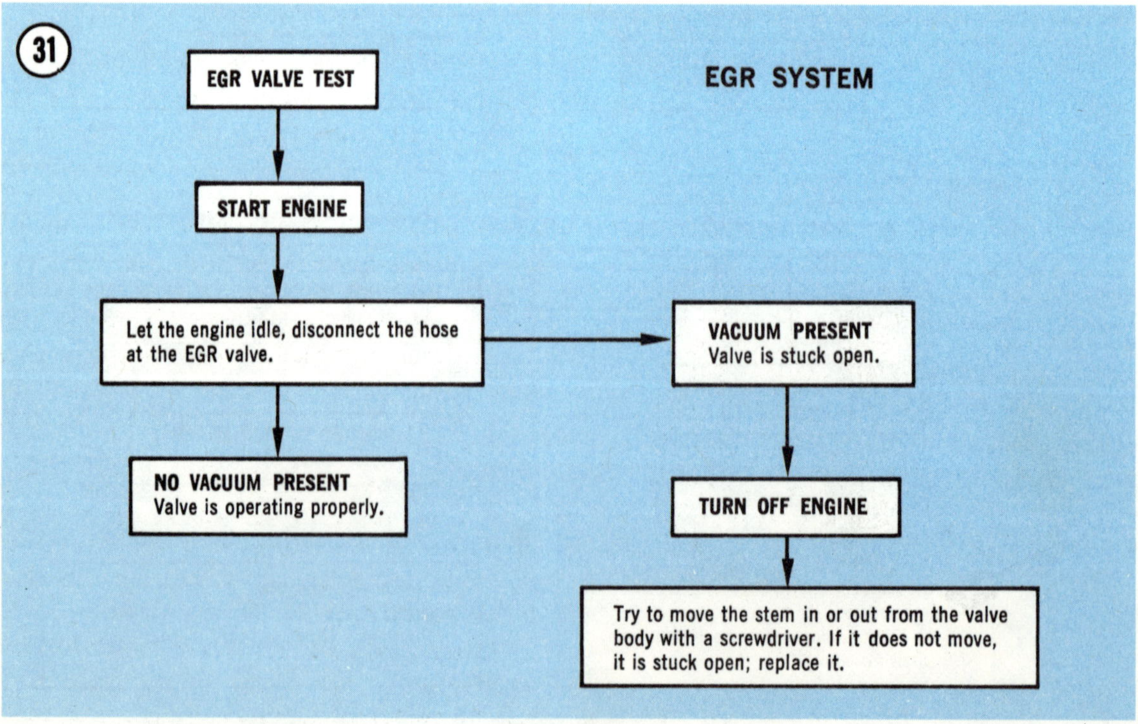

sounds emanating from that area. The first time you do this, you may be horrified at the strange noises coming from even a normal engine. If you can, have an experienced friend or mechanic help you sort the noises out.

Clicking or Tapping Noises

Clicking or tapping noises usually come from the valve train, and indicate excessive valve clearance.

If your vehicle has adjustable valves, the procedure for adjusting the valve clearance is explained in Chapter Three. If your vehicle has hydraulic lifters, the clearance may not be adjustable. The noise may be coming from a collapsed lifter. These may be cleaned or replaced as described in the engine chapter.

A sticking valve may also sound like a valve with excessive clearance. In addition, excessive wear in valve train components can cause similar engine noises.

Knocking Noises

A heavy, dull knocking is usually caused by a worn main bearing. The noise is loudest when the engine is working hard, i.e., accelerating hard at low speed. You may be able to isolate the trouble to a single bearing by disconnecting the spark plugs one at a time. When you reach the spark plug nearest the bearing, the knock will be reduced or disappear.

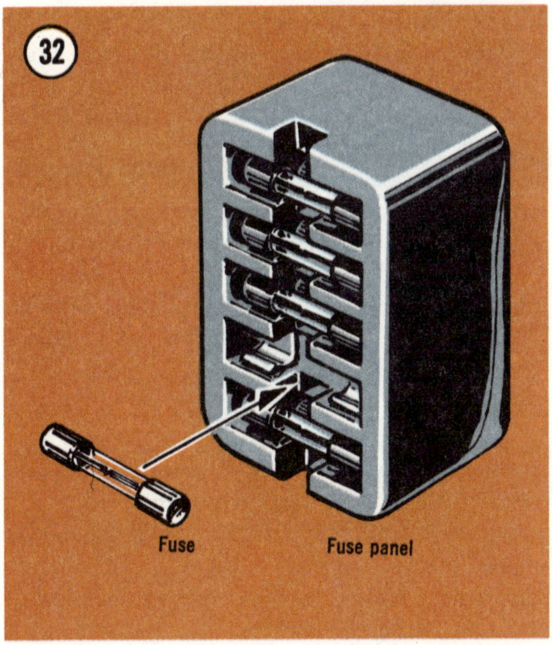

Worn connecting rod bearings may also produce a knock, but the sound is usually more "metallic." As with a main bearing, the noise is worse when accelerating. It may even increase further just as you go from accelerating to coasting. Disconnecting spark plugs will help isolate this knock as well.

A double knock or clicking usually indicates a worn piston pin. Disconnecting spark plugs will isolate this to a particular piston, however, the noise will *increase* when you reach the affected piston.

A loose flywheel and excessive crankshaft end play also produce knocking noises. While similar to main bearing noises, these are usually intermittent, not constant, and they do not change when spark plugs are disconnected.

Some mechanics confuse piston pin noise with piston slap. The double knock will distinguish the piston pin noise. Piston slap is identified by the fact that it is always louder when the engine is cold.

ELECTRICAL ACCESSORIES

Lights and Switches (Interior and Exterior)

1. ***Bulb does not light*** — Remove the bulb and check for a broken element. Also check the inside of the socket; make sure the contacts are clean and free of corrosion. If the bulb and socket are OK, check to see if a fuse has blown or a circuit breaker has tripped. The fuse panel (**Figure 32**) is usually located under the instrument panel. Replace the blown fuse or reset the circuit breaker. If the fuse blows or the breaker trips again, there is a short in that circuit. Check that circuit all the way to the battery. Look for worn wire insulation or burned wires.

If all the above are all right, check the switch controlling the bulb for continuity with an ohmmeter at the switch terminals. Check the switch contact terminals for loose or dirty electrical connections.

2. ***Headlights work but will not switch from either high or low beam*** — Check the beam selector switch for continuity with an ohmmeter

at the switch terminals. Check the switch contact terminals for loose or dirty electrical connections.

3. ***Brake light switch inoperative*** — On mechanically operated switches, usually mounted near the brake pedal arm, adjust the switch to achieve correct mechanical operation. Check the switch for continuity with an ohmmeter at the switch terminals. Check the switch contact terminals for loose or dirty electrical connections.

4. ***Back-up lights do not operate*** — Check light bulb as described earlier. Locate the switch, normally located near the shift lever. Adjust switch to achieve correct mechanical operation. Check the switch for continuity with an ohmmeter at the switch terminals. Bypass the switch with a jumper wire; if the lights work, replace the switch.

Directional Signals

1. ***Directional signals do not operate*** — If the indicator light on the instrument panel burns steadily instead of flashing, this usually indicates that one of the exterior lights is burned out. Check all lamps that normally flash. If all are all right, the flasher unit may be defective. Replace it with a good one.

2. ***Directional signal indicator light on instrument panel does not light up*** — Check the light bulbs as described earlier. Check all electrical connections and check the flasher unit.

3. ***Directional signals will not self-cancel*** — Check the self-cancelling mechanism located inside the steering column.

4. ***Directional signals flash slowly*** — Check the condition of the battery and the alternator (or generator) drive belt tension (**Figure 4**). Check the flasher unit and all related electrical connections.

Windshield Wipers

1. ***Wipers do not operate*** — Check for a blown fuse or circuit breaker that has tripped; replace or reset. Check all related terminals for loose or dirty electrical connections. Check continuity of the control switch with an ohmmeter at the switch terminals. Check the linkage and arms for loose, broken, or binding parts. Straighten out or replace where necessary.

2. ***Wiper motor hums but will not operate*** — The motor may be shorted out internally; check and/or replace the motor. Also check for broken or binding linkage and arms.

3. ***Wiper arms will not return to the stowed position when turned off*** — The motor has a special internal switch for this purpose. Have it inspected by your dealer. Do not attempt this yourself.

Interior Heater

1. ***Heater fan does not operate*** — Check for a blown fuse or circuit breaker that has tripped. Check the switch for continuity with an ohmmeter at the switch terminals. Check the switch contact terminals for loose or dirty electrical connections.

2. ***Heat output is insufficient*** — Check the heater hose/engine coolant control valve usually located in the engine compartment; make sure it is in the open position. Ensure that the heater door(s) and cable(s) are operating correctly and are in the open position. Inspect the heat ducts; make sure that they are not crimped or blocked.

COOLING SYSTEM

The temperature gauge or warning light usually signals cooling system troubles before there is any damage. As long as you stop the vehicle at the first indication of trouble, serious damage is unlikely.

In most cases, the trouble will be obvious as soon as you open the hood. If there is coolant or steam leaking, look for a defective radiator, radiator hose, or heater hose. If there is no evidence of leakage, make sure that the fan belt is in good condition. If the trouble is not obvious, refer to **Figures 33 and 34** to help isolate the trouble.

Automotive cooling systems operate under pressure to permit higher operating temperatures without boil-over. The system should be checked periodically to make sure it can withstand normal pressure. **Figure 35** shows the equipment which nearly any service station has for testing the system pressure.

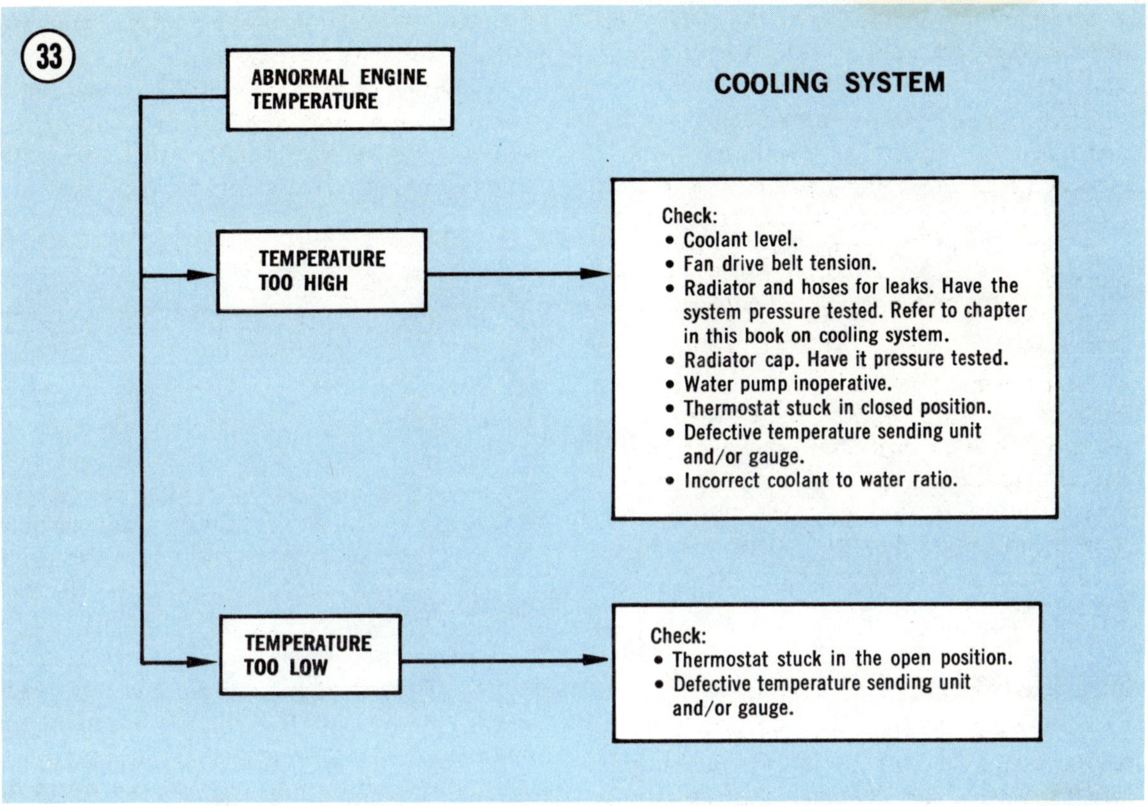

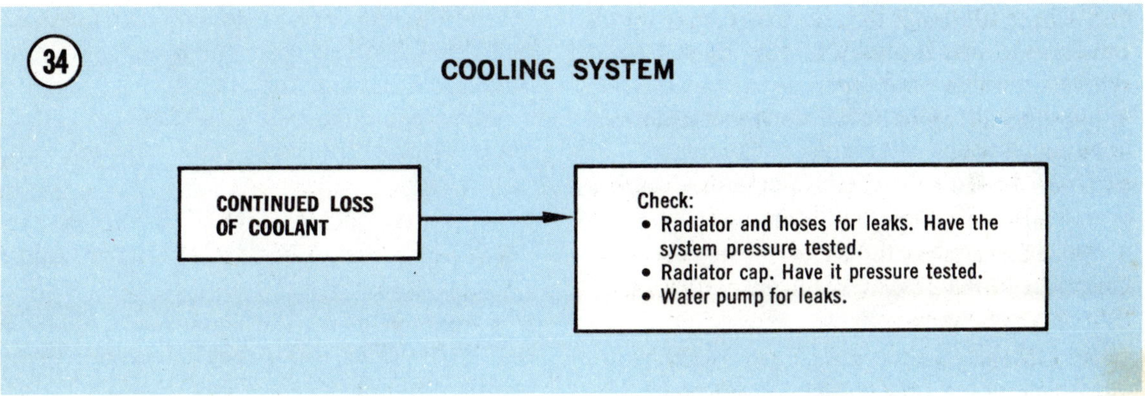

CLUTCH

All clutch troubles except adjustments require transmission removal to identify and cure the problem.

1. ***Slippage*** — This is most noticeable when accelerating in a high gear at relatively low speed. To check slippage, park the vehicle on a level surface with the handbrake set. Shift to 2nd gear and release the clutch as if driving off. If the clutch is good, the engine will slow and stall. If the clutch slips, continued engine speed will give it away.

Slippage results from insufficient clutch pedal free play, oil or grease on the clutch disc, worn pressure plate, or weak springs.

2. ***Drag or failure to release*** — This trouble usually causes difficult shifting and gear clash, especially when downshifting. The cause may be excessive clutch pedal free play, warped or bent pressure plate or clutch disc, broken or

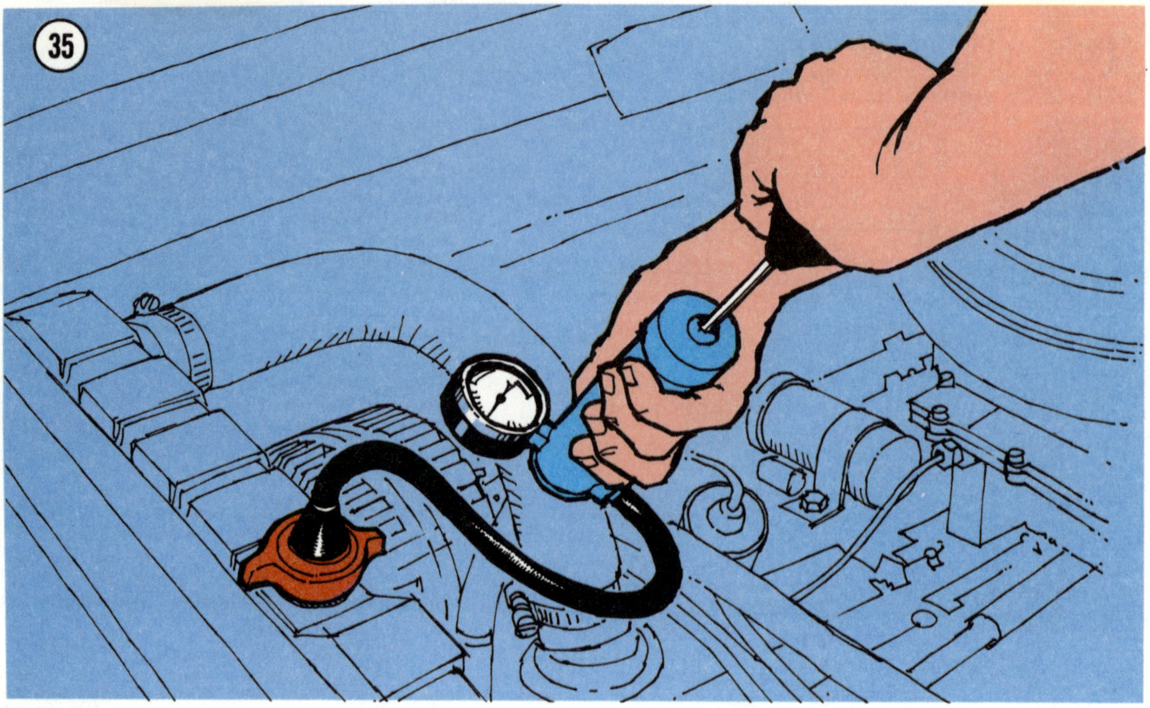

loose linings, or lack of lubrication in pilot bearing. Also check condition of transmission main shaft splines.

3. ***Chatter or grabbing*** — A number of things can cause this trouble. Check tightness of engine mounts and engine-to-transmission mounting bolts. Check for worn or misaligned pressure plate and misaligned release plate.

4. ***Other noises*** — Noise usually indicates a dry or defective release or pilot bearing. Check the bearings and replace if necessary. Also check all parts for misalignment and uneven wear.

MANUAL TRANSMISSION/TRANSAXLE

Transmission and transaxle troubles are evident when one or more of the following symptoms appear:

a. Difficulty changing gears
b. Gears clash when downshifting
c. Slipping out of gear
d. Excessive noise in NEUTRAL
e. Excessive noise in gear
f. Oil leaks

Transmission and transaxle repairs are not recommended unless the many special tools required are available.

Transmission and transaxle troubles are sometimes difficult to distinguish from clutch troubles. Eliminate the clutch as a source of trouble before installing a new or rebuilt transmission or transaxle.

AUTOMATIC TRANSMISSION

Most automatic transmission repairs require considerable specialized knowledge and tools. It is impractical for the home mechanic to invest in the tools, since they cost more than a properly rebuilt transmission.

Check fluid level and condition frequently to help prevent future problems. If the fluid is orange or black in color or smells like varnish, it is an indication of some type of damage or failure within the transmission. Have the transmission serviced by your dealer or competent automatic transmission service facility.

BRAKES

Good brakes are vital to the safe operation of the vehicle. Performing the maintenance speci-

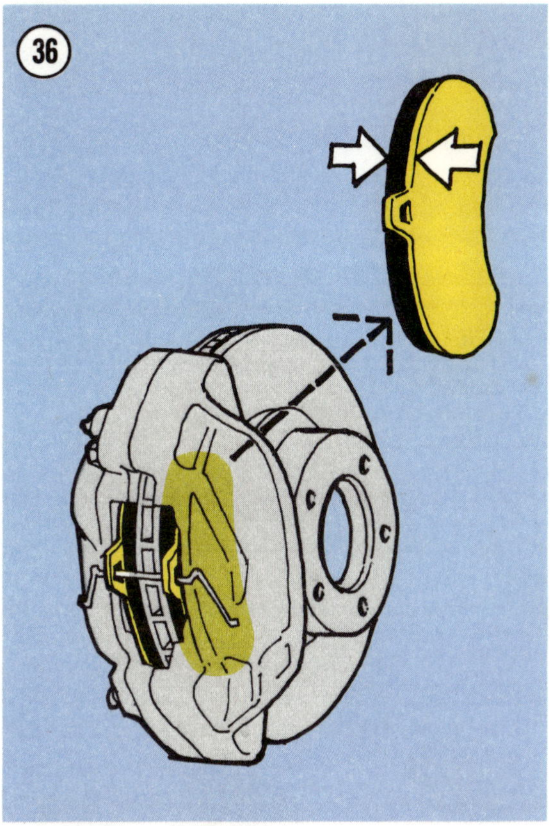

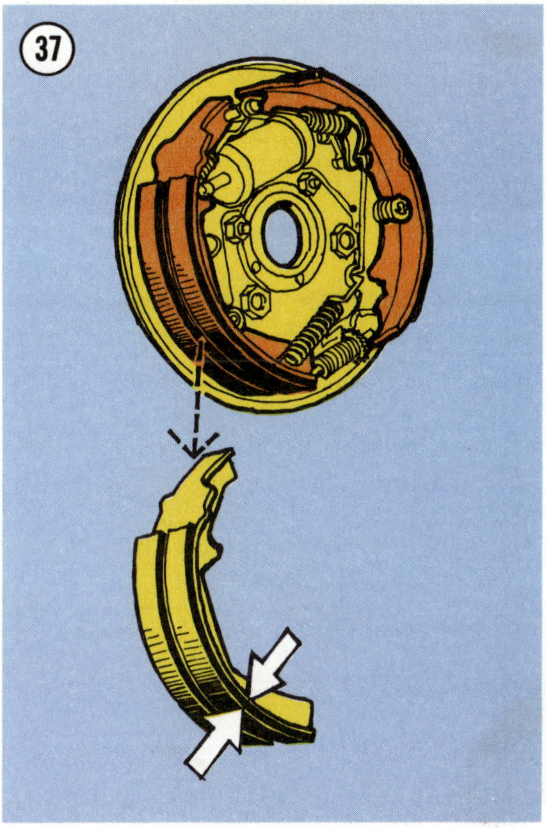

fied in Chapter Three will minimize problems with the brakes. Most importantly, check and maintain the level of fluid in the master cylinder, and check the thickness of the linings on the disc brake pads **(Figure 36)** or drum brake shoes **(Figure 37)**.

If trouble develops, **Figures 38 through 40** will help you locate the problem. Refer to the brake chapter for actual repair procedures.

STEERING AND SUSPENSION

Trouble in the suspension or steering is evident when the following occur:

a. Steering is hard
b. Car pulls to one side
c. Car wanders or front wheels wobble
d. Steering has excessive play
e. Tire wear is abnormal

Unusual steering, pulling, or wandering is usually caused by bent or otherwise misaligned suspension parts. This is difficult to check without proper alignment equipment. Refer to the suspension chapter in this book for repairs that you can perform and those that must be left to a dealer or suspension specialist.

If your trouble seems to be excessive play, check wheel bearing adjustment first. This is the most frequent cause. Then check ball-joints as described below. Finally, check tie rod end ball-joints by shaking each tie rod. Also check steering gear, or rack-and-pinion assembly to see that it is securely bolted down.

TIRE WEAR ANALYSIS

Abnormal tire wear should be analyzed to determine its causes. The most common causes are the following:

a. Incorrect tire pressure
b. Improper driving
c. Overloading
d. Bad road surfaces
e. Incorrect wheel alignment

38

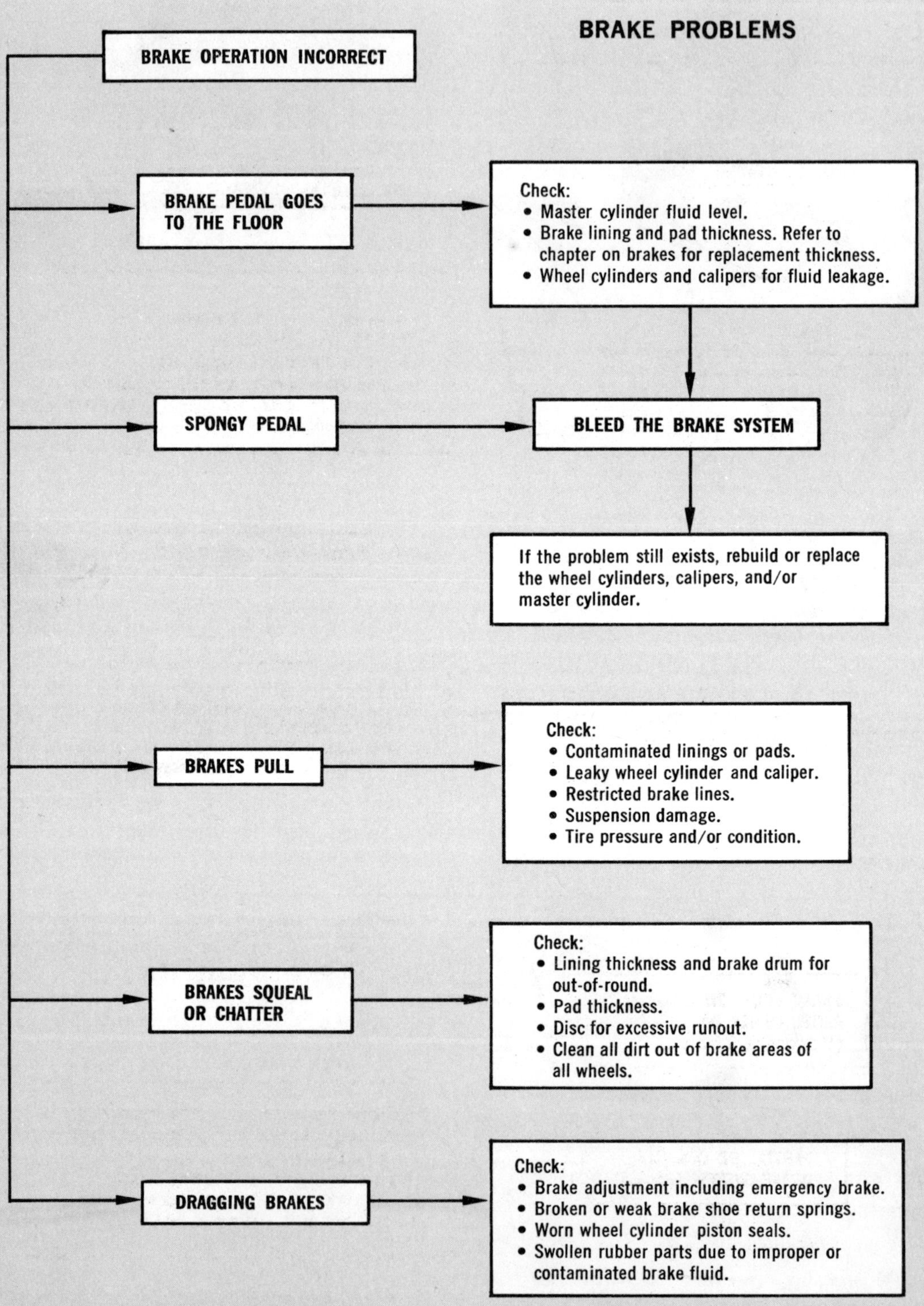
BRAKE PROBLEMS
BRAKE OPERATION INCORRECT
BRAKE PEDAL GOES TO THE FLOOR
Check:
• Master cylinder fluid level.
• Brake lining and pad thickness. Refer to chapter on brakes for replacement thickness.
• Wheel cylinders and calipers for fluid leakage.
SPONGY PEDAL
BLEED THE BRAKE SYSTEM
If the problem still exists, rebuild or replace the wheel cylinders, calipers, and/or master cylinder.
BRAKES PULL
Check:
• Contaminated linings or pads.
• Leaky wheel cylinder and caliper.
• Restricted brake lines.
• Suspension damage.
• Tire pressure and/or condition.
BRAKES SQUEAL OR CHATTER
Check:
• Lining thickness and brake drum for out-of-round.
• Pad thickness.
• Disc for excessive runout.
• Clean all dirt out of brake areas of all wheels.
DRAGGING BRAKES
Check:
• Brake adjustment including emergency brake.
• Broken or weak brake shoe return springs.
• Worn wheel cylinder piston seals.
• Swollen rubber parts due to improper or contaminated brake fluid.

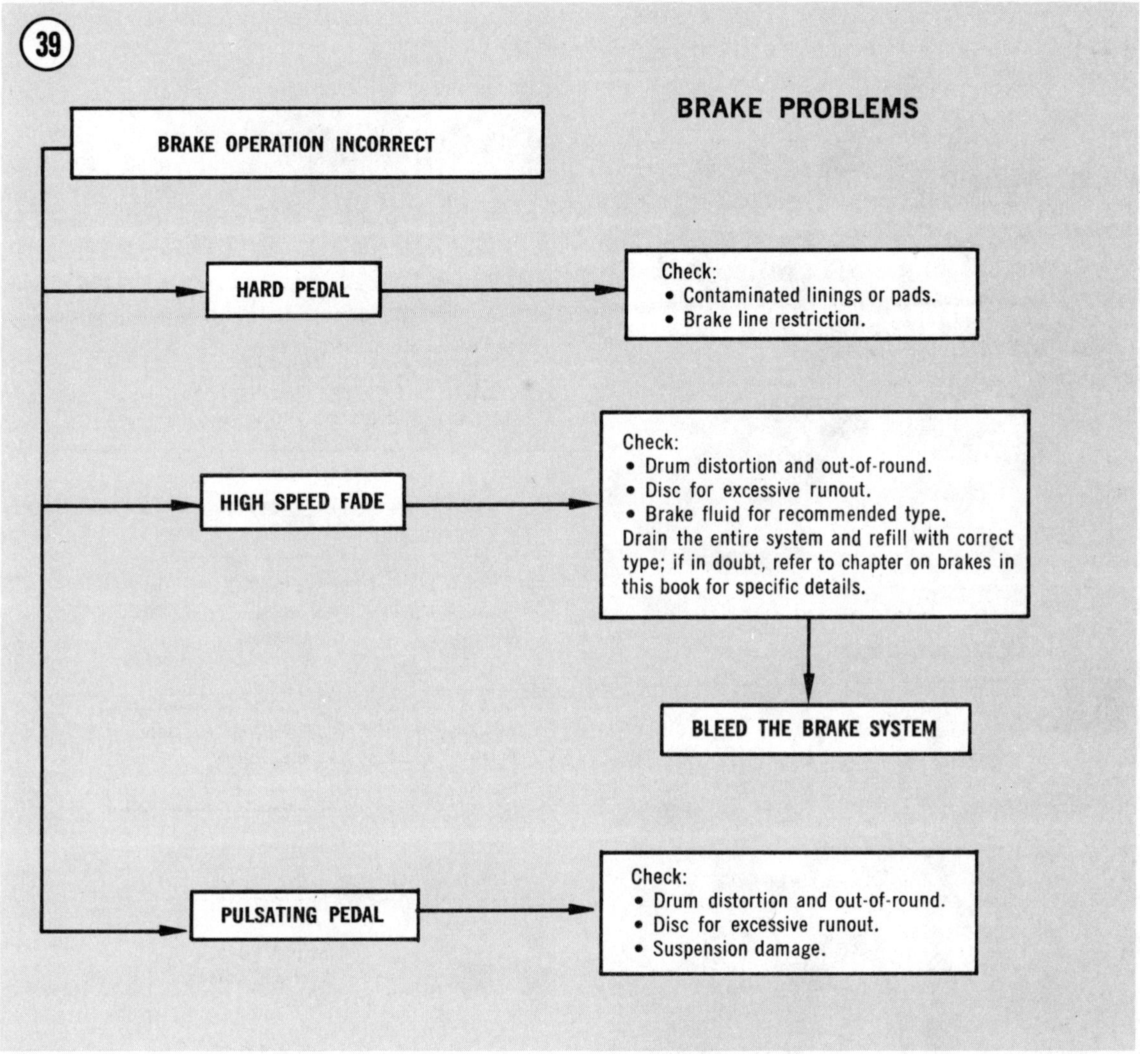
39
BRAKE PROBLEMS
BRAKE OPERATION INCORRECT
HARD PEDAL
Check:
• Contaminated linings or pads.
• Brake line restriction.
HIGH SPEED FADE
Check:
• Drum distortion and out-of-round.
• Disc for excessive runout.
• Brake fluid for recommended type.
Drain the entire system and refill with correct type; if in doubt, refer to chapter on brakes in this book for specific details.
BLEED THE BRAKE SYSTEM
PULSATING PEDAL
Check:
• Drum distortion and out-of-round.
• Disc for excessive runout.
• Suspension damage.

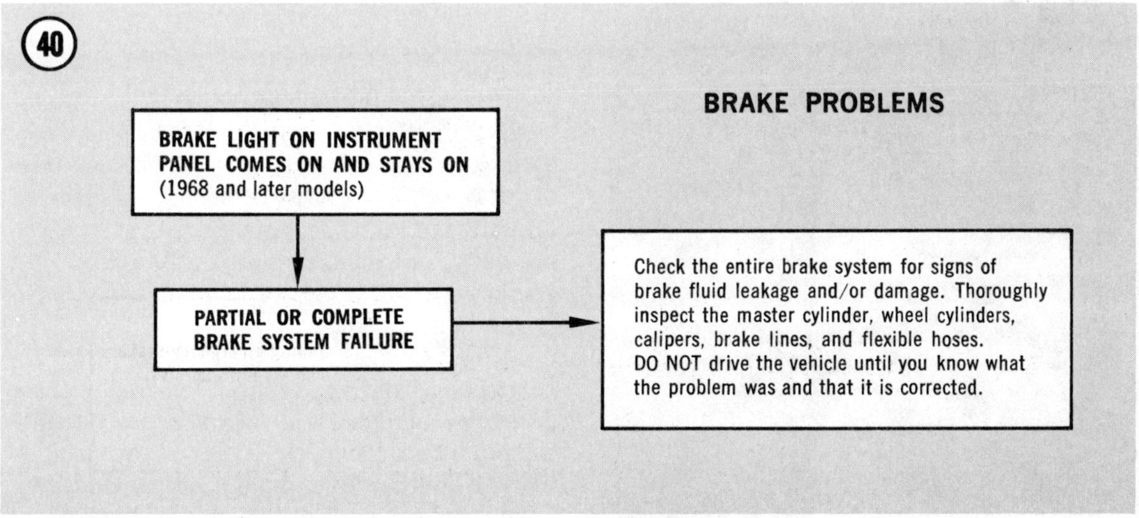
40
BRAKE PROBLEMS
BRAKE LIGHT ON INSTRUMENT PANEL COMES ON AND STAYS ON (1968 and later models)
PARTIAL OR COMPLETE BRAKE SYSTEM FAILURE
Check the entire brake system for signs of brake fluid leakage and/or damage. Thoroughly inspect the master cylinder, wheel cylinders, calipers, brake lines, and flexible hoses.
DO NOT drive the vehicle until you know what the problem was and that it is corrected.

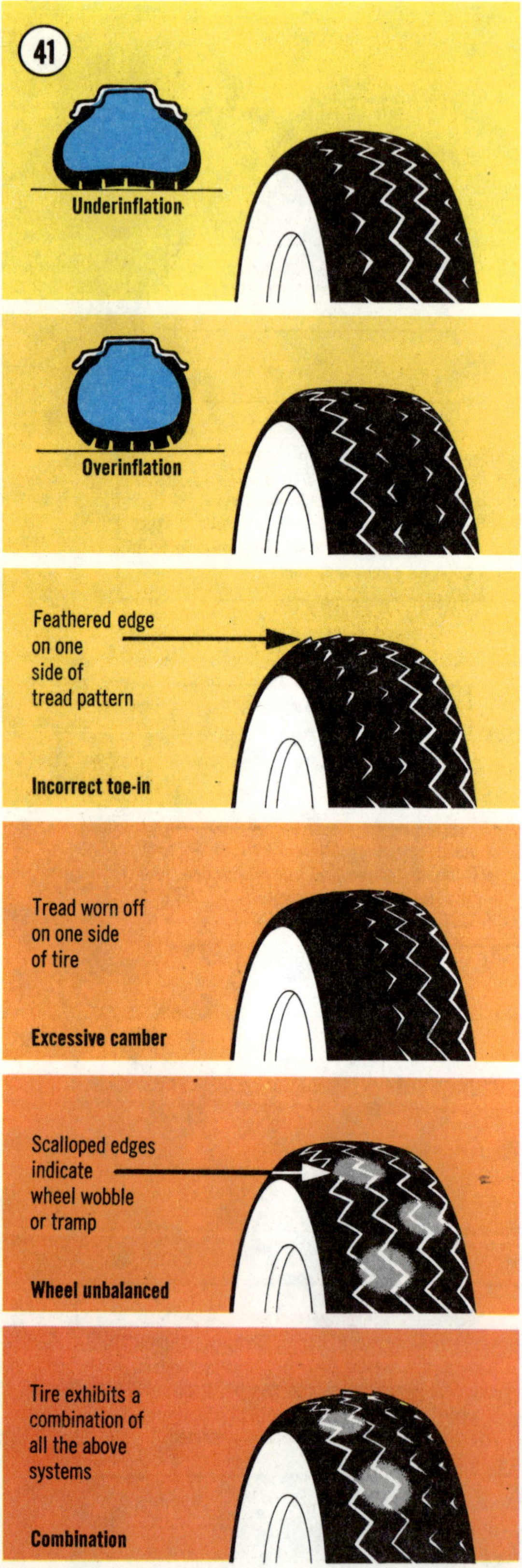

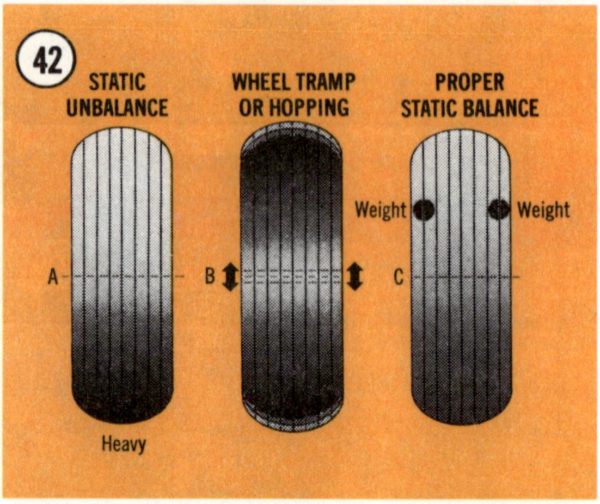

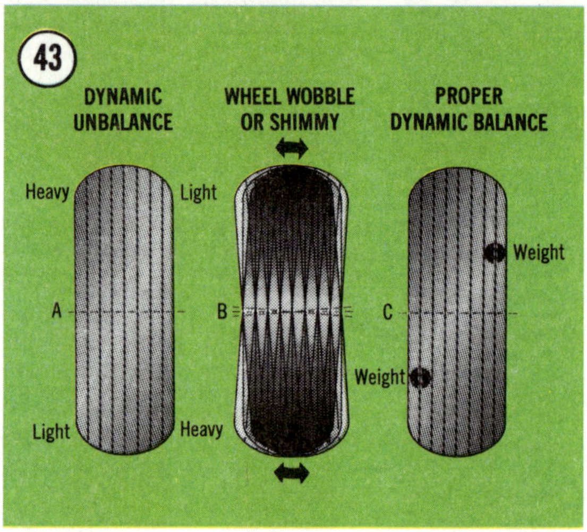

Figure 41 identifies wear patterns and indicates the most probable causes.

WHEEL BALANCING

All four wheels and tires must be in balance along two axes. To be in static balance **(Figure 42)**, weight must be evenly distributed around the axis of rotation. (A) shows a statically unbalanced wheel; (B) shows the result — wheel tramp or hopping; (C) shows proper static balance.

To be in dynamic balance **(Figure 43)**, the centerline of the weight must coincide with the centerline of the wheel. (A) shows a dynamically unbalanced wheel; (B) shows the result — wheel wobble or shimmy; (C) shows proper dynamic balance.

CHAPTER THREE

3

LUBRICATION, MAINTENANCE, AND TUNE-UP

To ensure good performance, dependability, and safety, regular preventive maintenance is necessary. This chapter outlines periodic lubrication and maintenance for a car driven by an average owner. A car driven more than average may require more frequent attention, but even without use, rust, dirt, and corrosion cause unnecessary damage. Whether performed by the owner or a dealer, regular routine attention helps avoid expensive repairs.

The recommended schedule in this chapter includes routine checks which are easily performed at each fuel stop, periodic checks to be performed at each oil change, and periodic maintenance to prevent future trouble. The last part of this chapter suggests a systematic engine tune-up procedure which simplifies this important task. **Table 1** summarizes all periodic maintenance required in an easy-to-use form.

ROUTINE CHECKS

The following simple checks should be performed at each fueling stop.

1. *Check engine oil*—Oil should be checked with the engine warm and on level ground. Level should be between the 2 marks on the dipstick; never above or never below. Top up if necessary.

2. *Check battery electrolyte level*—If it is below the indicator, fill it with distilled water only up to the indicator.

3. *Check brake fluid level*—It must be between the minimum and maximum marks. See **Figure 1**. Top up if necessary with brake fluid clearly marked SAE 1703, DOT 3, or DOT 4 only.

4. *Check drive belt tension* and condition for the alternator, air compressor, and air injection pump. Tension is correct when the belt can be depressed 3/8-9/16 in. (10-15mm) under slight thumb pressure. See **Figure 2**.

a = 3/8 - 9/16 in. (10-15mm)

5. *Check tire pressure* when the tires are cold. See **Table 2**.

6. *Check windshield washer container level.*

7. *Check coolant level.* This check should be made when the engine is cold. Level should be between the minimum (cold) and maximum (warm) marks in the expansion tank.

> NOTE: *The expansion tank is externally located on 1975 models and is built into the radiator on 1976 and later models.*

PERIODIC CHECKS

These checks are performed less frequently than routine checks. Recommended intervals are discussed below and are summarized in Table 1. Many require that the automobile be on a hoist or jackstands.

> WARNING
> *Do not use the tire jack when working under the car. Use only jackstands made specifically for this purpose.*

Air Pump Drive Belt

On models equipped with air injection pumps, check drive belt tension and condition frequently. When tension is correct the belt should deflect about 3/8-9/16 in. (10-15mm) under light thumb pressure.

To adjust or replace a belt, loosen the 2 bolts shown in **Figure 3**. Push down on pump to relieve belt tension and remove old belt. Install

Table 1 MAINTENANCE SUMMARY

Every 5,000 miles or 6 months (1975)
Change engine oil
Every 7,500 miles or 6 months (1976-on)
Change engine oil
Change oil filter[2]
Every 15,000 miles or 12 months
Replace engine oil filter[1]
Replace spark plugs[1]
Adjust valve clearance
Replace breaker points[1]
Adjust timing[1]
Check compression
Check tension and condition of belts
Check EGR system visually[1]
Clean PCV valve[1]
Check exhaust system
Clean air filter element
Replace EGR air filter element[1]
Check clutch adjustment
Check engine idle speed
Check CO content of exhaust[1]
Check ATF level in automatic
Check charcoal filter and hoses for damage[1]
Check injection pump timing[2]
Replace injector heat shields[2]
Check oil pump drive gear[2]
Replace fuel filter and bleed fuel system[2]
Check radiator and heating/cooling systems
Every 30,000 miles
Replace catalytic converter[1]
Replace air filter element
Change automatic transmission fluid
Fuel filter (1976 and later)[1]
Every 45,000 miles
Replace spur belt[2]

1. Gasoline engines only
2. Diesel engines only

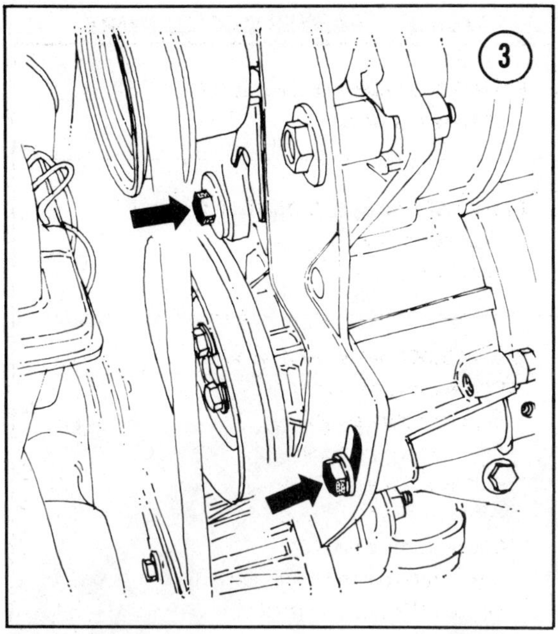
3

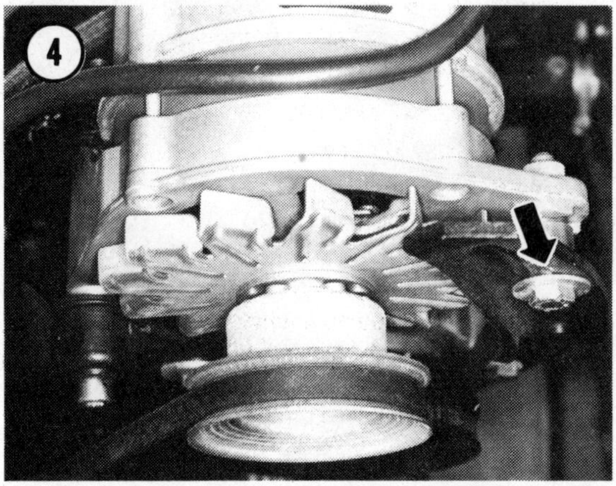
4

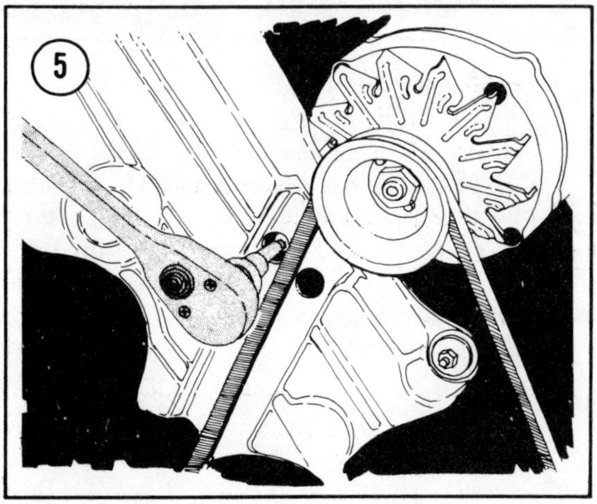
5

Table 2 TIRE PRESSURES

	145-13, 155-13 155 SR 13 Front	145-13, 155-13 155 SR 13 Rear	175/70 SR 13 Front	175/70 SR 13 Rear
Partial load	27	27	27	27
Fully loaded	27	27	27	27[1]

NOTE: Add 3 psi front and rear for sustained high-speed driving.
1. 31 psi on 1977 and later.

a new one. Pull up on the pump and tighten the bolts when tension is correct.

Alternator Drive Belt

Since drive belt tension and condition affect battery charging, it is important to check it frequently. When correct, the belt should deflect about 3/8-9/16 in. (10-15mm) under light thumb pressure. See Figure 2. Check condition of the belt also; if worn or cracked, replace it.

To adjust or replace a belt, loosen adjusting bolt shown in **Figure 4** and also the alternator mounting bolt, accessible through the timing belt cover. See **Figure 5**. If installing a new belt, move the alternator as far to the right as possible and slip the old belt off the pulleys. Install a new belt. Tighten by moving alternator to the right.

Belt tension is adjusted by pushing the alternator to the right until the belt can be deflected as described earlier. Tighten the bolts in this position.

Compression Check

Every 15,000 miles, check cylinder compression. The procedure is fully described in Chapter Three for gasoline engines and later in this chapter for diesel engines (see *Diesel Checks and Adjustments*). Record the results and compare them at the next 15,000-mile check. A running record will show trends in deterioration so that corrective action can be taken before complete failure.

Engine Compartment Check

Every 15,000 miles, check entire engine compartment for leaking or deteriorated oil and

Table 3 EXHAUST EMISSION LEVELS (GASOLINE ENGINES)

Carbon Monoxide (CO)		Idle RPM	Ignition Timing
1975	2.0 ± 0.5%[1] by volume	925 ± 75	3°ATDC
1976	1.5 ± 0.7%[1] by volume[2]	925 ± 75	3°ATDC
1977 and later	1.5% maximum[3 4 5]	925 ± 75	3°ATDC

1. Air pump disconnected, transmission in neutral, measured ahead of catalytic converter.
2. 1.0 ± 0.7% by volume for cars equipped with automatic transmission.
3. 0.3% maximum for all cars first sold in California, measured at tailpipe.
4. 1.0% maximum for 49 states models with automatic transmissions. For 1978 models equipped with 34 PICT-5 carburetors adjust to 1.5 ± 0.7%.
5. 0.5-0.9% for 1979 Scirocco first sold in California.

fuel lines. Check electrical wiring for breaks in insulation caused by deterioration or chafe. Check for loose or missing bolts, nuts, and screws.

Exhaust Emission Control Check (Gasoline Engines)

After every engine tune-up (see later section), check carbon monoxide (CO) content of exhaust gas. Use a good quality exhaust gas analyzer following the manufacturer's instructions. With engine idling, CO content should be within values shown in **Table 3**, measured ahead of the catalytic converter. See Chapter Five for procedure.

Steering and Suspension

Every 15,000 miles, check entire steering and suspension systems. Check ball-joint and tie rod end dust seals. Check tie rods for tightness and damage. Check tire wear which may indicate damaged or worn suspension parts. Check shock absorbers for oil streaks indicating leaks; replace if necessary.

Jack up the front wheels. Move front wheels by hand. The steering wheel should turn as soon as the wheels turn; there should be no free play.

Automatic Transmission Check

Every 15,000 miles, check the automatic transmission fluid level. The transmission must be thoroughly warmed up, the engine idling, selector in NEUTRAL, and the parking brake applied. Pull out the dipstick, wipe it with a clean cloth and reinsert the dipstick. Pull the dipstick

out again and check that the level is between the 2 marks. If necessary, add fluid but do not overfill. If level is above the top mark, fluid must be drained to restore proper level or seals may be damaged.

Check fluid in final drive as described under *Manual Transaxle and Final Drive Check*.

Manual Transaxle and Final Drive Check

Every 15,000 miles, check oil level in transaxle. To do this, remove filler plug **(Figure 6)** and make sure that oil level reaches to the bottom of the hole. If the level is low, top up with gear oil recommended in **Table 4**.

Wheel Bearings

Every 15,000 miles, check rear wheel bearing adjustment as described in Chapter Eleven. Ball

Table 4 RECOMMENDED LUBRICANTS AND FUEL

	Temperature Range	Recommended Type	Capacity
Engine oil (gasoline engines)[1]			
Single grade oil	Above +68°F	SAE 40	3.2 quarts*
	+32° to +78°F	SAE 30	
	+15° to +50°F	SAE 20W20	
	−5° to +25°F	SAE 10W	
Multi-grade oil	+15° to +80°F	SAE 20W40	
		SAE20W50	
	−5° to +50°F	SAE 10W30	
		SAE 10W40	
	Consistently below +15°F	SAE 5W20	
Manual transaxle	All temperatures	SAE 80 (MIL-L-2105)	1.3 quarts
Automatic final drive	All temperatures	SAE 90 (MIL-L-2105B)	0.8 quarts
Automatic transaxle	All temperatures	ATF (DEXRON)	6.4 quarts (dry) 3.2 quarts (refill)
Fuel	All temperatures	91 octane, unleaded	9.5 gal.

*Add 1 pint for filter change.
1. Use only engine oil marked "Service API/SE"

bearings are used on the front wheels and do not require adjustment.

Disc Brakes

Every 10,000 miles, check brake pad thickness. Brake pads should be replaced if thickness is less than 0.08 in. (2mm). If necessary, replace all 4 pads to keep pads balanced. Never replace pads on one wheel only.

> NOTE: *Front wheel disc brake pads on Rabbits with automatic transmissions and on all Scirocco models have wear indicators that cause the brake pedal to pulsate when the pads need changing.*

Drum Brakes

Every 10,000 miles, remove the wheels and brake drums as described in Chapter Nine and check the brake shoes. Replace the riveted linings if worn to less than 0.10 in. (2.5mm) thick or if soaked with oil or brake fluid. Replace bonded linings if worn to less than 0.06 in. (1.5mm).

Windshield Wiper Blades

Long exposure to weather and road film hardens the rubber wiper blades and destroys their effectiveness. When blades smear or otherwise fail to clean the windshield, they should be replaced.

Tire and Wheel Inspection

Every 15,000 miles, check the condition of all tires. Check local traffic regulations concerning minimum tread depth. Most recommend replacing tires when tread depth is less than $\frac{1}{32}$ in. Original equipment tires have tread wear indicators molded into the bottom of the tread grooves. Tread wear indicators appear as $\frac{1}{2}$ in. bands (**Figure 7**) when tread depth becomes $\frac{1}{16}$ in. Tires should be replaced at this point.

Check lug nuts for tightness.

Clutch

Every 10,000 miles, check pedal free play on manual shift cars. See **Figure 8**. Depress pedal by hand. Free play should be about $\frac{5}{8}$ in. (15mm). See Chapter Eight for adjustment.

Exhaust System

Every 10,000 miles, examine the mufflers, tailpipes, and exhaust header for rust, holes, and other damage. Replace any damaged parts.

3

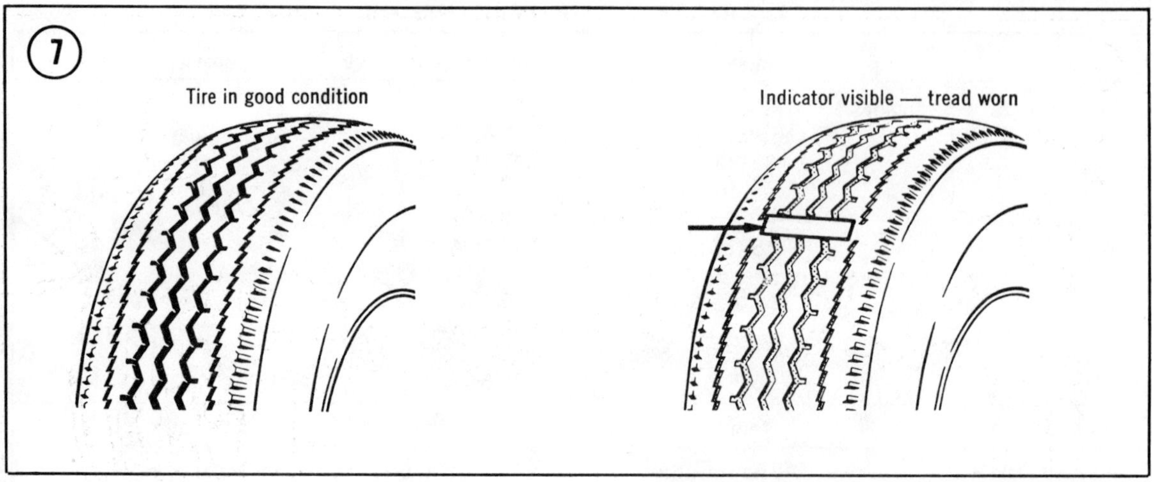

PERIODIC MAINTENANCE

Engine Oil Change

The oil change interval varies depending on the type of driving you do. For normal driving, including some city traffic, change the oil every 5,000 miles (7,500 miles for diesel engines). If driving is primarily short distance, with considerable stop-and-go traffic, change oil more frequently. Change oil at least twice a year if the car is driven only a few hundred miles a month.

Any oil used in gasoline engines must be rated "For API Service SD or SE." Non-detergent oils are not recommended. Refer to Table 4 for recommended oil grades. See Table 6 for diesel engine recommendations.

To drain oil:

1. Warm engine to operating temperature.
2. Remove drain plug from crankcase. See **Figure 9**.
3. Let oil drain for at least 10 minutes.
4. Install oil drain plug.
5. Change oil filter. See procedure below.
6. Remove oil filler cap. See **Figure 10**. Refill with 3.7 U.S. quarts (3.5 liters).
7. Check level on dipstick.
8. Install oil filler cap.

Engine Oil Filter

Every 15,000 miles, replace the oil filter. This should be done after oil is drained, and before new oil is poured in.

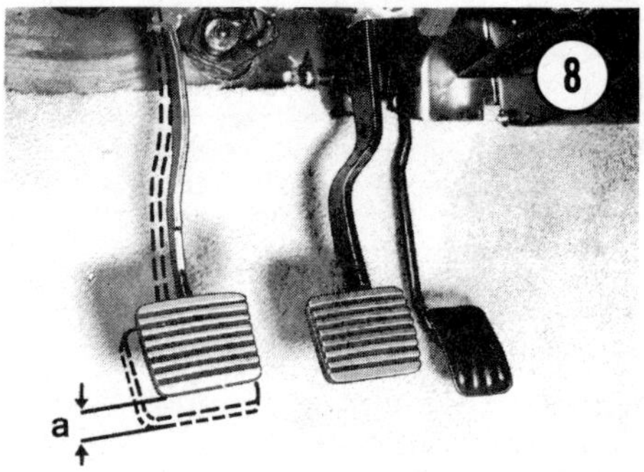

To remove the filter, unscrew it by hand or use a filter wrench. See **Figure 11**. Wipe the gasket at the base with a clean, lint-free cloth. Coat the neoprene gasket on the new filter with clean oil. Screw the filter on by hand until the gasket just touches the base. Then tighten ½ turn by hand; do not use a filter wrench.

After adding engine oil, start the engine and check for leaks. Also check the oil level and adjust if necessary.

The specified filter is VW 056-115-561B. Substitutes include FRAM PH-2870 and Lee LF-213FC.

EGR System (Gasoline Engines)

Every 15,000 miles, check the entire EGR system visually. See Chapter Five for a description of the system. Make sure connecting hoses are attached and in good condition. In addition, replace the EGR air filter element on 1975 models. To do this:

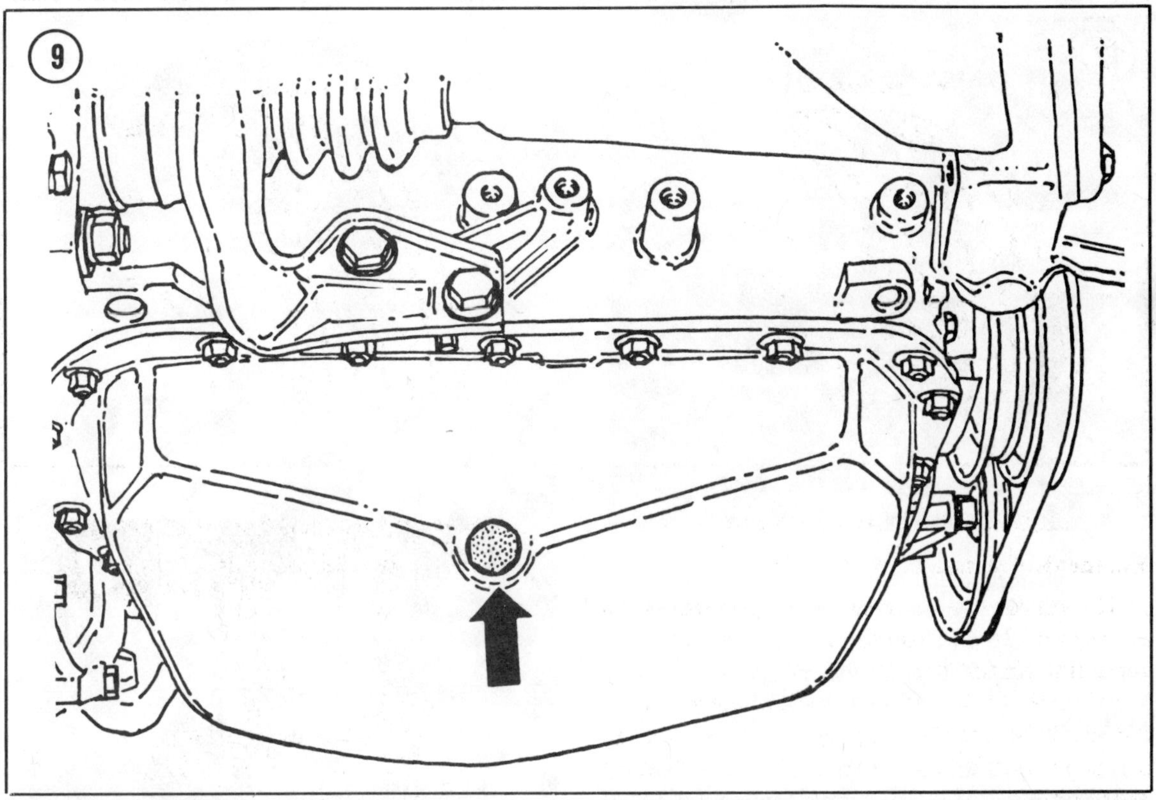

1. Locate the air filter which is behind the radiator near the engine oil filter.
2. Remove wing nut on bottom of air filter.
3. Remove old element and install new one.
4. Tighten wing nut.

NOTE: *1976 and later cars are not equipped with* EGR *filters.*

PCV System

Every 15,000 miles, remove the PCV valve on 1975 models and clean it in solvent. Blow dry and install valve. See **Figure 12**.

NOTE: *On 1976 and later models the* PCV *valve was replaced with a deflector in the air intake elbow **(Figure 13)** and a*

*7mm (approximately) restrictor in the connection hose (**Figure 14**). These elements should be cleaned when the air cleaner is serviced (see below).*

Air Cleaner

Every 15,000 miles, remove and clean the air cleaner element. In very dusty areas, clean filter element frequently, even daily if necessary.

Replace the element every 15,000 miles on fuel injection models.

Every 30,000 miles (more frequently if the vehicle is driven in very dusty areas), replace the filter element on carburetted and diesel models.

To clean the filter element, release the 4 clips and remove the cover. See **Figure 15**. Remove the filter element and thoroughly clean the inside of the air cleaner housing with a lightly oiled lint-free cloth. Tap the filter lightly against your hand to shake dirt out. Under no circumstances may the filter element be cleaned or soaked with gasoline, solvents, or oil.

Automatic Transmission

Every 30,000 miles, drain and replace the automatic transmision fluid (ATF) on models in normal use. If the vehicle is driven under severe operating conditions such as trailer towing, constant stop-and-go traffic, continuous mountain driving, or driving in very high temperatures, the ATF should be changed every 15,000 miles. If in doubt, consult with the dealer in your area.

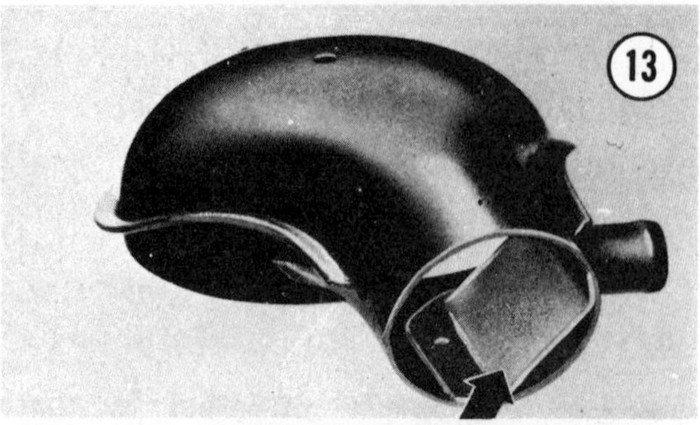

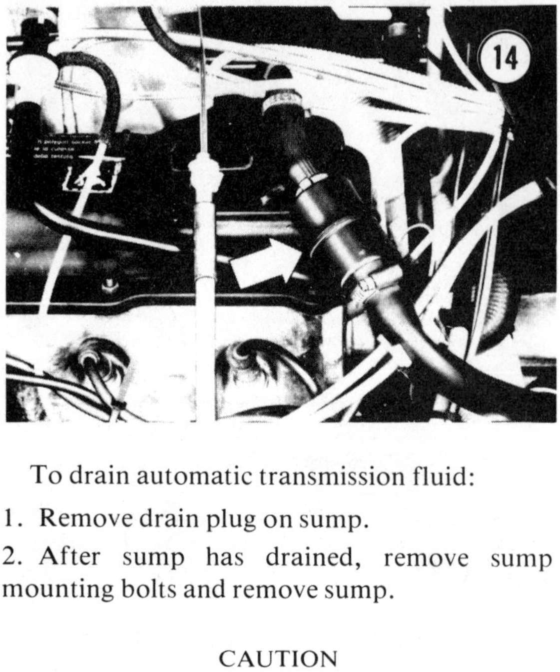

To drain automatic transmission fluid:

1. Remove drain plug on sump.
2. After sump has drained, remove sump mounting bolts and remove sump.

CAUTION

Do not remove sump if you must work outdoors. Cleanliness is very important when working with an automatic transmission. Blowing dust can settle on internal transmission parts and cause serious damage. Let your dealer or local repair shop change the oil if you don't have access to a clean garage.

3. Clean sump thoroughly with solvent and wipe dry.
4. Install sump with new gasket. Torque mounting bolts to 14 ft.-lb. (2 mkg). After 5-10 miles, retorque bolts, as the gasket will settle.

CAUTION

Do not start the engine or move the vehicle with the ATF drained.

6. Pour in 5 U.S. pints of ATF through the dipstick opening.

7. Start engine and shift transmission lever through all positions several times.

8. Check ATF level with dipstick. The ATF level should reach the tip of the dipstick. If not, add ATF until the level just reaches the tip.

9. After a short test drive, fill the transmission with ATF until the level is between the marks on the dipstick. Do not overfill. Excess ATF must be drained.

10. Retorque the sump mounting bolts once again to 7 ft.-lb. (1 mkg).

Catalytic Converter (Gasoline Engines)

Every 30,000 miles, replace the catalytic converter with a new one. See the procedure in Chapter Five.

Brake Fluid

Every 2 years, drain and replace brake fluid. To do this:

1. Siphon brake fluid from reservoir with a siphon used exclusively for brake fluid.

2. Connect a drain hose to each bleeder valve. Open the valves one at a time and have an assistant pump the brake pedal until no more brake fluid emerges. Catch the brake fluid in a container and then discard it.

3. Fill reservoir with new, unused brake fluid which is clearly marked SAE J1703, DOT 3, or DOT 4 only.

4. Bleed brakes in the sequence described in Chapter Nine.

Fuel Filter

All gasoline-powered Rabbits after Chassis No. 175 3 394 505 and all Sciroccos after Chassis No. 535 2 052 618 are equipped with a replaceable inline fuel filter (**Figure 16**). This filter can be installed on earlier models, if desired. The filter should be changed every 30,000 miles (15,000 miles on fuel injection models), or more often if required. When installing filter, be sure arrow points in direction of fuel flow (Figure 16).

See *Diesel Engine Maintenance*, later in this chapter, for diesel fuel filter maintenance.

ENGINE TUNE-UP (GASOLINE ENGINE)

In order to maintain a car in perfect running condition, the engine must receive periodic tune-ups. The procedures outlined here are performed every 15,000 miles. **Table 5** summarizes tune-up specifications. Since different systems in an engine interact to affect overall performance, tune-up must be accomplished in the following order:

a. Valve clearance adjustment
b. Ignition adjustment and timing
c. Fuel system adjustment

Valve Adjustment

Valve clearance for your engine must be carefully determined while the engine is warm

Table 5 TUNE-UP SPECIFICATIONS

Valve clearance[1]	
Intake	0.008-0.012 in. (0.20-0.30mm)
Exhaust	0.016-0.020 in. (0.40-0.50mm)
Ignition timing	3° ATDC[2] @ 925 ± 75 rpm
Spark plug type	
Carburetted engine	Bosch W200T30; Beru 200/14/3A1
Full injected engine	Bosch W175T30; Beru 175/14/3A
Spark plug gap	0.024-0.028 in. (0.6-0.7mm)
Breaker point gap	0.016 in. (0.4mm)
Dwell angle	47 ± 3°
Firing order	1-3-4-2
Idle speed	925 ± 75 rpm (diesel: 820 ± 50 rpm)

1. Warm engine, subtract 0.002 in. (0.05mm) for cold engine.
2. Vacuum advance disconnected. On special FX engine, set timing to 7.5° BTDC with vacuum hose connected.

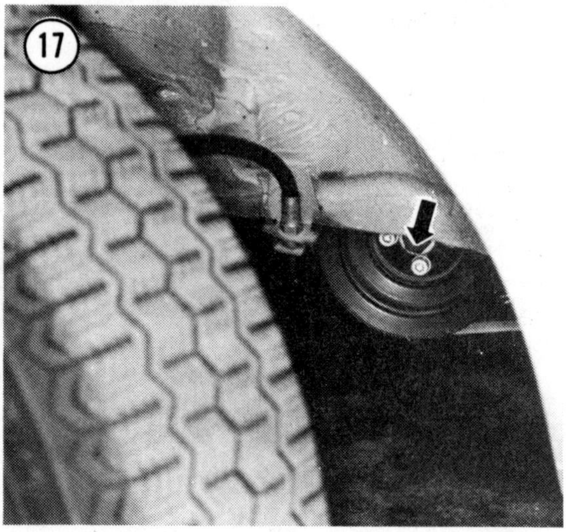
17

(95°F coolant temperature). If the clearance is too small, the valves may be burned or distorted. Large clearance results in excessive noise. In either case, engine power is reduced.

Before adjusting valves, remove valve cover and all spark plugs. This makes the engine much easier to turn by hand; plugs require replacement at this time anyway.

> NOTE: *After cylinder head repairs, the valve adjustment should be rechecked after 600 miles. Readjust if necessary.*

To adjust valve clearance:

1. Turn crankshaft with socket wrench (**Figure 17**) until the cam lobes for cylinder No. 1 no

18

longer rest on the tappets, i.e., intake and exhaust valve for cylinder No. 1 are closed.

2. Insert feeler gauge between cam lobes and tappets (**Figure 18**) and measure clearance very carefully. Quickly write measured clearance on piece of paper or on cylinder head with felt tip marker or crayon.

3. Turn crankshaft until intake and exhaust valves for cylinder No. 3 are closed. Measure and record valve clearance as in Step 2, above.

4. Rotate crankshaft as necessary to measure valve clearance for cylinder No. 4, then cylinder No. 2, in the same manner.

5. For each valve, subtract measured clearance from specified clearance. If difference is less than 0.002 in. (0.05mm), no adjustment is necessary. If difference is greater than this, replace

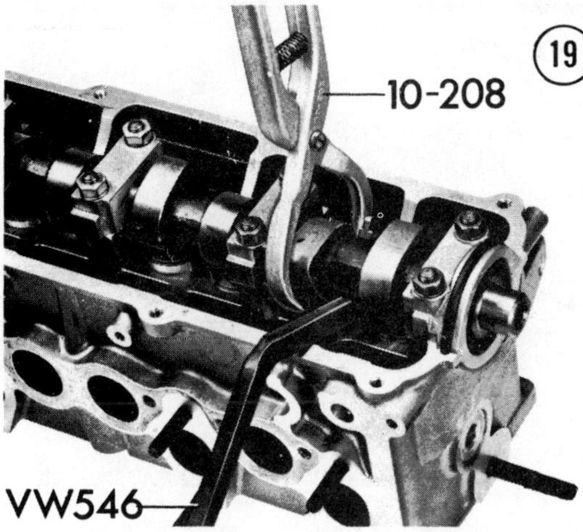

Table 6 TAPPET DISCS

Thickness, mm	Part No.
3.00	056 109 555
3.05	056 109 556
3.10	056 109 557
3.15	056 109 558
3.20	056 109 559
3.25	056 109 560
3.30	056 109 561
3.35	056 109 562
3.40	056 109 563
3.45	056 109 564
3.50	056 109 565
3.55	056 109 566
3.60	056 109 567
3.65	056 109 568
3.70	056 109 569
3.75	056 109 570
3.80	056 109 571
3.85	056 109 572
3.90	056 109 573
3.95	056 109 574
4.00	056 109 575
4.05	056 109 576
4.10	056 109 577
4.15	056 109 578
4.20	056 109 579
4.25	056 109 580

tappet clearance disc with a different one to bring clearance within specifications.

Here is an example to determine which size clearance disc must be installed. Suppose that measured clearance for exhaust valve is 0.0118

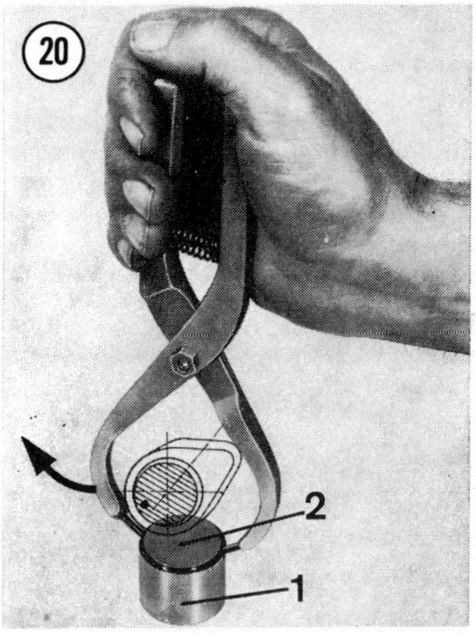

1. Tappet 2. Tappet clearance disc

in. (0.299mm). Subtracting this from the specified clearance, 0.0156 in. (0.396mm), yields a difference of 0.004 in. (0.1mm). Since this difference is greater than 0.002 in. (0.05mm), a smaller tappet clearance disc is required. If the present disc is 4.05mm thick, replace it with a new disc 3.95mm thick, i.e., 0.1mm thinner. **Table 6** shows tappet clearance discs available.

CAUTION

Special tools are required to change the tappet discs. Due to the possibility of damage, improvised tools are not recommended. Your dealer can order special tools 10-208 and VW546 for you.

To change tappet clearance discs:

1. Press valve tappet down with VW546 as shown in **Figure 19**.
2. Engage tool 10-208 in tappet openings. See Figure 19 and **Figure 20**.
3. Lift the clearance disc up with tool 10-208. Rotate it around the camshaft and out.

NOTE: *It will probably be necessary to rotate the tappets after depressing them so that their openings are at right angles to the camshaft.*

4. Installation is the reverse of these steps.

3

(21)

SPARK PLUG CONDITION

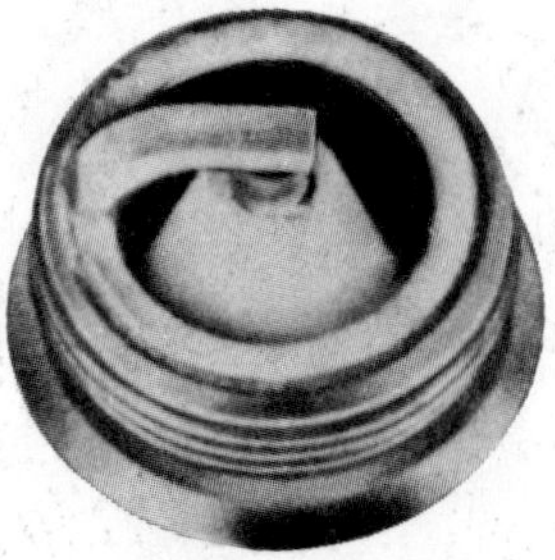

NORMAL

- Identified by light tan or gray deposits on the firing tip.
- Can be cleaned.

GAP BRIDGED

- Identified by deposit buildup closing gap between electrodes.
- Caused by oil or carbon fouling. If deposits are not excessive, the plug can be cleaned.

OIL FOULED

- Identified by wet black deposits on the insulator shell bore electrodes.
- Caused by excessive oil entering combustion chamber through worn rings and pistons, excessive clearance between valve guides and stems, or worn or loose bearings. Can be cleaned. If engine is not repaired, use a hotter plug.

CARBON FOULED

- Identified by black, dry fluffy carbon deposits on insulator tips, exposed shell surfaces and electrodes.
- Caused by too cold a plug, weak ignition, dirty air cleaner, defective fuel pump, too rich a fuel mixture, improperly operating heat riser, or excessive idling. Can be cleaned.

LEAD FOULED

- Identified by dark gray, black, yellow, or tan deposits or a fused glazed coating on the insulator tip.
- Caused by highly leaded gasoline. Can be cleaned.

WORN

- Identified by severely eroded or worn electrodes.
- Caused by normal wear. Should be replaced.

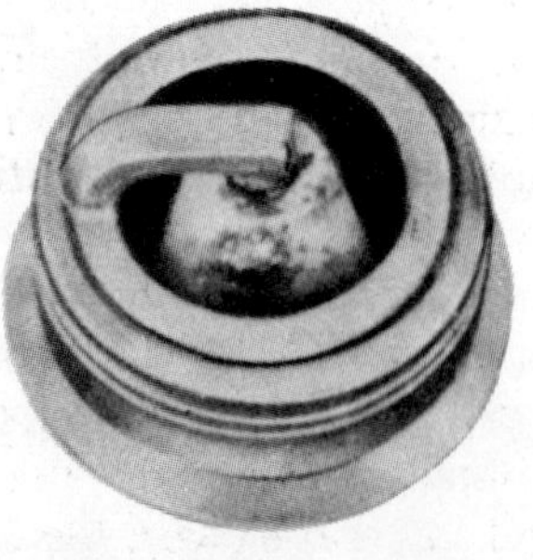

FUSED SPOT DEPOSIT

- Identified by melted or spotty deposits resembling bubbles or blisters.
- Caused by sudden acceleration. Can be cleaned.

OVERHEATING

- Identified by a white or light gray insulator with small black or gray brown spots and with bluish-burnt appearance of electrodes.
- Caused by engine overheating, wrong type of fuel, loose spark plugs, too hot a plug, low fuel pump pressure, or incorrect ignition timing. Replace the plug.

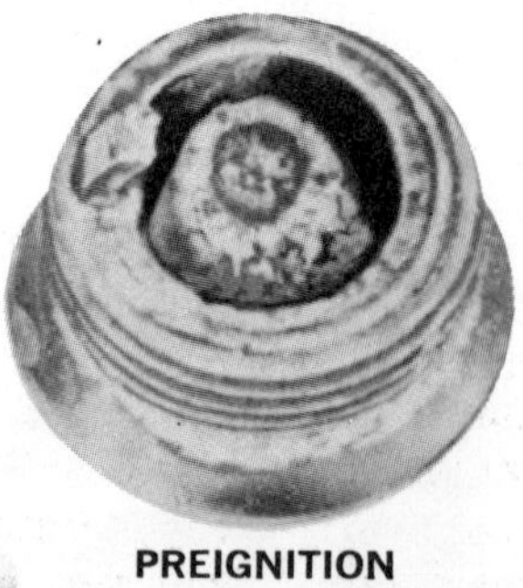

PREIGNITION

- Identified by melted electrodes and possibly blistered insulator. Metallic deposits on insulator indicate engine damage.
- Caused by wrong type of fuel, incorrect ignition timing or advance, too hot a plug, burned valves, or engine overheating. Replace the plug.

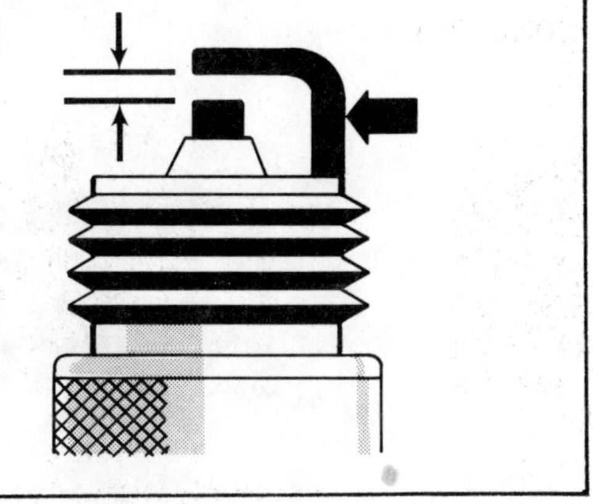

22

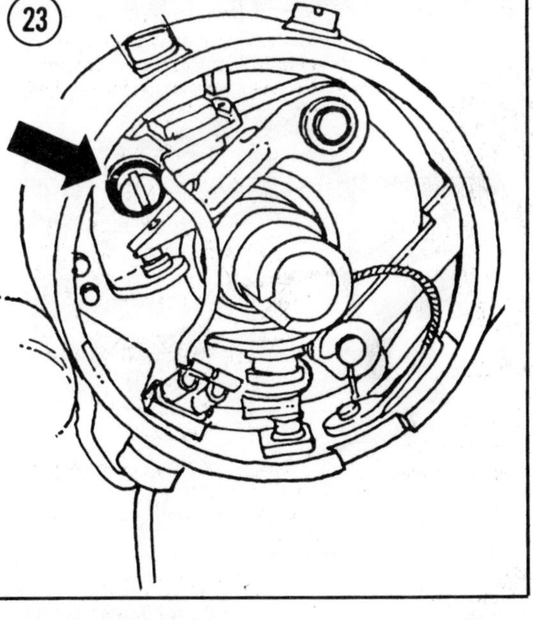

23

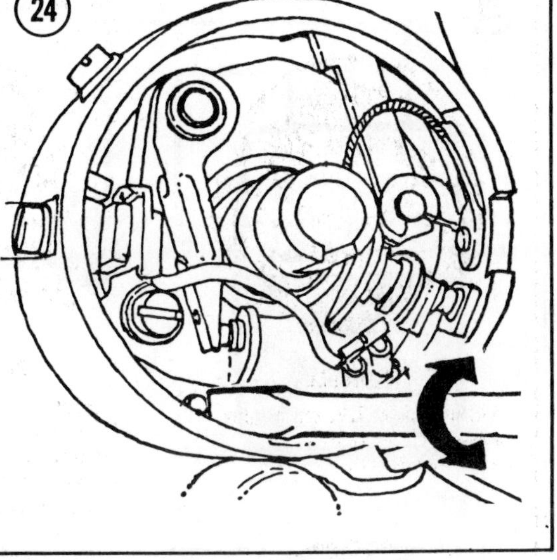

24

Spark Plug Replacement

Once valve clearance is properly adjusted, work on the ignition system. Examine the spark plugs and compare their appearance with **Figure 21**. Electrode appearance is a good indication of performance in each cylinder and permits early recognition of trouble. Remove plugs in order. That way, you will know which cylinder is malfunctioning should such be the case. Gap new plugs to 0.023-0.031 in. (0.6-0.8mm). See **Figure 22**. Use a wire type feeler gauge. Bend negative electrode as necessary to adjust gap. Apply a drop of engine oil to the threads of each spark plug. Install the plugs and torque to 22 ft.-lb. (3 mkg).

Breaker Point Replacement

Every 15,000 miles, replace the breaker points and condenser. Remove distributor cap and rotor. Remove screw securing points. See **Figure 23**. Remove old points and install new points. Turn crankshaft until a distributor cam lobe opens the contacts fully. Loosen retaining screw, insert a 0.016 in. (0.4mm) feeler gauge. Move fixed contact base with a screwdriver as shown in **Figure 24** to set point gap. Tighten screw. Install rotor in distributor cap.

More accurate measurement of breaker point gap is possible by measuring dwell angle. To measure the dwell angle, connect a dwell meter to the engine, following the manufacturer's instructions. Start the engine and allow it to warm up, then read the dwell angle from the meter while the engine is idling at 1,000 rpm. Dwell angle should be 44-50 degrees. If adjustment is required, stop the engine, remove the distributor cap, the rotor, and the shield plate. Use a screwdriver to adjust the points as described above. Widen the gap to decrease, or narrow the gap to increase, the angle. Replace the plate, rotor, and cap and recheck the dwell angle. Repeat as required until dwell is within specification. Increase engine speed to 2,000 rpm and recheck dwell. If it varies more than one degree from the measurement made at 1,000 rpm, the distributor is worn and should be replaced.

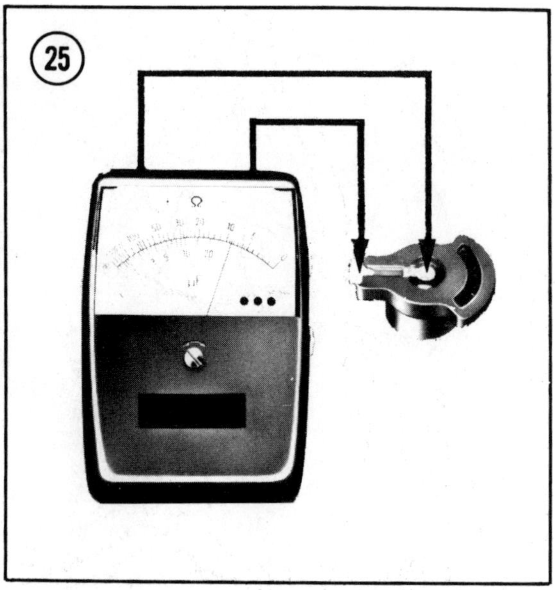

25

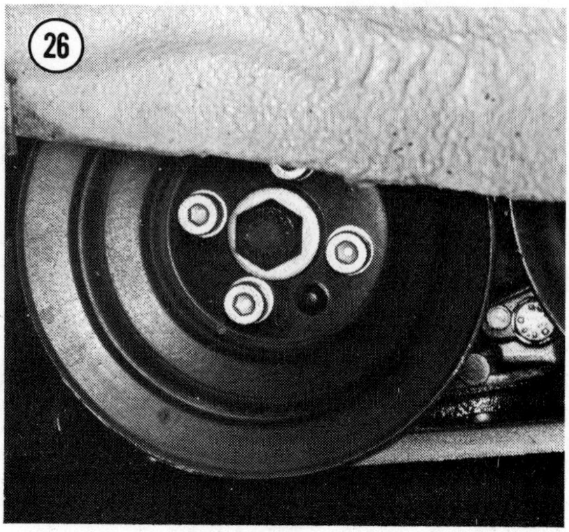

26

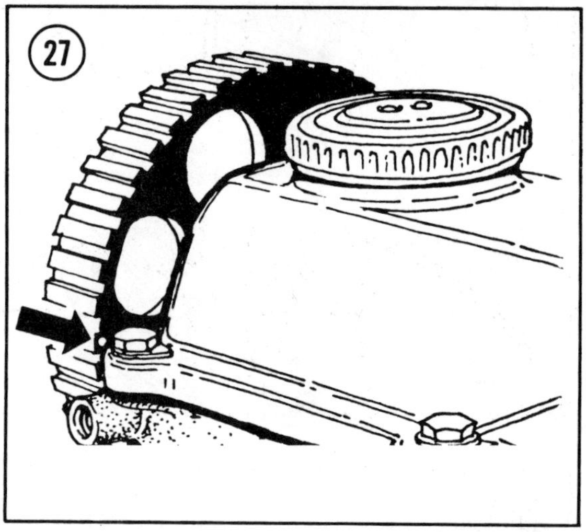

27

Rotor and Distributor Cap

As part of each tune-up, wipe off any dirt or corrosion on the distributor cap. Examine inside of the cap for wear and signs of carbon tracks (arcing). Replace the cap if carbon tracks are evident. Remove the rotor and inspect for excessive wear or burning around the metal contact surfaces. Also measure resistance of rotor as shown in **Figure 25**. Replace rotor if damaged, or if resistance is greater than 10 kilohms.

Ignition Timing Adjustment

After adjusting breaker point gap, set the ignition timing. Timing is set in 2 stages:

a. Static timing with test lamp
b. Dynamic timing with strobe

Static Timing

1. Remove distributor cap.
2. Unscrew the TDC sensor with special tool US4463.

> NOTE: *If tool US4463 is not available, try to locate a combination lug and spark plug socket that formerly was supplied with the VW Beetle tool kit. The lug nut end of this tool can be used to remove the TDC sensor.*

3. Rotate crankshaft with socket wrench (**Figure 26**) until mark on cam pulley aligns with

28

rocker arm cover (**Figure 27**) and TDC mark on flywheel aligns with timing mark on transmission case opening (**Figure 28**).

4. Loosen distributor housing clamp bolt. See **Figure 29**.

29

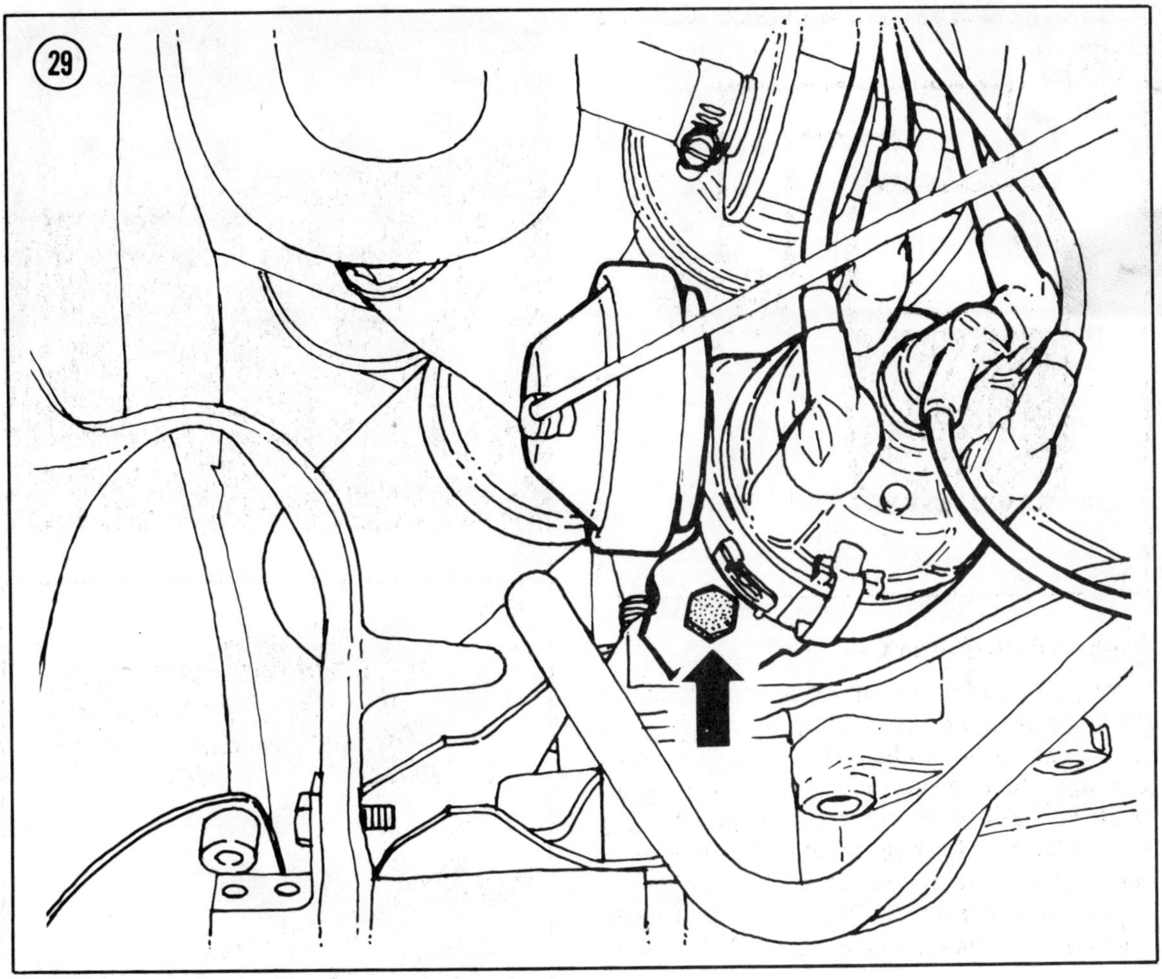

30

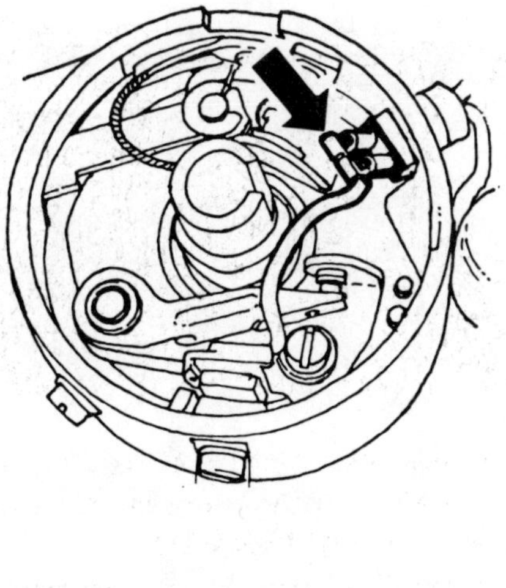

5. Connect 12-volt test lamp from primary lead on the distributor to ground **(Figure 30)**.

6. Switch ignition on.

7. Rotate distributor body until the test lamp goes off (points closed). Slowly rotate the distributor in the opposite direction until the light just goes on (points open). Tighten the distributor in this position.

8. Disconnect the test lamp and reinstall the distributor cap.

Dynamic Timing

1. Remove the TDC sensor with special tool US4463. (See NOTE in *Static Timing*.)

2. Connect timing light to spark plug No. 1, following manufacturer's instructions.

3. Warm engine to normal operating temperature (oil temperature: 176°F, 80°C).

4. Run engine at 925 rpm with vacuum advance connected.

5. Loosen distributor housing and turn it until timing mark on transmission case aligns with 3° ATDC mark on flywheel when illuminated by timing light. See **Figure 31**.

> NOTE: *The 3° ATDC mark is a small notch filed in the flywheel 1/4 inch to the right of the TDC mark.*

6. Tighten distributor clamp when adjustment is correct to 14 ft.-lb. (1.9 mkg).

7. Install TDC sensor.

31

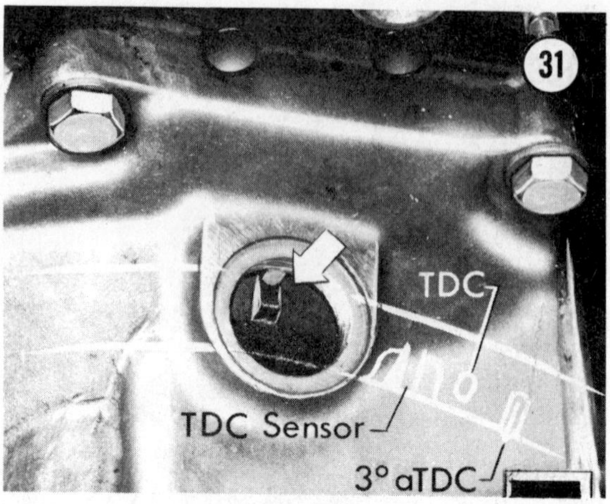

Carburetor Adjustment

> NOTE: *A number of 1978 models (49-states models) were equipped with Solex 34 PICT-5 carburetors. Service procedures for this carburetor are located in Chapter Five.*

Accurate carburetor adjustment requires a tachometer with a 0-2,000 rpm range and an exhaust gas analyzer capable of measuring 1-2% CO content. This procedure explains how to adjust CO content *approximately* without an analyzer, but it should be checked on calibrated and approved equipment as soon as possible.

CAUTION

Excessively low CO values will cause an abnormally lean mixture which could damage the engine.

1. All hoses *except* the hose from the charcoal filter must be connected.

2. Verify that all electrical connections are on and tight. Reconnect the battery ground wire if this has not already been done.

3. Air cleaner and hoses must be in place.

4. Back the idle adjustment screw out about 3 turns. See **Figure 32**. Start the engine. If it will not idle, adjust the idle screw accordingly.

5. Operate the engine until warm or at operating temperature. The point when the thermostatically controlled fan comes on is a good indication.

6. Connect a tachometer and a calibrated CO meter.

32

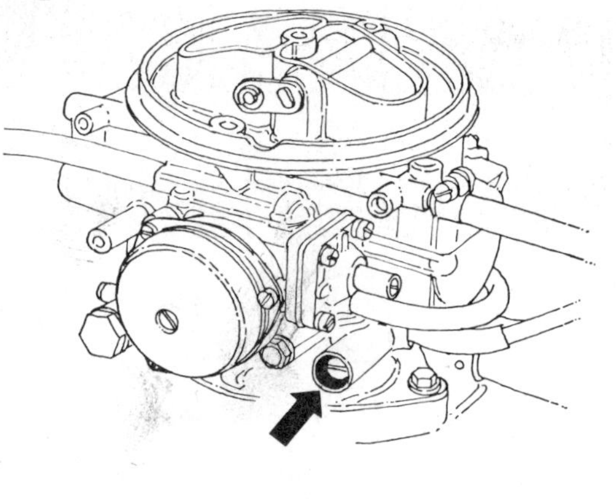

33

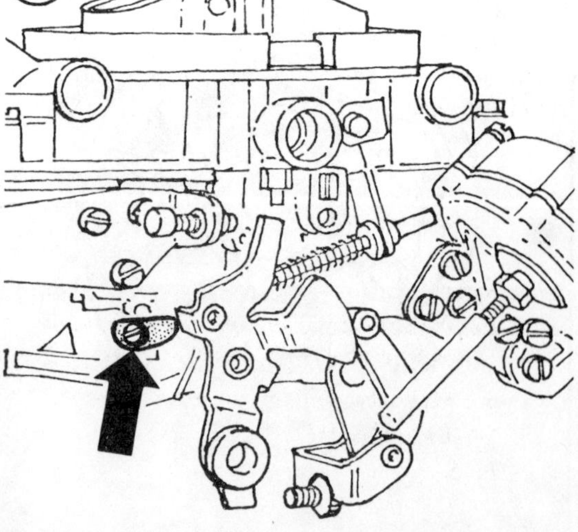

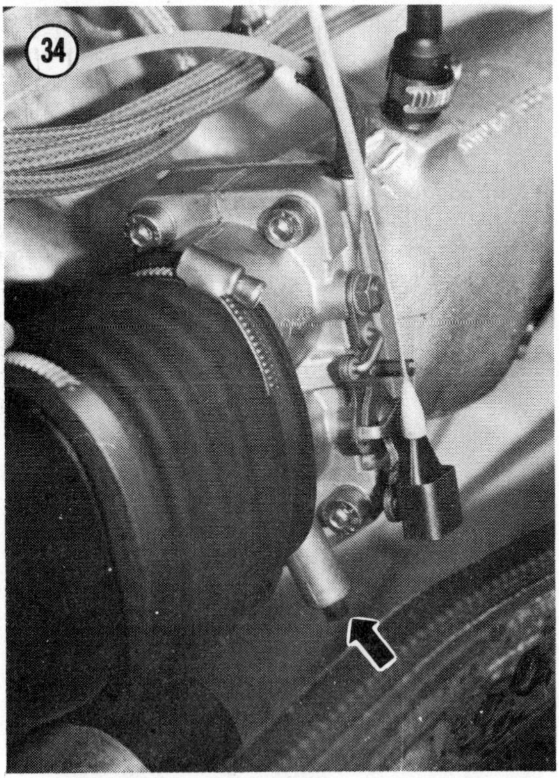

NOTE: CO meter must be connected ahead of catalytic converter on cars so equipped.

7. Ensure that idle speed is 950 ± 50 rpm. Adjust the idle speed screw (arrow, Figure 32) if necessary.

8. Read CO content on exhaust gas analyzer, and compare to Table 3. If necessary, adjust idle mixture screw (arrow, **Figure 33**).

9. Readjust idle speed if necessary, then recheck CO content until both are within specifications.

NOTE: Do not adjust throttle stop screw to change idle speed; use idle speed screw (Figure 32).

NOTE: In the event that a CO meter is unavailable it is still possible to make a close estimate of CO:

a. With the engine warm verify the valve adjustment as being correct.

b. Set the timing exactly *with a strobscopic timing light.*

c. Adjust idle speed to exactly *900 rpm.*

d. Connect a manifold pressure (vacuum) gauge to the intake manifold. The line leading to the brake booster reservoir is convenient.

e. Place a small load on the engine. Headlights on high beam work fine.

f. Adjust the CO screw until the vacuum gauge reads between 14 and 16 in. Hg (inches of mercury).

10. Reconnect the charcoal filter line and remove all test instruments.

CIS Fuel Injection CO/Idle Adjustment

1. Warm the engine to normal operating temperature.

2. With engine idling at about 925 rpm, check ignition timing and adjust, if needed, to 3 degrees after top dead center (ATDC). Vacuum hoses should be left connected.

3. Using a tachometer connected according to manufacturer's instructions, check idle speed and adjust, if required, to 925 ± 75 rpm. Use idle adjusting screw (arrow, **Figure 34**).

4. Remove the charcoal filter hose from the air cleaner. Turn on headlights and switch to high beam. Air conditioner, if equipped, should not be running. Install accurate exhaust analyzer, using manufacturer's instructions.

NOTE: Analyzer must be installed in the tailpipe on all models.

5. Remove the plug located between fuel distributor and air flow sensor and install tool P377 or equivalent (**Figure 35**). Turn screw clockwise to raise and counterclockwise to lower the percentage of carbon monoxide (CO). The percentage should be 0.3 maximum for all vehicles first sold in California (those equipped with a catalytic converter); 1.5 percent maximum for manual transmission models, and 1.0 percent maximum for automatic transmission models first sold elsewhere in the United States and Canada.

CAUTION

Do not press down on the tool while adjusting CO, and do not accelerate the engine with the tool in place. Remove

3

tool after each adjustment, then accelerate engine briefly before reading the CO percentage.

NOTE: *If an exhaust gas analyzer is not available, an accurate vacuum gauge, properly adjusted for altitude, can be used to approximate the correct setting. Connect the gauge to the intake manifold system and use the CO adjustment procedure above to obtain a manifold vacuum of 14-16 in. Hg, needle steady, at sea level. This procedure should be used only in an emergency, however.*

DIESEL ENGINE DESCRIPTION

The Volkswagen diesel engine was developed from the standard 1471cm³ Rabbit gasoline engine, and uses similar, but modified, engine block and cylinder head assemblies. The electrical breaker point ignition system used on the gasoline engine has been eliminated. Instead, the diesel engine relies on the heat generated by air compression within the combustion chamber for ignition. A fuel injection system has replaced the conventional carburetor.

The cylinder head no longer has combustion chamber recesses, and valves are now flush mounted. Fuel injectors and heat shields are mounted in the holes formerly used for spark plugs. Glow plugs are fitted into the holes which were used for air injection tubes (from the emission control air pump) on carburetted gasoline engines.

The camshaft has been modified by eliminating the keyway on the geared end of the shaft. This end is now cone-shaped to permit precise adjustment of the valve train timing to the fuel pump timing (the fuel pump is driven by the same spur belt that drives the camshaft). This adjustment is extremely critical.

The diesel engine block is identical to the gasoline engine block except that a number of machined openings (for mounting the distributor, fuel pump, etc.) have been sealed with metal plates. Also, different pistons and a different oil pump are used. Otherwise the lower end remains the same with a strong, 5-main-bearing crank.

Pistons have been "dished" or "relieved" to provide combustion chambers. By eliminating the recesses in the cylinder head and relieving the pistons, a compression ratio of 23.5:1 is achieved.

CAUTION

Although many diesel engine parts are similar, they are not necessarily identical to those in gasoline engines. Always order parts with numbers that apply to diesel engines.

The intake manifold is a simple casting, with the openings to the 4 matched channels covered by a common air filter. Air intake is not controlled by venturis, throttle valves, or other means.

Components that have been added include a different fuel filter, a new mechanical fuel pump, a hand fuel pump, a different spur belt, glow plugs, a fuel shut-off valve, and fuel injectors. See **Figure 36**.

Fuel filtration is more critical with diesel engines than with gasoline engines; therefore, the filter element should be changed more often.

The mechanical fuel pump meters fuel to the injectors at very high pressure (1,849 psi). The spring-loaded injectors open at precisely the correct instant during the compression stroke, and the pressurized fuel is sprayed into the cylinder. Heat generated by the compression of air within the cylinder causes spontaneous combustion of the air/fuel mixture.

1. Hand pump
2. Fuel filter
3. Spur (timing) belt
4. Fuel injectors
5. Glow plug
6. Fuel shut-off valve
7. Mechanical fuel pump

The hand fuel pump, mounted on the fuel filter housing, was used for bleeding the fuel system and to prime the mechanical fuel (injector) pump if the fuel supply had been interrupted. The hand pump was eliminated on later models, and fuel system bleeding is not required on any model including those equipped with hand pumps.

Glow plugs are used to electrically pre-warm the combustion chambers for starting cold engines.

The electrically operated (solenoid) fuel shut-off valve is used to stop the engine.

DIESEL ENGINE MAINTENANCE

Most of the routine maintenance jobs for diesel engines (see Table 1) can be performed by anyone with a modest amount of mechanical aptitude and a well-stocked tool box. Other tasks, such as injector pump timing, require special measuring tools and the ability to take accurate readings from such tools. Also required is the ability to make delicate adjustments. If the special tools are not available, and/or you have any doubts as to your abilities or do not fully understand what is required by a procedure, then it is best to take such jobs to your Volkswagen dealer.

Engine Oil and Filter Change

Procedures for changing engine oil and filter are identical to those given earlier in this chapter for gasoline engines. The diesel engine requires a different type of engine oil, however, and only oil designated "Service API/CC" should be used. This oil can be obtained at truck stops if it is not available at your local service station. See **Table 7** for some of the trade names available, and consult the *Quick Reference Data* pages at the front of this book for the oil weights to use at various temperatures. Engine oil and filter should be changed every 7,500 miles.

Fuel Filter Service

Bleeding of the fuel system, once thought to be necessary every 7,500 miles, is no longer considered necessary. Should it be necessary to bleed the system, however, the following procedure may be used.

1. On early models equipped with a priming pump atop the fuel filter housing (**2, Figure 37**), loosen the bleeder vent screw (1) and wrap the filter with rags. Place a suitable container under the engine to catch spilled fuel. Operate priming pump until emerging fuel is free of bubbles. Hold down pump plunger and tighten vent screw. Loosen fuel line connectors at 2 injectors.

2. On models without priming pump, loosen fuel line connectors at all four injectors.

3. Without using glow plugs, crank engine until fuel emerges from all loosened fuel line connectors, then tighten connectors to 2.5 mkg (18 ft.-lb.).

4. Start engine (using glow plugs) and make sure it runs without stumbling or stalling.

Water should be drained from the filter every 7,500 miles. Open the vent screw, if so equipped. If the fuel filter does not have a vent screw, disconnect the fuel return line from the filter. Open the water drain plug at the bottom of the filter housing and catch the water in a suitable container. Let the fuel flow until it runs clean, then close and tighten the drain plug.

Table 7 DIESEL ENGINE OIL RECOMMENDATIONS

Capacity: 3.2 U.S. qt. + 1 U.S. pint with filter change		
Brand	**Type***	**Viscosity**
B.P.	B.P. Vanellus Multigrade	SAE 20W-40 All year around
Castrol	Castrol SAE 20W-20 or Castrol SAE 30	Winter — SAE 20W-20 Summer — SAE 30
Exxon	"Exxon plus" Mono Grade HDX plus ①	Winter — SAE 20W-20 Summer — SAE 30
Mobil	Mobil Oil Super	SAE 10W-40 All year around
Shell	Shell "Rotella" "Rotella" Mono ①	Winter — SAE 20W-20 Summer — SAE 30
Texaco	Texaco Oil ED	Winter — SAE 20W-20 Summer — SAE 30
American Oil	Permalube Motor Oil Amoco 200 ①	Mono Grade 10W-20, 20W-30, 30W-40, etc.
Chevron	Chevron Special Chevron Delo, 100, 200, 400 ①	Mono Grade 10W-20, 20W-30, 30W-40, etc. Multi Grade
Gulf	Gulf Super Duty, Gulf Lube XHD, Gulf Lube Multi Viscosity Gulf Super duty ①	10W-20, 20W-30, 30W-40, etc. Mono Grade
Sunco	Sun Fleet XL, Super Fleet Special Sun Fleet Super ①	10W-40 Multi Duty 10W-20, 30, 40 Mono Grade

* Use only oil marked "Service API/CC."
① May be sold under this label at truck stops.

1. Bleeder vent screw
2. Hand pump

Close the vent screws or reinstall the fuel return line, then start the engine and let it run a few minutes to remove air from the system.

To replace the filter element, loosen it with a band-type filter wrench and unscrew it by hand. If a suitable wrench is not available, remove the entire filter from the fuel line and the car. Then use an open end wrench on the hexagon boss on the bottom of the filter to separate the element from the flange. Lubricate the new filter seal with diesel fuel and screw it onto the flange hand tight. Do not tighten with a wrench. If assembly was removed from the car, reinstall it.

CHECKS AND ADJUSTMENTS

Preliminary Procedure

Use the following procedure to remove certain components before performing the check and adjustment procedures given in this section. See **Table 8** for tightening torques.

1. Remove air cleaner hose. Release 4 clips and remove air cleaner cover and paper filter element.
2. Use a 13mm wrench to remove the spur belt cover.

NOTE: *Volkswagen has a special angled 13mm wrench for this purpose.*

3. Verify that ignition key is OFF and remove red wire from fuel shut-off valve on top of mechanical fuel pump.

Table 8
DIESEL ENGINE TIGHTENING TORQUES

Tightening Torques	Mkg	Ft.-lb.
Tensioner	4.5	33
Camshaft gear	4.5	33
Injection pump gear	4.5	33
Upper and lower parts of injectors	7.0	51
Injector/cylinder head	7.0	51
Injection pump	2.5	18
Injection lines	2.5	18
Adapters on injection pump	2.5	18
Fuel shutoff valve/pump	4.5	33
Glow plug/cylinder head	2.0	14
Cylinder head bolts		
Hot/warm	9.5	69
Cold	8.5	61

4. Remove short black hoses between fuel injectors. Remove and plug the long black hose at injector No. 1.
5. Loosen nuts on steel injector lines at fuel pump and injectors and remove all 4 lines as a unit, using a 17mm wrench.
6. Remove the 4 injectors, using a deep-well 27mm socket wrench.
7. Use a magnet to remove the 4 injector heat shields from the injector bores.

NOTE: *Injector heat shields should not be reused.*

CAUTION
Removal of the heat shields is important. If the engine is cranked while the injectors are removed and the heat shields are still in place, the shields may be drawn into the engine at high speed. If this happens, cylinder head will have to be removed and damage to engine could result.

8. Remove valve cover bolts with a 10mm wrench and remove valve cover.

3

9. Remove wire connected to glow plugs. **Figure 38** shows engine after above steps have been performed.

10. Torque head bolts to 61 ft.-lb. (8.5 mkg) if engine is cold, or 69 ft.-lb. (8.5 mkg) if hot, tightening center bolts first and continuing diagonally from the center out.

Valve Adjustment

The procedure for adjusting valve clearance is identical to that given in *Valve Adjustment*, in the *Engine Tune-up (Gasoline Engine)* section earlier in this chapter, with the following exceptions: in Step 1, before depressing the cam followers with special tool VW546, turn crankshaft so that piston is lowered approximately one inch from TDC position. This must be done at each cylinder for which a tappet disc is changed. Set intake valve clearance to 0.008-0.012 in. (0.20-0.30mm) and exhaust clearance to 0.016-0.020 in. (0.40-0.50mm).

CAUTION

Failure to follow the above precautionary instruction will result in damage to the valve and/or piston.

Compression Check

NOTE: *A special tool, VW1323, and adapter, VW1323/2, are required for this test. This tool is a compression test gauge with a range large enough to read the high pressures involved (398-483 psi). The usual gasoline compression gauge reads to approximately 300 psi. The adapter is required to fit the injector openings.*

1. Verify that all injector heat shields have been removed and that injector openings are clean. Inspect threads for carbon deposits or damage, especially if undue force was required to remove injectors.

2. Install a used injector heat shield in the opening at cylinder No. 1, then install special adapter (VW1323/2) in the hole. Install compresion tester (VW1323) in the adapter. See **Figure 39**.

3. Close tester thumbscrew and crank engine for 10 seconds, using ignition key. Record

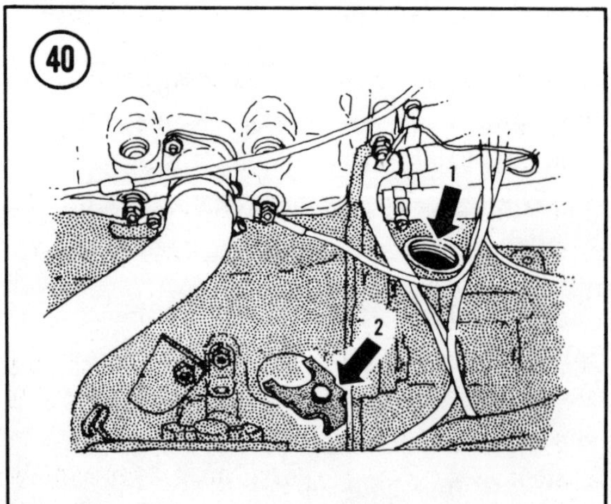

reading and release pressure by turning thumbscrew counterclockwise. Remove tester and adapter.

4. Repeat Steps 2 and 3 for the remaining cylinders. At sea level, the pressure should be between 483 and 398 psi (33.31 and 27.45 kg/cm²), with no more than about 70 psi (4.90 kg/cm²) between the high and low cylinders.

NOTE: *For each 1,000 feet above sea level, subtract about 12 psi (0.80 kg/cm²) from the maximum and minimum limits, i.e., 425 psi (29.31 kg/cm²) maximum at 5,500 feet above sea level.*

5. If an abnormally low reading is obtained for any cylinder, or if the difference in the reading for the high and low cylinders exceeds 70 psi, refer to *Diesel Engine Troubleshooting,* this chapter.

Spur Belt Tension Check/Adjustment

1. Remove the timing plug from the bell housing at rear of engine (1, **Figure 40**).

2. Use 19mm socket on crankshaft pulley bolt to turn engine clockwise until TDC mark on flywheel is aligned with reference mark in bell housing hole.

3. Strike spur belt a sharp blow with rubber mallet halfway between cam gear and fuel pump gear.

4. Install VW210 tool as shown in **Figure 41**. Turn tension tester handle to align both marks on scale and record the reading.

5. Remove the tester.

6. Turn crankshaft one full turn and realign the flywheel TDC mark with the bell housing reference mark.

7. Repeat Steps 3, 4, and 5, and average the 2 readings. The average reading must be between 12 and 13.

8. If the average reading does not fall within the specified range, loosen the belt tensioner (see *Camshaft Timing Belt*, Chapter Four) and adjust tensioner to obtain correct tension. Hold tensioner in position with a wrench and tighten the locknut.

9. After adjustment, repeat Steps 3 through 7 to verify correct tension. Repeat Step 8 if tension still is not correct.

CAUTION
Incorrect belt tension will affect fuel pump and valve timing and will result in a poorly operating engine.

Fuel Pump Timing Check and Adjustment

CAUTION
This procedure requires the use of a special tool, VW2066, and a dial gauge reading in millimeters. If you do not have these tools, and/or you are not experienced in making precision measurements with a dial gauge, take your car to your dealer for injection timing.

NOTE: *Injectors and fuel lines should not be installed for this procedure. See* Preliminary Checks and Adjustments *procedure, elsewhere in this section, for removal instructions.*

1. Remove small plug from rear face of fuel pump (plug is centered between the 4 fuel outlets).

2. Install threaded adapter, VW2066, in hole from which plug was removed. Install tracer pin extension to dial gauge.

3. Slide the tracer pin extension into adapter (VW2066) until the dial gauge reads 2.5mm preload. Secure the dial gauge by tightening the

3

threaded cap on the end of the adapter. Figure 40 shows the dial gauge installed.

4. Turn the crankshaft counterclockwise until the dial gauge needle stops moving.

5. Loosen adapter threaded cap and reset dial gauge small needle to read 1mm. Tighten the cap to secure the gauge and verify the reading. Turn bezel (outer ring) of dial gauge to set large needle to zero.

6. Turn crankshaft clockwise until TDC for cylinder No. 1 is reached. Verify that flywheel TDC mark is aligned with bell housing reference mark.

7. Verify that alignment mark on fuel pump gear is in line with mark on pump support and pump housing (black arrow, **Figure 42**).

8. Read dial gauge. Reading must be exactly 0.83mm. If not, loosen 4 bolts (white arrows, **Figure 43**) and turn pump body until gauge reads 0.83mm. Retighten bolts and recheck reading.

9. Check spur belt tension and readjust if necessary, using the procedure given elsewhere in this chapter.

10. Remove dial gauge and adapter and replace plug in pump housing.

Oil Pump Drive Gear Check

1. Remove bolt and hold-down bracket, then remove distributor-bore plug (2, Figure 40).

2. Use a flashlight to carefully inspect oil pump drive gear teeth for wear or damage.

3. If gear is in good condition, replace plug and bracket and tighten bolt. If teeth are worn or damaged, replace the gear. See *Intermediate Shaft,* Chapter Four.

Alternator Belt Tension

Adjustment of the alternator/water pump V-belt is identical to the gasoline engine procedure. See *Alternator Drive Belt,* in the *Periodic Checks* section earlier in this chapter.

Fuel Injectors

Testing, cleaning, and adjustment of fuel injectors requires special tools and skills. Servicing of these components should be left to your Volkswagen dealer.

42

43

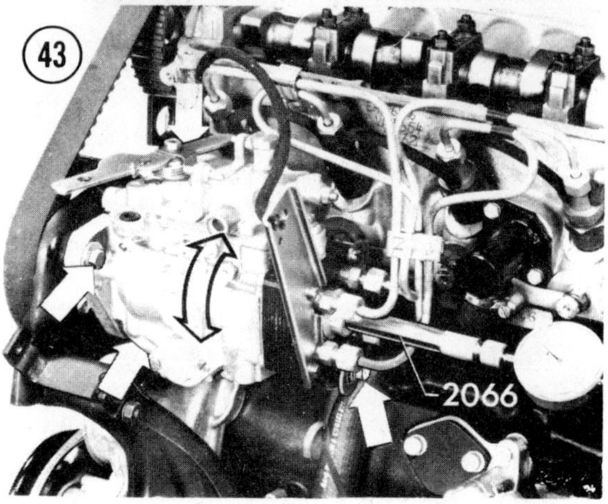

Timing Belt Removal/Installation

> NOTE: *Special tools are required for this procedure to hold the camshaft and fuel pump in place while the timing belt is being replaced. Replacement should not be attempted if these tools (VW2064 and VW2065) are not available. Also, if belt is being replaced during normal maintenance, replace belt before adjusting pump timing.*

1. Remove timing belt cover, valve cover, air cleaner cover, and air cleaner element as described in *Preliminary Checks and Adjustments Procedure,* earlier in this chapter.

2. Turn crankshaft to TDC for the No. 1 cylinder. Verify that the flywheel TDC mark is aligned with the reference mark on the bell housing (1, Figure 40).

3. Secure camshaft in position by installing tool VW2065 in the groove at the rear of the camshaft. See **Figure 44**.

4. Secure fuel pump gear with tool VW2064 (white arrow, Figure 42).

5. Loosen belt tensioner nut and turn tensioner with wrench to relieve belt tension.

6. Loosen camshaft gear retaining bolt ½ turn. Use rubber mallet to tap camshaft gear off taper.

7. Slide old timing belt off gears and remove.

8. Check alignment of marks on fuel pump gear, bracket, and housing (Figure 42). If not aligned, loosen 4 bolts (Figure 43) and rotate pump housing to bring into alignment. Tighten bolts.

9. Install new timing belt on gears and adjust tension as described elsewhere in this section, using tool VW210.

10. Tighten camshaft gear retaining bolt to 33 ft.-lb. (4.5 mkg), and remove tools VW2064 and VW2065.

11. Turn crankshaft clockwise for 2 complete turns and reset No. 1 cylinder to TDC. Verify that TDC mark on flywheel is aligned with reference mark on bell housing.

12. Recheck timing belt tension and readjust to specifications, if required.

13. Torque belt tensioner nut to 33 ft.-lb. (4.5 mkg).

Post-adjustment Procedure

1. Install new heat shields in injector bores. Concave side of each heat shield must face upward, toward injectors.

2. Install injectors and tighten each to 51 ft.-lb. (7.0 mkg).

3. Connect steel injector lines to fuel pump and injectors. Tighten fittings to 18 ft.-lb. (2.5 mkg). Do not overtighten.

4. Unplug and replace long flexible hose from top of injector pump to injector at No. 1 cylinder. Reinstall short flexible hoses between injectors.

5. Connect wire to electric fuel shut-off valve on top of fuel pump.

6. Install timing belt cover and tighten nut.

CAUTION

Make sure timing belt cover is not touching the timing belt at any point. Premature wear and possible engine damage could result if belt is touching the cover.

7. Clean air cleaner housing, clean air filter element with compressed air, and install filter element and air cleaner cover. Make sure all clips are correctly positioned. Install valve cover.

8. Install air inlet hose and tighten clamp.

9. Connect heavy gauge wire to glow plug bar.

10. Start engine and check for leaks in the fuel and water systems. Correct if necessary.

Idle Speed Adjustment

NOTE: *Tachometers designed for use with gasoline engines will not work on the diesel engine, as a rule. Volkswagen has a tachometer and special adapter (VW1342) that may be available through your dealer. Other diesel tachometers are available.*

1. Mount tool VW1342, which is magnetic based, on center of engine valve cover and connect tachometer leads as indicated on the tool. If another diesel tachometer is used, mount according to manufacturer's instructions.

2. Start engine, allow engine to warm up, and check idle speed. Adjust to 820 (± 50) rpm, if necessary, using idle speed adjustment screw (1, **Figure 45**). Loosen locknut on screw and turn clockwise to increase speed or counterclockwise to decrease. When adjusted to 820 (± 50) rpm, carefully tighten locknut and remove tachometer.

3

Maximum Engine Speed Adjustment

1. Connect diesel tachometer, following manufacturer's instructions. Start engine and allow to warm up to operating temperature.

2. Manually pull speed adjustment lever (2, Figure 45) until it rests against rpm maximum adjustment screw (3, Figure 45).

3. Adjust maximum engine speed to 5,400 rpm, if required, using rpm maximum adjustment screw. Loosen locknut, turn screw to adjust to proper rpm, and carefully tighten locknut. Remove tachometer.

Altitude Correction

NOTE: *Many diesel engine fuel pumps are equipped with an altitude correction cell that automatically corrects fuel metering at different altitudes. Cars so equipped should not be adjusted manually. Other engines are factory calibrated to operate satisfactorily at all altitudes below 5,000 feet. If your car is not equipped with an altitude correction cell, does not operate properly at altitudes above 5,000 feet, and prolonged high altitude operation is anticipated, the following adjustments can be made.*

1. Loosen the locknut on the fuel quantity adjustment screw (4, Figure 45) and insert an Allen wrench in the end of the adjustment screw.

2. Turn the Allen wrench exactly 90 degrees counterclockwise and carefully tighten locknut while holding screw in position with Allen wrench. This will reduce fuel quantity by 20 percent.

3. Adjust idle speed to 820 rpm, if required.

CAUTION

Pump must be reset to original position when returning to altitudes below 5,000 feet, or poor performance will result and engine damage may occur.

DIESEL ENGINE TROUBLESHOOTING

The following troubleshooting guide is intended only for diesel engine systems. Other

1. Idle speed adjustment screw
2. Speed adjustment lever
3. RPM maximum adjustment screw
4. Fuel quantity adjustment screw

systems, which are common to all Rabbit and Scirocco cars, are discussed in Chapter Two.

Incorrect or Uneven Idle Speed

The engine should be warmed up to normal operating temperature before attempting to discover the problem.

1. *Linkage adjustment*—Check for loose or incorrectly set idle screw and, if necessary, adjust and tighten screw to obtain 850 rpm. Check accelerator cable for looseness, tightness, binding, etc., and correct as required. Check for loose governor lever on fuel injection pump.

2. *Air in fuel system*—Bleed the injection system, using the procedure given in this chapter under *Diesel Engine Maintenance, Fuel Filter Service.*

3. *Fuel restriction*—Check the system for blocked fuel lines, bent or kinked lines, overtightened connections, and blocked fuel filter. Repair or replace, as required.

4. *Injection problems*—Check injection pump timing and timing belt tension, using the procedures given in this chapter. Also check for damaged injector heat shields, dirty or corroded injectors, and correct fuel pressures. Replace or correct, as required.

5. *Engine mechanical problems*—Check valve clearances and engine compression, using the procedures given in this chapter. Also check for proper engine mounting.

Engine Will Not Start

Make sure that there is adequate fuel in the tank, and that the starter is cranking the engine at normal speed (at least 150 rpm) before proceeding.

1. *Defective throttle and engine stop controls*—Check all throttle controls for damage and freedom of movement, and repair or replace as required. Verify that the fuel shut-off solenoid valve on the fuel injection pump is operating properly. Make sure that the electrical wire to the switch is attached and is in good condition.

2. *Malfunctioning glow plugs*—Check for voltage by connecting a test lamp between the No. 4 cylinder glow plug and ground and turning the ignition switch to PREHEAT. If test lamp does not light, check wire for open or shorted circuit. Remove connecting bar from glow plugs and connect test lamp between wire from ignition switch and each plug in turn. Turn ignition switch to PREHEAT and check each plug. If lamp does not light when checking any plug (and ignition wire is known to be conducting), replace that glow plug. If ignition wire is OK, but does not deliver current to plugs, check ignition switch, plug relay, and relay plate on fuse box.

3. *Fuel system fault*—Determine if fuel is being delivered to the injectors by loosening the fuel line to one injector and cranking engine. Verify that all fuel lines are connected to the proper injectors. Also check for leaking or blocked fuel lines, and blocked fuel filter. Bleed the system, using the procedure given in this chapter, *Fuel Filter Service*. In cold weather, check for ice or wax in fuel lines.

4. *Injection system fault*—Check the injection pump timing and correct, if necessary, using the procedure in this chapter, *Fuel Pump Timing Check and Adjustment*. Remove injectors and check for defective heat shields. Take injectors to your dealer and have them checked. If these measures fail to correct injection problems, it may be necessary to replace the injection pump.

5. *Engine mechanical fault*—Check valve clearances and adjust as required, using the procedures given in this chapter. Also check engine compression, using the procedure given in this chapter. Any faults found should be eliminated.

Smoking Exhaust

Black smoke usually indicates that excessive fuel is reaching the combustion system, while blue or gray smoke indicates burning oil. White smoke is usually water vapor (steam), and could result from a leak in the cooling system. Visible exhaust gases that occur when the engine is cold, but go away when the engine warms up, may, as a rule, be ignored. The exhaust also may "smoke" when the engine is being "lugged down" in an incorrect gear. This "smoking" also may be ignored in most cases. Some common causes of diesel engine visible exhaust are discussed below.

1. *Dirty air cleaner or fuel filter*—Clean or renew air cleaner element, or replace fuel filter element.

2. *Injection system fault*—Check and correct, if required, injection pump timing, using the procedure given in this chapter. Check maximum engine speed and adjust to 5,400 rpm if out of adjustment. Have your dealer check injection pressure and condition of injectors (sticking, leaking, and other damage). Also check for defective injector heat shields, and/or defective fuel injection pump.

3. *Engine mechanical fault*—Check valve clearance adjustment, using the procedures given in this chapter. Also check for leaking valves, defective valve stem seals, and worn valve guides. May also be caused by sticking or worn piston rings, or worn cylinders and/or pistons. Also check for leaking head gasket.

Excessive Fuel Consumption

One of the most common causes of excessive fuel consumption is a dirty air filter. Before proceeding, it is a good idea to check the filter element and clean or replace it. Also check the fuel system for leaks and blockages; correct them if found.

1. *Injection system fault*—Make the checks described in Step 2, *Smoking Exhaust*, elsewhere in this chapter.

2. *Engine mechanical fault*—Make the checks described in Step 3, *Smoking Exhaust*, elsewhere in this chapter.

Lack of Power

Lack of power can be caused by a number of conditions. Before proceeding, verify that the speedometer/odometer is in good working order, the car is equipped with standard size tires and wheels that are properly inflated, brakes are not binding, clutch is in good condition and properly adjusted, and that the accelerator pedal, cable, and the pump governor lever are not restricted, loose, or improperly adjusted. Also verify that the air cleaner element is not restricted. Clean or replace the element, if required.

1. *Fuel system fault*—Check for clogged fuel lines, clogged fuel filter, air in fuel system, kinked injector lines, loose injector connections, and injector lines connected in improper order. Also check for system leaks. Correct as required and bleed system, if needed.

2. *Injection system fault*—Check injector pump timing and correct, if required, using the procedure given in this chapter, *Fuel Pump Timing Check and Adjustment.* Check adjustment of maximum speed stop screw, using the procedure under *Maximum Engine Speed Adjustment*, this chapter. Check for damaged injectors and heat shields, and/or defective fuel injection pump.

3. *Engine mechanical fault*—Most likely causes are valves and pistons. Check valve clearances, using the procedure given in this chapter. Check for sticking or leaking valves. Also check for sticking or worn piston rings and damaged pistons.

EMISSION CONTROL SYSTEMS

Harmful emissions are minimized by three systems:

a. Crankcase ventilation
b. Exhaust emission control
c. Fuel evaporation control

The positive crankcase ventilation (PCV) system scavenges emissions (e.g., piston blow-by) from the valve cover and directs them to the air intake. Eventually, they can be reburned in the normal combustion process.

Exhaust emission control is more complex. Harmful exhaust emissions consist mainly of carbon monoxide, unburned hydrocarbons, and oxides of nitrogen. The relative amounts of these emissions depend on carburetor air/fuel mixture ratio, ignition timing, engine temperature and condition. Exhaust emission control therefore depends on proper ignition and carburetor adjustment.

Even with a properly tuned engine, excessive emissions are produced when coasting downhill or decelerating. Special air injection techniques described in Chapter Five ensure adequate air/fuel mixture to minimize unburned fuel in the exhaust.

Fuel evaporation control eliminates emission of fuel into the atmosphere. Fuel vapor forms in the fuel tank of a parked car in the hot sun. This vapor is stored until the engine is started and the vapor can be burned in the engine. Chapter Five describes the system in detail.

DIAGNOSTIC SERVICE

A special diagnostic service is available from your dealer. Your car receives a thorough examination in a special stall equipped for this purpose. A trained diagnostician checks items on a diagnosis test report and indicates repairs and maintenance needed depending on mileage and condition of the car. The diagnostician, who is also a top mechanic, can explain each item to you if necessary.

When the diagnosis is complete, you receive a copy of the test report and a cost estimate. The dealer will repair the items after getting your approval or, of course, you may fix them yourself. In either case, you know exactly the condition of your car and have the opportunity to keep it in top shape.

You should also consider dealer diagnosis when buying a used car. Insist on a test report when buying from a dealer. If you buy from someone else, the small cost of the diagnosis may save you from a costly mistake.

CHAPTER FOUR

4

ENGINE

The engine is a water-cooled, 4-cylinder with a single overhead camshaft. Five main bearings support the fully counterweighted, forged steel crankshaft in the cast-iron cylinder block. A toothed rubber belt drives the single camshaft in the aluminum head. Cylinder head design eliminates piston-valve collision if the drive belt breaks. Cam lobes work directly on cup-shaped followers over the valve ends. The cam belt also drives the intermediate shaft which in turn operates the fuel pump, oil pump, and distributor. **Figure 1** shows a cutaway view of the engine. **Table 1** provides engine specifications and **Table 2** provides torque specifications. Both are at the end of the chapter.

SERVICE NOTES

1. Although cylinder bore was increased in 1976 and stroke was decreased in 1978 (and were increased again for Scirocco in 1979), basic engine design remains essentially the same as that used in 1975 models. The procedures in this chapter apply to all engines, unless specifically noted otherwise.

2. Although the Volkswagen diesel engine is quite similar to the Rabbit gasoline engine, except for the ignition and fuel systems, owner disassembly of the diesel engine is not recommended at this time, especially if the vehicle is still under the manufacturer's warranty. The procedures given in this chapter may be used if emergency repairs are necessary and no other source of information or help is available.

3. On a conventionally-mounted engine, the timing gear end of the engine is the front and the flywheel end is the rear, since these ends face that way in the car. Transverse-mounting of the Rabbit/Scirocco engine makes these terms misleading. However, since most mechanics are used to conventional terminology, it is used throughout this chapter. That is, "front" means the timing gear end and "rear" means the flywheel end.

ENGINE REMOVAL/INSTALLATION

The engine and transaxle may be removed as a unit, or the transaxle can be removed separately. The engine cannot be removed separately, however, without first removing the transaxle.

> NOTE: *If so equipped, remove air conditioner components before attempting engine removal. Do not loosen any refrigerant hose connections. Loosen bolts on compressor support, then remove compressor (K,* ***Figure 2****). Then remove cooling fan, air ducts, and*

1

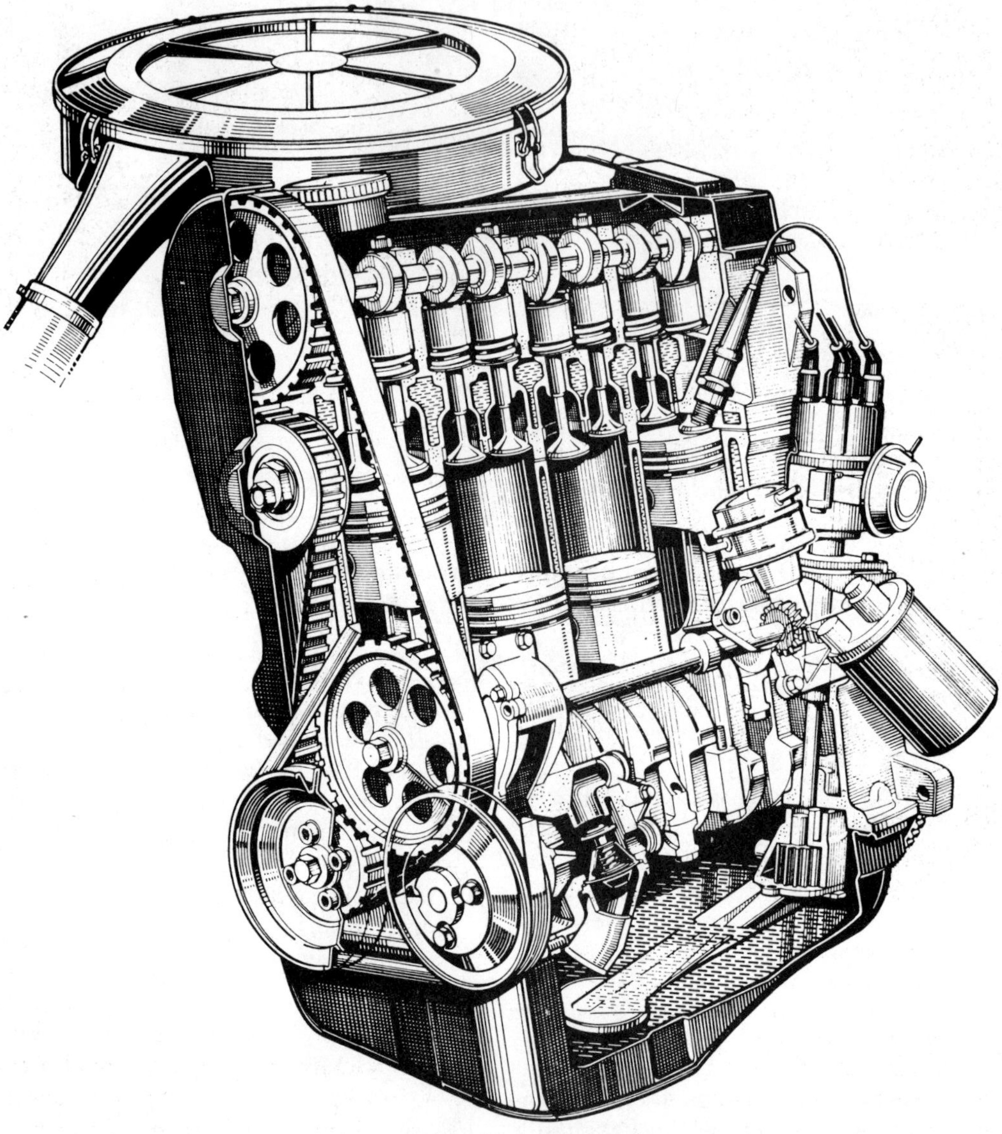

CUTAWAY VIEW OF ENGINE

radiator. Remove condenser (C, Figure 2) and place compressor and condenser, with hoses attached, on a shop cart or other moveable support. After engine installation, reinstall air conditioner components, making sure that pulleys are aligned and belt tension is correct: 3/8-9/16-in.(10-15mm) deflection.

On 1978 and later models, turn on ignition switch (without starting engine) and turn on air conditioner to engage magnetic clutch. Remove V-belt by removing bolt from center of magnetic clutch and using a 5/8-in. x 18 UNF bolt in the center hole to press off the clutch from the compressor shaft. Then remove compressor and condenser as described in paragraph above.

Engine With Manual Transmission

1. Remove hood, described in Chapter Twelve.
2. Disconnect battery ground cable.
3. Drain coolant and remove radiator as described in Chapter Six.
4. On gasoline models, disconnect wiring at points shown in **Figure 3**.
5. On cars with carburetors, disconnect fuel line, coolant hoses, and accelerator cable at points shown in **Figure 4**. On gasoline-powered engines with fuel injection, pull the injectors out of their tubes and disconnect all fuel lines except the injector lines from the fuel distributor. Remove mixture control unit, air cleaner, and intake air duct. Disconnect the fuel return line and the electric plug from the control pressure regulator. On diesel engines, detach the fuel filter and place it out of the way. Detach the fuel supply and return lines and the cold start line from the injection pump. Without detaching the accelerator cable, remove the cable bracket from the pump and place it out of the way. Remove wires from stop control, glow plug buss, oil pressure switch, starter, back-up light switch, and coolant temperature sensor. On injected and diesel engines, remove coolant hoses at points shown in Figure 4.
6. Remove air cleaner and connecting hose.
7. Disconnect speedometer cable, clutch cable, and engine mount shown in **Figure 5**.
8. Remove drive shafts from transmission and hang them up with wire.

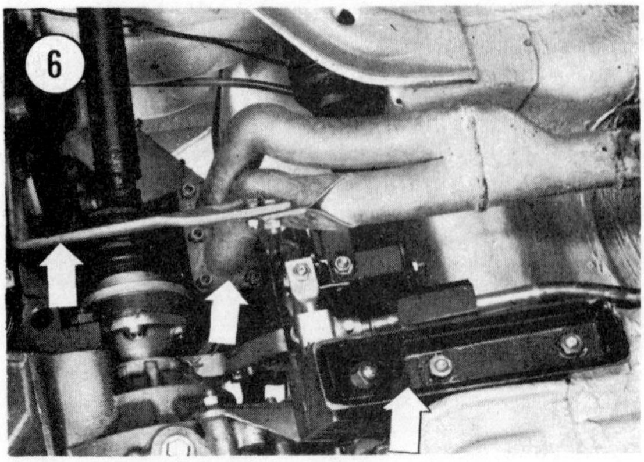

9. Detach exhaust pipe from manifold and remove exhaust pipe support. See upper arrows, **Figure 6**.

10. Remove rear transmission support. See lower arrow, Figure 6.

11. Move transmission ground strap between transmission and body.

12. Remove gearshift linkage from relay lever (a, **Figure 7**) and short rod at transmission (b, Figure 7).

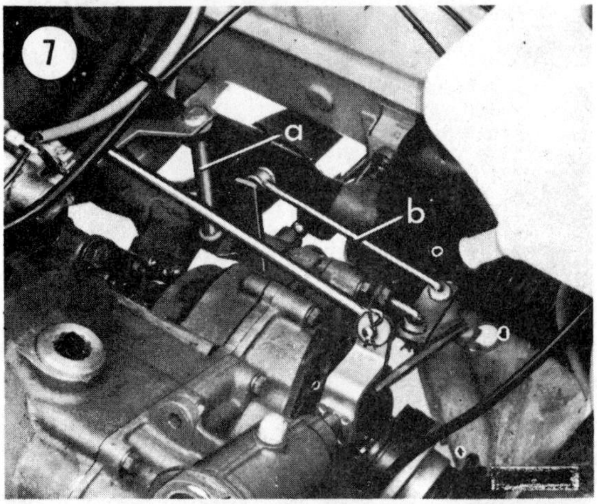

13. Connect chain hoist to engine as shown in **Figure 8**. Lift engine/transmission just enough so that the hoist bears their weight.

14. Remove engine carrier from body.

15. Remove left transmission carrier.

16. Carefully lift engine/transmission assembly out of the body.

17. Installation is the reverse of these steps. Do not tighten any engine or transmission carrier bolts until the engine is aligned properly.

> NOTE: *Engine/transmission mounts and exhaust pipe hangers must be free of tension when the engine/transmission is installed. Loosely install bolts in front mount (A,* **Figure 9***), left mount (B, Figure 9), and rear mount (C, Figure 9). Move engine/transmission assembly from side to side to align rear mount, then tighten nuts. Then move assembly from front to rear until left mount is centered in bracket and tighten bolt. Push front mount upward to center rubber core in housing and tighten bolts. Make sure exhaust pipe and muffler hangers are free of strain before tightening bolts.*

Accelerator Cable Adjustment (Manual Transmission/Carburetted Engine)

> NOTE: *Accelerator cable must be perfectly straight between carburetor*

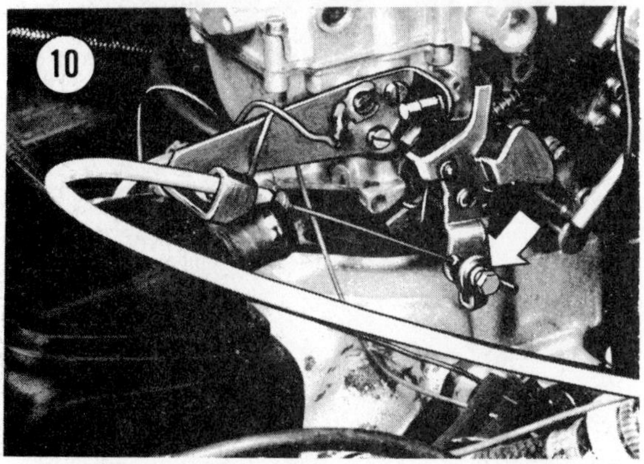

support bracket and carburetor throttle lever. If necessary, bend support bracket for alignment.

1. Install support bracket on carburetor and loosely install accelerator cable in clamp bolt (arrow, **Figure 10**) on throttle lever.
2. Have an assistant press accelerator pedal to the stop on the floor.
3. Move throttle valve lever until throttle valve just reaches the fully open position, and then tighten cable clamp bolt. Throttle valve play must not exceed 0.04 in. (1mm).

Engine With Automatic Transmission

1. Remove hood, described in Chapter Twelve.
2. Disconnect battery ground cable.
3. Drain coolant and remove radiator as described in Chapter Six.
4. Disconnect wiring at points shown in Figure 3.
5. Disconnect fuel line from fuel pump and coolant hoses from right end of engine block.
6. Remove accelerator bracket from carburetor. See **Figure 11**.
7. Move shift lever to P.
8. Disconnect selector cable (1, **Figure 12**).
9. Disconnect accelerator link at (2, Figure 12) and cable at (3, Figure 12).
10. Remove bracket bolts (4, Figure 12).

4

11. Remove drive shafts from transmission and hang them up with wire.

12. Detach exhaust pipe from manifold.

13. Remove rear transmission mount from body. See **Figure 13**.

14. Remove 3 bolts securing torque converter to drive plate. See **Figure 14.**

15. Remove alternator. See Chapter Seven.

16. Connect chain hoist to engine as shown in **Figure 15**. Lift engine/transmission just enough so that the hoist bears their weight.

17. Disconnect front engine mount.

18. Remove left transmission carrier.

19. Remove right engine carrier.

20. Carefully lift engine/transmission assembly out of the body.

21. Installation is the reverse of these steps.

> NOTE: *Observe alignment instructions given in note at end of procedure above,* Engine with Manual Transmission.

Accelerator Cable Adjustment (Automatic Transmission/Carburetted Engine)

After engine has been installed and accelerator cable bracket has been attached to carburetor, adjust cable as follows.

1. Operate throttle lever on carburetor to close throttle. Choke should be open and cam out of action.

2. Place throttle (relay) lever on transmission to end position (toward accelerator cable).

3. Adjust tension nut on carburetor bracket until there is no play in the cable. Verify that transmission lever is still in end position. If ball socket on cable can be pressed onto ball on relay lever without tensioning cable, adjustment is correct.

4. Have an assistant depress the accelerator pedal to the stop on the floor (A, **Figure 16**).

5. Loosen the locknut (arrow, Figure 16), and eliminate play at relay lever (B, Figure 16) by turning knurled nut. Retighten locknut.

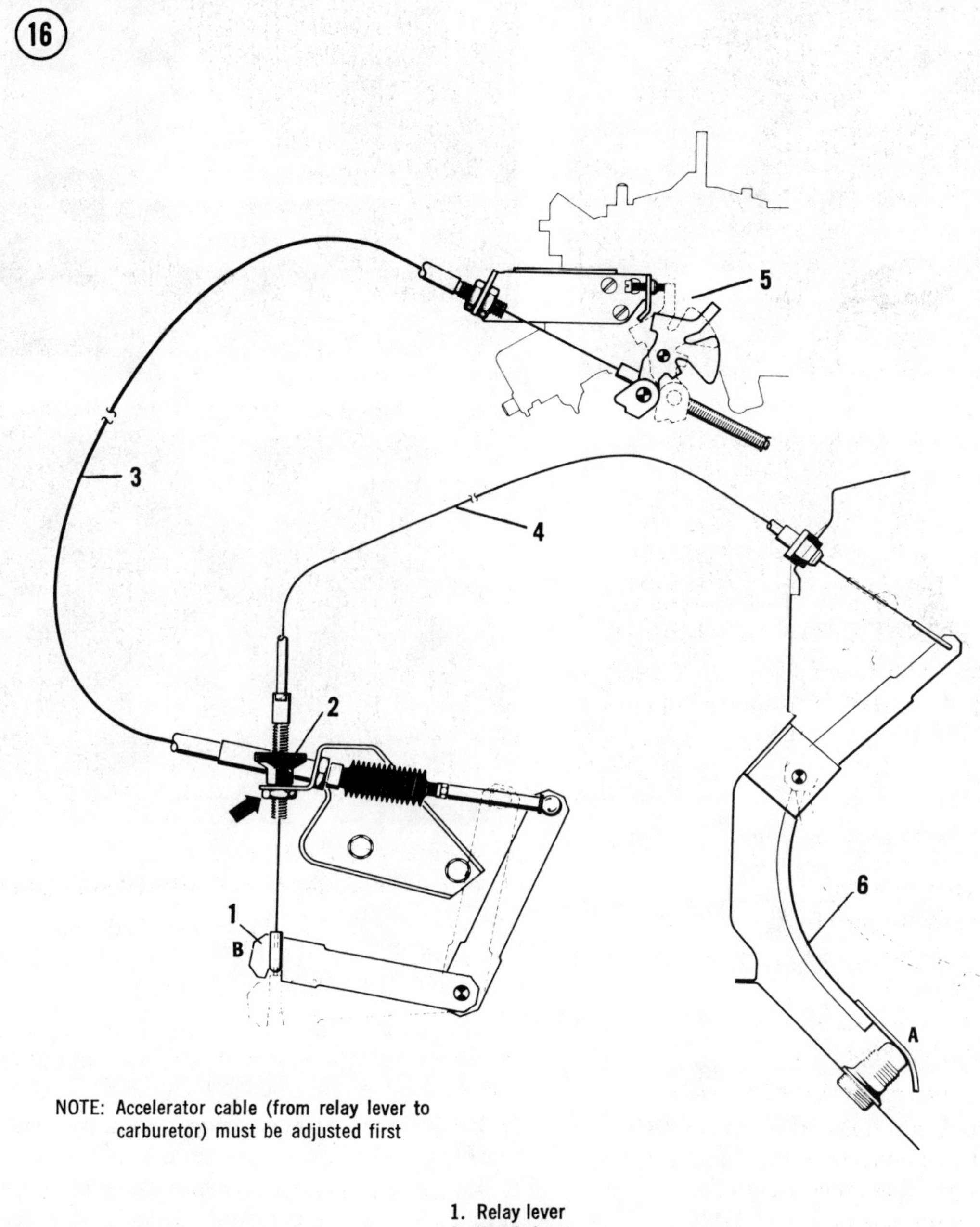

NOTE: Accelerator cable (from relay lever to carburetor) must be adjusted first

1. Relay lever
2. Knurled nut
3. Accelerator cable
4. Pedal cable
5. Carburetor
6. Accelerator pedal

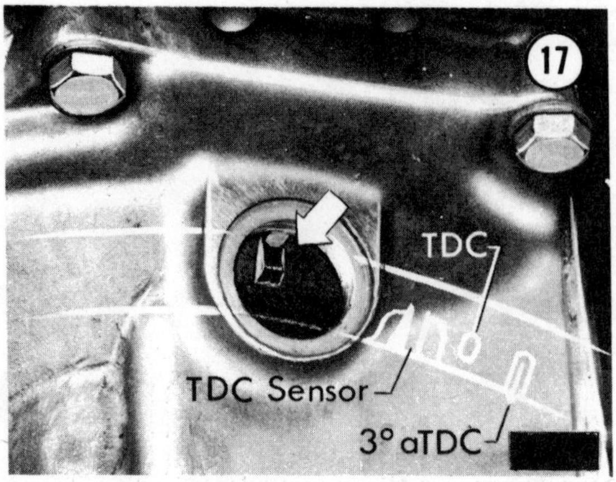

6. Check adjustment by operating accelerator pedal several times. Hold accelerator pedal in kickdown position and check again for play. Readjust if required.

SEPARATING ENGINE/TRANSAXLE

1. Rotate crankshaft with a socket wrench on the pulley nut until the mark shown in **Figure 17** aligns with the transaxle mark.
2. Remove cover plate over drive shaft flange. See **Figure 18**.
3. Remove bolts securing engine to transaxle, and remove the transaxle cover plate.
4. Pull the transaxle straight away from the engine until the transaxle drive shaft and the clutch pushrod clear the clutch and flywheel.

CAUTION

Do not let the engine tilt or let engine weight put any load on the transaxle drive shaft or clutch pushrod. The drive shaft, pushrod, or other clutch parts could be seriously damaged.

JOINING ENGINE/TRANSAXLE

Joining the engine and transaxle is the reverse of the separation procedure. Keep these points in mind when joining the two:

a. Before joining them, rotate the crankshaft so that the flywheel recess is adjacent to the drive shaft flange, shown in **Figure 19**.
b. Lubricate the drive shaft spline and the end of the clutch pushrod (protruding from the transaxle drive shaft) with multipurpose grease.
c. Torque bolts which join engine to transaxle to 40 ft.-lb. (5.5 mkg).

OIL PAN

1. Drain oil as described in Chapter Three.
2. Remove Allen bolts securing pan to block. See **Figure 20**.
3. Installation is the reverse of these steps. Be sure that you remove all traces of old gasket from the block and the oil pan. Use a new gasket and tighten oil pan bolts to 7 ft.-lb. (1.0 mkg) on 1975 cars and 14 ft.-lb. (2.0 mkg) on 1976 and later models.

OIL PUMP

The oil pump may be removed and installed without removing the engine. Refer to **Figure 21** for these procedures.

20

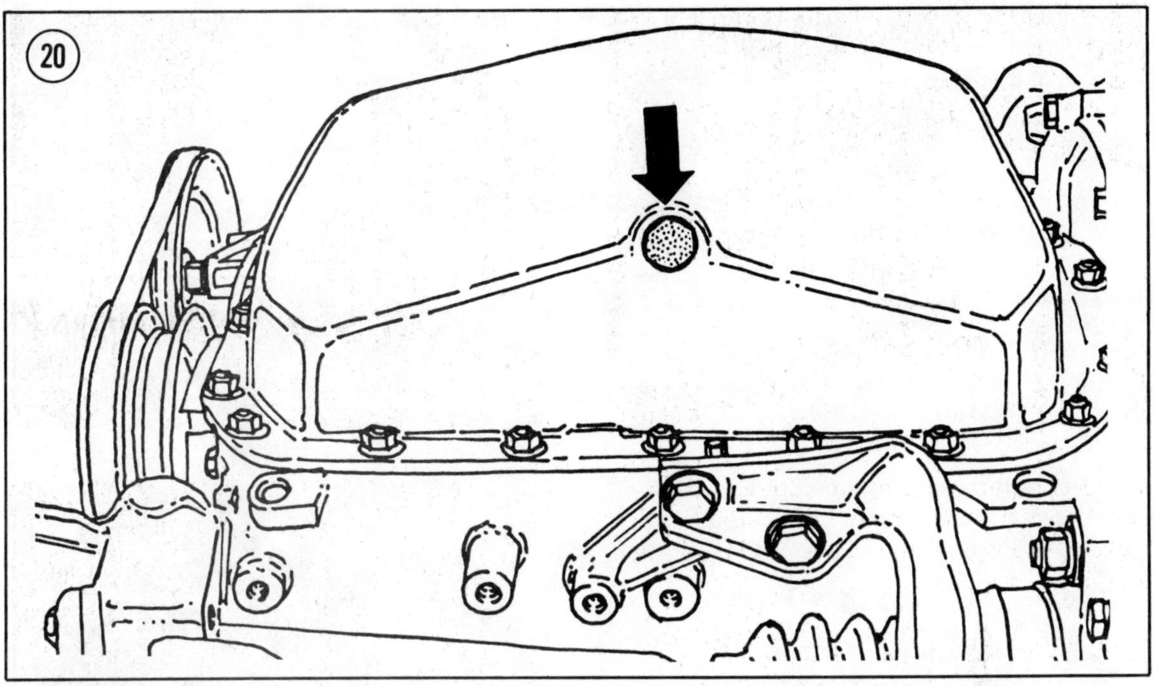

22

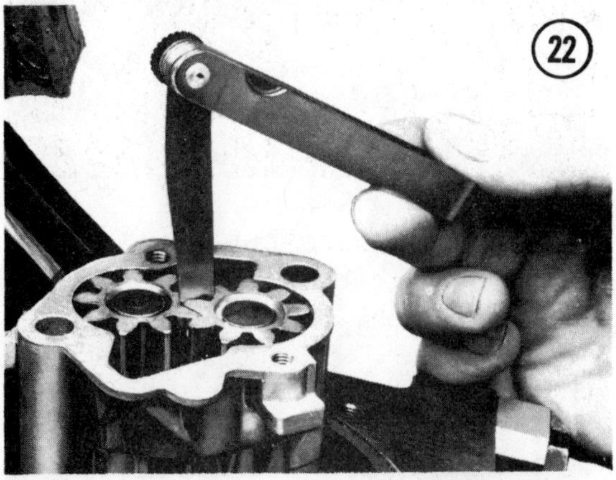

23

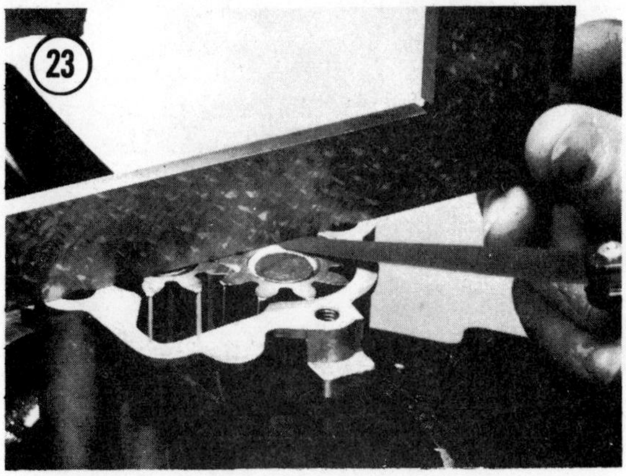

Removal/Installation

1. Remove oil pan as described earlier.
2. Remove mounting bolts and lower the oil pump.
3. Installation is the reverse of these steps.

Disassembly/Assembly

Refer to Figure 21 for this procedure.

1. Remove oil pump as described above.
2. Remove 2 bolts securing upper and lower halves and separate them.
3. Remove drive shaft and gear from upper half.
4. Clean all parts with solvent. If very dirty, bend up edges of suction head and remove suction head and filter screen for cleaning.
5. Install pump gears in body. Check backlash by inserting a feeler gauge between gear teeth as shown in **Figure 22**. Backlash should be 0.002-0.008 in. (0.05-0.20mm).
6. Place a square over the body and insert a feeler gauge as shown in **Figure 23**. Maximum end play allowable is 0.006 in. (0.15mm).
7. Remove gears from body.
8. Install suction head and filter screen if they were removed.

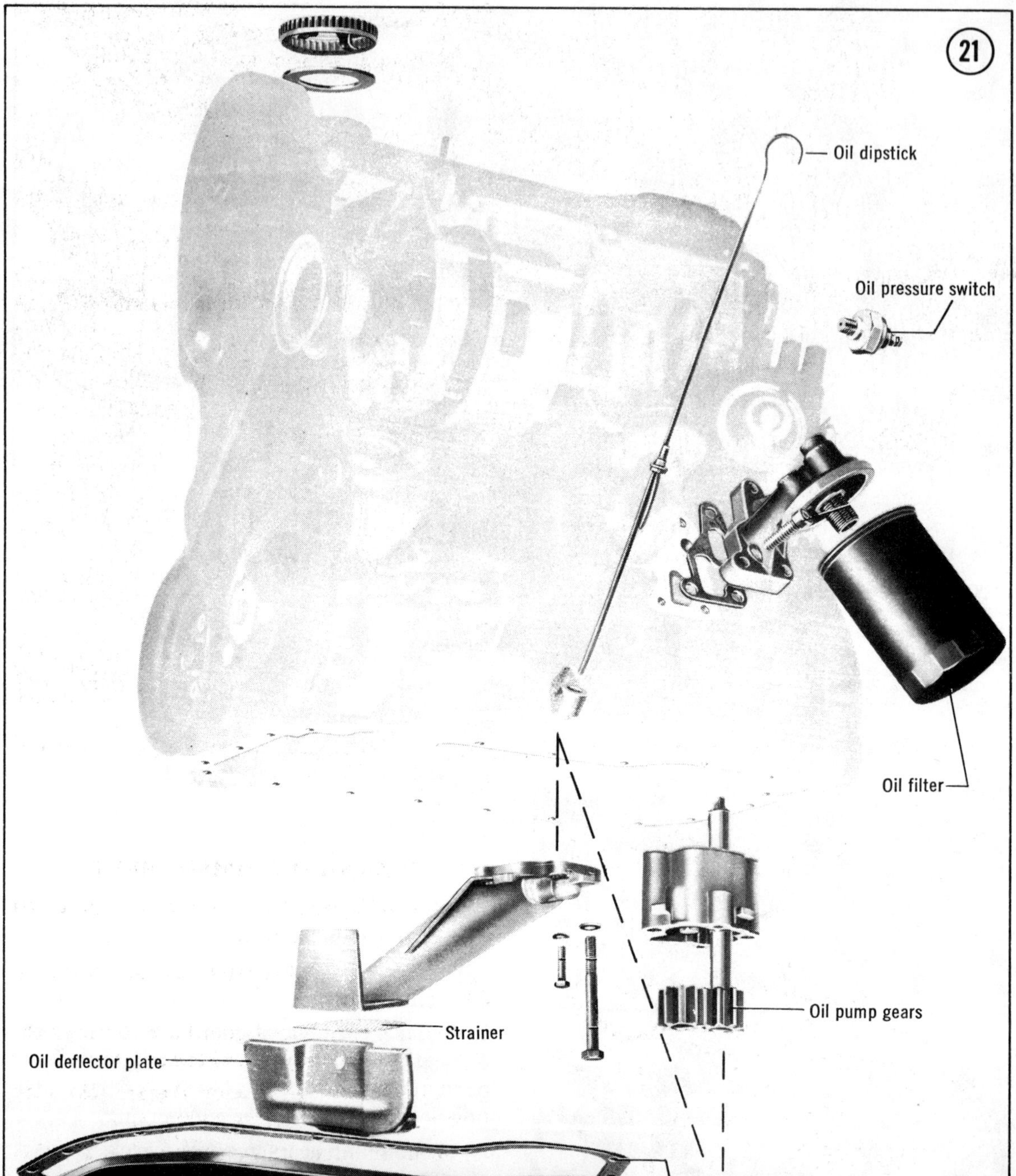
21
Oil dipstick
Oil pressure switch
Oil filter
Oil pump gears
Strainer
Oil deflector plate
Oil pan gasket
OIL PUMP

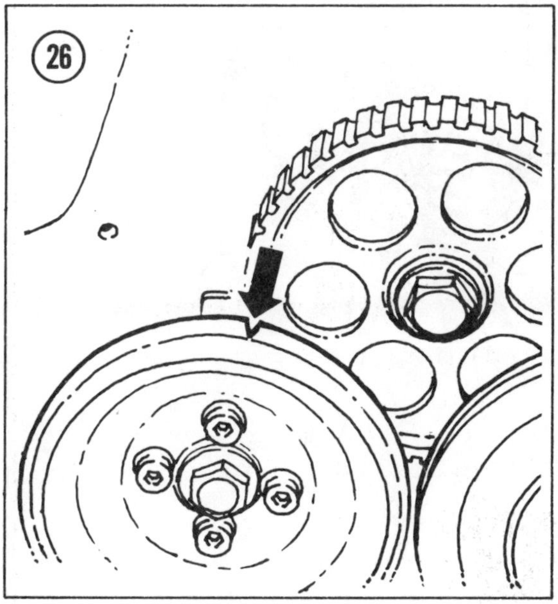

9. Lubricate drive shaft and gear with assembly lubricant and install them in the upper half.

10. Bolt upper and lower halves together and torque to 6-9 ft.-lb. (0.8-1.2 mkg).

11. Rotate drive shaft by hand to ensure that it turns freely and smoothly.

CAMSHAFT TIMING BELT

Refer to **Figure 24A** (gasoline) or **Figure 24B** (diesel) for this procedure.

1. Remove the alternator as described in Chapter Seven.

2. Remove sheet metal guard over timing belt. On diesel, remove cylinder head cover.

3. Remove the TDC sensor **(Figure 25)** with special tool US4463, if so equipped.

4. Turn the crankshaft sprocket with a socket wrench until piston No. 1 is at TDC on its compression stroke. This is evident when the TDC mark aligns with the mark in the transmission case opening. At the same time, the rotor in the distributor (gasoline engines) must point to the notch on the rim of the distributor housing. Finally, ensure that the notch in the crankshaft pulley aligns with the punch mark on the intermediate shaft sprocket **(Figure 26)** and the

24 A

Note: All parts shown in this illustration can be removed and installed with the engine in car

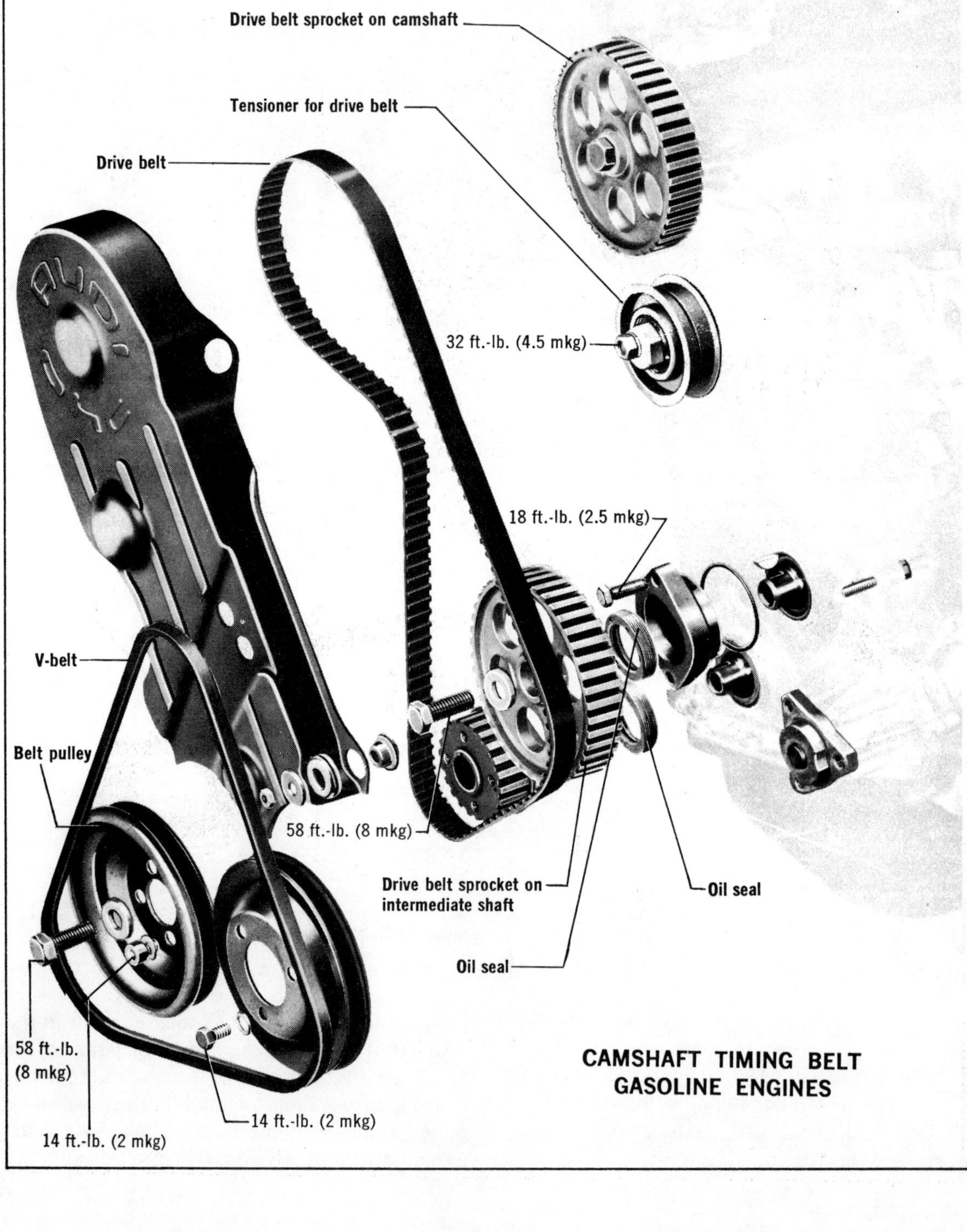

CAMSHAFT TIMING BELT
GASOLINE ENGINES

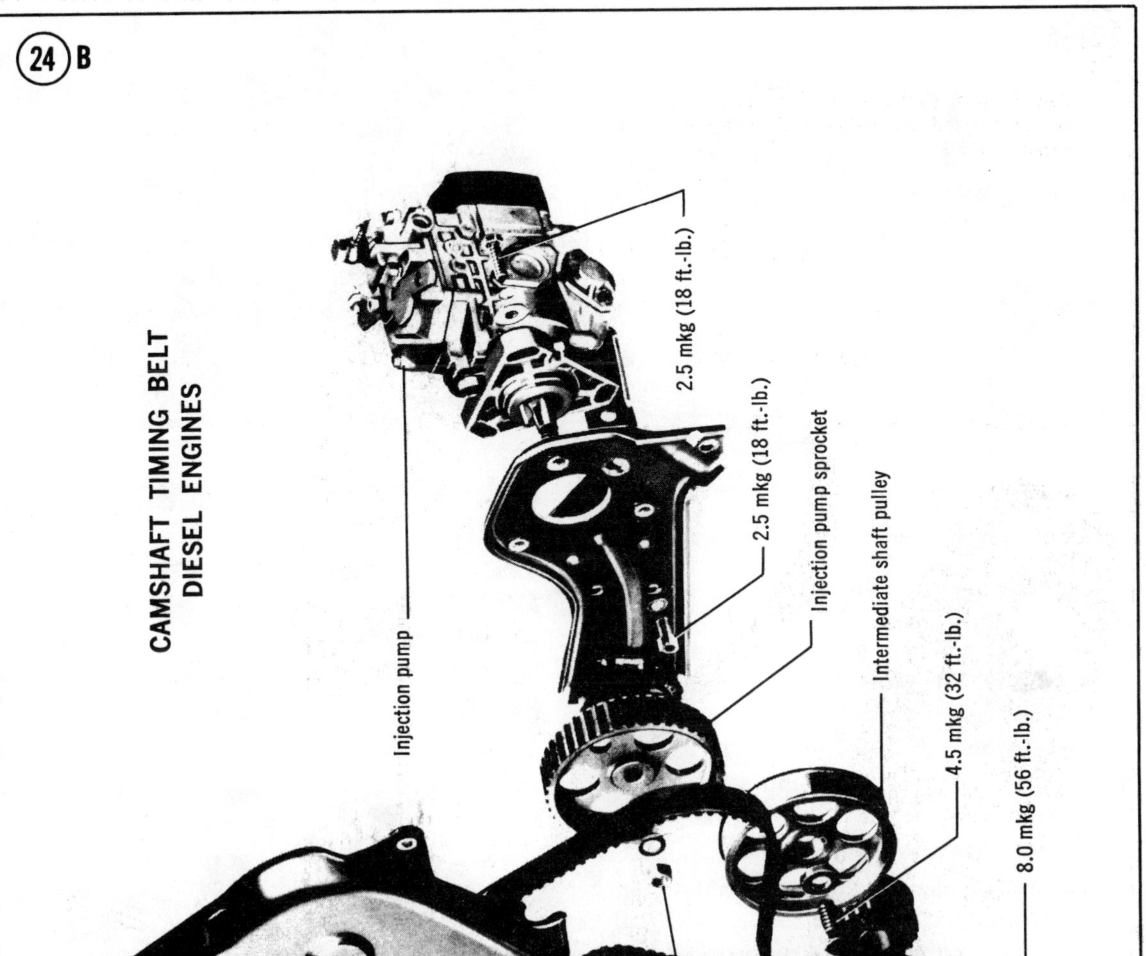

(24) B

CAMSHAFT TIMING BELT
DIESEL ENGINES

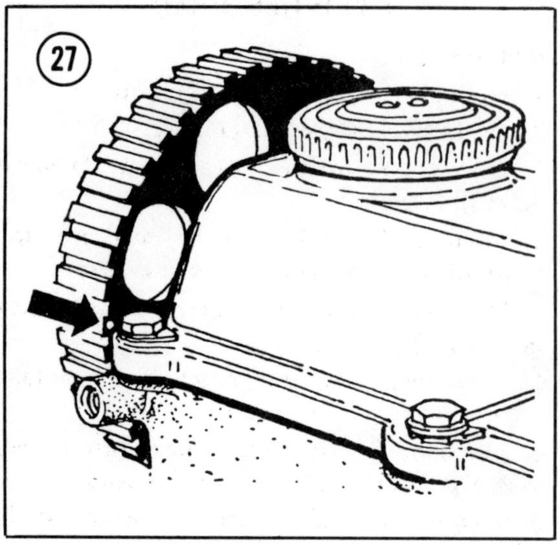

punch mark on the camshaft sprocket is in line with valve cover (**Figure 27**). On diesel, hold injection pump sprocket in place with special tool 2064 (**Figure 28**) and hold the camshaft with tool 2065 (**Figure 29**).

5. Loosen tensioner as shown in **Figure 30** to release belt tension (diesel is similar).

6. Slide the timing belt forward, off camshaft sprocket as shown in **Figure 31**.

7. On gasoline engine, make certain that punch mark on camshaft sprocket aligns with valve cover, and intermediate shaft sprocket punch mark aligns with the crankshaft pulley notch. On diesel engine, make certain marks on pump sprocket, pump mounting and pump are aligned. If necessary, align marks by turning pump. Loosen camshaft sprocket bolt ½ turn and loosen gear from camshaft.

CAUTION

Very accurate alignment of these marks is necessary as this sets the basic valve timing of the engine. Failure to align these marks can result in a very poorly running engine.

8. Install new timing belt under intermediate shaft sprocket and crankshaft sprocket, then slide it over the top of the camshaft sprocket.

CAUTION

Be absolutely certain that the sprockets do not move while sliding the belt into place. If necessary, reposition the

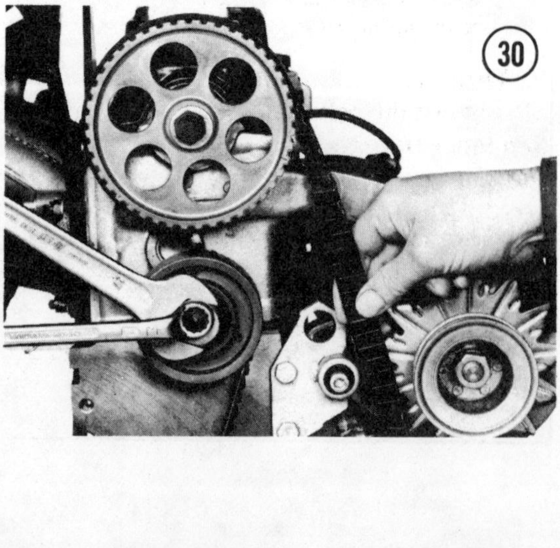

31

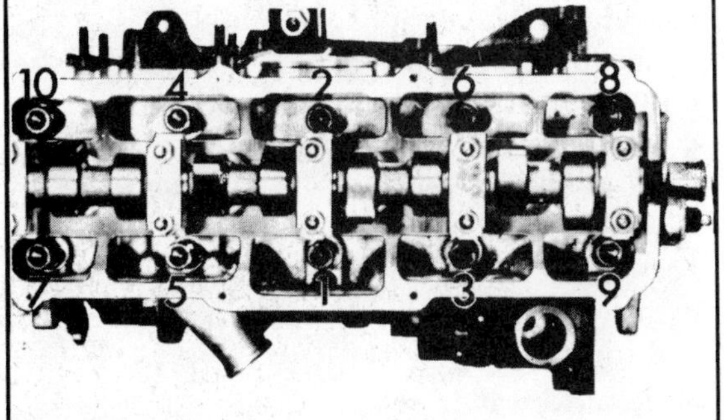

32

sprockets as described in Step 4, then reinstall the belt.

9. Turn the belt tensioner until it is just possible to twist the belt about 90° with your thumb and index finger at a point midway between the camshaft and intermediate shaft sprockets. Hold the tensioner in this position and tighten locknut. On diesel engine, tighten camshaft sprocket bolt to 32 ft.-lb. (4.5 mkg).
10. Install the timing belt guard.
11. Install the alternator as described in Chapter Seven.
12. Install TDC sensor, if so equipped.

CYLINDER HEAD

Removal

1. Disconnect the battery ground cable.
2. Drain coolant. See Chapter Six.
3. Disconnect exhaust header at exhaust manifold flange.
4. Remove the carburetor or fuel injection components as described in Chapter Five.
5. Disconnect accelerator cable and carburetor bracket.
6. Disconnect coolant hoses from intake manifold and cylinder head.
7. Disconnect wires from temperature sender and oil pressure sender on cylinder head.
8. Remove the alternator as described in Chapter Seven.
9. Remove camshaft timing belt as described in this chapter.

CAUTION
Be sure to align crankshaft and camshaft as described in Step 4 of Camshaft Timing Belt Removal *procedure.*

10. Loosen cylinder head bolts a turn at a time by reversing the sequence shown in **Figure 32**. That is, bolt 10 should be loosened first and bolt one last.
11. Tap cylinder head lightly with a plastic or wooden mallet to loosen the head. Lift the cylinder head off with intake and exhaust manifolds attached.

Installation

1. Be sure the cylinder head, block, and cylinder bores are clean.
2. Install a new cylinder head gasket on the block so that the word TOP (OBEN) faces toward the cylinder head. See **Figure 33**.

NOTE: *Never reuse a cylinder head gasket.*
On diesel engines, piston projection must be measured as shown in **Figure 34** *in order to determine thickness of head gasket. Four thicknesses are available. See* **Table 3** *to determine thickness required.*

4

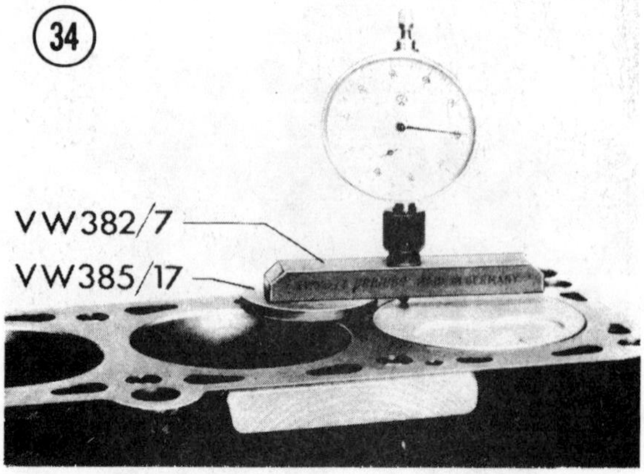

Table 3 DIESEL CYLINDER HEAD GASKET THICKNESSES

Piston projection mm (in.)	Thickness of gasket mm (in.)	Identification (number of notches)	Part No.
0.43-0.63 (0.017-0.025)	1.3 (0.051)	2	068 103 383
0.63-0.82 (0.025-0.032)	1.4 (0.055)	3	068 103 383 C
0.82-0.92 (0.032-0.036)	1.5 (0.059)	4	068 103 383 G
0.92-1.02 (0.036-0.040)	1.6 (0.063)	5	068 103 383 H

3. After positioning the cylinder head gasket exactly, install the cylinder head and the cylinder head bolts. First, tighten bolts 7 and 8 finger-tight. Then tighten the remaining bolts finger-tight.

4. Tighten the cylinder head bolts ½ turn at a time in the sequence shown in Figure 3 until reaching a final torque of 54 ± 6 ft.-lb. (7.5 ± 0.8 mkg) for a cold engine or 61 ± 6 ft.-lb. (8.5 ± 0.8 mkg) for a warm engine. On diesel, torque to 61 ft.-lb. (8.5 mkg) cold or 69 ft.-lb. (9.5 mkg) warm.

VALVE AND VALVE SEATS

Removal

1. Remove cylinder head.

2. Remove intake and exhaust manifolds from cylinder head.

3. Remove camshaft from cylinder head as described later.

CAUTION

To prevent bending, the camshaft must be removed exactly as described in the procedure later in this chapter.

4. Remove valve tappets (**Figure 35**) and store them in a holder marked so they may be reinstalled in their original positions.

5. With special tool VW541 or equivalent, push down on the valve spring retainers and remove the valve locks with needle-nose pliers. See **Figure 36**. Slowly release spring tension with tool. Then remove valve spring retainers and springs.

6. Remove valves from head. Store all parts so they may be reinstalled in their original positions.

7. Remove the valve spring seats as shown in **Figure 37**.

CAUTION

Remove any burrs from valve stem grooves before removing the valves. Otherwise, the valve guides will be damaged.

Inspection

1. Clean valves with a wire brush and solvent. Discard burned, warped, or cracked valves.

2. Measure the valve stems for wear. Compare with specifications. See **Figure 38**.

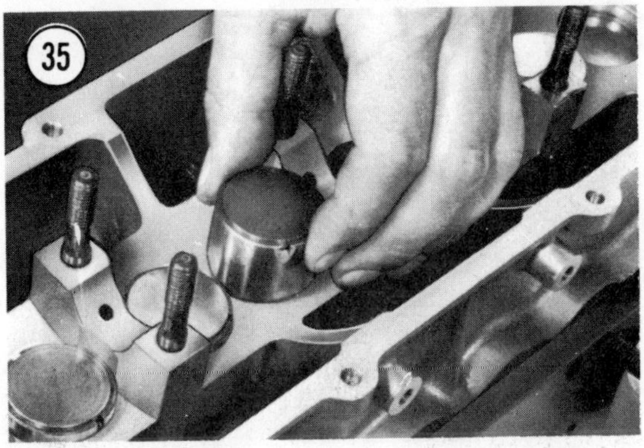

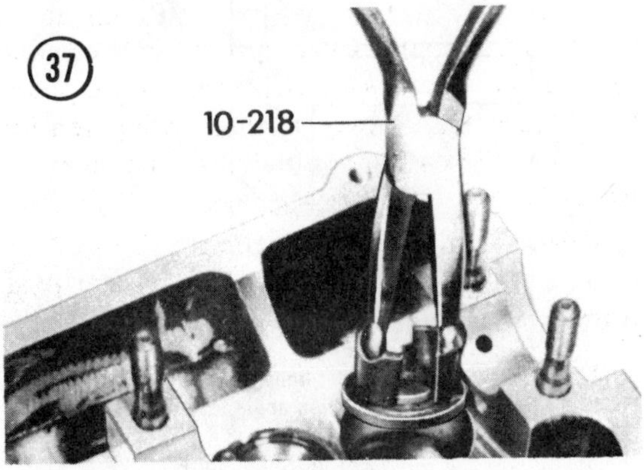

3. Remove all carbon and varnish from the valve guides with a stiff spiral wire brush.

4. Insert each valve in its guide. Hold the valve just slightly off its seat and rock it sideways. If it rocks more than slightly, the guide is probably worn and should be replaced. As a final check, take the head to a dealer and have the valve guides measured with special tool VW 689.

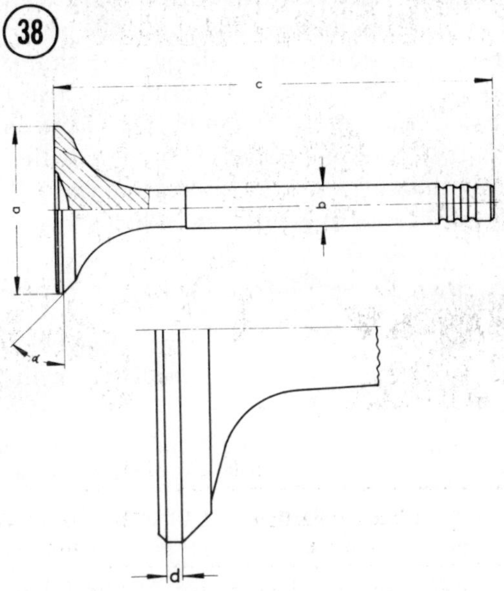

INTAKE AND EXHAUST VALVES—MEASUREMENTS

Intake valve:
a — 1.338 in. (34.0mm) diameter
b — 0.314 in. (7.97mm) diameter
c — 3.886 in. (98.70mm)[1]
d — min. 0.02 in. (0.5mm)
α — 45°

Exhaust valve:
a — 1.220 in. (31.0mm) diameter
b — 0.313 in. (7.95mm) diameter
c — 3.878 in. (98.50mm)[2]
d — min. 0.02 in. (0.5mm)
α — 45°

CAUTION
Do not rework **exhaust valves** on a machine; **grind by hand only.**

1. 4.125 in. (104.8mm) on diesel.
2. 4.117 in. (104.6mm) on diesel.

5. Measure the valve heights. All should be of equal length, with no bends or other distortion. Replace defective springs.

6. Check the valve spring retainer and valve locks. If they are in good condition, they may be reused.

7. Inspect valve seats. If worn or burned, they must be reconditioned. This should be performed by your dealer or local machine shop, although the procedure is described later in this section. Seats and valves in near-perfect condition can be reconditioned by lapping with fine carborundum paste. Lapping, however, is always inferior to precision grinding.

Installation

1. Coat the valve stems with molybdenum disulphide paste and insert them into cylinder head.
2. Install bottom spring retainers and new seals.
3. Install valve springs and upper valve spring retainers.
4. Push down on upper valve spring retainers with special tool VW541 and install valve locks.

Valve Guide Replacement

When guides are worn so that there is excessive stem-to-guide clearance or valve tipping, they must be replaced. Replace all, even if only one is worn. This job should only be done by a dealer, as special tools are required.

Valve Seat Reconditioning

This job is best left to your dealer or local machine shop. They have the special equipment and knowledge required for this exacting job. The following procedure is provided in the event you are not near a dealer and the local machine shop is not familiar with the engine.

Valve seats are shrunk into the cylinder heads. Damaged or burned seats may be reconditioned until the bottom edge of the 60° chamfer exceeds refinishing depth indicated in **Figure 39** (gasoline) or **Figure 40** (diesel). After this point is reached, the cylinder head must be replaced.

1. Using a 45° valve seat cutter or special tool, cut the 45° face. Do not take off any more metal than necessary to provide a clean, concentric seat. See Figure 39 or 40 and **Figure 41**.
2. Narrow the width of the 45° valve seat by cutting the top of the seat with a 30° (15° on diesel) cutter or stone. See Figure 39 or 40.

39

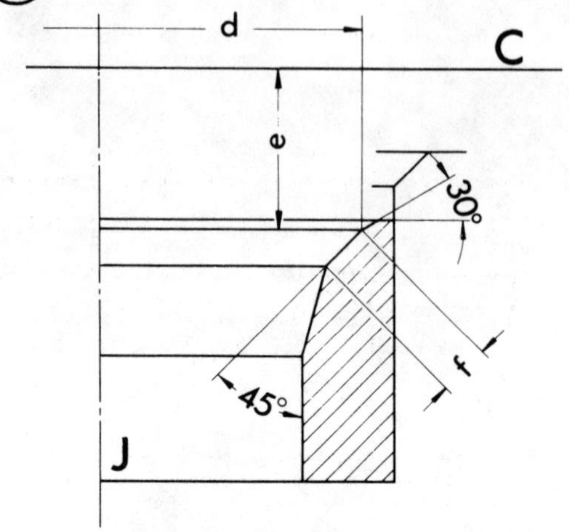

C — cylinder head, lower edge
30° — correction angle, upper
45° — valve seat angle
d — 1.306 in. (33.20mm)
e — 0.354 in. (9.00mm)
f — 0.069 in. (2.00mm)

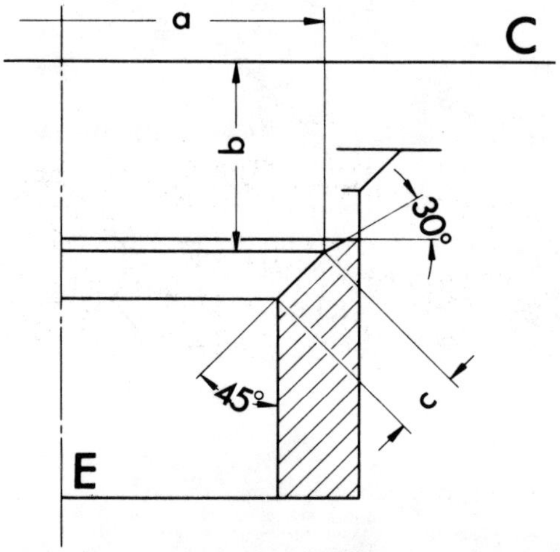

C — cylinder head, lower edge
30° — correction angle, upper
45° — valve seat angle
a — 1.212 in. (30.80mm)
b — 0.378 in. (9.60mm)
c — 0.094 in. (2.40mm)

Table 1 at the end of this chapter shows intake and exhaust seat width for your engine.

3. Coat the corresponding valve face with Prussian blue.
4. Insert the valve into the guide.
5. Rotate the valve under light pressure approximately ¼ turn.

40

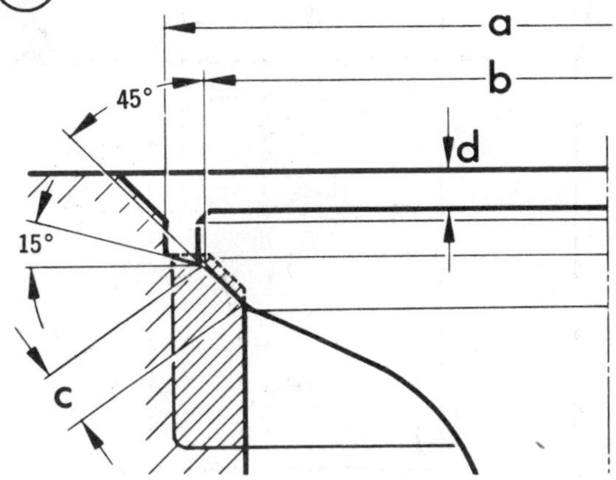

Valve seat angle = 45°
Correction angle = 15°
Dimension d: be sure "d" is not more than 1.5mm (0.059 in.)

Intake

a = 35.2mm (1.384 in.)
b = 32.8mm (1.290 in.)
c = 2.0mm (0.078 in.)

Exhaust

33.2mm (1.306 in.)
30.4mm (1.196 in.)
2.4mm (0.44 in.)

41

42

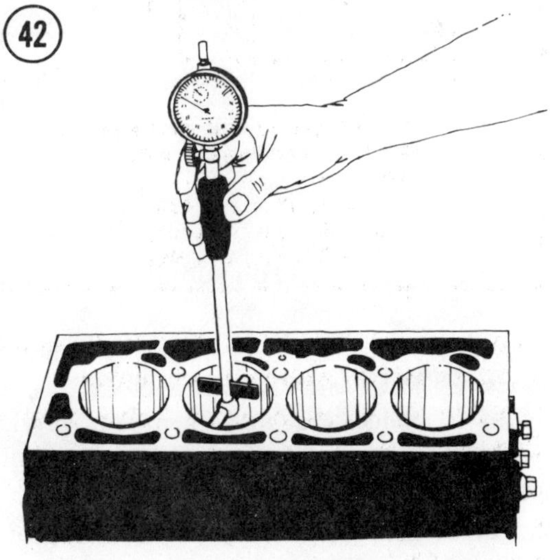

6. Lift the valve out. If the valve seats properly, and blue will transfer to valve seat face evenly.

CYLINDER BLOCKS

Inspection

1. Check cylinder block for cracks in the cylinder walls, water jacket, and main bearing webs.

2. Check cylinder walls for taper, out-of-round, or excessive ridge at the top of ring travel. Use a dial gauge as shown in **Figure 42**. Check at points shown in **Figure 43**.

Reconditioning

Cylinder walls may be reconditioned by honing only or boring and honing to correct out-of-round and taper.

If only slight wear is evident, bores may be lightly honed and high-limit standard size pistons fit to maintain proper piston-to-cylinder clearance. Measure piston clearance as described later.

If wear is more excessive, cylinder should be bored and honed for oversize pistons. Measure piston clearance as described later.

Tables 4 and 5 indicate available oversizes for 1975 (and all diesels) and 1976 and later models, respectively. Actual cylinder bore is coded in Table 4 as *Honing Group*. The honing

Table 4 PISTON OVERSIZES
(1975 GASOLINE AND ALL DIESEL)

	Piston dia. (mm)	Cylinder bore (mm)	Honing group
Basic dimension	76.48	76.51	651
	76.49	76.52	652
	76.50	76.53	653
Repair stage 1	76.73	76.76	676
	76.74	76.77	677
	76.75	76.78	678
Repair stage 2	76.98	77.01	701
	76.99	77.02	702
	77.00	77.03	703
Repair stage 3	77.48	77.51	751
	77.49	77.52	752
	77.50	77.53	753

Table 5 PISTON OVERSIZES
(1976 AND LATER GASOLINE)

	Piston diameter (mm)	Cylinder bore (mm)
Basic dimension	79.48	79.51
	79.49	79.52
	79.50	79.53
Repair stage 1	79.73	79.76
	79.74	79.77
	79.75	79.78
Repair stage 2	79.98	80.01
	79.99	80.02
	80.00	80.03
Repair stage 3	80.48	80.51
	80.49	80.52
	80.50	80.53

group, used mostly by European mechanics, is stamped on the engine block of 1975 models (**Figure 44**). Use of the honing group was discontinued on 1976 and later models imported into the U.S.A.

PISTONS AND CONNECTING RODS

NOTE: *New (higher) pistons are used beginning with 1978 models. New pistons cannot be retrofitted in earlier gasoline models, but earlier diesel engines can use the new diesel pistons if all 4 pistons are replaced.*

43

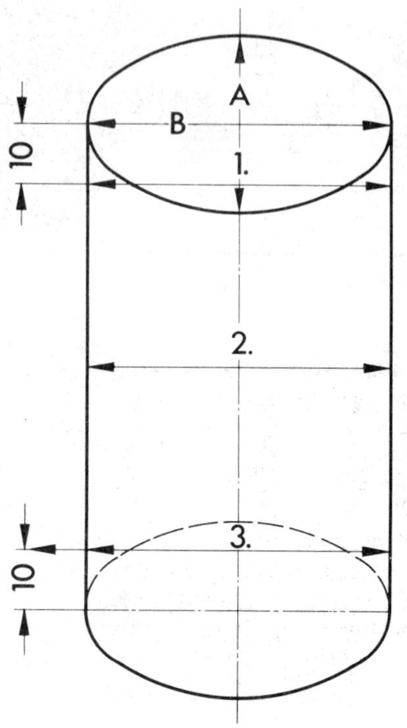

CYLINDER MEASURING POINTS
at 3 points crosswise ⅜ in. (10mm) from top and bottom and middle of cylinder wall—first in direction "A" and then in direction "B".

Removal

1. Remove oil pan and oil pump.
2. Remove cylinder head.
3. Rotate crankshaft until piston is at bottom of travel. Place an oil-soaked cloth over the piston to collect cuttings, then remove ridge and/or deposits from upper edge of cylinder bore with a ridge remover.
4. Turn crankshaft until piston is at top of its stroke, remove cloth and cuttings.

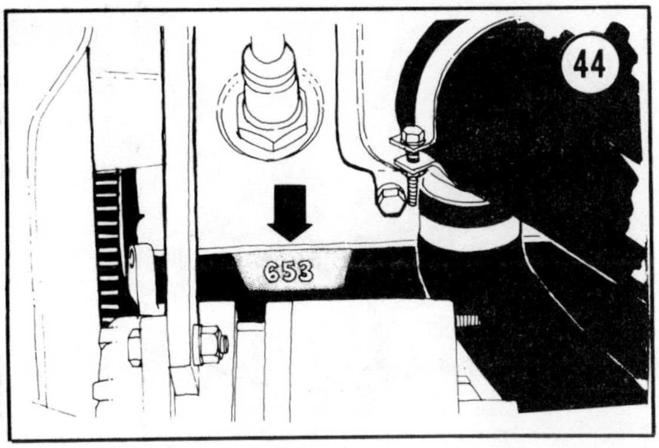

44

45

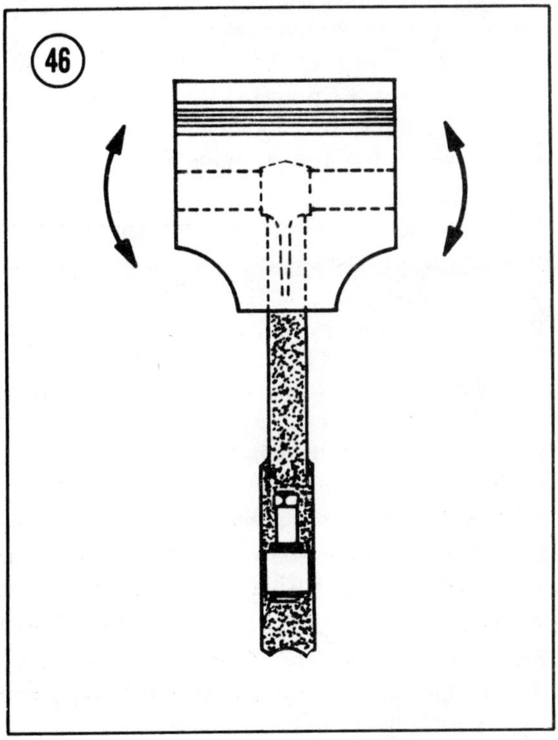

46

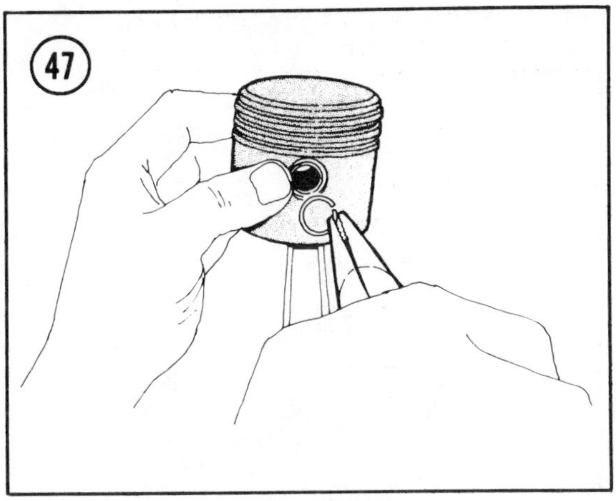

47

5. Repeat Steps 3 and 4 for all other pistons to be removed.

6. Mark pistons, connecting rods, and connecting rod bearing caps 1-4, working from front to rear. See **Figure 45**.

7. Remove connecting rod bolts.

8. Tape bottom end of rod to prevent damage to cylinder walls, and push piston/rod assembly out top of cylinder bore with a piece of hardwood or hammer handle.

9. Remove bearing shells from connecting rods and bearing caps. Mark the backs of the bearings with the cylinder number from which they were removed and whether they were the upper or lower bearing.

> NOTE: *Bearing shells may be reused if they are in good condition, but they must be reinstalled in their original positions.*

Disassembly

1. Remove rings with a ring expander tool.

2. Before removing the piston pin, hold the rod tightly and rock the piston as shown in **Figure 46**. Any rocking movement (do not confuse with sliding motion) indicates wear in the piston pin, rod bushing, pin bore, or more likely, a combination of all three. Mark the piston, pin, and rod for further examination later.

3. Remove the snap rings at each end of the piston pin. See **Figure 47**.

4. Heat the piston and pin with a small butane torch. The piston pin will probably drop right out, but may need coaxing with a brass rod.

48

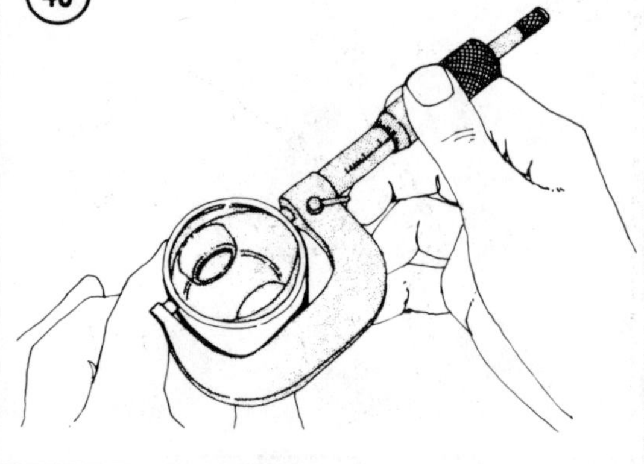

Heat the piston to about 140°F (60°C), i.e., until it is too warm to touch, but not excessively hot.

Inspection

1. Clean pistons thoroughly in solvent. Scrape carbon deposits from the top of the piston and ring grooves. Do not damage the pistons.

CAUTION
Do not wire brush piston skirts.

2. Examine each ring groove for burrs, dented edges, and side wear. Pay particular attention to the top compression ring groove, as it usually wears more than the others.

3. Measure piston-to-cylinder clearance as described below.

4. If damage or wear indicate piston replacement, select a new piston as described under *Piston Clearance* procedure.

5. Measure any parts marked in Step 2 of the disassembly procedure with a micrometer and dial bore gauge to determine which part or parts are worn. Any machinist can do this for you if you do not have micrometers. Replace piston/pin set as a unit if either or both are worn.

Piston Clearance

1. Make sure the piston and cylinder walls are clean and dry.

2. Measure the inside diameter of the cylinder bore at a point ½ in. (13mm) from the upper edge with a bore gauge.

49

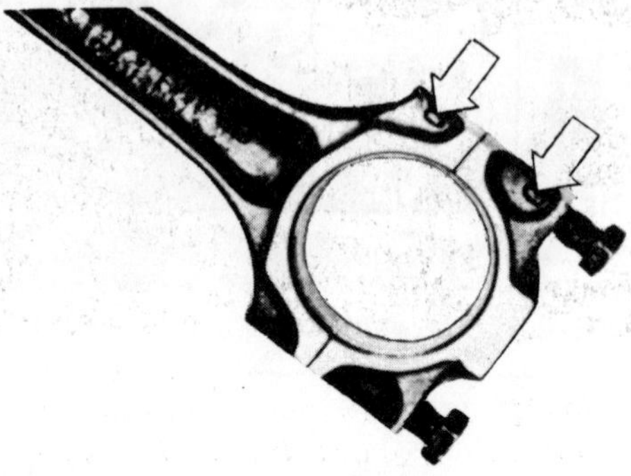

3. Measure the outside diameter of the piston at a point ⅝ in. (16mm) from the lower edge of the piston 90° to the piston pin axis. See **Figure 48**.

4. If the difference in the 2 readings exceeds 0.0016 in. (0.04mm), piston must be replaced.

Assembly

1. Insert snap ring in either end of piston.

2. Coat the connecting rod bushing, piston pin, and piston holes with assembly lubricant.

3. Place the piston over the connecting rod with the top arrow pointing toward the front of the engine and the cast bosses on the connecting rod toward the intermediate shaft. See **Figure 49**.

4. Insert the piston pin and tap it with a plastic hammer until it starts into the connecting rod bushing. If it does not slide in easily, heat the piston until it is warm to the touch, but not too hot (about 140°F/60°C). Continue to drive the piston pin in while holding the piston so that the rod does not have to take any shock. Otherwise, it may be bent. Drive the pin in until it touches the snap ring.

5. Insert the other snap ring.

6. Install rings as described in Steps 3-8 under *Piston Ring Replacement*.

7. Insert bearing shells in connecting rod in the bearing cap with the locating tangs facing toward the cast boss on the connecting rod and cap. See Figure 49.

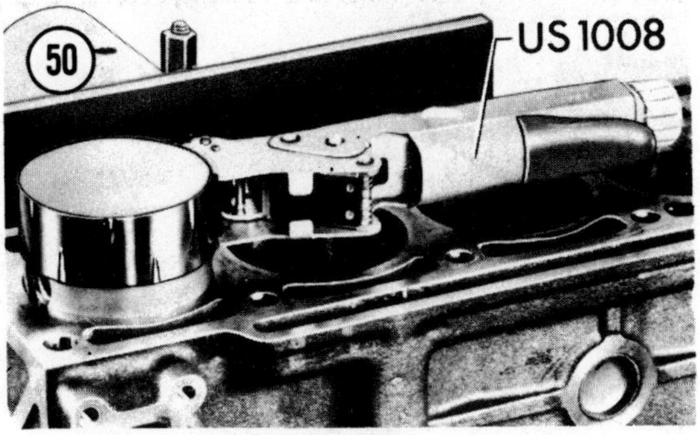

NOTE: *If old bearings are reused, be sure they are installed in their exact original locations.*

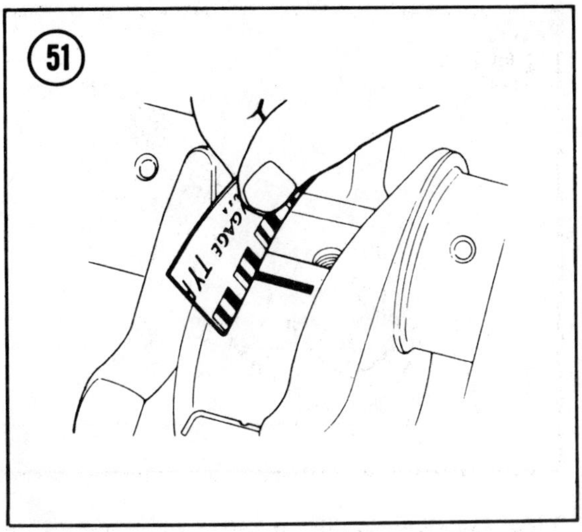

Installation

1. Coat pistons, rings, and cylinder walls with light engine oil.
2. Tape bottom end of connecting rods to prevent damage to the cylinder walls.
3. Insert piston/rod assemblies in their respective bores with the piston arrows pointing toward the front of the engine. See Figure 45.
4. Compress rings with a ring compressor tool and press pistons into bores with a hammer handle. See **Figure 50**.
5. Remove tape from connecting rod end and guide connecting rod onto journal.
6. Loosely install bearing caps, matching marks made during removal.
7. Check bearing clearances as described later in *Bearing and Crankpin Inspection*.

CONNECTING ROD BEARINGS

Bearing and Crankpin Inspection

1. Remove oil pan and oil pump.
2. Remove connecting rod bearing caps. Be sure to mark them so they may be reinstalled in their original positions.
3. Push piston/rod assembly toward head just far enough to gain access to crankpin.

CAUTION
Do not force piston high enough so that top ring contacts ridge at top of cylinder.

4. Wipe bearing inserts and crankpins clean. Check bearing inserts and crankpins for evidence of wear, abrasions, or scoring.
5. Place a piece of Plastigage on one crankpin parallel to the crankshaft.
6. Install rod cap and tighten connecting rod bolt evenly to 25-32 ft.-lb. (3.5-4.5 mkg).

CAUTION
Do not rotate crankshaft while Plastigage is in place.

7. Remove bearing cap.
8. Measure width of flattened Plastigage according to the manufacturer's instructions. See **Figure 51**. Measure at both ends of the Plastigage strip. A difference of 0.001 in. or more indicates a tapered crankpin. Confirm with a micrometer. If bearing is not over 0.004 in. (0.12mm), or less than 0.001 in. (0.03mm), then bearing insert is good. Otherwise, replace bearing insert.
9. Remove Plastigage strip.
10. Repeat Steps 5-9 for each of the other rods.
11. Lubricate bearings and crankpins and install rod caps. Tighten the nuts to 25-32 ft.-lb. (3.5-4.5 mkg).
12. Rotate crankshaft to be sure bearings are not too tight.
13. Insert feeler gauge between connecting rods and crankshaft. Axial clearance should be less than 0.015 in. (0.37mm). See **Figure 52**.

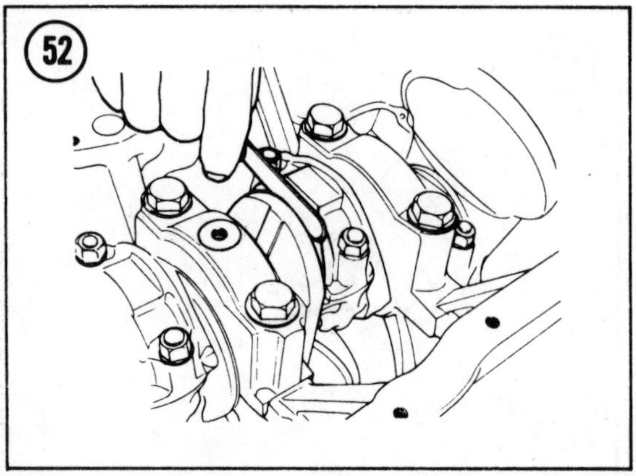

52

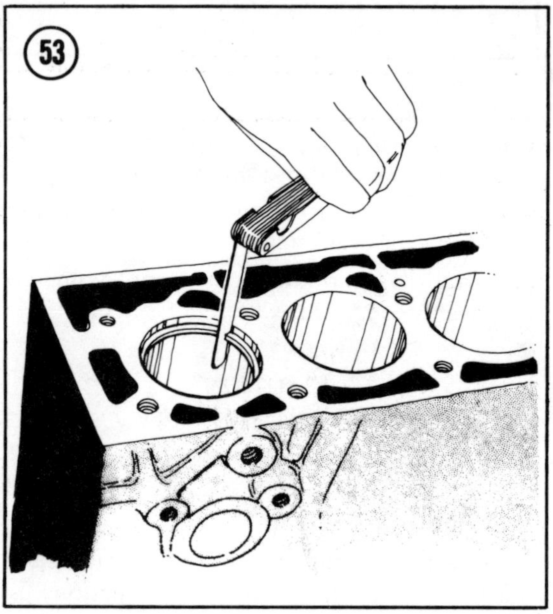

53

Table 6 RING GAP

	Ring gap	Wear limit
Upper piston ring	0.3-0.45mm	1.0mm
Lower piston ring	0.3-0.45mm	1.0mm
Scraper ring	0.25-0.40mm	1.0mm

PISTON RINGS

1. Remove old rings with a ring expander tool.

2. Carefully remove all the carbon from ring grooves. Inspect grooves carefully for burrs, nicks, or broken and cracked lands. Recondition or replace piston if necessary.

3. Check end gap of each ring. To check ring, insert it in the cylinder bore and square it with the wall by tapping with the piston. The ring should be in about ⅝ in. (15mm). Insert a feeler gauge as shown in **Figure 53**. Compare gap with **Table 6**. If the gap is smaller than specified, hold a small file in a vise, grip the ends of the ring with your fingers, and enlarge the gap. See **Figure 54**.

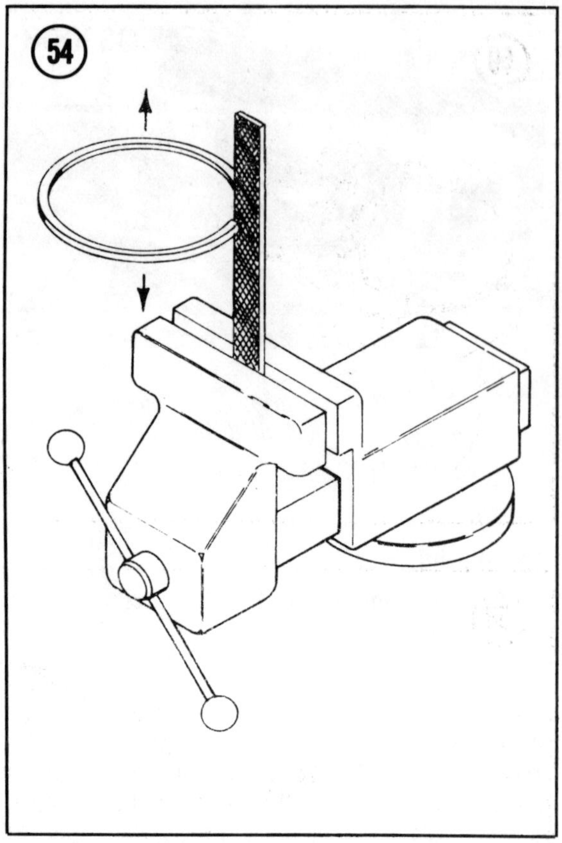

54

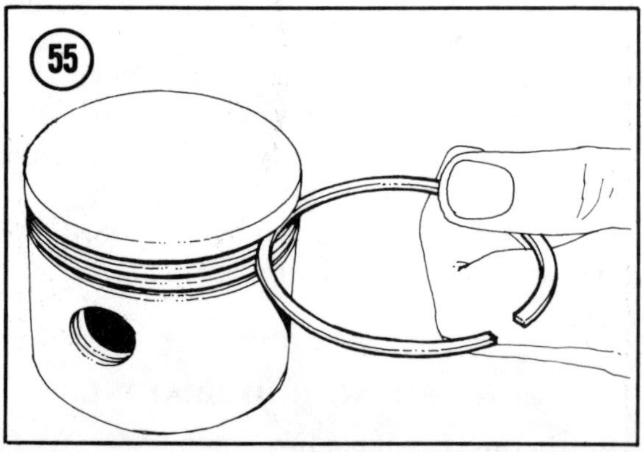

55

4. Roll each ring around its piston groove as shown in **Figure 55** to check for binding. Minor binding may be cleaned up with a fine cut file.

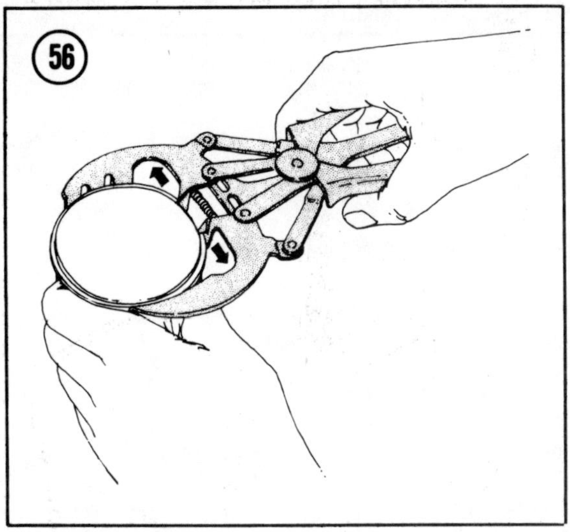

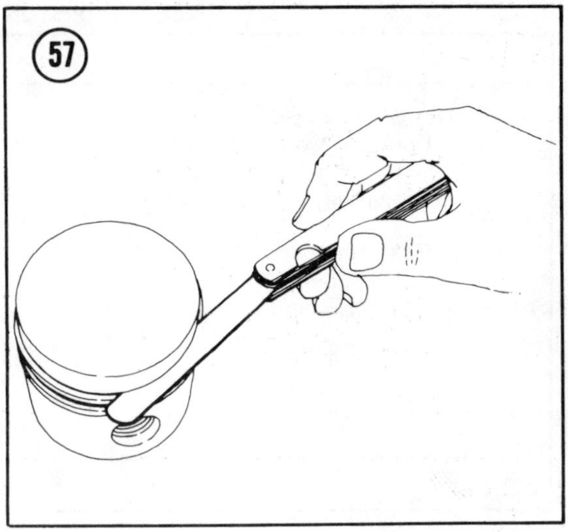

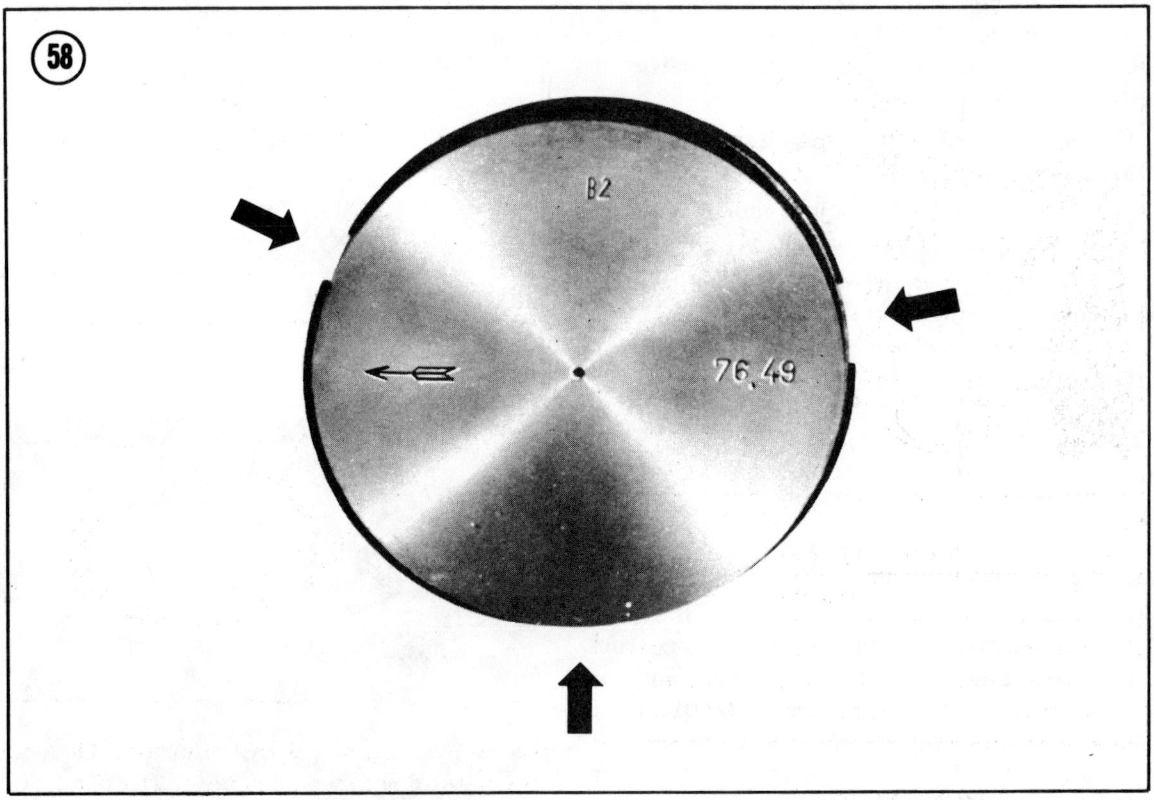

5. Install oil ring in oil ring groove with a ring expander tool. See **Figure 56**.

6. Install 2 compression rings carefully with a ring expander tool.

7. Check side clearance of each ring as shown in **Figure 57**. Compare with specifications for your engine in **Table 7**.

8. Distribute ring gaps around piston as shown in **Figure 58**.

CRANKSHAFT

Bearing and Journal Inspection

Generally, the lower bearing halves wear more rapidly than the upper halves. If the lower

Table 7 PISTON RING SIDE CLEARANCES

	Clearance	Wear Limit
Gasoline Engines		
Upper ring	0.02-0.05mm (0.0008-0.002 in.)	0.15mm (0.006 in.)
Lower ring	0.02-0.05mm (0.0008-0.002 in.)	0.15mm (0.006 in.)
Oil scraper ring	0.02-0.05mm (0.0008-0.002 in.)	0.15mm (0.006 in.)
Diesel engines		
Upper ring	0.06-0.09mm (0.0024-0.0035 in.)	0.2mm (0.008 in.)
Lower ring	0.05-0.08mm (0.002-0.003 in.)	0.2mm (0.008 in.)
Oil scraper ring	0.03-0.06mm (0.001-0.0024 in.)	0.15mm (0.006 in.)

halves are good, it is safe to assume upper halves are good also. If new lower halves are required, replace corresponding upper halves at the same time.

1. Remove rear bearing cap and wipe oil from journal and bearing cap.
2. Check bearing insert in journal for evidence of wear, abrasion, and scoring.
3. Place a piece of Plastigage under the journal, parallel to the crankshaft.
4. Install bearing cap and tighten retaining bolts evenly to 47 ft.-lb. (6.5 mkg).

CAUTION
Do not rotate the crankshaft while Plastigage is in place.

5. Remove bearing cap.
6. Measuring the width of the flattened Plastigage according to manufacturer's instructions. See **Figure 59**. Measure at both ends of Plastigage strip. A difference of 0.001 in. or more indicates a tapered journal. Confirm with a micrometer. If bearing clearance is not over 0.007 in. (0.17mm), or less than 0.001 in. (0.03mm), the bearing insert is good. Otherwise, replace bearing insert.
7. Remove Plastigage strip.
8. Repeat Steps 1-7 for each of the other bearings.
9. Install all bearing shells and caps and tighten bolts to 47 ft.-lb. (6.5 mkg).

59

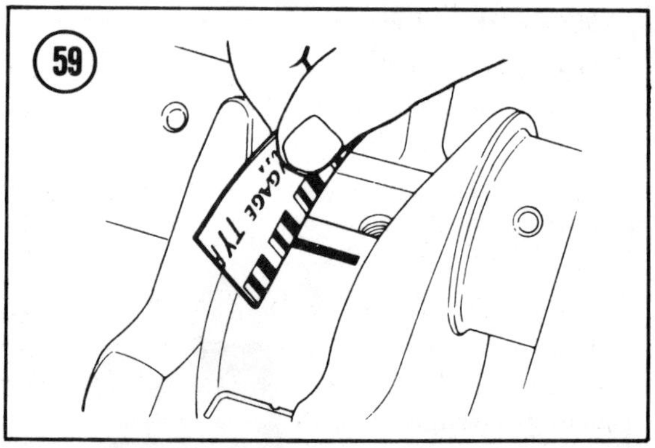

60

10. Force crankshaft as far forward as possible. Insert feeler gauge between the cap for main bearing No. 3 and the crankshaft as shown in **Figure 60**. End play should be 0.0027-0.0067 in. (0.07-0.17mm). If greater than 0.015 in. (0.37mm), replace bearing No. 3 (thrust bearing).

Main Bearing Replacement

Main bearings may be replaced with the engine installed or not. Replace bearings in sets.

Engine Installed

1. Remove oil pan.
2. Remove rear bearing cap and remove bearing insert from cap.
3. Insert long cotter pin into crankshaft journal oil hole. Rotate crankshaft to roll bearing out.
4. Clean crankshaft journal, insert unnotched side of bearing into notched side of block. Using same technique as for removal, roll new bearing insert into place.

> NOTE: *Only the upper bearing insert has an oil hole.*

5. Install new bearing insert cap.
6. Install cap with strip of Plastigage and measure clearance as described in Steps 3-7, *Bearing and Journal Inspection*.
7. If bearing clearance is satisfactory, lubricate journal and bearing halves with assembly lubricant.
8. Install bearing cap and tighten to 10-12 ft.-lb. (1.4-1.6 mkg).
9. Repeat Steps 2-8 for other main bearings.
10. Tap crankshaft rearward with a lead hammer to locate bearing caps in bearings.
11. Tighten main bearing cap bolts to 47 ft.-lb. (6.5 mkg).
12. Force crankshaft as far forward as possible. Insert feeler gauge between main bearing No. 3 and crankshaft as shown in Figure 56. End play should be 0.0027-0.0067 in (0.07-0.17mm) with a new bearing No. 3.
13. Install oil pan and refill with engine oil.

Engine Removed

If the engine is removed, simply follow the crankshaft removal and installation procedures below.

Crankshaft Removal

1. Remove oil pan and oil pump.
2. Mark all main bearing caps and connecting rod caps so that they will be reinstalled in exactly the same location. See **Figure 61**.
3. Remove connecting rod bearing caps. Push piston/rod assemblies toward the heads.
4. Remove main bearing caps.
5. Remove front and rear seal flanges from cylinder block.
6. Carefully lift the crankshaft out of the cylinder block.
7. Remove main bearing inserts from cylinder block and main bearing caps. If they are reusable, mark their location on the back of the insert with a pencil.
8. Remove connecting rod bearing inserts from rods and rod caps. If they are reusable, mark their location on the back of the insert with a pencil.

Crankshaft Inspection

1. Check connecting rod side clearance and bearing clearance as described earlier.
2. Clean crankshaft thoroughly with solvent. Clean oil holes with rifle cleaning brushes; flush thoroughly and blow dry with air. Lightly oil all journal surfaces immediately to prevent rust.
3. Carefully inspect each journal for scratches, ridges, scoring, nicks, etc. Very small nicks and scratches may be removed with crocus cloth. More serious damage must be removed by grinding, a job for a machine shop.
4. If the surface finish on all journals is satisfactory, take the crankshaft to your dealer or local machine shop. They can check out-of-roundness, taper, and wear on the journals. They can also check crankshaft alignment and inspect for cracks.

Crankshaft Installation

1. Make sure the cylinder block bearing saddles, bearing caps, bearing inserts, and crankshaft journals are perfectly clean. A small piece of grit behind a bearing insert could deform the bearing and lead to very early failure.

2. Install new upper main bearing inserts in cylinder block. Upper halves have an oil hole. The lower halves do not. Make sure that the bearing tang fits in the cutout in the block. See **Figure 62**.

CAUTION

Do not file bearings or bearing saddles to get a better fit. The ends of the bearings normally protrude slightly. This bearing crush causes the bearing to be forced tightly against the saddle and cap when the caps are tightened down. See ***Figure 63****, which is exaggerated for clarity.*

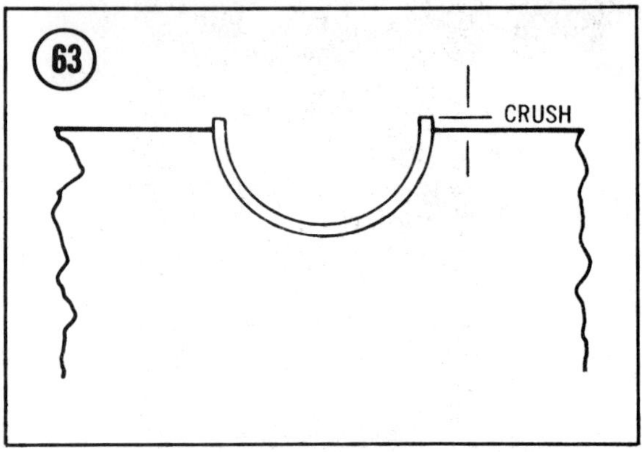

3. Install new lower bearing inserts in the main bearing caps. Make certain that the bearing tang fits in the cutout in the cap and observe the caution above.

4. Install new bearing inserts in connecting rod caps.

5. Carefully lower crankshaft into place. Be careful not to damage the bearing or journal surfaces.

6. Check clearance of each main bearing following Steps 4-8, *Bearing and Journal Inspection*.

7. If bearing clearance is satisfactory, lubricate the journal and bearing halves with assembly lubricant.

8. Install bearing caps and tighten to 47 ft.-lb. (6.5 mkg).

9. Tap crankshaft rearward with a lead hammer to locate bearing caps in bearings.

10. Tighten main bearing cap bolts to 47 ft.-lb. (6.5 mkg).

11. Force crankshaft as far forward as possible. Insert feeler gauge between main bearing No. 3 and crankshaft as shown in Figure 56. End play should be 0.0027-0.0067 in. (0.07-0.17mm).

12. Install rods on crankshaft as described in *Connecting Rod* section.

CAMSHAFT

It is not necessary to remove the cylinder head in order to remove the camshaft.

1. Remove valve cover from cylinder head if not previously done.

2. Remove bearing caps 1, 3, and 5. See **Figure 64** (gasoline engine shown; diesel similar).

3. Loosen diagonally opposite nuts on bearing caps 2 and 4 a turn at a time to gently relieve valve spring pressure.

CAUTION

Camshaft can be bent by spring pressure unless bearing caps are removed exactly as described.

4. Remove camshaft bearing cap mounting nuts when all pressure is relieved.

5. Lift out the camshaft.

6. Installation is the reverse of these steps. Tighten diagonally opposite nuts on bearing

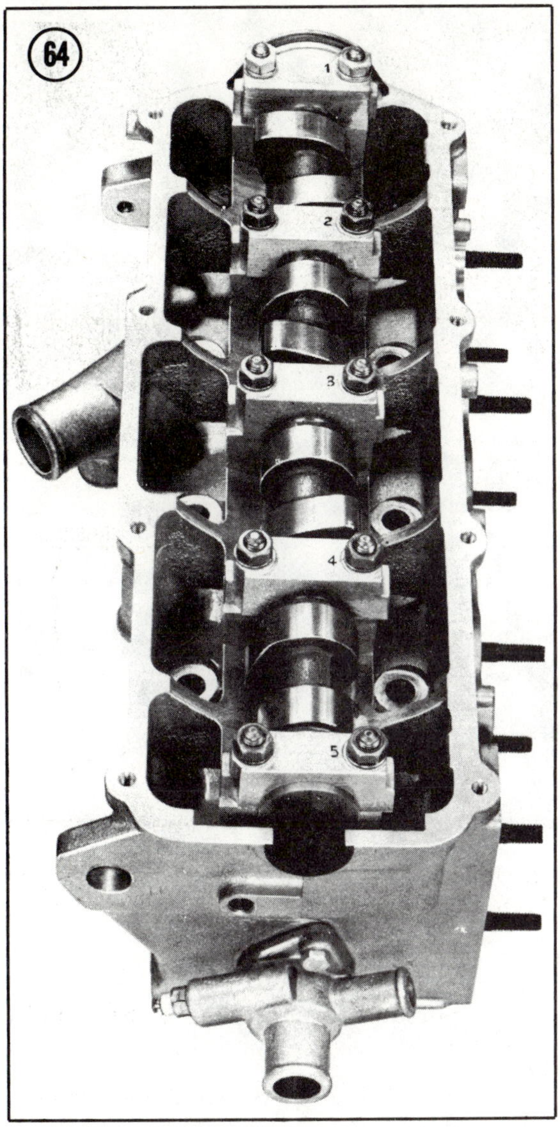

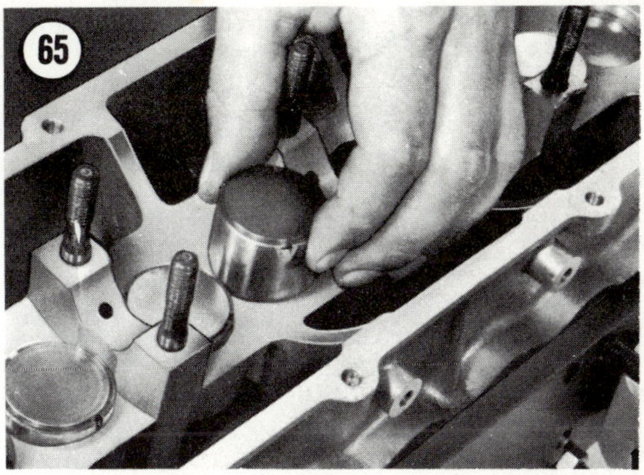

caps 2 and 4 a turn at a time. Then install bearing caps 1, 3, and 5. Torque all nuts to 13-15 ft.-lb. (1.8-2.2 mkg).

VALVE TAPPETS

1. Remove camshaft as described earlier.

CAUTION
Follow the camshaft removal and installation procedure exactly to prevent distortion of the camshaft.

2. Lift out tappets as shown in **Figure 65**. Store them so that they may be reinstalled in their original positions.

3. When installing tappets, apply a light coat of oil before insertion in the cylinder head. Install tappets in their original positions only.

INTERMEDIATE SHAFT

1. Remove camshaft timing belt as described elsewhere.
2. Remove timing gear from intermediate shaft.
3. Remove fuel pump (1975-1976 models only) and distributor.
4. Remove intermediate shaft bearing flange and seal.
5. Pull intermediate shaft out of block. See **Figure 66**.
6. Pry the old oil seal from the intermediate shaft flange.
7. Insert intermediate shaft into block.
8. Install intermediate shaft flange.
9. Press new seal into flange with special tool 10-203 or equivalent.
10. Install timing gear.
11. Install fuel pump (1975-1976 models) and distributor.
12. Install camshaft timing belt as described elsewhere.

CRANKSHAFT SEAL (FLYWHEEL SIDE)

Replacement (Engine Removed)

1. Remove flywheel.
2. Remove rear bearing flange.
3. Press old seal out of flange.

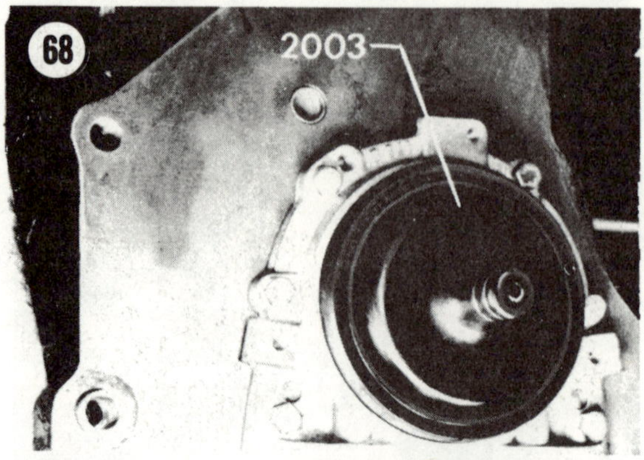

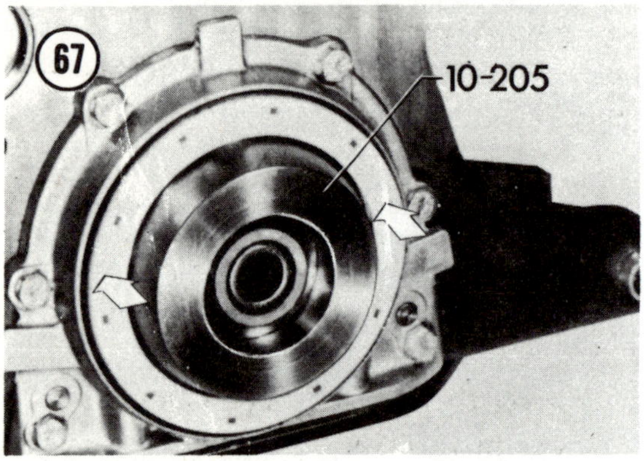

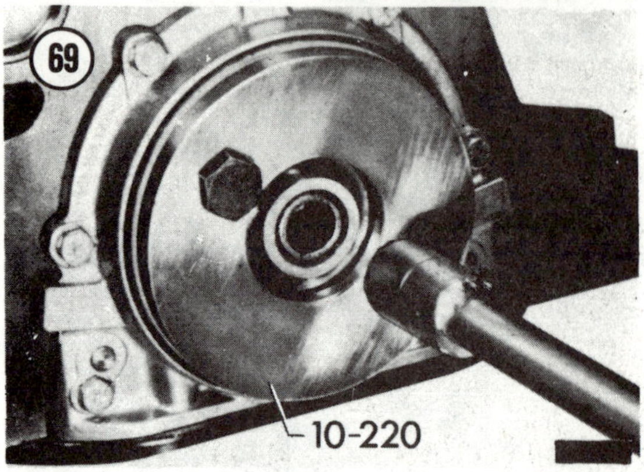

4. Clean flange and mating surface on cylinder block thoroughly. Be sure to remove all traces of old gasket.

5. Bolt flange onto the cylinder block with a new gasket.

6. On very early models having 3.228 in. (82mm) flywheel flange, install the special tool 10-205 (**Figure 67**) and slide a new seal over the special tool as far as possible. Remove the tool. On later models having a 3.346 in. (85mm) flywheel flange, center new seal using one part of 2-part tool 2003 as shown in **Figure 68**.

7. On early models, press the seal in completely with tool 10-220 by tightening both bolts alternately as shown in **Figure 69**. On later models, use second part of tool 2003 as shown in **Figure 70**.

Replacement (Engine In Vehicle)

1. Remove the transmission as described in Chapter Eight.

2. Remove flywheel.

3. Pry old seal out with a screwdriver as shown in **Figure 71**.

4. Clean seal cavity in flange thoroughly.

5. Perform Steps 6 and 7 of the replacement procedure above.

CRANKSHAFT SEAL (TIMING GEAR SIDE)

Replacement (Engine Removed)

1. Remove camshaft timing belt as described elsewhere.

2. Remove timing gears from crankshaft and intermediate shaft.

3. Remove front crankshaft flange.

4. Press old seal from flange.

5. Clean flange and mating surface on cylinder block thoroughly. Remove all traces of the old gasket.

6. Install the flange on the cylinder block with a new gasket.

7. Install new seal in flange with special tool

10-203 as shown in **Figure 72**. Press it in until it is flush with the flange.

Replacement (Engine In Vehicle)

1. Remove camshaft timing belt as described elsewhere.
2. Hold crankshaft at TDC, using a screwdriver against the flywheel, accessible through an opening in the transmission case.

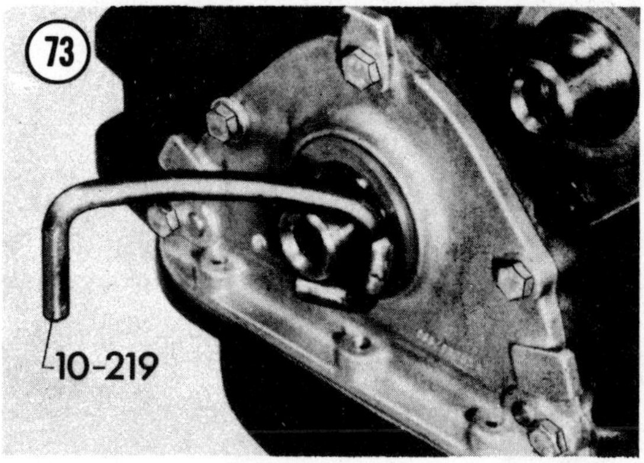

3. Remove the crankshaft pulley belt.
4. Remove the pulley.
5. Pry old seal out with special tool 10-219. See **Figure 73**.

CAUTION
This special tool must not fit between the seal and the crankshaft. Instead, the special tool cuts through the dust lip and over the inner edge of the support ring of the seal.

6. Clean out the seal cavity thoroughly.
7. Press in new seal with special tool 10-203 until it is flush. See Figure 72.
8. Install crankshaft pulley but do not tighten mounting bolt.
9. Install camshaft timing belt exactly as described elsewhere. Tighten the crankshaft pulley bolt after the timing belt is in place.

FLYWHEEL

Removal

Remove flywheel and clutch disc as described in Chapter Eight.

Inspection

1. Check ring gear teeth for wear or damage.
2. Check clutch friction surface of flywheel for cracks and grooves. If necessary, recondition or replace flywheel.

Installation

Mount flywheel and clutch disc as described in Chapter Eight.

4

Table 1 ENGINE SPECIFICATIONS

		FC, FG, 1975	FN, 1976
Type		4-cylinder, four-stroke, in line	4-cylinder, four-stroke, in line
Fuel grade		Unleaded (minimum 91 RON)	Unleaded (minimum 91 RON)
Bore		3.01 in. (76.5mm)	3.13 in. (79.5mm)
Stroke		3.15 in. (80.0mm)	3.15 in. (80.0mm)
Swept volume		1470cc	1588cc
Compression ratio		8.2:1	8.2:1
Output SAE HP		70 @ 5,800 rpm	71 @ 5.600 rpm
Torque SAE		81 ft.-lb. @ 3,500 rpm	86 ft.-lb. @ 3,000 rpm
Tappet clearance:	Intake	Warm 0.008 to 0.012 in. (0.20 to 0.30mm)*	Warm 0.008 to 0.012 in. (0.20 to 0.30mm)*
		Cold 0.006 to 0.010 in. (0.15 to 0.25mm)	Cold 0.006 to 0.010 in. (0.15 to 0.25mm)
	Exhaust	Warm 0.016 to 0.020 in. (0.40 to 0.50mm)*	Warm 0.016 to 0.020 in. (0.40 to 0.50mm)*
		Cold 0.014 to 0.018 in. (0.35 to 0.45mm)	Cold 0.014 to 0.018 in. (0.35 to 0.45mm)
Valve timing (1mm valve stroke at 0 tappet clearance)			
Intake opens		4° BTDC	4° BTDC
Intake closes		47° ABDC	47° ABDC
Exhaust opens		43° BBDC	43° BBDC
Exhaust closes		7° ATDC	7° ATDC
Piston play		0.0012 in. (0.03mm)	0.0012 in. (0.03mm)
Oil pressure, minimum		14 psi (1.0 kg/cm^2) at idle & 176° F/80°C	14 psi (1.0 kg/cm^2) at idle & 176°F/80°C
Oil pressure, maximum		100 psi (7.0 kg/cm^2) from 5,000 rpm	100 psi (7.0 kg/cm^2) from 5,000 rpm
Idle speed		925 ± 75 rpm	925 ± 75 rpm
Maximum speed		6,500 rpm	6,500 rpm
Point gap		0.016 in. (0.4mm)	0.016 in. (0.4mm)
Dwell angle		44-50°	44-50°
Ignition timing		3° ATDC	3° ATDC
Firing order		1-3-4-2	1-3-4-2
Spark plugs:	Bosch	W200T30	W200T30
	Beru	200/14/3A1	200/14/3A1
Electrode gap		0.028 in. (0.7mm)	0.028 in. (0.7mm)
Idle CO content		2.0 ± 0.5%	1.5 ± 0.7% (1.0 ± 0.7% on auto. trans., except California)

*Coolant temperature 95°F (35°C)

(continued)

Table 1 **ENGINE SPECIFICATIONS** (continued)

		EE, EF, 1976-1977; EH, 1978
Type		4-cylinder, four-stroke, in line
Fuel grade		Unleaded (minimum 91 RON)
Bore		3.13 in. (79.5mm)
Stroke		3.15 in. (80.0mm)[1]
Swept volume		1588cc[2]
Compression ratio		8.0:1
Output SAE HP		78 @ 5,000 rpm (76, California)[3]
Torque SAE		84.1 ft.-lb. @ 3,200 rpm (82.7, California)[4]
Tappet clearance:	Intake	Warm 0.008 to 0.012 in. (0.20 to 0.30mm)*
		Cold 0.006 to 0.010 in. (0.15 to 0.25mm)
	Exhaust	Warm 0.016 to 0.020 in. (0.40 to 0.50mm)*
		Cold 0.014 to 0.018 in. (0.35 to 0.45mm)
Valve timing		
(1mm valve stroke at 0 tappet clearance)		
Intake opens		4° BTDC
Intake closes		47° ABDC
Exhaust opens		43° BBDC
Exhaust closes		7° ATDC
Piston play		0.0012 in. (0.03mm)
Oil pressure, minimum		28 psi (2.0 kg/cm²) at 2,000 rpm and 140°F/60°C
Oil pressure, maximum		100 psi (7.0 kg/cm²) from 5,000 rpm
Idle speed		925 ± 75 rpm
Maximum speed		6,500 rpm
Point gap		0.016 in. (0.4mm)
Dwell angle		44-50°
Ignition timing		3° ATDC
Firing order		1-3-4-2
Spark plugs:	Bosch	W175T30
	Beru	175/14/3A
Electrode gap		0.028 in. (0.7mm)
Idle CO content		1.5% max., man. trans. (0.3% California)
		1.0% max., auto. trans. (0.3% California)

*Coolant temperature 95°F (35°C)

1. EH = 2.89 in. (73.4mm)
2. EH = 1457cc
3. EH = 75 @ 5,800 rpm (California slightly less)
4. EH = 73 ft.-lb. @ 3,500 rpm (California slightly less)

(continued)

Table 1 ENGINE SPECIFICATIONS (continued)

		DIESEL
Type		4-cylinder, four-stroke, in line
Fuel grade		Diesel fuel
Bore		3.01 in. (76.5mm)
Stroke		3.15 in. (80.0mm)
Swept volume		1470cc
Compression ratio		23.5:1
Output SAE HP		48 @ 5,000 rpm
Torque SAE		58 ft.-lb. @ 2,500 rpm
Tappet clearance:	Intake	Warm 0.008 to 0.012 in. (0.20 to 0.30mm)*
		Cold 0.006 to 0.010 in. (0.15 to 0.25mm)
	Exhaust	Warm 0.016 to 0.020 in. (0.40 to 0.50mm)*
		Cold 0.014 to 0.018 in. (0.35 to 0.45mm)
Piston play		0.0012 in. (0.03mm)
Oil pressure, minimum normal		28 psi (2.0 kg/cm^2) at 2,000 rpm & 176 °F/80 °C
Idle speed		820 ± 50 rpm
Maximum speed		5,400-5,450 rpm
Firing order		1-3-4-2

*Coolant temperature 95 °F (35 °C) or higher

Table 2 TIGHTENING TORQUES

Engine	Ft.-lbs.	Mkg
Gasoline Engine		
Cylinder head to engine block (M 11)	54.2 cold/61.5 warm	7.5 cold/8.5 warm
Crankshaft bearing caps to engine block (M 10)	47	6.5
Flywheel to crankshaft (M 10 x 1)	36	5.0
Sprocket to intermediate shaft (M 12 x 1.5)	57.8	8.0
Connecting rod (M 9 x 1)	25.3	3.5-4.5
Water pump to engine block (M 8)	14.4	2.0
Flange to engine block (M 6)	7.2	1.0
Fuel pump to engine block (M 8)	12.3	1.7-2.2
Intermediate shaft guide to engine block (M 8)	18.0	2.5
Pulley to crankshaft (M 12 x 1.5)	57.8	8.0
Distributor clamp to engine block (M 8)	14.4	2.0
Alternator bracket to engine block (M 8)	23.8	3.3
Alternator to bracket (M 8)	18.0	2.5
Alternator adjuster to cylinder head and alternator (M 8)	14.4	2.0
Water drain plug (M 10 x 1)	25.3	3.5
Pulley to cam belt pulley (M 8)	18.0	2.5
Oil pump cover (M 6)	5.8	0.8-1.2
Oil pump to engine block (M 8)	13.0	1.8-2.2
Oil pan plug (M 14 x 1.5)	18.0	2.5
Oil pan to engine block (M 6)	7.2[1]	1.0[1]
Oil filter bracket to engine block (M 8)	18.0	2.5
Oil filter to oil filter bracket	18.0	2.5-3.5
Bearing housing to water pump housing (M 6)	7.2	1.0
Water pump pulley to hub (M 8)	14.4	2.0
Cover to water pump housing (M 6)	7.2	1.0
Carburetor stud to intake manifold (M 8)	14.4	2.0
Bracket to intake manifold (M 8)	14.4	2.0
Exhaust manifold stud to cylinder head (M 8)	16.6	2.3
Camshaft bearing cap to cylinder head (M 8)	13.0	1.8-2.2
Exhaust manifold to cylinder head (M 8)	18.0	2.5
Intake manifold to cylinder head (M8 x 80)	18.0	2.5
Sprocket to camshaft (M 12 x 1.5)	57.8	8.0
Tensioner to cylinder head (M 10)	32.5	4.5
Cylinder head cover to cylinder head (M 6)	5.8	0.8
Carburetor to intake manifold (M 8)	14.4	2.0
Plug in cylinder head (M 26)	43.4	6.0
Water adaptor to cylinder head (M 6)	7.2	1.0
Heater flange to cylinder head (M 6)	7.2	1.0
Guard to exhaust manifold (M 8)	14.4	2.0
Intake manifold support to intake manifold (M 8)	14.4	2.0
Oil pressure switch	8.6	1.2
Spark plug (M 14)	21.7	3.0
Intake manifold support to exhaust manifold (M 8)	18.0	2.5

(continued)

4

Table 2 TIGHTENING TORQUES (continued)

Engine	Ft.-lbs.	Mkg
Gasoline Engine (cont'd)		
Cam belt guard	6.5	0.9
Clutch to flywheel (M 8)	23.8	3.3
Engine to transmission (12)	39.8	5.5
Engine support to engine block (M 10)	31.8	4.4
Clutch pressure plate to flywheel (M 8)	23.1	3.2
Diesel Engine[2]		
Tensioner	33	4.5
Camshaft gear	33	4.5
Injection pump gear	33	4.5
Upper and lower parts of injectors	51	7.0
Injector/cylinder head	51	7.0
Injection pump	18	2.5
Injection lines	18	2.5
Adapters on injection pump	18	2.5
Fuel shutoff valve/pump	33	4.5
Glow plug/cylinder head	14	2.0
Cylinder head bolts		
Hot/warm	69	9.5
Cold[2]	61	8.5

1. 14.4 ft.-lb. (2.0 mkg) on 1976 models.
2. Values not listed here are same as those for gasoline engines.

CHAPTER FIVE

FUEL, EXHAUST, AND EMISSION CONTROL SYSTEMS

5

CARBURETTED SYSTEM (1975-1976)

This section contains repair and replacement procedures for the carburetted fuel, exhaust, and emission control systems. The fuel system consists of a rear mounted tank, mechanical fuel pump, and a 2-barrel Zenith carburetor. The exhaust system uses a muffler, catalytic converter and interconnecting pipes. The emission control system includes air injection and exhaust gas recirculation to minimize harmful emissions. In addition, fuel evaporation control prevents emission of gasoline vapor while the car is parked. All of these systems are described in detail.

Further emission control is provided by a temperature valve that shuts off vacuum to the distributor advance system until the engine is warmed up to 130-142°F (55-61°C). This holds the distributor in the retarded position, which speeds warm-up of the engine and the catalytic converter. The temperature valve opens the vacuum supply after warm-up, allowing normal operation of the vacuum advance system.

Carburetors on 1976 models have a cold-idle enrichment valve. A temperature valve opens when coolant temperatures are below 55-68°F (13-20°C). This supplies vacuum to open the cold-idle enrichment valve to supply extra fuel during idling until the engine warms up, at which time the temperature valve shuts off the vacuum supply to the enrichment valve. This allows the idle system to function in a normal manner.

A temperature-controlled accelerator pump is used on 1976 models. This system allows maximum fuel delivery by the accelerator pump when the engine is cold, i.e. 113-141°F (45-61°C), but restricts the delivery of the pump above this temperature.

Additional temperature valves control automatic choke pull down and second-stage throttle operation on 1976 models.

The complexity and interdependence of these systems, and the special tools and knowledge required to work on them, indicate that most emission problems should be referred to your Volkswagen dealer.

FUEL SYSTEM

The fuel system consists of a rear mounted fuel tank connected through a line to the fuel pump. An eccentric cam on the intermediate shaft, driven by the camshaft drive belt, operates the mechanical fuel pump which delivers fuel to a 2-barrel Zenith carburetor.

AIR CLEANER

The air cleaner should be cleaned every 15,000 miles and replaced every 30,000 miles. Refer to Chapter Three. To remove the air cleaner housing and connecting hoses:

1. Release clip securing housing to body.
2. Disconnect warm air hose at base of housing. See **Figure 1**.
3. Remove nut at top of carburetor (Figure 1).
4. Disconnect crankcase ventilation hose. See Figure 1.
5. Remove housing complete with hose.
6. Installation is the reverse of these steps.

ZENITH 32/32-2B2 CARBURETOR

To work on the carburetor, you must have a clean work area and use the proper tools and cleaning agents. Many of the carburetor passages are small. Any restrictions for the flow of either air or fuel will result in adjustment difficulties and poor engine performance. In some cases setting CO and hydrocarbon levels will be impossible.

Due to the extremely critical adjustments made and the large number of parts changes from the 1975 to 1976 models, approach rebuilding and adjustments in the following manner:

1. Read this section through *completely* before starting to work.
2. Select a clean work area. It should have a large flat space, good lighting and good ventilation. Extinguish any pilot lights within 50 feet of the work area or where gasoline is present.
3. Allow ample time, 3 hours at least.
4. Visually inspect the carburetor prior to removal. Look for fuel leaks at hoses, cracks in vacuum lines, obvious worn parts, etc. This will save additional trips for parts.
5. Refer to **Table 1** for needed overhaul parts.
6. Use only high quality carburetor cleaner and solvent.
7. Only one "special" tool is required: A 0-25cc calibrated glass vial. It is sometimes difficult to acquire one so order from a druggist first.

Removal

1. Disconnect the battery ground cable.
2. Remove hoses at the black carburetor cover.

1. Warm air hose 2. Air cleaner nut 3. PCV hose

Table 1 CARBURETOR OVERHAUL PARTS

Gasket between body and throttle plate
Accelerator pump discharge arm
Accelerator pump spring (new design)
Carburetor top gasket — 1975
Carburetor top gasket — 1976
Secondary throttle linkage (w/ball)
Secondary diaphragm operating rod
Accelerator pump thermostat valve kit
Choke housing w/open circuit heating valve
Thermostat for pre-heat flap, air cleaner

Remove air cleaner connection at top of carburetor. See Figure 1.

3. Remove nut holding cover in place. Remove cover and rubber gasket.

4. Remove the 3 choke housing screws. *Do not* remove the water lines from the choke housing. This is a sealed unit and no leakage should occur.

WARNING

If the engine is hot the cooling system is under 15 lb. pressure.

5. Remove fuel line clamp and fuel line. Plug line.

6. Remove accelerator cable linkage. On vehicles with automatic transmissions, do not lose the small retaining pin at the extreme end of the cable.

7. Remove all vacuum hoses from the carburetor body. Each connection has a color coded plastic ring to identify where the vacuum line connects in the engine compartment. As each hose is removed:

   a. Mark the hose for identification.
   b. Refer to **Figures 2 and 3** to verify that they were correctly connected *before* removal.

8. Remove black wires at the choke heater and the electro-magnetic idle circuit cutoff valve.

9. Remove the brown ground wire attached to the carburetor top with a bolt.

10. Completely loosen the 4 carburetor mounting bolts. Remove the closest to the front of the car. The rear bolts must be removed with the carburetor as they will not clear the firewall.

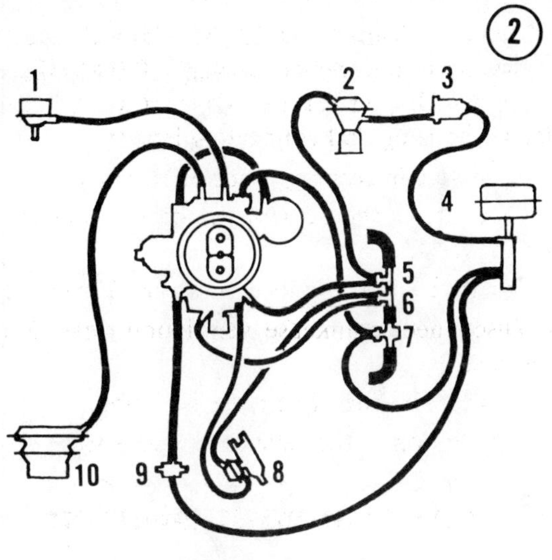

1. Anti-backfire valve
2. EGR valve
3. Two-way valve
4. Brake booster
5. EGR temperature valve
6. Vacuum advance temperature valve
7. Accelerator pump temperature valve
8. Distributor
9. Vacuum delay valve
10. Diverter valve

11. Lift the carburetor off of its rubber manifold mount and set on workbench.

CAUTION

Cover the intake manifold openings. Small parts such as screws or nuts could fall unnoticed and damage the engine.

Disassembly/Inspection

Refer to **Figures 4 and 5** to help identify parts.

1. If possible support the carburetor so that both hands can be used. A bolt held in a vise makes a suitable support.

2. Remove the cotter key holding the choke rod to the plate. See **Figure 6**. When withdrawing the rod do not lose the plastic bushing or washers.

3. Using a screwdriver, gently pry the accelerator pump rod out of its plastic bushing. See **Figure 7**.

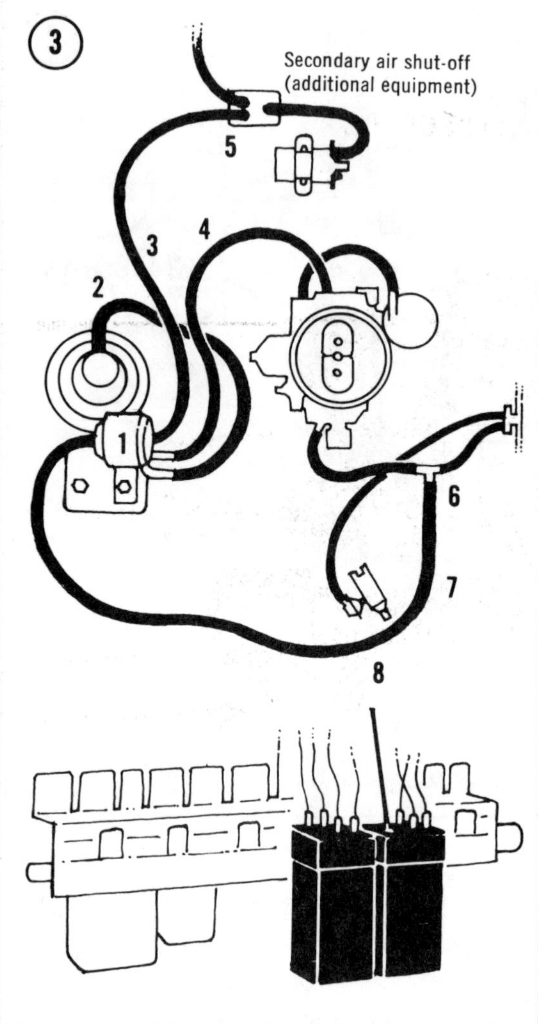

4. Pull the secondary diaphragm rod downward until the rod is released from its ball socket. Check the ball for flat spots or out-of-round condition. Check pull rod at ball seat end for signs of wear. Replace necessary parts.

5. Remove the carburetor top screws. *Do not* discard the thin metal numbered plate. This number is necessary for the ordering of all carburetor parts.

6. Gently tap the sides of the carburetor top to loosen from the gasket and remove top. Set on bench upside down to keep from damaging floats.

7. Remove the floats by pushing the hinge pins toward the outside. If very tight tap with a thin stiff wire.

8. Inspect seats and needles. Needles are spring loaded ball type. Check for spring tension. Check tip of needle for grooves or wear. Check seats for burrs. Replace as necessary.

9. Remove all threaded jets. See **Figure 8**.

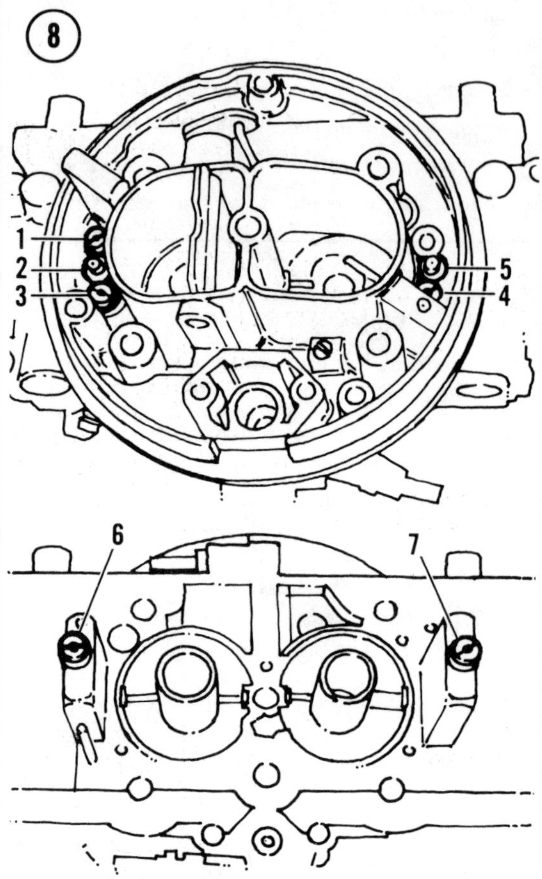

1. First stage auxiliary air and fuel jet
2. Air correction jet
3. First stage air mixture and fuel jet
4. Second stage air mixture and fuel jet
5. Air correction jet
6. Second stage main jet
7. First stage main jet

10. Check movement of choke plate and inspect for possible air leaks between housing and choke pivot rod shaft.

11. Place carburetor top in carburetor cleaner.

12. Remove screws holding vacuum diaphragm unit to carburetor body.

13. On California cars remove micro-switch.

14. Remove dashpot assembly complete.

4

ZENITH 32/32-2B2 CARBURETOR

5

5

ZENITH 32/32-2B2 CARBURETOR

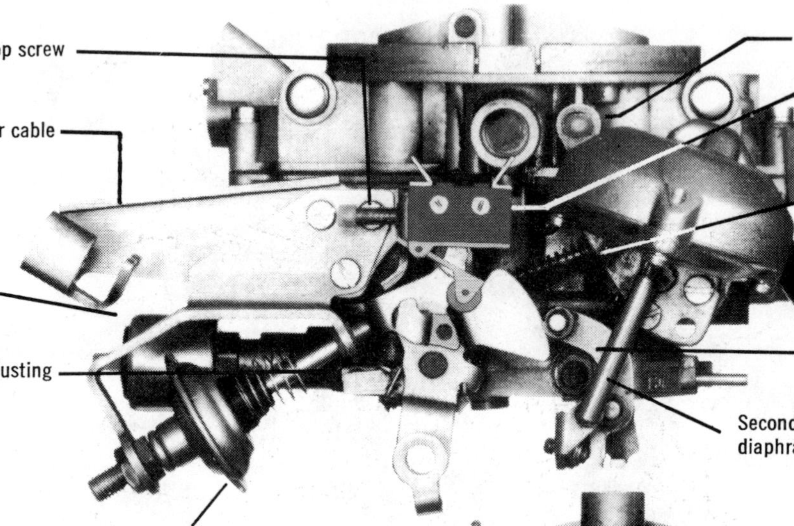

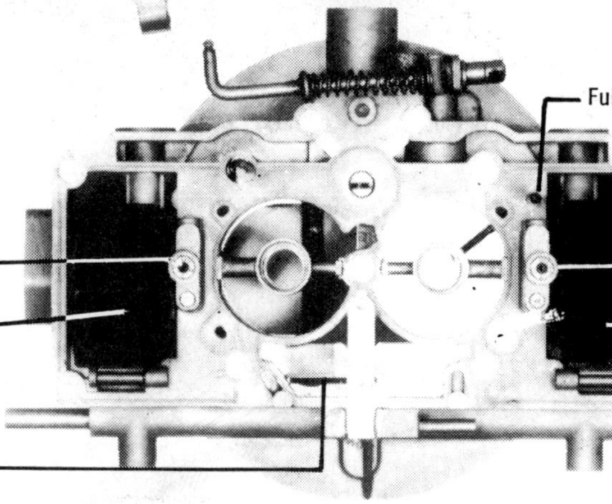

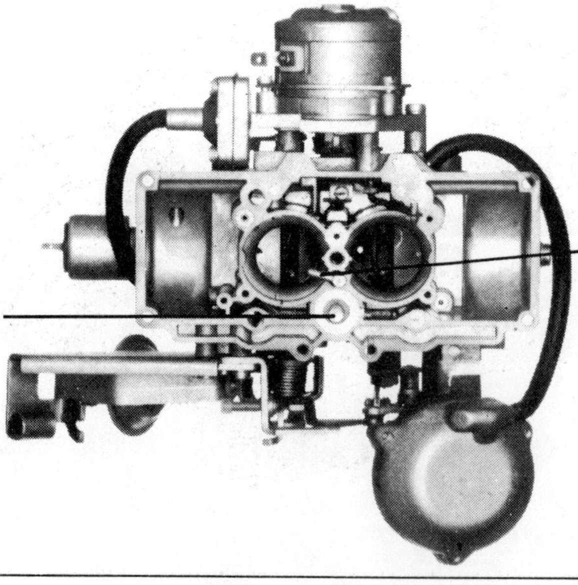

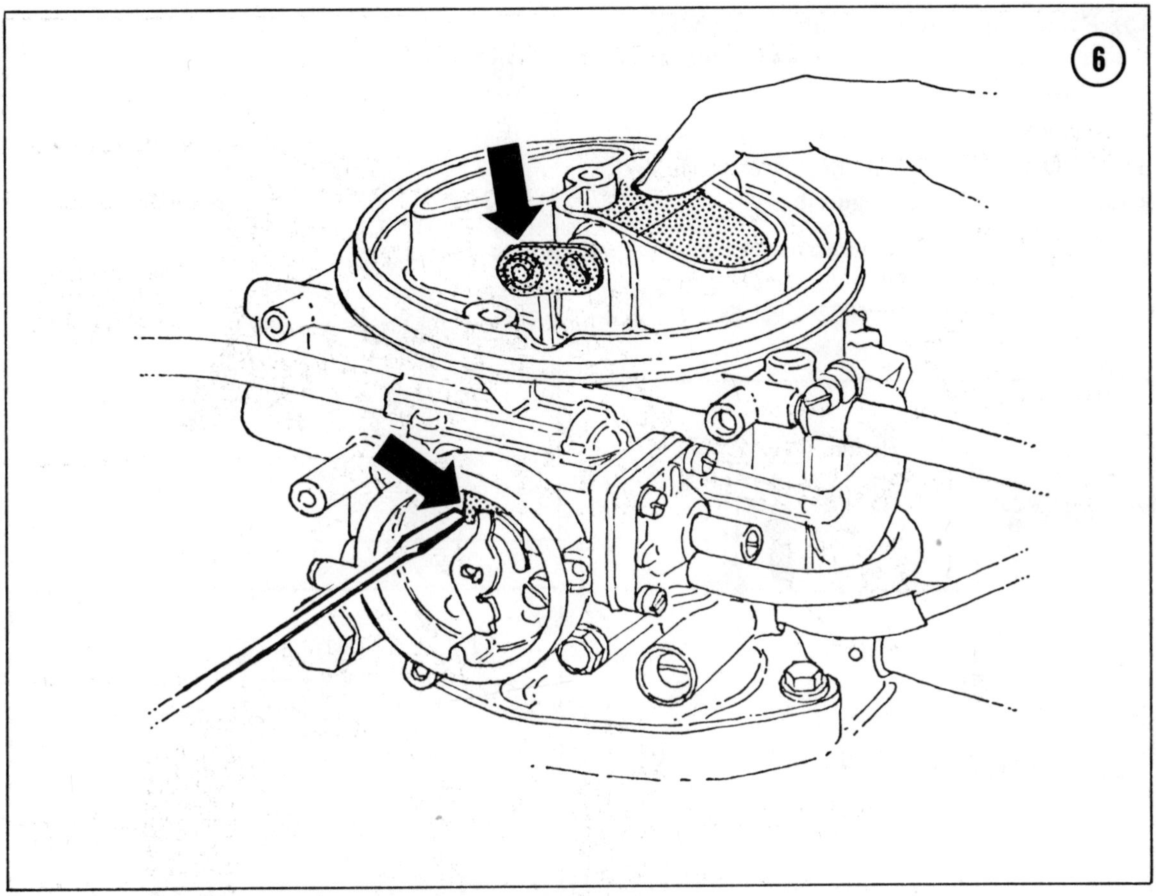
6

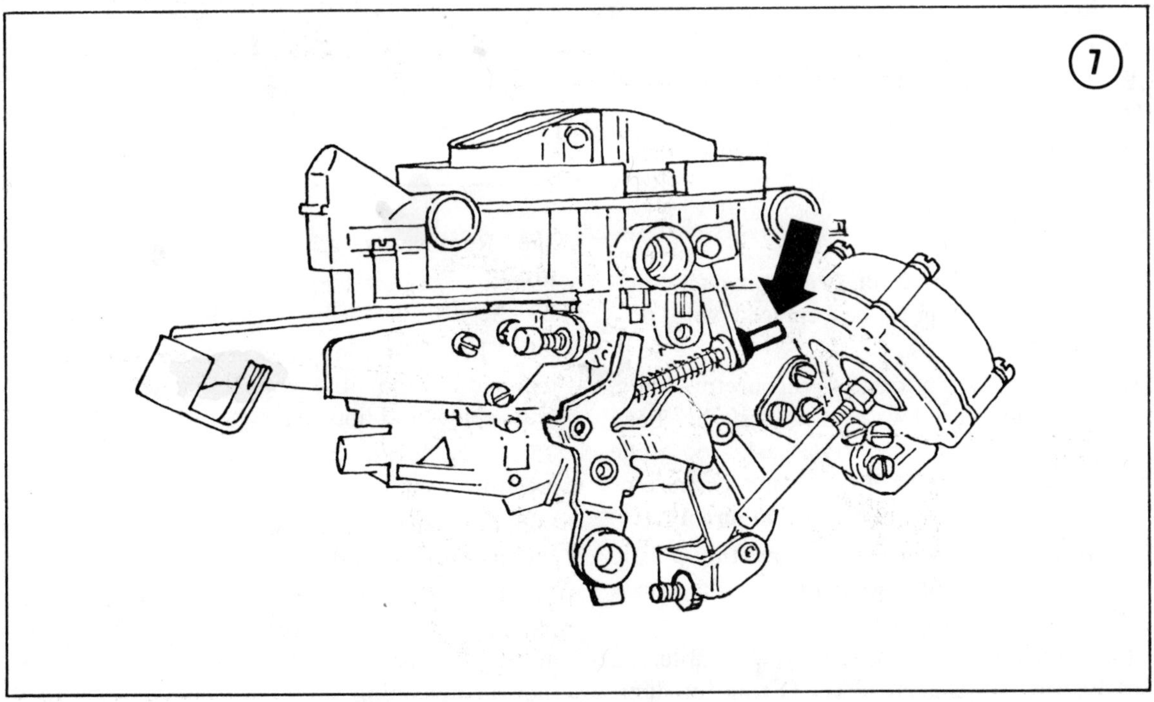
7

15. Remove the 4 screws holding the choke unloader diaphragm cover and and remove the diaphragm.

16. Remove the accelerator pump discharge nozzle. Determine if it is the newest style with an additional hole. See **Figure 9**.

NOTE: *1976 carburetors have a discharge nozzle that is tapered at the bottom. Inspect the rubber O-ring for damage.*

9

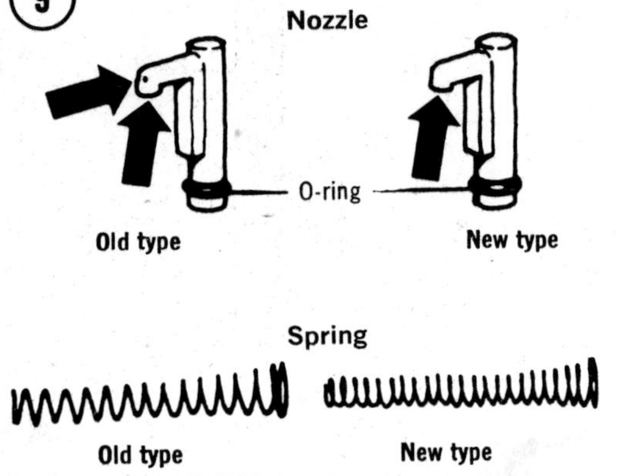

17. Remove accelerator pump piston. Inspect the metal tip for damage. Inspect the rubberized pump seal for damage. Remove accelerator pump spring.

18. Remove carburetor from holding device and turn upside down. Remove screw holding throttle plate assembly to body and separate them.

19. Remove gasket from guide pins and discard. This gasket must be replaced with new style. See parts list.

20. Looking at bottom of carburetor body, check that additional water drain hole has been added. If not, mount new style gasket on guide pins and drill a 1/16 in. hole through carburetor base. Use gasket as a guide. See **Figure 10**.

21. Turn body upright and remove thin plastic retaining ring holding accelerator pump check ball. Remove check ball.

22. Remove large idle speed screw completely. See **Figure 11**. Inspect rubber O-ring for damage. Remove CO adjustment screw. See **Figure 12**.

10

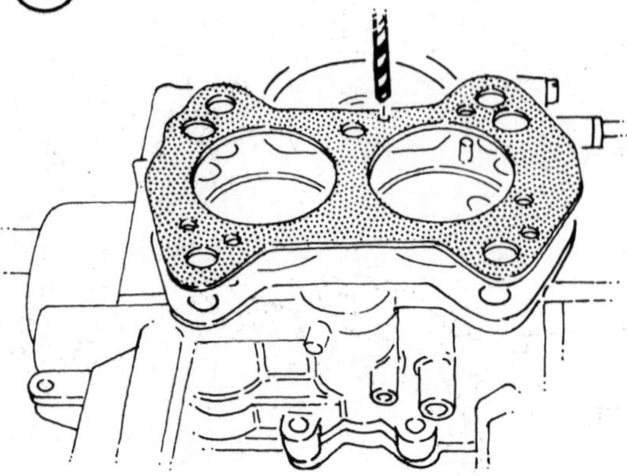

11

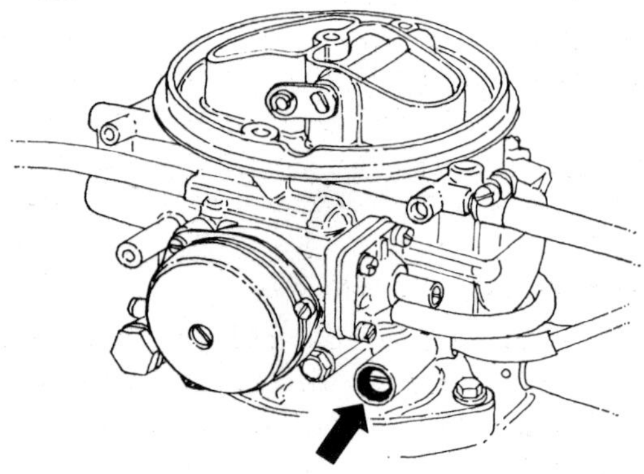

23. Set carburetor body in cleaner.

24. Check throttle plate assembly for visible damage and possible air leaks between throttle plate shafts and housing.

25. Place throttle plate assembly in cleaner.

26. Place all small metal parts in small container or screen strainer with closed lid (to avoid accidental loss) and set in cleaner.

27. Follow manufacturer's instructions on use of specific cleaner used. In general, approximately one hour should be sufficient time for thorough cleaning.

28. Remove carburetor parts from cleaner. Wash all parts in *clean* solvent. All air and fuel passages should be checked for free flow with high pressure air. Dry all parts with high pressure air. Should this be impossible use only clean lint free cloths. Dry passages with pipe cleaners.

Assembly and Adjustments

1. With carburetor body upside down, install new base gasket on guide pins and set throttle plate in place. *Be sure* that all parts are correctly aligned before tightening holding screw.
2. Mount carburetor in upright position on holding fixture.
3. Install idle speed screw. Spray O-ring with silicone lubricant first.
4. Install co adjustment screw. *Do not* overtighten or tip may be damaged.
5. Install accelerator pump spring and piston. Apply 2 drops of high grade machine oil on felt O-ring to keep plastic shaft of piston lubricated.

> NOTE: *Plastic centering ring on pump shaft should be set flush to the housing. If further depressed, the accelerator pump may either stick or produce incorrect quantity on discharge.*

6. Install accelerator pump check ball and plastic retainer.
7. Set accelerator pump discharge nozzle in place. Use care not to damage the rubber O-ring.
8. Check all carburetor body plugs and threaded drain openings for signs of leakage and tight fit. Correct as necessary.
9. Set carburetor top upside down and install needle valves and floats.
10. Adjust float height *without gasket*. See **Figure 13**.

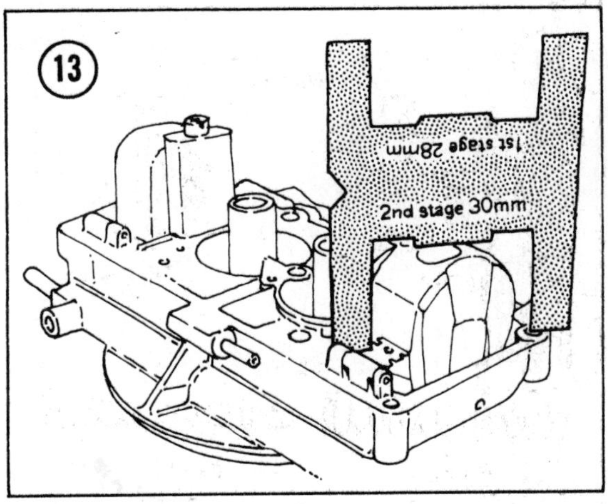

11. Install body to top gasket on carburetor body.

> CAUTION
> *1975 and 1976 carburetors have* different gaskets. *They are* not *interchangeable.*

12. Install carburetor top on body.

> CAUTION
> *The choke rod must be held upright and placed through a hole in the carburetor top to avoid damage to the rod.*

13. Insert holding screws and tighten securely. Do not forget the number tag and the ground wire holder.
14. Install the choke rod with washers and plastic bushing. Use new cotter key.

External Carburetor Adjustments

1. Throttle stop screw: Open choke plate fully and allow primary throttle to close completely.

Turn screw counter-clockwise until there is a small gap between the screw end and the stop arm. Hold a thin piece of paper or cellophane between the two and carefully turn the screw clockwise until the paper is just held. Remove the paper and turn the screw one-quarter turn clockwise. See **Figure 14**.

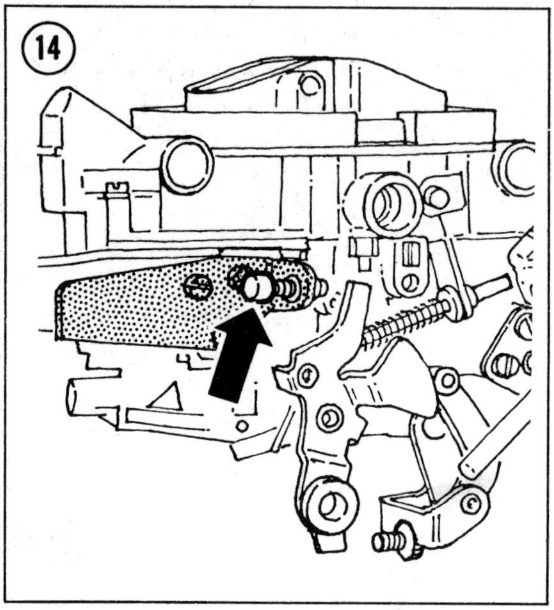

2. Dashpot: With the primary throttle closed (screw seated against stop arm) pull the dashpot rod down fully against its diagram. The clearance between the rod end and the arm must be 0.120 in. (.03mm). If clearance is incorrect loosen the locknut holding the dashpot and turn the dashpot on its threads in or out until the correct dimension is reached. Tighten the locknut. See **Figure 15**.

3. Primary throttle, fast idle: Open primary throttle plate and close choke fully. With the choke fully closed, turn carburetor upside down and test primary throttle to bore clearance. Throttle gap should be 0.020 in. (0.50mm). See **Figure 16**. If throttle gap is incorrect adjust screw as indicated in Figure 16.

4. Choke gap: Set carburetor upright and on holding fixture. Open primary throttle and close choke. There should be a large gap between the throttle stop screw and the throttle arm. Referring to **Figure 17**, place tip of small screwdriver against end of choke unloader diaphragm arm

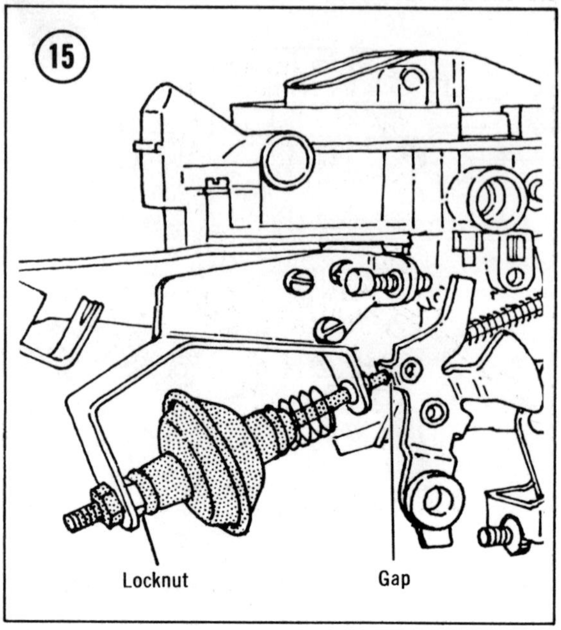

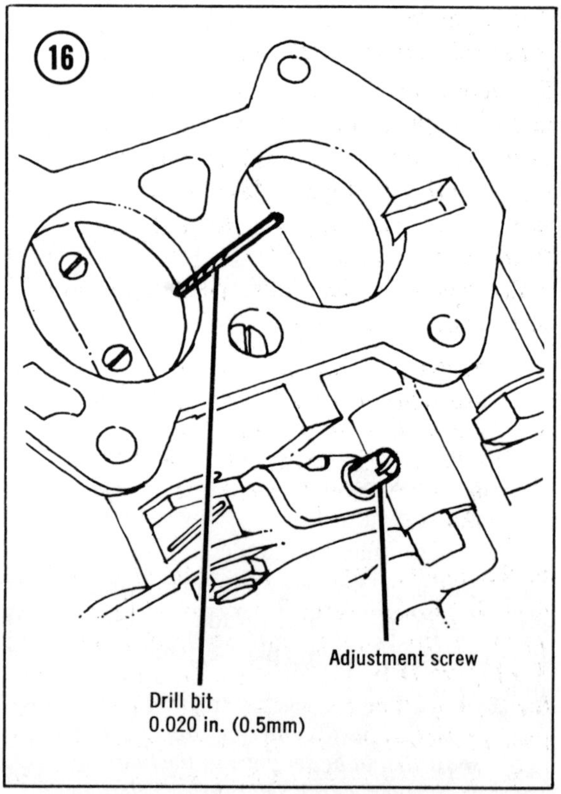

and push arm in direction as shown. Holding the choke unloader arm in this position, measure choke gap between plate and upper bore as shown. Gap should be 5/32 in. (4.20mm). A

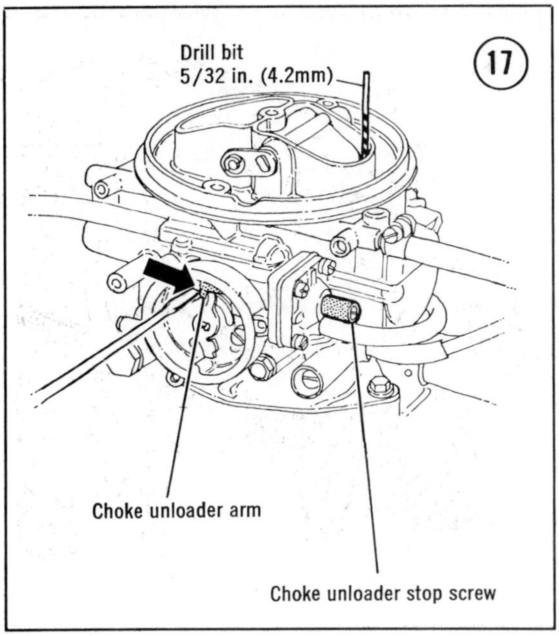

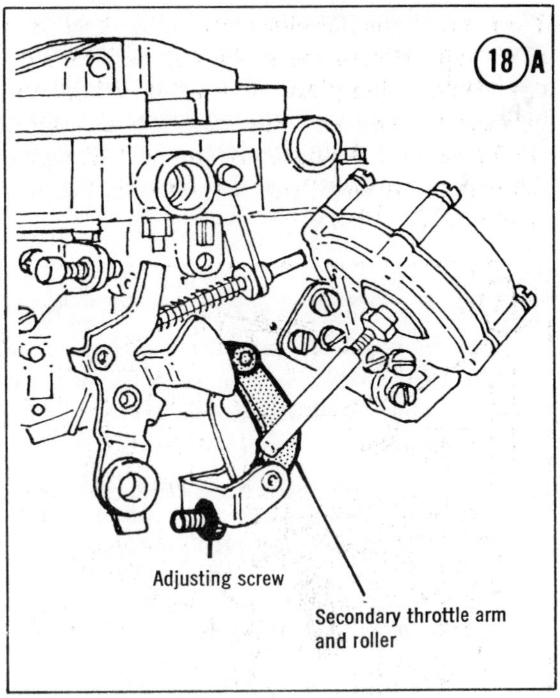

drill bit makes an excellent gauge. If adjustment is needed, turn the choke unloader stop screw.

5. Second stage throttle: open primary throttle and open choke plate. With choke in full open position, allow throttle to close fully against stop screw. Refer to **Figure 18A**. Unscrew adjustment screw until there is some clearance between screw and stop. Turn screw in until lever roller has zero clearance. Turn screw out ¼ turn from this position.

> NOTE: *If roller is adjusted* too tight, *the roller will bind, causing the vehicle to have a "flat spot." If roller is adjusted* too loose, *the vehicle will have a "surge" condition at part throttle.*

6. Secondary diaphragm operating rod: disconnect diaphragm throttle rod by pulling downward on the housing until the ball is released. See **Figure 18B**. The housing has a metal "seat" for the ball. The top of the "seat" should be between 0.040-0.080 in. (1-2mm) *above* the bottom of the ball. To adjust: pull the housing down against its spring tension and hold the rod with pliers. Loosen the 5.5mm locknut. Turn the rod and re-check the measurement. Tighten the locknut and install the pullrod housing on the ball.

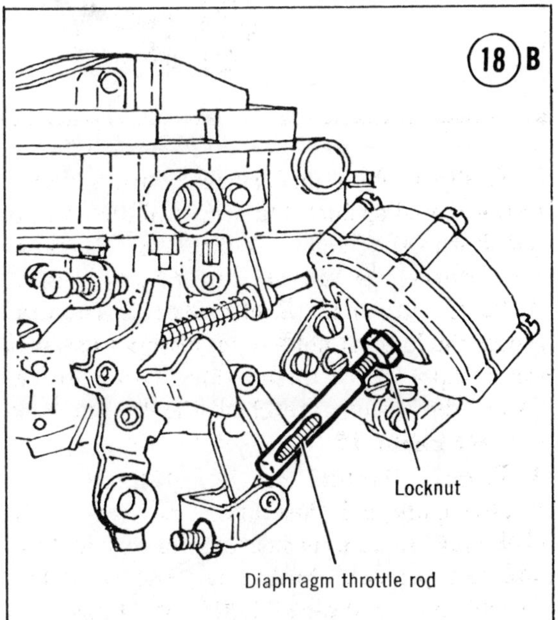

7. Accelerator pump quantity: fill carburetor with solvent or gasoline. Solvent is recommended as the danger of fire or explosion is minimized. Use a short piece of fuel line and a funnel. If not convenient, attach the engine fuel line to the carburetor directly, connect a

ground wire to terminal No. 1 of the coil and crank the engine approximately 20 seconds. *Holding the choke open*, operate the throttle until fuel is sprayed from the accelerator pump nozzle. Place a suitable container under the carburetor and operate the throttle ten (10) strokes. Allow one to two seconds between each stroke. Carefully pour the liquid into a calibrated vial. Read the quantity and divide by 10. Each stroke should equal 0.85cc-1.05cc. If adjustment is required, turn the adjustment nut (**Figure 19A**) clockwise to increase quantity per stroke, counterclockwise to decrease quantity per stroke.

> NOTE: *This nut often comes loose after adjustment. Either paint the nut/threads or crimp the nut. In the event that the nut falls off and is lost completely, use the long threaded nut that is on the end of a Bosch spark plug as a substitute.*

> NOTE: *On cars with automatic transmission, a special temperature valve changes the quantity of accelerator pump discharge based on coolant temperature. See* **Figure 19B**. *To adjust accelerator pump fuel quantity on this carburetor, attach a short piece of tight fitting hose and* plug the end *so that the valve is not linked to atmospheric pressure. Adjust quantity as indicated in Step 7.*

19A

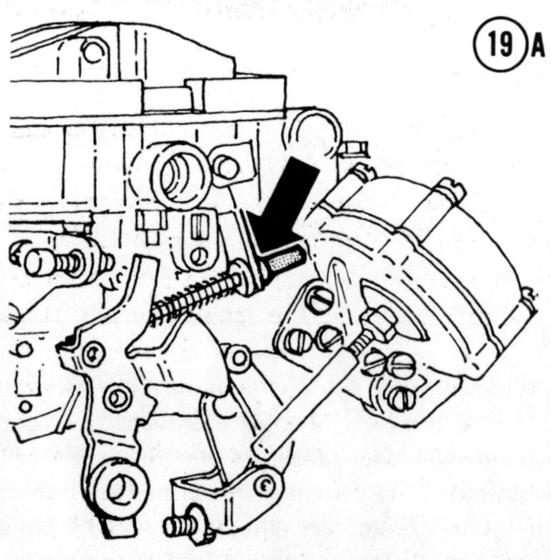

19B

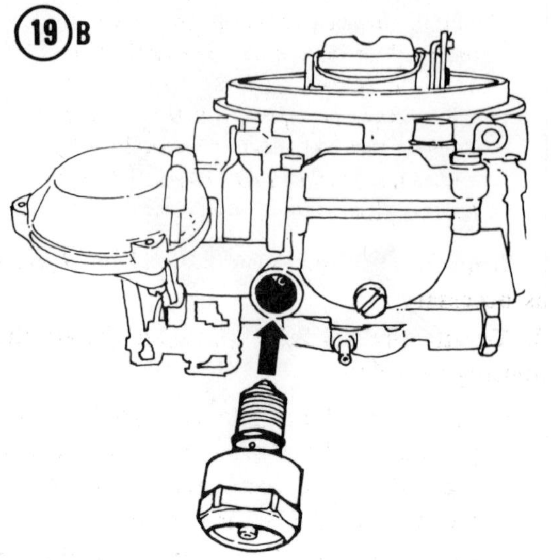

Installation

1. Place the four attaching screws through the carburetor housing *before* setting the carburetor on its mount.
2. Attach the throttle cable prior to setting the carburetor in place.
3. Set carburetor on manifold and tighten screws to 7.2 ft.-lb. (1 mkg) in a diagonal pattern.
4. Inspect choke cover and choke spring. **Figure 20** shows a distorted spring; this unit must be replaced with the newer style that has a temperature-controlled electrical heater shutoff valve.

20

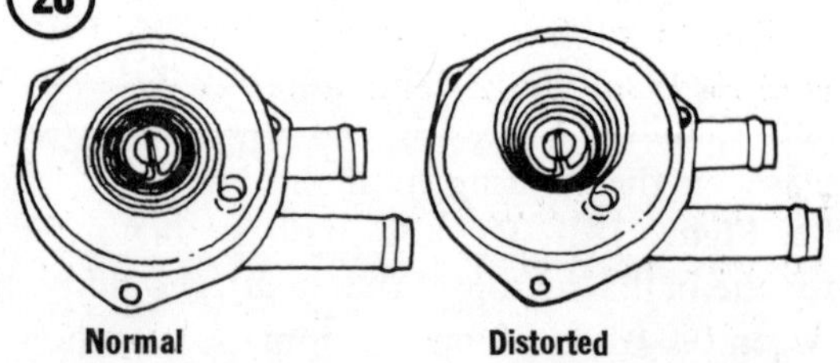

5. Install the choke cover. Do not overtighten the screws.
6. Connect all wires and hoses. Refer to Figures 2 and 3.

NOTE: *All vacuum lines that are routed through temperature valves in the coolant lines must be checked for hose* direction. *These temperature valves have two pipes on top. One is straight and one is set at an angle. The* vacuum side *must be connected to the* angled pipe.

7. Inspect the paper element air filter. Replace as necessary.
8. Test the preheat valve located in the air filter housing as follows:
   a. Light a match and heat the "gold" colored preheat rod housing. After a few seconds the rod must expand out of the housing and close off the preheater pipe.
   b. Cool the housing. The flap covering the preheater pipe must open and allow preheated air to enter the air cleaner housing.

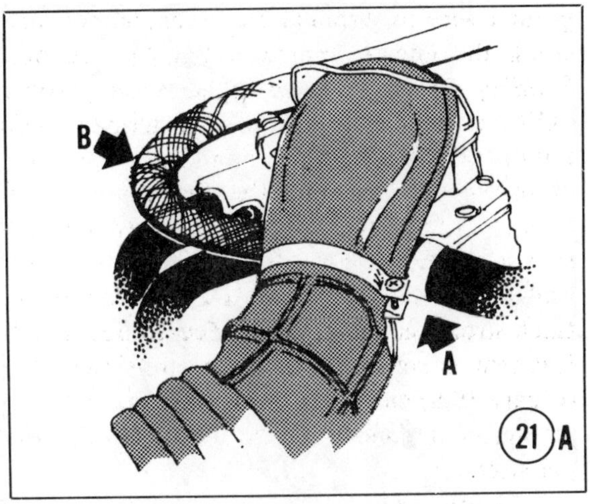

3. Remove the air injection hose (arrow, **Figure 21B**) at the air cleaner and plug the hose. Install a tachometer, using the manufacturer's instructions.

4. Make sure all of the car's electrical equipment (lights, radio, etc.) is off.
5. Adjust idle speed to 850-1,000 rpm, using the idle adjustment screw (A, **Figure 22**).
6. Install the probe of an accurate CO meter in the tailpipe, using the manufacturer's instructions. If the CO content of the exhaust is not between 0.8 and 2.2 percent, turn the CO adjusting screw (B, **Figure 22**) until the content falls within the specified range. Recheck idle speed and adjust if needed.
7. Remove the test equipment and plugs and reconnect the hoses to their original positions.

SOLEX 34 PICT-5 CARBURETOR

Some 1978 49-states versions of the Rabbit were equipped with the Solex 34 PICT-5 carburetor. Service of this carburetor by the home mechanic should be limited to adjustment of idle speed and the air/fuel mixture. The latter should be attempted only if an accurate carbon monoxide (CO) meter is available. Other service should be referred to your Volkswagen dealer.

If the carburetor must be removed for any reason, be sure to clearly identify all hoses, connectors, cables, etc., so they can be returned to their original positions. Be especially careful not to interchange the fuel supply and return hoses.

The tune-up specifications for 34 PICT-5 equipped cars are given in Chapter Three.

Idle Speed and Air/Fuel Mixture Adjustment

1. Start the engine and allow it to warm up until the oil temperature reaches approximately 140°F (60°C).
2. Remove the charcoal filter hose (B, **Figure 21A**) from the intake air elbow and plug the connector. Do not remove hose marked A in the figure.

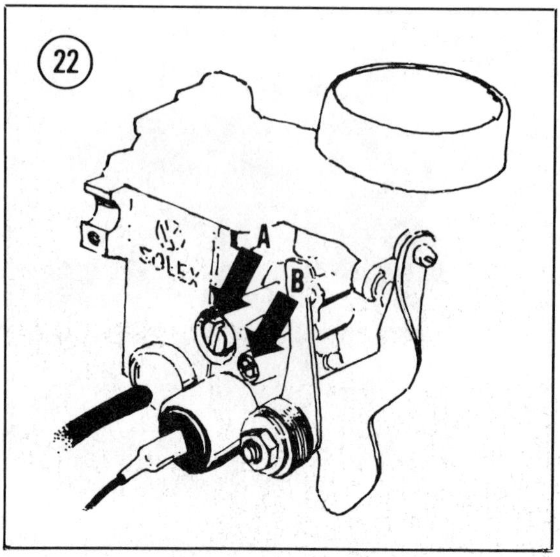

FUEL PUMP (CARBURETTED ENGINES)

Removal/Installation

Refer to **Figure 23** for this procedure.

1. Disconnect the fuel lines from the fuel pump.

2. Remove mounting bolts.
3. Lift off the pump with the plastic flange.
4. Installation is the reverse of these steps. Use a new seal.

Disassembly/Assembly

The only service possible on the fuel pump is replacement of the fuel filter. This is described in Chapter Three under *Preventive Maintenance*. The pump should not be disassembled any further. If the pump is defective, replace it as a unit.

INTAKE MANIFOLD

1. Remove air cleaner hose from carburetor.
2. Remove carburetor.
3. Disconnect engine coolant lines from intake manifold.
4. Disconnect accelerator cable from bracket on intake manifold.
5. Remove bolts securing intake manifold to cylinder head. Remove intake manifold.
6. Installation is the reverse of these steps. Use new gaskets; torque bolts to 18 ft.-lb. (2.5 mkg).

EXHAUST SYSTEM

The exhaust system consists of a catalytic converter, muffler, and interconnecting exhaust pipes all connected in series.

Catalytic Converter Replacement

The catalytic converter must be replaced every 30,000 miles. A light on the dash signals at these intervals to remind you.

1. Raise car on hoist or jackstands.
2. Remove shielding which covers converter.
3. Remove bolts on flanges at each end of converter.
4. Remove converter from the vehicle.
5. Install new converter with new gaskets.
6. Tighten bolts uniformly.
7. Turn off catalytic converter warning light by pressing reset button (see Figure 69 later in this chapter).

Muffler Replacement

NOTE: *Different muffler arrangements are used on different models. Early exhaust systems usually must be adapted to available replacement mufflers. (As a rule, new mufflers and pipes should not be adapted to fit existing systems.) See your dealer regarding available replacements and instructions for your car. The following procedure is general in nature.*

1. Loosen clamp at front of muffler or at intermediate pipe (later models).
2. Disconnect rubber mounting at front and rear of muffler. See **Figure 24**.

3. Separate defective muffler from system. Use penetrating oil liberally at connection. If necessary, use pipe cutting chisel to free muffler.

> NOTE: *If muffler is defective, chances are very good that other components are too. Consider replacing the entire system up to the exhaust header.*

4. Install new muffler in place. Tighten clamp.
5. Reconnect rubber mounts. If rubber loops are deteriorated, replace them.
6. Run engine and check for leaks.

EXHAUST GAS RECIRCULATION

The exhaust gas recirculation (EGR) system reduces oxides of nitrogen. **Figure 25** shows the 1975 system. **Figure 26** shows the 1976 system (except California), and **Figure 27** shows the California system. A similar, but simplified system, is used on the 1977 and later fuel injected models. All these systems are designed to help limit the formation of oxides of nitrogen (NOx) by introducing metered amounts of exhaust gases into the intake manifold where it mixes with the air/fuel mixture. This air/fuel/exhaust gas mixture causes peak flame temperatures in the cylinders to be lowered. Since the production of NOx is directly related to heat, lowering the peak temperatures limits formation of these pollutants. The system does not operate when the engine is cold or under certain operating conditions, such as idling, because the introduction of the exhaust gases under these conditions would cause the engine to run roughly. The EGR filter, shown in Figure 25, was discontinued on 1976 models.

Filter Replacement (1975)

1. Disconnect union at exhaust header and EGR valve. See **Figure 28**.
2. Remove exhaust headed nuts securing EGR filter and remove filter.
3. Installation is the reverse of these steps.

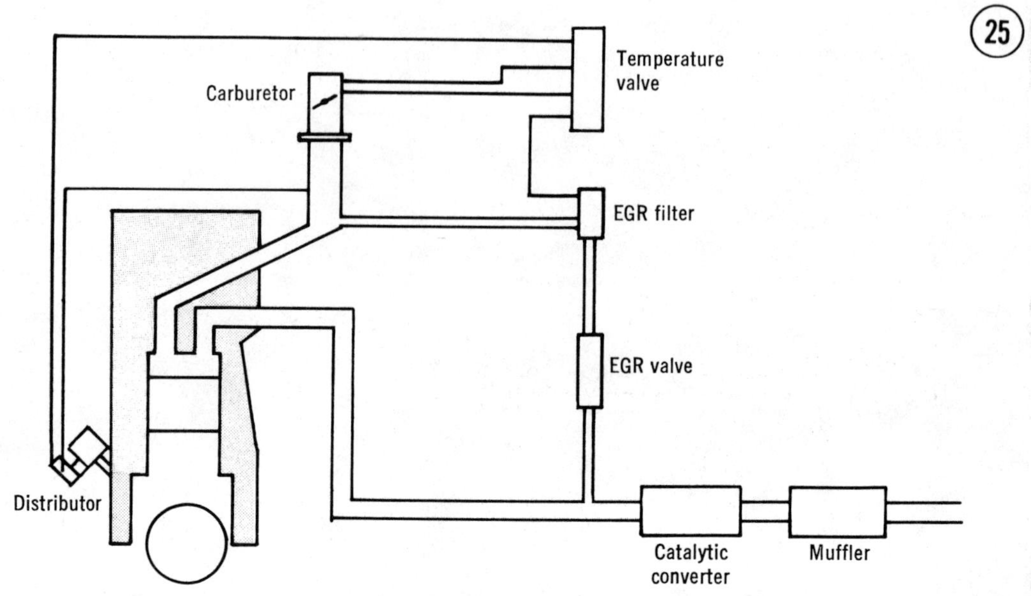

EGR SYSTEM — 1975

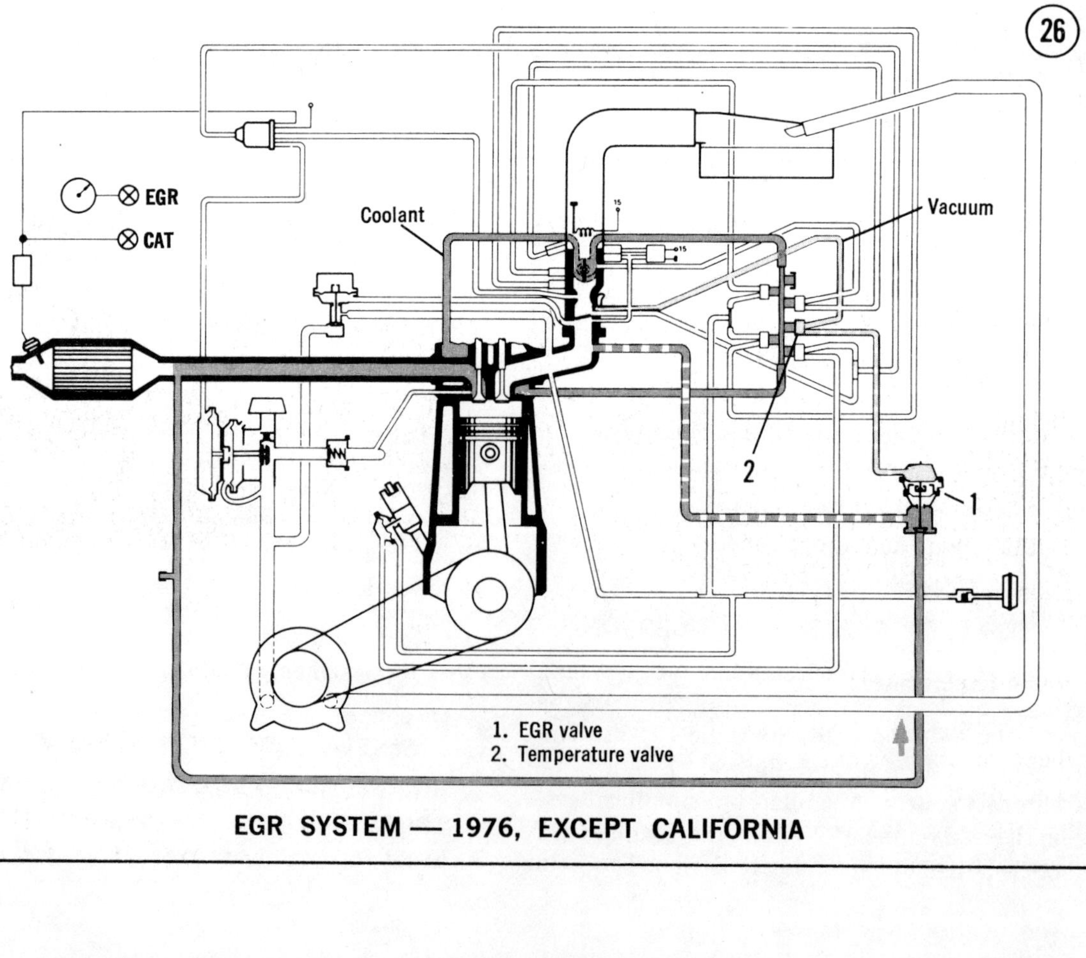

EGR SYSTEM — 1976, EXCEPT CALIFORNIA

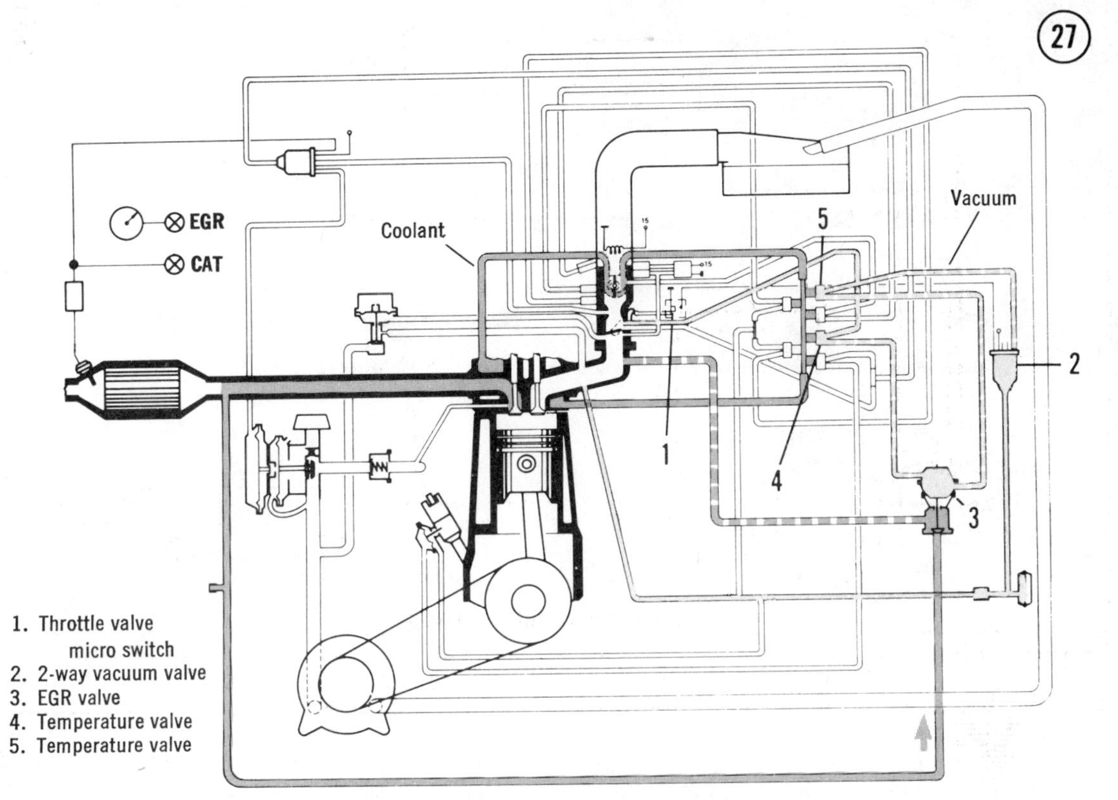

EGR SYSTEM — 1976 CALIFORNIA

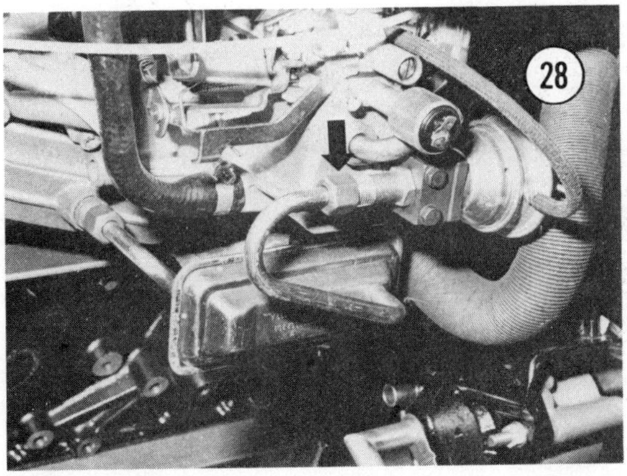

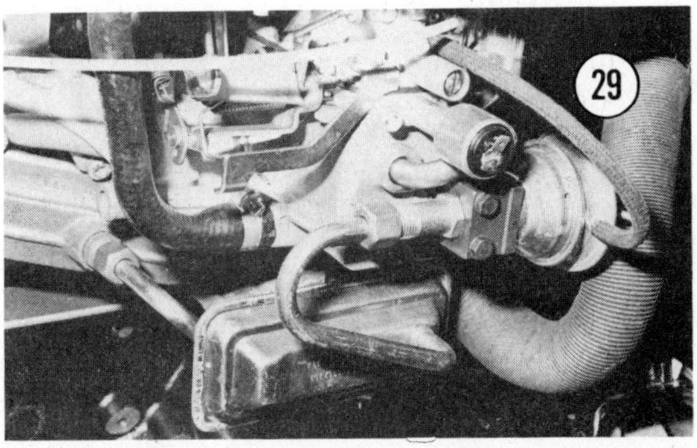

Valve Replacement

1. Disconnect vacuum lines from valve. Mark them so they cannot be interchanged when reinstalled.

2. Disconnect line from EGR filter (**Figure 29**), if so equipped.

3. Remove bolts securing valve to manifold. See **Figure 30**.

4. Installation is the reverse of these steps.

AIR INJECTION SYSTEM

Most carburetted models use an exhaust "after burner" system. See **Figure 31**. This system reduces pollution by oxidizing hydrocarbons

and carbon monoxide as they leave the combustion chamber; harmful carbon monoxide (CO) changes to harmless carbon dioxide (CO_2) in the process.

The engine driven air pump (Figure 31) compresses filtered air through a check valve to the exhaust port of each cylinder. This fresh air mixes with the unburned gases in the exhaust and promotes further burning in the catalytic converter. The check valve prevents exhaust gases from entering and damaging the air pump if the pump becomes inoperative, e.g., from a drive belt failure. Under normal conditions, the pump delivers sufficient air pressure to prevent exhaust gases from entering the pump.

The diverter valve senses sharp decreases in manifold vacuum such as during closed-throttle deceleration. Increased vacuum opens the control valve, admitting fresh air into the intake manifold. This leans out the air/fuel mixture and prevents exhaust system backfire.

Air Injection Filter Replacement

On 1975 models, the air injection filter is located behind the radiator, near the engine oil filter (**Figure 32**). The 1976 models do not have an air injection filter.

1. Remove the wing nut on the bottom of the filter housing.
2. Remove cover and filter.
3. Installation is the reverse of these steps.

Diverter Valve Replacement

The diverter valve is mounted on the top edge of the radiator. **Figure 33** shows the location. **Figure 34** shows the 1976 two-stage diverter valve used on cars first sold in California.

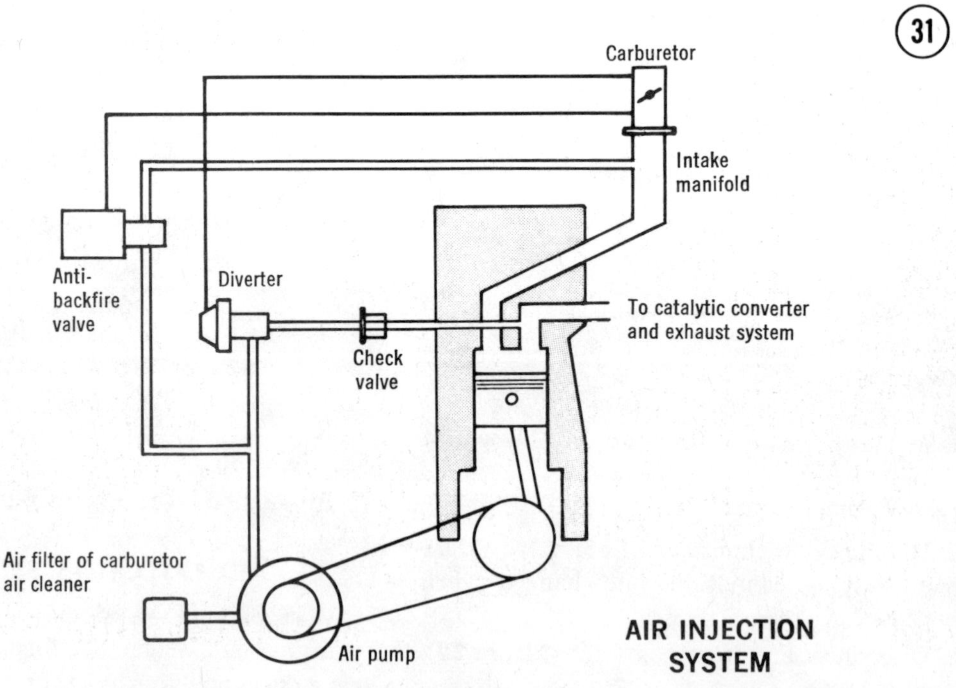

AIR INJECTION SYSTEM

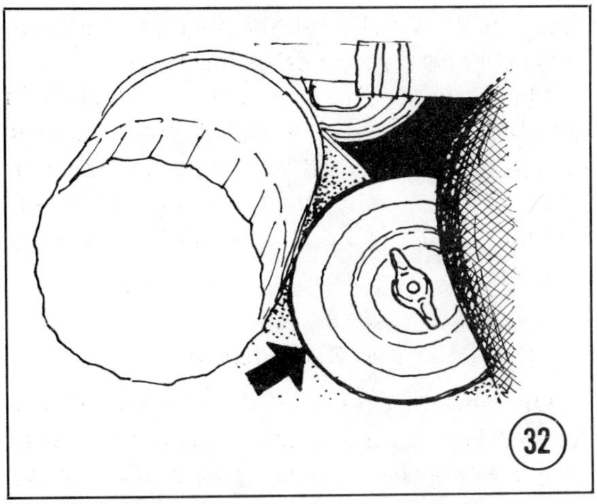

1. Disconnect air hoses at diverter valve.
2. Disconnect vacuum lines from valve.
3. Remove bolts securing valve to radiator.
4. Installation is the reverse of these steps.

Anti-backfire Valve Replacement

The anti-backfire valve is located on the right side of the engine compartment. See **Figure 35**.

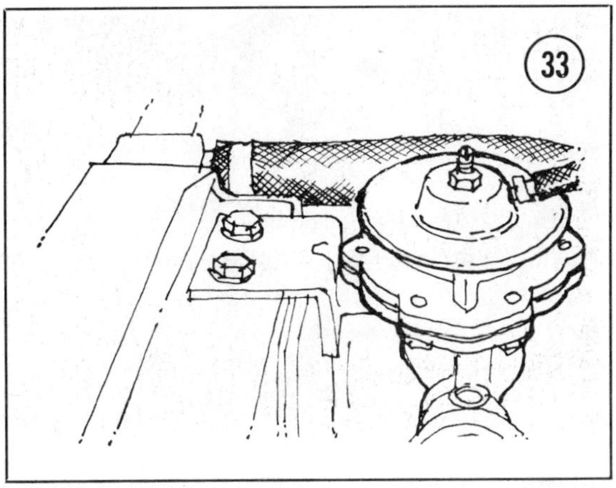

1. Disconnect the air hoses and vacuum line from valve.
2. Remove bolts securing valve to body and remove valve.
3. Installation is the reverse of these steps.

Check Valve Replacement

The check valve is located near the distributor. See **Figure 36**.

1. First stage diverter valve
2. Second stage diverter valve (California only)

1. Disconnect air hose from valve.
2. Unscrew check valve from injector manifold.
3. Installation is the reverse of these steps.

Air Pump Removal/Installation

1. Loosen the two mounting bolts as shown in **Figure 37**.
2. Remove drive belt.
3. Disconnect air hoses.
4. Remove mounting bolts and remove pump from underneath.
5. Installation is the reverse of these steps.
6. Adjust belt tension (see Chapter Three).

FUEL EVAPORATIVE CONTROL SYSTEM

The fuel evaporative control system prevents release of fuel vapor into the atmosphere.

Refer to **Figure 38**. Fuel vapor from the fuel tank passes through the separator to the acti-

vated charcoal filter. When the engine runs, the fuel vapor is drawn into the air cleaner. Instead of being released into the atmosphere, the fuel vapor takes part in the normal combustion process.

There is no preventive maintenance other than checking the tightness and condition of the lines connecting parts of the system. The separator is an integral part of the fuel tank. The activated charcoal filter is located on the left side of the engine compartment. See **Figure 39** for location on 1975 models and **Figure 40** for location on 1976 models.

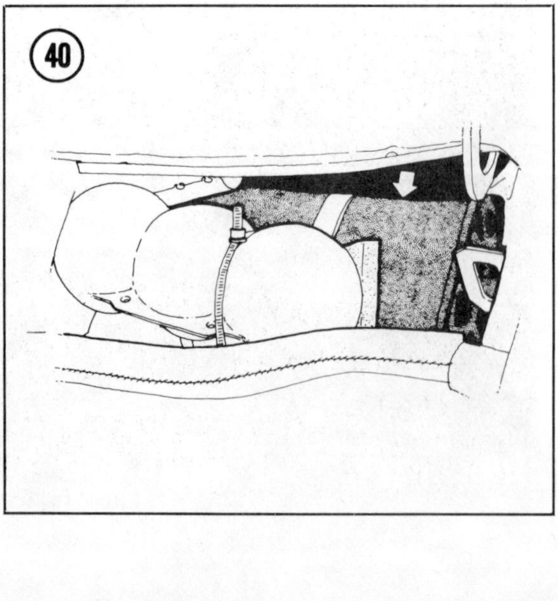

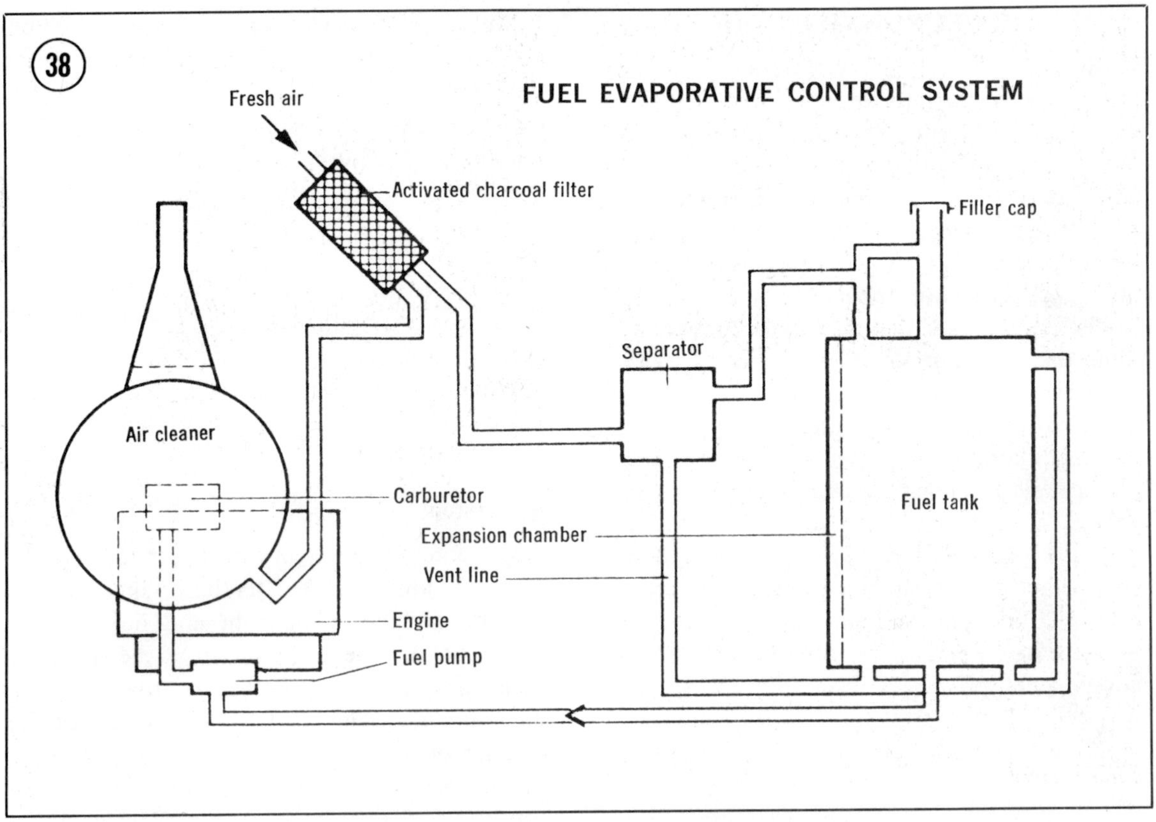
38
FUEL EVAPORATIVE CONTROL SYSTEM
Fresh air
Activated charcoal filter
Filler cap
Separator
Air cleaner
Carburetor
Expansion chamber
Vent line
Engine
Fuel pump
Fuel tank

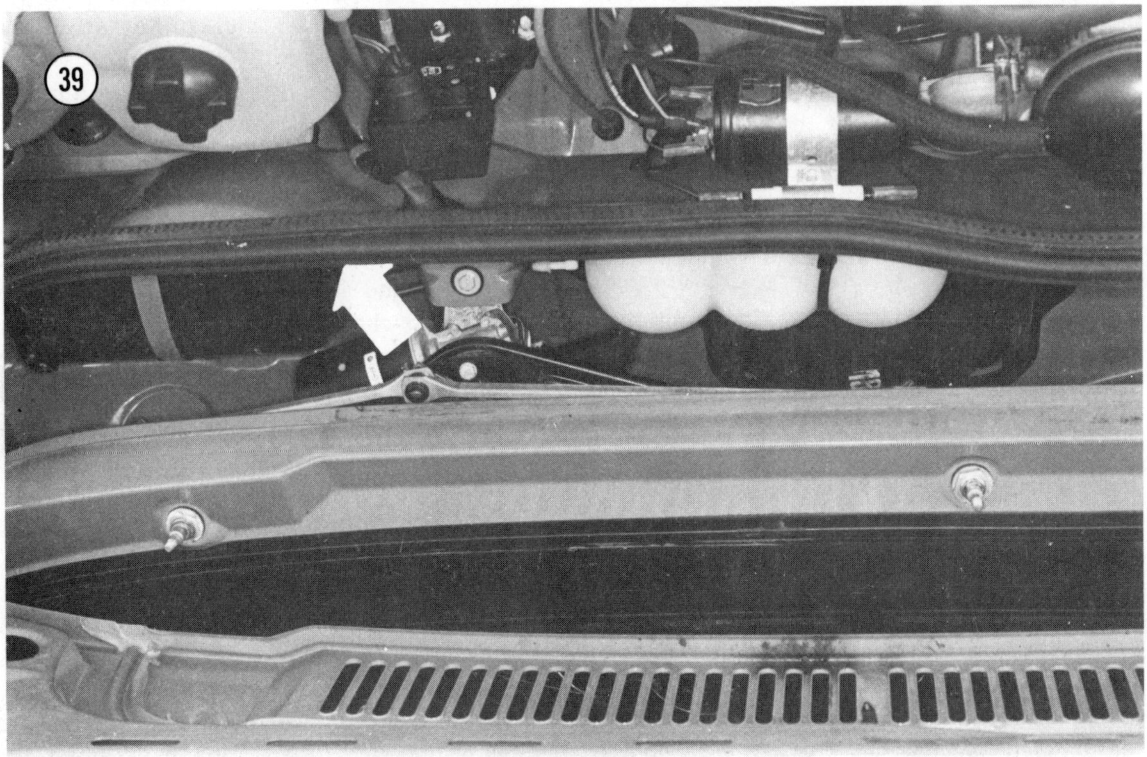
39

5

CIS FUEL INJECTION

Most 1977 and later gasoline-powered Rabbits and Sciroccos are equipped with the Bosch Continuous Injection System (CIS) fuel injection. This system, which is operated by vacuum and hydraulic forces, is much simpler and easier to check and maintain than the electronic computer controlled injection system used on some other Volkswagen products.

The CIS consists of fuel and air delivery systems and appropriate controls. Most system components are not repairable and must be replaced if defective. Maintenance and repairs are not difficult, if the system is fully understood and a few special tools, such as a fuel pressure gauge, are available. However, no attempt should be made to repair or disassemble the system unless a clean, protected work area is available. Even a small amount of dust or contamination can cause malfunctioning of some components.

Fuel System

Gasoline from the sealed fuel tank is fed through a fuel damper or silencer (to prevent gurgling) to the electric fuel pump. This pump, which is controlled by a special transducer relay, feeds the fuel at high pressure to the accumulator, which smoothes out the pressure pulses caused by the pump. The accumulator also serves as a check valve when the fuel pump is turned off to maintain a ready supply of fuel available for easier starting. Fuel from the accumulator is fed through a fine-mesh filter to the fuel distributor, which helps regulate fuel pressure and feeds fuel to the injectors for the individual cylinders. Surplus fuel is returned to the fuel tank by a pressure relief valve in the distributor. A control pressure regulator provides counter-pressure on the fuel distributor to help maintain constant fuel pressure. A temperature-controlled amount of fuel is permitted to "leak" back to the fuel tank, with a lesser amount being allowed to escape when the engine is cold. This allows more fuel to be present at the injectors for cold starts, a function which can be compared roughly to choke action on a conventional carburetted fuel system.

An electro-mechanical temperature-controlled (thermo-time switch) auxiliary injector, mounted on the intake manifold, operates at coolant temperatures below 90°F to provide additional fuel for cold starts.

The fuel injectors, one for each cylinder, open when the fuel pressure reaches about 43.5 psi and all four injectors remain open at all times when the engine is operating. A vibrating pin in each injector tip atomizes the fuel, which is sprayed in a conical pattern. When an intake valve is closed, the fuel is "stored" near the valve until it reopens.

Air System

Air enters the system through the air cleaner assembly and is ducted to the intake manifold via the air sensor housing and auxiliary air regulator. A plate in the throat of the air sensor housing venturi is deflected or raised by the incoming air. This plate is connected by the balance beam to the fuel distributor piston. As the air lifts the sensor plate, the balance beam lifts the fuel distributor piston. The height of the piston determines the amount of fuel fed to the injectors. The higher the piston the greater the fuel quantity (fuel pressure to the injectors remains constant; only the quantity changes).

The venturi of the air sensor housing has a three-dimensional design. This permits a slightly rich air/fuel mixture, which is adjustable, at idle speed, a lean mixture under partial-load conditions, and a richer mixture at full load or full throttle when maximum power is required. Idle speed mixture is controlled by the carbon monoxide adjustment screw. Under other conditions or loads, the mixture is controlled entirely by the design of the venturi.

The auxiliary air regulator is a temperature-controlled barrel valve that is open when the engine is cold, allowing some additional air to bypass the primary throttle valve and enter the intake manifold. The valve closes as the engine warms up, and the dual throttle system takes over the air regulation job.

On models with manual transmissions, a vacuum-operated deceleration valve holds the throttle partially open when the engine is decelerating (except on models equipped with catalytic converters). This valve helps reduce harmful emissions.

CIS MAINTENANCE, TESTING, AND ADJUSTMENT

Maintenance

CIS periodic maintenance is limited to air and fuel filter replacement and idle/CO adjustment, as described in Chapter Three. The system also should be checked for leaks, faulty air and vacuum lines, and other visible damage whenever other maintenance is performed.

CIS components have proven to be every reliable and seldom require replacement or adjustment. When troubleshooting an engine, always check out all other possibilities (ignition timing, valve clearances, spark plugs, timing belt tension, etc.) before touching the fuel injection system. See troubleshooting procedures at the end of this chapter. **Figures 41 and 42** show the location of the system components. **Figure 43** shows the fuel pump and accumulator.

Air Flow Sensor Checks and Adjustment

1. Start the engine and operate at idle speed. Remove the intake air boot from the air sensor housing.
2. Use magnet as shown in **Figure 44** to lift air sensor plate as high as possible. No change in resistance should be felt.

> NOTE: *Make sure sensor plate is properly centered in venturi. Plate position can be adjusted by loosening bolt slightly and running a 0.004 in. (0.10mm) gauge around the perimeter of the plate. Retighten bolt when plate is centered.*

3. If resistance is felt when sensor plate is quickly moved up and down, air sensor must

1. Vacuum booster
2. Plug for CO adjustment
3. Fuel distributor
4. Fuel filter
5. Air flow sensor

5

41

1. Auxiliary air regulator (see inset)
2. Cold start valve
3. EGR valve
4. Fuel injectors
5. Idle adjustment screw
6. Thermo-time switch
7. Deceleration valve (not present on automatic transmissions or California cars)
8. Control pressure regulator
9. EGR temperature control valve
10. Distributor
11. Ignition coil

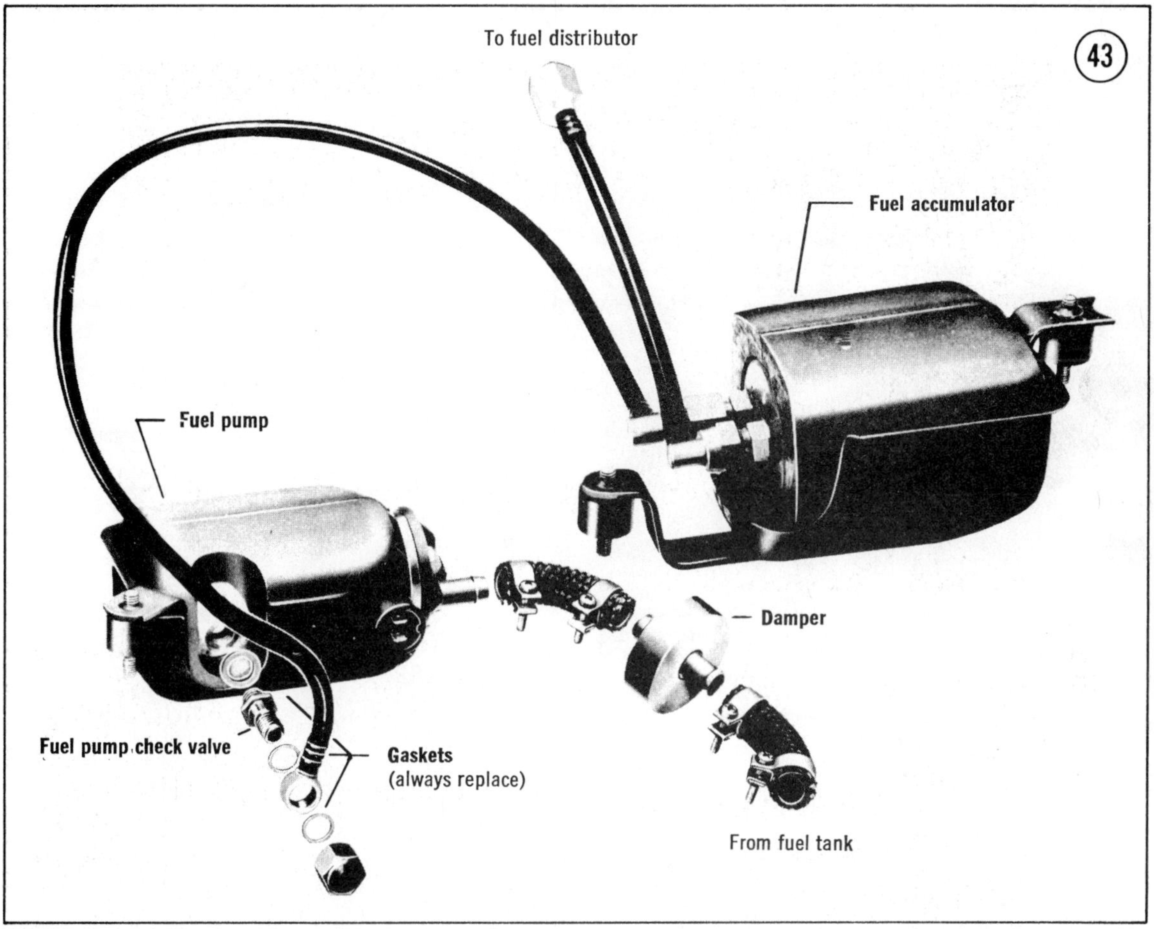

be replaced. If plate is hard to move up, but can be moved down easily, control plunger in fuel distributor is sticking. Remove distributor and clean plunger in solvent and reinstall distributor. If this does not solve the problem, replace fuel distributor with new one.

Sensor Plate Rest Position Check and Adjustment

1. Install pressure gauge VW1318 or P378 between fuel distributor and control pressure regulator. Open valve lever (position A, **Figure 45**). Remove rubber boot from air flow sensor housing.

2. Remove fuel pump relay from fuse/relay panel and install tool US 4480/3 as shown in **Figure 46**. Place tool switch in ON position and wait until gauge reads 49-54 psi (3.4-3.8 bar).

> NOTE: *It is not necessary to turn ignition switch on for this test.*

3. Turn tool switch off. Pressure now must read 28-37 psi (2.0-2.6 bar).

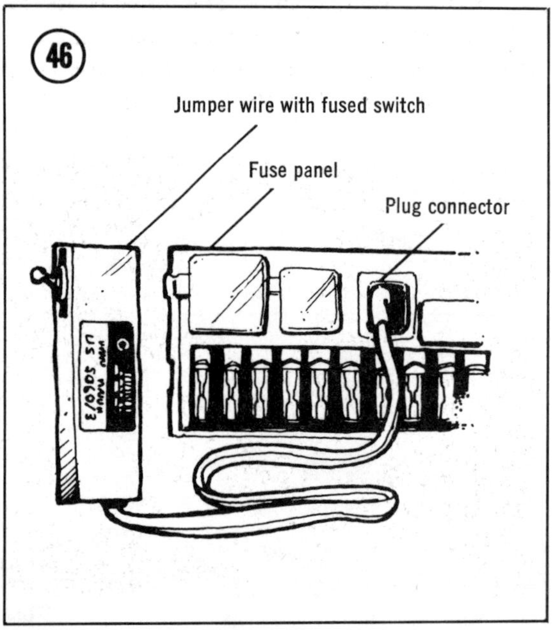

4. Check position of sensor plate. Upper edge must be even with bottom of air cone taper (**Figure 47**), or no more than 0.020 in. (0.5mm) below bottom. Adjust plate height, if required, by bending clip (lower arrow, Figure 47).

5. Recheck pressure readings after adjusting plate height.

6. Remove test equipment and install fuel pump relay. Check idle speed and exhaust CO content, and adjust as required.

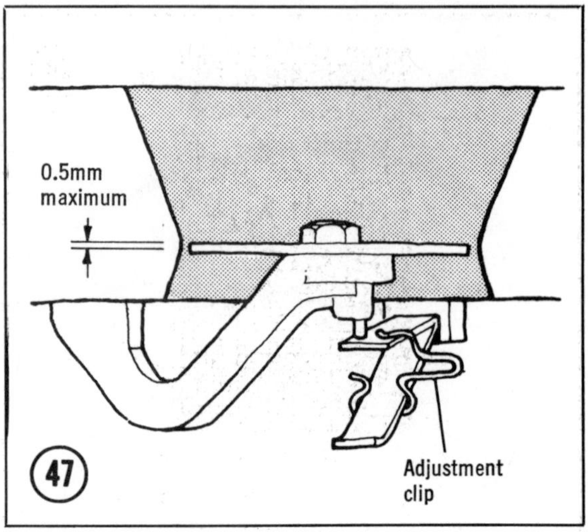

Fuel Pressure Tests

> NOTE: *VW tool 1318 or P378 is required for these tests. A substitute can be made by using a valve, a fluid pressure gauge (100-150 psi), and tube fittings. See Figure 45.*

1. Install pressure gauge tool in fuel line between fuel distributor and control pressure regulator and open valve lever (position A, Figure 45). Remove connector from control pressure regulator. See **Figure 48**.

2. If engine is cold, start engine and operate at idle speed for no more than one minute. Note the reading on the pressure gauge and compare with the tolerance range shown in **Figure 49** of 18-24 psi (1.3-1.7 bar) at 68°F (20°C). If pressure is not within the range for the outside air temperature, the control pressure regulator should be replaced.

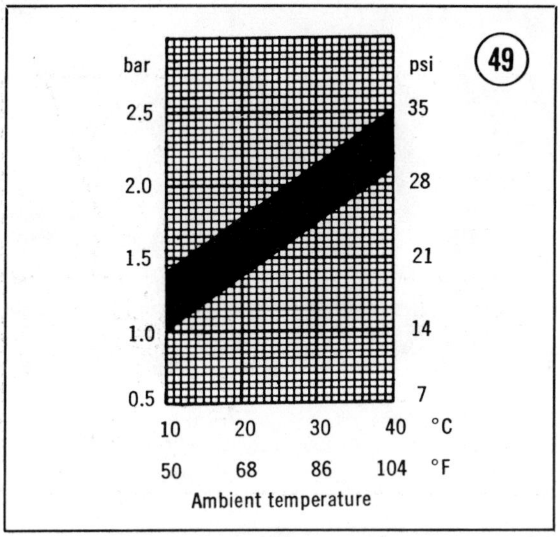

3. If engine is at normal operating temperature, operate the engine at idle speed until the pressure gauge stabilizes and read the pressure. Reading must be between 49 and 54 psi (3.4-3.8 bar). If not, replace control pressure regulator.

Fuel Pump Delivery Test

1. Check fuel filter and replace if filter restricts flow of fuel.

2. Connect a jumper wire from ignition coil terminal No. 1 to ground to prevent engine starting.

CAUTION

Perform this test in a well-ventilated area in which no open flames are present (pilot lights, burners, etc.). Do not allow smoking in the area while the test is in progress. Have a fire extinguisher approved for fuel fires at hand.

3. Remove the fuel return line (**Figure 50**) and hold the end in a one-quart or larger measuring cup or other container. Operate the starter for 30 seconds. If less than ¾ quart (750 cm^3) for pumps with wires attached with flat connectors or 9/10 quart (900 cm^3) of fuel is delivered for pumps with wires attached with nuts, the fuel pump should be replaced.

System Pressure Test

NOTE: *Fuel delivery and fuel filter should be checked and corrected, if necessary, before proceeding with this test.*

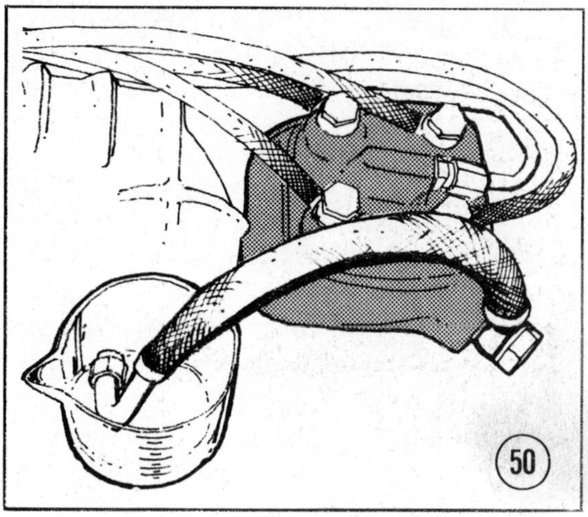

1. Connect pressure gauge and valve as shown in Figure 45 (in fuel line between fuel distributor and control pressure regulator) and turn valve lever to closed position (B, **Figure 51**).

2. Start engine and operate at idle speed. Pressure gauge should register between 66 and 74 psi (4.5 and 5.2 bar). If out of tolerance, clean distributor relief valve using the procedure given later in this chapter.

3. Repeat the test. If still not within the limits given in Step 2, replace the fuel distributor.

4. Set valve lever to open position (A, Figure 45) and allow engine to warm up to normal operating temperature. Pressure reading should be between 48 and 54 psi (3.4-3.8 bar).

5. Turn off engine and wait 10 minutes. Reading should be at least 25 psi (1.8 bar) after 10 minutes. If the reading is 25 psi or higher, wait another 10 minutes and recheck the gauge. Reading should be at least 23 psi (1.6 bar).

6. If pressure drops below 23 psi after 20 minutes, close the valve lever (B, Figure 51) and repeat Steps 4 and 5. If pressure does not drop below 25 psi after 10 minutes or 23 psi after 20 minutes, replace the control pressure regulator. However, if the pressure does drop below these limits, check for fuel line leaks, or faulty fuel distributor, injectors, cold start valve, and fuel pump. Replace defective component.

Fuel Pump Electrical Check

1. Operate starter and listen at right rear of car for sound of fuel pump. If pump is not running, check fuse on front of fuel pump relay on relay panel under dash (**Figure 52**).

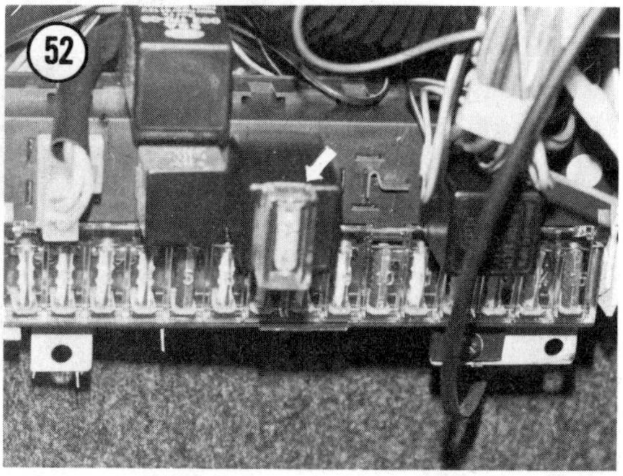
52

2. If fuse is OK, replace fuel pump relay. If pump still does not run, replace pump (arrow, **Figure 53**).

53

Thermo-Time Switch Check

NOTE: *Make this check with engine cold (coolant temperature below 95°F).*

1. Remove harness connector from cold start valve and connect test lamp between connector plug terminals.

2. Connect jumper between coil terminal No. 1 and ground to prevent starting, and operate starter.

3. If test lamp does not light up for 1-8 seconds, replace thermo-time switch (**Figure 54**).

54

Cold Start Valve Check

1. Remove connector from cold start valve (arrow, **Figure 55**), but do not disconnect the fuel line.

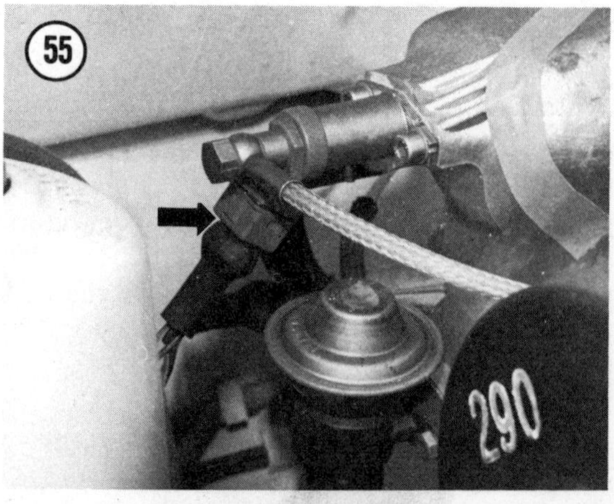
55

2. Remove the cold start valve from the manifold (2 bolts) and hold nozzle over a suitable container (**Figure 56**).

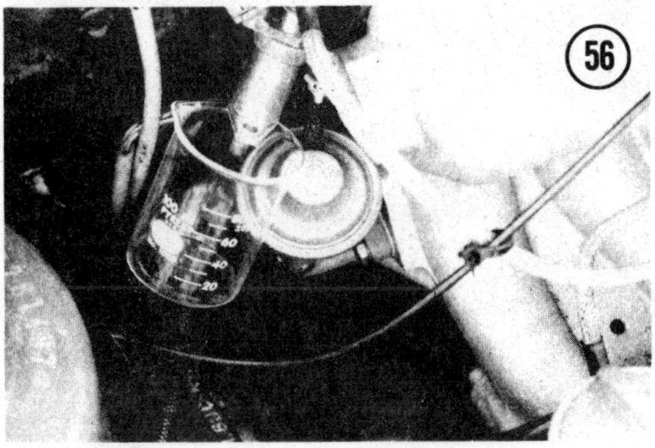

3. Connect a jumper wire between terminal No. 15 of the ignition coil and one terminal of the cold start valve. Connect the other valve terminal to ground.

4. Remove pump relay and install fused (8 amp) jumper wire between relay plate terminals L13 and L14 (**Figure 57**).

5. Turn ignition switch on and observe cold start valve spray pattern, which must be cone shaped and steady.

6. With fuel pump still running, turn ignition switch off. Wipe cold start valve dry and observe one minute for leakage. If fuel drops form, valve is defective.

Auxiliary Air Regulator Check

> NOTE: *Engine must be cold for this check (coolant temperature below 95°F).*

1. Remove and plug auxiliary air regulator hose (arrow, **Figure 58**).

2. Use a mirror to observe gate valve in auxiliary air regulator (**Figure 59**). Gate valve must be open.

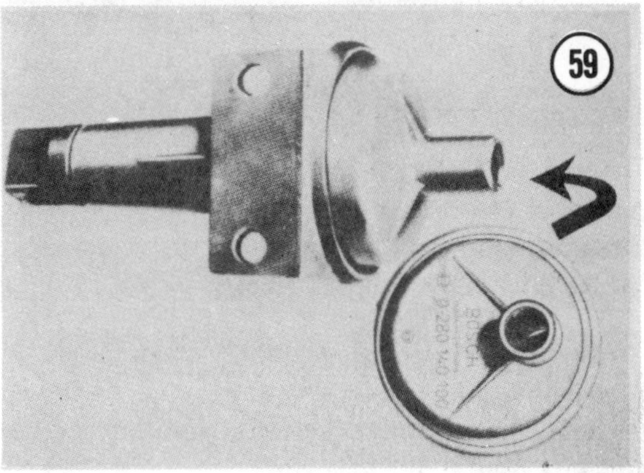

5

3. Start engine and run at idle speed for five minutes, then check gate valve with mirror again. Valve must be closed. Replace valve if not functioning properly.

Control Pressure Regulator Check

1. Remove connector from control pressure regulator. See **Figure 60**.

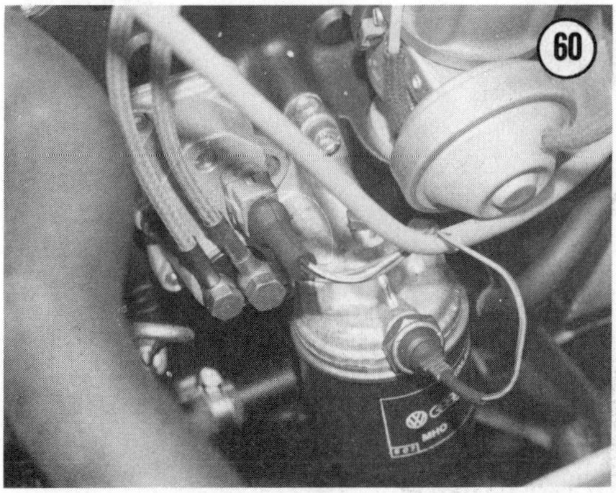

2. Connect an ohmmeter across contacts in regulator socket. Resistance should be approximately 20 ohms. If not, replace regulator.

Fuel Injector Check

1. Remove a fuel injector, leaving it attached to fuel line (**Figure 61**). Hold injector in a suitable container.

2. Remove fuel pump relay and connect a fused (8 amp) jumper wire between terminals L13 and L14. See Figure 57.

3. Remove the bellows from the air intake sensor and turn on the ignition switch.

4. Lift the sensor plate with magnet or pliers (**Figure 62**) and observe the fuel injector that was removed in Step 1. Spray pattern must be even and cone shaped.

5. Turn off ignition, clean injector, and hold injector horizontally. Injector must not drip.

6. If faults are found during Step 4 or 5, replace injector.

7. Repeat check for each injector.

NOTE: *One or all injectors may be checked at the same time, if desired.*

Fuel Injector Installation

1. Moisten rubber seal with fuel prior to installation.

2. Press injector fully into seat.

Fuel Filter Installation

1. Remove and discard old fuel filter.

2. Install new filter with arrow pointing as shown in **Figure 63**. Securely tighten all connections, start engine, and check connections for leaks.

Fuel Distributor Removal/Installation

1. Clean and remove all fuel lines from fuel distributor.

2. Remove retaining bolts (arrows, **Figure 64**).

3. Remove the distributor carefully, watching underneath to keep the control plunger from falling out.

> NOTE: *If control plunger falls out or is removed, clean and moisten with gasoline before reinstalling. Be sure small shoulder is inserted first.*

4. Installation is the reverse of removal. Be sure to use new O-rings.

Fuel Pump Check Valve Replacement

1. Raise vehicle and remove right rear wheel. Remove fuel tank cap to relieve pressure in tank.
2. Thoroughly clean fuel line connection at fuel pump, and disconnect fuel line.
3. Remove the screw connector that holds the check valve (arrow, **Figure 65**) and replace it with a new part, using a new seal washer. Torque the connector to 14-18 in.-lb. (16-20 cm/kg). Do not over-torque.
4. Reconnect fuel line, using new seal washers.

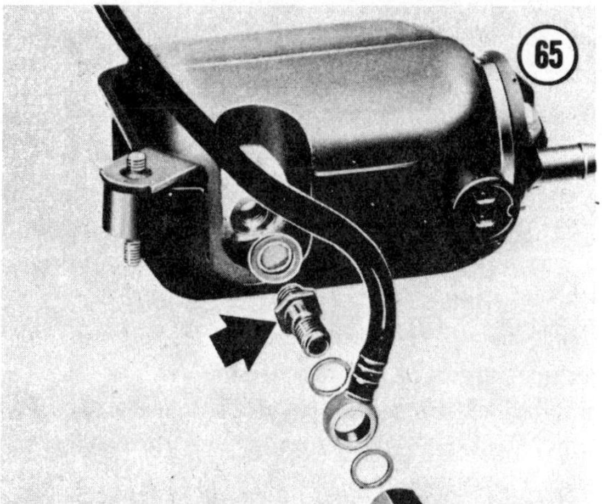

Exhaust Gas Recirculation Valve Check

Figure 66 shows the location of the exhaust gas recirculation (EGR) valve. The EGR valve is controlled by a temperature valve (arrow, **Figure 67**).

1. Warm engine to operating temperature and run engine at idle speed.
2. Check line between EGR valve and exhaust pipe for leaks. Replace line if leaks are found.
3. Remove vacuum line from EGR valve and replace with vacuum line from brake booster.

> NOTE: *This can be accomplished by installing a T-fitting in the vacuum line to the retard side of the distributor diaphragm and running a vacuum hose from the T-fitting to the* EGR *valve.*

4. The EGR valve is OK if the idle speed drops or the engine stalls. If engine speed does not change, EGR valve or line is dirty, blocked, or damaged. Locate the fault and clean or replace part, as indicated.

EGR Temperature Control Valve Check

1. Warm engine to operating temperature and run at idle speed.
2. Attach vacuum gauge bewteen EGR valve and temperature control valve. See **Figure 68**. If gauge indicates 2-4 in. Hg (50-90mm Hg), temperature control valve is OK. If outside these limits, replace valve.

EGR Indicator Light

The EGR indicator light is controlled by the speedometer cable and lights after 15,000 miles as a reminder for EGR valve maintenance. After maintenance is completed, reset the indicator light by pressing the button (arrow, **Figure 69**). Light should go out.

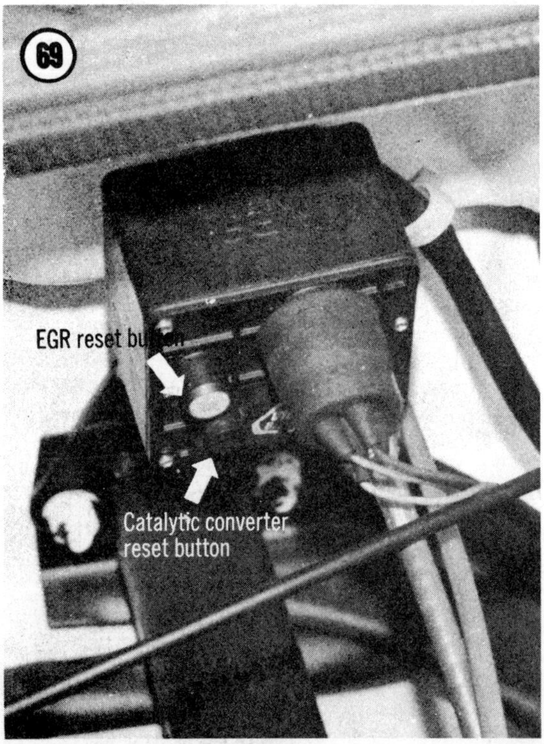

Deceleration Valve Check (Manual Transmission Only)

1. Remove and plug hose from deceleration valve (arrow, **Figure 70**).

2. Start engine and run at about 3,000 rpm for a few seconds, then let throttle valve snap closed. At the same time, check with finger for vacuum at deceleration valve hose connection.
3. Remove vacuum hose from T-connector and plug T-connector.
4. Run engine at about 3,000 rpm and check for suction with finger at hose connection of deceleration valve. If suction is felt, replace the valve.

DIESEL FUEL INJECTION SYSTEM

Operation of the diesel fuel injection system and the procedures for maintaining the system are described in Chapter Three. Disassembly, repair work, and adjustments beyond the procedures given in Chapter Three are not recommended. Such work should be performed by your Volkswagen dealer, especially if the vehicle is still under warranty.

Diesel engines do not have air pollution control devices, as the engines do not produce emissions in amounts that are considered harmful.

CIS TROUBLESHOOTING

Troubleshooting the CIS fuel injection system requires more thought, experience, and know-how than any other part of the vehicle. A logical approach and proper test equipment are essential to successfully find and fix these troubles.

It is best to leave injection troubles to your dealer. In order to isolate a problem to the injection system or to find a problem in an emergency, use the troubleshooting diagrams referred to under the appropriate problem. The following symptoms and probable causes summarize the information in the troubleshooting diagrams. Test and adjustment procedures are given in Chapter Three.

Engine Will Not Start

Refer to **Figure 71** and check the following:

a. Defective fuel pump
b. Sticky air flow sensor plate
c. Leaky air intake system
d. Sensor plate stop too low
e. Low fuel line pressure
f. Defective cold start system

Cold Engine Will Not Start

Refer to **Figure 72** and check the following:

a. Improper starting procedure
b. Hand throttle not properly adjusted
c. Defective cold start system
d. Defective control pressure regulator

Warm Engine Will Not Start

Refer to **Figure 73** and check the following:

a. System pressure drops too suddenly
b. Leaky injector(s)
c. Defective cold start system
d. Sensor plate stop too low

Idle Rough

Refer to **Figure 74** and check the following:

a. Incorrect idle CO adjustment
b. Leaky air intake system
c. Leaky cold start valve
d. Clogged injector(s)

Poor Performance

Refer to **Figure 75** and check the following:

a. Throttle valve does not open fully
b. Sensor plate sticky
c. Co adjustment not correct
d. Low fuel pump delivery
e. Fuel tank vent blocked

Engine Surges at Constant Speed

Refer to **Figure 76** and check the following:

a. Soft sensor plate spring
b. Throttle valve improperly adjusted
c. Control pressure too high

Excessive Fuel Consumption

Refer to **Figure 77** and check the following:

a. Mixture too rich (high CO)
b. Defective control pressure regulator or wiring
d. Defective cold start system
c. Blocked return line

5

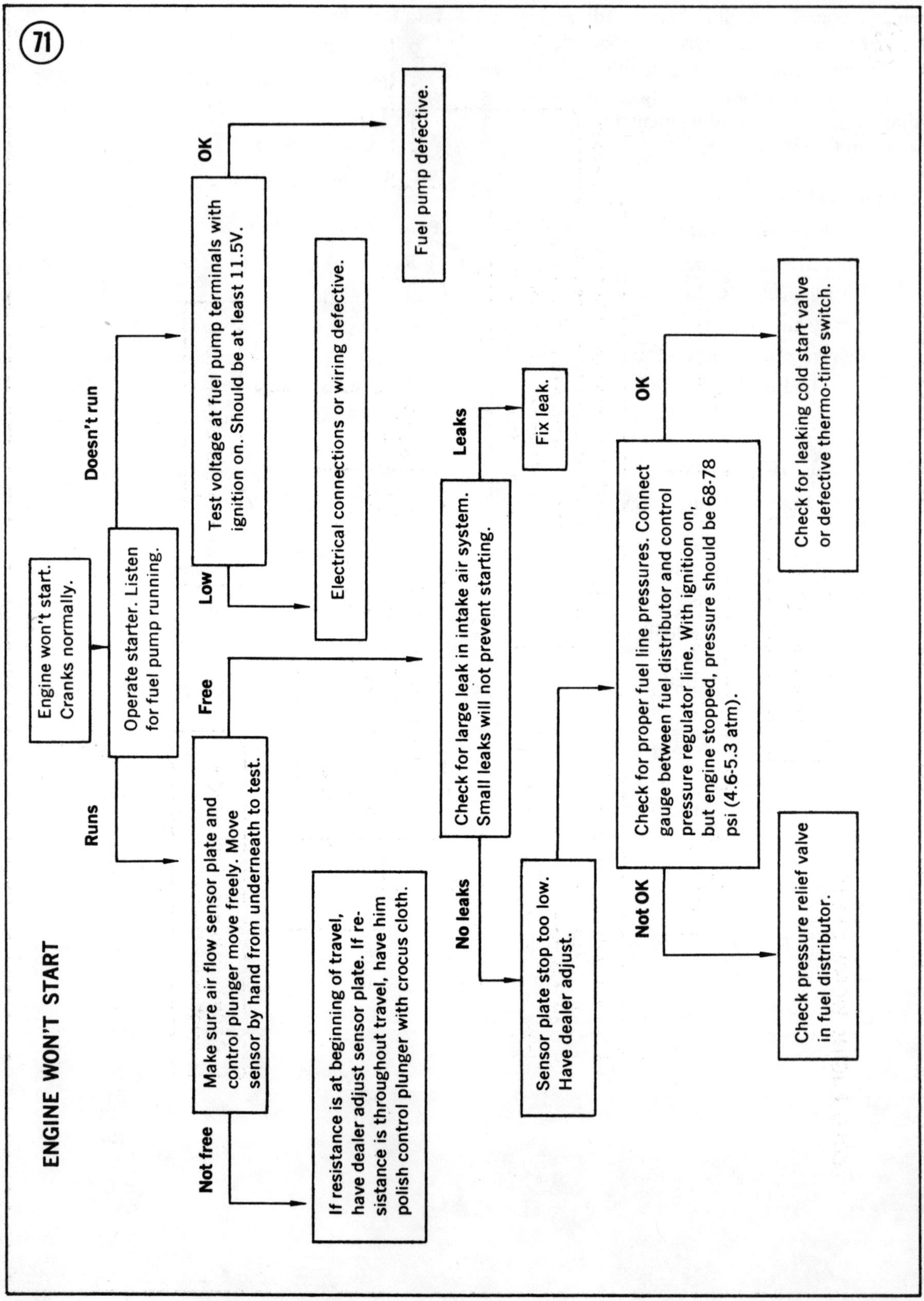
71
ENGINE WON'T START
Engine won't start. Cranks normally.
Operate starter. Listen for fuel pump running.
Runs
Doesn't run
Make sure air flow sensor plate and control plunger move freely. Move sensor by hand from underneath to test.
Not free
Free
If resistance is at beginning of travel, have dealer adjust sensor plate. If resistance is throughout travel, have him polish control plunger with crocus cloth.
Test voltage at fuel pump terminals with ignition on. Should be at least 11.5V.
Low
OK
Electrical connections or wiring defective.
Fuel pump defective.
Check for large leak in intake air system. Small leaks will not prevent starting.
No leaks
Leaks
Fix leak.
Sensor plate stop too low. Have dealer adjust.
Check for proper fuel line pressures. Connect gauge between fuel distributor and control pressure regulator line. With ignition on, but engine stopped, pressure should be 68-78 psi (4.6-5.3 atm).
Not OK
OK
Check pressure relief valve in fuel distributor.
Check for leaking cold start valve or defective thermo-time switch.

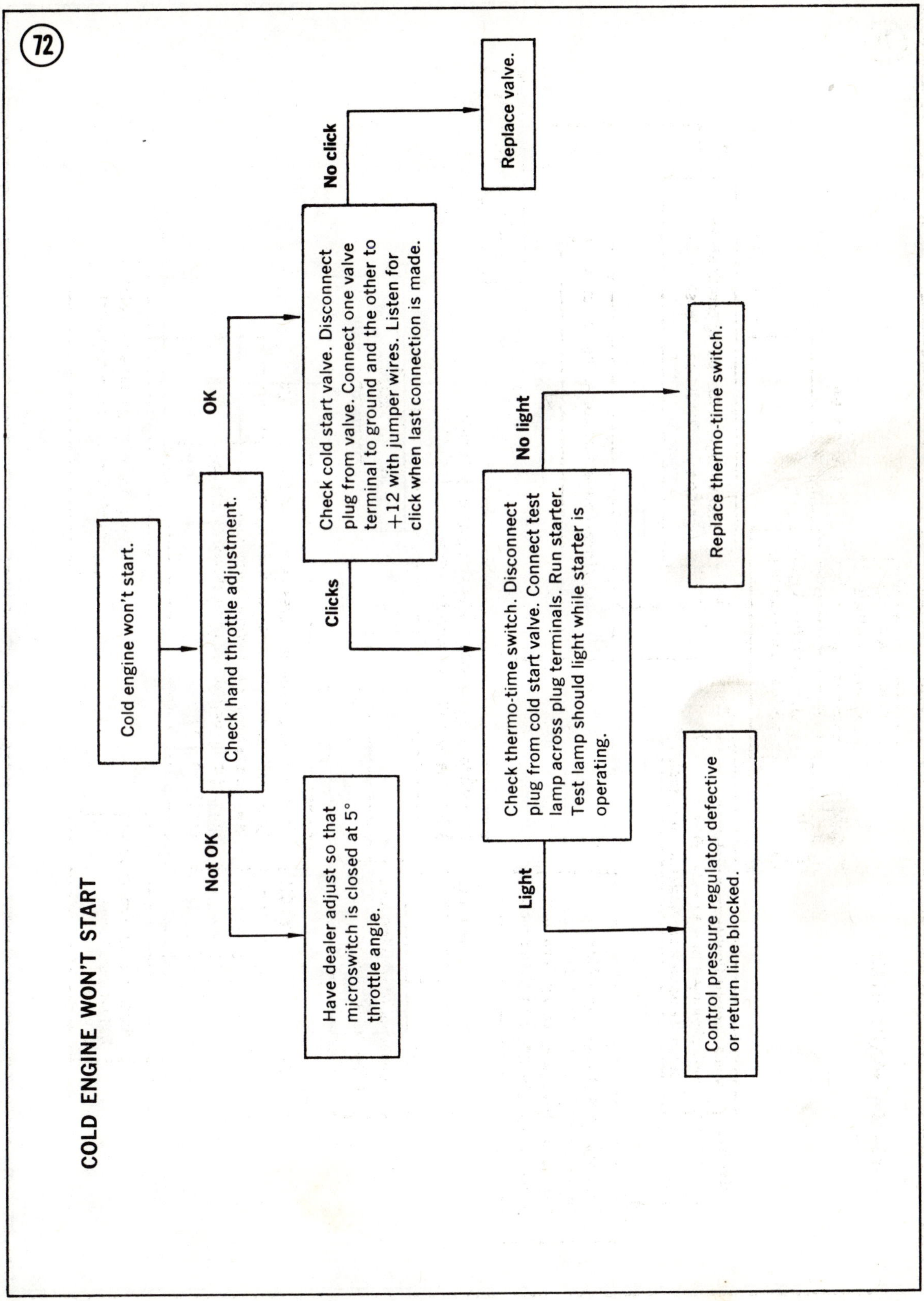
72
COLD ENGINE WON'T START
Cold engine won't start.
Check hand throttle adjustment.
Not OK
Have dealer adjust so that microswitch is closed at 5° throttle angle.
OK
Check cold start valve. Disconnect plug from valve. Connect one valve terminal to ground and the other to +12 with jumper wires. Listen for click when last connection is made.
No click
Replace valve.
Clicks
Check thermo-time switch. Disconnect plug from cold start valve. Connect test lamp across plug terminals. Run starter. Test lamp should light while starter is operating.
No light
Replace thermo-time switch.
Light
Control pressure regulator defective or return line blocked.

73

WARM ENGINE WON'T START

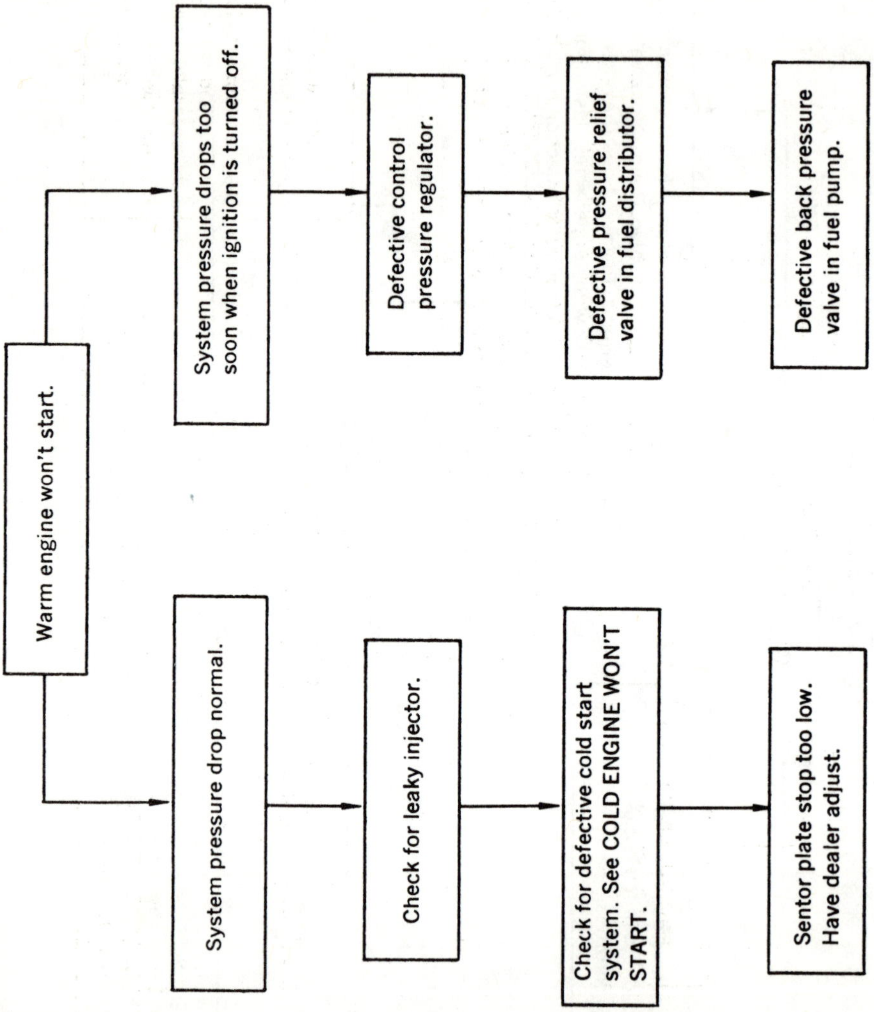

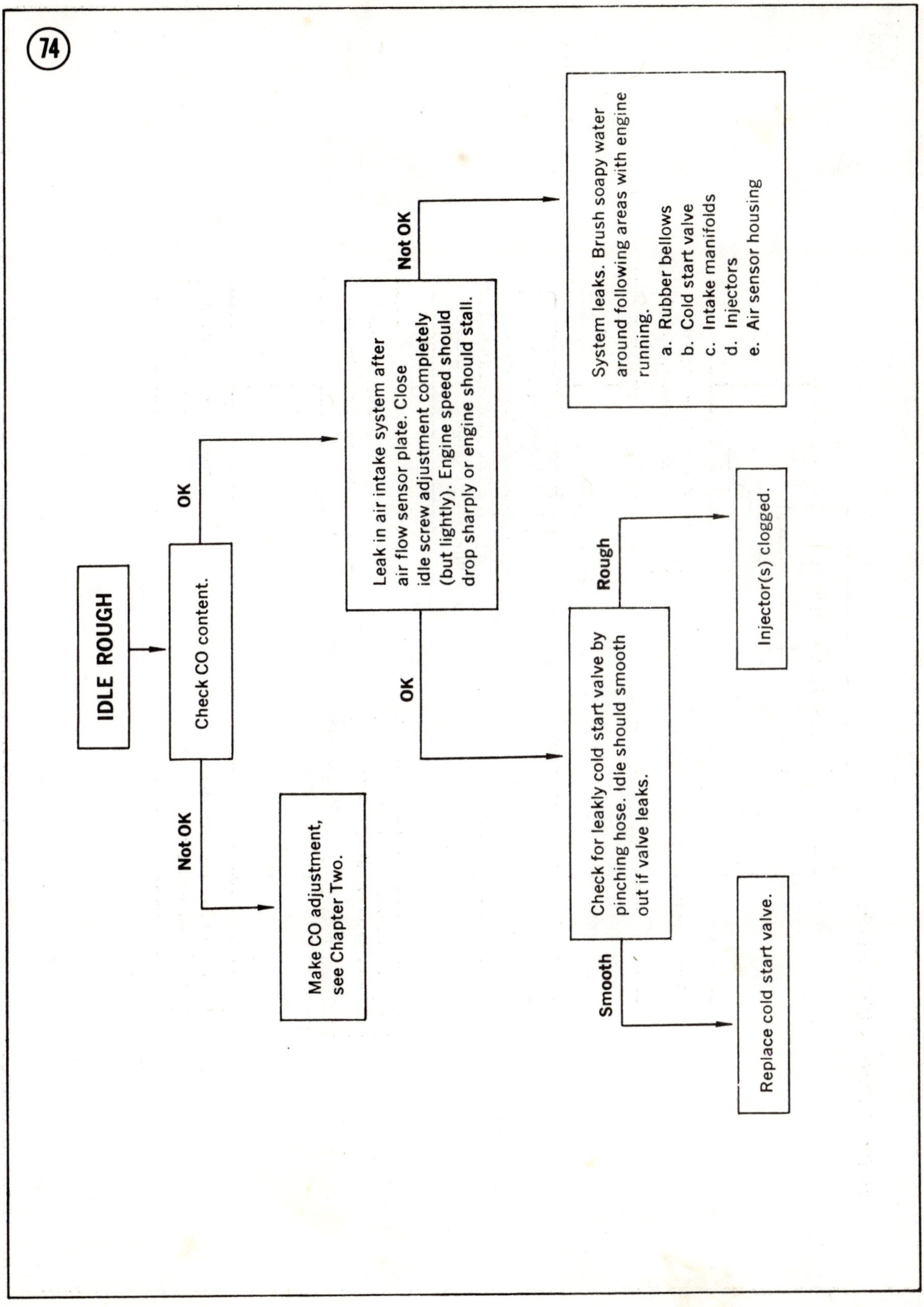
74
IDLE ROUGH
Check CO content.
OK
Not OK
Make CO adjustment, see Chapter Two.
Leak in air intake system after air flow sensor plate. Close idle screw adjustment completely (but lightly). Engine speed should drop sharply or engine should stall.
OK
Not OK
System leaks. Brush soapy water around following areas with engine running.
a. Rubber bellows
b. Cold start valve
c. Intake manifolds
d. Injectors
e. Air sensor housing
Check for leakly cold start valve by pinching hose. Idle should smooth out if valve leaks.
Rough
Smooth
Injector(s) clogged.
Replace cold start valve.

5

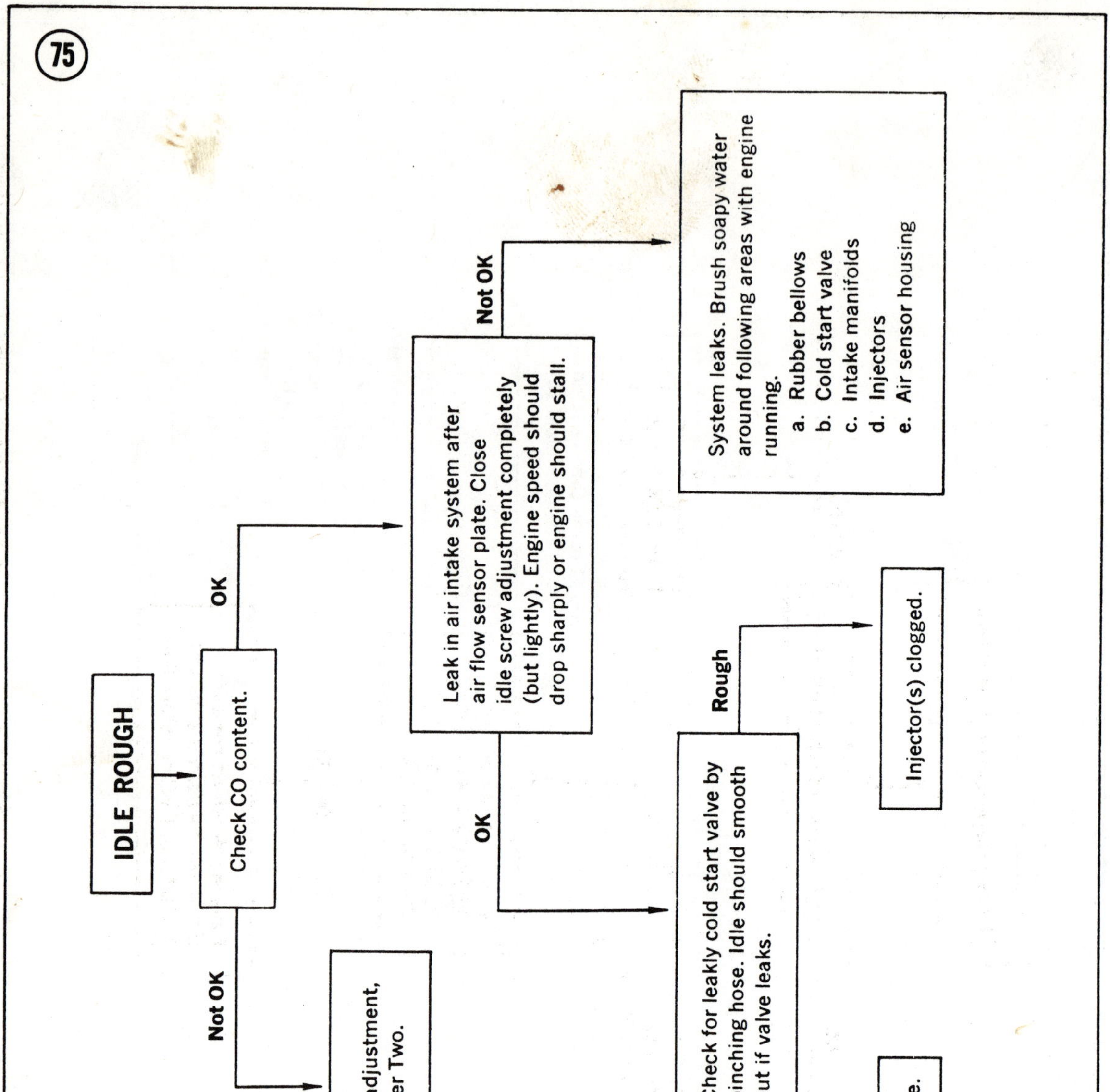
75
IDLE ROUGH
Check CO content.
OK
Not OK
Make CO adjustment, see Chapter Two.
Leak in air intake system after air flow sensor plate. Close idle screw adjustment completely (but lightly). Engine speed should drop sharply or engine should stall.
Not OK
System leaks. Brush soapy water around following areas with engine running.
a. Rubber bellows
b. Cold start valve
c. Intake manifolds
d. Injectors
e. Air sensor housing
OK
Check for leakly cold start valve by pinching hose. Idle should smooth out if valve leaks.
Rough
Injector(s) clogged.
Smooth
Replace cold start valve.

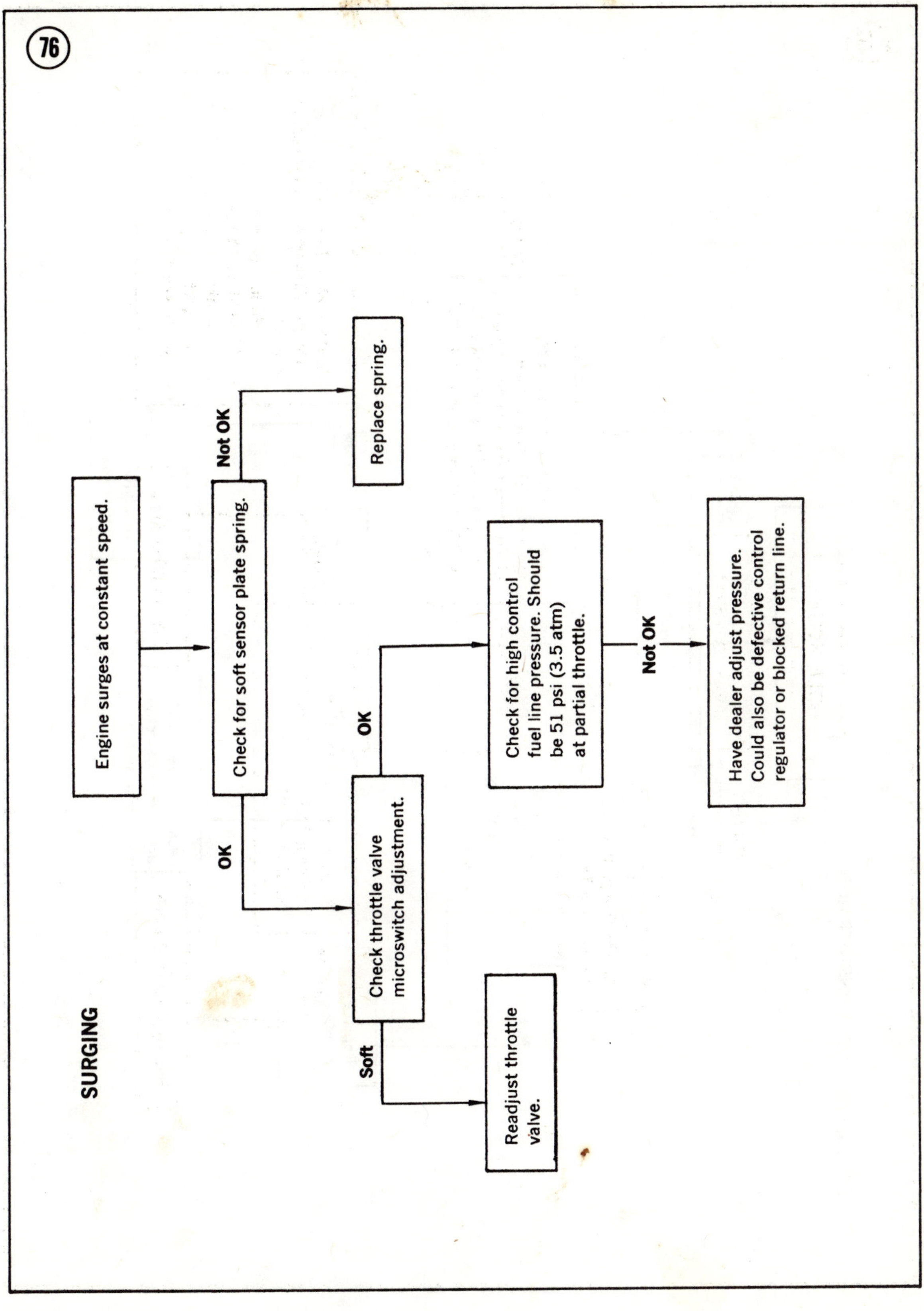
76
SURGING
Engine surges at constant speed.
Check for soft sensor plate spring.
Not OK
Replace spring.
OK
Check throttle valve microswitch adjustment.
Soft
Readjust throttle valve.
OK
Check for high control fuel line pressure. Should be 51 psi (3.5 atm) at partial throttle.
Not OK
Have dealer adjust pressure. Could also be defective control regulator or blocked return line.

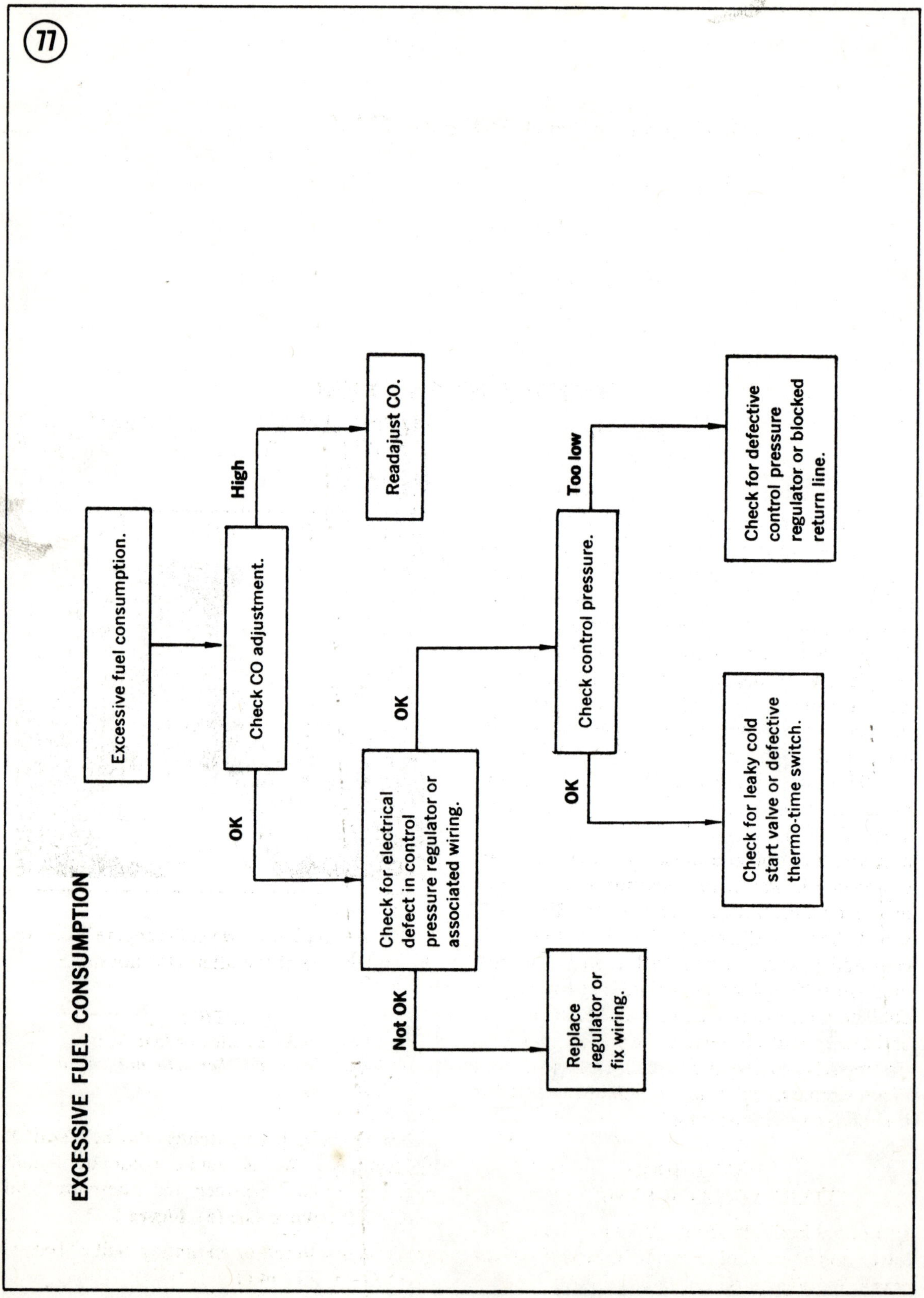
77
EXCESSIVE FUEL CONSUMPTION
Excessive fuel consumption.
Check CO adjustment.
High
Readjust CO.
OK
Check for electrical defect in control pressure regulator or associated wiring.
Not OK
Replace regulator or fix wiring.
OK
Check control pressure.
Too low
Check for defective control pressure regulator or blocked return line.
OK
Check for leaky cold start valve or defective thermo-time switch.

CHAPTER SIX

COOLING SYSTEM

The cooling system is shown in **Figure 1**. Engine coolant is cooled by the radiator and an electric fan. A thermoswitch grounds the fan motor, turning it on when engine coolant reaches 194°F (90°C) and it turns it off at 185°F (85°C). Of course, the fan can only be energized when the ignition is on. Engine coolant is circulated by a water pump mounted on the side of the engine block. A single drive belt drives both the water pump and the alternator. The thermostat, also mounted on the side of the block, controls coolant flow through the radiator. When the engine is cold, the thermostat bypasses the coolant around the radiator. When the engine is warm, the thermostat opens and directs coolant through the radiator. **Figures 2 and 3** show the direction of coolant flow for a cold and a warm carburetted engine. The figures are self-explanatory. Note that the engine coolant controls the automatic choke on the carburetor and also heats the intake manifold on models so equipped. CIS-equipped and diesel engine coolant flow is similar, except for fuel intake system heating.

DRIVE BELT TENSION ADJUSTMENT

1. Loosen both alternator mounting bolts. The lower bolt is accessible through the timing belt cover. See **Figure 4**.

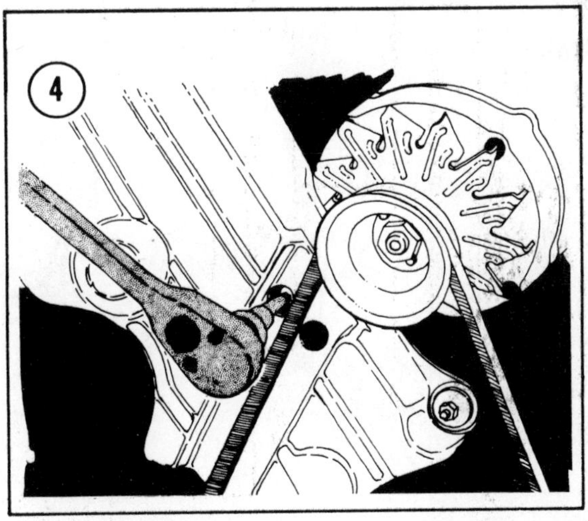

2. Insert a pry bar between the engine block and the pulley side of the alternator housing.

CAUTION

Use a hardwood stick or long hammer handle as a pry bar. Do not use a metal pry bar.

3. Using the pry bar, tighten the belt until it deflects about ½ in. under moderate thumb pressure applied between the alternator and crankshaft pulleys. See (a), **Figure 5**.

4. Tighten alternator mounting bolts. Torque to 14 ft.-lb (2.0 mkg).

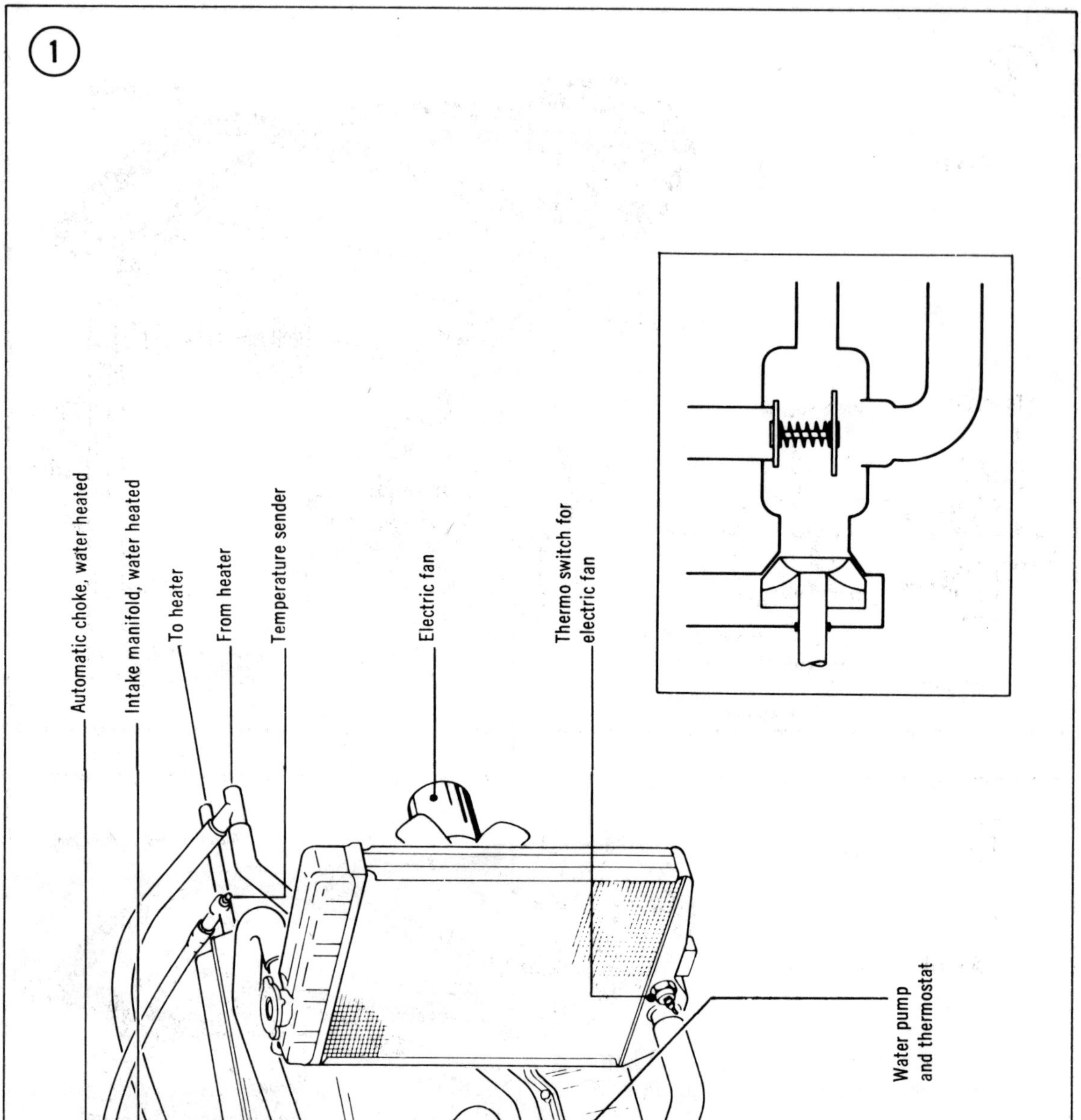

1

COOLING SYSTEM

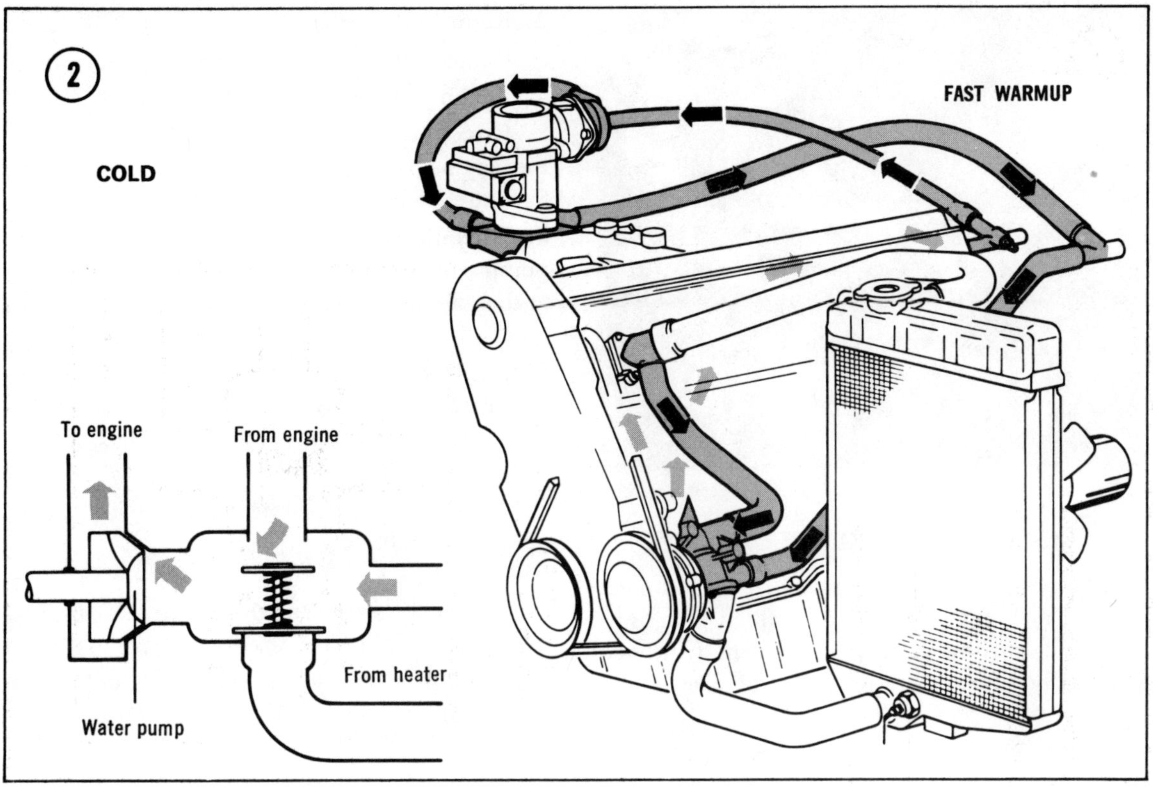
2
COLD
FAST WARMUP
To engine
From engine
From heater
Water pump

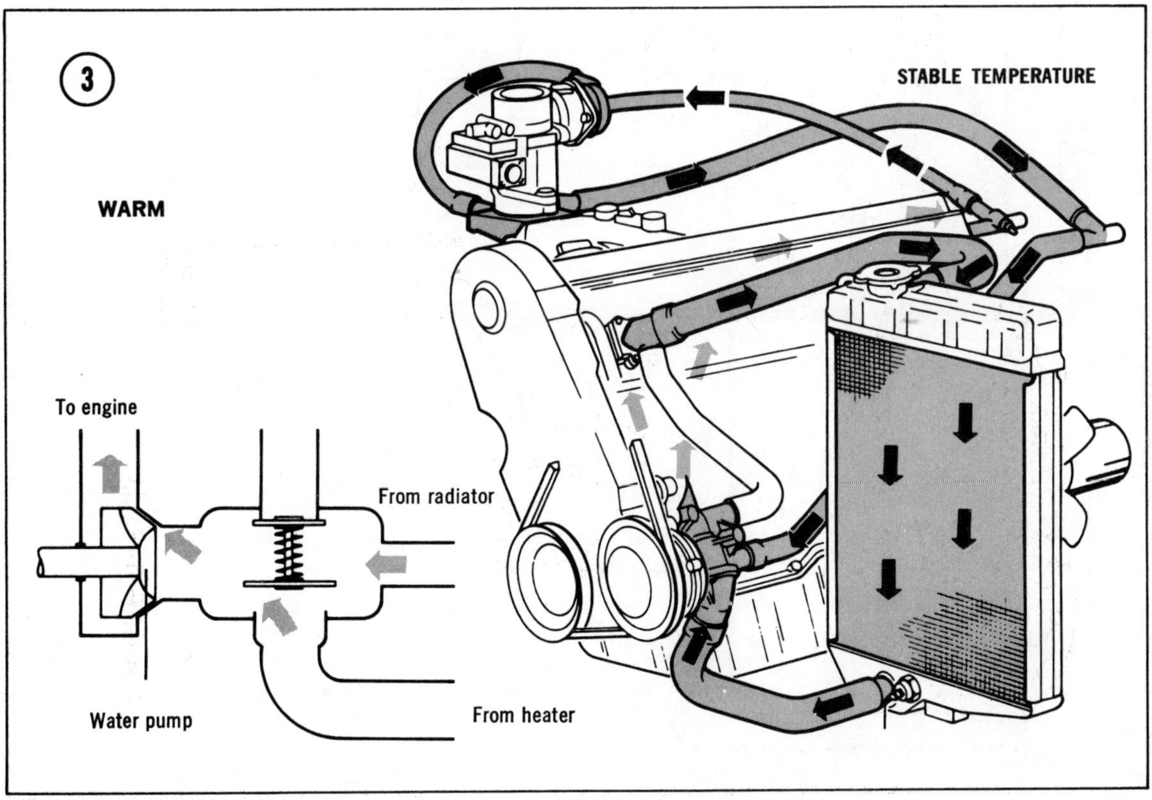
3
WARM
STABLE TEMPERATURE
To engine
From radiator
Water pump
From heater

5

COOLING SYSTEM FLUSHING

The cooling system should be drained, flushed with clean water, and refilled with anti-freeze at least every 2 years. The best method is described below and shown in **Figure 6**.

Flushing

1. Drain the cooling system by removing the lower radiator hose.
2. Remove the radiator cap.
3. Remove the thermostat and the water pump.
4. Reconnect the lower radiator hose.
5. Disconnect the upper radiator hose from the engine block. This will be a drain during flushing.
6. Disconnect the small hose between the water pump and the upper engine block connection at the engine block.
7. Connect a water supply, for example, from a garden hose, to the end of the small hose disconnected in Step 6. This does not have to be a positive connection as long as most of the water enters the engine.
8. Turn the heater control on the instrument panel to maximum.
9. Turn the water on and flush for 3-5 minutes. It is not necessary to run the engine. For the last minute of flushing, repeatedly squeeze the lower radiator hose to expel any trapped coolant.
10. Turn the water off and reconnect the 2 water hoses.
11. Drain the entire system by removing the drain plug in the bottom of the radiator. When completed, close the drain.

6

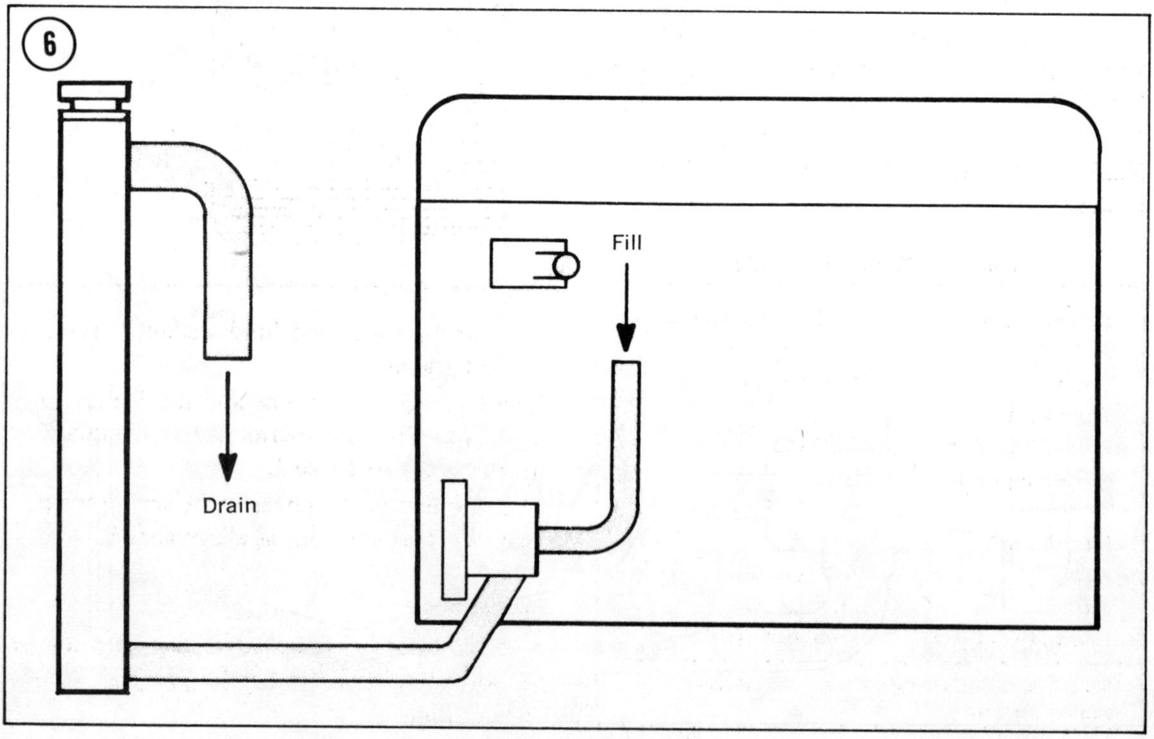

Refilling

1. Be sure all hoses are connected.
2. Set the heater control on the instrument panel to maximum.
3. Remove the radiator cap, fill the system with a 50/50 mixture of ethylene glycol and water even if you live in a climate which does not require this degree of freeze protection. The antifreeze makes a good rust inhibitor. When the system is full, replace the radiator cap.
4. Run the engine at a fast idle and recheck the coolant in the radiator. Top up if necessary. Also check the system for leaks.
5. After driving several miles, recheck the coolant level; it takes some time for all the air to be removed from the system.

PRESSURE CHECK

If the coolant system requires frequent topping up, chances are there is a leak. Not only may coolant be lost, but without proper pressure, the coolant recovery system cannot function properly.

To check the system, proceed as follows.

1. Remove the radiator cap.
2. Dip the cap in water and attach to a cooling system pressure tester, using suitable adapters supplied with the instrument.
3. Pump the pressure to that specified in **Table 1**. If the cap fails to hold pressure, replace it.

Table 1 COOLING SYSTEM

System pressure	17-19 psi (1.2-1.35 atm)
Capacity	6.8 U.S. qts. (6.5 liters)[1]
Coolant	50/50 ethylene glycol
Thermostat	
Opening begins	176°F (80°C)
Opening stroke	0.27 in. (7mm) @ 194°F (90°C)
Electric fan	
On	194°F (90°C)
Off	185°F (85°C)
Drive belt deflection	3/8-9/16 in. (10-15mm)

[1] 4.9 U.S. qts. (4.6 liters) on models without expansion tanks.

4. Attach the pressure tester to the filler hole on the radiator.
5. Pump the system to the pressure specified in Table 1. There should be no noticeable pressure drop in 30 seconds. If pressure falls off, there is a leak which must be found and sealed.

THERMOSTAT

Removal and Testing

1. Drain the radiator by disconnecting lower radiator hose at water pump.
2. Remove 2 bolts securing thermostat housing to water pump.
3. Remove thermostat and seal.
4. To test, slip a 0.002 in. feeler gauge between the valve and its seat.
5. Submerge the thermostat in water with a thermometer as shown in **Figure 7**.

7

6. Heat the water and hold a slight tension on the feeler gauge.
7. When the valve opens and the feeler gauge slips out, read the thermometer. Compare to specifications in Table 1.
8. If the thermostat opens at the wrong temperature, or does not open at all, replace it.

Installation

1. Test the new thermostat as described above.
2. Install the thermostat in position in the water pump.

3. Position the thermostat housing using a new gasket.
4. Tighten cap screws to 7 ft.-lb. (1.0 mkg).
5. Connect radiator hose and fill system with a 50/50 mixture of ethylene glycol and water.

WATER PUMP

A defective water pump is usually evident when the engine overheats and there is no other apparent reason. Quite often, the water pump will give some warning before it fails completely. When the water pump begins to make noise or fails, replace with a new pump. The pump should not be rebuilt since there is considerable risk of cracking the aluminum pump housing when replacing the seals. However, the water pump may be disassembled to replace the gasket between the water pump body and cover (6, **Figure 8**).

Removal/Installation

1. Drain coolant by removing lower radiator hose from radiator.

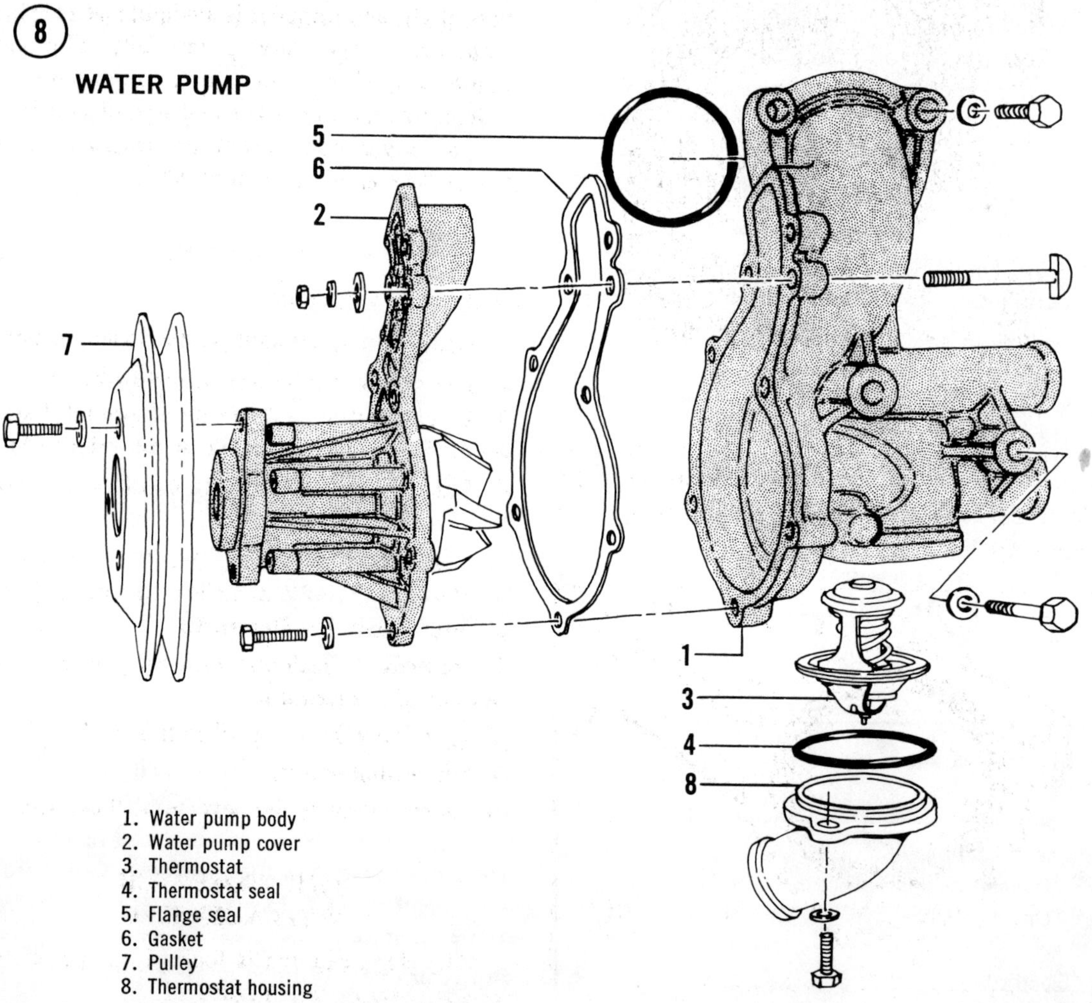

1. Water pump body
2. Water pump cover
3. Thermostat
4. Thermostat seal
5. Flange seal
6. Gasket
7. Pulley
8. Thermostat housing

2. Remove the alternator as described in Chapter Seven.
3. Remove timing belt cover as described in Chapter Four.
4. Disconnect 3 coolant hoses from water pump.
5. Remove water pump mounting bolts circled in **Figure 9**.

6. Lift water pump out.
7. Installation is the reverse of these steps. Use a new seal between the water pump and the block and be sure it is seated properly. See **Figure 10**.

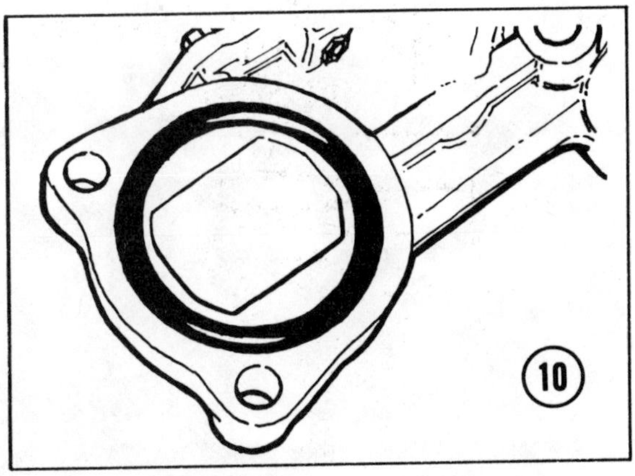

Cover Gasket Replacement

The cover gasket can be replaced if it is leaking. Further disassembly of the water pump is not recommended.

1. Remove the water pump as described above.
2. Remove the drive pulley.
3. Remove the water pump cover shown in Figure 8.
4. Install new gasket with waterproof gasket sealer.
5. Install water pump cover and torque the bolts to 7 ft.-lb. (1 mkg).
6. Install the drive pulley and torque the bolts to 14 ft.-lb. (2 mkg).

Water Pump Cover Replacement

The water pump cover which includes the hub, shaft, and impeller is available as a replacement part if the water pump fails. The water pump body should not require replacement.

Remove the old cover and gasket and install a new cover and gasket as described under *Cover Gasket Replacement,* above.

RADIATOR

Removal/Installation

1. Drain engine coolant as described earlier.
2. Disconnect upper and lower radiator hoses.
3. Disconnect wires from thermoswitch located on the left side of the radiator. See **Figure 11**.
4. Disconnect line going to overflow reservoir. See **Figure 12**.
5. Disconnect fan motor plug. See Figure 12.
6. Remove 2 bolts securing the air injection diverter valve. See **Figure 13**.
7. Remove 2 radiator mounting nuts at the bottom of the radiator.
8. Remove wire at top of radiator.
9. Lift radiator out.
10. Installation is the reverse of these steps.

THERMOSWITCH REPLACEMENT

The thermoswitch is located on the left side of the radiator. See Figure 11.

1. Drain coolant as described earlier.
2. Disconnect wires from thermoswitch.
3. Unscrew thermoswitch from radiator.
4. Installation is the reverse of these steps.

11

12

13

CHAPTER SEVEN

ELECTRICAL SYSTEM

This chapter includes service procedures for the battery, starter, charging system, lighting system, fuses, instruments, and windshield wipers. Specifications are given in **Table 1** at the end of the chapter.

BATTERY

The battery is located in the engine compartment. See Table 1 for battery specifications.

> NOTE: *Make sure battery ground connections are properly made* (**Figure 1**). *Poor connections can cause illumination of brake warning lamp, or result in speedometer needle not returning to zero, because of improper current flow. When disconnecting battery, always remove ground cable at battery (Z, Figure 1) first. When connecting ground cables, make X-Y connection first, then make connection Z. Make certain that all contact surfaces are clean, bright, bare metal, and that all connector bolts are tightened securely.*

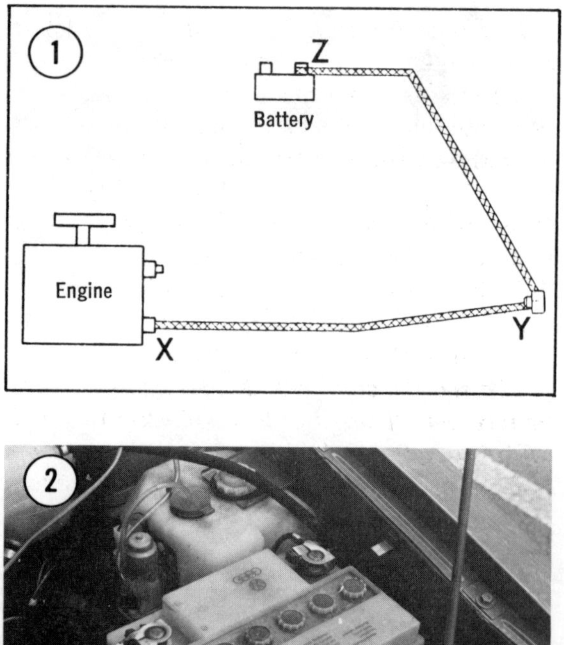

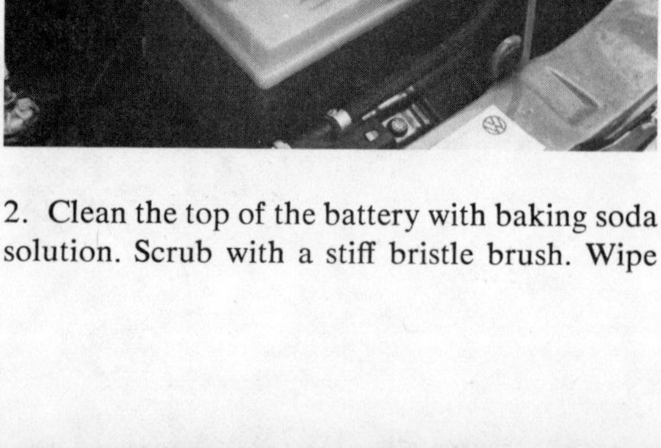

Care and Inspection

1. Disconnect both battery cables and remove the battery. See **Figure 2**.

2. Clean the top of the battery with baking soda solution. Scrub with a stiff bristle brush. Wipe

battery clean with a cloth moistened in ammonia or baking soda solution.

CAUTION

Keep cleaning solution out of battery cells or the electrolyte will be seriously weakened.

3. Clean battery terminals with a stiff wire brush or one of the many tools made for this purpose.
4. Examine entire battery case for cracks.
5. Install the battery and reconnect cables.

NOTE: *Observe polarity when reconnecting cables.*

6. Coat battery connections with light mineral grease or Vaseline after tightening.
7. Check the electrolyte level and top up if necessary.

Testing

Hydrometer testing is the best way to check battery condition. Use a hydrometer with numbered graduations from 1.100 to 1.300 rather than one with color coded bands. To use the hydrometer, squeeze the rubber ball, insert the tip in the cell and release the ball (**Figure 3**). Draw enough electrolyte to float the weighted float inside the hydrometer. Note the number in line with the surface of the electrolyte; this is the specific gravity for this cell. Return the electrolyte to the cell from which it came.

The specific gravity of the electrolyte in each battery cell is an excellent indication of that cell's condition. A fully charged cell will read 1.275-1.380, while a cell in good condition may read from 1.250-1.280. A cell in fair condition reads from 1.225-1.250, and anything below 1.225 is practically dead.

If the cells test in the poor range, the battery requires recharging. The hydrometer is useful for checking the progress of the charging operation. A reading from 1.200 to about 1.225 indicates a half charge; 1.275-1.380 indicates a full charge.

CAUTION

Always disconnect both *battery connections before connecting charging equipment.*

3

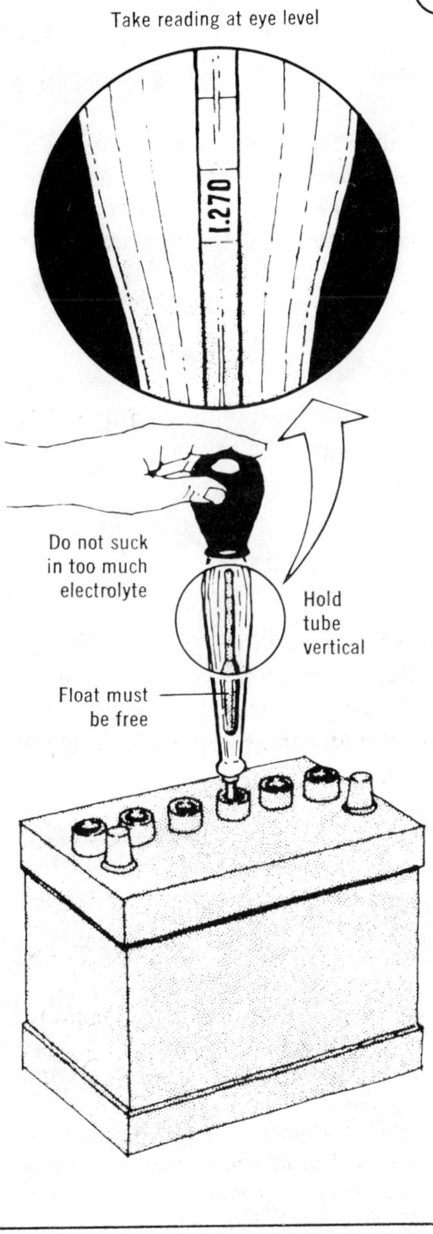

STARTER

NOTE: *A new type of starter is used on cars produced in July, 1975, and later. This starter cannot be used on earlier models, although removal and repair procedures remain unchanged. If starter replacement is necessary, make sure you have the proper starter for your car.*

7

Removal/Installation

1. Disconnect battery ground cable.
2. Disconnect starter wires, shown in **Figure 4**.
3. Remove starter mounting bolts and remove starter. See **Figure 5**.
4. Installation is the reverse of these steps. Torque mounting bracket bolts and nuts to 11 ft.-lb. (1.6 mkg). Torque brace bracket-to-transmission bolt to 11 ft.-lb. With starter under no strain, tighten brace bracket-to-starter nuts to 4 ft.-lb. (0.6 mkg).

Brush Replacement

Starter must be removed and partially disassembled to replace brushes.

1. Remove starter.
2. Perform Steps 2-4 of the *Disassembly* procedure to expose the brushes.
3. Brushes must be at least ½ in. (13mm) long. If less, replace them.

> NOTE: *Brushes cannot be replaced separately. If worn, replace entire field coil assembly and/or brush holder assembly.*

4. Examine the commutator before assembling. If it is dirty or oily, clean it with a cloth moistened in solvent. If it is scored, burned, or worn down to the mica strips, overhaul the starter.
5. Reassemble by reversing Steps 2-4 of the *Disassembly* procedure.

Solenoid Replacement

1. Disconnect the large connecting wire between the starter and solenoid. See **Figure 6**.

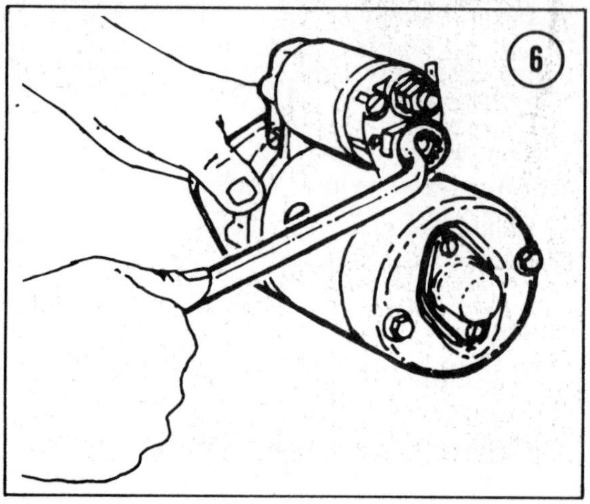

2. Remove 2 screws securing solenoid to the mounting bracket. See **Figure 7**.

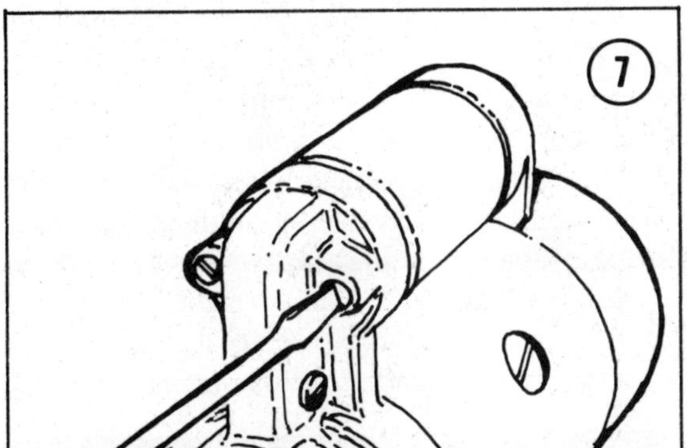

3. Lift solenoid pullrod free of the operating lever and remove the solenoid. See **Figure 8**.

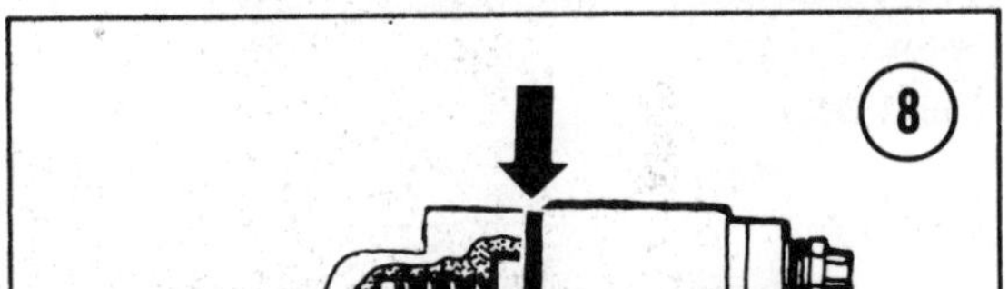

4. Place strip of VW D14 plastic sealer on the outer edge of the solenoid face.

5. Pull the drive pinion to bring the operating lever back toward the solenoid opening. Connect the pullrod to the operating lever.

6. Secure solenoid with mounting screws and reconnect large wire from the starter.

Disassembly

See **Figure 9** for this procedure.

1. Remove solenoid as described earlier.
2. Remove end caps and seal shown in **Figure 10**.

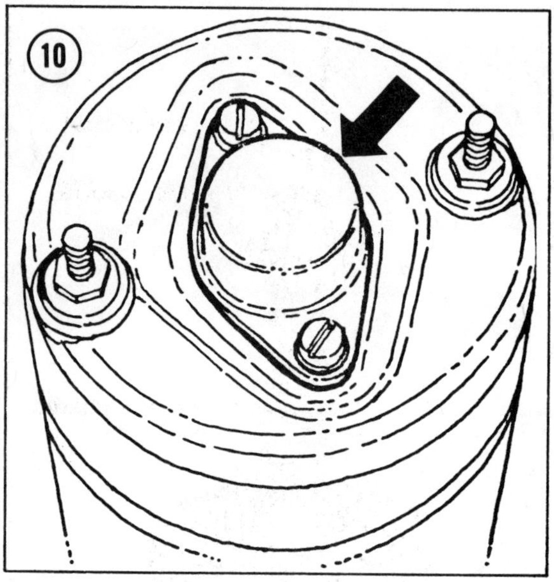

3. Pry out the lock ring (7, **Figure 11**) and remove shims.

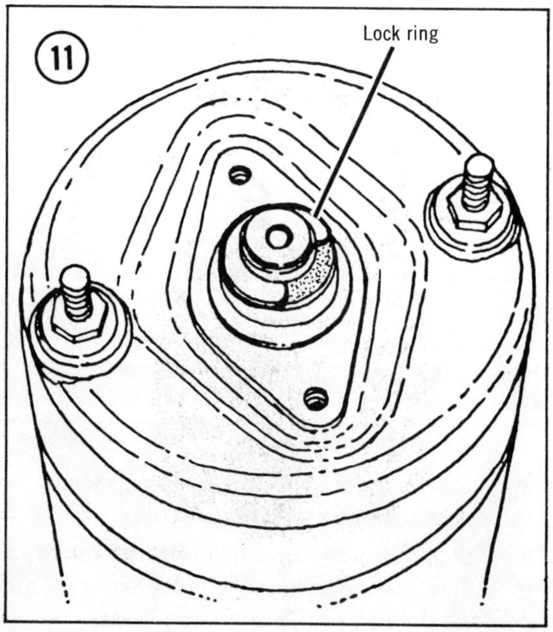

4. Remove the cover nuts (arrows, Figure 9) and cover.
5. Lift brushes out of holder.
6. Remove brush holder.
7. Remove housing from the armature/mounting bracket assembly.
8. Hold the armature in a vise with soft jaws (copper, wood blocks), commutator end down. With a hollow drift, tap stop ring down, away from lock ring.
9. Pry off lock ring and slide the stop ring off.
10. Remove any burrs around the lock ring groove. Slide mounting bracket and pinion assembly off the armature.
11. Remove the operating lever pin from the mounting bracket and remove pinion assembly.

Cleaning

Do not immerse starter parts in cleaning solvent. Solvent can permanently destroy insulation on the field housing or armature. Wipe these parts with a clean cloth. Other parts not containing insulated wiring may be cleaned with a brush moistened in solvent, then wiped dry with a clean cloth.

Inspection

1. Examine the armature for obvious mechanical damage such as burned windings, bent or worn shaft, or scored commutator. Scored or unevenly worn commutators may be turned on a lathe. Minimum diameter permissable is 1.357 in. (34.5mm). After turning, undercut the mica strips, separating the brass about 1.64 in. (0.4mm). **Figure 12** shows right and wrong undercuts. Use a short piece of hacksaw blade or a special tool made for this purpose.

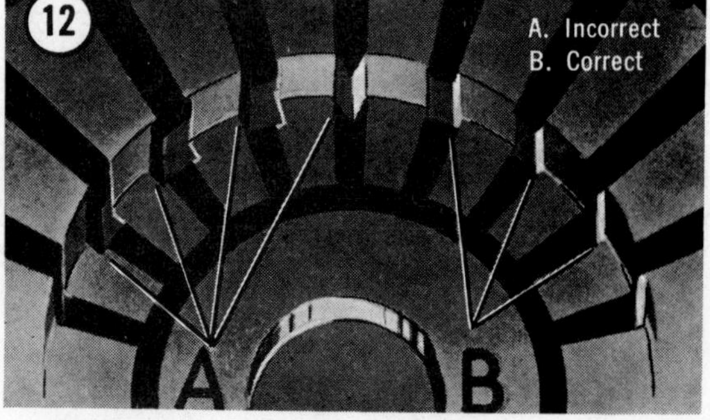

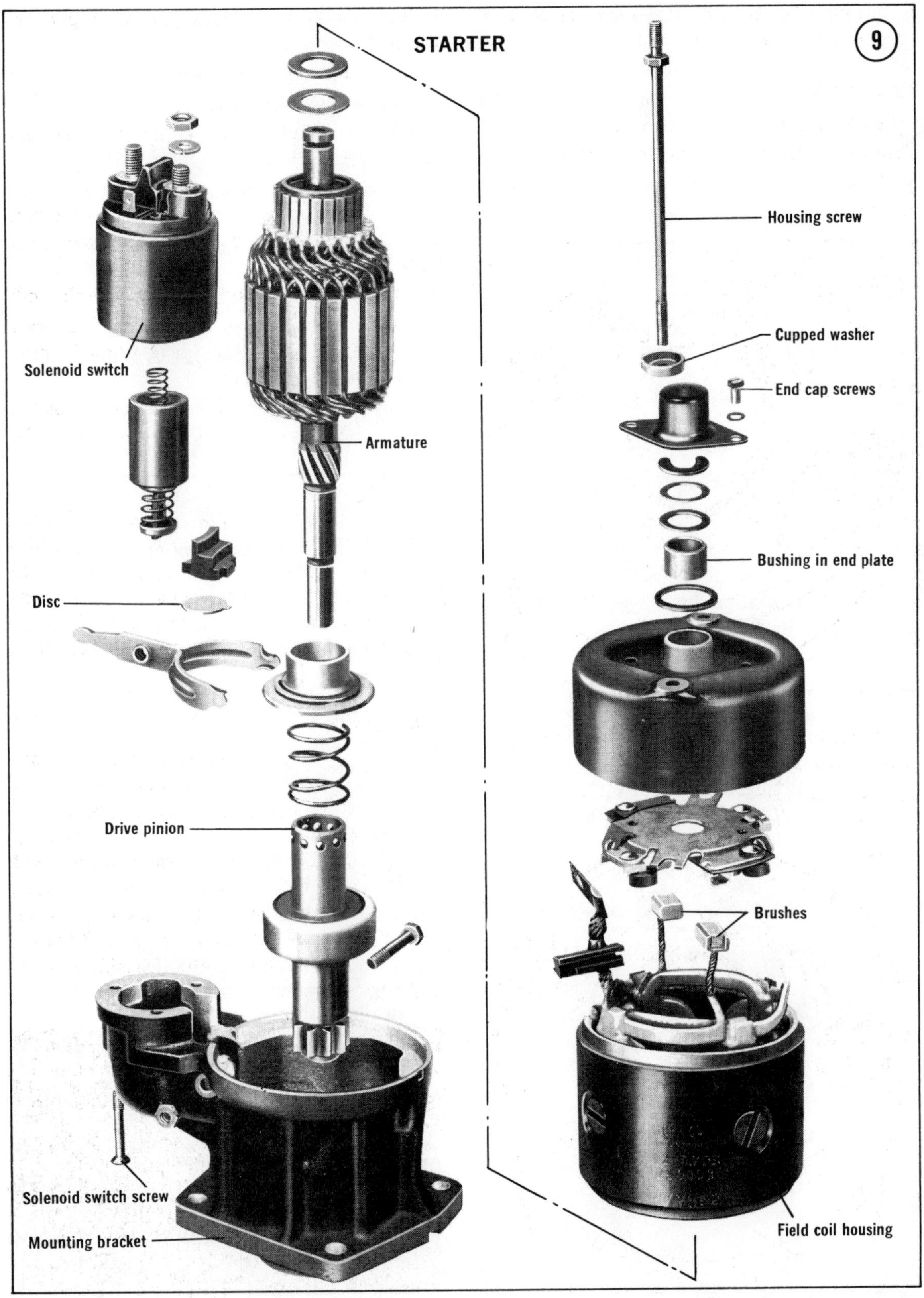
STARTER
9
Housing screw
Cupped washer
End cap screws
Solenoid switch
Armature
Bushing in end plate
Disc
Drive pinion
Brushes
Solenoid switch screw
Mounting bracket
Field coil housing

2. Check armature for shorts to ground with an ohmmeter or other continuity tester. Connect one test prod to the armature core, connect the other test prod to each commutator bar. See **Figure 13**. If continuity occurs on any bar, replace the armature.

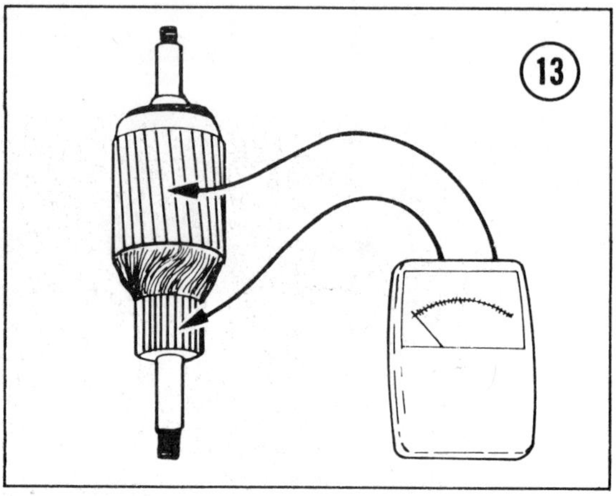

3. Check armature for opens. Usually these are evidenced by burn marks between commutator bars caused by the brushes bridging the open circuit.

4. Check armature for winding shorts. To do this, insert the armature in a growler. Turn the growler on and hold hacksaw blade slightly above, but not touching, the armature. See **Figure 14**. Rotate the armature slowly; if the blade vibrates and is attracted to the armature, a winding is shorted. If visual inspection does not reveal a short which can be fixed, replace the armature.

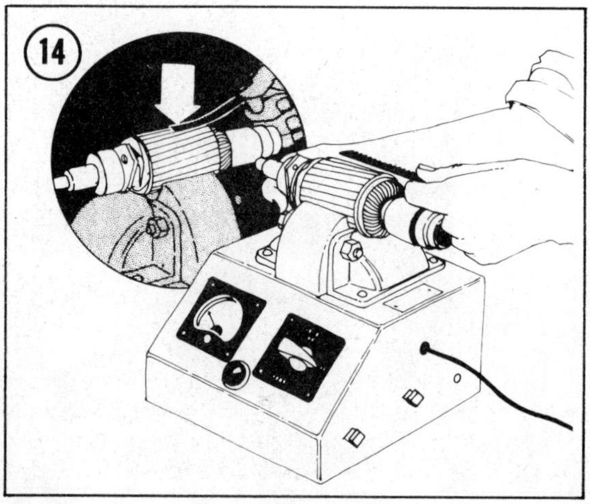

5. Check field windings for shorts to ground. To do this, connect an ohmmeter or other continuity tester between a field winding lead (coil end) and the field housing. See **Figure 15**. If continuity occurs, the field winding is shorted. The entire field coil and the brushes must be replaced.

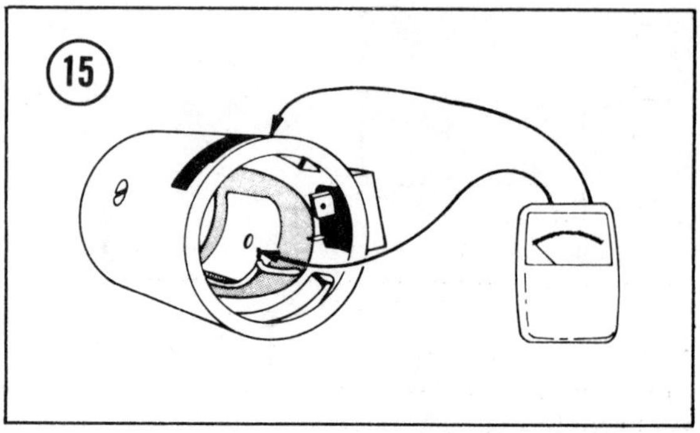

6. Examine all other parts for wear, particularly bushings. Replace any that are worn or questionable.

Assembly

Refer to Figure 9 for this procedure.

1. Mount the drive pinion with operating lever on mounting bracket with operating lever pin.

2. Grease all bearing surfaces with universal grease and guide the armature shaft into the drive pinion.

3. Push on the stop ring and install the lock ring. Pull the stop ring over the lock ring. It should be possible to turn the stop ring on the shaft without jamming.

4. Install rubber seat in mounting bracket and fit the starter housing. Ensure that the tab on the housing locates in the mounting bracket slot. Use sealing compound at (D), **Figure 16**.

5. Slide steel washer and fiber washer on the armature shaft.

6. Install the brush holder on the commutator and insert the brushes.

7. Lubricate the bushing in the end cover with oil. Install the end cover on the housing and secure it with nuts. Use sealing compound at (B) and (C), Figure 16. Ensure that the rubber grommet on the wire to the solenoid fits properly in the cover.

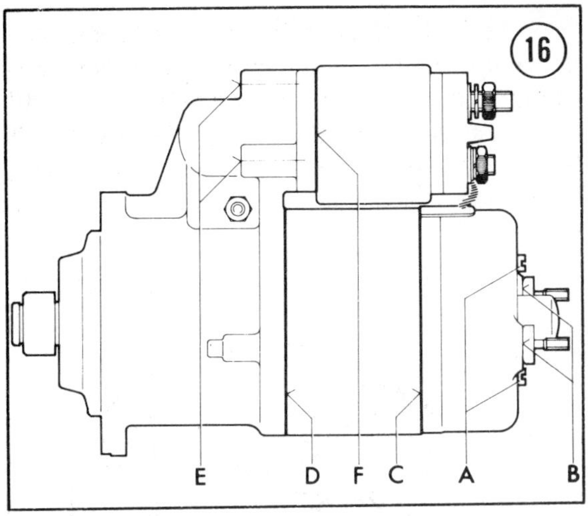

8. Install shims and lock ring. Shaft end play should be 0.004-0.012 in. (0.1-0.3mm). Adjust by adding or removing shims.

9. Install a new seal and install the end cap. Use sealing compound at (A), Figure 16.

10. Install solenoid as described earlier.

ALTERNATOR

The alternator generates alternating current (AC) which is converted to direct current (DC) by 6 internal silicon diodes. The alternator consists of the rotor, stator, end plate, housing, and drive pulley. Refer to Table 1 for specifications.

Removal/Installation

1. Open the hood and disconnect the battery ground cable.

2. Disconnect electrical plug at rear of alternator. See **Figure 17**.

3. Remove the top adjusting bolt shown in **Figure 18**. Loosen bolt at other end of bracket and swing out of the way.

4. Remove drive belt.

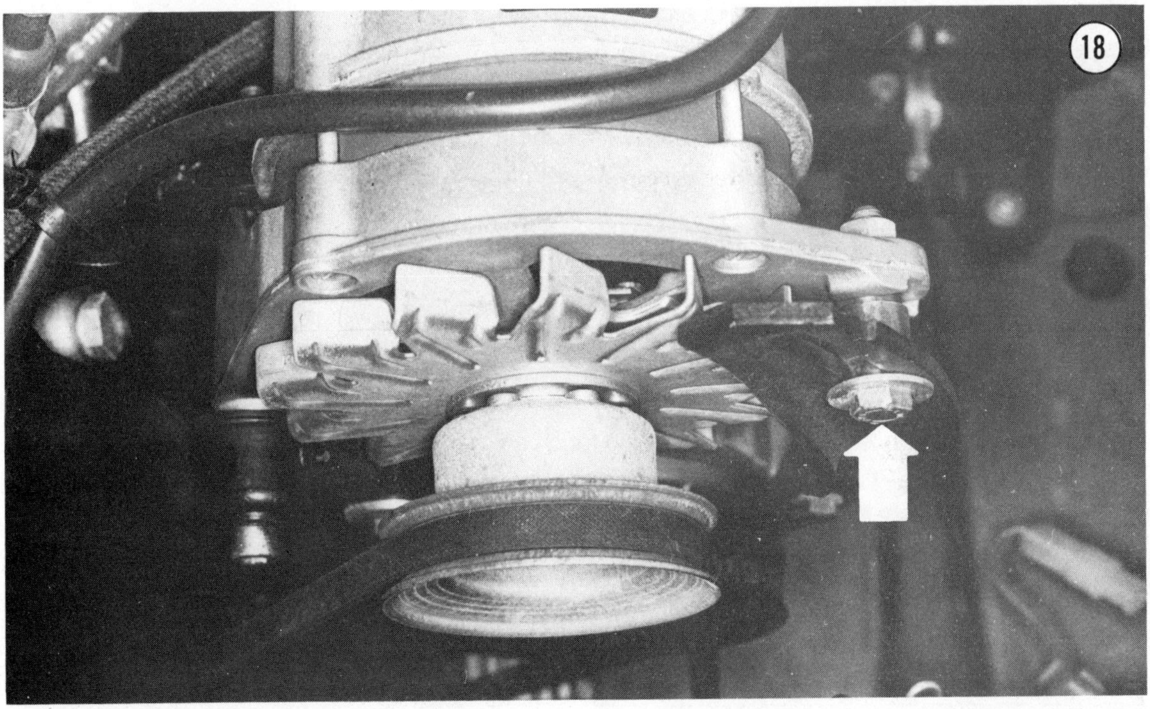

5. Remove lower bolt and nut securing alternator. This Allen bolt is accessible through the timing belt cover. See **Figure 19**.

6. Lift alternator out.

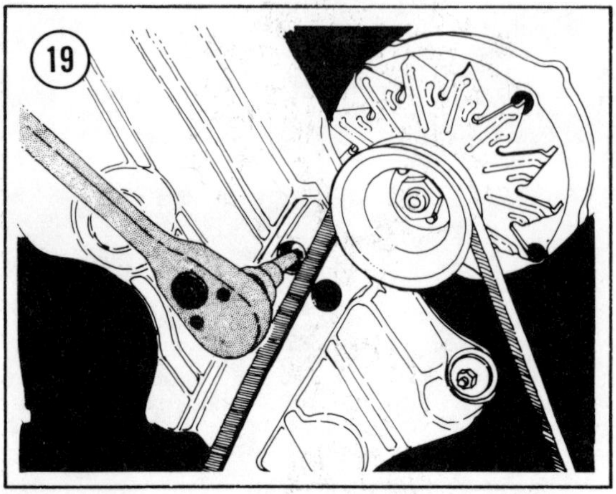

7. Installation is the reverse of these steps. Adjust belt tension as described in Chapter Three.

Disassembly/Assembly

See **Figure 20** for this procedure.

NOTE: *The 1977 model alternators have a slightly different mounting flange shape and hole pattern than earlier models.*

1. Mark the end plate and housing to make reassembly easier.

2. Remove voltage regulator/brush holder.

3. Hold pulley in a vise with soft jaws as shown in **Figure 21**. Remove pulley nut and pulley. Remove Woodruff key.

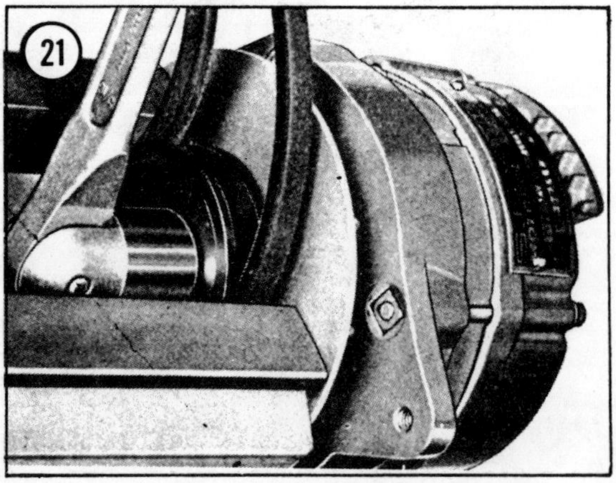

4. Remove spacers and fan.

5. Remove through-bolts and carefully separate end plate/rotor assembly from the stator/housing assembly. If necessary, pry them apart carefully with a screwdriver.

CAUTION

Do not insert screwdriver more than 1/16 in. (2mm) or the stator windings may be damaged.

6. Press the rotor out of the end plate as shown in **Figure 22**.

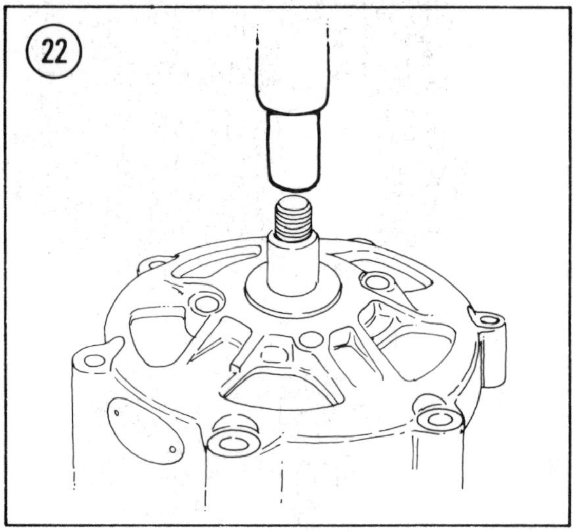

7. Remove screws holding bearing retainer plate. Remove plate and press bearing out.

8. Pull bearing off rear end of rotor. Use a pulley which grips the inner race. If you must use a puller which grips only the outer race, discard the bearing and reassemble with a new bearing.

9. Unsolder stator wires from diode carrier. Mark the leads and make a rough sketch to facilitate reassembly.

CAUTION

Use longnose pliers as a heat sink to draw away excessive heat.

10. Lift out stator assembly.

11. Remove screws securing diode carrier and lift carrier assembly out.

12. Assembly is the reverse of these steps. If a new rotor is installed, new bearings must be used.

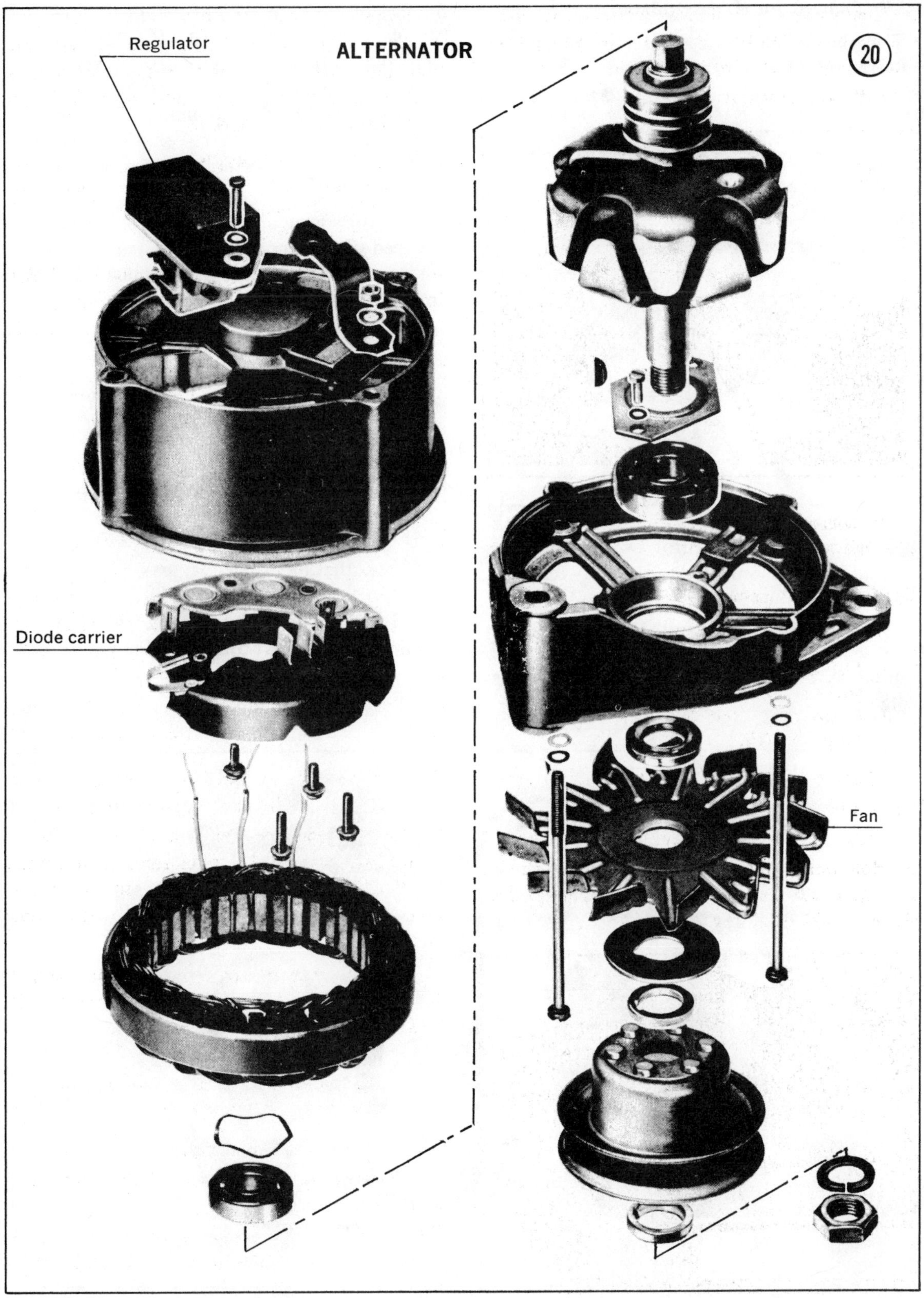

7

Testing Alternator (Disassembled)

For the following test, use an ohmmeter powered by a 3-volt battery (no more), or make a small continuity tester wired as shown in **Figure 23**.

23

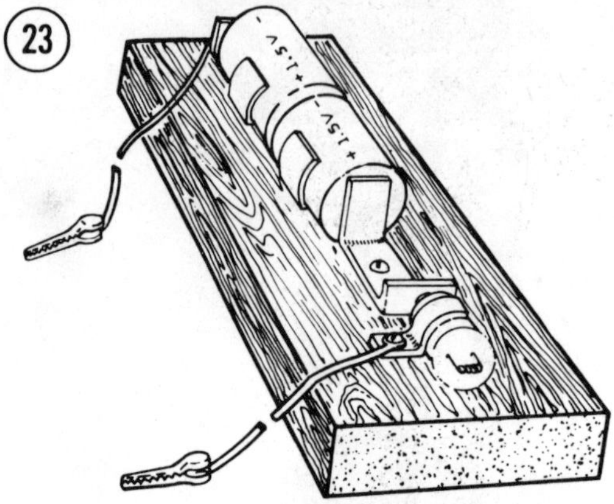

1. Test for a grounded rotor by touching one test lead of the ohmmeter or continuity tester to the rotor shaft and the other test lead to each of the slip rings (**Figure 24**). If the ohmmeter reads a low resistance or the lamp lights, the winding is grounded and the rotor must be replaced.

2. Test for an open circuited rotor by touching one test lead to each slip ring (**Figure 25**). The lamp should light if using the continuity tester. If using an ohmmeter, the resistance should be about 4 ohms. If it reads infinity, the winding is open. If it reads less than 4 ohms, the winding is shorted. In the latter 2 cases, replace the rotor.

3. Test for a grounded stator by connecting one test lead of an ohmmeter to the frame and the other test lead to any grounded stator lead (**Figure 26**). A low resistance indicates a grounded stator. Replace the stator.

CAUTION

Do not use 110 volts to test the stator as recommended for some other alternator makes.

4. Test for open stator winding by measuring resistance between successive pairs of stator leads. Resistance should be about 1.26 ohms.

5. Check the slip rings. If the slip rings are scored or otherwise damaged, they may be turned down on a lathe. Do not turn down to less than 1.24 in. (31.5mm) in diameter.

6. To test diodes for opens and shorts, proceed as follows: connect one test lead of the ohm-

24

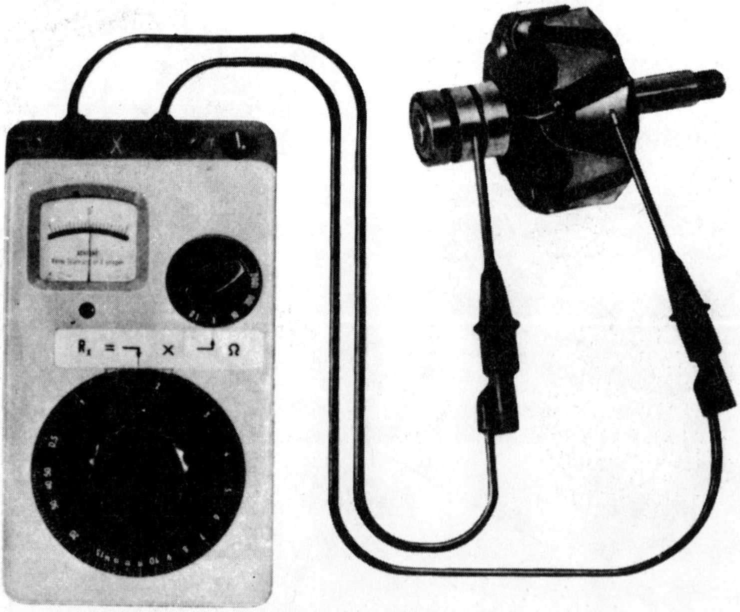

25

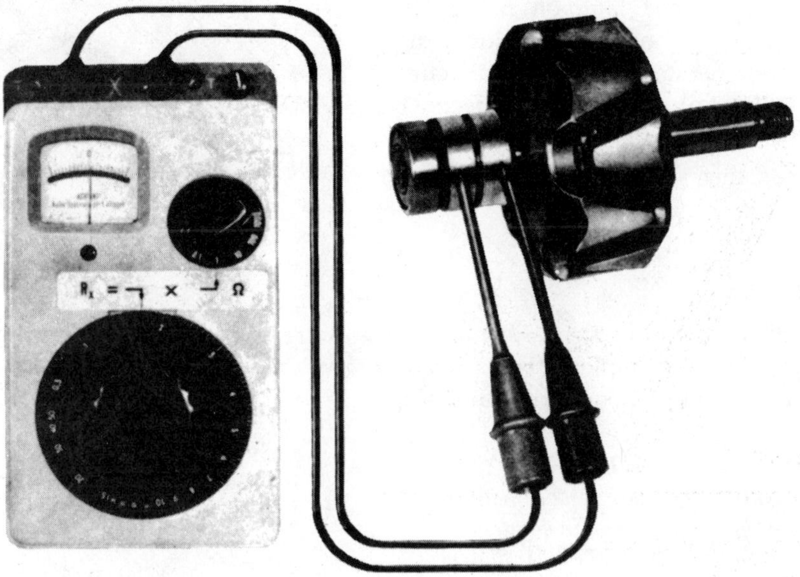

26

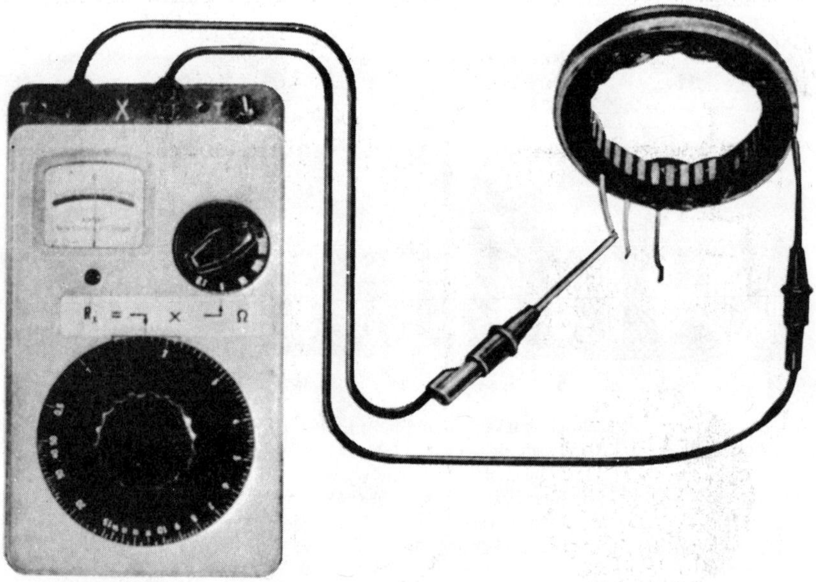

meter to a diode mounting base and the other test lead to the diode terminal. Note the reading, then reverse the test leads and note the reading again. A high resistance (lamp out) in one direction, but a low resistance (lamp on) in the other direction indicates a good diode. A low resistance or a high resistance in both directions indicates a shorted or open diode, respectively, and the entire diode carrier must be replaced.

7. Check the other set of diodes in the same manner.

Replacing Diodes

On some alternators it is permissible to press out individual diodes to replace them. On this alternator, replace entire diode carrier assembly.

> NOTE: *Diodes may be damaged by voltage surges. If diode replacement is required, install suppression condenser (VW Part. No. 059 035 271) as shown in* **Figure 27** *to prevent future damage of this nature.*

VOLTAGE REGULATOR

The alternator voltage regulator is mounted on the rear of the alternator. It is not necessary to remove the alternator in order to replace the voltage regulator.

1. Disconnect the battery ground cable.
2. Remove screws securing voltage regulator to rear of alternator and lift regulator off.
3. Install new regulator by reversing these steps.

FUSES

The fuse box is located on the left side under the dash. See **Figure 28** (typical).

Whenever a fuse blows, ascertain the reason for the failure before replacing fuse. Usually, the trouble is a short circuit in the wiring. This

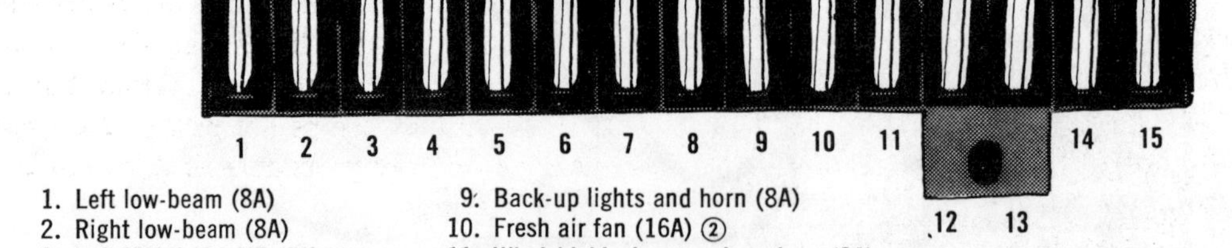

1. Left low-beam (8A)
2. Right low-beam (8A)
3. Left high-beam; high-beam warning light (8A)
4. Right high-beam (8A)
5. Rear window defogger (16A) ①
6. Stoplights and emergency flasher (8A)
7. Interior lights, lighter, clock (8A)
8. Turn signals and indicators (8A)
9. Back-up lights and horn (8A)
10. Fresh air fan (16A) ②
11. Windshield wipers and washers (8A)
12. Rear license plate light (8A)
13. Right parking, tail, and side marker lamps (8A)
14. Left parking, tail, and side marker lamps (8A)
15. Radiator fan (16A) ③

① 8A on 1975 cars
② 8A on 1975-1976 cars
③ Vacant on 1975 cars

may be caused by worn-through insulation or a wire which works its way loose and shorts to ground. Carry several spare fuses in the glove compartment.

CAUTION
Never substitute tinfoil or wire for a fuse. An overload could result in fire and complete loss of the automobile.

HORN

If the horn works, but not loudly or not at the correct pitch, make sure that it is not touching the body. Horn pitch and loudness can be adjusted by removing the seal on the rear of the horn and turning the adjusting screw.

When the horn does not work at all, check the wiring to the horn and check the horn switch. To service the switch:

1. Disconnect the battery ground cable.
2. Pry horn cover off by hand.
3. Remove 3 screws securing switch to steering wheel.
4. Clean contact points with fine crocus cloth.

NOTE: *If carbon brush is broken, the entire steering wheel must be replaced.*

5. Installation is the reverse of these steps.

Horn Replacement

The horn is mounted at the front end, near the radiator. See **Figure 29**.

29

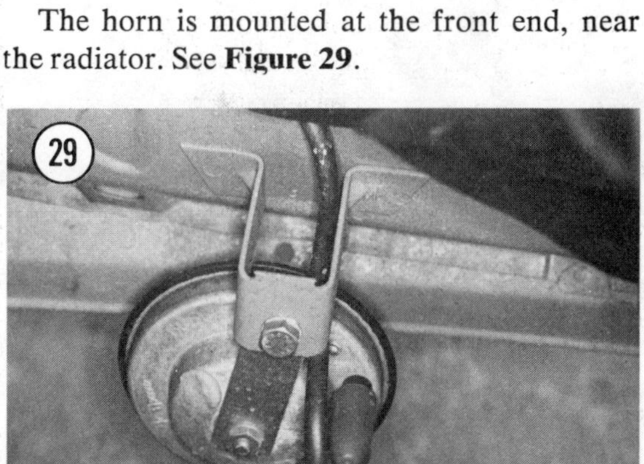

1. Disconnect battery ground cable.
2. Remove nut securing horn to bracket. See Figure 29.
3. Disconnect wires from horn.
4. Installation is the reverse of these steps. Make sure that the horn does not touch the body.

DIRECTIONAL SIGNAL SYSTEM

The directional signal system consists of the steering column mounted switch, flasher, and indicator lamps.

Switch Removal/Installation

1. Disconnect battery ground cable.
2. Remove steering wheel as described in Chapter Eleven.
3. Remove upper and lower trim panels.
4. Disconnect multi-pin connector for directional switch lever and windshield wiper switch lever.
5. Remove 4 screws securing directional signal switch to switch housing and remove switch from housing. See **Figure 30**.
6. Installation is the reverse of these steps.

Flasher Relay Replacement

The flasher relay is mounted on the fuse box. See **Figure 31**. To replace the relay, remove the relay marked J2 and plug in a new one.

NOTE: *The Rabbit model is not equipped with the windshield washer/wiper relay J31 shown in Figure 31. In this model, a jumper wire is used between terminals 19 and 21.*

Lamp Replacement

Front directional signal lamps are behind the same lenses as parking lights. See *Front Parking Turn Signal Lights* procedure in this chapter.

Rear directional lamps are part of the brake lamps. See *Taillight* procedure in this chapter.

INSTRUMENT CLUSTER

Removal/Installation

1. Disconnect battery cables at battery.
2. Remove trim plate over heater/fresh air controls.
3. Remove radio if installed.

7

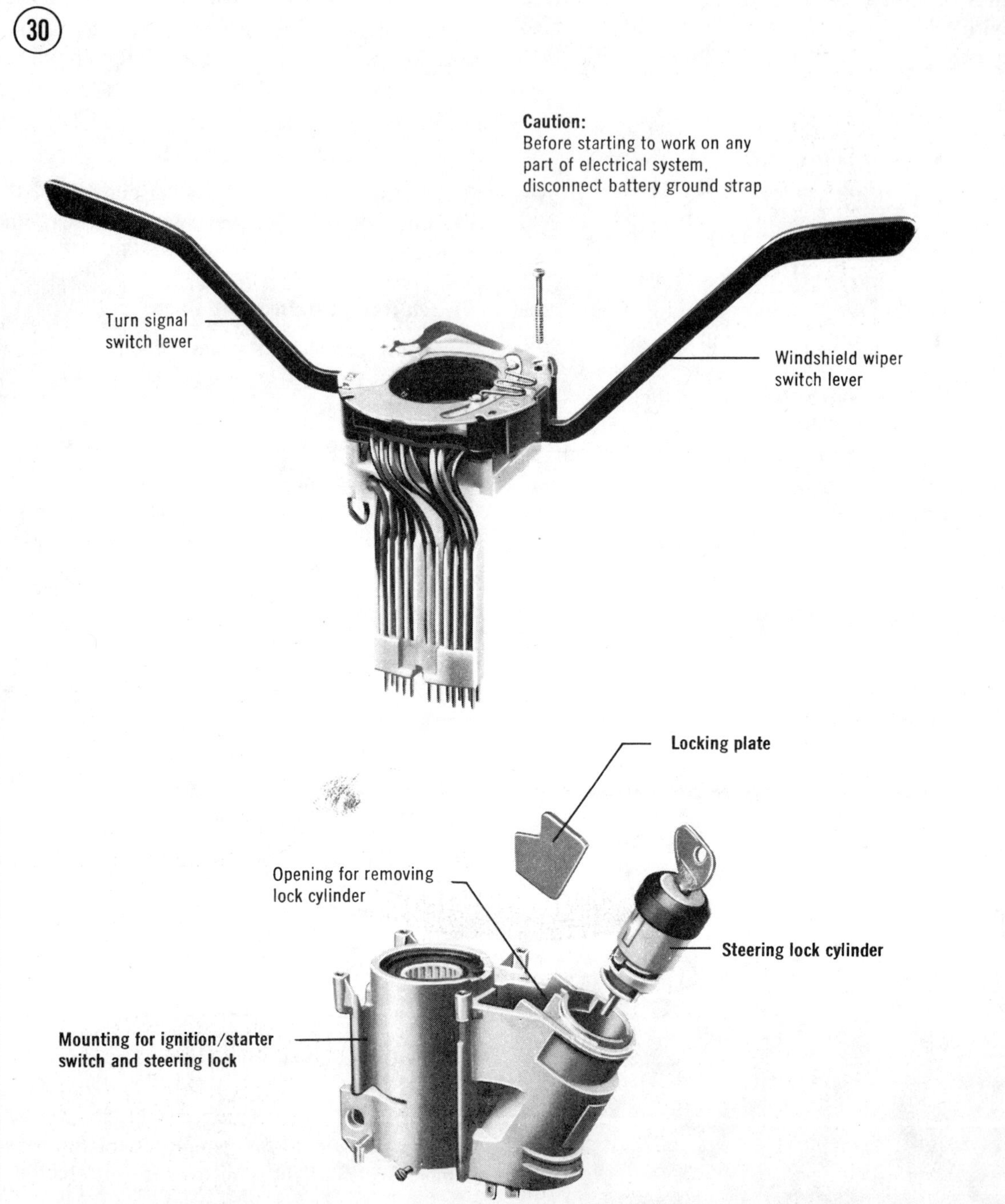

IGNITION SWITCH AND COLUMN CONTROLS

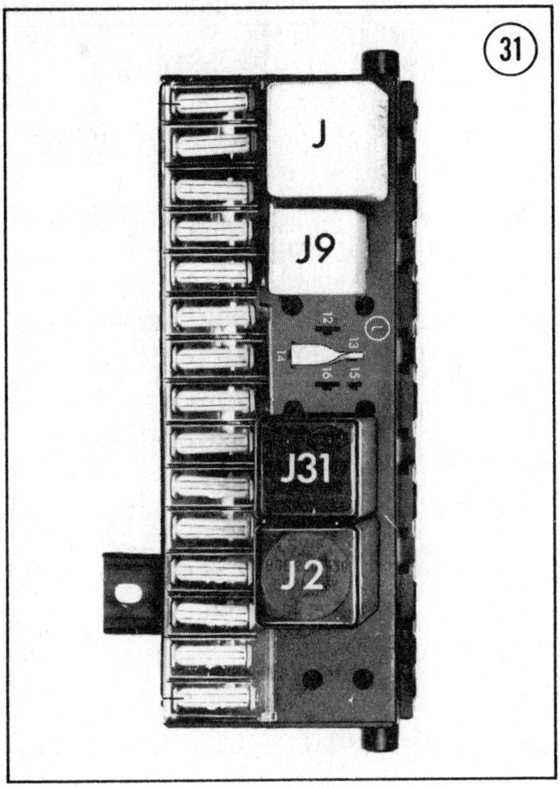

NOTE: *Installations vary considerably. If mounting method is not evident, check with your dealer.*

4. Disconnect cable from rear of speedometer.
5. Remove screw shown in **Figure 32**.

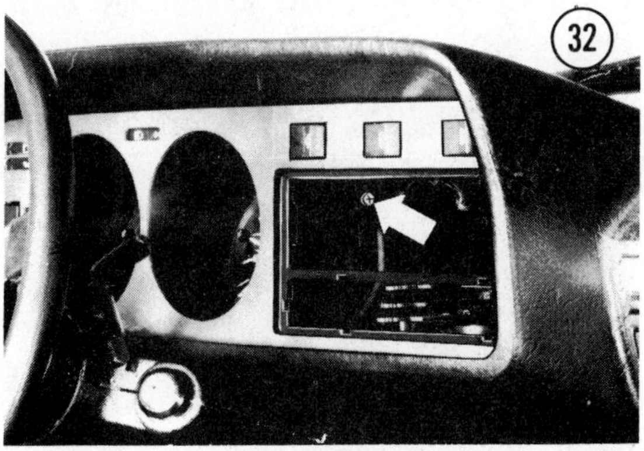

6. Pull entire cluster forward.
7. Carefully mark and disconnect other wires to switches.
8. Installation is the reverse of these steps.

Instrument Replacement

1. Remove the entire instrument cluster as described above.
2. Remove screws securing instrument to back of cluster.
3. Lift out instrument.
4. Installation is the reverse of these steps.

Fuel Gauge Sender Replacement

The fuel sender is mounted on the right side of the tank and is accessible from underneath the car.

1. Disconnect *both* battery cables.
2. Drain fuel tank.
3. Disconnect wires from sender.
4. Disconnect fuel line from sender.
5. Unscrew sender with special tool which fits the 4 cutouts in the sender.

WARNING
Fuel remaining in the tank is exposed when sender is removed. Avoid open flames or cigarettes until the sender is replaced. Do not reconnect battery until sender is fully installed.

6. Installation is the reverse of these steps.

WINDSHIELD WIPER SYSTEM

NOTE: *The 1976 Scirocco has only one center mounted wiper arm. Procedures below apply to both one- and two-arm systems.*

Motor Removal/Installation

1. Disconnect battery ground cable.
2. Lift up protective caps on wiper arms and remove wiper arm nuts. Pull wiper arms off.
3. Remove large nuts around wiper shaft.
4. Disconnect the multi-pin connector on the wiper motor.
5. Remove mounting bolt near motor. See **Figure 33**.
6. Push wiper assembly down and out of holes in body and remove motor with wiper frame.
7. Installation is the reverse of these steps.

7

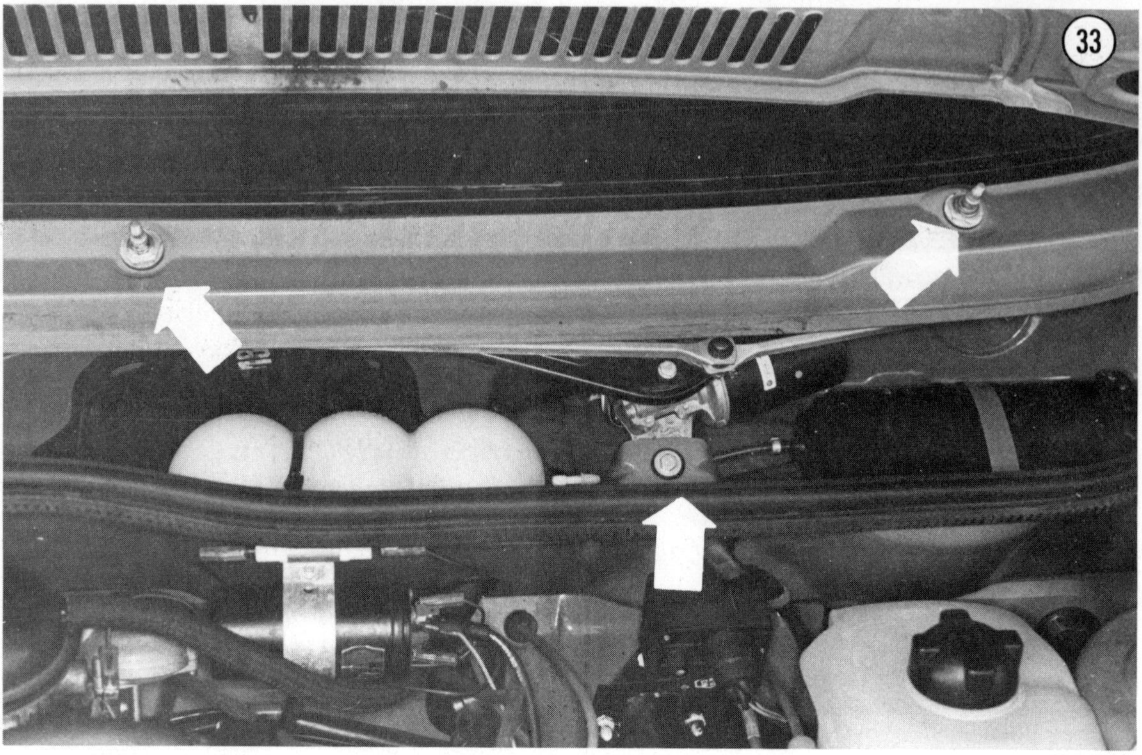

Switch Removal/Installation

The wiper switch is part of the directional signal switch. See *Directional Switch Removal/Installation*.

Washer Pump Replacement

1. Disconnect wire cable from motor.
2. Disconnect plastic water lines.
3. Pull motor off plastic lugs on container.
4. Installation is the reverse of these steps.

IGNITION SYSTEM (GASOLINE ENGINES)

The ignition system consists of the battery, ignition switch, ignition coil, distributor, spark plugs, and associated wiring. The following procedures describe the replacement of these components.

Ignition Lock Replacement

Refer to Figure 30 for this procedure.

1. Disconnect battery ground cable.
2. Remove steering wheel.
3. Remove directional signal and windshield switches.
4. Remove upper and lower trim panels around ignition lock.
5. On 1976 and earlier models, pull out locking plate with pliers. Insert ignition key in lock. Turn key clockwise about the thickness of the key and pull out the lock.
6. On 1977 models, drill a 1/8 in. deep hole as indicated in **Figure 34**. Remove lock cylinder by pressing down on spring through the newly-drilled hole.
7. Insert new lock without inserting key.
8. Install locking plate and tap it down lightly with a hammer.
9. Complete installation by reversing Steps 1-4.

Ignition Switch Replacement

1. Disconnect battery ground cable.
2. Remove steering wheel.
3. Remove directional signal and windshield switches.

34

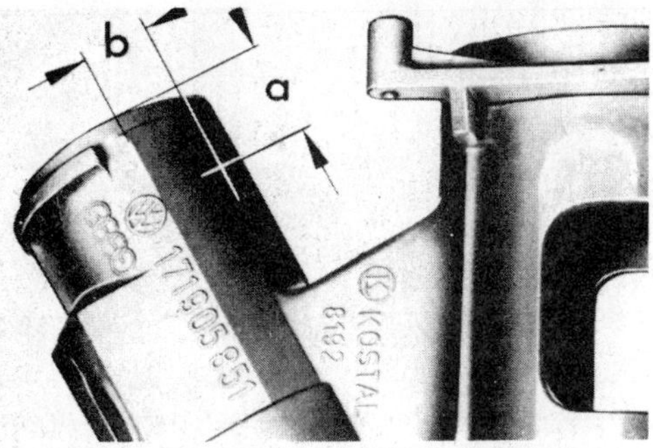

a = 12mm (0.472 in.) b = 10mm (0.393 in.)

4. Remove upper and lower trim panels around ignition lock.

5. Remove Allen bolt from bottom of steering lock assembly.

6. Disconnect connector from ignition switch and pull lock assembly off.

7. Remove setscrew shown in **Figure 35** and remove switch.

8. Installation is the reverse of these steps. Be sure that hole in starter switch aligns with setscrew.

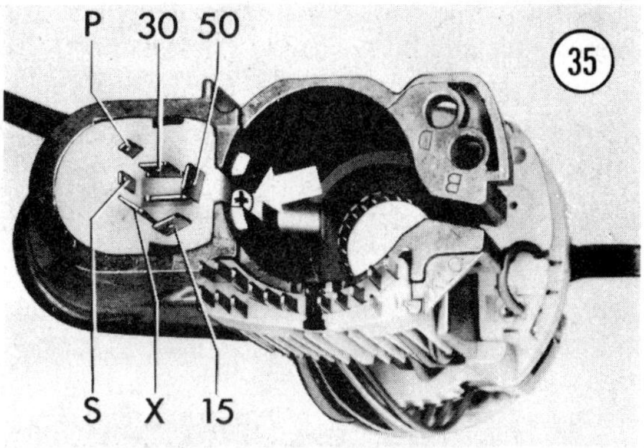

Ignition Coil Replacement

A defective ignition coil must be replaced. Disconnect primary and secondary wires from coil and remove it from bracket. See **Figure 36**. Install new coil, tighten bracket, and connect the wires.

Distributor Removal

1. Remove the distributor cap, but leave the wires connected.

7

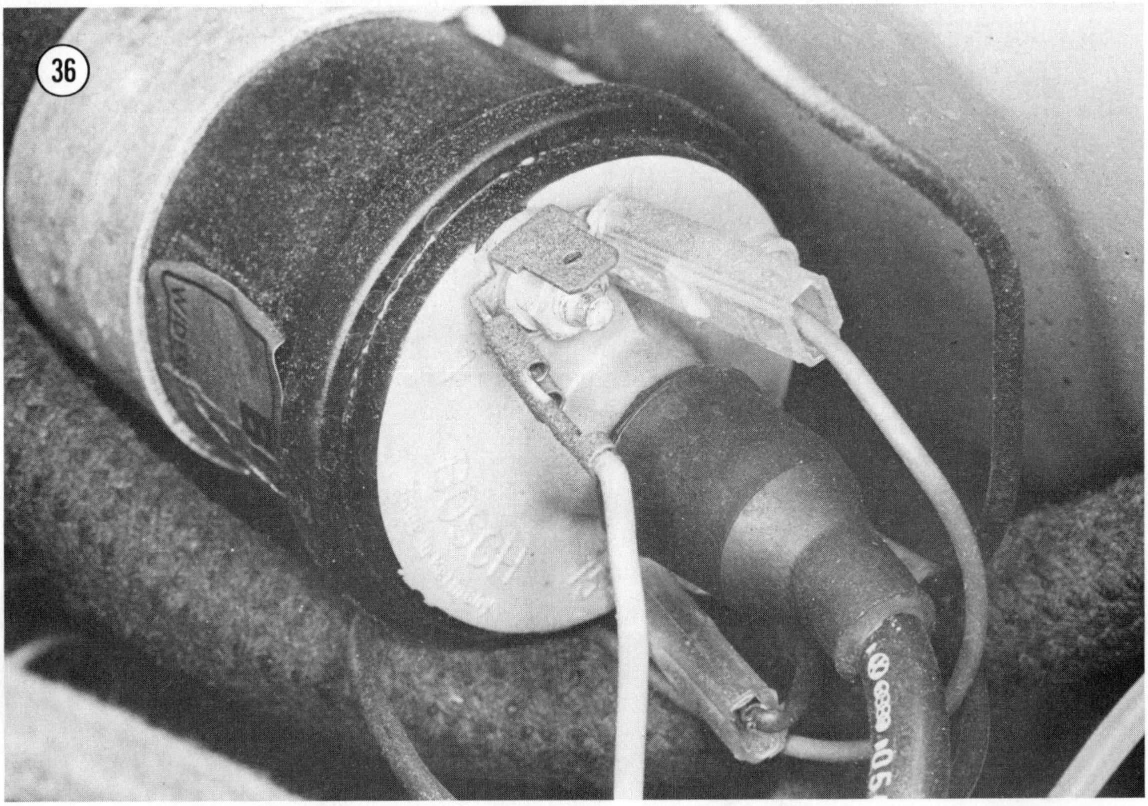

2. Remove TDC sensor with special tool US4463. See **Figure 37**.

3. Turn engine crankshaft over until the mark in the TDC sensor opening aligns with the TDC mark on the flywheel (**Figure 38**) and the rotor points at the notch on the distributor housing rim. See **Figure 39**.

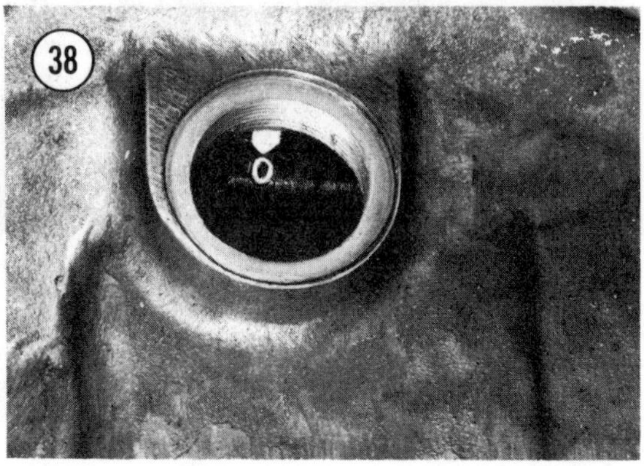

4. Disconnect primary lead from terminal 1 of ignition coil.

5. Remove distributor clamp bolt. See arrow, **Figure 40**.

6. Lift distributor out.

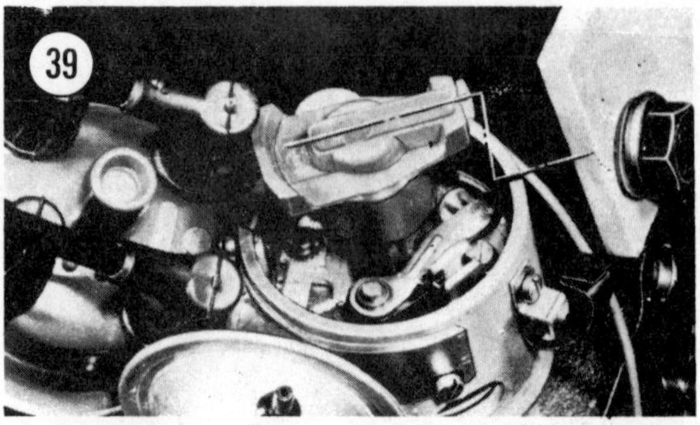

Distributor Installation

1. Ensure that piston No. 1 is still at TDC on a compression stroke.

2. Make sure oil pump shaft is positioned as shown in **Figure 41** (parallel to crankshaft). Reposition with screwdriver, if necessary.

3. Install the distributor so that the vacuum advance unit faces to the left and the distributor shaft engages in the oil pump shaft.

4. Rotate the distributor housing until the notch on the rim aligns with the rotor.

5. Tighten the clamp nut.

6. Install distributor cap and adjust ignition timing as described in Chapter Three.

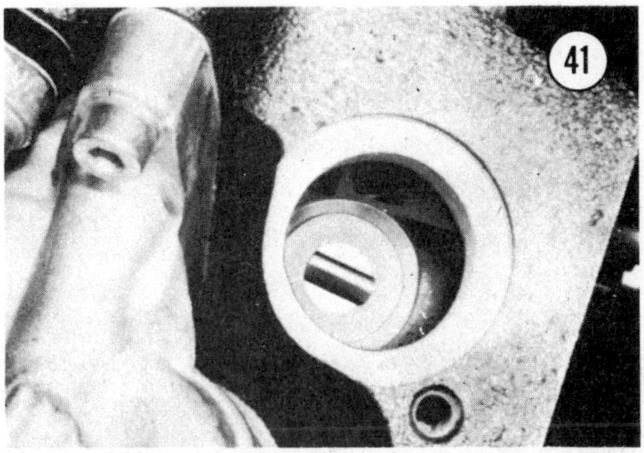

LIGHTING SYSTEM

Headlight Replacement

1. Remove front grille. See Chapter Twelve.
2. Remove 3 screws securing retaining ring. See **Figure 42**.
3. Pull sealed beam out.
4. Disconnect plug from sealed beam.
5. Installation is the reverse of these steps.
6. Adjust the headlights according to the local traffic regulations. Adjustments are shown in **Figure 43**.

Headlight Dimmer Relay Replacement

The dimmer relay is mounted on the fuse box. See **Figure 44**. To replace the relay, remove the relay marked J and plug in a new one.

43

44

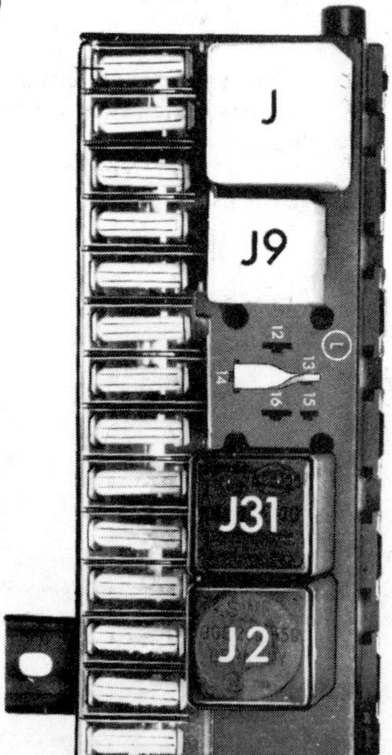

Headlight Switch Replacement

Refer to **Figure 45** for this procedure.

1. Perform Steps 1-5 of *Instrument Cluster Removal/Installation* procedure elsewhere in this chapter.

2. Squeeze tabs on headlight switch to release them and pull the switch out of the rear of the cluster.

3. Disconnect one wire at a time from the old switch and connect it to the corresponding terminal on the new switch.

4. Insert the new switch into the cluster and push it until the tabs lock in place.

5. Install the instrument cluster by reversing Steps 1-5 of the *Instrument Cluster Removal/Installation* procedure.

Front Parking and Turn Signal Lights

Front parking and turn signal lights are located in the front bumper. To replace the lamp, remove 2 screws securing the lens and lift it off. Replace the lamp and secure the lens. See **Figure 46**.

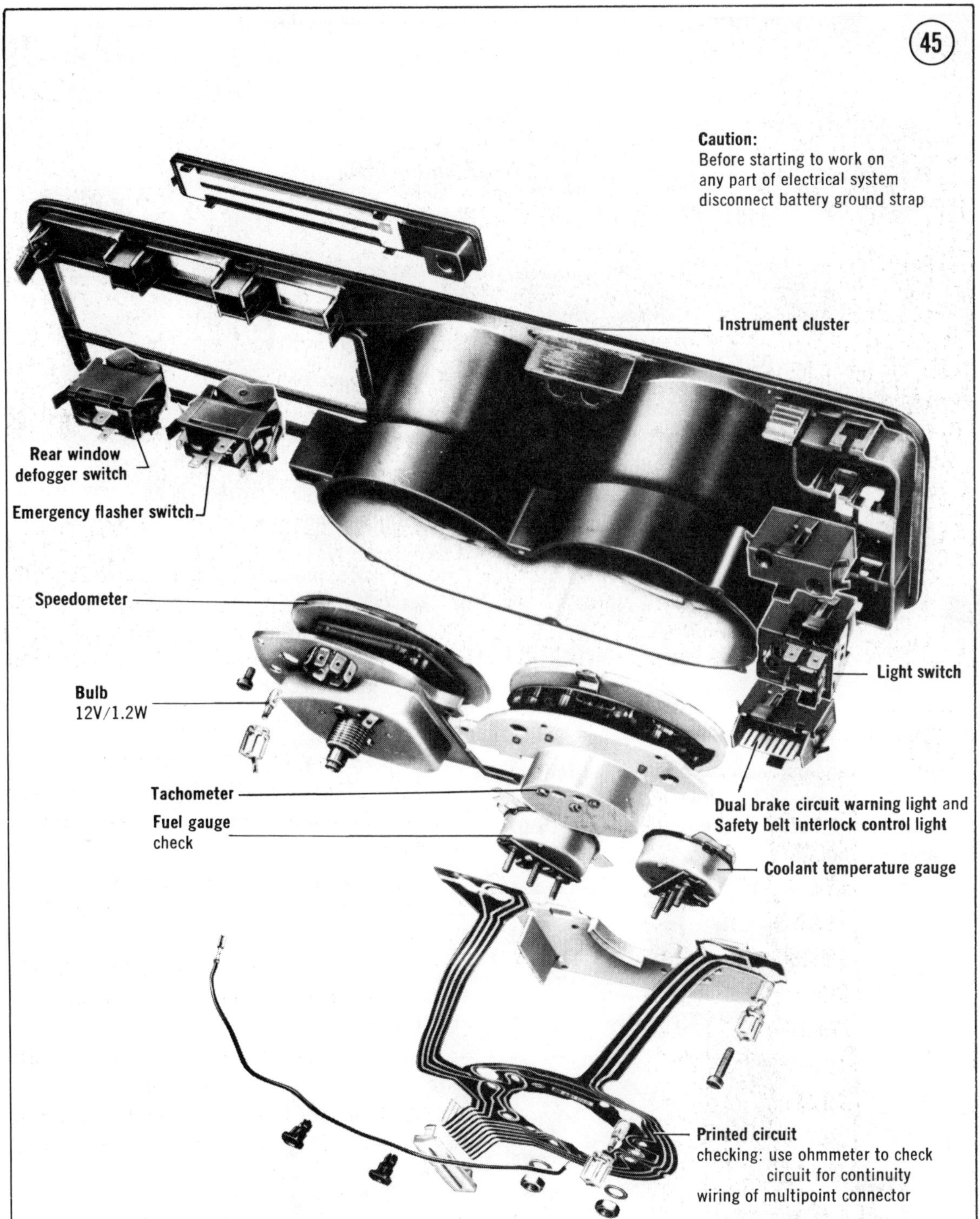

INSTRUMENTS

Taillights

To replace the rear taillight, brake, turn signal, or back-up lamps, unscrew knurled knob on back of taillight assembly and lift out the assembly.

> NOTE: *A new mounting hole pattern in the rear panel for taillights and also a new taillight assembly were introduced during the 1976 production year. The new assembly can be fitted to the old type panel by using a self-tapping screw.*

Side Marker Lamps

Side marker lamps are located in the fender mounted assemblies. To replace the lamps, remove 2 screws securing the lens and lift it off. **Figures 47 and 48**.

License Plate Lights

To replace a lamp, remove screw(s) securing the lens and lift it off. Replace the lamp and secure the lens.

Interior Light

To replace the interior lamp, pull the entire assembly out of the roof member. Replace the lamp and reinstall holder back in the roof. Do not damage the headliner.

Back-up Light Switch

Several types of back-up light switches have been used on the Rabbit and Scirocco manual transmission models. See **Figures 49, 50, and 51**. To replace a switch, disconnect the wires, remove the old switch, install new switch, and reconnect the wires. Torque screw-in models (Figures 49 and 51) to 14 ft.-lb. (2.0 mkg). Adjust blade model (Figure 50) by moving bracket (1).

On models with automatic transmission, the back-up light switch is part of the neutral safety switch in the selector lever assembly. Refer to Chapter Eight for replacement.

WIRING DIAGRAMS

Wiring diagrams are located at the rear of this book.

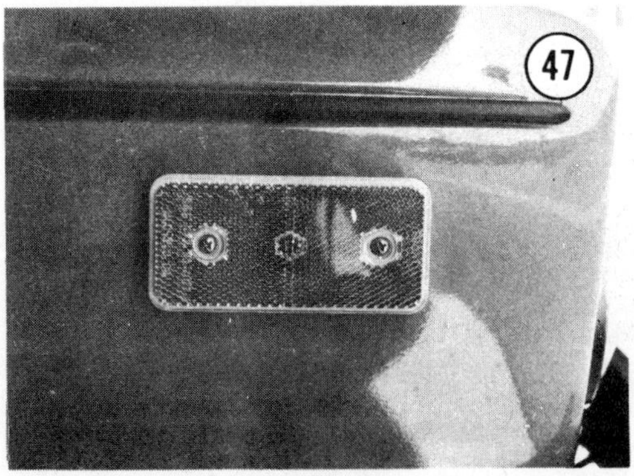

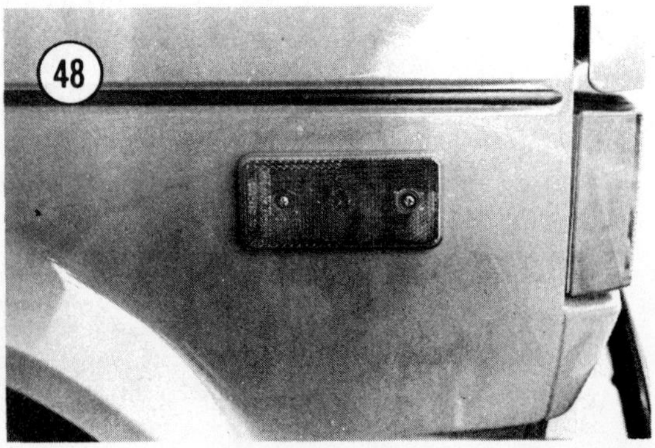

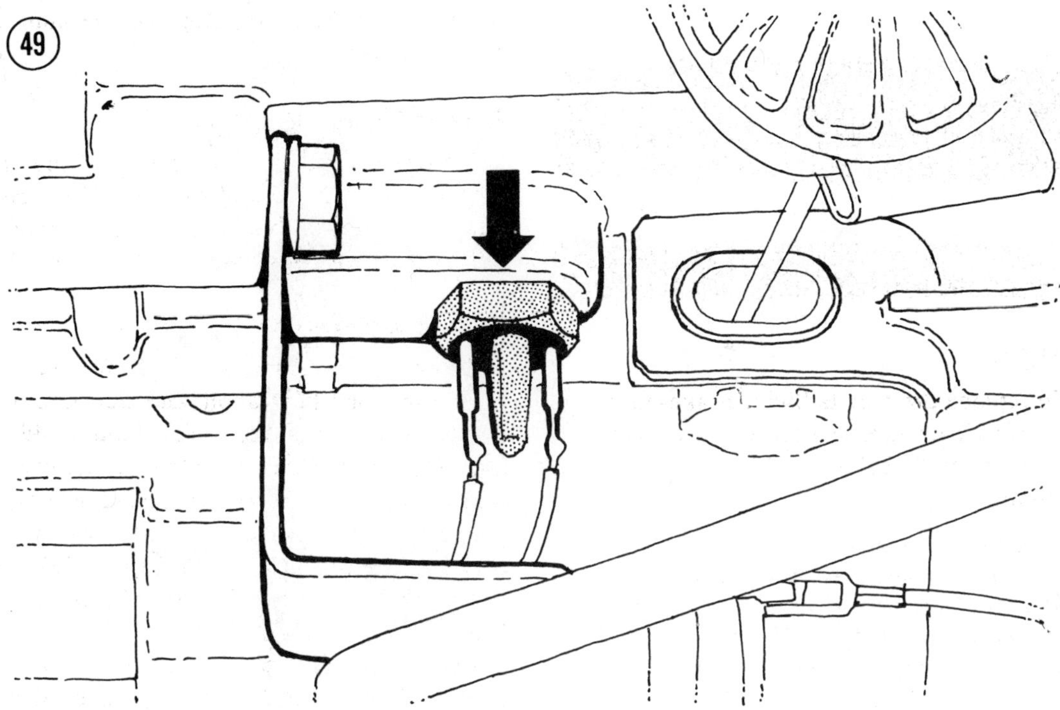
49

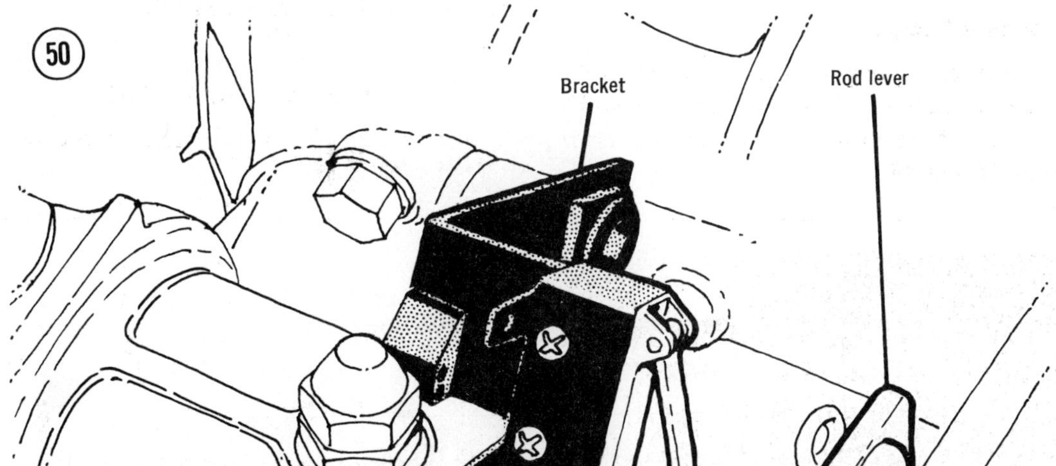
50
Bracket
Rod lever

51

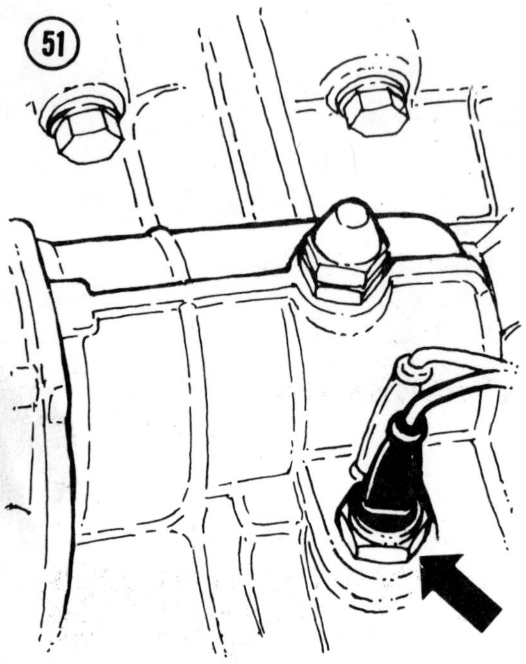

Table 1 ELECTRICAL SPECIFICATIONS

Battery	
Voltage	12V
Capacity	45Ah (54Ah w/air cond.)
Ground terminal	Negative
Alternator	
Model	K1 14 55A (Bosch)[1]
Voltage	14V
Current	55A[2]
Voltage regulator	
Model	EE 14 Bosch (p/o alternator)
Type	Transistorized
Starter	
Model	EF 12 (Bosch)
Voltage	12V
Horsepower	0.7 hp
Distributor	
Model	JFU 4 (Bosch)
Ignition control	Vacuum & centrifugal

1. Some models are equipped with Motorola alternators. Specifications are similar and testing is identical.
2. 65A on 1977 and later models with air conditioning.

CHAPTER EIGHT

CLUTCH AND TRANSMISSION

CLUTCH

The clutch is a single plate, dry disc type, mounted on the flywheel. The pressure plate has a diaphragm spring. The clutch is mechanically operated through an adjustable wire cable.

Clutch Free-play Adjustment

Clutch adjustment involves taking up cable slack caused by cable stretch and lining wear. To check clutch free-play, depress the clutch pedal by hand. Free-play should be about ⅝ in. (15mm). See **Figure 1**. If more or less than this, adjust the cable. To increase free-play, loosen the lower nut and tighten the upper nut on the clutch cable stop bracket. See **Figure 2**. To decrease free-play, do just the opposite. Loosen the upper nut and tighten the lower nut. when free-play is correct, tighten whichever nut was loosened.

Clutch Cable Replacement

1. Disconnect clutch cable from clutch pedal.
2. Loosen both clutch adjusting nuts.
3. Slide clutch cable out of clutch bracket.
4. Disconnect clutch cable from operating lever.
5. Installation is the reverse of these steps. Adjust free-play as described above.

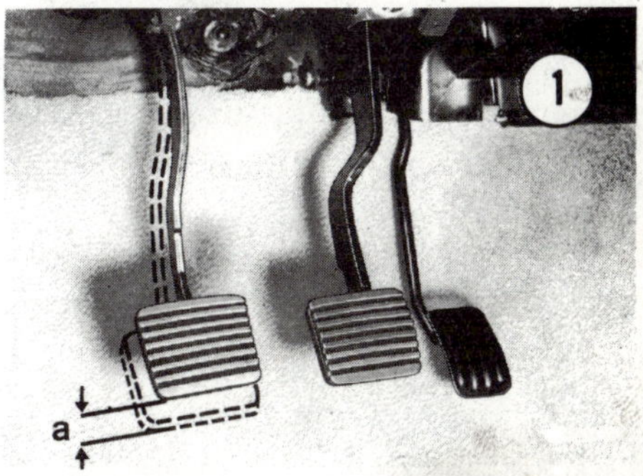

Clutch Removal

Refer to **Figure 3** for this procedure.

1. Remove the transmission as described later.
2. Prevent flywheel from turning with special tool VW558 or equivalent. See **Figure 4**.

8

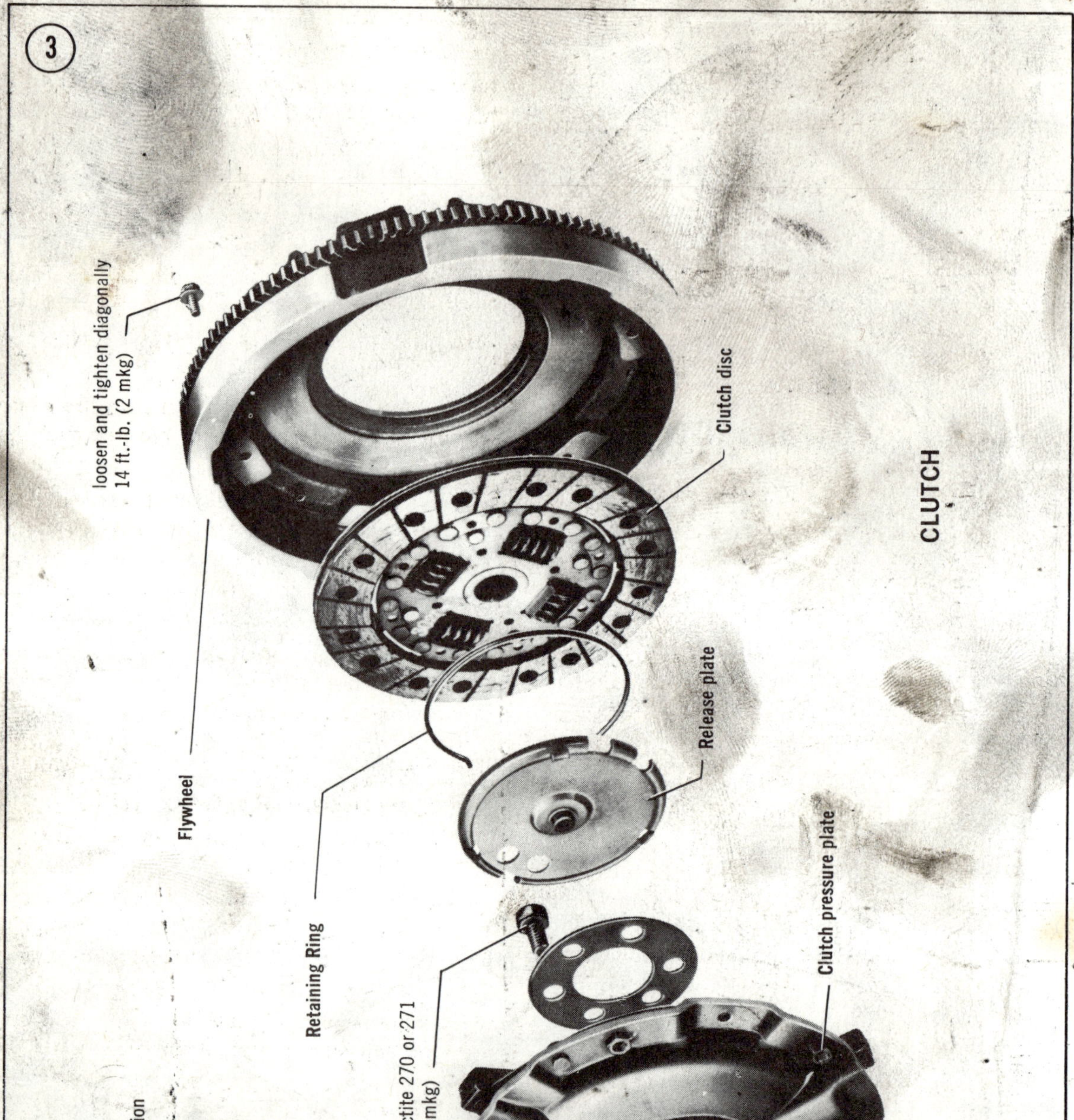
3
loosen and tighten diagonally
14 ft.-lb. (2 mkg)
Flywheel
Clutch disc
Retaining Ring
Release plate
insert with Loctite 270 or 271
54 ft.-lb. (7.5 mkg)
Clutch pressure plate
Note:
For clutch repairs transmission
must be removed
CLUTCH

3. Unscrew bolts securing flywheel to pressure plate one turn at a time. Unscrew bolts diagonally opposite from one another, rather than working directly around the flywheel. This insures that heavy spring pressure will not warp the pressure plate.

4. Once spring tension is relieved, unscrew each bolt entirely and remove the flywheel.

5. Remove the clutch disc.

6. Pry retaining ring off with screwdriver.

7. Remove release plate.

8. Prevent pressure plate from turning with special tool VW558 or equivalent. See **Figure 5**.

9. Remove bolts securing pressure plate to crankshaft and remove pressure plate from engine.

Clutch Inspection

Never replace clutch parts without giving thought to the reason for failure. To do so only invites repeated troubles.

1. Clean the flywheel face and pressure plate assembly in a non-petroleum cleaner such as trichlorethylene.

2. Check the friction surface of the flywheel for cracks and grooves. Attach a dial indicator and check runout. Compare with specifications for your engine. If necessary, have the flywheel reground; replace it in cases of severe damage.

3. Check the pressure plate for cracked or broken springs, evidence of heat, cracked or scored friction surface, and looseness. Check spring fingers for wear. See **Finger 6**. Also check tightness of rivets. If there is any damage, replace pressure plate assembly.

4. Check the clutch disc lining for wear, cracks oil, and burns. Check for loose rivets and cracks in the spring leaves and carrier plate. Ensure that the disc slides freely on the transmission spline without excessive radial play. If the disc is defective, replace it with a new one.

5. Check the release plate for wear to determine if it caused the original trouble.

8

Clutch Installation

1. Wash your hands *clean* before proceeding.

2. Sand the friction surface of the flywheel and pressure plate with medium-fine emery cloth. Sand lightly across the surfaces, not around, until they are covered with fine scratches. This breaks the glaze and aids seating a new clutch disc.

3. Clean the flywheel and pressure plate with trichlorethylene or equivalent.

4. Apply Loctite to mounting bolts, and install pressure plate on crankshaft. Tighten diagonally opposite bolts to 54 ft.-lb. (7.5 mkg).

5. Apply multipurpose grease to contact surface and pushrod socket of release plate. Install release plate. Secure with retaining ring. Make sure that ring ends rest between 2 slots as shown in **Figure 7**.

6. Place the clutch disc and the flywheel over pressure plate.

7. Install bolts finger-tight. Center disc with special tool VW547 as shown in **Figure 8**. This tool is easily improvised. See **Figure 9** for one method.

8. With centering tool in place, tighten diagonally opposite bolts a few turns at a time until they are torqued to 14 ft.-lb. (2 mkg). Remove the centering tool.

9. Install transmission as described elsewhere.

MANUAL TRANSAXLE

The standard manual transaxle has four forward speeds and one reverse. The gears are in constant mesh and all forward speeds are fully synchronized. An optional 5-speed transmission became available on 1979 models.

Although disassembly and assembly procedures are included in this chapter, the use of these procedures involves special skill and requires a large number of special tools. Many of these tools are required for holding and aligning parts and subassemblies. As the cost of these tools far exceeds the cost of a professionally rebuilt transaxle, and their proper use requires skill and experience, disassembly and assembly of the transaxle by the home mechanic is not recommended.

7

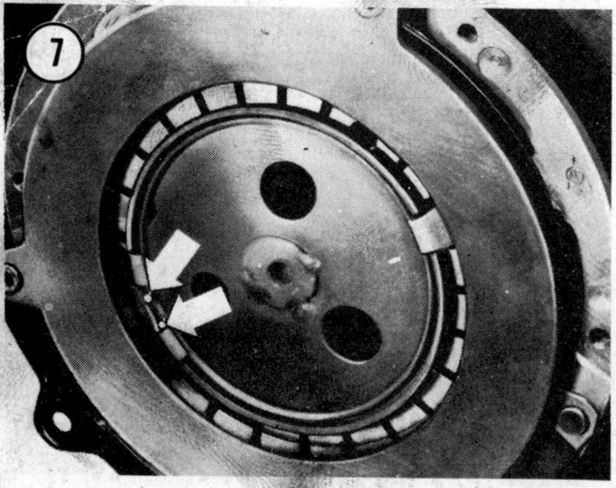

A clean work area is also a necessity.

The disassembly and assembly procedures provided apply only to the 4-speed manual transaxle. Disassembly and assembly of the 5-speed transaxle is not recommended.

Considerable money can be saved by removing the old transaxle and installing a new or rebuilt one yourself. This chapter includes removal and installation procedures, plus other simple repairs. See **Table 1** at the end of this chapter for specifications and tightening torques. See Chapter Three for lubrication and preventive maintenance.

Removal/Installation

The transaxle can be removed without removing the engine.

8

9

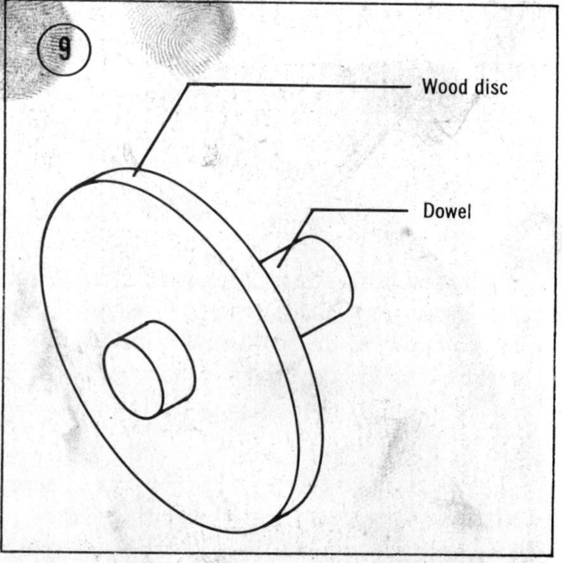

1. Disconnect battery cables (1, **Figure 10**).

2. Improvise a tool similar to that shown in Figure 10 (item 2) to lift up on the cast hole in the cylinder head. This supports the engine when the transaxle is removed.

CAUTION

Make sure that the improvised tool bears on the insides of the fenders as shown in Figure 10 and not on the tops of the fenders which could be dented.

3. Remove left mount (3, Figure 10).

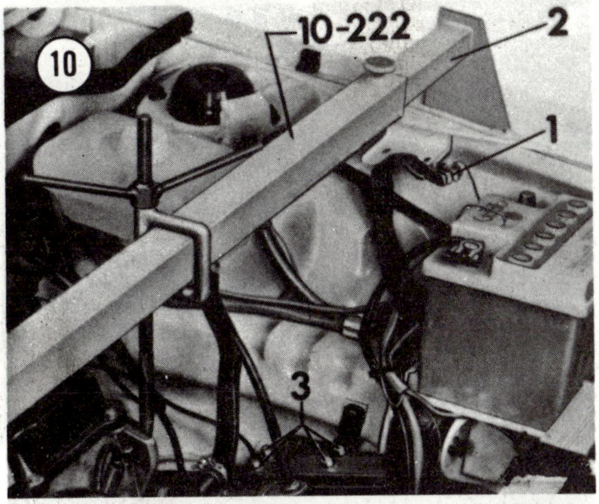

4. Remove the TDC sensor with special tool US4463. See **Figure 11**.

5. Rotate engine crankshaft with socket wrench at pulley until lug on flywheel appears in sensor hole. See 4, **Figure 12**.

NOTE: *The transaxle and engine cannot*

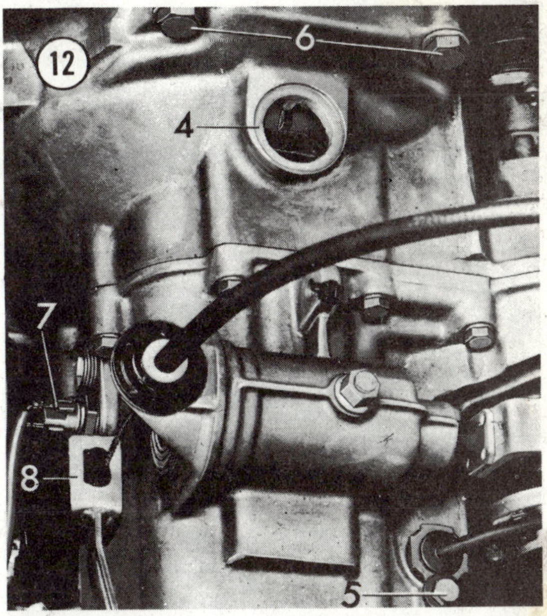

8

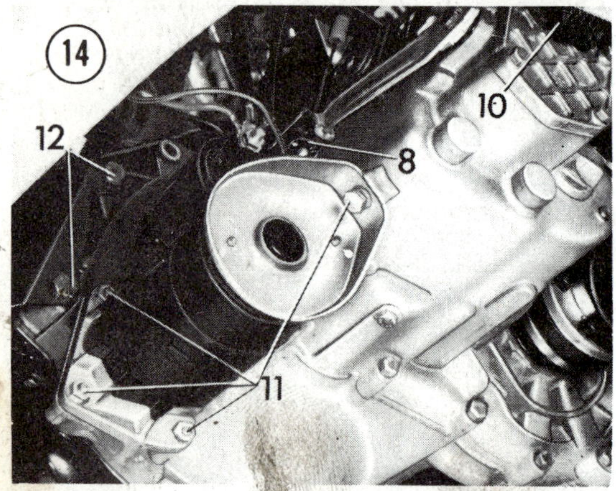

be separated unless the lug is aligned in the hole.

6. Disconnect the speedometer cable from the transaxle (5, Figure 12).

7. Remove upper bolts securing transaxle to engine. See 6, Figure 12.

8. Disconnect back-up light wires (7, Figure 12).

9. Disconnnect clutch cable from transaxle (8, Figure 12).

10. Disconnect shift linkage from transaxle. See **Figure 13**.

11. Disconnect ground strap between body and transaxle (10, **Figure 14**).

12. Remove starter as described in Chapter Seven (11, Figure 14).

13. Remove engine mounting support (12, Figure 14).

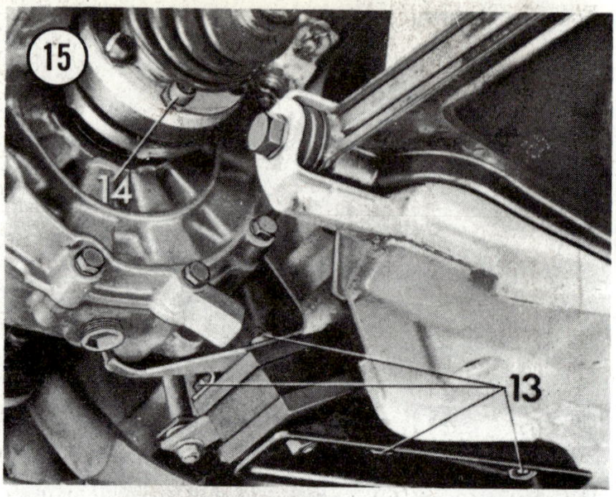

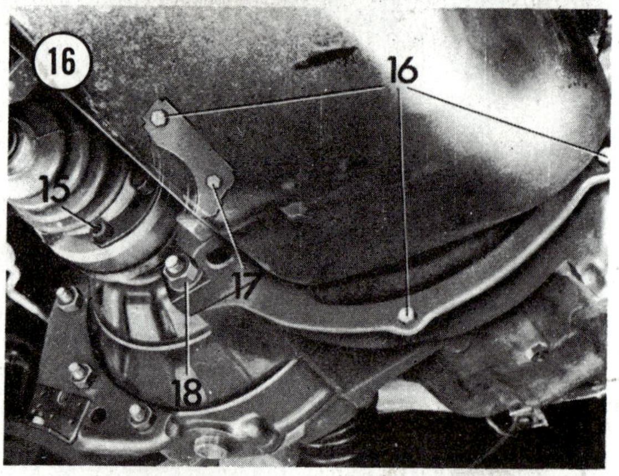

14. Remove lower transaxle mount. (See 13, **Figure 15**).

15. Remove drive shafts from transaxle as described in Chapter Ten. Hang up ends with wire.

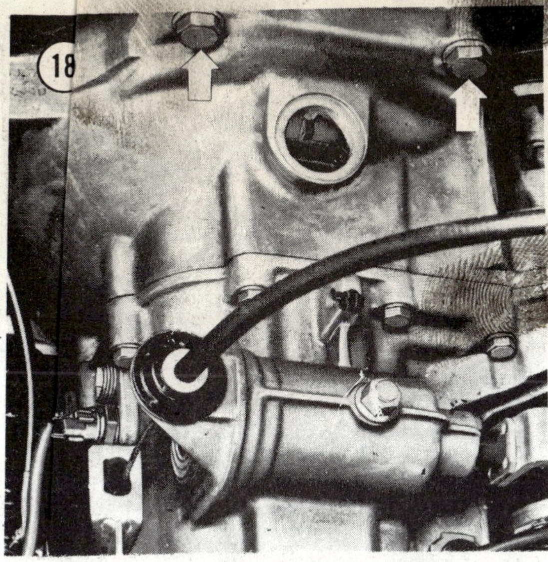

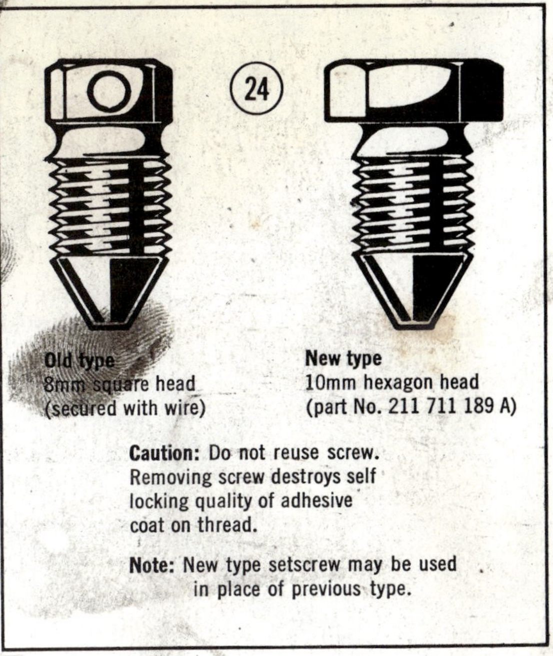

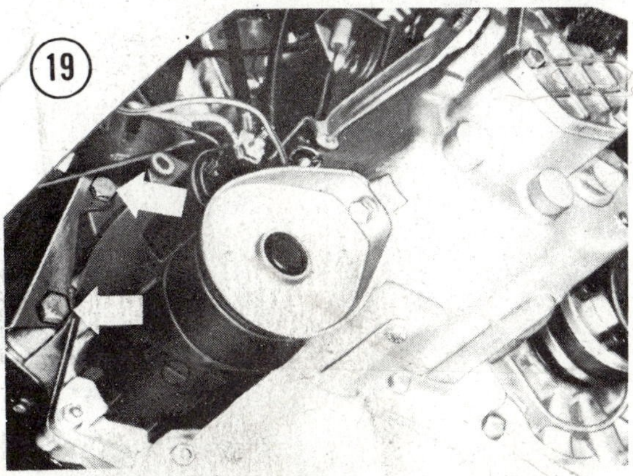

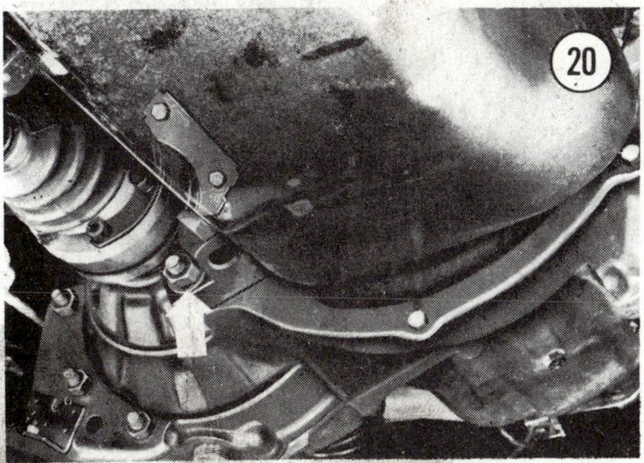

16. Remove bolts on large cover plate. See 16, **Figure 16** . The plate remains on the engine.

17. Remove small cover plate (17, Figure 16).

18. Remove nut (18, Figure 16).

19. Support the bottom of the transaxle on a garage-type jack.

20. Slide transaxle to the left and lower through the bottom.

21. Installation is the reverse of these steps. Keep the following points in mind:

   a. Recess in flywheel must be positioned adjacent to drive shaft. See **Figure 17**.
   b. Tighten upper mounting bolts to 39 ft.-lb. (5.5 mkg). See **Figure 18**.
   c. Tighten lower mounting bolts (**Figure 19**) to 39 ft.-lb. (5.5 mkg).
   d. Tighten nut in **Figure 20** to 39 ft-lb. (5.5 mkg).

Gearshift Linkage

Figure 21 and 22 show details of the gearshift linkage used on early 1975 models. New shift linkage was introduced on Chassis Nos. 175 3 108 888 and 535 2 020 020 (**Figure 23**), including a new hex head setscrew (**Figure 24**) that must be replaced with a new one whenever it is removed. The newer linkage can be installed on older models if all new type parts are used. Different linkage is used on 1976 and later models (**Figure 25 and 26**). This linkage provides a different pattern for reverse shifting (down and to the left).

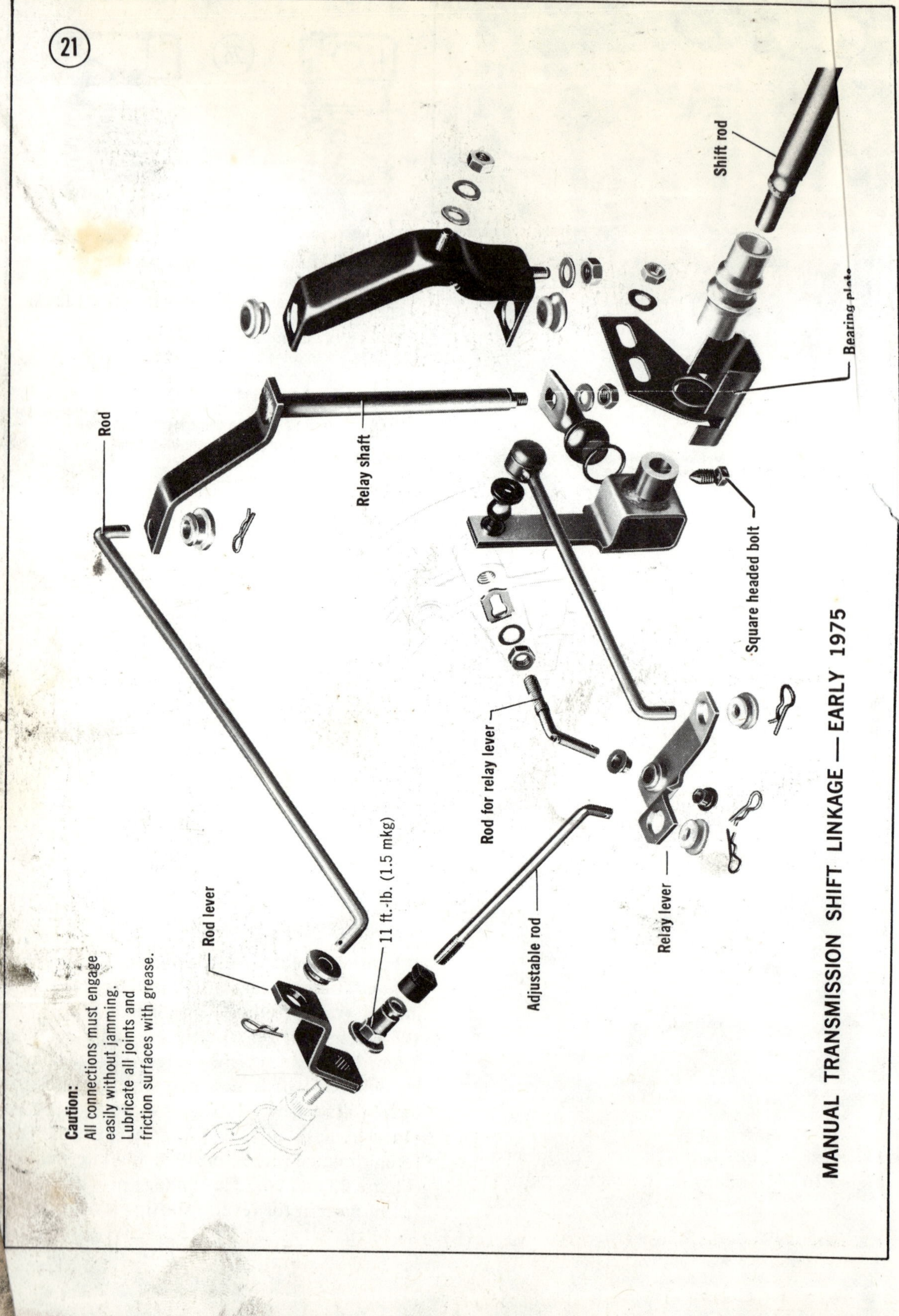

Caution:
All connections must engage easily without jamming. Lubricate all joints and friction surfaces with grease.

MANUAL TRANSMISSION SHIFT LINKAGE — EARLY 1975

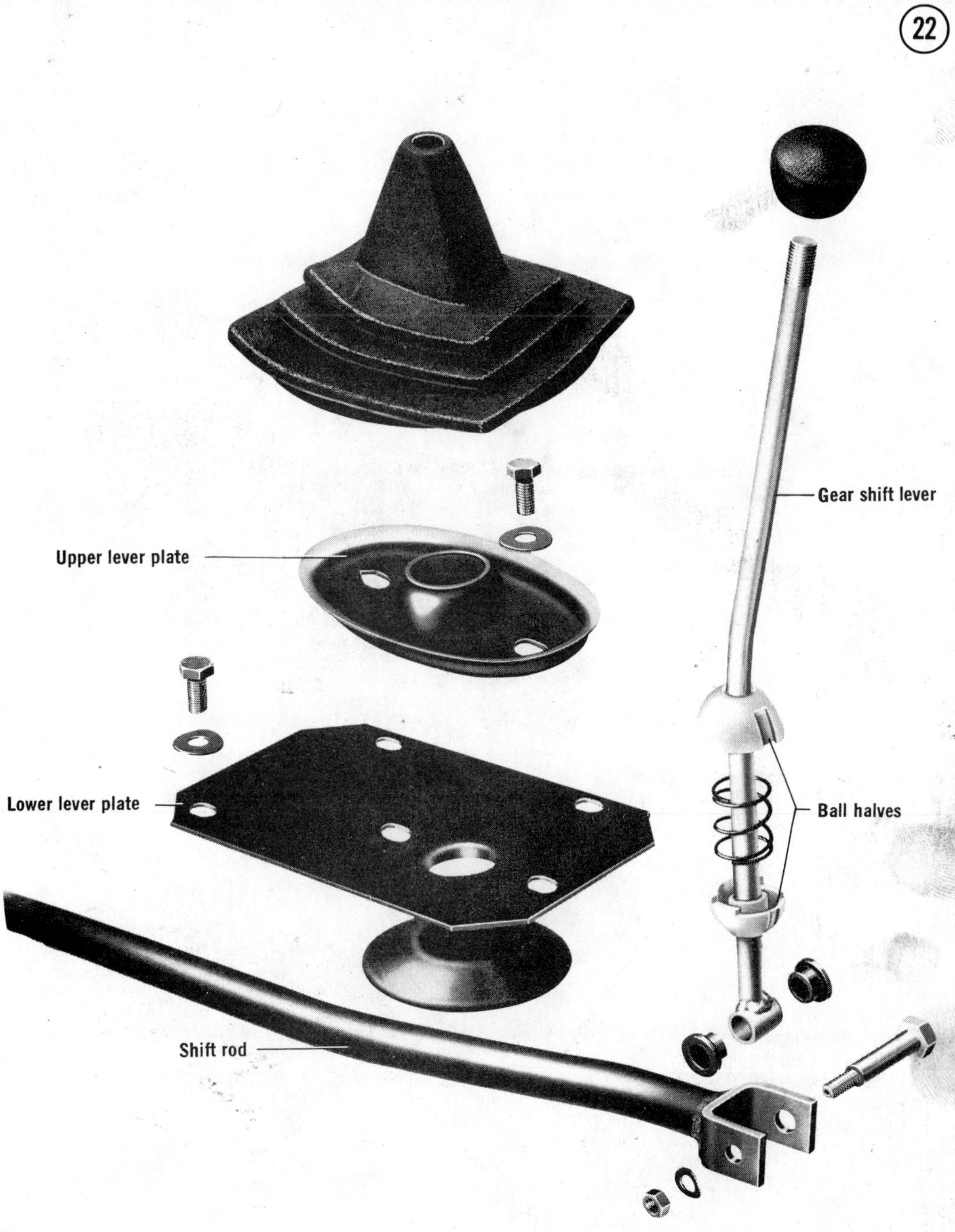

MANUAL TRANSMISSION
SHIFT LEVER
(EARLY 1975)

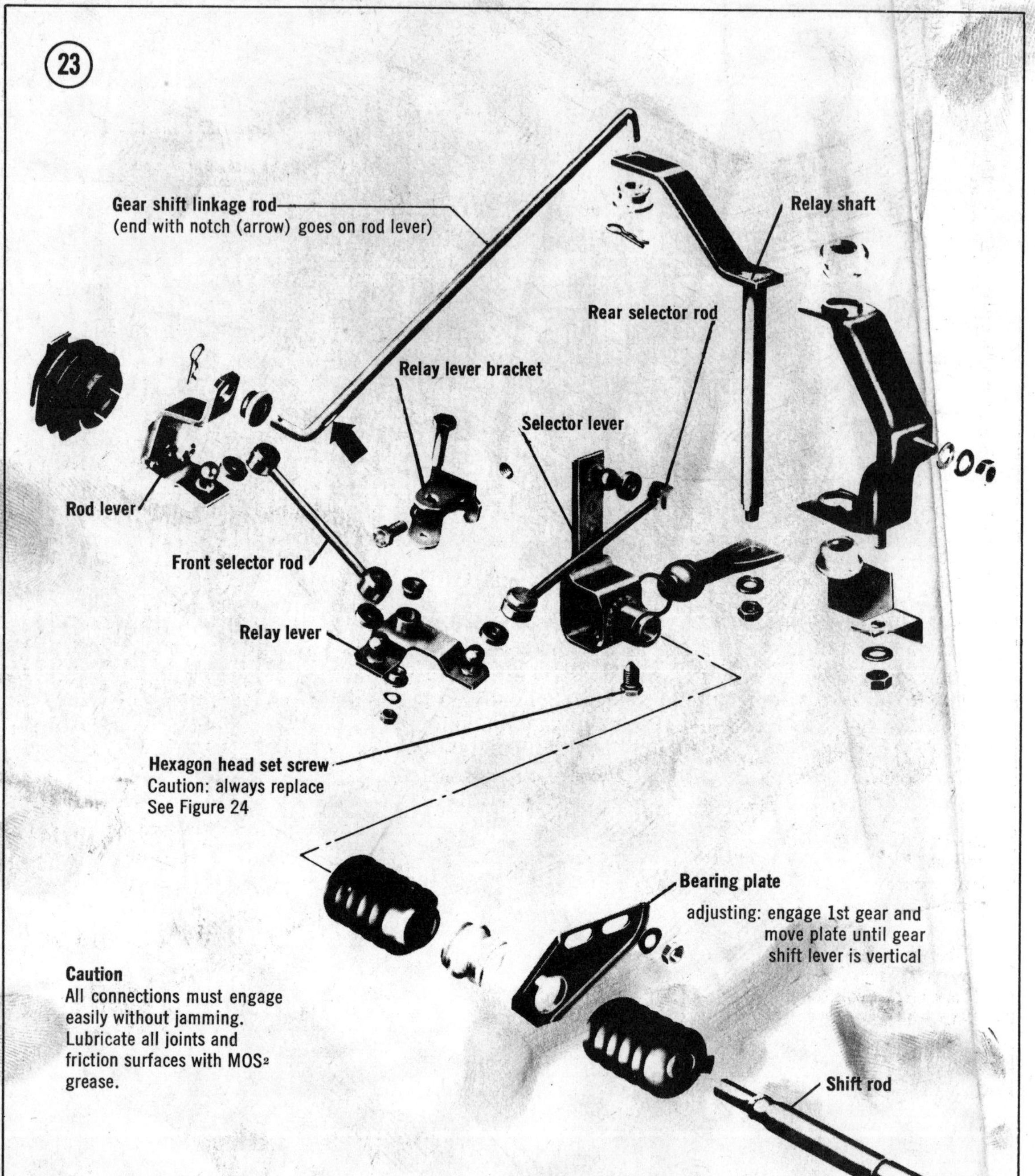

MANUAL TRANSMISSION SHIFT LINKAGE — LATER 1975

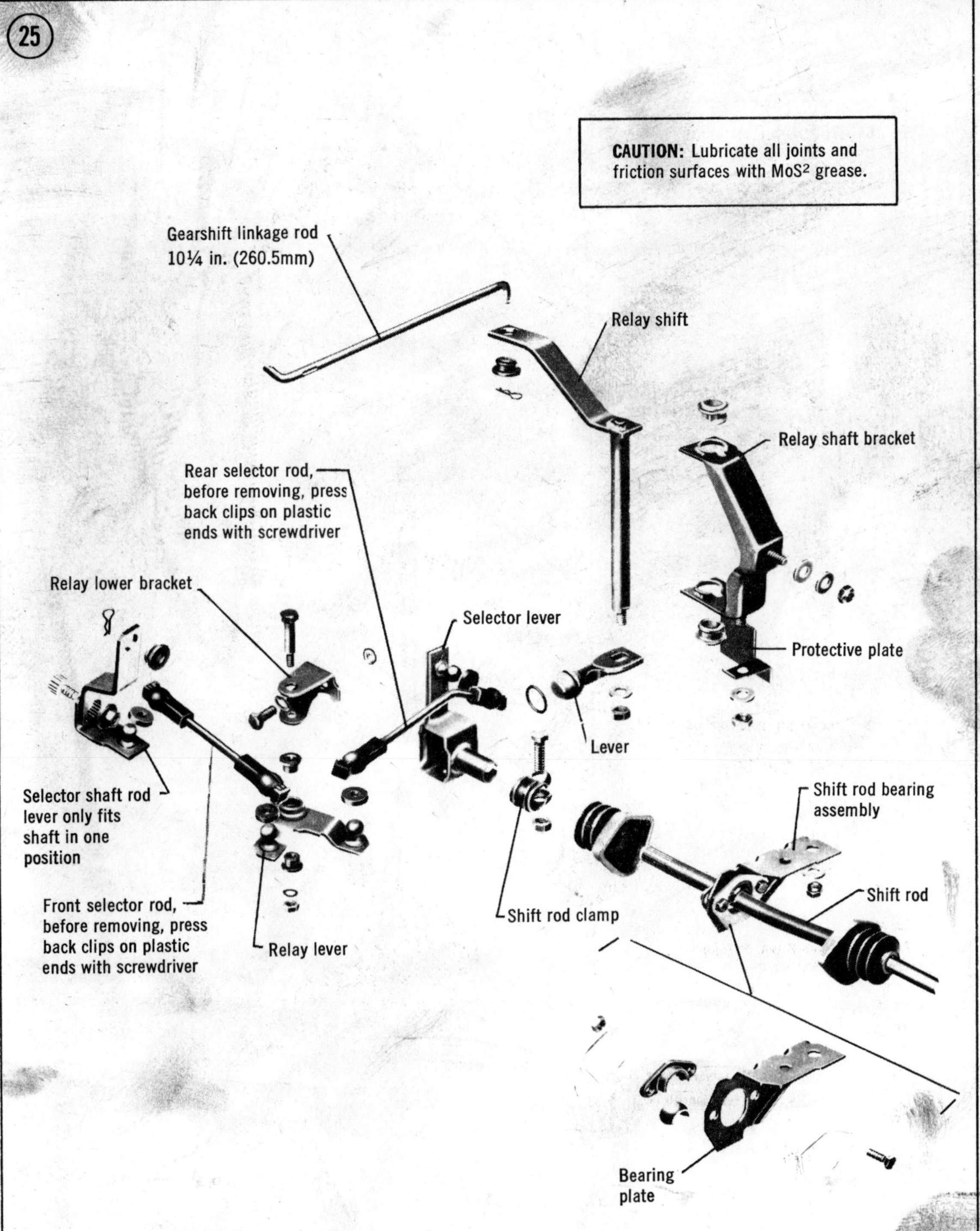

MANUAL TRANSMISSION SHIFT LINKAGE — 1976 AND LATER

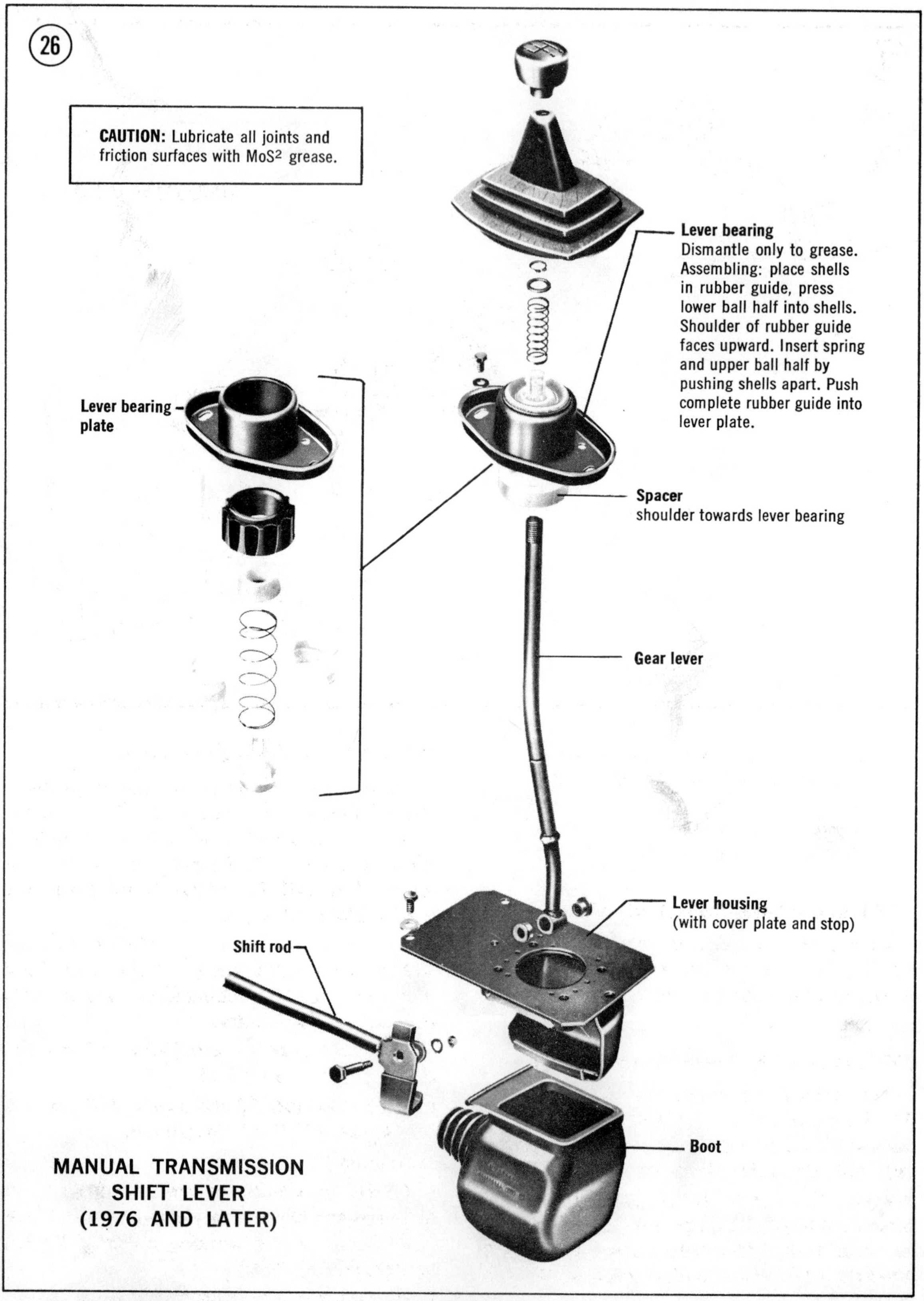

MANUAL TRANSMISSION
SHIFT LEVER
(1976 AND LATER)

27

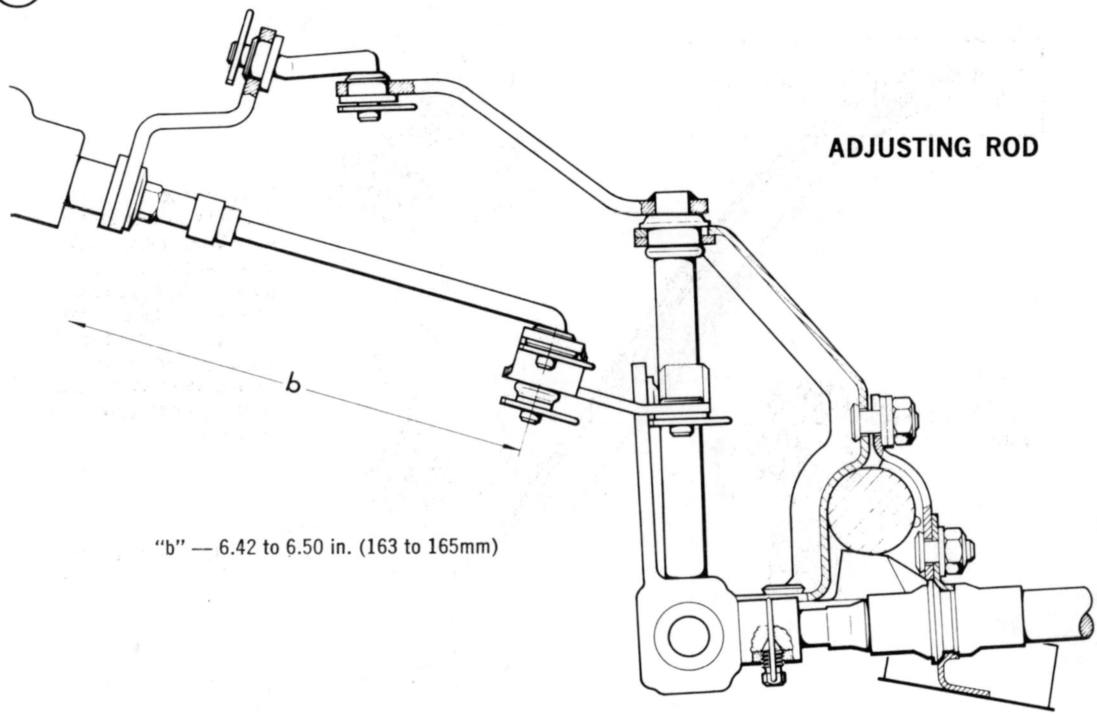

NOTE: *The gear shift linkage rod has one end bent to 90 degrees and the other to 95 degrees. The 95 degree end is marked with an arrow. This marked end must be inserted in the rod lever.*

1975 Linkage Adjustment (Early Models)

After replacing any linkage parts or after installing the transaxle, adjust the rods as shown in **Figure 27 and 28** to dimensions specified.

1975 Linkage Adjustment (Later Models)

New linkage introduced as of Chassis Nos. 175 3 108 888 and 535 2 020 020 eliminated the adjustable feature of the front selector rod and replaced the relay lever rod with a fixed bracket. See Figure 23. Adjustment is made after installing the linkage (making sure all connections engage freely) by engaging first gear and moving the bearing plate until the rear shift is vertical.

1976 and Later Linkage Adjustment

1. Make sure shift lever bearing is properly aligned (**Figure 29**). Holes in lever housing cover must align with holes in lever bearing plate (A, Figure 29). Tapped holes must be in center of slots (B, Figure 29). If not, turn lever bearing plate 180 degrees.
2. Loosen shift clamp rod (**Figure 30**) until selector lever moves easily on shift rod. Push boot out of way, loosening lever housing cover plate screws if necessary.
3. Refer to **Figure 31** and adjust shift finger until distances "x" are equal.
4. Refer to **Figure 32** and adjust shift rod end until distance "a" is ¾ in. (20mm).
5. Tighten shift rod clamp.
6. Check adjustment by shifting through all gears and making sure they engage easily. Make sure reverse catch is working properly. Repeat procedure if necessary.
7. Replace boot and tighten all screws.

28

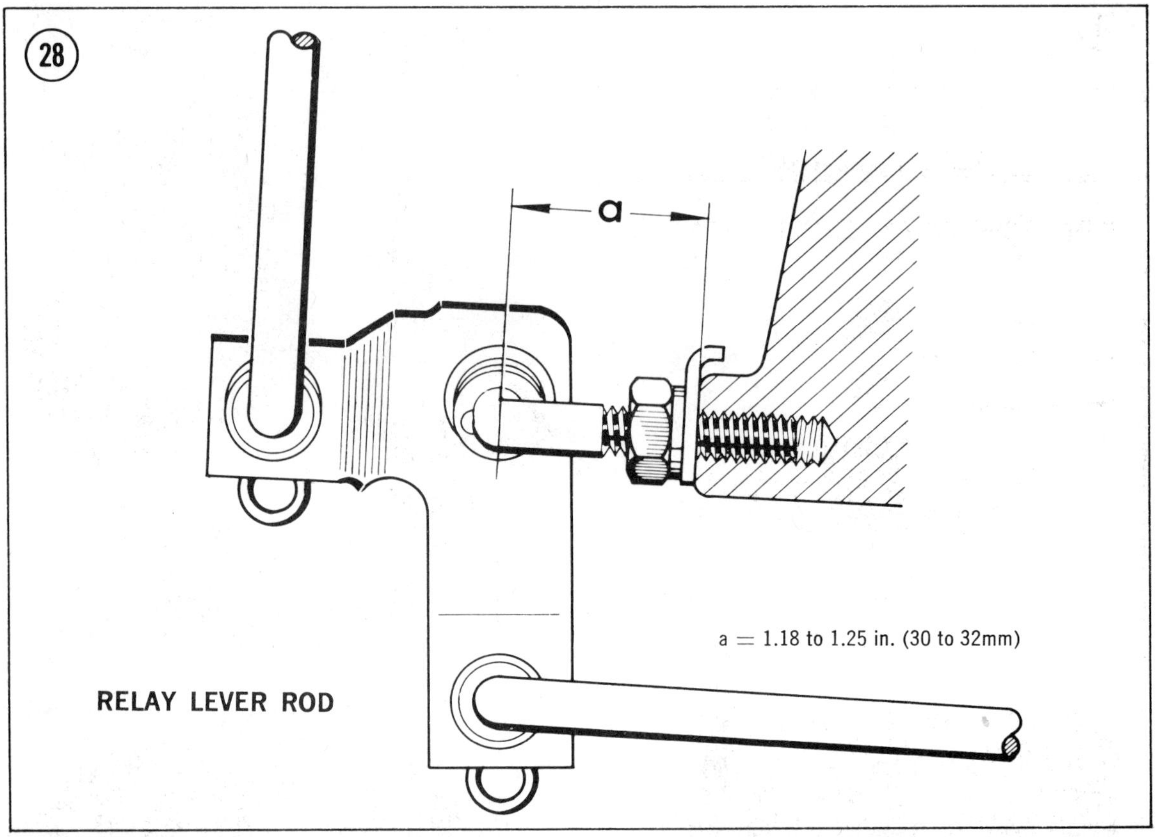

29

30

Disassembly

CAUTION

Do not attempt this procedure unless you have all of the necessary special tools — substitutions are risky — and are sure of your mechanical skills. Read the procedure until you understand exactly what is required in each step. If you do not fully understand any part of the procedure, do not attempt it. Considerable damage to the transaxle could result.

Refer to **Figure 33** for this procedure.

1. Drain the oil from the transmission and remove it from the vehicle as described in *Removal/Installation*, this section. Mount the transmission on a suitable stand **(Figure 34)**.

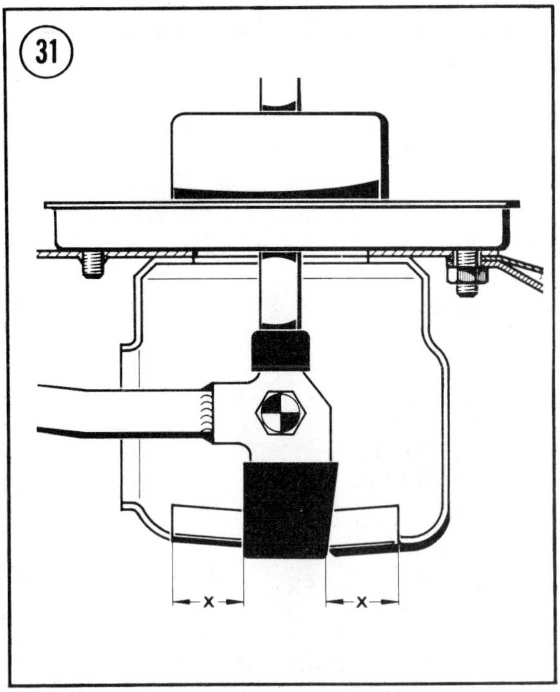

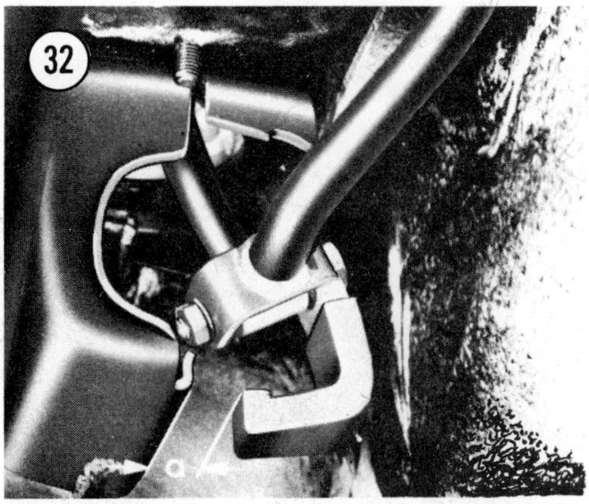

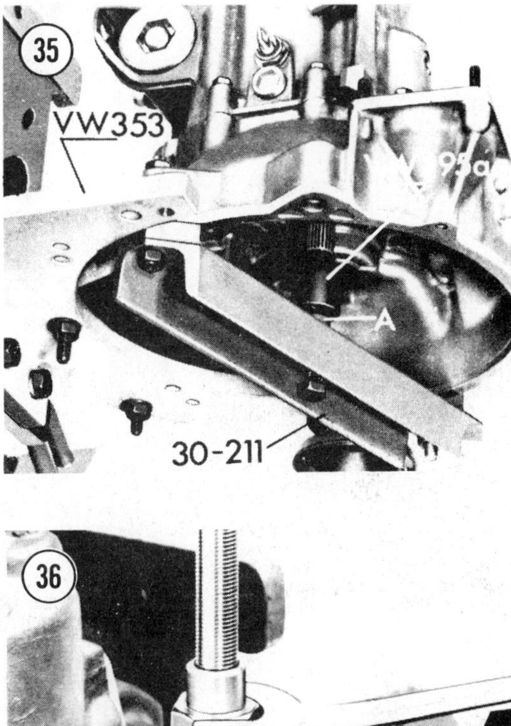

2. Remove the clutch pushrod by pulling it downward and install special tool 30-211 as shown in **Figure 35** to support the main shaft, using spacer VW295a and locknut (A, Figure 35) to support the shaft.

3. Remove the cap, circlip, and spring washer from the drive shaft flange. See Figure 33.

4. Install tool VW 391 and remove the drive shaft flanges. See **Figure 36**. Remove the release bearing cover and pry off the circlips from the clutch release shaft. Remove the clutch release shaft, clutch lever, return spring, release bearing, and guide sleeve.

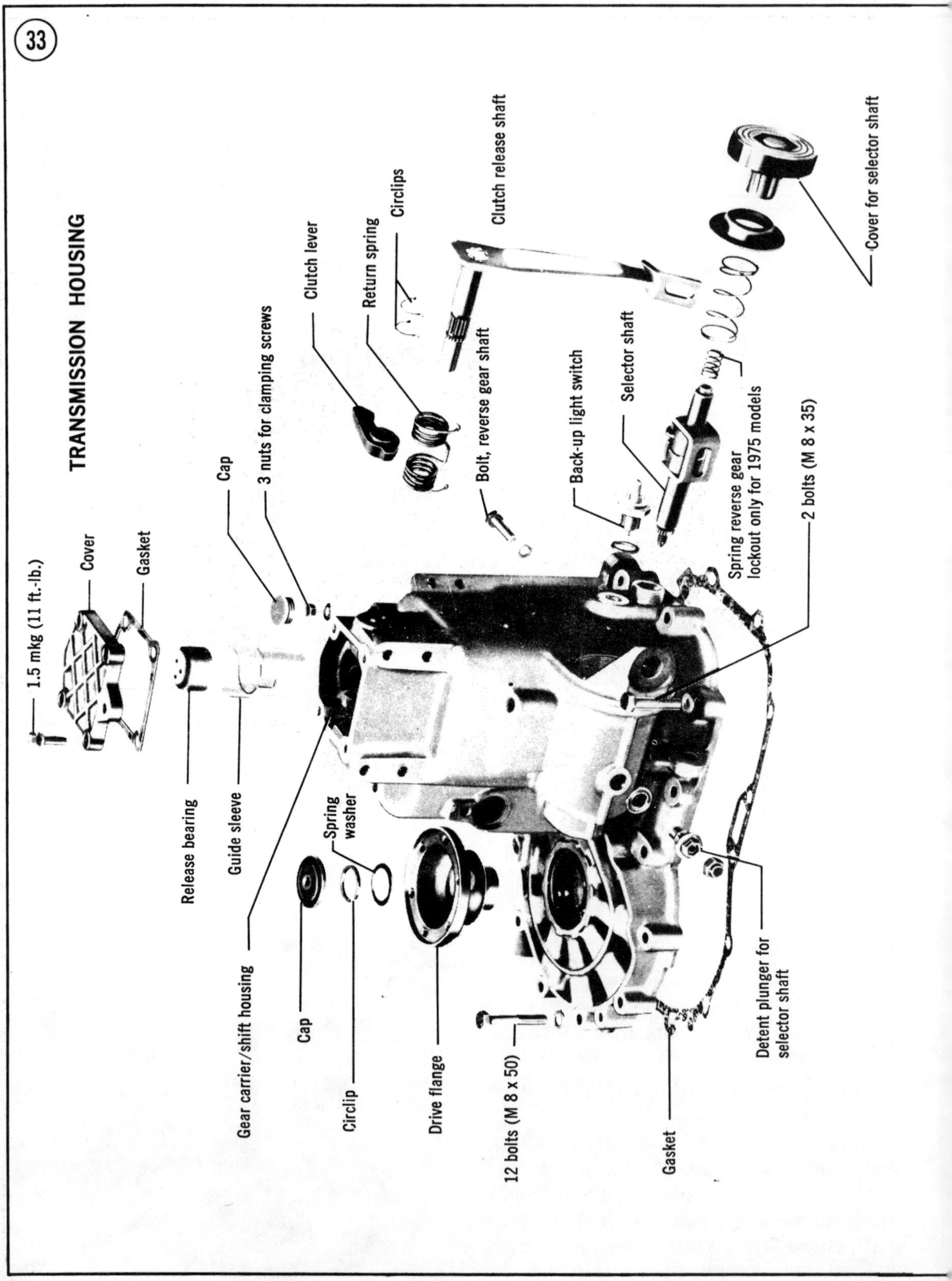
33
TRANSMISSION HOUSING
1.5 mkg (11 ft.-lb.)
Cover
Gasket
Release bearing
Guide sleeve
Cap
3 nuts for clamping screws
Gear carrier/shift housing
Spring washer
Cap
Circlip
Drive flange
12 bolts (M 8 x 50)
Gasket
Clutch lever
Return spring
Circlips
Clutch release shaft
Bolt, reverse gear shaft
Back-up light switch
Selector shaft
Spring reverse gear lockout only for 1975 models
2 bolts (M 8 x 35)
Cover for selector shaft
Detent plunger for selector shaft

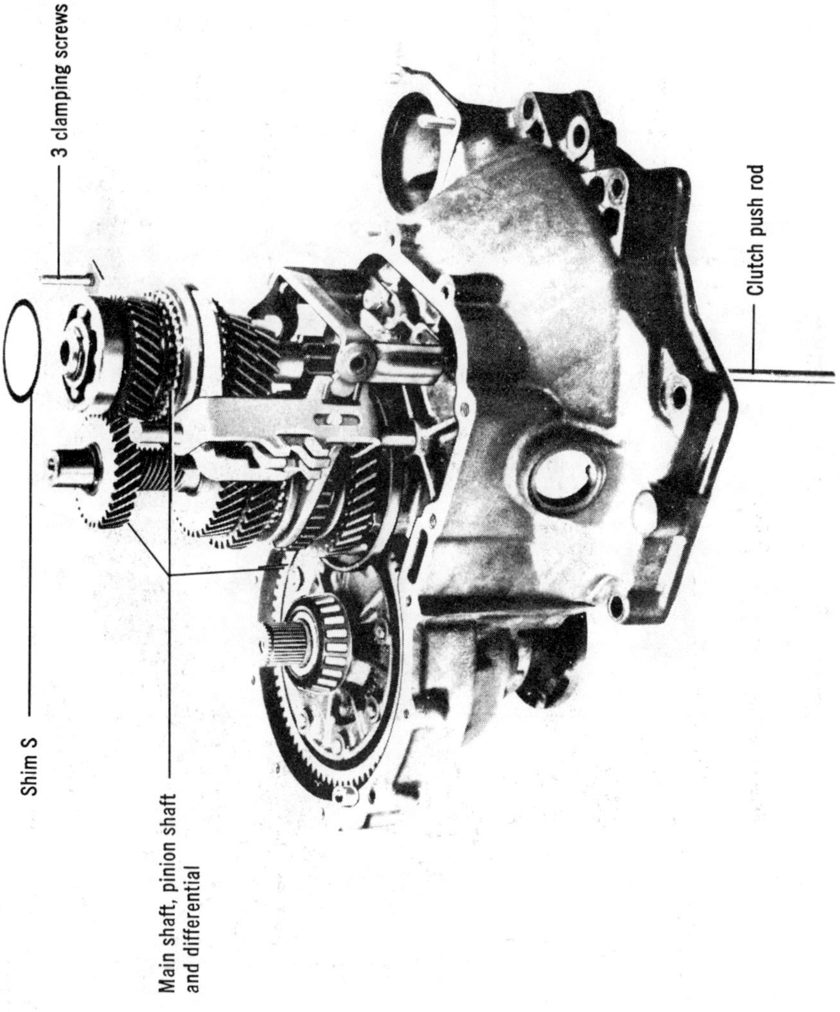
3 clamping screws
Clutch push rod
Shim S
Main shaft, pinion shaft and differential

NOTE: *Only one circlip was used on the clutch release shaft on transmissions between serial No. 15 03 5 and 17 03 7. If the clutch release shaft is to be replaced, use the newer type having two circlips, regardless of the type removed from the transaxle.*

5. Remove the plastic caps (arrows, **Figure 37**) and remove the 3 nuts from the clamping screws. Remove selector shaft detent plunger, the retaining bolt for the reverse gear shaft, and the back-up light switch.

6. Remove the selector shaft cover, using tool US4463 (A, **Figure 38**). Place the shift forks in neutral.

NOTE: *If the shift forks connot be place in neutral and the selector shaft cannot be removed, perform Step 7. Otherwise, proceed to Step 8.*

7. Remove the circlip (2, **Figure 39**) from the selector shaft and then drive or press out the selector shaft (1) in the direction indicated by the arrow. Do not remove the shift fork rail (3), shifting finger (4), or the sleeve (5) from the case (6).

NOTE: *The circlip was not used on 1975 models. To remove the selector shaft, drive or press it out.*

37

38

39

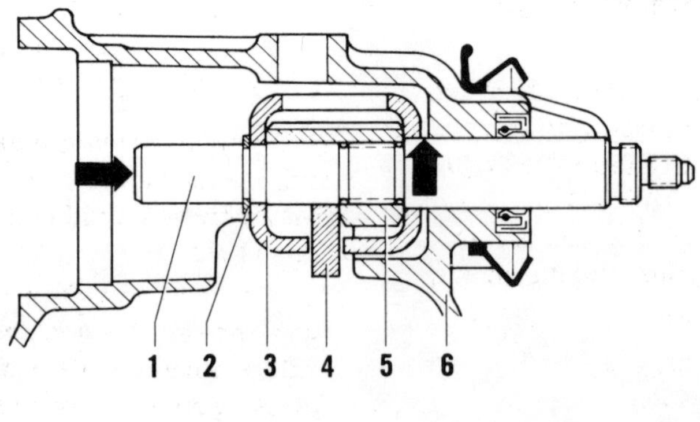

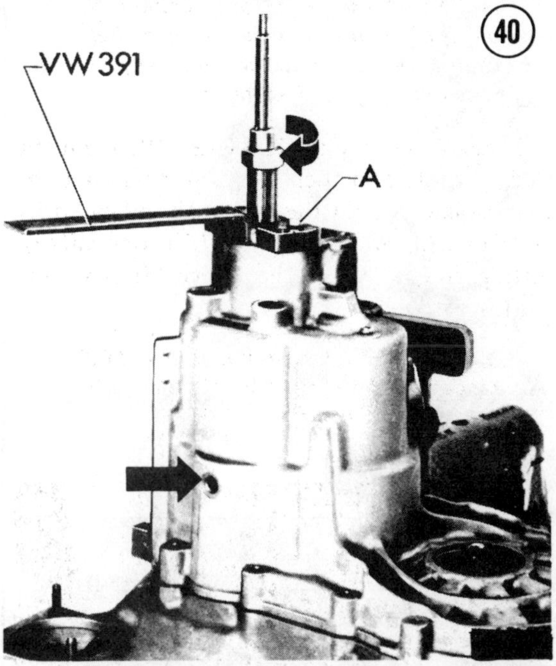

8. Remove the 14 attaching bolts holding the gear case to the final drive case and remove the reverse sliding gear shaft support bolt (arrow **Figure 40**). Mount tool VW 391 as shown in Figure 40, using two M7 x 30 bolts (A), and turn in the direction indicated by the curved arrow to remove the gear case.

CAUTION

Do not attempt to pry the cases apart by forcing a tool between them. To do so will result in damage to one or both of the cases which could lead to a serious lubricant leak.

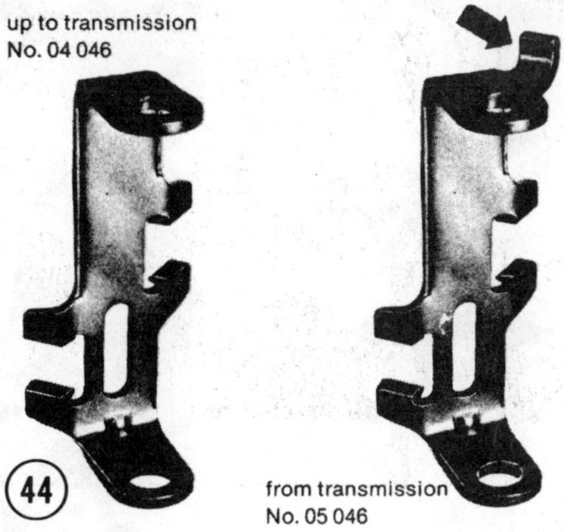

NOTE: *When the gear case is removed, the main shaft bearing should pull out of the case and remain on main shaft.*

9. Remove the main shaft bearing spacing shim and the clamping screws (arrow, **Figure 41**). These screws should pull out of the case when it is removed.

10. Use a screwdriver to remove the circlips from the shift fork assembly **(Figure 42 and 43)** and remove the shift fork assembly. If the reverse gear shift fork requires repairs, unbolt and remove it.

NOTE: *Two types of reverse gear shift fork have been used. See* ***Figure 44****).*

8

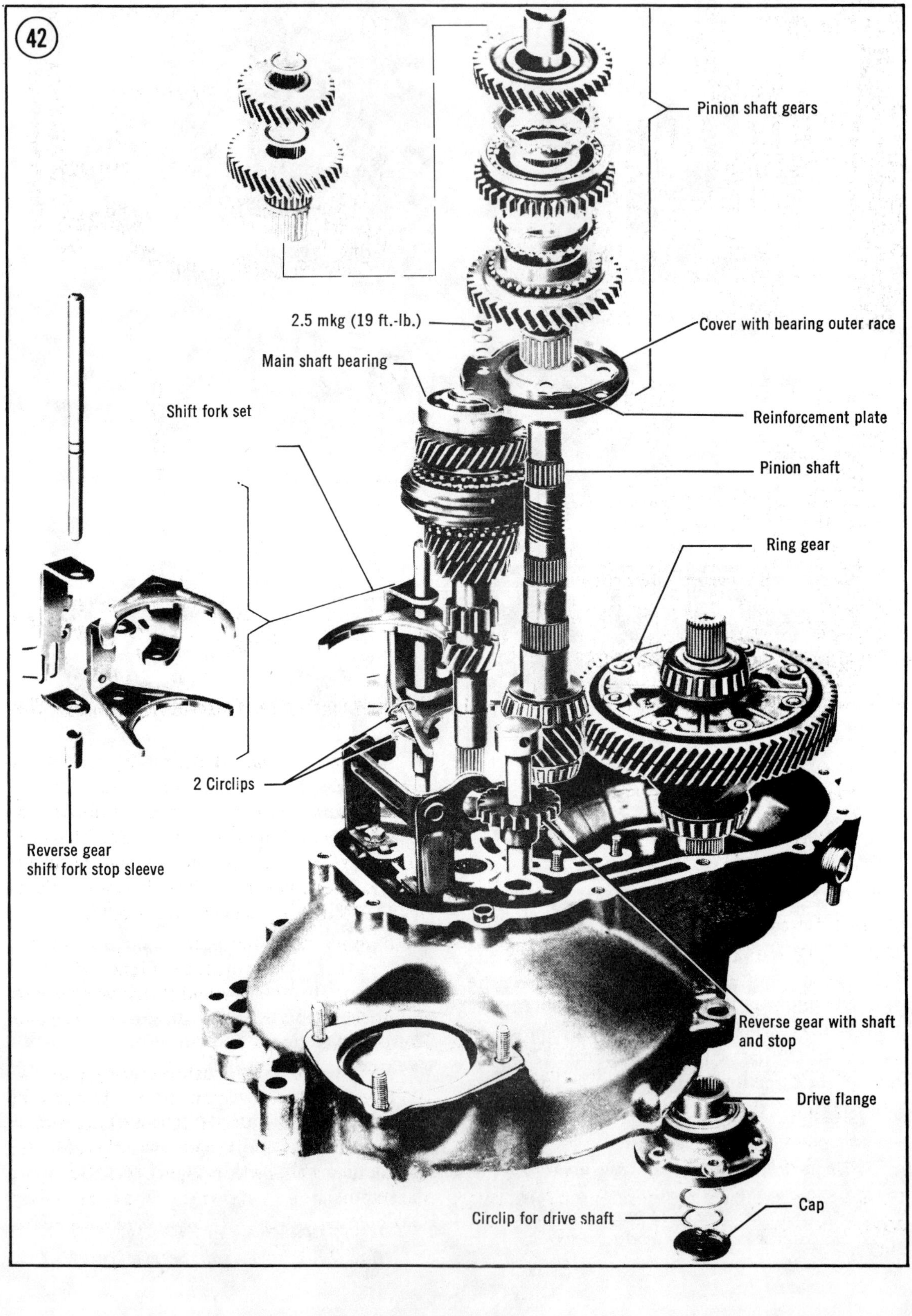
42
Pinion shaft gears
2.5 mkg (19 ft.-lb.)
Cover with bearing outer race
Main shaft bearing
Shift fork set
Reinforcement plate
Pinion shaft
Ring gear
2 Circlips
Reverse gear
shift fork stop sleeve
Reverse gear with shaft
and stop
Drive flange
Cap
Circlip for drive shaft

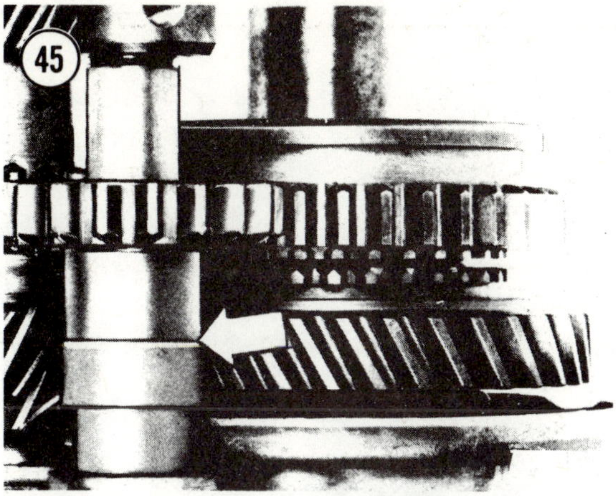

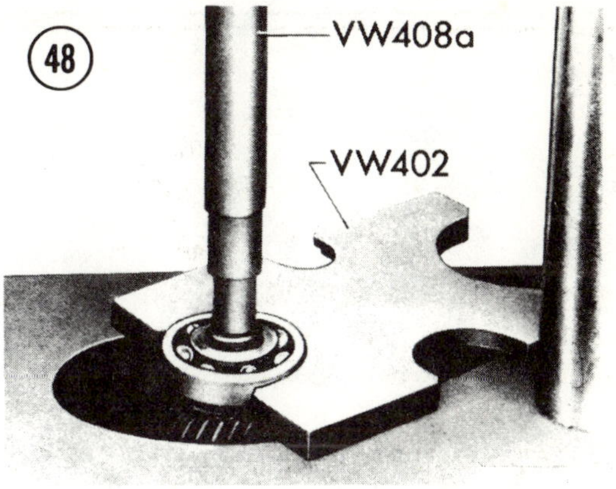

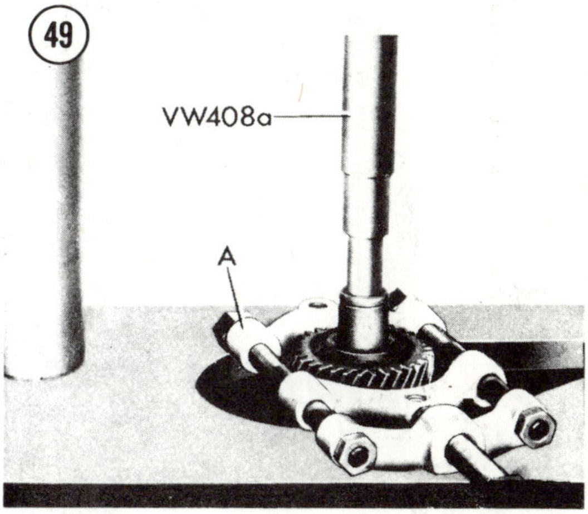

The fork on the left was used through transmission No.04 046 and the one on the right, which has a tab to operate the back-up lights switch, was used on later transmissions.

11. Lift out the reverse gear with its shaft and stop, if so equipped.

> NOTE: *The stop was a sleeve on the shaft in transmissions through 15 065. See* **Figure 45**. *On later transmissions, the stop was a tab on the pinion shaft bearing cover plate. See* **Figure 46**. *When installing a new pinion shaft bearing cover plate in an early transmission, do not install the sleeve.*

12. Remove the circlip from the end of the drive pinion shaft and remove the 4th gear from the shaft.

13. Lift out the main shaft, taking care not to damage gear teeth, seals and bearings. Remove the circlip and use a press to remove the bearing from the end of the main shaft. See **Figure 47 and 48**. When removing the bearing, be sure to support the inner race. The bearing will be ruined if the outer race only is supported.

14. Remove the other gears and synchronizer. See Figure 47 for sequence. **Figure 49** shows removal of the 4 th gear and thrust washer, and **Figure 50** shows removal of the synchronizer hub and 3rd gear.

15. Remove the clutch pushrod bushing and oil seal. **Figure 51** shows removal of the old style (up to transmission No. 26 107) bushing and oil seal. On later models, remove the oil seal with a special tool as shown in **Figure 52**, then drive out the bushing as shown in Figure 51. Use a drift rod (A, Figure 51) approximately 10mm (3/8 in.) in diameter.

47

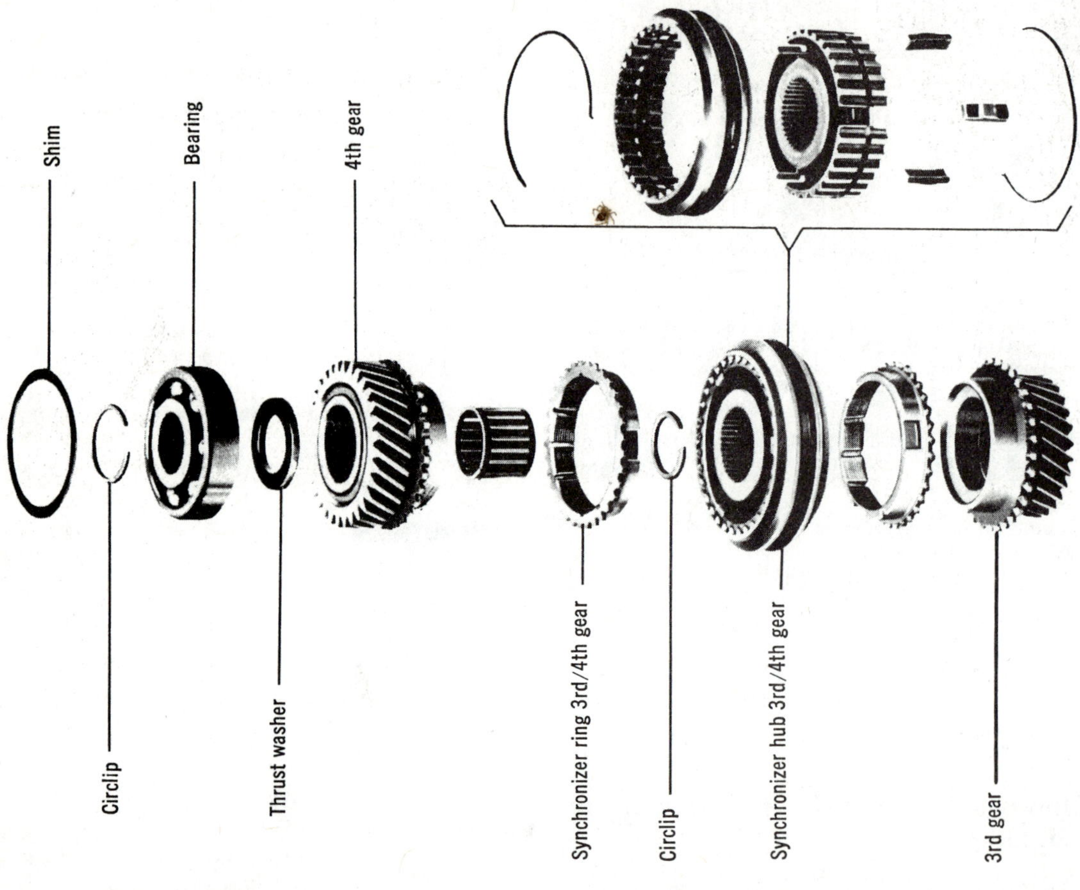
Shim
Circlip
Bearing
Thrust washer
4th gear
Synchronizer ring 3rd/4th gear
Circlip
Synchronizer hub 3rd/4th gear
3rd gear

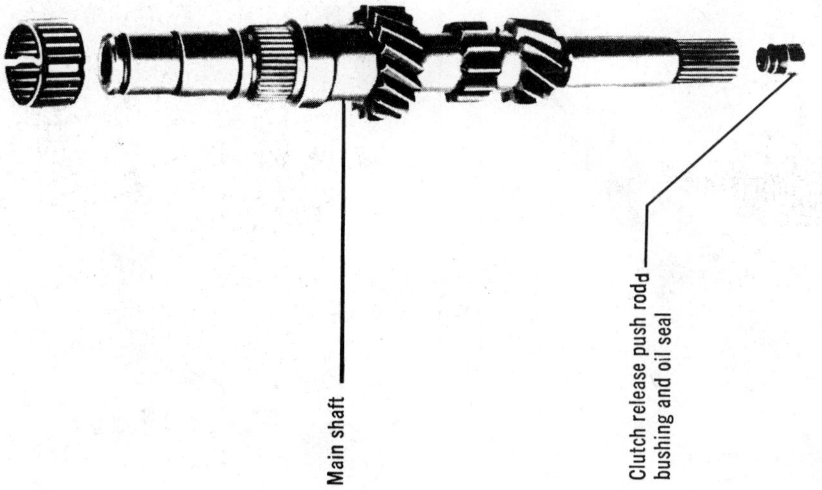
Main shaft
Clutch release push rod
bushing and oil seal

50

51

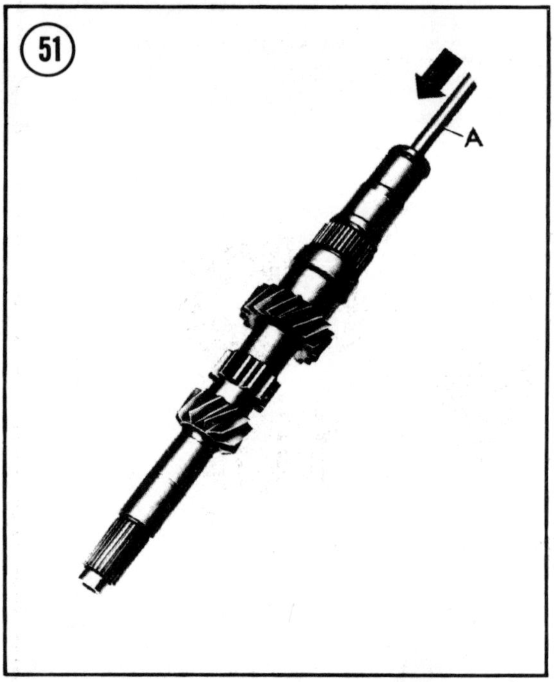

52

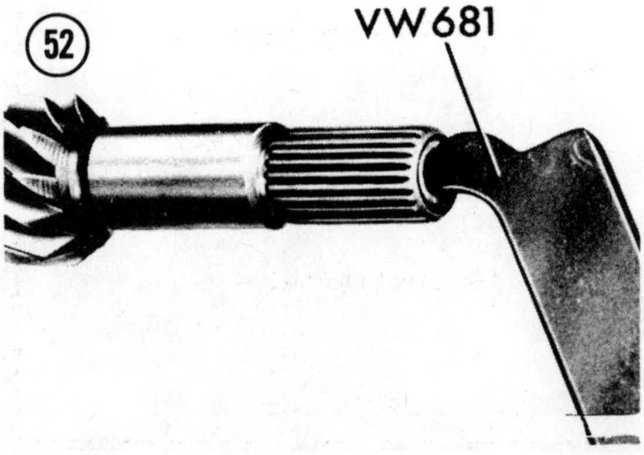

16. Remove the circlip and lift off the 3rd gear (4th gear was removed in Step 11), 2nd gear, 2nd gear needle bearing, and the second gear synchronizer ring. See **Figure 53**.

17. Use a puller tool as shown in **Figure 54** to remove the synchonizer hub, 1st gear synchronizer ring, and the 1st gear. Remove the 1st gear needle bearing and the thrust washer.

18. If disassembly of the synchronizer hub is planned, refer to Figure 53. Check to see if index marks are on the hub parts (arrow, **Figure 55**). If not (they were discontinued during the 1977 model year), scribe marks as shown before starting disassembly. Disassemble by removing the springs and separating the parts.

54

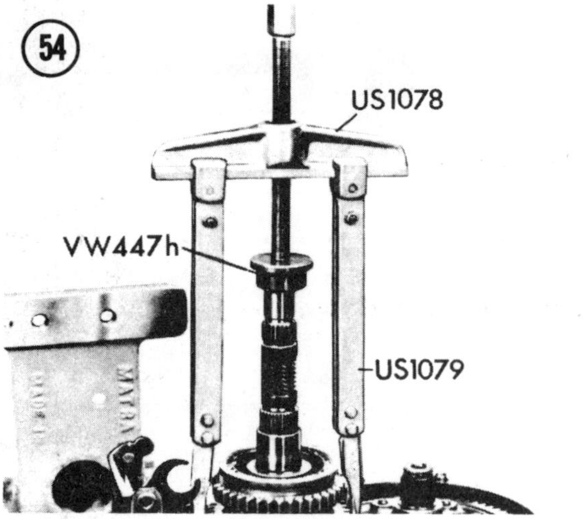

55

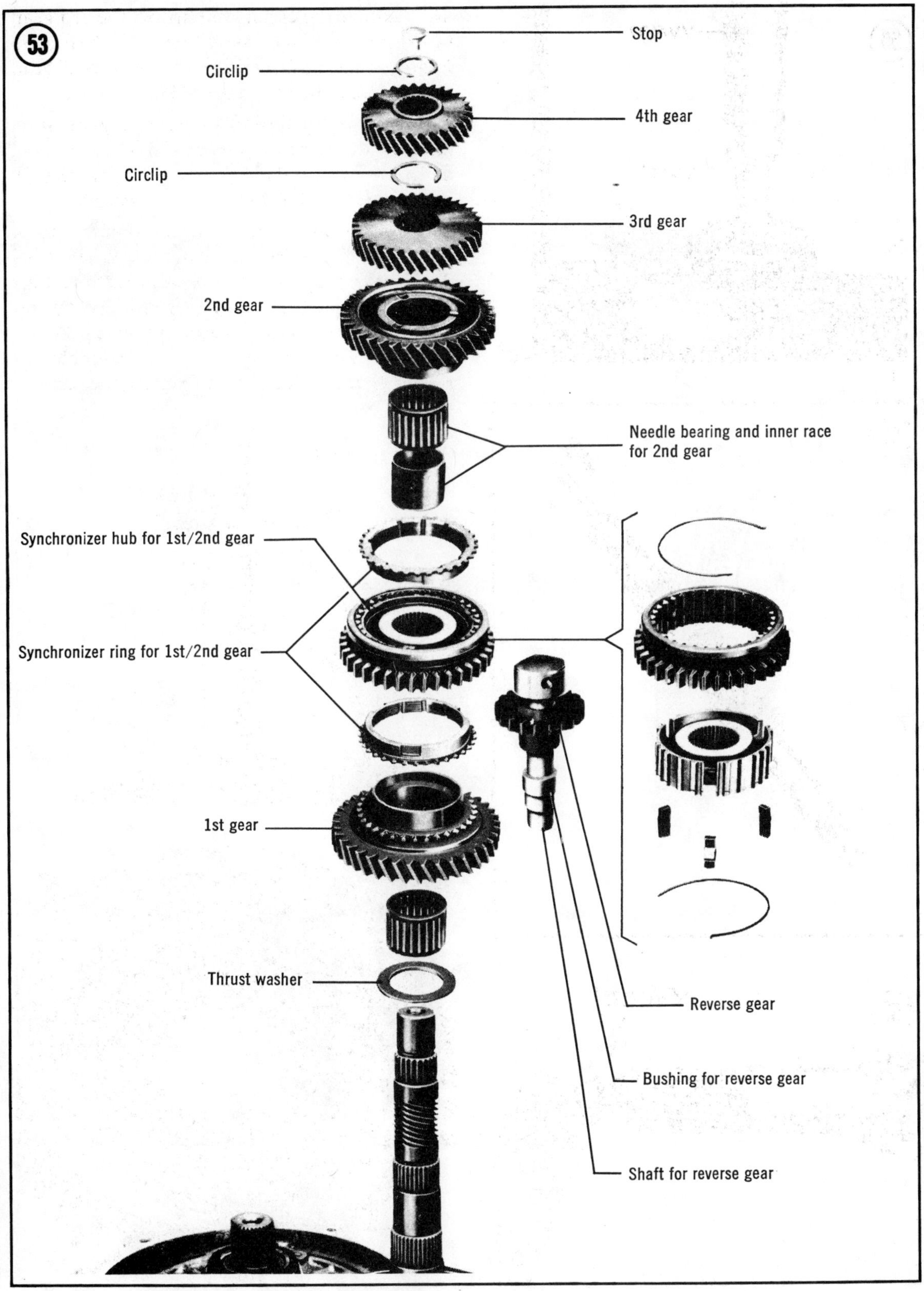
53
Stop
Circlip
4th gear
Circlip
3rd gear
2nd gear
Needle bearing and inner race for 2nd gear
Synchronizer hub for 1st/2nd gear
Synchronizer ring for 1st/2nd gear
1st gear
Thrust washer
Reverse gear
Bushing for reverse gear
Shaft for reverse gear

56

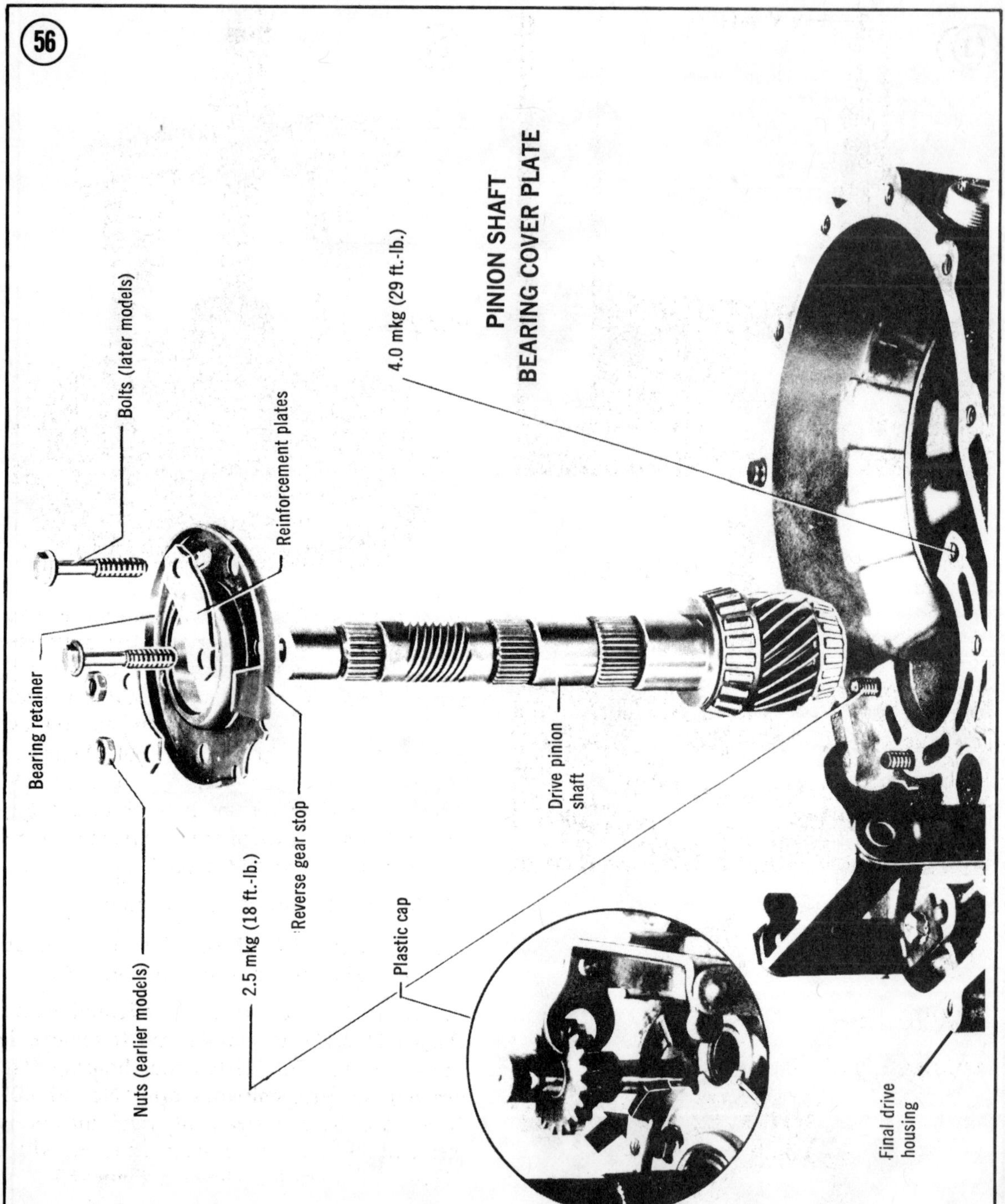
PINION SHAFT
BEARING COVER PLATE
Bolts (later models)
Reinforcement plates
Bearing retainer
Nuts (earlier models)
2.5 mkg (18 ft.-lb.)
Reverse gear stop
Plastic cap
4.0 mkg (29 ft.-lb.)
Drive pinion shaft
Final drive housing

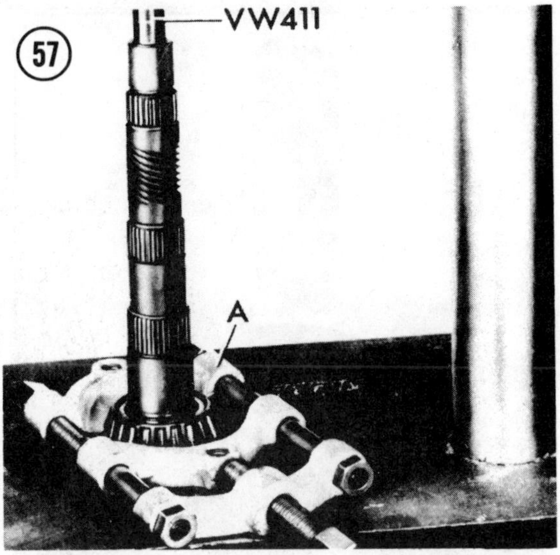

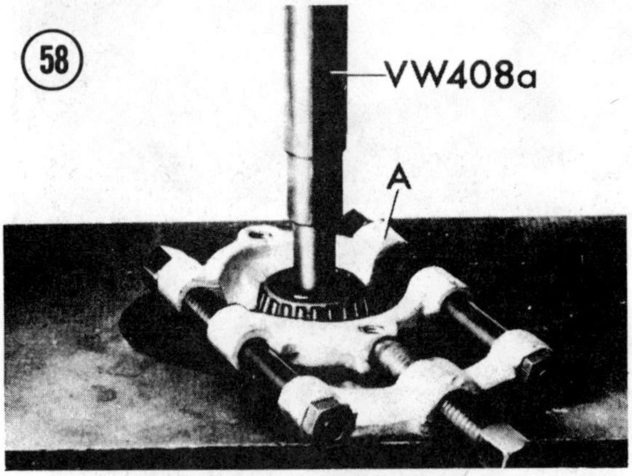

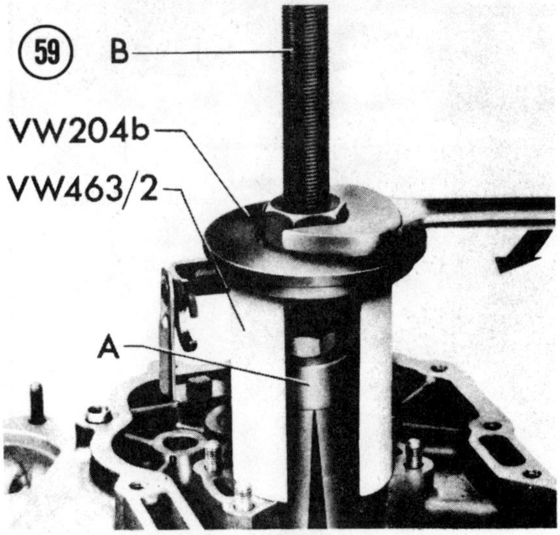

A = puller US 1099
B = spindle with internal thread

19. If removal of the drive pinion shaft is planned, remove the attaching nuts or bolts (see **Figure 56**) from the bearing retainer and remove the retainer. Lift out the shaft and bearings. If bearing removal is planned, remove them with a press and suitable tools. **Figure 57** shows removal of the large bearing, **Figure 58** shows removal of the small bearing, and **Figure 59** shows removal of the race from the case. "A" in Figure 57 and 58 is tool US4439.

20. Lift out the differential assembly.

21. If differential disassembly is required, remove the bearings as shown in **Figure 60**.

22. On 1975 models, remove the retaining bolts **(Figure 61)** and use a suitable tool to remove the ring gear from the differential housing **(Figure 62)**. On transmissions after No. 07 085, rivets are used instead of retaining bolts. Remove the rivets by drilling them out with a 12mm (15/32 in.) drill as shown in **Figure 63**.

23. Remove the circlips from ends of the differential pinion shaft and use a drift bar to drive out the shaft.

24. Remove the circlips holding the side gears to the drive flange shafts and remove the shafts. Then remove the pinions, side gears, and the thrust washers of thrust cage.

8

61

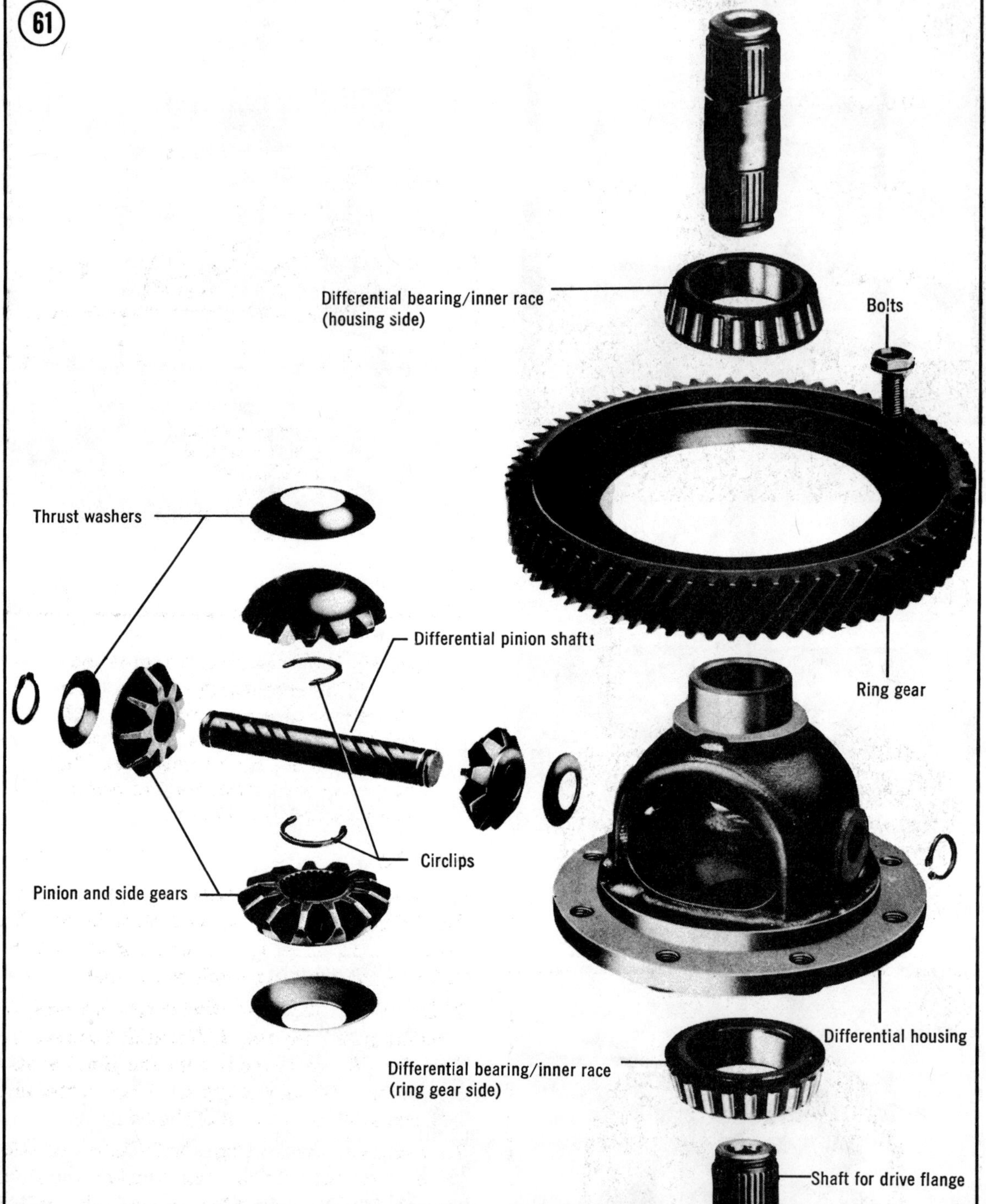
Differential bearing/inner race
(housing side)
Bolts
Thrust washers
Differential pinion shaftt
Ring gear
Circlips
Pinion and side gears
Differential housing
Differential bearing/inner race
(ring gear side)
Shaft for drive flange

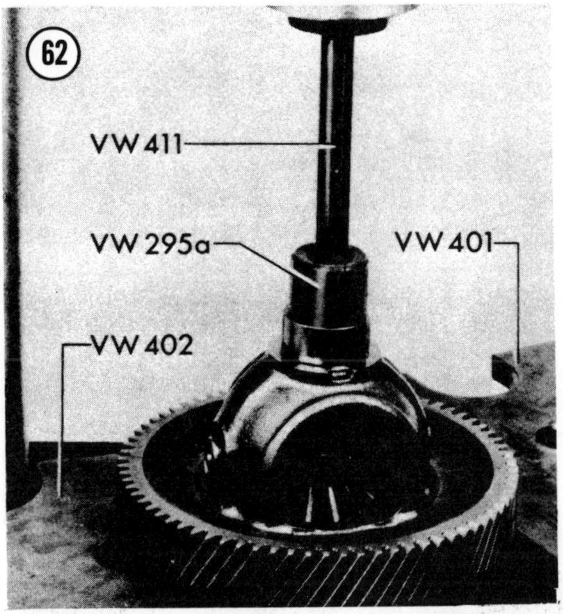

63

64

Part No. 020 409 170 A

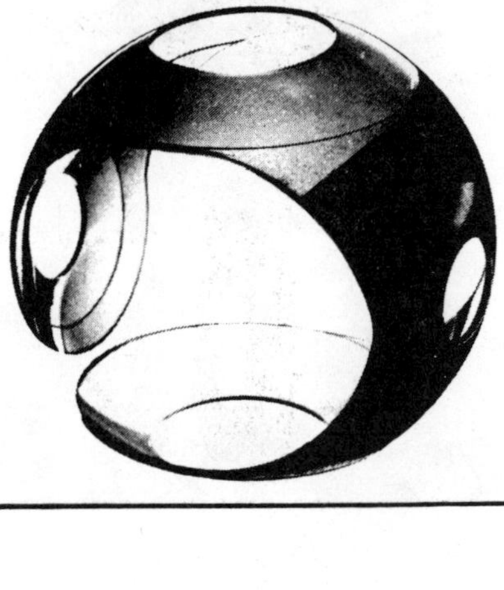

65

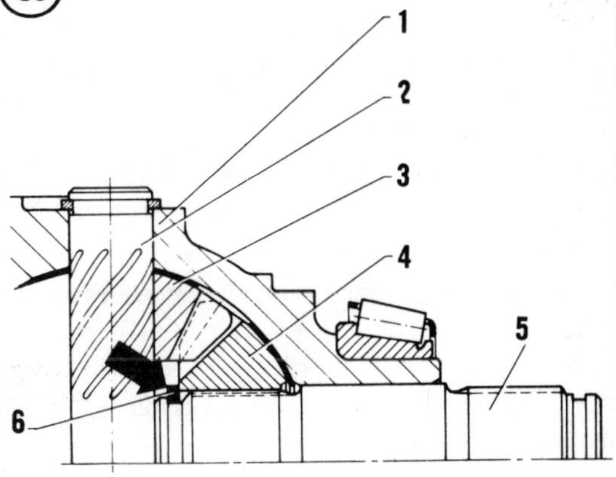

1. Differential housing
2. Pinion gear shaft
3. Pinion gear
4. Side gear
5. Drive flange shaft
6. Circlip

NOTE: *Differentials up to transmission No. 12 126 were equipped with thrust washers as shown in Figure 61. Differentials from No. 13 126 were equipped with thrust cages* ***(Figure 64)****. The cage consists of thrust washers embedded in a molded plastic cage.*

Assembly

1. Install the thrust washers or thrust cage in the differential housing, and then install the pinions. Then drive in the pinion shaft and install new circlips on the ends of the shaft.

2. Insert the side gears (and thrust washers, if so equipped) into the differential housing so that the side gears mesh with the pinions and are located 180 degrees apart. Then rotate the side gears into position in the housing.

3. Insert the drive flange shafts into the side gears and then install the thicket possible circlips. See **Figure 65**. Circlips available are 2.0 and 2.3mm.

4. Install new ring attaching bolts in the differential housing. If the ring gear was originally attached with rivets, obtain a special bolt kit for refastening from your VW dealer.

5. Heat the ring gear to approximately 100°C (212°F) and then install the heated ring on the differential housing (**Figure 66**). The gear can be heated in an oven. Tighten the bolts on older differentials having tapped holes to 36 ft.-lb. (5.0 mkg) and those that were originally riveted to 51 ft.-lb. (7.0 mkg). **Figure 67** shows a cross section of the newer differentials with the replacement bolts and washers.

6. Install the roller bearing inner races on the differential housing. Heat the bearings to approximately 100°C (212°F) before installing them and then press them into place as shown in **Figure 68**.

> NOTE: *(1) Remove the drive flange shafts before installing the bearings.*
>
> *(2) Adjustment of the drive flange shafts is required whenever any of the following parts is replaced: transmission housing, final drive housing, differential housing, or differential bearings.*
>
> *(3) If bearings are replaced on the differential housing, be sure not to mix the bearing outer races, as each bearing is matched to its race. When installing the race in the final drive housing (**Figure 69**), install a 1mm shim (S_2) between the race and the housing as a spacer. If the old shim is in good condition, it can be reused.*

7. To adjust the differential, install the bearing outer race and shim S_2 in the final drive housing. Remove the bearing outer race and shim S_1 from the gear housing and reinstall the race without the shim. Install the differential assembly in the final drive housing and then install the gear housing on the final drive housing. Install the attaching bolts and tighten them to 14 ft.-lb. (2.0 mkg). Install a dial indicator as shown in **Figure 70** and zero the indicator with a 1mm preload. Move the differential assembly up and down and note the displacement on the indicator dial. Add 0.40mm to the reading to obtain the correct thickness for shim S_2. (For example, if the reading is 0.90mm, add 0.40mm to obtain 1.30mm as the correct shim thickness.) Remove the bolts and the gear housing and then remove the bearing outer race from the gear housing.

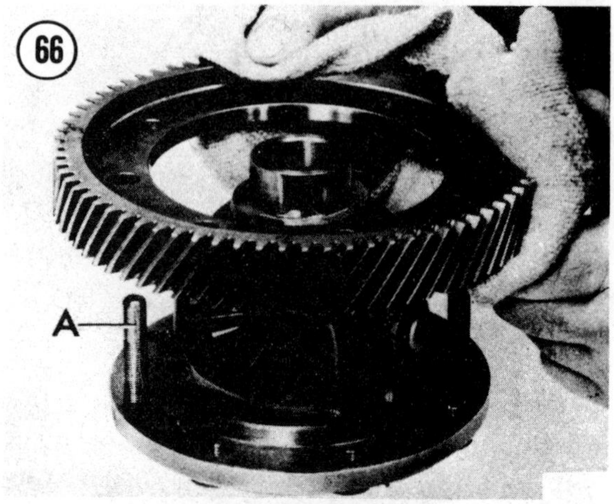

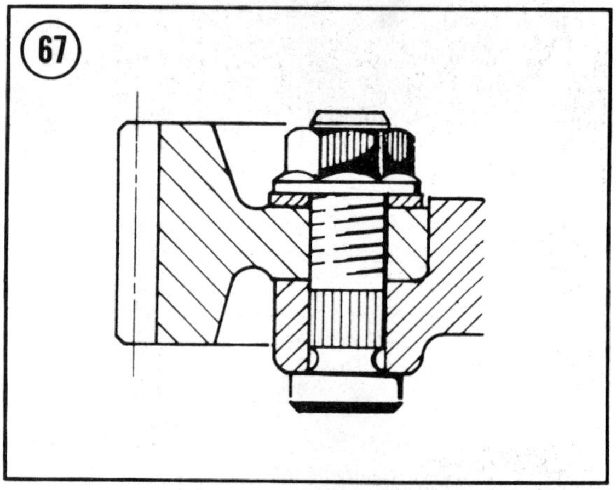

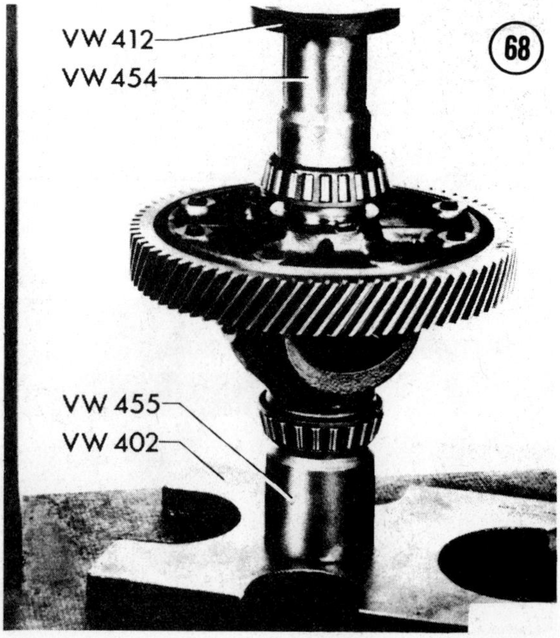

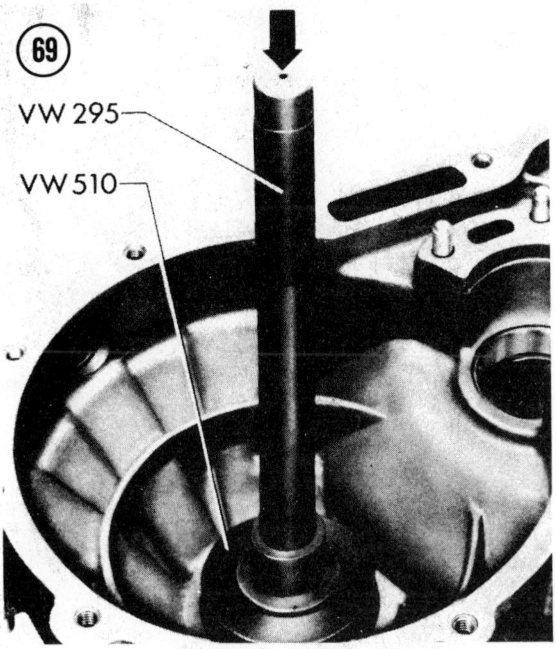

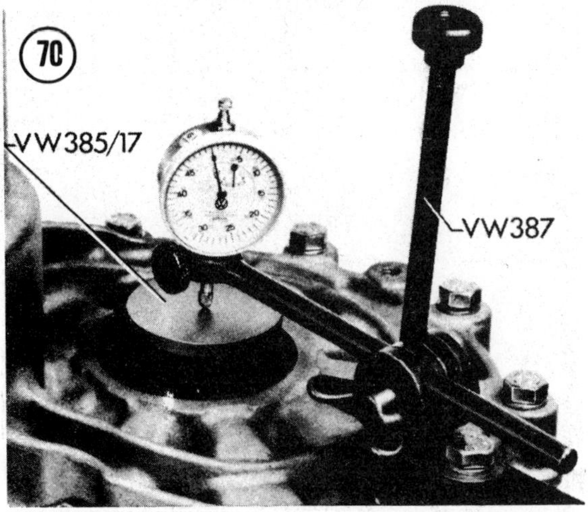

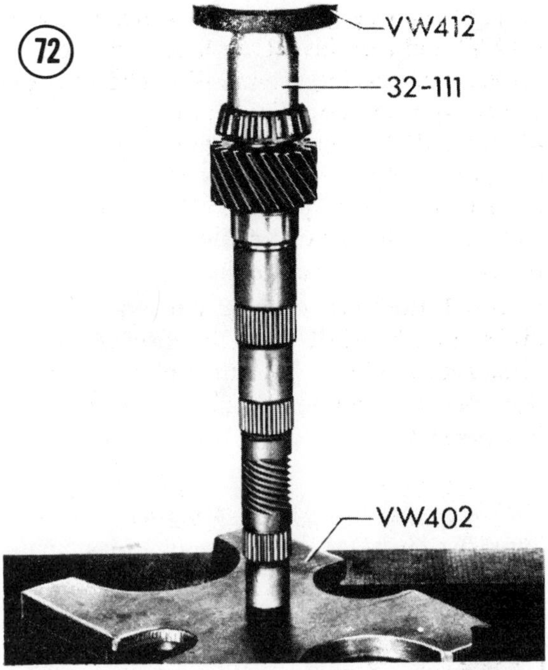

Install shim S_1 of the proper thickness and reinstall the bearing outer race in the gear housing. Shims are available in the following thickness 0.15, 0.30, 0.60, 0.70, 0.80, and 1.00mm. If necessary, use two or more shims to obtain the correct thickness. Lubricate the differential with transmission oil and reinstall the differential in the final drive housing and install the gear housing, tightening the bolts to 14 ft.-lb. (2.0 mkg). Install a torque gauge (**Figure 71**) with a range of 0-26 in.-lb. (0-30 cmkg) and turn the differential several turns in each direction, noting the torque required. New bearings should require 10-22 in.-lb. (12-25 cmkg). If less than this for new bearings, or less than 2.7 in.- lb. (3 cmkg) for used bearings, check all assembly steps for possible errors and reselect shim S_1 if bearings are new. Install new bearings if used bearings can be turned with less than the specified torque.

NOTE: *The pinion shaft must be adjusted whenever any of the following are replaced: final drive housing, ring gear and pinion, or pinion shaft tapered roller bearings.*

8. Install the small tapered bearing on the pinion shaft as shown in **Figure 72**. Install the large

8

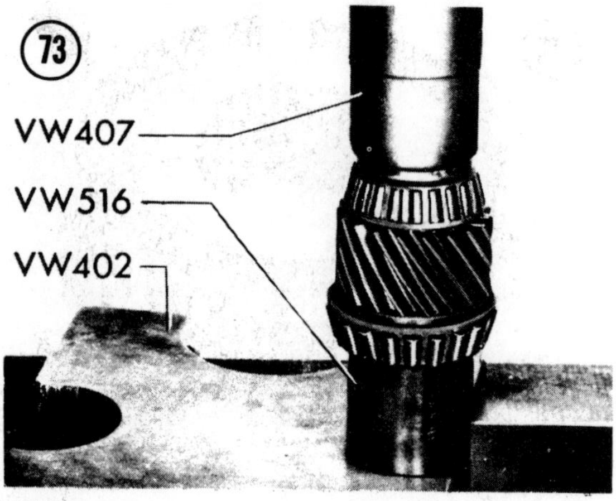

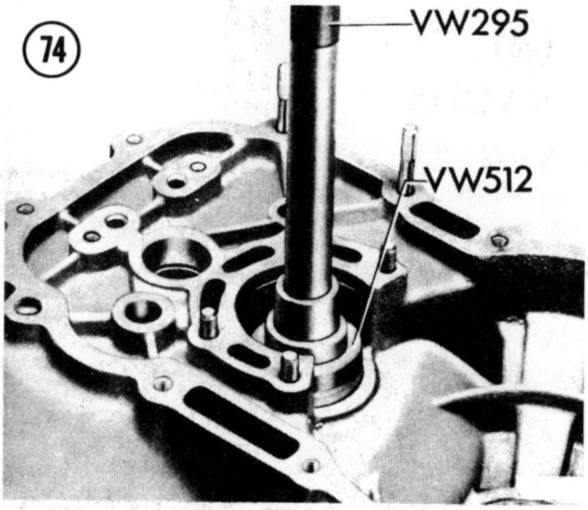

bearing on the shaft as shown in **Figure 73**. Heat the bearings to approximately 100°C (212°F) before installing them.

9. Install a 0.65mm shim in the bearing housing in the final drive housing and install the outer race for the small tapered pinion shaft bearing as shown in **Figure 74**. Install the pinion shaft in the housing and tighten bearing cover retaining nuts to 18 ft.-lb. (2.5 mkg). If the cover is retained by bolts instead of nuts, tighten the bolts to 29 ft.-lb. (4.0mkg). See Figure 56. Install a dial indicator as shown in **Figure 75** and zero the indicator with a 1mm preload. Move the pinion shaft up and down without rotating it and observe the reading on the indicator. Add the reading to the valve of the shim already installed (0.65mm) and then add a preload factor of 0.20mm. (For example, if the reading was 0.30mm, add this to 0.65mm and 0.20mm to obtain a correct shim thickness of 1.15mm.) Remove the dial indicator and then remove the pinion shaft. Remove the small bearing outer race from the final drive housing as shown in **Figure 76.** "A" in the figure is puller US1099, "B" is a spinkle with an internal thread. Remove the 0.65mm shim and replace it with one of the correct value. Install the bearing outer race. Lubricate the pinion shaft bearings with transmission oil and reinstall the pinion shaft as described earlier. If new bearings were installed, check the turning torque with a torque gauge as shown in **Figure 77**. The torque should be between 4.5 and 13 in.-lb. (5-15 cmkg). If not within this range, reselect the shim as described earlier. Available

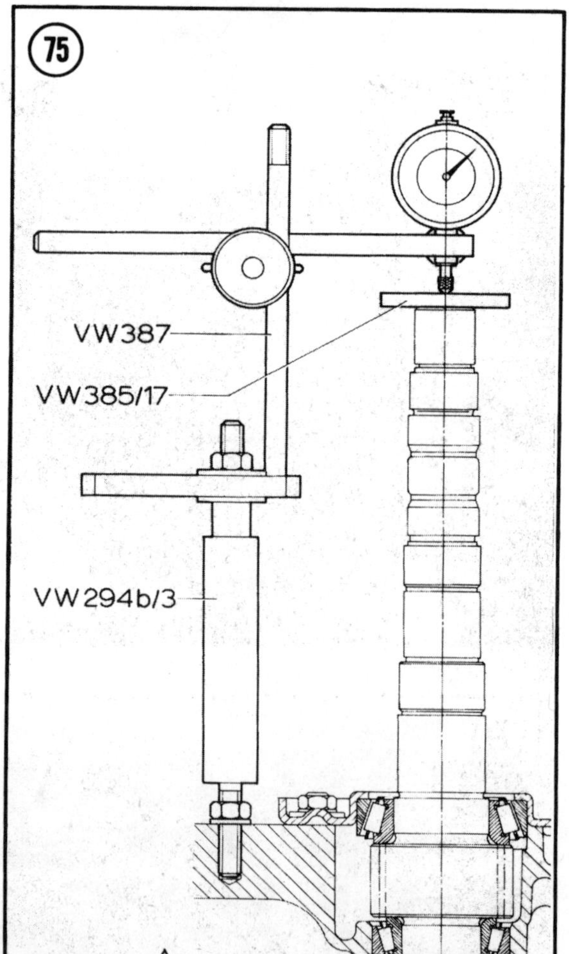

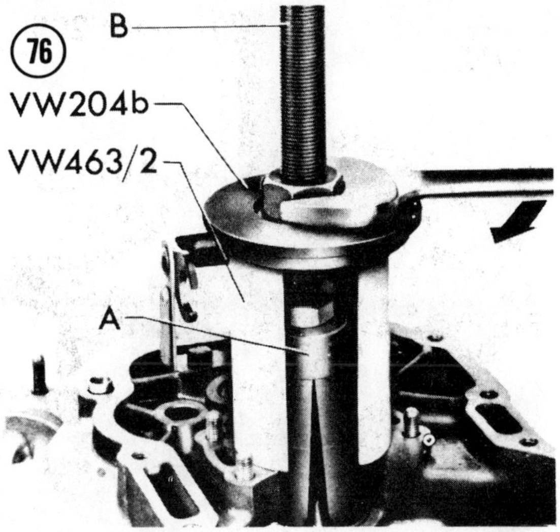

shim thicknesses range from 0.65 to 1.40mm, in 0.05 intervals.

10. Press the synchronizer ring onto the 1st gear as shown in **Figure 78** and measure gap "a." The gap for a new part should be between 1.1 and 1.7mm (0.042-0.066 in.). If gap is less than 0.5mm (0.019 in.), install new parts. Repeat the check, using the 2nd gear and its synchronizer ring.

11. Reassemble the 1st/2nd gear synchronizer hub with the groove (white arrow, **Figure 79**, on transmissions up to 26 076; black arrow from 27 076 on) facing 1st gear. Make sure the scribe marks (arrow, Figure 55) are aligned, then install the keys and springs 120 degrees offset. Angled ends must engage the hollow key.

12. Assemble the thrust washer, 1st gear needle bearing, 1st gear, and 1st gear synchronizer ring on the pinion shaft.

13. Heat the synchronizer hub assembly to approximately 120°C (238°F) and press it onto the shaft as shown in **Figure 80**. Make sure the grooves (see Step 10) face 1st gear.

14. Press the 2nd gear needle bearing inner race onto the pinion shaft, using the tooling set-up shown in **Figure 81**. These tools must be used to make sure the race is properly seated.

15. Install the needle bearing, the 2nd gear synchronizer ring, 2nd gear, and 3rd gear. Make sure the collar on 3rd gear is facing 2nd gear.

16. Install a circlip of the proper thickness to obtain a clearance between the circlip and 3rd gear of between zero and 0.20mm (0-0.008 in.), measured as shown in **Figure 82**. Circlips are available in the following sizes: 2.5mm (brown), 2.6mm (black), 2.7mm (shiny), 2.8mm (copper), 2.9mm (brass), and 3.0mm (blue). The clearance should be kept as low as possible.

17. Install the stop in the end of the pinion shaft (Figure 53) but do not install the 4th gear and its circlip at this time.

> NOTE: *Some changes in gear ratios have been made over the years. As a general rule, if a gear is replaced on either the pinion shaft or the main shaft, the gear with which it will mesh on the other shaft also must be replaced. Consult your dealer's parts department for proper replacement gears for your car.*

18. Press the synchronizer ring onto 3rd gear and measure gap "a" (**Figure 83**). For new parts the gap should measure 1.15-1.75mm (0.045-0.068 in.), with a service limit of 0.5mm (0.019 in.). Repeat the check for 4th gear and its synchronizer ring. Gap should measure 1.30-1.90mm (0.051-0.074 in.), with a service limit of 0.5mm (0.019 in.). Replace parts if gap is smaller than the service limit.

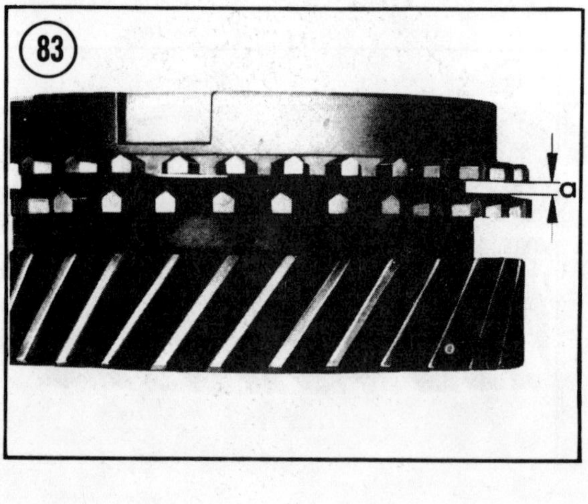

84

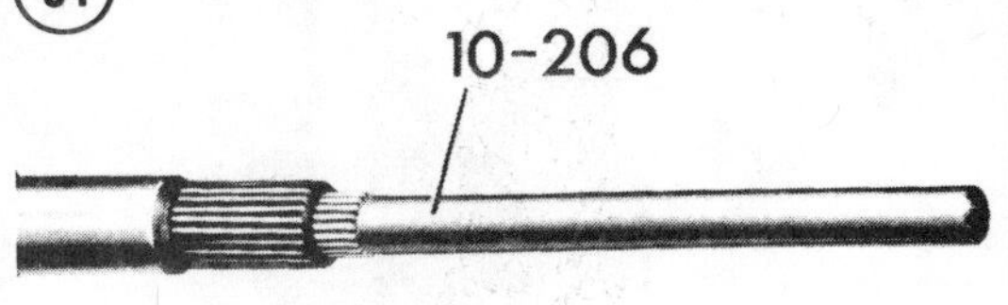

85

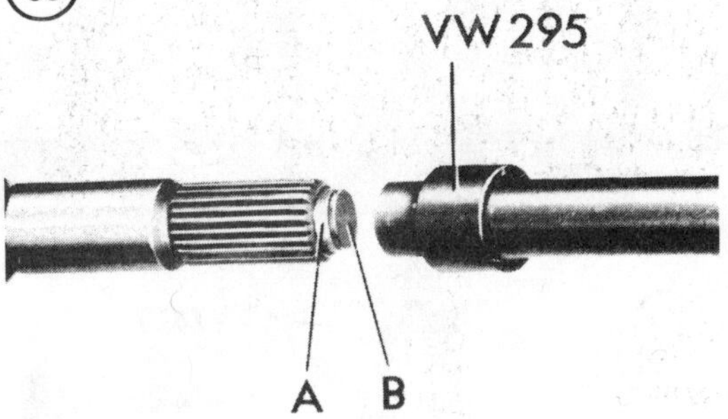

86

87

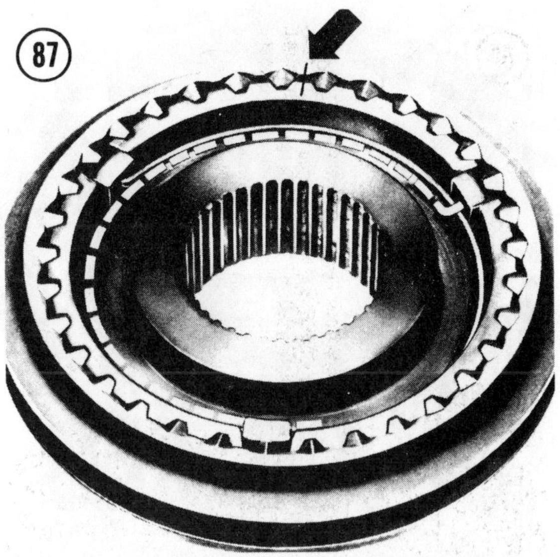

19. Install the clutch pushrod bushing in the main shaft as shown in **Figure 84**. Install the clutch pushrod oil seal in the shaft as shown in **Figure 85**. Make sure the bushing is fully seated. Drive the seal (A, **Figure 85**) in until the plug (B) is flush, then remove the plug and lightly lubricate the lip of the seal.

20. Assemble the 3rd/4th gear synchronizer hub components as shown in **Figure 86**. The chamfer on the inner hub splines (black arrow, **Figure 86**) should face toward 3rd gear. On transmission No. 19 025 and later, the groove (white arrow) should face 4th gear. Also, make sure the scribe marks (arrow, **Figure 87**) are aligned. Install the keys, and then install the springs 120° offset with angled ends engaged in hollow keys.

> NOTE: *A new type of synchronizer hub, with a slightly offset retaining groove in splines to prevent 4th gear from jumping out, was introduced with transmission No. 04 085. See* **Figure 88**. *The new hub has either a circular groove on the 4th gear side (white arrow), or lengthwise grooves on each spline (black arrow).*

21. Install the 3rd gear needle bearing on the main shaft. Arrange the 3rd gear, 3rd gear synchronizer ring, and synchronizer hub in their proper relationship and install them on the

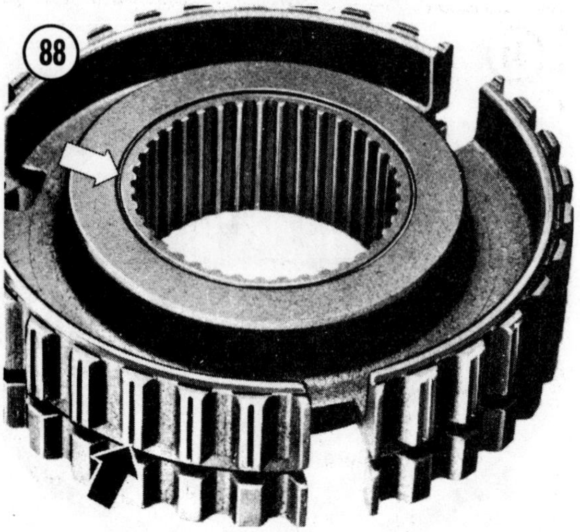

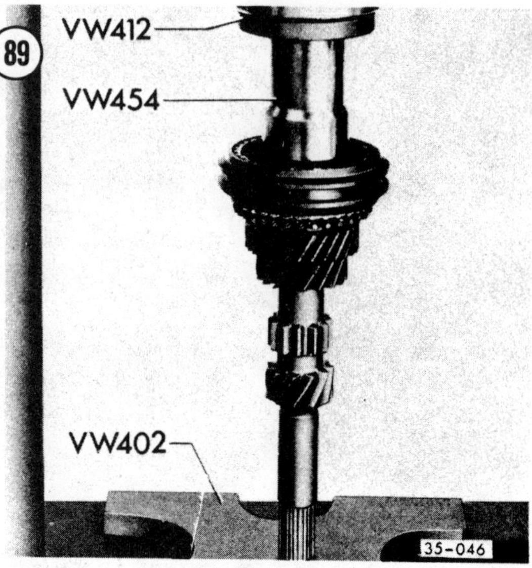

main shaft, using the tools shown in **Figure 89** and a press. Turn the synchronizer ring until the grooves are aligned with the shift keys, and make sure all splines are properly aligned. Install a new circlip on the shaft. Make sure the synchronizer hub is in firm contact with the circlip.

22. Install the 4th gear synchronizer ring on the synchronizer hub, making sure the grooves engage the keys of the synchronizer hub.

23. Install the 4th gear needle bearing on the main shaft and then install the 4th gear. Some 1975 models were equipped with a thrust washer. If your car is so equipped, press the thrust washer onto the main shaft as shown in **Figure 90**. Washer should firmly contact the shoulders on the main shaft.

24. Install the main shaft in the final drive housing, making sure that all gears mesh properly with the gears on the pinion drive shaft.

> NOTE: *Adjustment of the main shaft is required if any of the following parts were replaced: transmission housing, final drive housing, thrust washer for 4th gear, or the main shaft itself. If adjustment is required, follow the instructions in Step 24. If not, proceed to Step 25.*

25. Use the nut on the support bar spindle (A, **Figure 91**) to position the main shaft until the clearance between the 2nd gear on the pinion shaft and the 3rd gear on the main shaft is

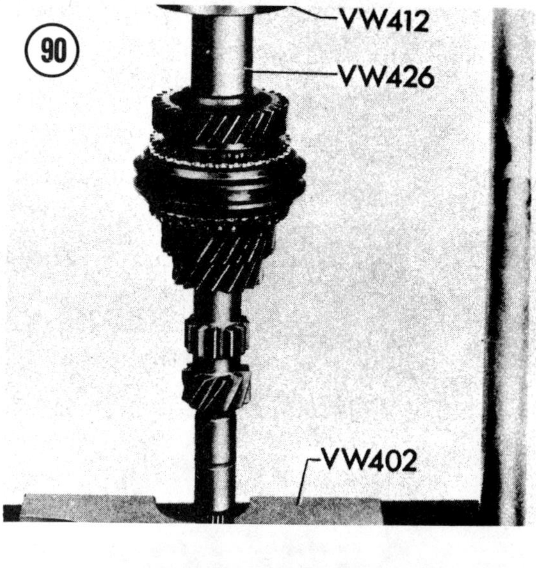

1.0mm (0.039 in.). See **Figure 92**. When clearance is correct, tighten the locknut and recheck the clearance to make sure the relationship had not changed. Install a dummy bearing and measuring sleeve (VW 549) on the main shaft as shown in **Figure 93**. If your car does not have a thrust washer, one must be inserted between 4th gear and the dummy bearing (A, **Figure 94**). Install the transmission housing without the main shaft bearing installed, using a new gasket. Tighten the bolts 14 ft.-lb. (2.0 mkg). Install a dial indicator as shown in **Figure 95** and zero the indicator with a preload of 3mm. Move the measuring sleeve up and down

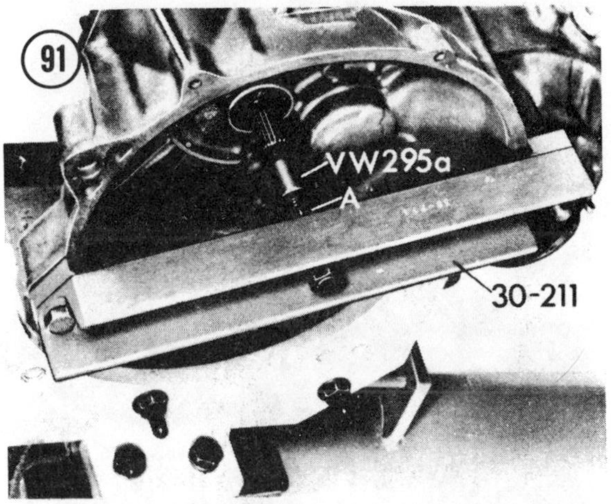

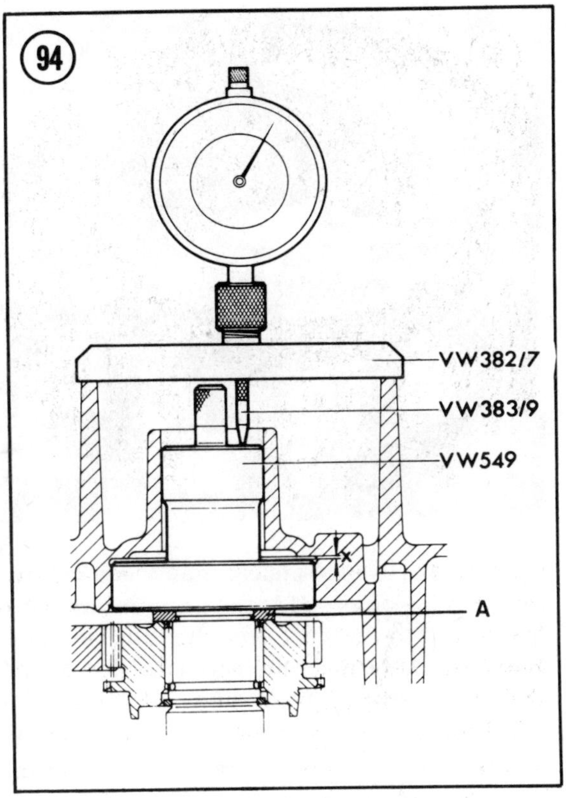

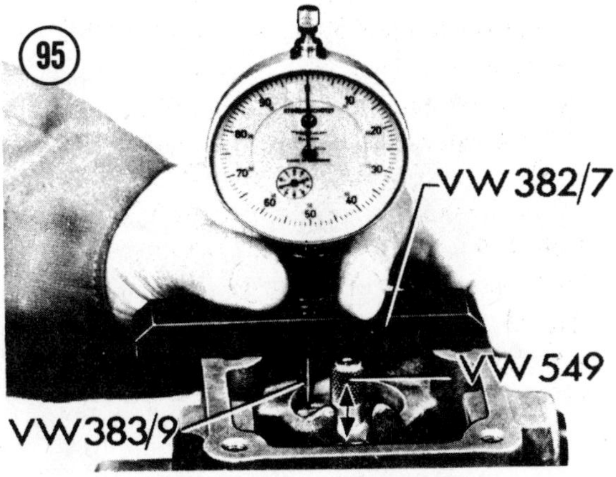

as far as it will go and observe the reading on the indicator to determine the correct size shim to be installed in the bearing housing. If the play is 0- 0.46mm, no shim is required. If play is 0.47- 0.75mm, use a shim thickness of 0.30mm; if play is 0.76-1.04mm, thickness should be 0.60; if play is 1.05-1.45mm, thickness of shim should be 0.90mm. Available thicknesses are 0.30mm and 0.60mm. Use two shims if thickness of 0.90mm is required.

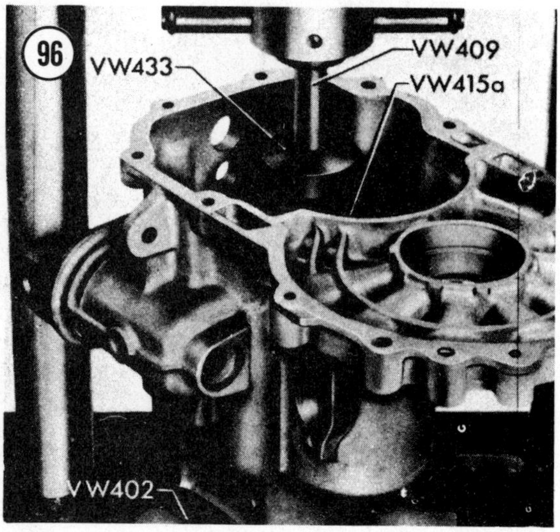

26. Remove the dial indicator and then remove the retaining bolts and remove the transmission housing from the final drive housing. Remove the dummy bearing and measuring sleeve (and the thrust washer, if not required).

27. Install shim(s) of the proper thickness in the bearing recesses in the transmission housing and then press the bearing into place. See **Figure 96**.

CAUTION

Bearing must be installed with the plastic cage toward the shim. Damage to the bearing will result if it is reversed.

NOTE: *If installing a newer type bearing having a thrust face in an older type transmission originally equipped with a thrust washer, remove and discard the old thrust washer.*

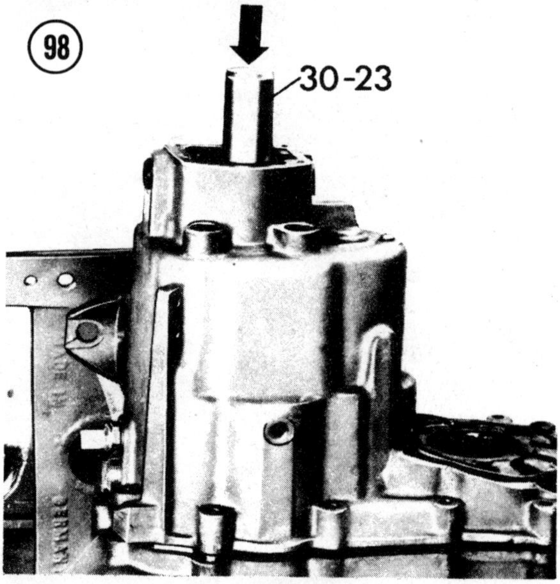

28. Install the bearing clamping screws as shown in Figure 41. Tighten the nuts to 11 ft.-lb. (1.5 mkg) and install the plastic caps.

29. Refer to note following Step 10 of *Disassembly* and install the reverse sliding gear and its shaft. Install the support bolt in the shaft (**Figure 97**) and align the shaft as shown in the figure so that the distances X are equal. Remove the support bolt.

30. Install the shift forks in the operating sleeves. Use screwdriver to install new circlips as shown in **Figure 43**. When installing reverse shift fork, tighten bolts to 11 ft.-lb. (1.5 mkg).

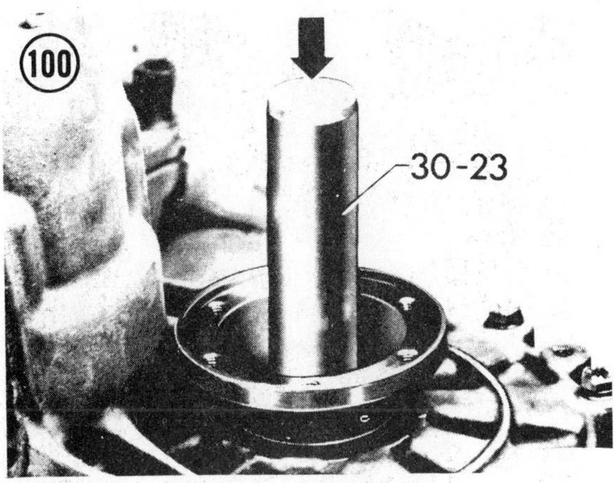

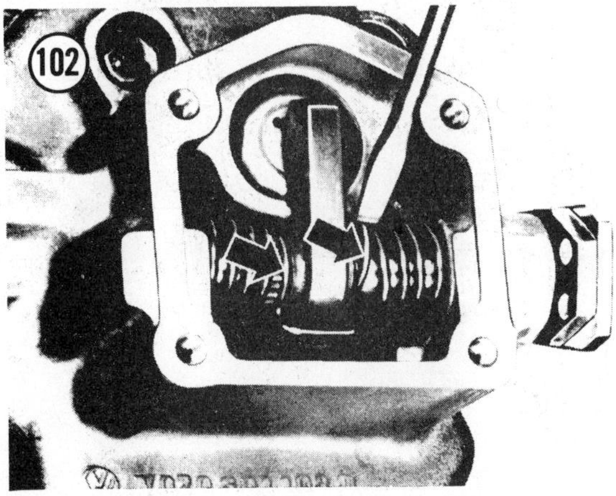

31. Install the 4th gear on the pinion drive shaft and secure it with a new circlip.

32. Using a new gasket, install the transmission housing on the final drive housing. Take care to align the transmission housing so that the main and pinion shafts enter their respective bearings and that mating dowels are aligned with their

holes. Use a tool as shown in **Figure 98** to press the case onto the supported main shaft. Install the attaching bolts and tighten them to 14 ft.-lb. (2.0 mkg).

33. Install the reverse sliding gear shaft support bolt through the hole in the transmission case (arrow, Figure 40) and tighten the bolt to 18 ft.-lb. (2.5 mkg).

NOTE: *If the attaching bolts are not fully threaded (as originally installed on 1975 and some 1976 models), obtain a set of the new fully threaded bolts and install them.*

34. Install a new circlip in the groove in the end of the main shaft, making sure it is fully seated. See **Figure 99** (starting the circlip) and **Figure 100** (pressing it in).

35. If drive flange oil seal replacement is needed, pry out the old seal and install a new one as shown in **Figure 101**.

36. Install the speedometer drive gear, making sure it meshes properly.

37. Pry out old and install new clutch lever oil seals. Lightly lubricate the release bearing shaft and install the guide sleeve, bearing, lever, return spring and shaft in the transmission housing as shown in **Figure 102**. Center of the spring must fit over the lever and the bent ends of the spring must contact the housing. Secure the shaft with new circlips (arrows, Figure 102). Install the cover and tighten the bolts to 11 ft.-lb. (1.5 mkg). Insert the clutch pushrod.

38. If the selector shaft oil seal requires replacement, pry out the old one **(Figure 103)** and install a new one **(Figure 104)**.

39. Make sure transmission is in neutral. Lightly lubricate the oil seal lips and the selector shaft. Install the shaft in the transmission housing. Install the control spring and the oil deflector plate. If so equipped, install the spring inside the cover and then install the cover, tightening it to 32 ft.-lb. (4.5 mkg). **Figure 105** is a cross section of the selector shaft and cover used on 1975 models, and **Figure 106** shows that used on later models (from transmission 25 085).

40. **Figure 107** shows the selector shaft adjuster used on early 1975 models, **Figure 108** shows that used on late 1975 models, and **Figure 109** shows the adjuster used on 1976 and later models. To adjust the early 1975 model, place the transmission in neutral and remove the protective cap from the adjuster. Turn the slotted plunger (1, Figure 107) until it bottoms (indicated by the nut starting to turn) and then back it off ¼ turn and install the plastic cap. On later 1975 models, place transmission in neutral and loosen the locknut (Figure 108) and turn the adjusting sleeve until a space can be seen between the lock ring and the adjusting sleeve. Loosen the adjusting sleeve ¼ turn and hold the sleeve while tightening the locknut. Install the plastic cap (not shown). On 1976 and later models, remove the plastic cap (not shown), make sure the treansmission is in neutral, and loosen the locknut (2, Figure 109). Turn the adjusting sleeve (1) until a gap can be seen between the sleeve and the lock ring (4). Turn the adjusting sleeve in the other direction until it barely touches the lock ring and tighten the locknut. Turn the shaft (3) slightly and make sure the lock ring lifts away from the adjusting sleeve as soon as the shaft is turned.

41. Remove the main shaft support tools (Figure 35) from the transmission and then remove then transmission from the workstand.

104

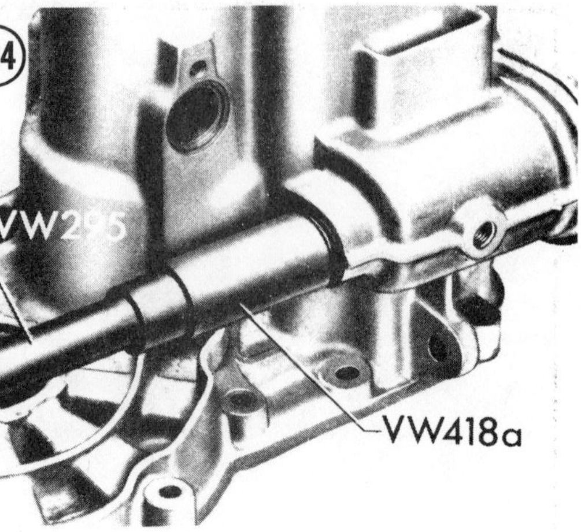

105

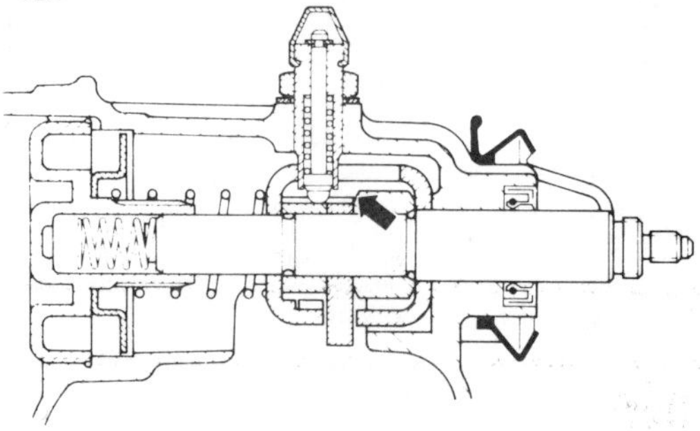

106

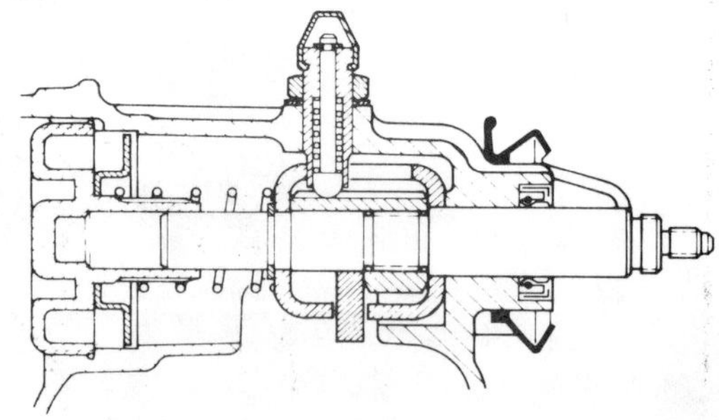

AUTOMATIC TRANSAXLE

The automatic transaxle contains a fully automatic, hydraulically controlled 3-speed transmission with a conventional torque converter. Gearshifts are automatic, depending on engine speed and accelerator position.

This section includes checks and adjustments to be performed with the transmission in the car. Many problems can be corrected with the adjustment procedures described here. Automatic transmission overhaul, however, requires

107

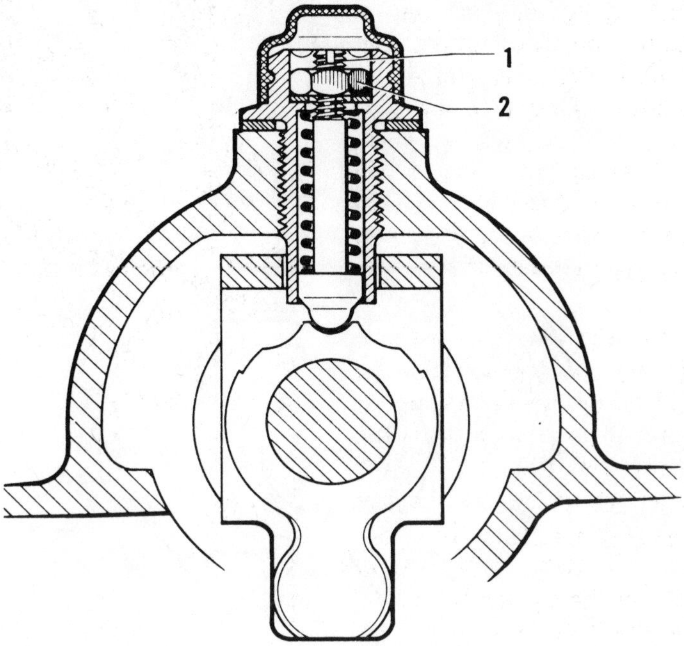

1. Plunger
2. Nut

108

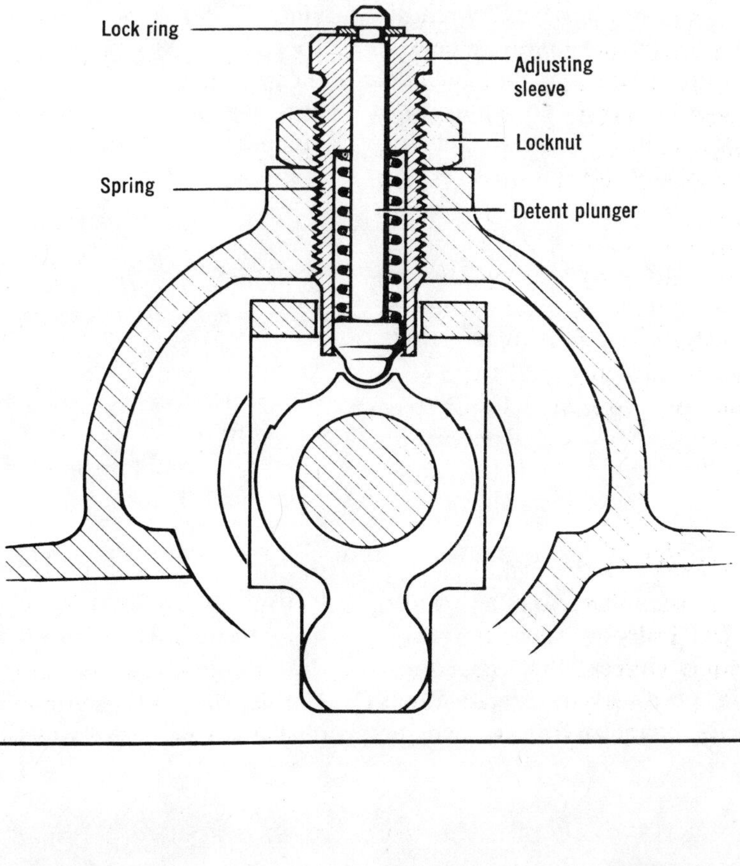

109

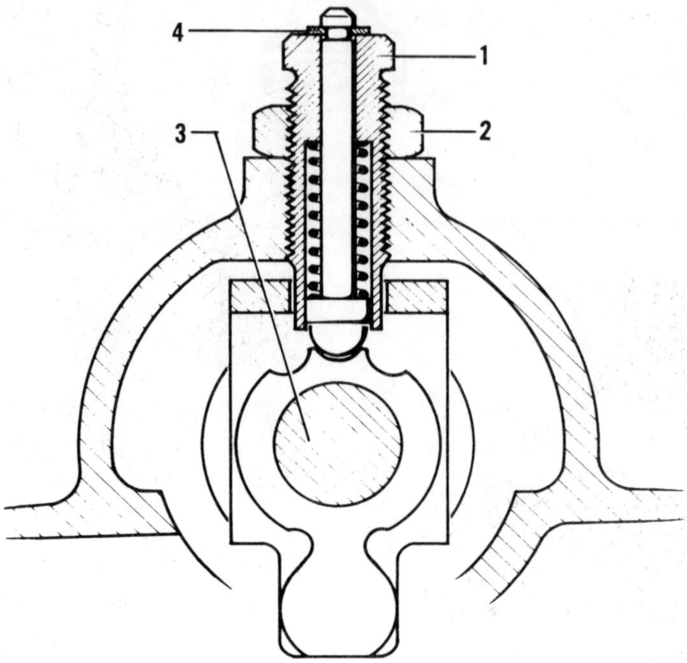

special skills, tools, and high standards of cleanliness not possessed by the average home mechanic.

Considerable money can be saved by removing the old transaxle and installing a new or rebuilt one yourself. This chapter includes removal and installation procedures, plus other simple repairs. See Chapter Three for lubrication and preventive maintenance.

Road Test

1. Check that starter operates only in P and N. Ensure that the back-up light operate only in R.
2. With the footbrake applied and the engine running at normal idle, move the selector from N to D, N to 2, N to 1, and N to R. The shift into each gear should be noticeable. If it is harsh, check the engine idle or kickdown cable adjustment.
3. Connect a tachometer to the engine. Jack up the rear wheels, set the handbrake, and warm up the engine. Fully depress the footbrake, engage D, and fully depress the accelerator. Compare the stall speed with the specifications in **Table 2** (end of chapter) for your engine type. If the stall speed indicated on the tachometer is more than 400 rpm below the specification, the torque converter or one-way clutch is defective and must be replaced. A stall speed up to 200 rpm below the specification indicates the engine is not delivering full output and probably needs a tune-up. A stall speed higher than specified indicates the transmission is slipping.

CAUTION
Do not run the engine at full load for more than 10 seconds or the transmission may be seriously damaged.

4. With the transmission at normal operating temperature, select D and slowly accelerate. Check for upshifts from 1-2 and 2-3.
5. Compare full throttle upshift and kickdown points with **Table 3**.
6. Come to a full stop, engage 1, and with full throttle, accelerate to 20 mph (30 kph). The transmission should not slip and there should be no upshift. If possible to do so safely, repeat the test in R.
7. Stop the car on a grade. With the brakes applied shift to P. Release the brake and check

Table 3 SHIFT POINTS—MPH

Shift	Full Throttle	Kickdown
1 - 2	20 - 23	36 - 39
2 - 3	51 - 55	68 - 69
3 - 2	31 - 36	64 - 65
2 - 1	15 - 17	32 - 35

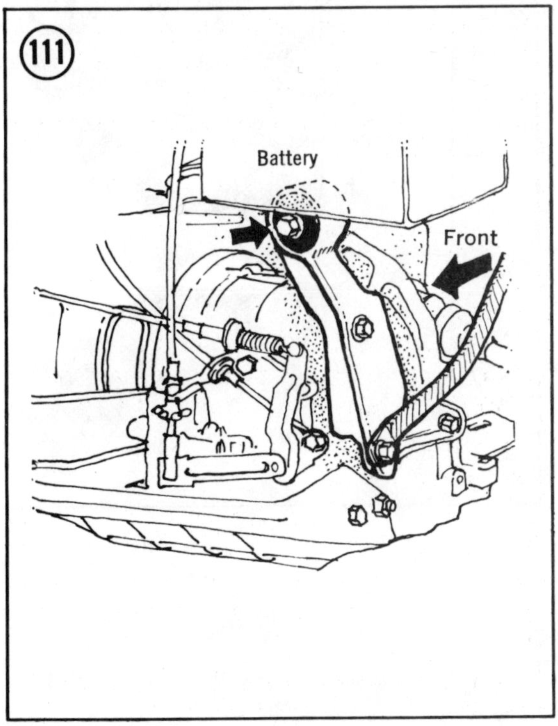

that the parking pawl holds the car. Test with the car facing up the hill and down the hill. Depress the brakes before shifting out of P.

Removal/Installation

The automatic transaxle can be removed without removing the engine.

1. Disconnect battery cables at battery.
2. Disconnect speedometer cable at transaxle.
3. Improvise a tool similiar to that shown in **Figure 110** to lift up on the cast hole in the cylinder head and support the engine.

CAUTION
Make sure that the tool bears on the insides of the fenders and not on the tops which could be dented.

4. Connect a chain hoist to the transaxle. See **Figure 110**.
5. Remove the transaxle side carrier. See (4), **Figure 111**.
6. Remove rear transaxle carrier. See **Figure 112**.
7. Disconnect drive shafts from transaxle as described in Chapter Ten and hang ends up with wire.
8. Remove starter.
9. Remove transaxle and torque converter cover plates.
10. Remove 3 bolts securing torque converter to drive plate. See **Figure 113**.
11. Move selector lever to P and disconnect cable at transaxle.

12. Remove bolts securing cable bracket to transaxle.

13. Disconnect side transaxle carrier from transaxle.

14. Disconnect side transaxle mount from transaxle.

15. Lift transaxle slightly with chain hoist.

16. Swing left drive shaft up.

17. Remove bolts securing transaxle to engine.

18. Pull transaxle to left and lower.

19. Secure torque converter with strap to keep it from falling out.

20. Installation is the reverse of these steps. Keep the following points in mind:

   a. Tighten nuts and bolts shown in **Figure 111** at points (3), (14), and (15) to 39 ft.-lb. (5.5 mkg).
   b. Tighten torque converter bolts to 22 ft.-lb. (3 mkg).
   c. Tighten drive shaft bolts to 32 ft.-lb. (4.5 mkg).
   d. Make sure that transmission carrier is centered as shown in **Figure 114**.
   e. Make sure torque converter is fully seated in support (arrow, **Figure 115**) and can be turned by hand. Distance (a) should be $1\frac{13}{16}$ in. (30mm).

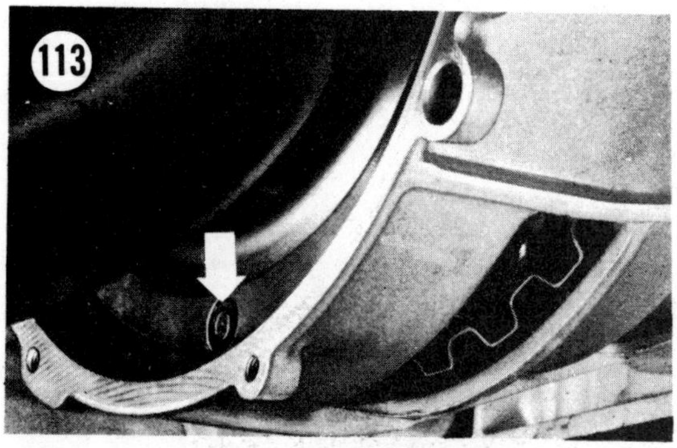

Selector Lever

Figure 116 shows details of the selector lever. After replacing any selector lever components, adjust the linkage as follows.

1. Shift lever into P and loosen the clamp screw on the transaxle end of the cable.

2. Move transaxle lever as far to left as possible and tighten clamp screw.

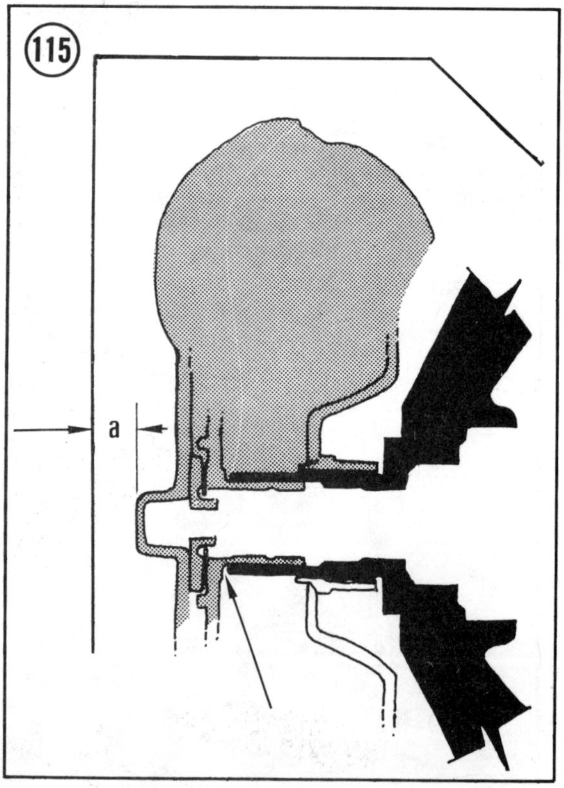

116

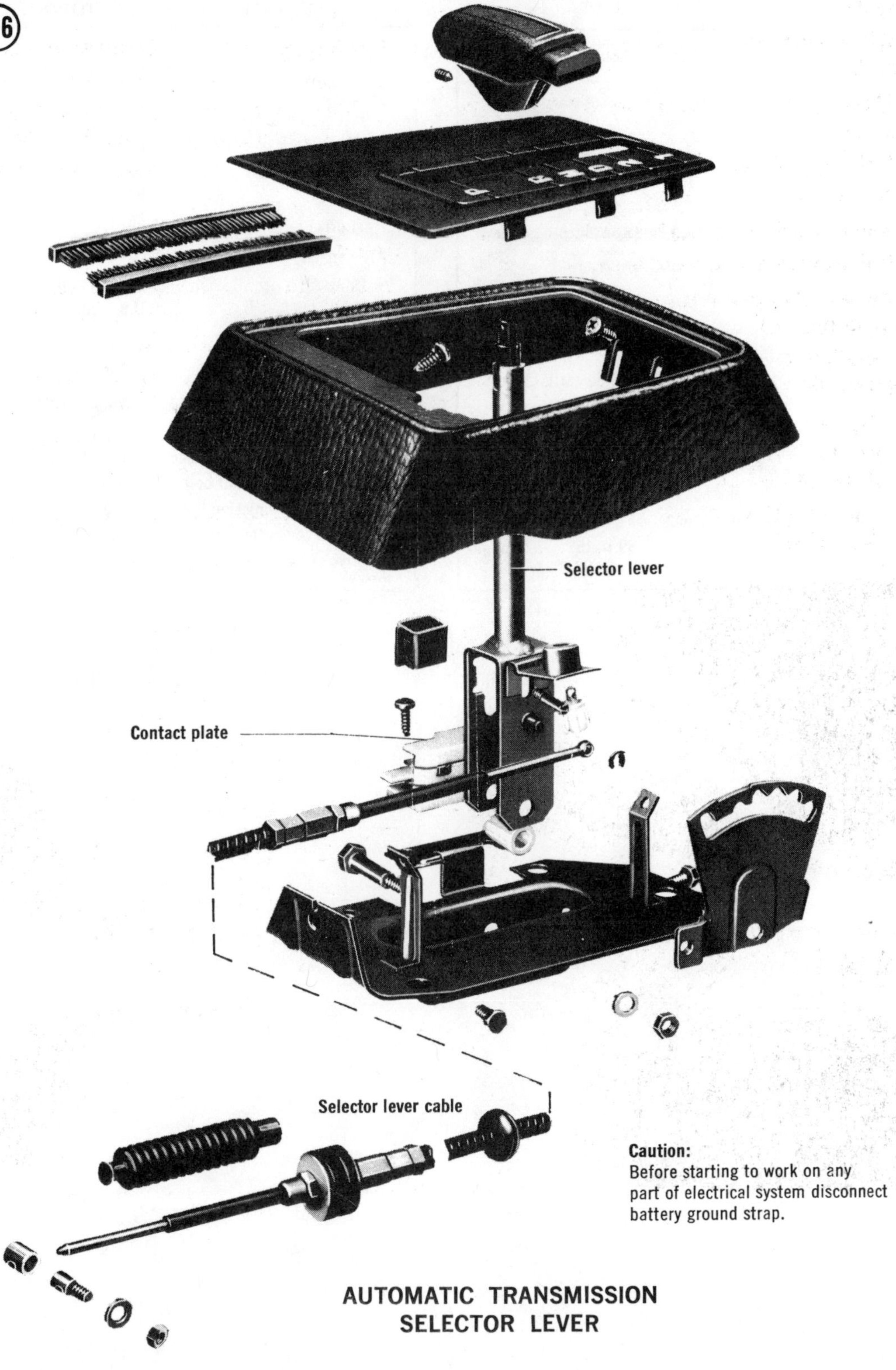

Caution:
Before starting to work on any part of electrical system disconnect battery ground strap.

AUTOMATIC TRANSMISSION SELECTOR LEVER

Table 1 MANUAL TRANSAXLE SPECIFICATIONS AND TORQUE VALUES

Item	Specification		
Gear ratios			
1st	3.45		
2nd	1.94		
3rd	1.37		
4th	0.97		
Reverse	3.17		
Final drive ratio	3.9		
Oil capacity	3.8 U.S. pints		
Lubricant	Hypoid SAE 80 (MIL-L2105)		
Torque values			
Flywheel retaining bolts		14 ft.-lb.	2.0 mkg.
Pressure plate retaining bolts		54 ft.-lb.	7.5 mkg.
Transmission-to-engine bolts		39 ft.-lb.	5.5 mkg.
Engine mounting support bolts		39 ft.-lb.	5.5 mkg.
Nut (Figure 20)		39 ft.-lb.	5.5 mkg.

Table 2 AUTOMATIC TRANSAXLE SPECIFICATIONS AND TORQUES

Item	Specification	
Gear ratios		
1st	2.65	
2nd	1.59	
Drive	1.00	
Reverse	1.80	
Final drive ratio	4.091	
ATF capacity		
Total	12.5 U.S. pints	
Refill	6 U.S. pints	
Final drive capacity	2.1 U.S. pints	
Lubricants	See Table 4, Chapter Two	
Converter stall speed	1,900-2,200 rpm	
Torque values		
Engine/transmission upper bolts	39 ft.-lb.	(5.5 mkg.)
Transmission mount bolts	39 ft.-lb.	(5.5 mkg.)
Engine/transmission lower bolts	39 ft.-lb.	(5.5 mkg.)
Torque converter bolts	22 ft.-lb.	(3.0 mkg.)
Drive shaft bolts	32 ft.-lb.	(4.5 mkg.)

CHAPTER NINE

BRAKES

The brake system has 2 independent circuits. Each independent brake circuit operates one front brake and one rear brake, diagonally opposite. See **Figure 1**. Therefore, in the event of complete failure in one circuit, the other circuit still provides 50% of the total brake effectiveness. Negative steering roll radius built into the front axle counteracts the tendency of the car to veer to one side if one brake circuit is defective.

The cable operated mechanical handbrake acts on the rear wheels when the hand lever is drawn up. The rear brake shoes expand to provide emergency or parking brakes.

This chapter describes repair procedures for all parts of the brake system. **Table 1** at the end of this chapter provides specifications.

MASTER CYLINDER

Removal/Installation

1. Place rags under the master cylinder to protect the body paint.
2. Remove brake fluid from reservoir with a siphon used exclusively for brake fluid.
3. Disconnect brake lines at master cylinder. See **Figure 2**.

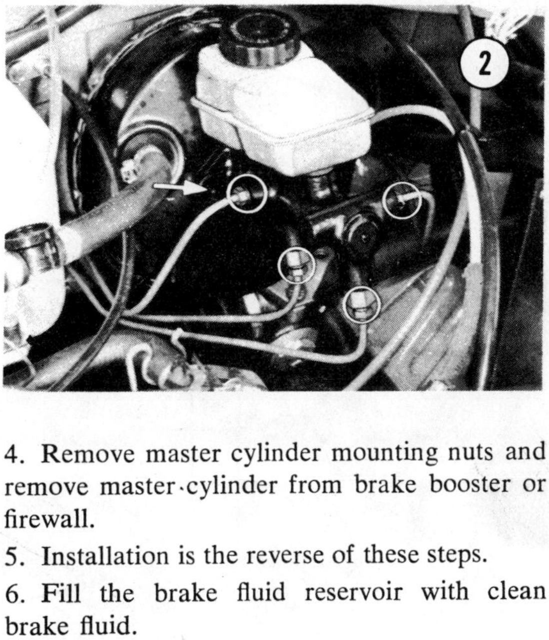

4. Remove master cylinder mounting nuts and remove master cylinder from brake booster or firewall.
5. Installation is the reverse of these steps.
6. Fill the brake fluid reservoir with clean brake fluid.
7. Bleed entire brake system as described later.

Disassembly

Refer to **Figures 3, 4, and 5** for the following procedure.

1. Hold the master cylinder in a vise. Pull the brake fluid reservoir straight up with both hands.

1

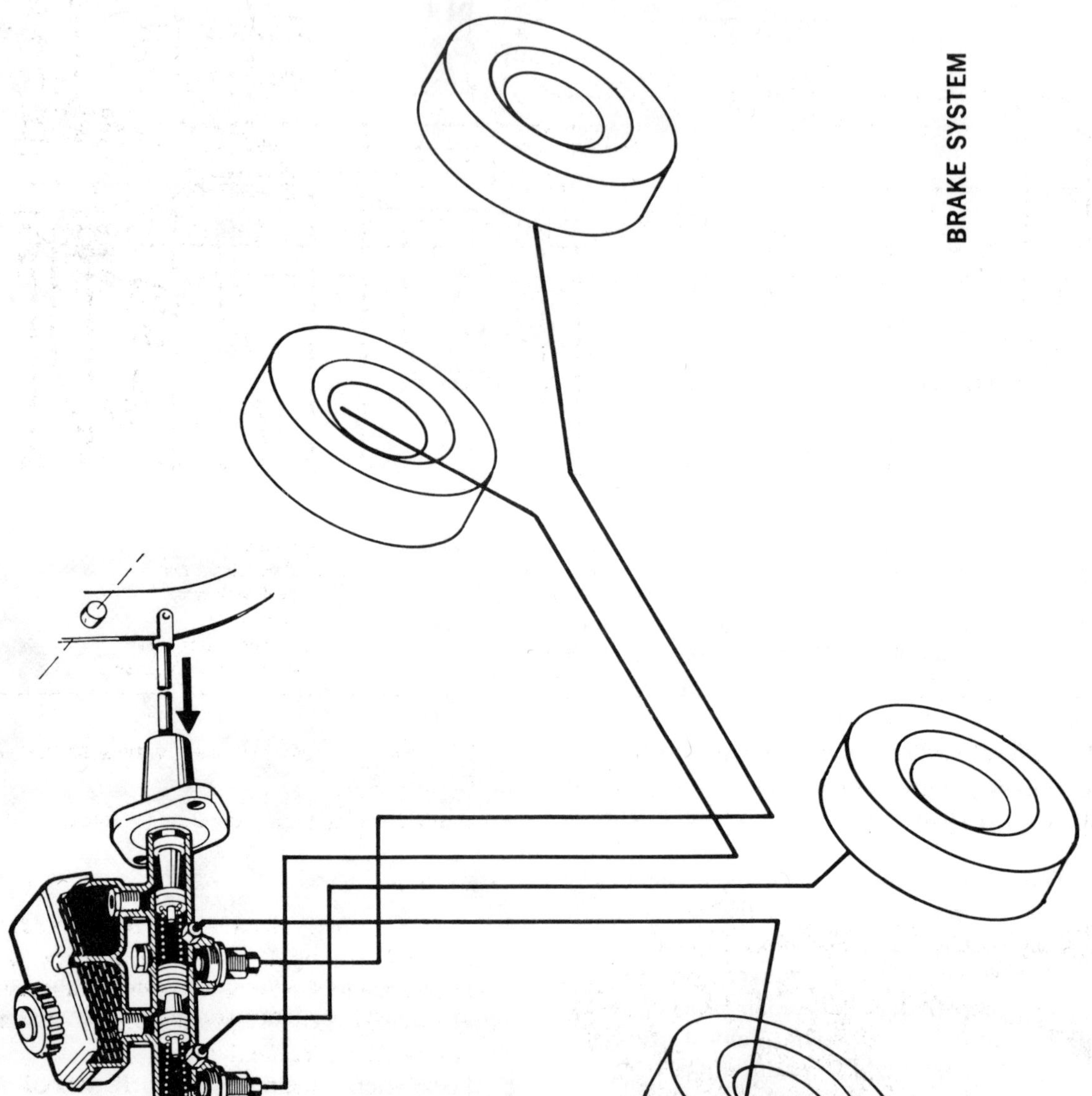

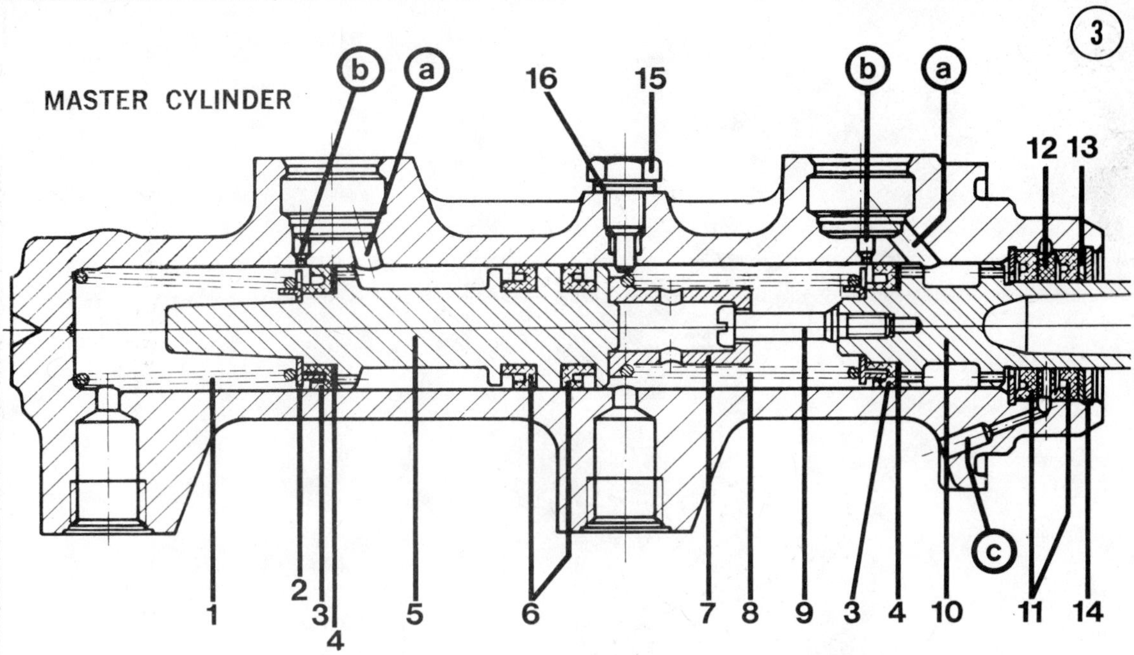

1. Secondary spring
2. Support disc
3. Primary cup
4. Filler disc
5. Intermediate piston
6. Separating cup
7. Stop sleeve
8. Primary spring
9. Inner stop screw
10. Pressure piston
11. Secondary cup
12. Intermediate cup
14. Circlip
15. Outer stop screw
16. Seal, stop screw
a. Filler bore
b. Compensating hole
c. Air compensating hole

2. Remove seal (C) shown in **Figure 6**.

3. Remove circlip from master cylinder as shown in Figure 6.

4. Loosen outer stop screw (A) shown in Figure 4.

5. Remove primary and secondary pistons. If the secondary piston does not shake out easily, blow it out with compressed air.

6. Unscrew residual pressure valves as shown in Figure 4.

7. Remove seals from secondary piston.

Inspection

Clean all parts in clean brake fluid or methylated spirits (denatured alcohol) which does not contain benzene. Do not use gasoline, kerosene, or trichlorethylene. If in doubt about a solvent, do not use it; use brake fluid.

Examine the cylinder walls. If scored or scratched, hone the cylinder with a brake hone, following manufacturer's instructions. Carefully clean the cylinder after honing and be sure all passages are clear.

Assembly

1. Assemble all parts for the secondary piston as shown in **Figure 7**. Use all new parts except for the piston itself. Be sure the seals face in the proper direction.

4

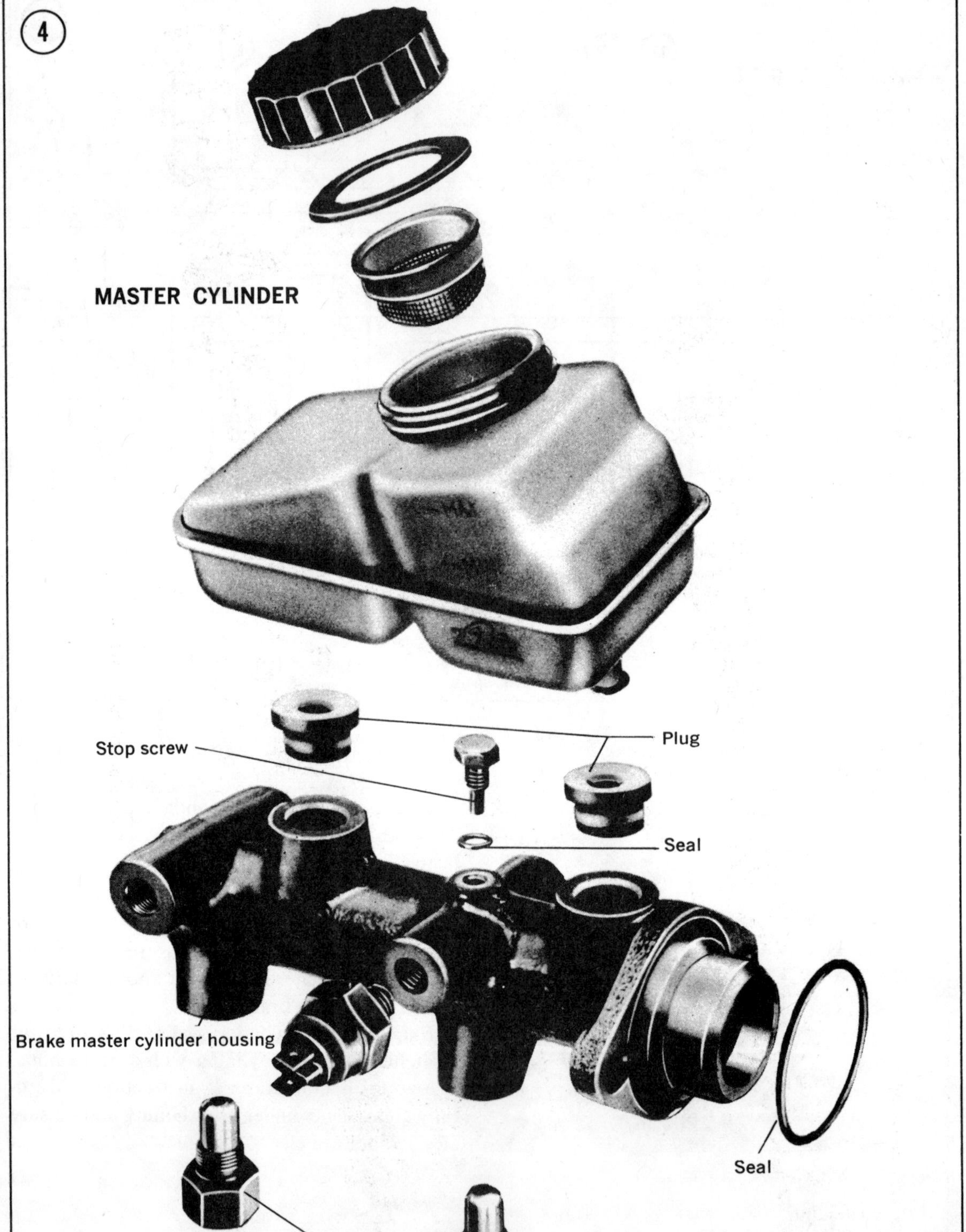
MASTER CYLINDER
Plug
Stop screw
Seal
Brake master cylinder housing
Seal
Residual pressure valves

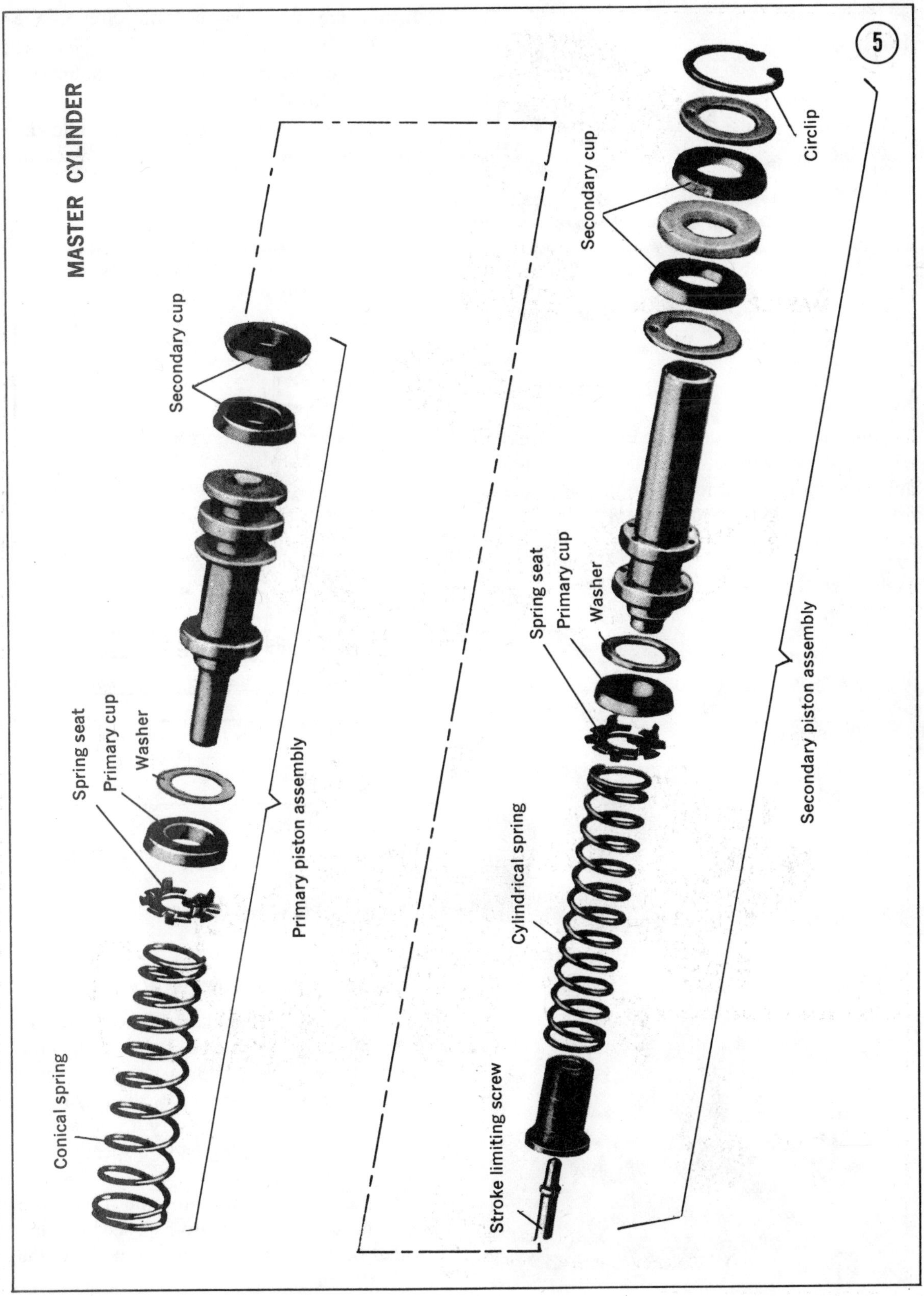
MASTER CYLINDER
5
Secondary cup
Spring seat
Primary cup
Washer
Primary piston assembly
Conical spring
Circlip
Secondary cup
Spring seat
Primary cup
Washer
Secondary piston assembly
Cylindrical spring
Stroke limiting screw

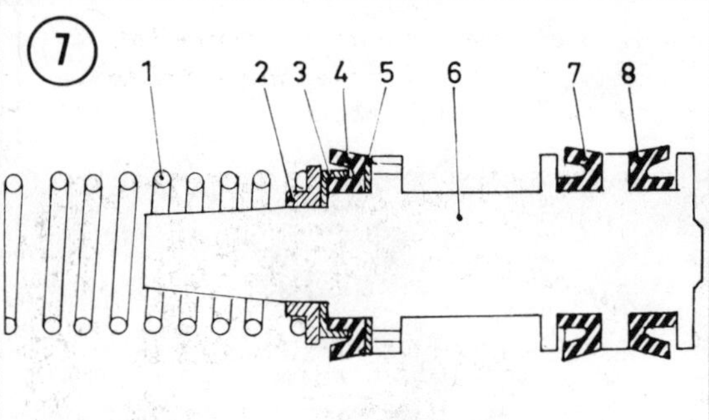

1. Spring
2. Spring plate
3. Back-up ring
4. Piston seal
5. Washer
6. Piston
7. Piston seal
8. Piston seal

2. Lubricate the cylinder with brake fluid. Dip the secondary piston assembly in brake fluid. Slide the spring on and insert the secondary piston in the cylinder. See **Figure 8**.

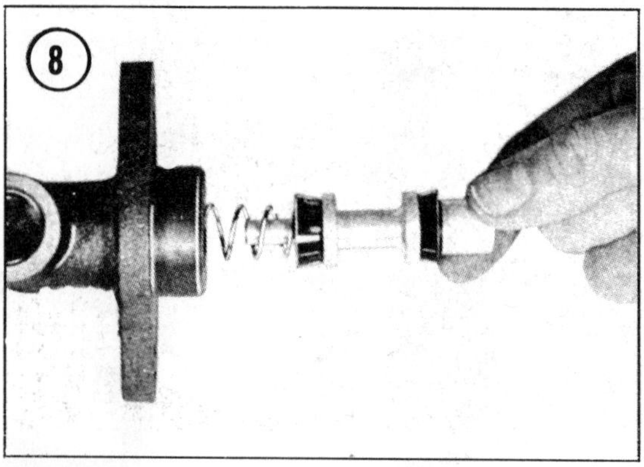

3. Dip a new primary piston in brake fluid and insert it in the cylinder. See **Figure 9**.

4. Install the stop washer and circlip. See Figure 4.
5. Install the stop screw and seal in the master cylinder. See Figure 4.
6. Insert a soft 25-gauge copper wire into the compensating holes to be sure they are clear. See **Figure 10**.

CAUTION
Do not use a drill bit or steel wire, as the holes may be enlarged.

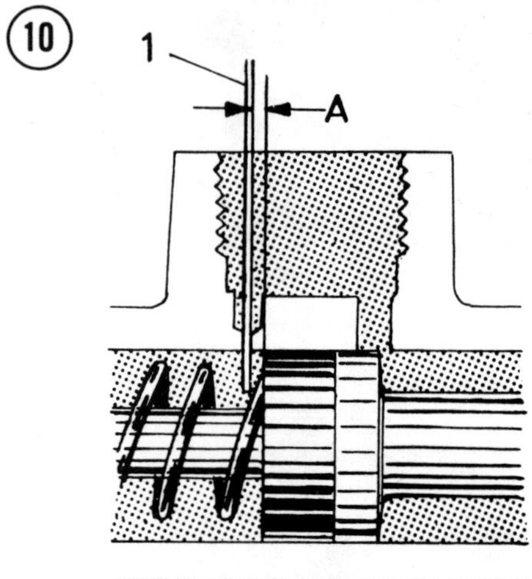

1.05mm (25 s.w.g.) soft copper wire
A = approx. 0.5mm (0.020 in.)

7. Install seal (Figure 4) on end of master cylinder.
8. Install the brake fluid reservoir.

BRAKE PAD REPLACEMENT

The brake pads should be inspected every 10,000 miles. They should be replaced when the lining thickness is ⅛ in. (3mm) or less. Never allow the linings to wear to less than 1/16 in. (1.5mm). It is rarely necessary to bleed the brakes after a simple pad inspection or replacement of pads.

Replacement procedures for the Teves and the Girling calipers vary. Both procedures are provided below. However, both calipers use the same brake pads.

Teves Caliper

1. Jack up the car on jackstands and remove front wheels.

2. Remove spring locks from retaining pins. See **Figure 11**.

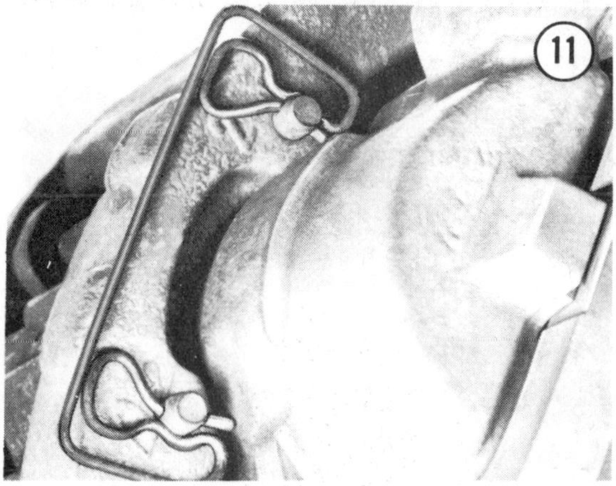

3. Drive out retaining pins with a punch. See **Figure 12.**

4. Remove the cross spring.

CAUTION
New cross springs are included in the repair kit and must always be installed when new pads are installed.

5. Pull brake pads out as shown in **Figure 13**. A piece of stiff wire bent in a loop with a hook in the 2 ends makes a suitable tool.

NOTE: *When removing the outer pad, the floating portion of the caliper must be pressed outward so the pad can be pulled out. See* **Figure 14**.

CAUTION
If brake pads are to be reinstalled, mark them so that they are installed in the same position.

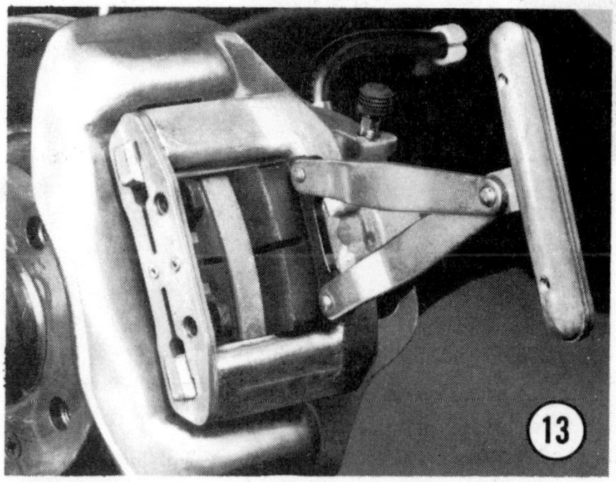

6. Carefully clean out the cavity which holds the brake pads. Inspect the rubber dust cover and if damaged, replace it. If dirt has penetrated the cylinder due to a damaged cover, recondition the brake caliper as described later.

7. Before installing new brake pads, push the pistons in as shown in **Figure 15**. Open the bleed valve to make this easier. The master cylinder may overflow when the pistons are pushed in. Draw some fluid out first to prevent this, and discard the fluid. Also, place rags under the master cylinder to protect the paint.

CAUTION
Do not let brake fluid spill on the brake pads or discs.

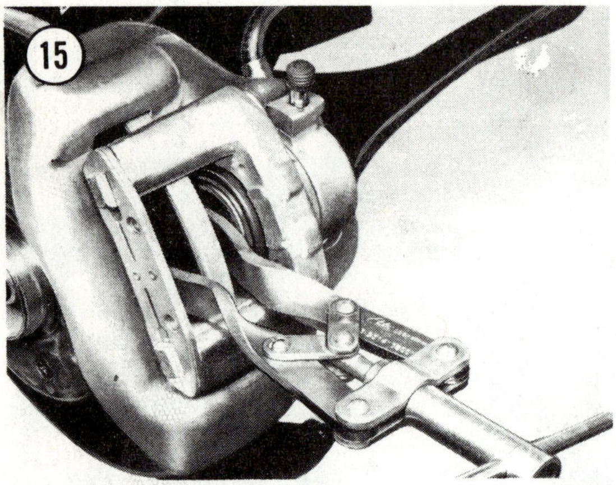

8. Be sure that the piston is at a 20° angle as shown in **Figure 16**. Use tool P-84 for this purpose. If necessary, reposition the piston.

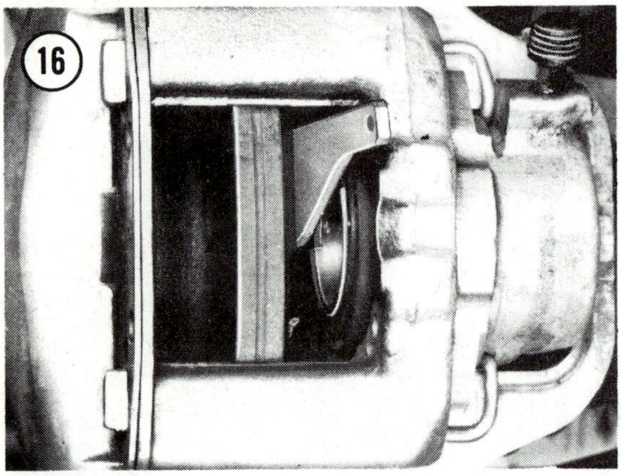

9. Install new brake pads. Make sure the dust cup in the brake cylinder is not damaged when installing the inner brake pad.

10. Install a new cross spring.

11. Install the pad retaining pins into the caliper. Drive the pin in with a hammer only, not a punch, so that the pin is not inadvertently driven in too far.

12. Press the brake pedal several times before driving the car so that the pads can assume correct alignment with respect to the brake disc.

Girling Caliper

1. Jack up the car on jackstands and remove the front wheels.

2. Pry off spreader spring with a screwdriver. See **Figure 17**.

3. Remove bolt and pull pad retainer out with pliers. See **Figure 18**.

4. Pull brake pads out as shown in **Figure 19**. A piece of stiff wire bent in a loop with a hook at the ends makes a suitable tool.

CAUTION

If brake pads are to be reinstalled, mark them so that they are installed in the same position.

5. Carefully clean out the cavity which holds the brake pads. Inspect the rubber dust cover and if damaged, replace it. If dirt has penetrated the cylinder due to a damaged cover, recondition the caliper as described later.

6. Before installing new pads, push pistons in as shown in Figure 15 (Teves caliper shown). Open the bleed valve to make this easier. The master cylinder may overflow when the pistons are pushed in. Draw some fluid out first to pre-

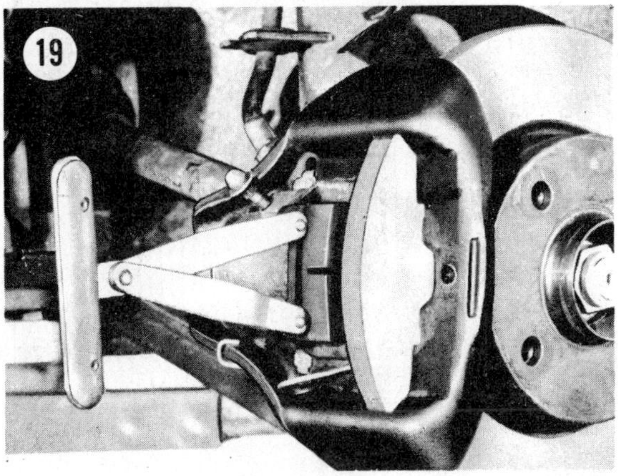

vent this, and discard the fluid. Also, place rags under the master cylinder to protect the paint.

CAUTION
Do not let brake fluid spill on brake pads, disc, or painted surfaces.

7. Install new brake pads. Do not damage the dust cover in the caliper when installing the inner pad.
8. Install pad retainer and secure with bolt. See **Figure 20**. Tighten bolt to 14 ft.-lb. (2 mkg).

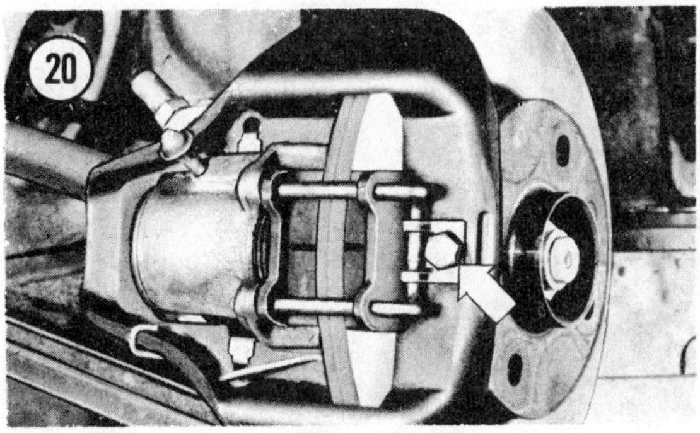

9. Install spreader spring with arrow pointing downward. See **Figure 21**.
10. Install wheels and lower car to ground.
11. Depress brake pedal several times before driving the car so that the pads can assume correct alignment with respect to the brake disc.

BRAKE CALIPERS

Removal/Installation

1. Jack up front of car on jackstands; remove front wheels.

2. Remove brake hose and cover end to prevent entry of dirt and moisture.
3. Remove mounting bolts. See **Figure 22**.
4. Remove the brake caliper.
5. Installation is the reverse of these steps. Tighten mounting bolts to 43 ft.-lb. (6 mkg).

Reconditioning Teves Caliper

The following procedure describes replacement of all parts included in the Teves caliper repair kit. Use all parts included in the kit. Refer to **Figure 23** for an exploded view of the caliper assembly.

NOTE: *Volkswagen recommends that the spring washers formerly used on retaining bolts be discarded when installing brake calipers. Tightening torque (Figure 23) remains unchanged.*

1. Remove brake pads as described earlier.
2. Pry mounting frame off floating frame. See **Figure 24**.
3. Drive brake cylinder and guide spring off floating frame. See **Figure 25**.
4. Remove clamp (**Figure 26**) from brake cylinder with appropriate pliers and remove the dust cap.
5. Pull piston out of cylinder. See **Figure 27**. If the piston is stuck, tighten the bleeder screw and force the piston out with compressed air introduced through the brake hose connection. See **Figure 28**. Even a bicycle tire pump should develop sufficient pressure.

9

(22)

DISC BRAKE ASSEMBLY
(Shown with Teves Caliper)

23

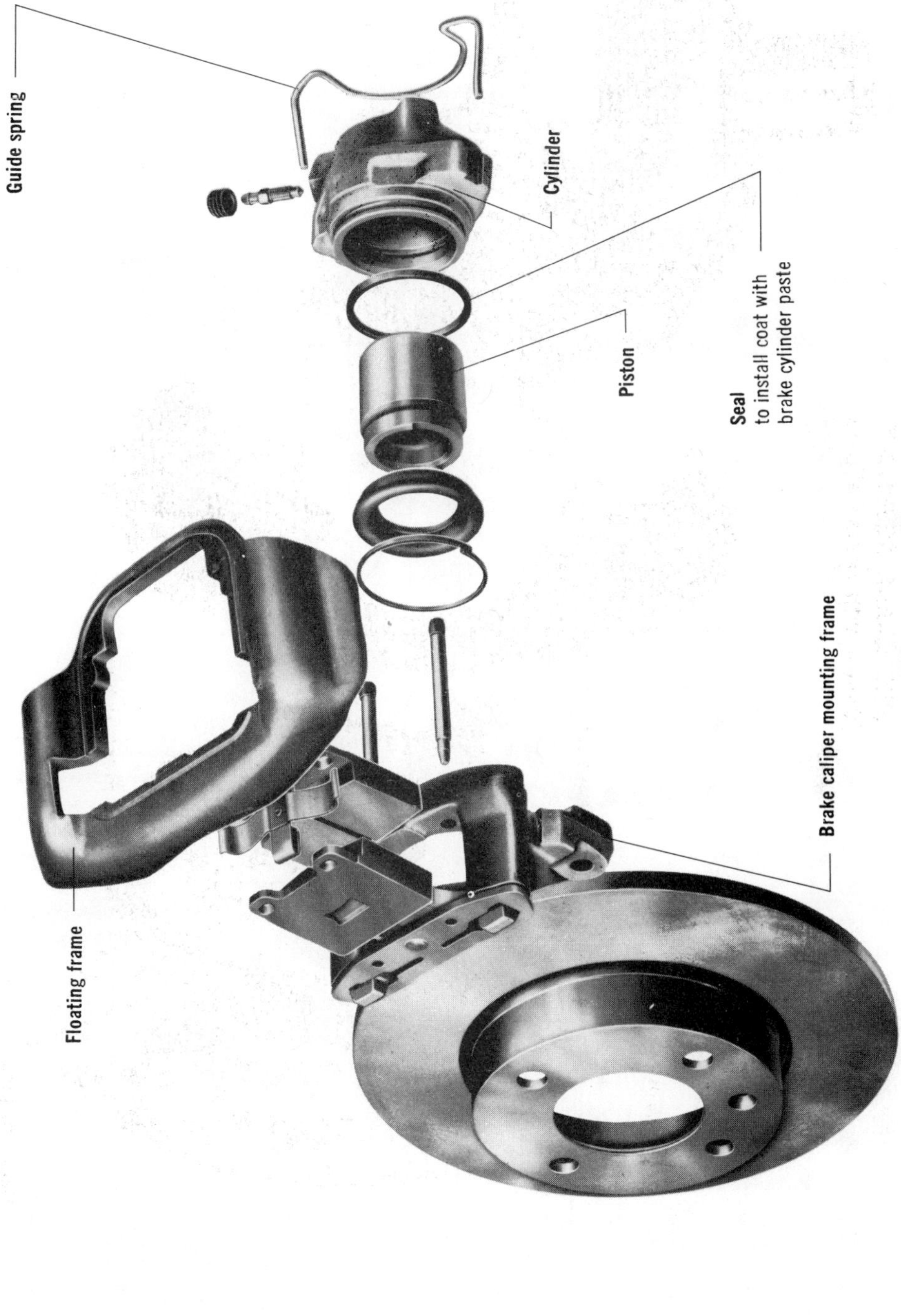

TEVES CALIPER ASSEMBLY

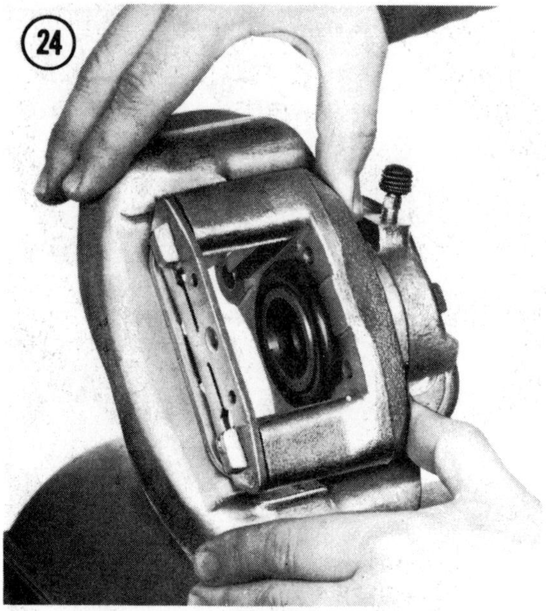

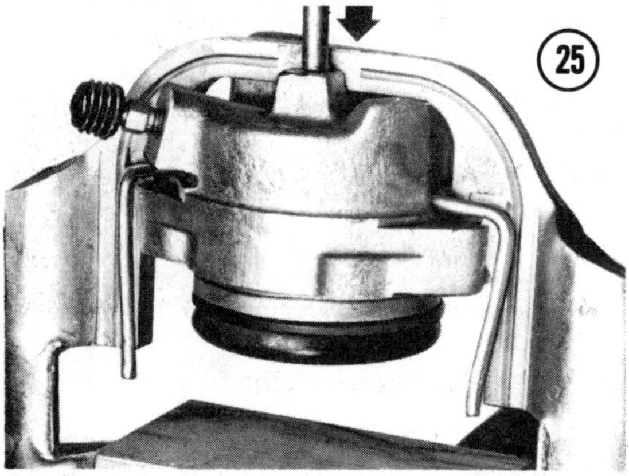

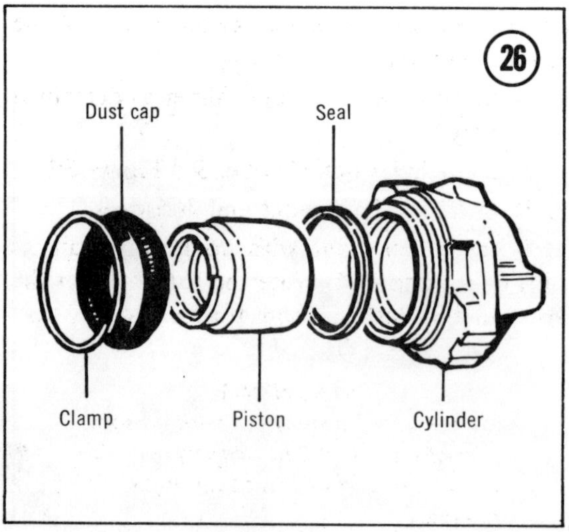

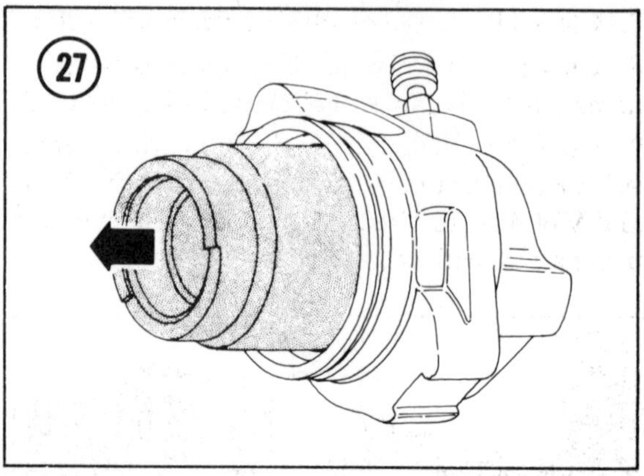

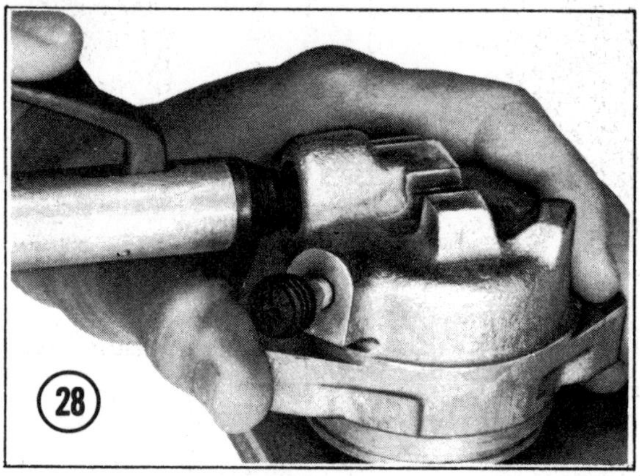

CAUTION

When using compressed air to force the piston out, support the piston on a wooden base because it flies out of the brake cylinder very suddenly and could be damaged.

6. Remove the seal from the brake cylinder. See **Figure 29**.

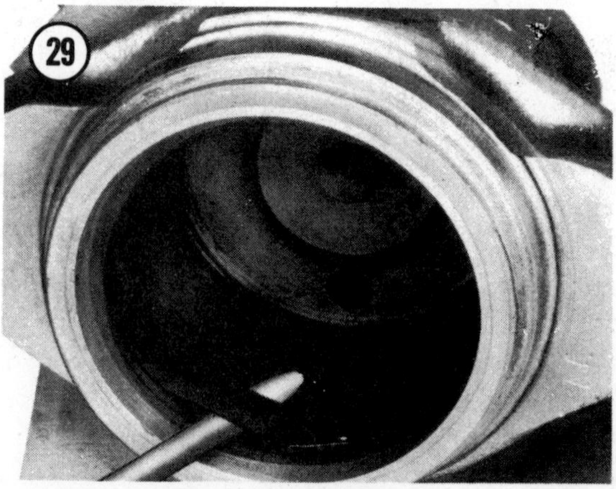

7. Clean all parts in alcohol or clean brake fluid.

8. Check parts for wear. If cylinder is worn or damaged, the complete caliper must be replaced.

9. Coat the rubber seal and piston with special ATE Brake Cylinder Paste available from Audi and VW dealers. Press the piston in the cylinder using a vise with soft jaws. See **Figure 30**.

10. Install a new dust cup over the piston. See Figure 26.

11. Place the guide pin in the groove of the brake cylinder and drive the brake cylinder on the floating frame with a brass drift (**Figure 31**).

12. Place the mounting frame in the guide spring and slide it on the floating frame. The mounting frame has grooves and is guided over the ribs of the floating frame. See **Figure 32**.

13. Insert tool P-84 and ensure that the piston recess inclines 20° from the lower guide area of the calipers. See **Figure 33**. Correct piston position if necessary.

Reconditioning Girling Caliper

The following procedure describes replacement of all parts included in the Girling caliper repair kit. Use all parts included in the kit. Refer to **Figure 34** for an exploded view of the caliper assembly.

1. Remove brake pads and caliper as described previously.

2. Press cylinder out of yoke. See **Figure 35**.

3. Remove retaining rings and dust caps.

4. Force pistons out with compressed air as shown in **Figure 36**. Note the soft jaws on the vise which act as backstops for the pistons.

WARNING

Do not force pistons out without some sort of backstop. They can fly out with considerable force causing injury or damage.

9

34

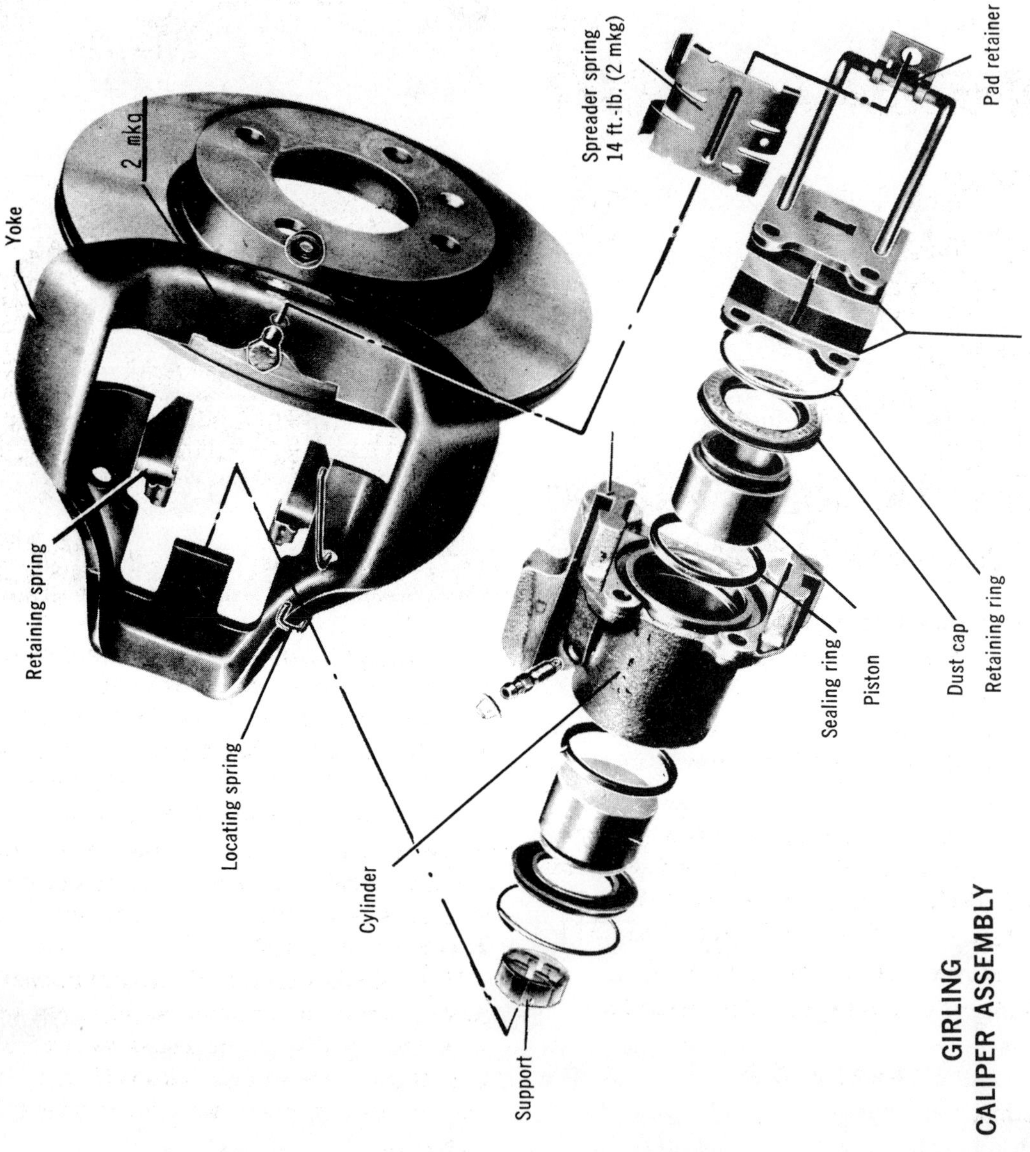

GIRLING
CALIPER ASSEMBLY

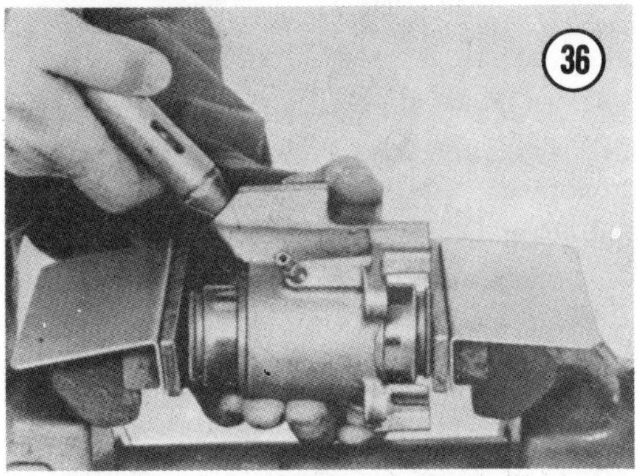

5. Remove seals from cylinder.
6. Clean all the parts in alcohol or in clean brake fluid.
7. Check all parts for wear. If cylinder is worn or damaged, the complete caliper must be replaced.
8. Coat the rubber seals and pistons with special ATE Brake Cylinder Paste available from Audi and VW dealers. Press the pistons in the cylinder using a vise with soft jaws. See **Figure 37**.
9. Install new dust caps over pistons.
10. Slide cylinder into yoke. See **Figure 38**.

BRAKE DISC

Inspection

Check the brake disc for deep scratches, excessive runout, and uneven thickness.

Small marks on the disc are not important, but deep radial scratches reduce braking effectiveness and increase pad wear.

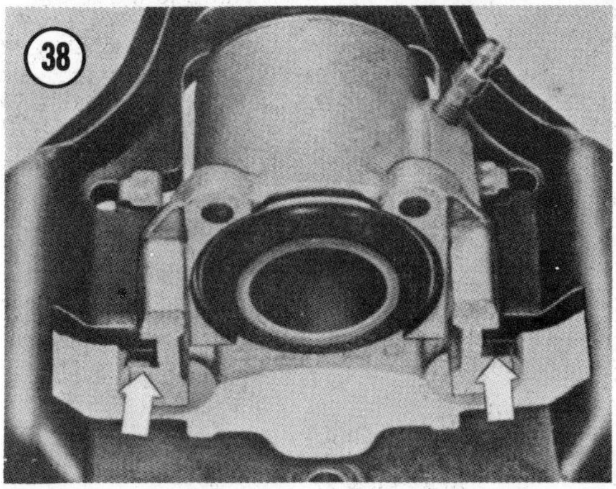

To check disc runout, mount a dial indicator as shown in **Figure 39** and rotate the disc; runout should not exceed 0.004 in. (0.1mm). This procedure assumes that the wheel bearings are in good condition. Check them if in doubt.

Check the thickness of the disc with a micrometer. Make about 12 measurements around the disc about one inch from the outer edge. Measurements should not vary more than 0.0008 in. (0.02mm).

If the disc has excessively deep scratches, excessive runout, or variation in thickness, renew or replace the disc. If the disc is renewed, minimum thickness must be at least 0.43 in. (11mm) and an equal amount must be removed from each side.

Removal/Installation

1. Raise front of vehicle on jackstands and remove wheels.

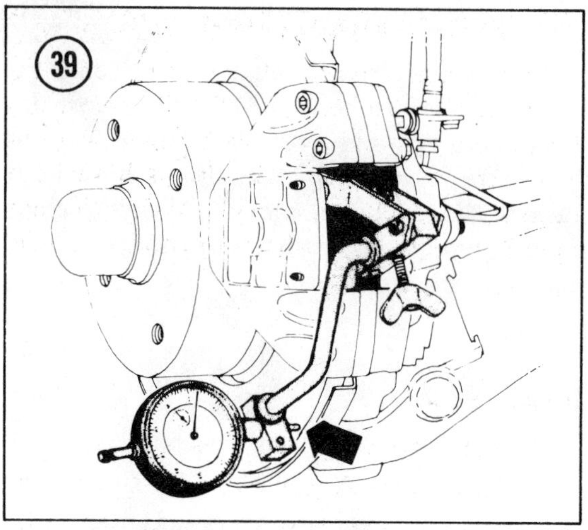

2. Remove caliper as described earlier, except leave brake hose attached and brake pads installed. Hang the assembly up with a piece of wire. See **Figure 40**.

3. Remove the small screw securing brake disc to the hub.

4. Pull off the brake disc. Do not use force, as force could cause damage.

5. Installation is the reverse of these steps.

FRONT BRAKE DRUMS (1975)

Removal/Installation

1. Put transmission in gear and pull up the handbrake.

2. Loosen the wheel lug bolts.

3. Raise front of car on jackstands.

4. Remove wheel lugs and wheel.

5. Remove screw securing drum. See **Figure 41**.

6. Pull drum off.

NOTE: *If necessary, loosen brake shoes with starwheel adjuster.*

7. Installation is the reverse of these steps.
8. Adjust brakes as described later.

Inspection

1. Blow brake dust and dirt from the brake drum. Remove grease and oil with cleaning solvent, blow dry.
2. Clean the drum braking surface with alcohol.
3. Inspect brake drums for scoring, cracking, taper, out-of-roundness, heat evidence, etc. Drums which are scored or worn should be turned by a dealer. Brake shoes must be replaced by oversized shoes. Cracked drums cannot be turned; replace them.
4. Remove glaze on serviceable drums with fine emery cloth.

FRONT BRAKE SHOES (1975)

Brake shoes require relining or replacement when linings are soaked with oil, grease, or brake fluid. In addition, replace linings worn to less than 1/16 in. If brake drums have been turned, use oversized linings. Always replace linings on both front wheels to ensure uniform braking.

Removal

Refer to **Figure 42** for this procedure.

1. Remove the brake drum as described earlier.
2. Remove 2 upper springs securing the shoes to the backing plate.
3. Remove the clips holding the shoes to the backing plate.
4. Lift off the shoes and the starwheel adjuster.
5. Separate shoes and lower springs.

Installation

Refer to Figure 42 for this procedure.

1. Mount brake shoes on backing plate with pins and clips.
2. Fit the starwheel adjuster between the shoes. Screw down the starwheel if necessary to fit it in. Make certain that the starwheel is over the adjustment hole in the backing plate.
3. Install 2 lower springs between shoes and backing plate.
4. Install 2 upper springs.
5. Install brake drum as described earlier.

Adjustment

1. Use screwdriver to turn starwheel adjuster clockwise until lining touches brake drum. See **Figure 43**.
2. Turn adjuster in opposite direction until wheel can be turned by hand. Slight rubbing or scraping noise is acceptable.
3. Back off adjuster an additional 2 notches. This will ensure that front wheels turn freely under all driving conditions.

43

REAR BRAKE DRUMS

Removal/Installation

Refer to **Figure 44** for this procedure.

> NOTE: *On 1979 models, before removing the wheel, remove one lug bolt and rotate the wheel until the hole from which the bolt was removed is at approximately the 11 o'clock position. Release the parking brake and insert a screwdriver through the hole.*

44

REAR BRAKE DRUM

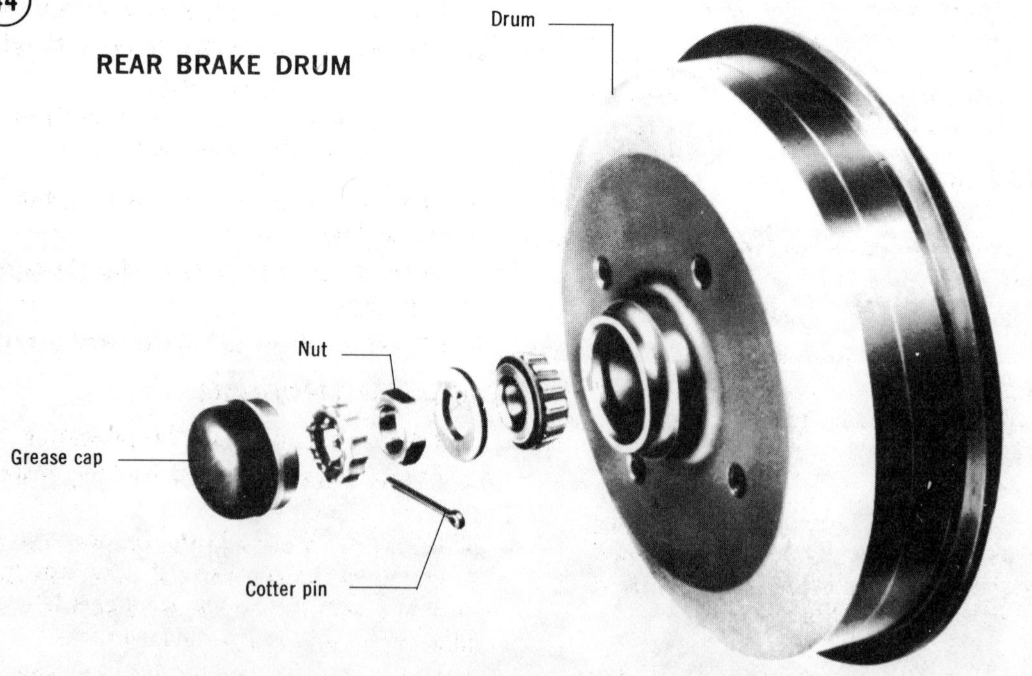

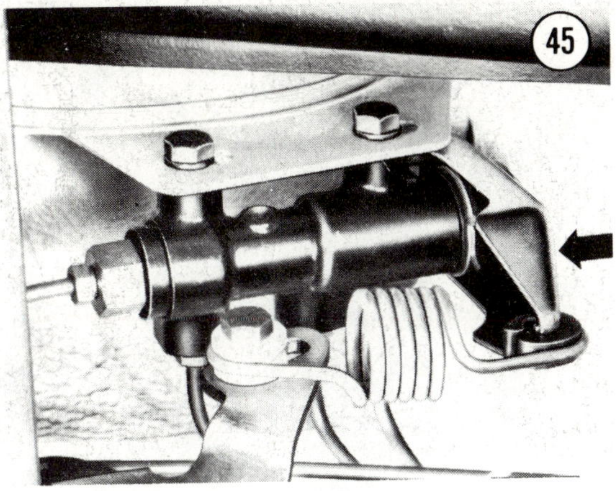

Push the adjusting wedge upward with the screwdriver until it reaches the stop. Then proceed as described in this procedure.

1. Put transmission in gear (manual) or PARK (automatic) and pull up the handbrake.
2. Loosen the rear wheel lug bolts.
3. Pry off dust cap on the wheel hub.
4. Remove the cotter pin and loosen the castellated nut on the axle stud.

CAUTION
Never loosen the nut unless all 4 wheels are firmly on the ground. The force required to loosen the nut is sufficient enough to knock the car off the jackstands.

5. Raise the rear of the car on jackstands and remove the rear wheels.
6. Remove the castellated nut, hex nut, and washer.
7. Release the parking brake.
8. Pull the brake drum off, making sure that the inner race of the outer bearing is not lost. Remove the inner race from the brake drum.

NOTE: *If removing the right rear brake drum, press the brake pressure regulator lever in the direction shown to relieve pressure in the right rear brake line. See* **Figure 45**.

9. Installation is the reverse of these steps.
10. Adjust brakes as described later.

Inspection

1. Blow brake dust and dirt from the brake drum. Remove grease and oil with cleaning solvent, blow dry.
2. Clean the drum braking surface with alcohol.
3. Inspect brake drums for scoring, cracking, taper, out-of-roundness, heat evidence, etc. Drums which are scored or worn should be turned by a dealer. Brake shoes must be replaced by oversized shoes. Cracked drums cannot be turned; replace them.
4. Remove glaze on serviceable drums with fine emery cloth.

REAR BRAKE SHOES

Brake shoes require relining or replacement when linings are soaked with oil, grease, or brake fluid. In addition, replace linings worn to less than 1/16 in. If brake drums have been turned, use oversized linings. Always replace linings on both rear wheels to ensure uniform braking.

Removal (1975-1978)

Refer to **Figure 46** for this procedure.

1. Remove the brake drum as described earlier.
2. Remove large U-shaped spring with pliers.

WARNING
Spring is under tension. Be careful that it does not fly out and injure you.

3. Remove 2 small springs securing the shoes to the backing plate.
4. Remove the clips holding the shoes to the backing plate.
5. Lift off the shoes and the starwheel adjuster.

Installation (1975-1978)

Refer to Figure 46 for this procedure.

1. Mount brake shoes on backing plate with pins and clips.
2. Fit the starwheel adjuster between the shoes. Screw down the starwheel if necessary to fit it in. Make certain that the starwheel is over the adjustment hole in the backing plate.
3. Install 2 small springs between shoes and backing plate.

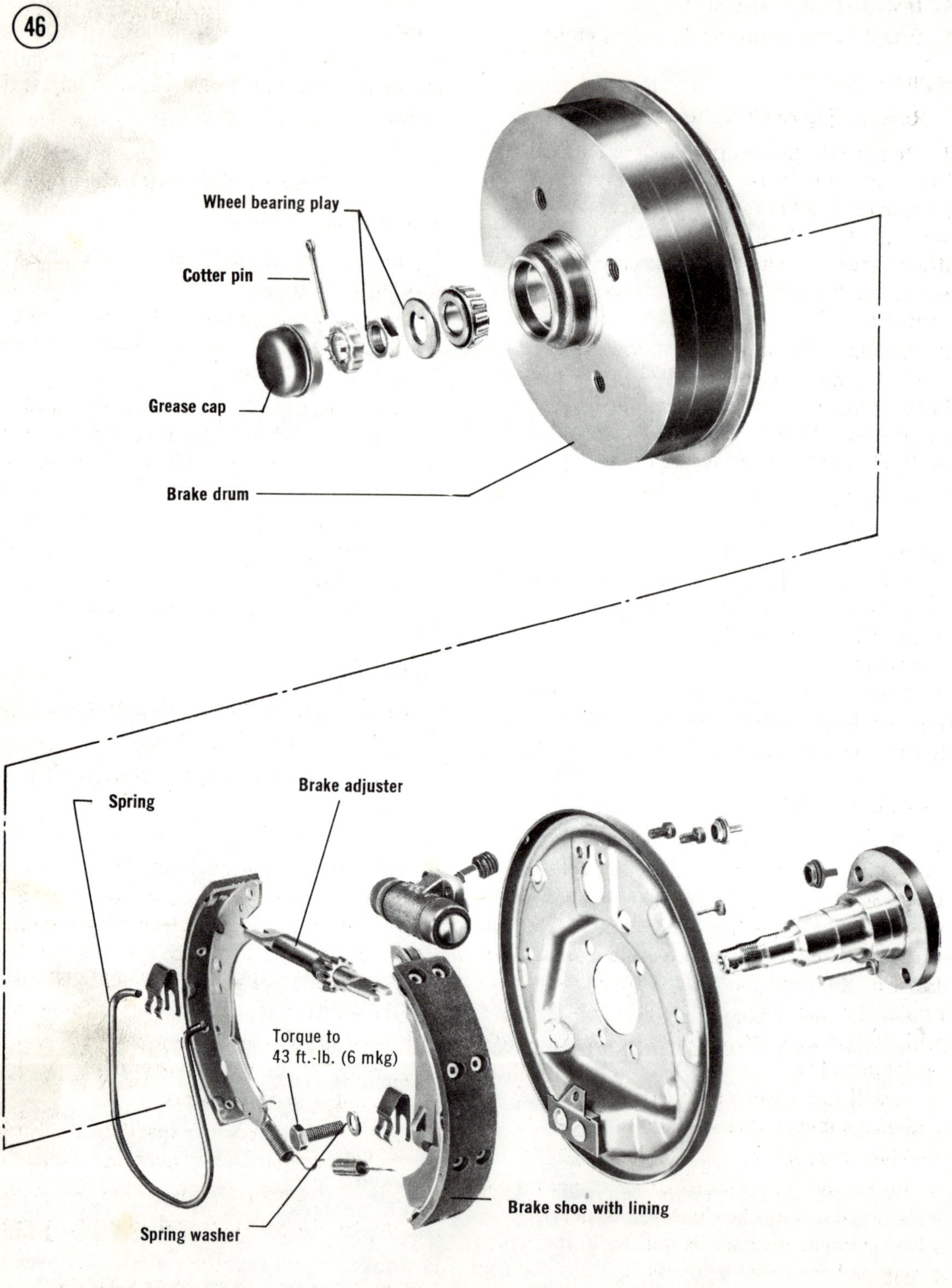

REAR BRAKE SHOES

4. Install large U-shaped spring.
5. Install brake drums as described earlier.

Removal (1979)

Refer to **Figure 47** for this procedure.

1. Remove the brake drum as described earlier. Make sure the brake pedal has not been depressed or handbrake has not been reset, as this will pull the adjusting wedge down again. If drum is hard to remove, push it up again as described in the NOTE preceding the drum removal procedure.
2. With the adjusting wedge pushed up as far as it will go, hold shoe retaining pins behind the backing plate and remove the spring retainers by pressing them in and turning them 90 degrees. Remove the springs and pins.
3. Carefully remove the brake shoes from the lower support and then remove the lower return spring.
4. Pull the parking brake lever attached to the shoe forward and detach the parking brake cable. Then unhook the spring from the adjusting wedge.
5. Remove the upper return spring and then remove the shoes from the car. Clamp the push bar in a vise and remove the tensioning spring.

Installation (1979)

1. Clamp the push bar in a vise and install the tensioning spring between the push bar and the brake shoe.
2. Install the adjusting wedge with the lug toward the backing plate, lubricate contact surfaces of the push bar with a small amount of brake lubricant, and then install the brake shoe with the parking brake lever to the other end of the push bar.
3. Install the upper return spring to the shoes and then connect the parking brake cable to the parking brake lever.
4. Install the shoes/push bar assembly on the backing plate with the shoes in contact with the wheel cylinder pistons. Install the lower return spring and then install the shoes on the lower support.
5. Connect the spring between the adjusting wedge and the brake shoe.
6. Install the retaining pins, springs, and retainers.
7. Install the brake drums as described earlier and then depress the brake pedal to adjust the brakes.

WHEEL CYLINDERS

Removal/Installation

1. Remove brake drum and brake shoes as described earlier.
2. Depress the brake pedal all the way and hold it with a support to close the compensating port in the master cylinder.
3. Disconnect the brake line at the wheel cylinder and cover it with the rubber cap from the bleeder screw to prevent entry of dirt and moisture.
4. Remove the bolts securing the wheel cylinder to the backing plate. Take the wheel cylinder off. See **Figure 48**.
5. Installation is the reverse of these steps.

Rebuilding

Refer to **Figure 49** for this procedure.

1. Remove rubber boots.
2. Remove pistons, cups, cup expanders, and springs.
3. Remove bleeder valve and adjusting screw.
4. Clean all parts in alcohol or clean brake fluid.
5. Examine the cylinder bore for scoring, pitting, or heavy corrosion. Very light scratches may be removed with crocus cloth. Flush out with alcohol and blow dry. Replace wheel cylinders which show more extensive damage.
6. Lubricate all parts with brake fluid or a thin coat of ATE Brake Cylinder Paste, available from Audi and VW dealers.
7. Install new cups, cup expanders, and springs provided in repair kit. Do not reuse old parts.
8. Install pistons and new rubber boots.
9. Install bleeder valve and adjusting screw.

FOOTBRAKE ADJUSTMENT

Only rear drum brakes require adjustment. Front disc brakes are self-adjusting.

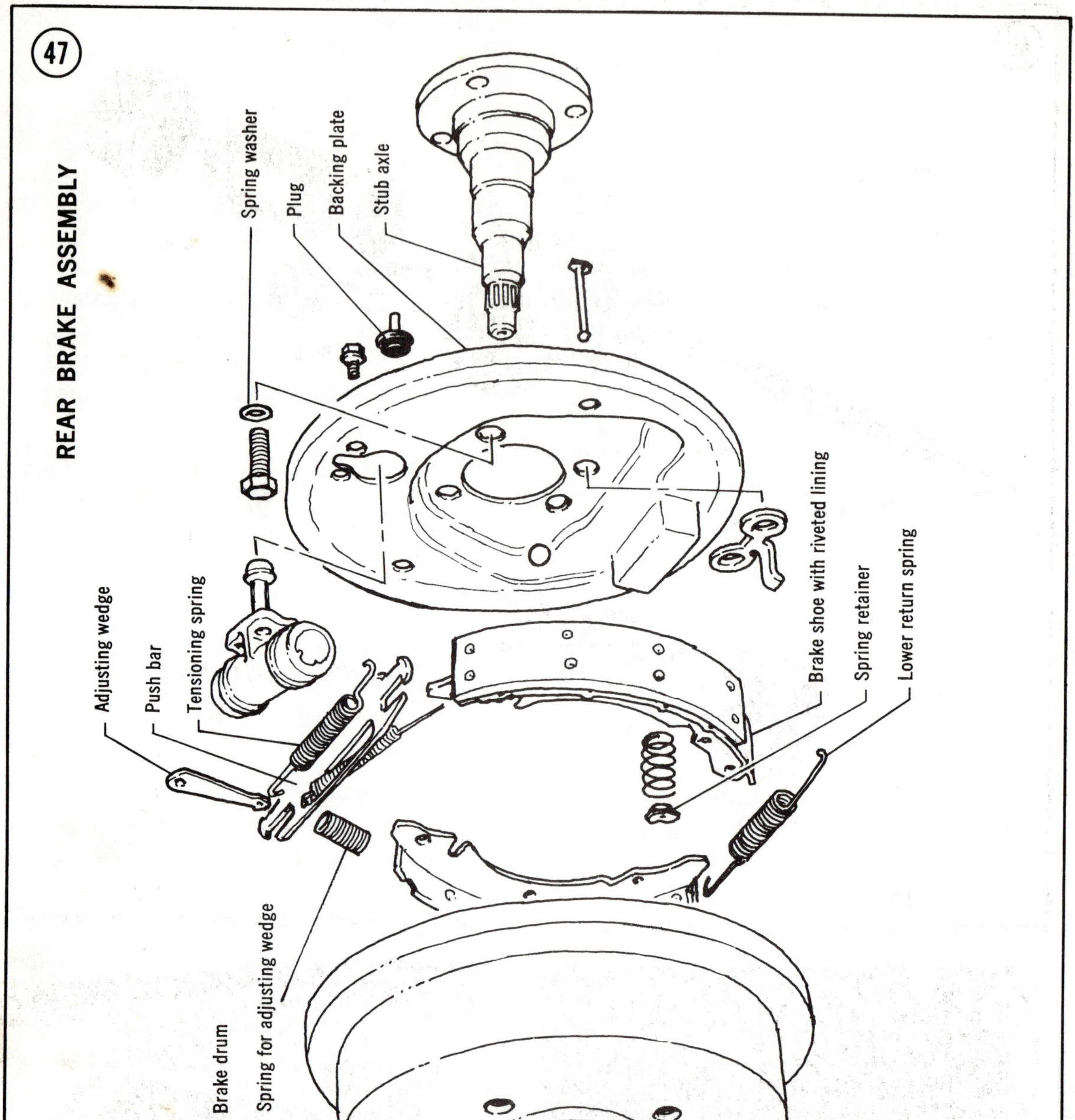

(47) REAR BRAKE ASSEMBLY

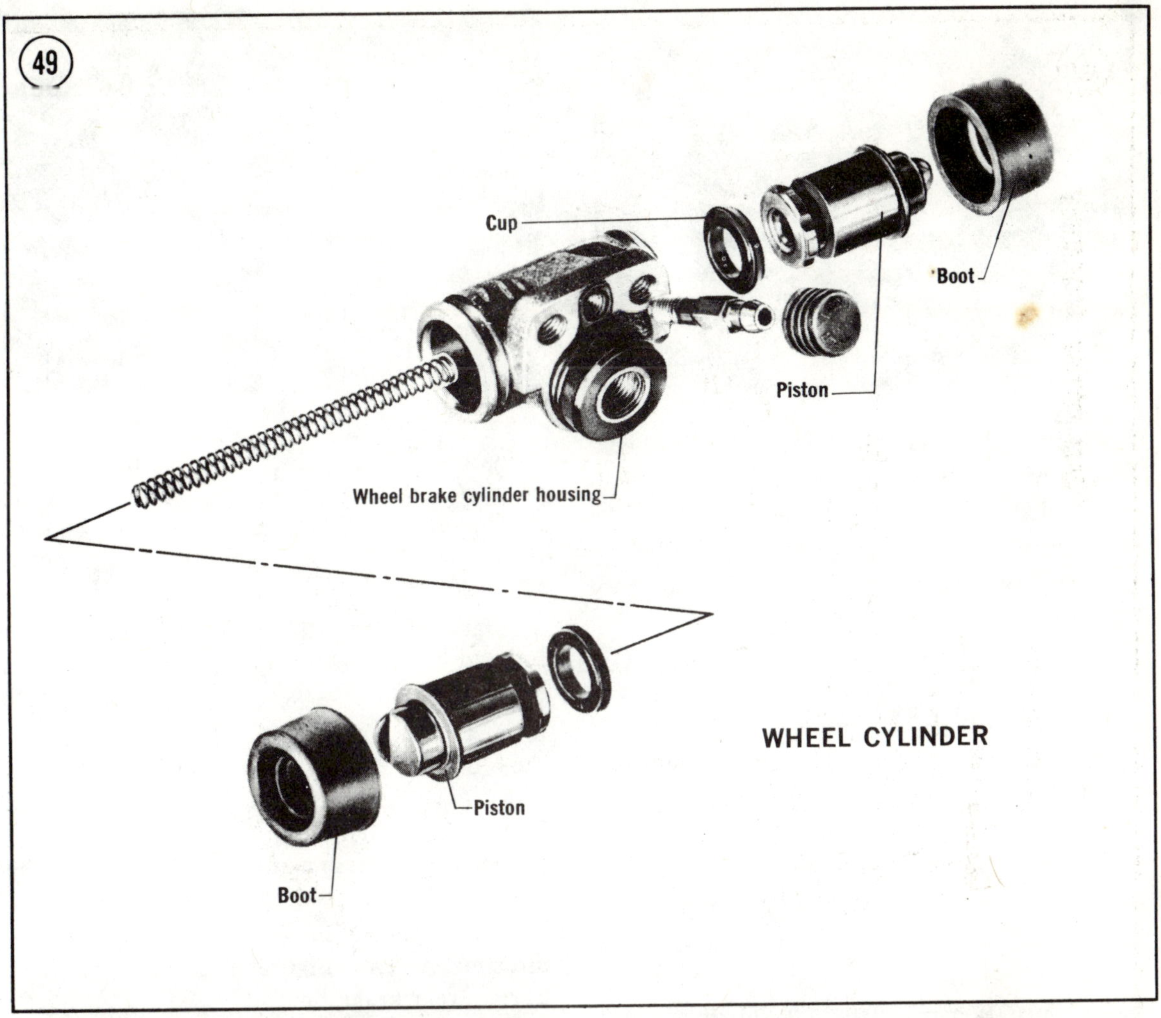

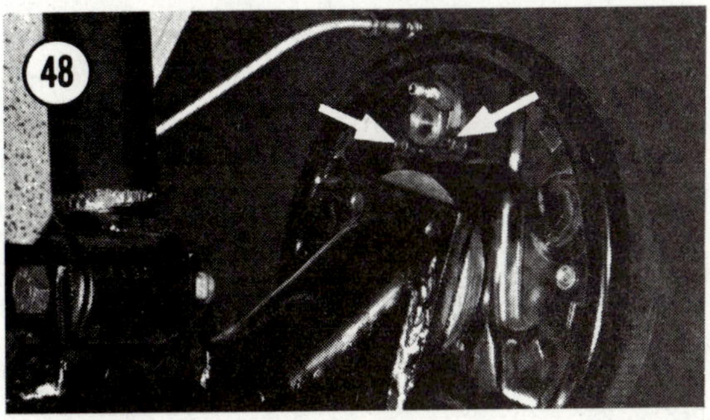

1. Raise the car on jackstands and release the handbrake.

2. Depress brake pedal several times to centralize the shoes in the drum.

3. Press lever on brake pressure regulator in direction shown in Figure 50 to release pressure in right rear brake line.

4. Turn the starwheel as necessary until the wheel can no longer be turned by hand. Back off the starwheel until the wheel can just be turned by hand.

5. Repeat these steps on the other wheel.

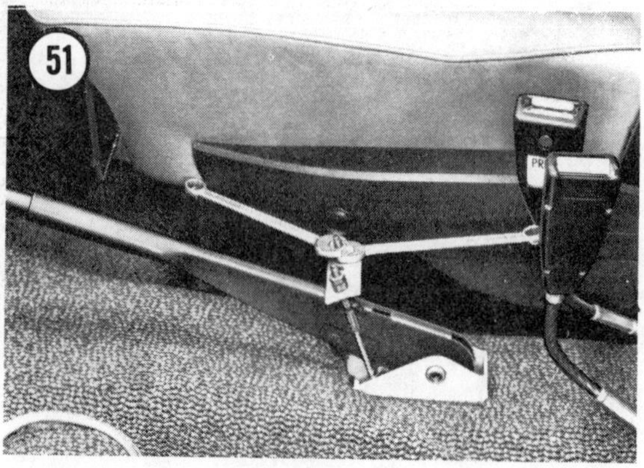

6. Operate footbrake several times and check that all wheels can just be rotated.
7. Check the brake fluid level and top up if necessary.
8. Road test the car. Check pedal free play and ensure that the car does not swerve to one side. If it does, recheck the adjustments.

HANDBRAKE ADJUSTMENT

1. Raise the rear of the car on jackstands and release the handbrake.
2. Loosen adjusting nuts shown in **Figure 51**.
3. Adjust footbrake as described earlier.
4. Pull parking brake lever up 2 notches.
5. Tighten adjusting nuts until neither rear wheel can be turned by hand.
6. Release the parking brake and make sure that both wheels rotate freely.
7. Tighten locknuts on adjusting nuts.
8. Lower vehicle.

BRAKE BLEEDING

Brakes require bleeding whenever air enters the system, lowering the effective braking pressure. Air can enter when the master cylinder or wheel cylinders are serviced or if the fluid in the reservoir runs dry. Air can also enter through a leaky brake line or hose. Find the leaking line and replace it before bleeding.

Whenever handling brake fluid, do not get any on the brake shoes, brake discs, calipers, or body paint. Brake shoes or brake pads will be permanently damaged, requiring replacement. Body paint can be damaged also unless you wipe the area with a clean cloth and wash it with a soapy solution immediately.

1. Make sure that the brake fluid reservoir is full and that the vent in the cap is open.
2. Connect a plastic or rubber tube to the bleeder valve on the right rear wheel. Suspend the other end of the tube in a jar or bottle filled with a few inches of brake fluid. See **Figure 52.** During the remaining steps, keep this end submerged at all times and never let the level in the brake fluid reservoir drop below ½ level.
3. Press lever on brake pressure regulator in direction shown in **Figure 50** to release pressure in right rear brake line.
4. Open the bleeder valve on the right rear wheel about one turn. Have an assistant depress the brake pedal slowly to the floor. As soon as the pedal is all the way down, close the bleeder valve and let the pedal up. Repeat this step as many times as necessary, i.e., until fluid with no air bubbles issues from the tube.
5. Bleed the remaining valves in the same manner as described in the steps above. Follow the sequence shown in **Figure 53**. Keep checking the brake fluid reservoir to be sure it does not run out of fluid.
6. When all wheels are bled, discard the brake fluid in the jar or bottle; never reuse such fluid. Top up the brake fluid reservoir with clean fluid.

53

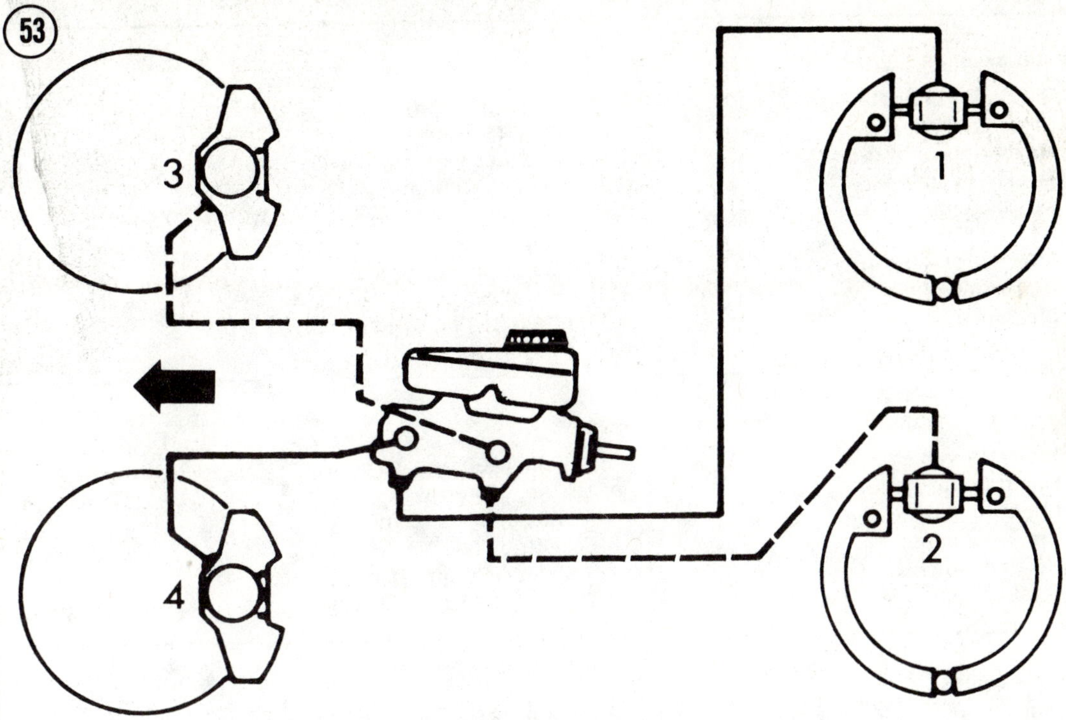

BRAKE BLEEDING

Bleeding sequence

1. Rear right wheel cylinder
2. Rear left wheel cylinder
3. Front right caliper
4. Front left caliper

After bleeding fill reservoir to maximum mark

Brake specifications and torques on next page.

Table 1 **BRAKE SPECIFICATIONS AND TORQUE VALUES**

Front brakes		
Disc brake diameter	9.41 in. (239mm)	
Disc thickness	0.47 in. (12mm)	
Maximum out of true	0.0023 in. (0.06mm)	
Thickness limits	0.0008 in. (0.02mm)	
Regrind dimension	0.43 in. (11.0mm) wear limit 0.41 in. (10.5mm)	
Brake cylinder diameter	1.73 in. (44mm)	
Effective braking area	16.25 sq. in. ($105cm^2$)	
Brake adjustment	Automatic	
Clearance	0.004-0.008 in. (0.1-0.2mm)	
Rear brakes		
Brake drum diameter	7.87 in. (200mm)	
Lining width	1.57 in. (40mm)	
Effective braking area	45.20 sq. in. ($292cm^2$)	
Brake adjustment	Eccentric	
Regrind dimension	7.89 in. (200.5mm) Wear limit 7.91 in. (201mm)	
Torque values		
Girling brake pad retainer bolts	14 ft.-lb.	2.0 mkg.
Caliper mounting bolts	43 ft.-lb.	6.0 mkg.
Spreader spring bolts	14 ft.-lb.	2.0 mkg.
Backing plate mounting bolts	43 ft.-lb.	6.0 mkg..

CHAPTER TEN

FRONT SUSPENSION AND STEERING

Specifications (**Table 1**) and tightening torques (**Table 2**) are found at the end of the chapter.

WHEEL ALIGNMENT

Several suspension angles affect running and steering. These angles must be properly aligned to maintain directional stability, ease of steering, and proper tire wear.

The angles involved define:

a. Caster

b. Camber

c. Toe-in

d. Steering axis inclination

e. Toe-out on turns

Only camber and toe-in are adjustable. Neither should be adjusted without a front-end rack. Other suspension angles, though not adjustable, should be measured on a front-end rack to check for bent suspension parts.

Pre-alignment Check

Several factors influence the suspension angles, or steering. Before any adjustments are attempted, perform the following checks.

1. Check tire pressure and wear.
2. Check the play in wheel bearings. Adjust if necessary.
3. Check play in ball-joints.
4. Check for broken springs or torsion bar (rear only).
5. Remove any excessive load.
6. Check shock absorbers.
7. Check steering gear adjustments.
8. Check play in tie rod parts.
9. Check wheel balance.
10. Check *rear* suspension for looseness.

A proper inspection of front tire wear can point to several alignment problems. Tires worn primarily on one side show problems with toe-in. If toe-in is incorrect on one wheel, the car probably pulls to one side or the other. If toe-in is incorrect on both wheels, the car probably is hard to steer in either direction. Incorrect camber may also cause wear on one side. Tire cupping (scalloped wear pattern) can result from worn shock absorbers, one wheel out of alignment, a bent spindle, or a combination of all. Tires which are worn in the middle, but not the edges; or worn nearly even on both edges, but not in the middle; are probably over-inflated or under-inflated, respectively; these conditions are not caused by suspension misalignment.

Camber

Camber is the inclination of the wheel from vertical, as shown in **Figure 1**. Note that angle (a) is positive camber, i.e., the top of the tire inclines outward more than the bottom.

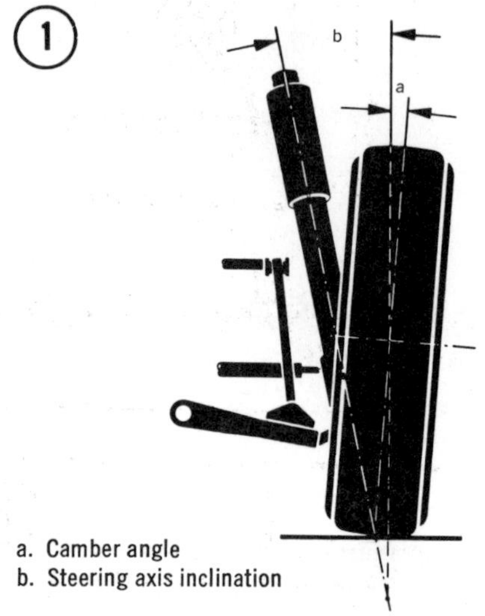

a. Camber angle
b. Steering axis inclination

Camber combines with steering axis inclination to determine steering roll radius as described later. Camber is easily adjusted on a front-end rack. Loosen the 2 bolts securing the steering knuckle to the suspension strut. The top bolt is an eccentric. See **Figure 2**. Rotate the top bolt as necessary to adjust camber. Tighten bolts to 58 ft.-lb. (8 mkg) without disturbing the adjustment.

Caster

Caster is the inclination of the axis through the suspension strut from vertical. Caster helps the wheels to return to a position straight ahead after a turn. It also prevents the car from wandering due to wind, potholes, or uneven road surfaces.

Caster is a function of wishbone design and cannot be adjusted.

Steering Axis Inclination

On very early automobiles, the front wheels pivoted on a vertical axis. The pivot point was

far from the centerline of the tire and caused the wheels to scuff and pull on irregular roads.

To combat this, automobile engineers tilted the steering axis inward (steering axis inclination) and tilted the top of the wheel outward (camber). See **Figure 3**. This placed the pivot point close to the centerline of the wheel.

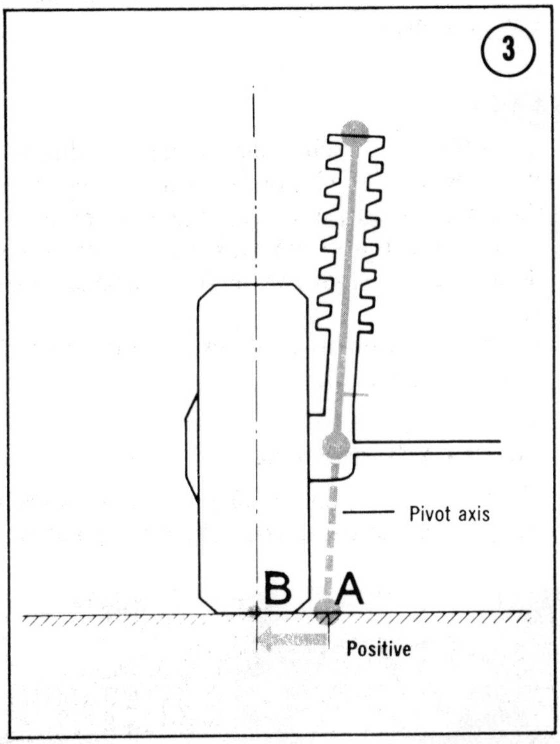

The actual difference between the pivot point and the wheel is called the steering roll radius. If the pivot point is inside the centerline of the wheel, the roll radius is positive. If the pivot point is outside the wheel centerline, the roll radius is negative. See **Figure 4**.

Steering axis inclination is a design function and is not adjustable.

Toe-in

Camber and rolling resistance tend to force the front wheels outward at their forward edge. To compensate for this tendency, the front edges are turned slightly inward when the car is at rest. This is toe-in. See **Figure 5**.

Toe-in is adjusted by lengthening or shortening the adjustable tie rod on the right side. The left tie rod is not adjustable.

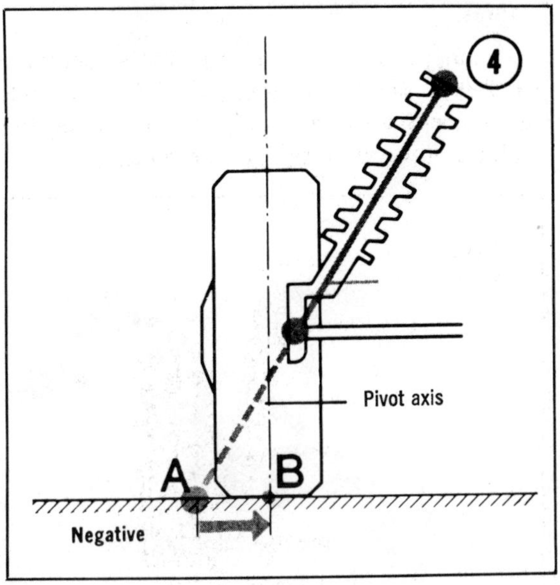

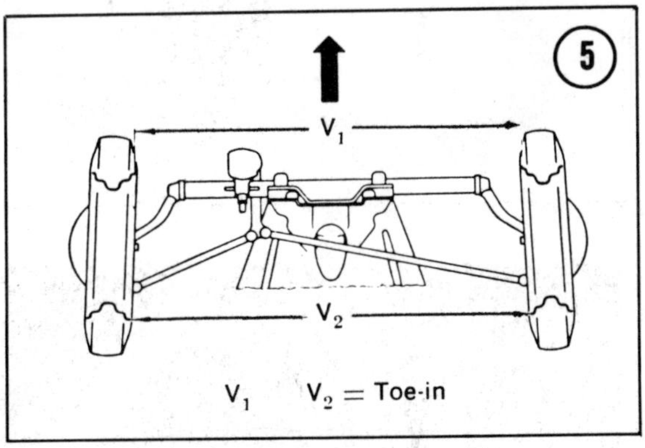

STEERING WHEEL

Refer to **Figure 6**.

1. Disconnect battery ground cable.
2. Pry horn cover off by hand.
3. Remove steering wheel nut and lockwasher.
4. Remove steering wheel.
5. Installation is the reverse of these steps. Tighten steering wheel nut to 36 ft.-lb. (5 mkg).

STEERING GEAR

The steering gear cannot be repaired. If it is defective, replace it as described below.

> NOTE: *The 1978 models have a new steering gear mounted with clamps and rubber bushings. The new gear cannot be used on earlier models.*

10

6

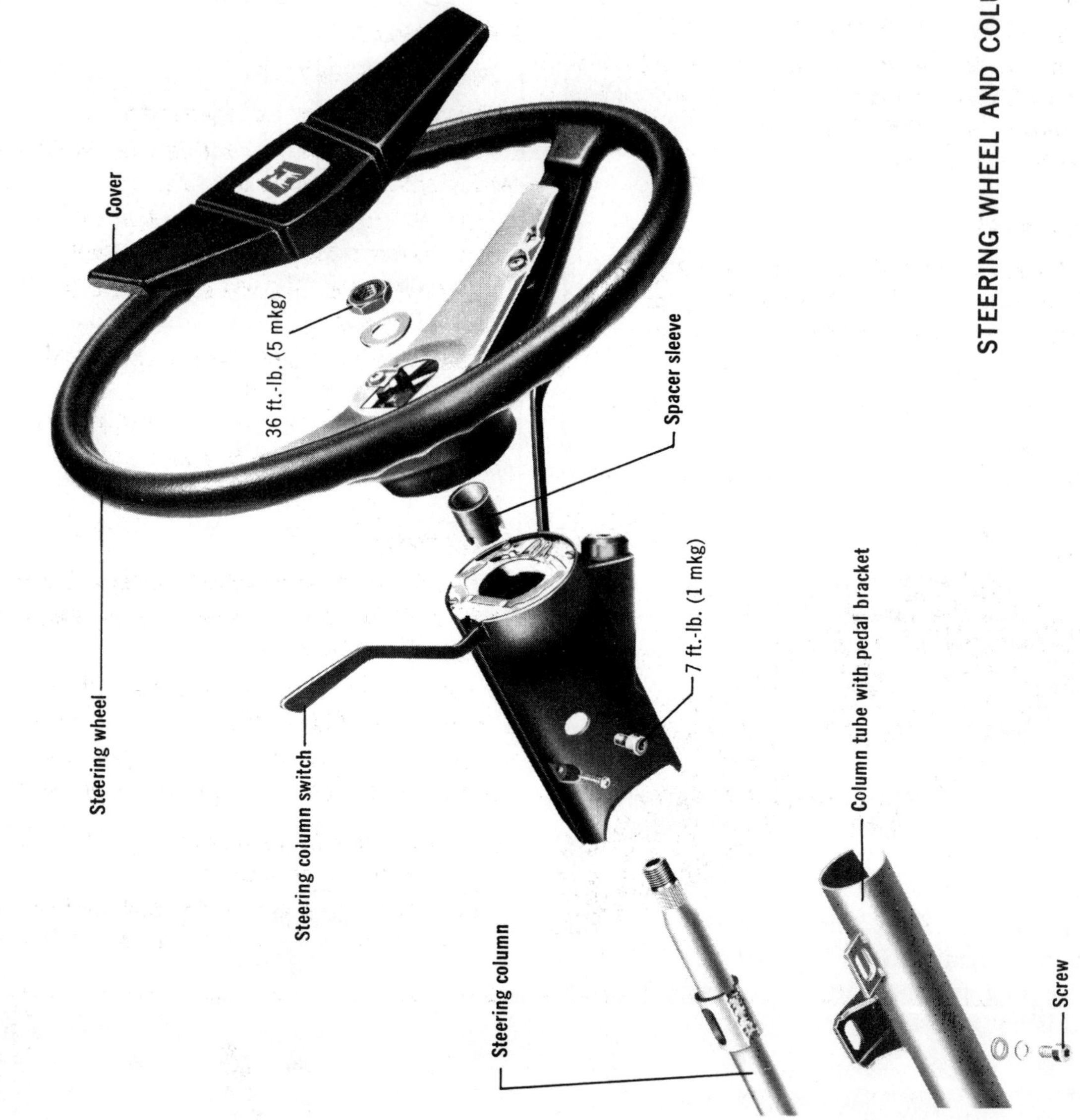

STEERING WHEEL AND COLUMN

Removal/Installation

Refer to **Figure 7**.

1. Remove both tie rods as described elsewhere.
2. Loosen clamp bolt securing universal joint shaft to steering gear.
3. Disconnect shift linkage from steering gear. Remove nuts and bolts which mount the steering gear and pull the assembly off the studs.
4. Installation is the reverse of these steps. Before installing tie rods, perform the adjustment procedure described under *Tie Rod Adjustment* later in this chapter.

Adjustment

If steering is too tight and wheel will not self-center, or if there is excessive play in the wheel, adjust the steering gear as follows.

1. Raise front of car on jackstands.
2. Loosen locknut on steering gear adjuster. See **Figure 8**.

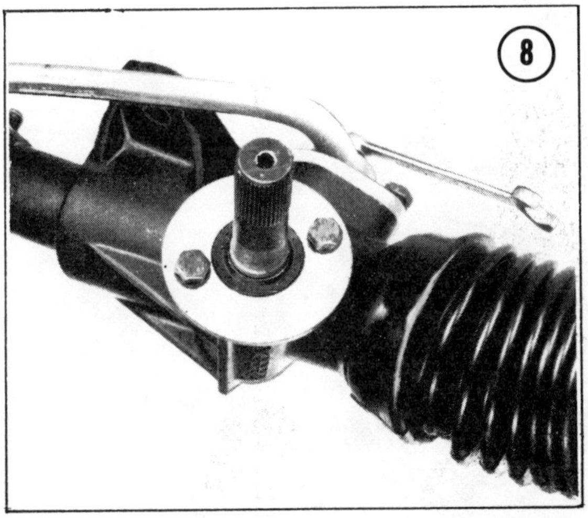

8

3. Back off adjuster 1-2 turns.
4. Turn adjuster in until it just touches the internal thrust washer.
5. Hold the adjuster in this position and tighten the locknut.

TIE RODS

Replacement

Refer to Figure 7.

1. Raise front of car on jackstands.
2. Pull rubber boot off steering gear. Slide it as far toward ball-joint as possible.
3. Loosen locknut at steering gear end of tie rod. Unscrew tie rod from steering gear.
4. Remove cotter pin and castellated nut from outer end of rod.
5. Loosen locknut at outer end of tie rod. Unscrew tie rod from ball-joint.
6. Installation is the reverse of these steps. Adjust tie rod length as described below.

Adjustment

1. Disconnect both tie rods at the steering gear.
2. Center rack so that dimension A, **Figure 9**, is the same at both ends.
3. Adjust tie rods to exactly 14.921 in. (379mm). See **Figure 10**. Tighten locknut.
4. Screw tie rods onto steering gear until dimention B, **Figure 11** (page 250), is as follows:
   a. On cars with manual transmission, 2.716 in. (69mm) at both ends.
   b. On cars with automatic transmission, left side (adjustable) tie rod to 2.716 in.

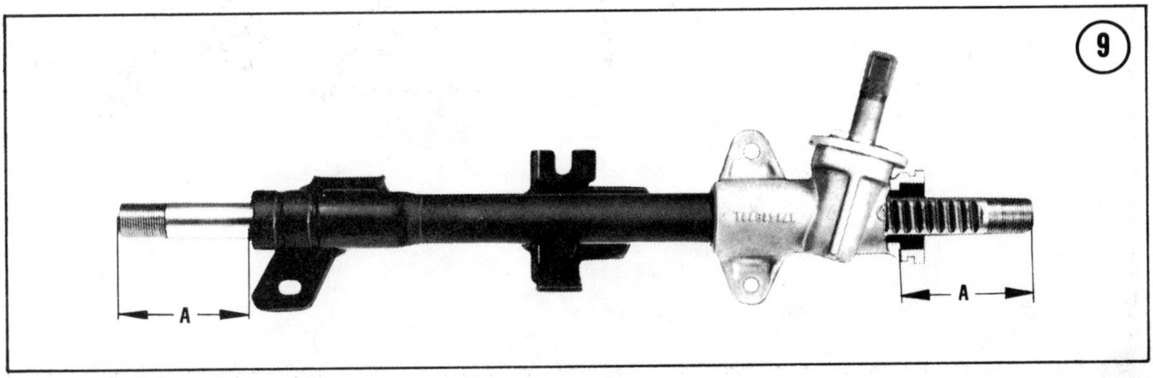

9

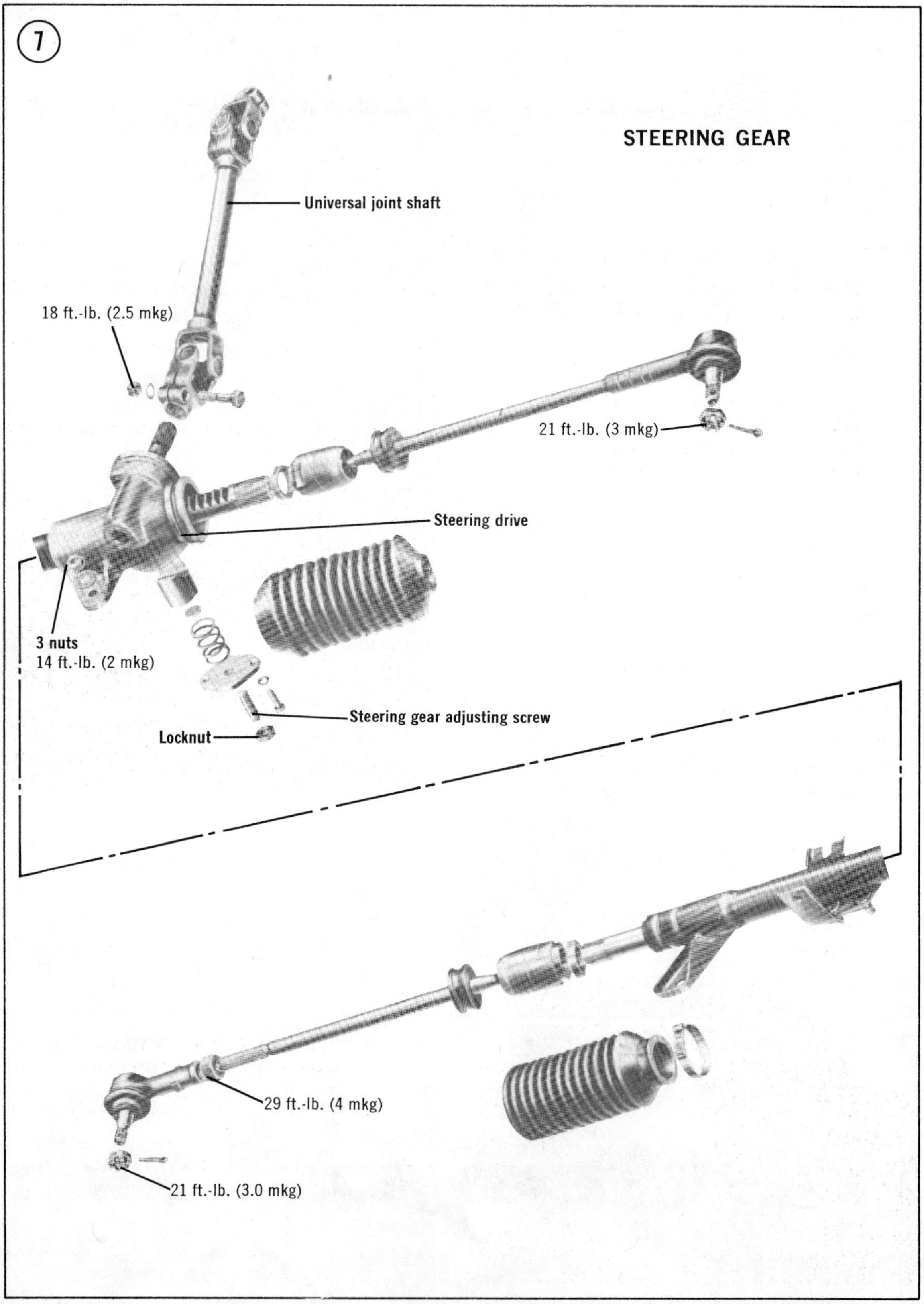
7
STEERING GEAR
Universal joint shaft
18 ft.-lb. (2.5 mkg)
21 ft.-lb. (3 mkg)
Steering drive
3 nuts
14 ft.-lb. (2 mkg)
Steering gear adjusting screw
Locknut
29 ft.-lb. (4 mkg)
21 ft.-lb. (3.0 mkg)

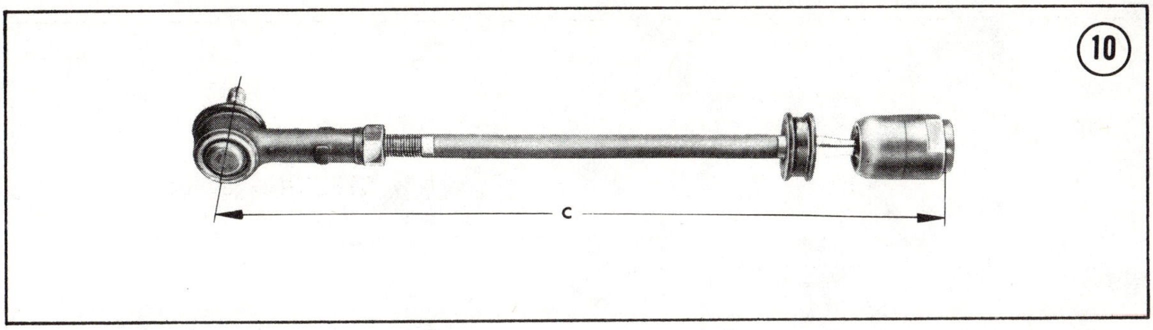

(69mm) and right side (non-adjustable) tie rod to 2.638 in. (67mm).

NOTE: *Only adjustable tie rods are available as spare parts. When replacing a non-adjustable rod with an adjustable one, measure and record dimension B. Adjust new rod to 14.921 in. (379mm) and tighten locknut. Attach rod and adjust dimesion B to the previously measured and recorded distance.*

5. Have wheel toe-in adjusted by a front-end specialist. Adjust with right tie rod.

DRIVE SHAFTS

Removal/Installation

1. Remove axle nut while car is still on the ground. See **Figure 12**. Use a long breaker bar if necessary.

CAUTION

Never loosen the nut unless all 4 wheels are firmly on the ground. The force required to loosen the nut is sufficient to knock the car off the jackstands.

2. Remove the bolts connecting the drive shaft to the transmission. See **Figure 13**.

3. Push drive shaft upward and lay it aside on the transmission.

4. Turn the front wheels to full steering lock and pull drive shaft out of steering knuckle. See **Figure 14**.

5. Installation is the reverse of these steps. Tighten new axle nut to 173 ft.-lb. (24 mkg) *after lowering the car.*

CAUTION

Always use new axle nut; do not reuse old one.

OUTER CONSTANT VELOCITY JOINT REPLACEMENT

Refer to **Figure 15** (page 252) for this procedure.

1. Remove drive shaft as described above.

2. Loosen rubber boot clamps and slide the boot back. See **Figure 16**.

3. Spread circlip securing outer constant velocity joint. See A, **Figure 17**.

10

11

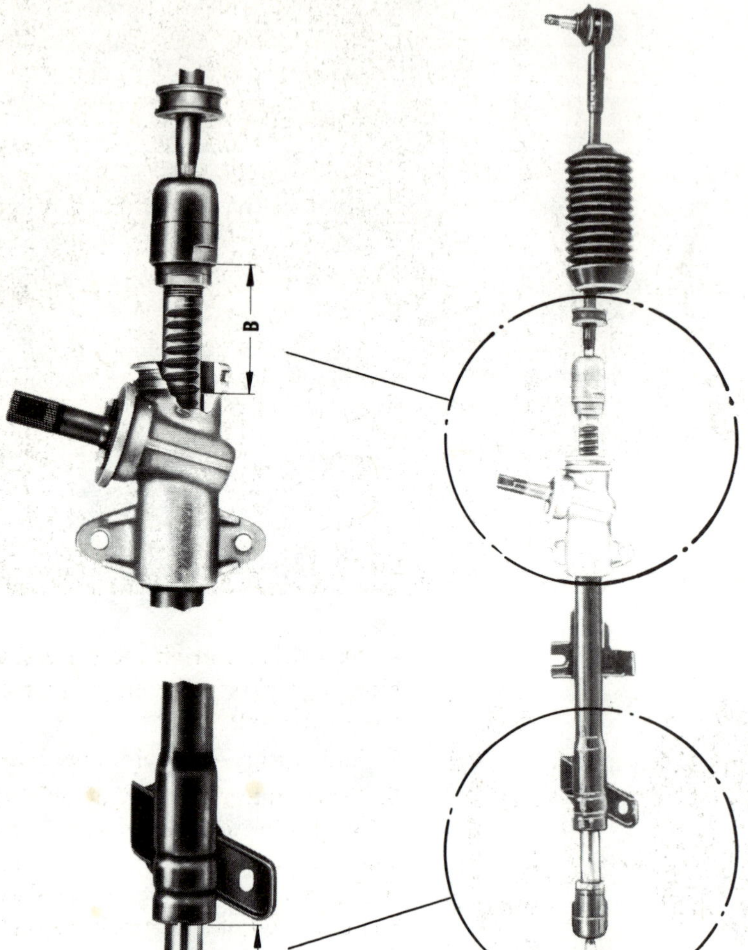

TIE RODS

4. Drive the joint off the drive shaft with light blows of a plastic or rubber hammer against the end of the axle.

5. Slide spring disc and rubber boot off the axle.

6. Wipe outer surfaces of axle and constant velocity joint with a clean cloth dipped in solvent. Do not immerse parts in solvent. Wipe rubber boot with denatured alcohol. Petroleum-based solvents could attack the rubber.

7. Slide the boot onto the drive shaft.

8. Slide the spring disc onto the drive shaft with the convex toward the joint. See **Figure 18**.

9. Install the outer constant velocity joint on the drive shaft and secure with the circlip and thrust washer. See Figure 18.

10. Slide the rubber boot into place. Tighten both clamps securing the boot. See **Figure 19**.

11. Install drive shaft as described previously.

INNER CONSTANT VELOCITY JOINT REPLACEMENT

Refer to Figure 15 for this procedure.

1. Remove drive shaft as described above.

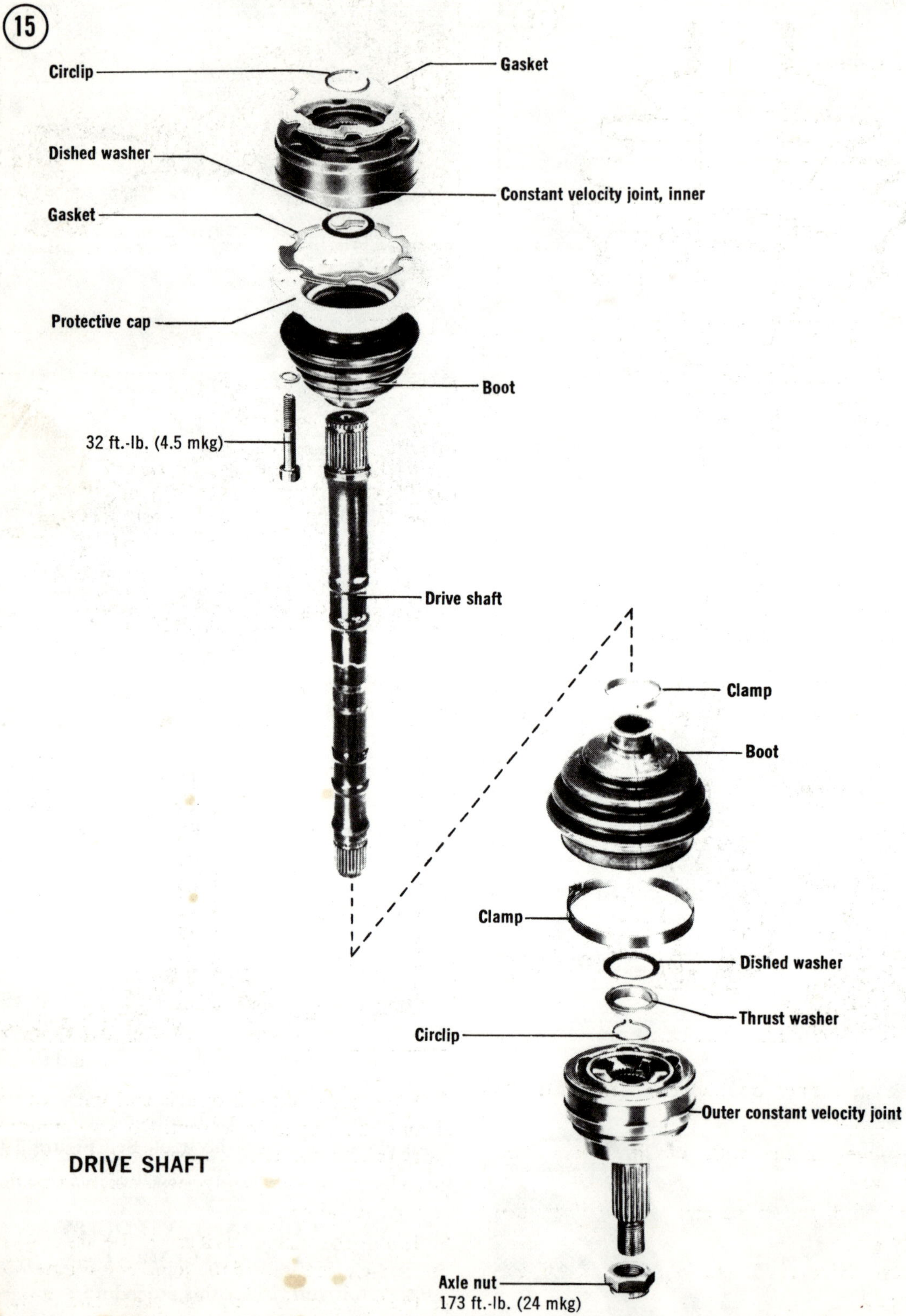
15
Circlip
Gasket
Dished washer
Constant velocity joint, inner
Gasket
Protective cap
Boot
32 ft.-lb. (4.5 mkg)
Drive shaft
Clamp
Boot
Clamp
Dished washer
Thrust washer
Circlip
Outer constant velocity joint
Axle nut
173 ft.-lb. (24 mkg)

DRIVE SHAFT

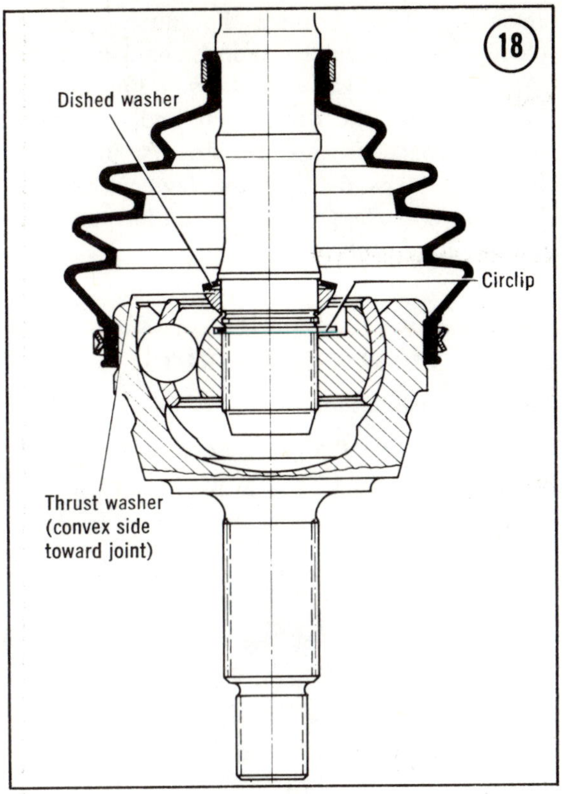

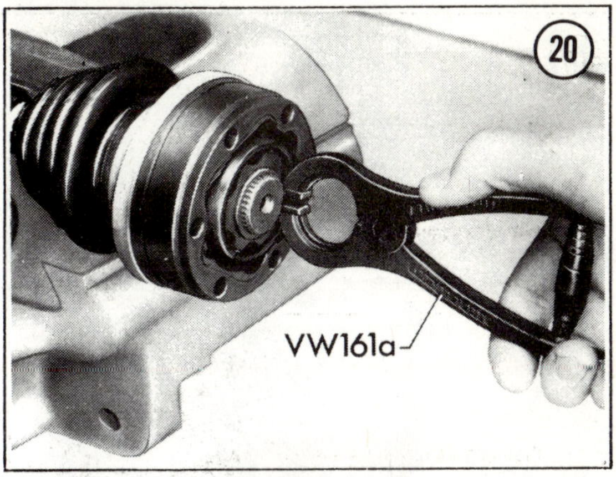

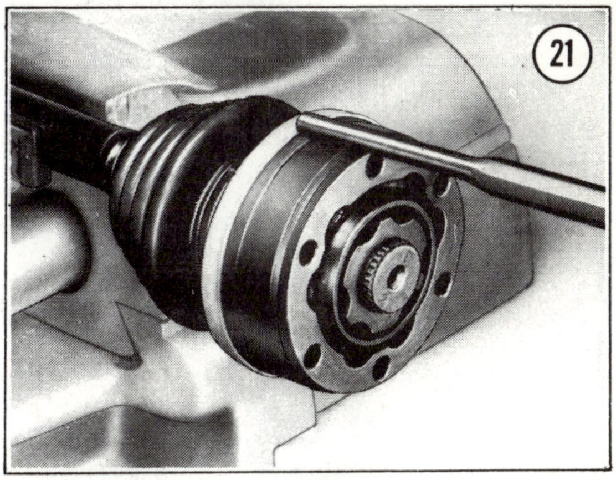

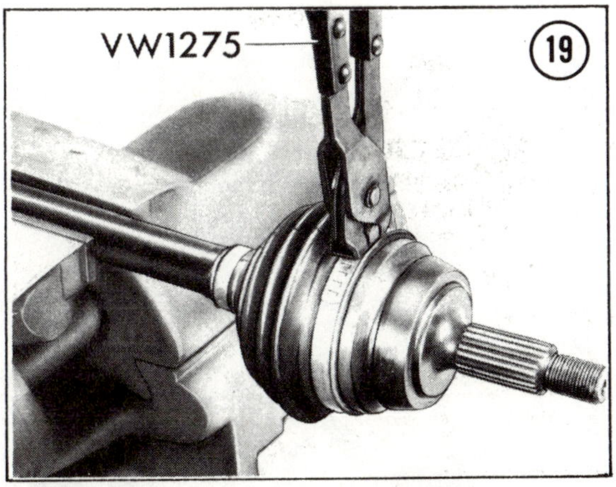

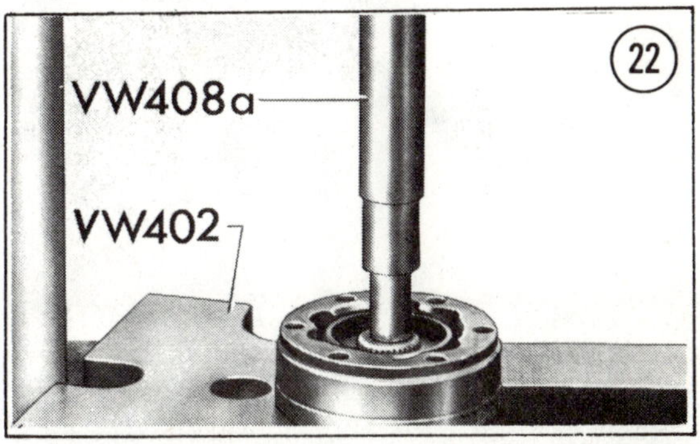

10

2. Loosen rubber boot clamps and slide the boot back.

3. Remove circlip with circlip pliers. See **Figure 20**.

4. Drive off protective cap with a drift. See **Figure 21**.

5. Press drive shaft out of inner joint. See **Figure 22**.

6. Remove dished washer from shaft.

7. Wipe outer surfaces of axle and joint with a clean cloth dipped in solvent. Do not immerse parts in solvent. Wipe rubber boot with denatured alcohol. Petroleum-based solvents could attack the rubber.

8. Install the dished washer on the shaft with the convex side toward the joint. See **Figure 23**.

9. Press the joint onto the shaft and install circlip over shaft. Dealers use the special tools

23

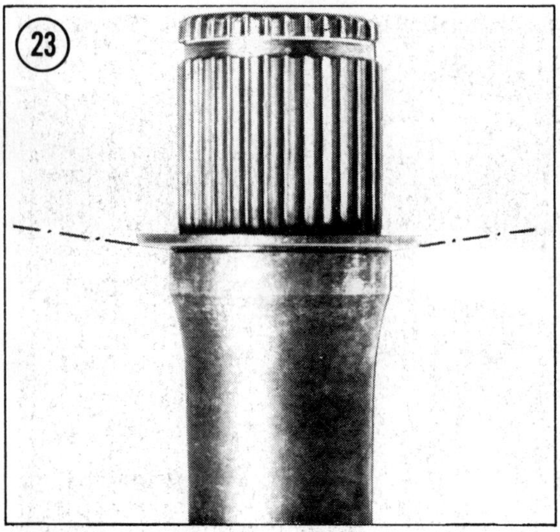

shown in **Figure 24**. Others are very easily improvised.

24

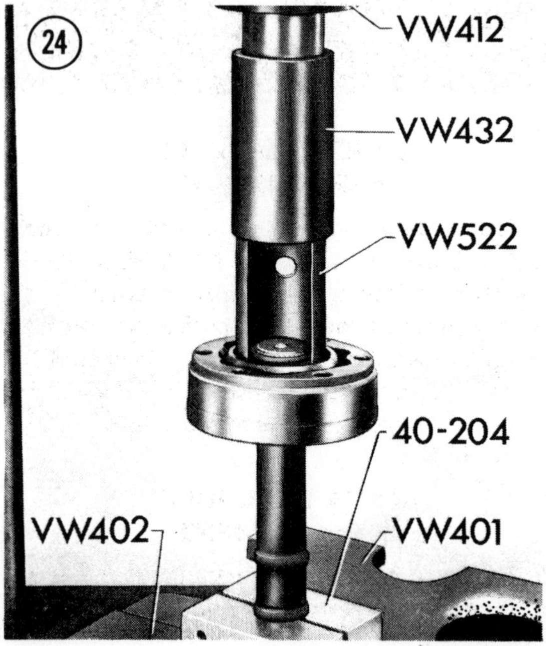

10. Tap the metal cap into place over the joint.
11. Slide the rubber boot over the metal cap. Tighten both clamps securing the boot.
12. Install the drive shaft.

RUBBER BOOT REPLACEMENT

To replace either rubber boot on the drive shaft, first remove the drive shaft as described previously. Then remove the outer constant velocity joint as described in Steps 1-4 of the *Outer Constant Velocity Joint Replacement.* Slide boots off the drive shaft and slide new ones into place. Reassemble drive shaft as described in Steps 6-11 of the *Outer Constant Velocity Joint Replacement* procedure and install the drive shaft.

SUSPENSION STRUTS

Removal/Installation

1. Remove drive shaft as described elsewhere.
2. Disconnect end of the brake hose. See (A), **Figure 25**.

25

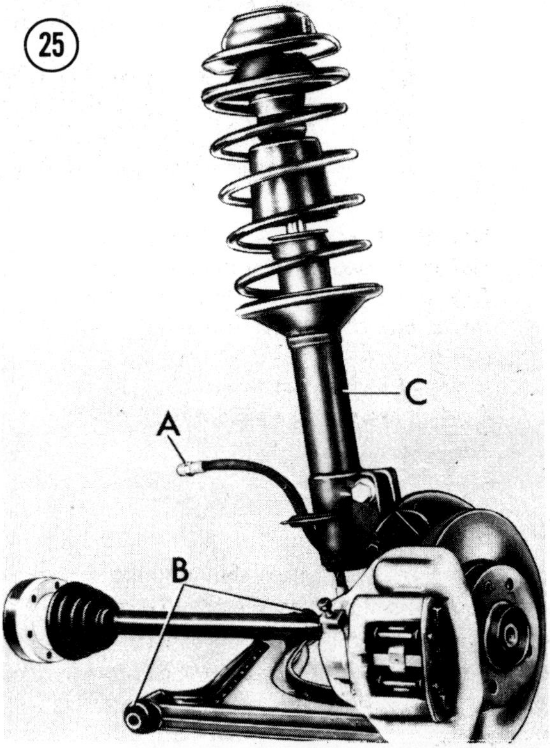

3. Remove bolt at forward end of wishbone and bracket at rear end (B, Figure 25).
4. Remove nuts at top of strut in the engine compartment. See **Figure 26**.
5. Lower strut from vehicle.
6. Installation is the reverse of these steps. Bleed brakes as described in Chapter Nine and have camber adjusted by front-end specialist.

NOTE: *Threads on wishbone bolts and nuts must be thoroughly cleaned before reassembly in order for true tightening torque to be achieved—43 ft.-lb. (6 mkg) for front bolts, 32 ft.-lb. (4.5 mkg) for rear bolts. Use locking compound on threads of front bolt.*

Disassembly/Assembly

This procedure is impossible without a special spring compressor tool; it would be dangerous to improvise a tool. Remove the strut and take it to your dealer as disassembly is required to replace the coil spring, shock absorber, or strut parts.

COIL SPRING REPLACEMENT

The coil spring is part of the suspension strut assembly. Since coil spring replacement requires disassembly of the suspension strut with a special tool, remove the strut assembly as described earlier and let a dealer replace the spring. Install the assembly following the same procedure.

SHOCK ABSORBER REPLACEMENT

The shock absorber fits inside the strut tube and is secured by a threaded cap. Since shock absorber replacement requires disassembly of the suspension strut with a special tool, remove the strut assembly as described earlier and let a dealer replace the shock absorber. Install the assembly following the same procedure.

STRUT BALL-JOINT REPLACEMENT

1. Raise front of car on jackstands.
2. Drill out rivets (**Figure 27**) with ¼ in. (6mm) drill bit.
3. Chisel rivet heads off.
4. Loosen top clamp bolt and remove ball-joint.
5. Install new ball-joint with M7x22 (7mm) bolts, nuts, and lockwashers. See **Figure 28**.
6. Torque clamp nut to 21 ft.-lb. (3 mkg) and torque new bolts to 18 ft.-lb. (2.5 mkg).

NOTE: *If only the ball-joint has been replaced, it is not necessary to adjust toe-in or camber.*

STEERING KNUCKLE

Refer to **Figures 29 and 30**.

1. Remove suspension strut as described elsewhere.
2. Remove brake disc or brake shoes as described in Chapter Nine.
3. Remove backing plate from steering knuckle.
4. Remove wishbone and strut from steering knuckle.
5. Press wheel hub out as shown in **Figure 31**.

CAUTION

Do not remove the bearing as described in Steps 6 and 7 unless you intend to replace it. Removal destroys the bearing.

6. Remove inner and outer circlips (Figures 29 and 30).
7. Pull inner race as shown in **Figure 32**. Press out outer race as shown in **Figure 33**.
8. Clean all parts except bearing in solvent. Wipe ball bearing with a clean cloth moistened lightly in solvent.

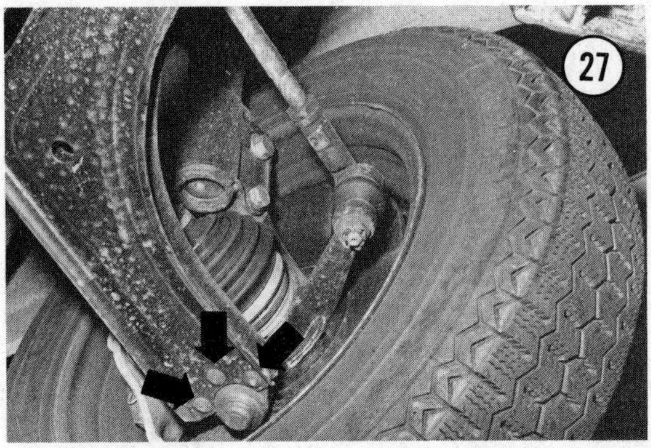

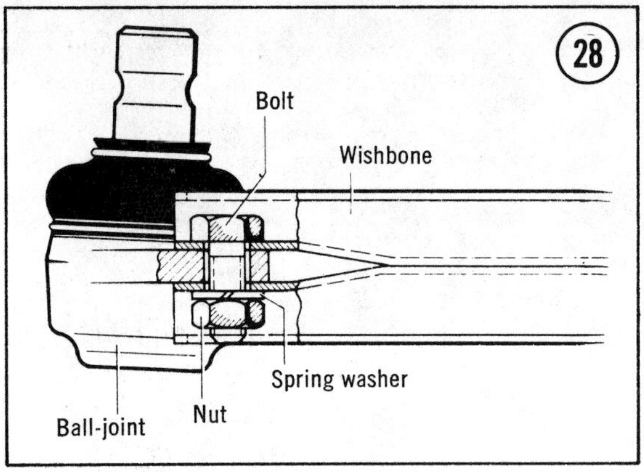

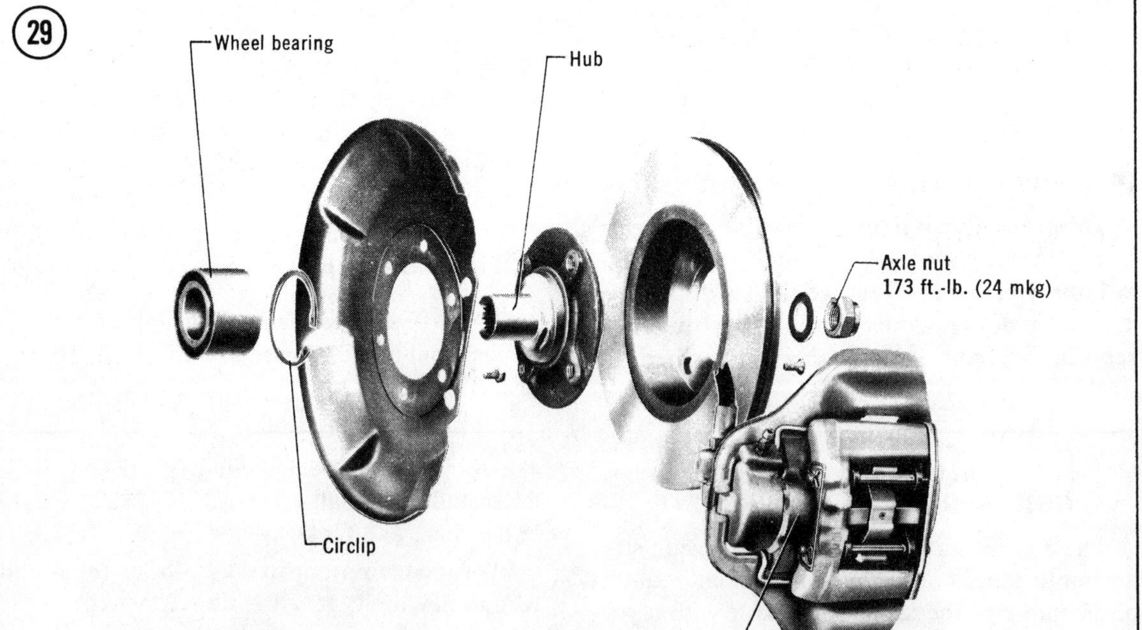

FRONT
BRAKE ASSEMBLY

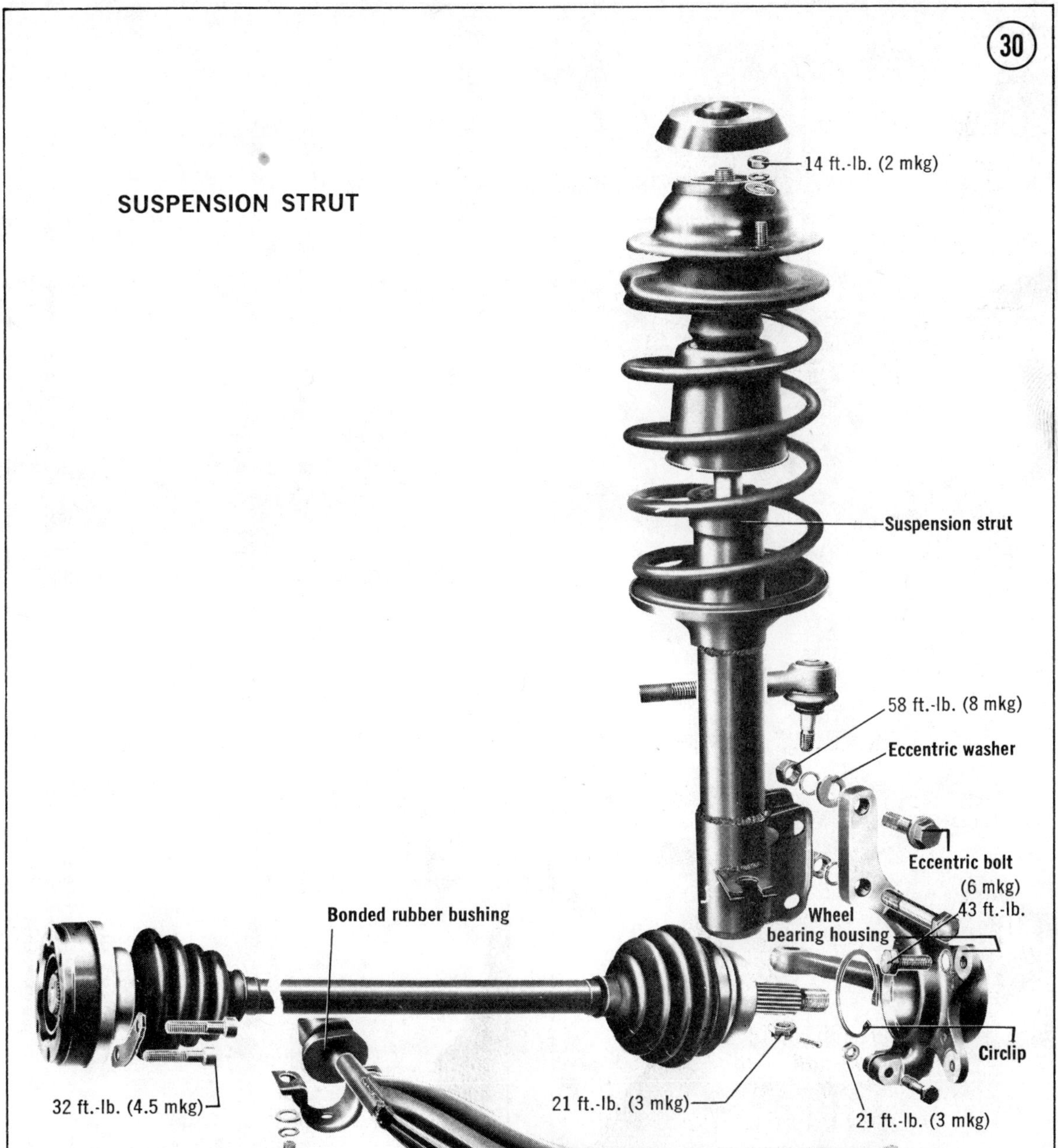
30
SUSPENSION STRUT
14 ft.-lb. (2 mkg)
Suspension strut
58 ft.-lb. (8 mkg)
Eccentric washer
Eccentric bolt
(6 mkg)
43 ft.-lb.
Wheel
bearing housing
Bonded rubber bushing
Circlip
32 ft.-lb. (4.5 mkg)
21 ft.-lb. (3 mkg)
21 ft.-lb. (3 mkg)
32 ft.-lb. (4.5 mkg)
Ball-joint
Bonded rubber bushing
Wishbone
43 ft.-lb. (6 mkg)

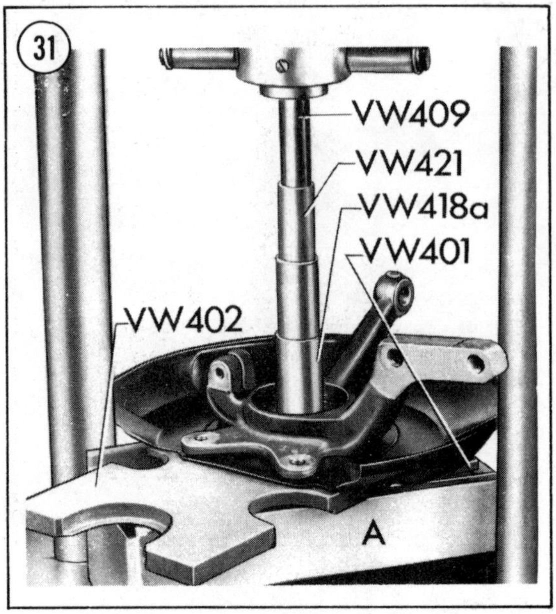

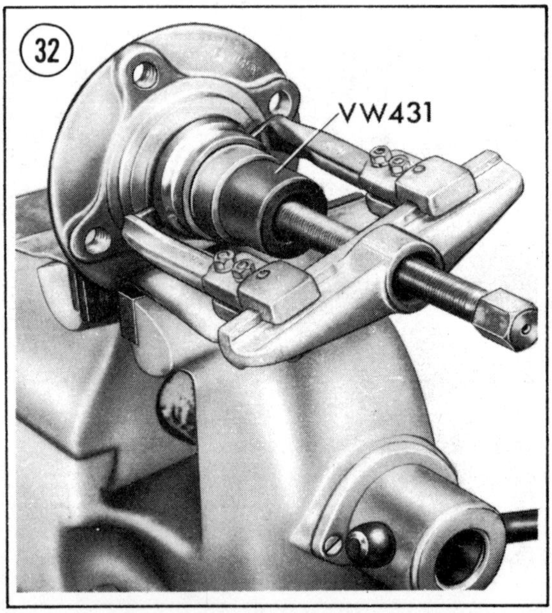

CAUTION
The bearing is pre-lubricated and sealed. Do not wash in solvent or bearing will be ruined. Wipe bearing with a clean cloth.

9. Hold the inner race of the ball bearing, lightly press the outer race against the inner race and rotate the outer race. If there is any noise or roughness, the bearing is defective and must be replaced.

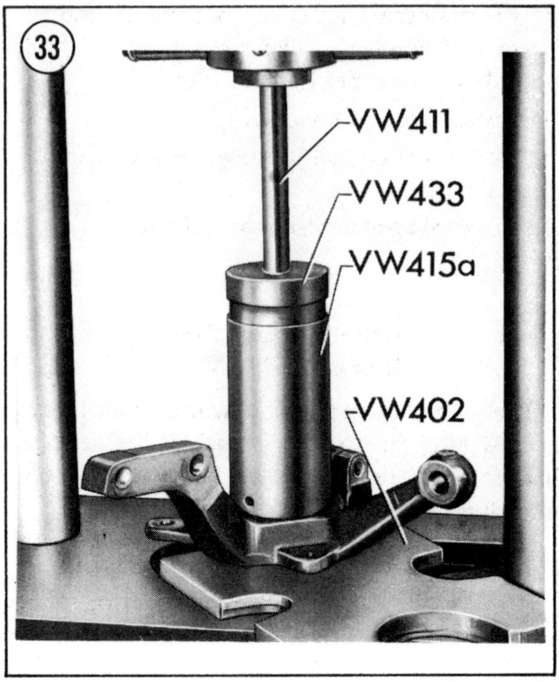

NOTE: *Steps 10 and 11 apply only if bearing was removed.*

10. Install outer circlip in groove.

11. Press in bearing until seated against circlip as shown in **Figure 34**.

12. Install inner circlip.

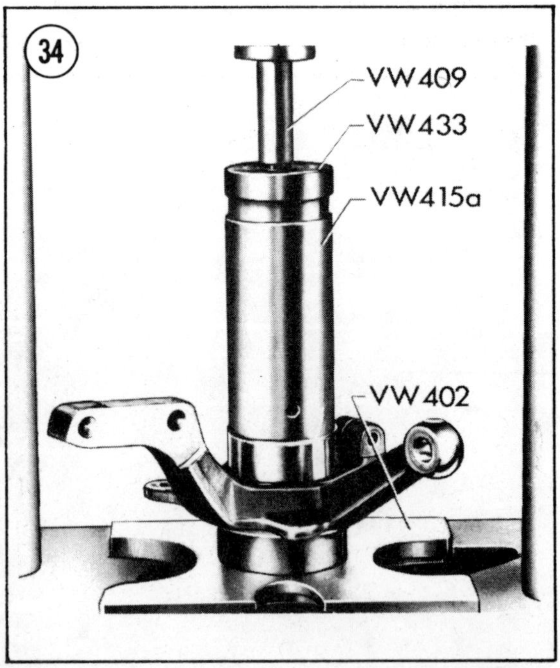

13. Press steering knuckle onto wheel hub as shown in **Figure 35**. The special tool should rest only on the inner bearing race.
14. Install strut on knuckle.
15. Install backing plate and brake disc or brake shoes.
16. Install suspension strut in vehicle.

35

WHEEL BEARING REPLACEMENT

The ball bearing type wheel bearing is pressed into the steering knuckle. To replace this bearing, refer to the *Steering Knuckle* procedure.

No adjustment of wheel bearing is necessary.

Table 1 SPECIFICATIONS

Item	1975-1976	1977-on
Front track	54.7 in. (1390mm)	54.7 in. (1390mm)
Camber	+ 30′ ± 30′	+ 20′ ± 30′
Toe	— 10′ ± 15′	— 15′ (+ 10′ — 15′)
Caster	+ 2° ± 30′	+ 1° 50′ ± 30′
Steering ratio	20.2-(1975), 20.8 (1976)	20.8
Steering wheel		
Turns lock-to-lock	3.94	3.94
Steering gear	Rack and pinion	Rack and pinion

Table 2 TIGHTENING TORQUES

	Ft.-lb.	Mkg
Front axle		
Wheel lugs	65	9
Drive shaft — wheel (M 18)	173	24
Coil spring-to-body (M 8)	14	2
Wishbone-to-body (M 10)	43	6
Wishbone bracket	32	4.5
Drive shaft-to-transmission (M 8)	32	4.5
Wishbone-to-steering knuckle (M 8)	21	3
Brake caliper-to-steering knuckle (M 10)	43	6
Brake disc wheel hub (M 6)	5	0.7
Brake disc guard-to-steering knuckle (M 6)	6	0.9
Steering		
Camber adjustment	58	8
Steering-gear-to-body (M 8)	14	2
Tie rod-to-tie rod lever (M 10)	21	3
Steering wheel-to-steering column (M 18)	36	5
Steering gear-to-steering column (M 8)	18	2.5

CHAPTER ELEVEN

REAR SUSPENSION

This chapter provides complete repair and replacement procedures for the rear suspension. Specifications (**Table 1**) and tightening torques (**Table 2**) are found at the end of the chapter. Except for wheel bearings, no maintenance or periodic adjustment is required.

CAUTION

If a hoist is used to raise the car, place additional weight on rear of car or secure car to hoist before removing heavy rear suspension components. This must be done to prevent tipping when center of gravity changes.

SHOCK ABSORBER REPLACEMENT

The rear shock absorbers are removed with the rear coil springs. To replace the shock absorbers, refer to the *Rear Coil Spring* section, below.

REAR COIL SPRINGS

Removal/Installation

Refer to **Figure 1**.

1. Raise rear wheels clear of the ground.
2. Remove cover from upper shock absorber mount.
3. Remove mounting nut, washer, and rubber disc shown in **Figure 2**.

4. Loosen the lower shock absorber mounting bolt (**Figure 3**) and remove the coil spring assembly.
5. Installation is the reverse of these steps. Tighten upper mounting nut to 25 ft.-lb. (3.5 mkg). Tighten lower bolt to 32 ft.-lb. (4.5 mkg).

Disassembly/Assembly

1. Loosen nut at top of shock absorber and release tension from spring. See **Figure 4**.

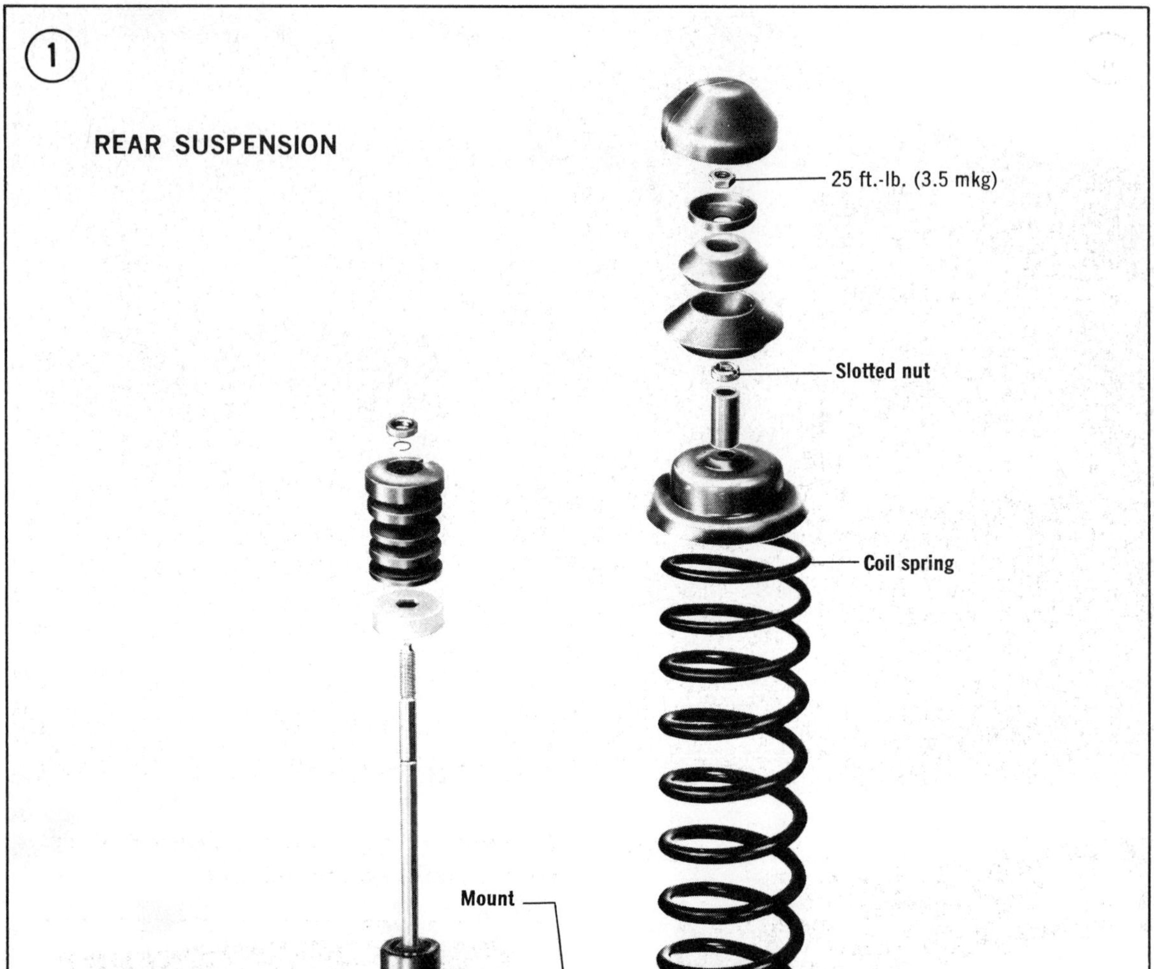
1
REAR SUSPENSION
25 ft.-lb. (3.5 mkg)
Slotted nut
Coil spring
Mount
Concaved washer
Flat washer
Parking brake cable holder
43 ft.-lb. (6 mkg)
Rear axle
Nut
32 ft.-lb. (4.5 mkg)
Shock absorber
32 ft.-lb. (4.5 mkg)

2. Remove all parts including coil spring from shock absorber.

3. Assembly is the reverse of these steps. Use a new shock absorber if the old one is worn and be sure that both coil springs have the same color code. Torque the slotted nut to 14 ft.-lb. (2.0 mkg).

STUB AXLE REPLACEMENT

1. Remove brake shoes and wheel cylinder as described in Chapter Nine.

2. Remove 4 bolts shown in **Figure 5**. Remove the backing plate and stub axle.

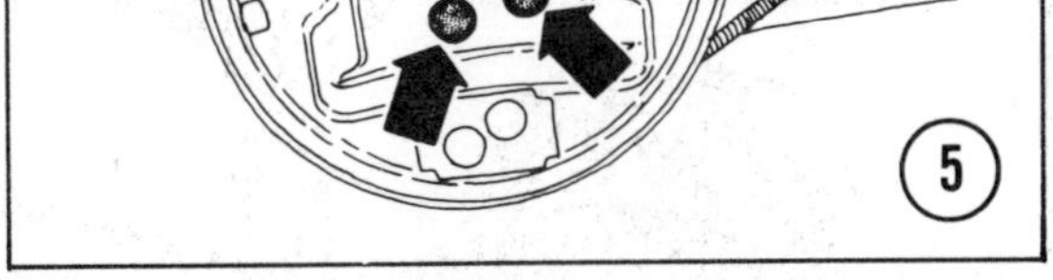

3. Installation is the reverse of these steps. Torque bolts to 22 ft.-lb. (3 mkg).

REAR AXLE REMOVAL

Refer to **Figure 6** for this procedure. See lifting caution at beginning of this chapter, if hoist is used instead of jackstands.

1. Raise rear of vehicle on jackstands.

11

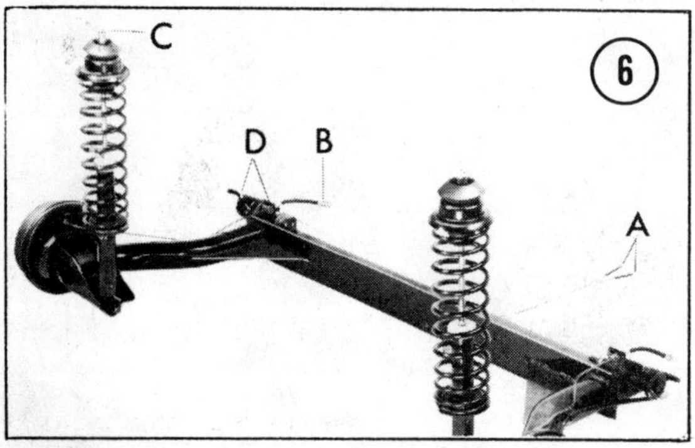

2. Remove both rear wheels.

3. Remove muffler and tailpipe between muffler and catalytic converter.

4. Disconnect parking brake cable from parking brake lever (A, Figure 6).

5. Disconnect brake line at (B, Figure 6).

6. Remove cover from upper shock absorber mount.

7. Remove mounting nut, washer, and rubber disc shown in Figure 2.

8. Support rear axle with a garage jack.

9. Remove 2 bolts securing rear axle to body. See (D), Figure 6, and Figure 1.

10. Lower rear axle clear of body.

11. Installation is the reverse of these steps. Refer to Table 2 (end of chapter) for tightening torques. Before tightening the mounting bolts at (D), Figure 6, make sure that upper edge (A), **Figure 7**, is approximately parallel to (B).

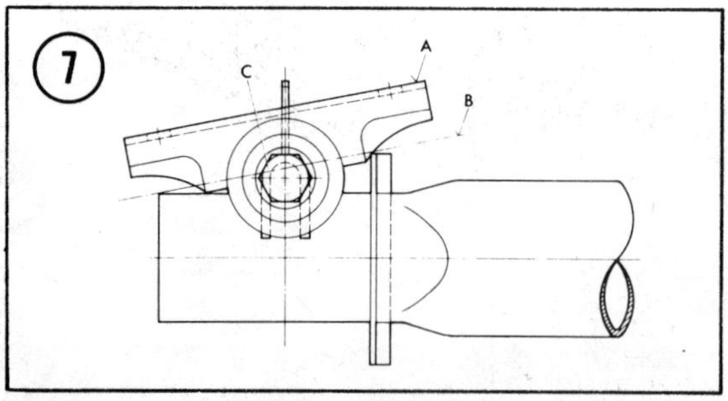

WHEEL BEARINGS

Wheel Bearing Replacement

Refer to **Figure 8** for this procedure.

1. Remove brake drums and wheel bearings as described in Chapter Nine.

2. Clean the wheel bearings thoroughly in solvent and blow dry. Check rollers for scores, wear, and evidence of overheating (bluish tint). Check bearing races in the brake drum. Do not mix up the bearings if they are good; they must be replaced on the same race.

3. If a bearing or a bearing race is damaged, the bearing and bearing race must be replaced.

4. Pack both wheel bearings with wheel bearing (lithium) grease. Press grease thoroughly into the cage and rollers.

5. Grease the stub axle lightly.

6. Install the inner race, bearing, and oil seal in the brake drum. The seal should be flush with, or slightly below, the hub.

7. Install the brake drum.

8. Install the outer race, bearing (packed in Step 4), and thrust washer.

9. Install the hub finger-tight, then adjust wheel bearings exactly as described below.

10. Adjust the brakes.

Wheel Bearing Adjustment

1. Raise rear of vehicle on jackstands.

2. Pry dust cap off.

3. Remove cotter pin and castellated nut.

4. Tighten hex nut to about 11 ft.-lb. (1.5 mkg) while rotating the wheel. This takes all slack out of the bearings.

5. Loosen hex nut just to point where thrust washer can be turned with a screwdriver. See **Figure 9**. This is equivalent to a bearing play of 0.0012-0.0027 in. (0.03-0.07mm).

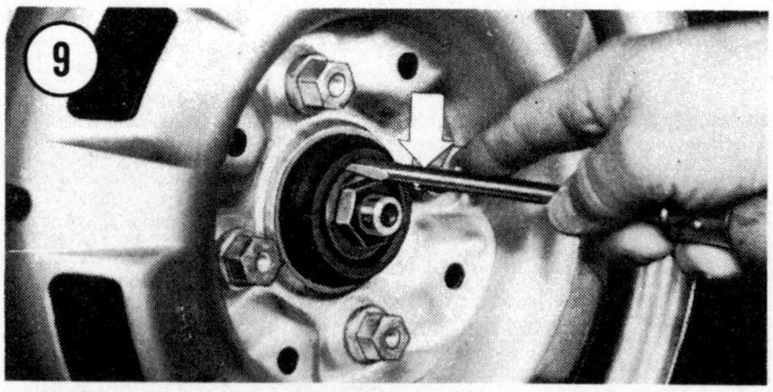

6. Install castellated nut, being sure not to disturb hex nut, and insert cotter pin.

7. Fill grease cup with multipurpose grease and press it on.

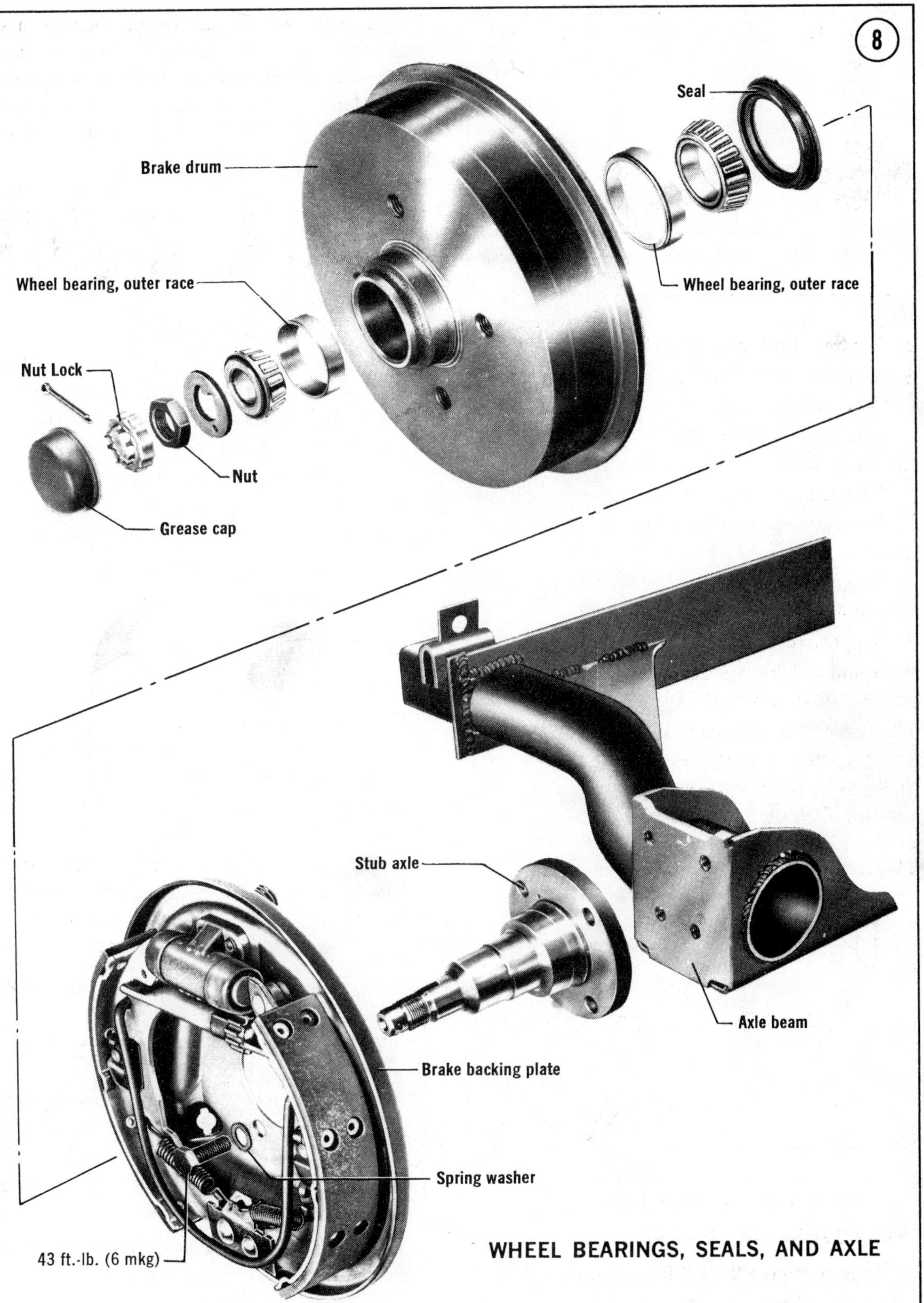

WHEEL BEARINGS, SEALS, AND AXLE

Table 1 SPECIFICATIONS

Type	Independent
Springing	Coil springs
Wheel alignment*	
Camber	—1° ± 30′
Toe (both wheels)	0° ± 15′
Rear track	53.1 in. (1,350mm)

* Not adjustable.

Table 2 TIGHTENING TORQUES

	Ft.-lb.	Mkg
Rear axle		
Piston rod to coil spring (M 10)	14	2.0
Coil spring to body (M 10)	25	3.5
Coil spring to rear axle (M 10)	32	4.5
Stub axle to rear axle	43	6.0
Rear axle to body (M 10)	43	6.0

CHAPTER TWELVE

BODY

This chapter includes replacement or repair procedures for the seats, doors, hoods, fenders, and bumpers. Other body repairs require special knowledge and/or tools and should be done by your dealer or local body repair shop.

SEATS

Front Seat Removal/Installation

1. Pry off cover shown in **Figure 1**.

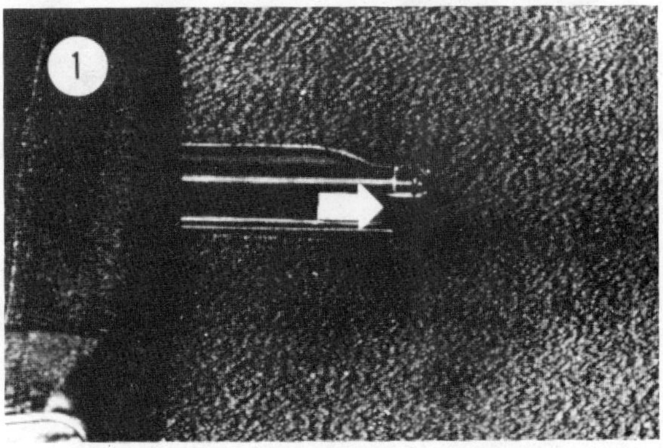

2. Push front seat backward into the next-to-last position.
3. Press stop ring down, using a screwdriver. See **Figure 2**.

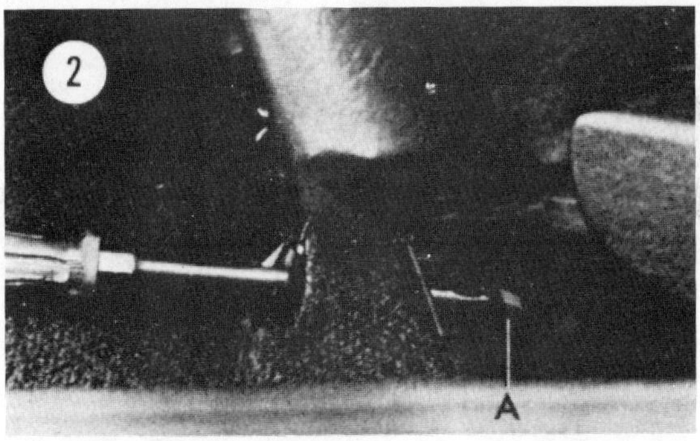

4. Still holding down stop ring (A), release the seat with control (B) and push it to the rear and out of the rails.
5. Installation is the reverse of these steps.

12

DOORS

Front Side Door Removal

1. Remove pin in check strap as shown in **Figure 3**.
2. Remove door panel as described later.
3. Scribe around hinges so that door can be reinstalled more easily.
4. Have an assistant support door, then remove hinge bolts from hinge pillar.

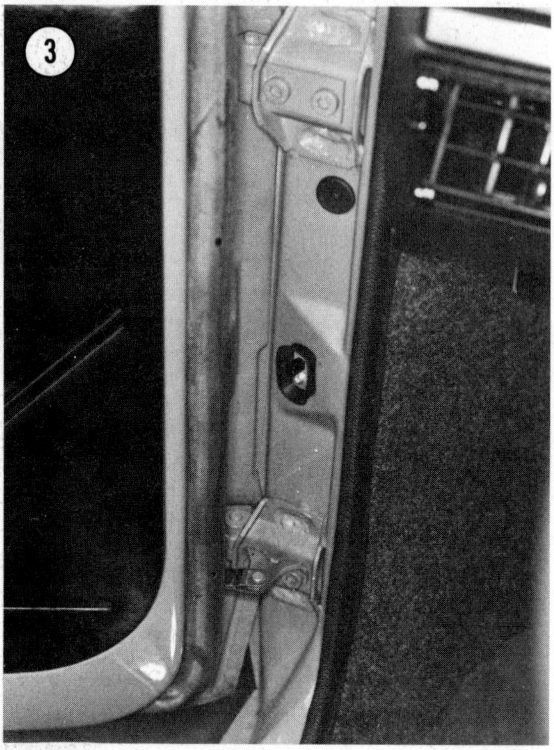

Front Side Door Installation

1. Check the door weatherstripping. Replace if damaged.

2. Remove door striker bolt from door frame. See **Figure 4**.

3. Install the door and secure hinges with bolts to hinge.

4. Ensure that the door can open and close without jamming and check alignment at the points shown in **Figure 5**. Loosen the door hinge screws and align the door if necessary.

5. Install the striker bolt in the door frame.

6. Oil the hinge pins.

7. Lubricate contact surfaces of the striker bolt and door bolt lightly with Vaseline or molybdenum disulfide paste.

Door Panel Removal/Installation

1. Carefully pry out cap from window crank. Remove Phillips screws securing crank and remove crank. See **Figure 6**.

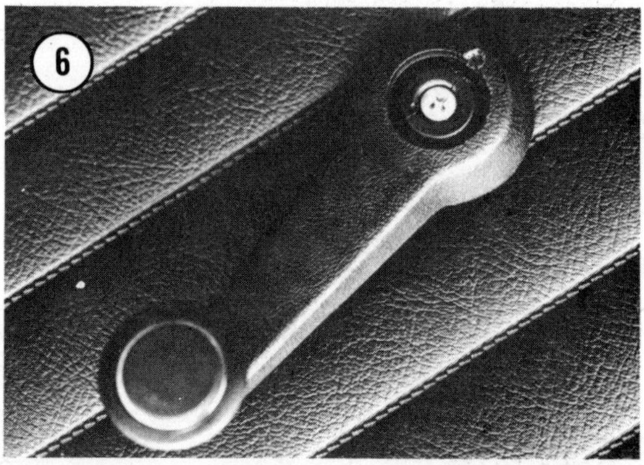

2. Remove screws securing arm rest.

3. Carefully pry door panel away from door, working slowly all around the edge until all clips are free.

4. Lift panel free from door.

5. Installation is the reverse of these steps.

DOOR LOCKS

Exterior Handle Replacement

1. Open door.

2. Remove door panel as described earlier.

3. Remove screws securing the rear edge of door handle to door. See **Figure 7**.

4. Pull rear edge of door handle outward and disengage front edge from door.

5. Installation is the reverse of these steps.

Lock Cylinder Replacement

1. Open door and remove door panel as described earlier.

2. Remove exterior door handle, as described above.

3. Insert key in lock cylinder.

CAUTION

Key must be inserted to prevent tumblers and springs from falling out.

4. Remove screws securing lock cylinder lever. Remove lever and spring.

5. Remove lock cylinder from door handle.

6. Installation is the reverse of these steps. Use new seal on the outside of the lock cylinder. See **Figure 8**.

Lock Replacement

1. Unscrew interior door lock button.

2. Remove door panel as described earlier.

3. Remove 2 screws shown in **Figure 9** securing lock to door.

4. Remove door lock with linkage.

5. Installation is the reverse of these steps.

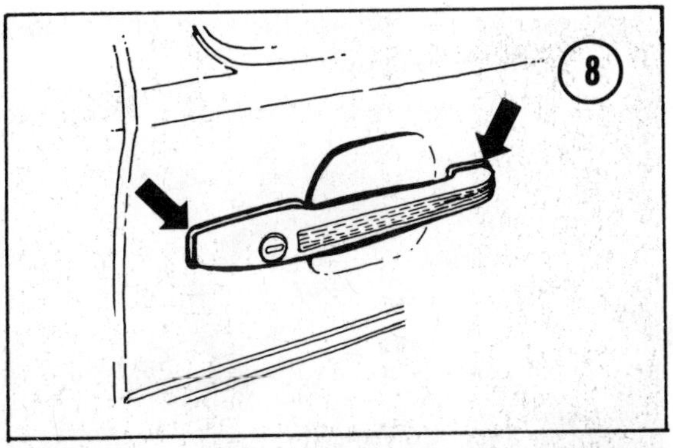

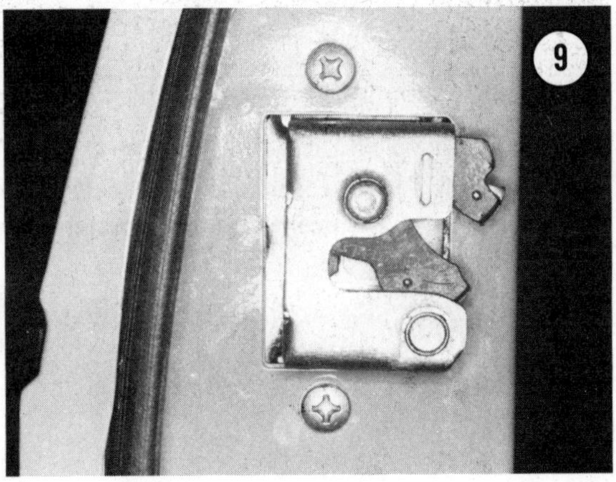

Make sure that operating lever (A) engages with the exterior door handle. See **Figure 10**.

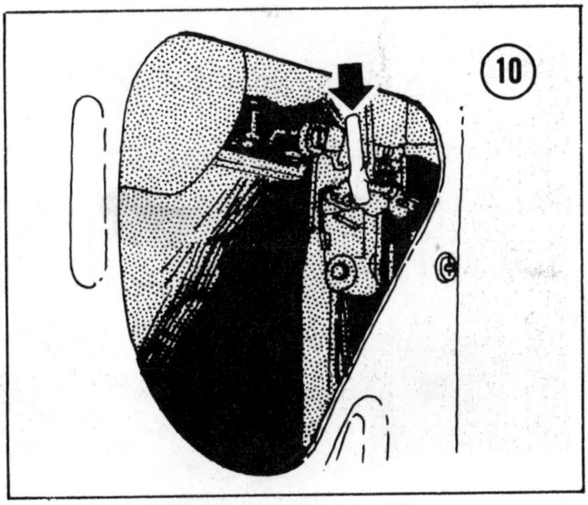

HOOD

1. Open the hood.

2. Scribe marks on the hood around the hinges to aid in reassembly.

3. Have a helper support the hood and remove hinge bolts. See **Figure 11**.

4. Lift the hood off.
5. Installation is the reverse of these steps. Line up scribe marks for proper hood alignment.

REAR LID

Removal/Installation

1. Open rear lid.
2. Disconnect rear tray straps.
3. Disconnect lid prop.
4. Remove covers in headliner over hinge bolts.
5. While a helper supports the lid, remove hinge bolts.
6. Lift lid off.
7. Installation is the reverse of these steps.

Lock Replacement

1. Open the lid.
2. Remove 3 screws securing upper part of lock to lid. See **Figure 12**.

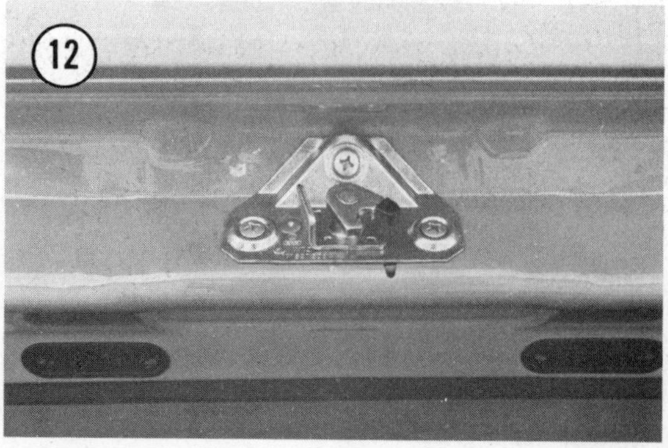

3. Unscrew nut securing lock cylinder and remove the lock cylinder. See **Figure 13**.

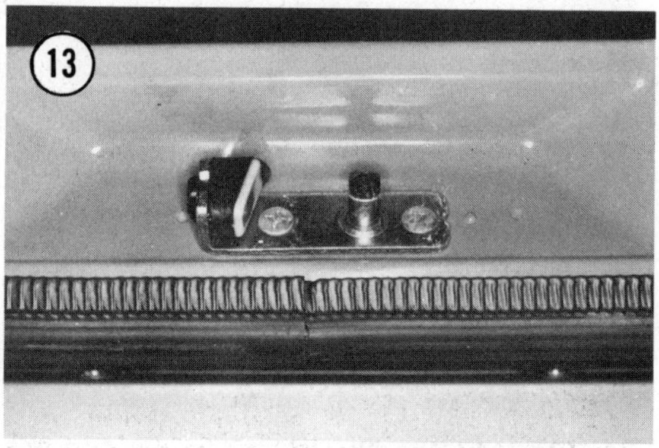

BUMPERS

1. Disconnect wires from the parking lights (front only).
2. Remove bolts securing energy absorbers to frame. See **Figure 14** (front) or **Figure 15** (rear).

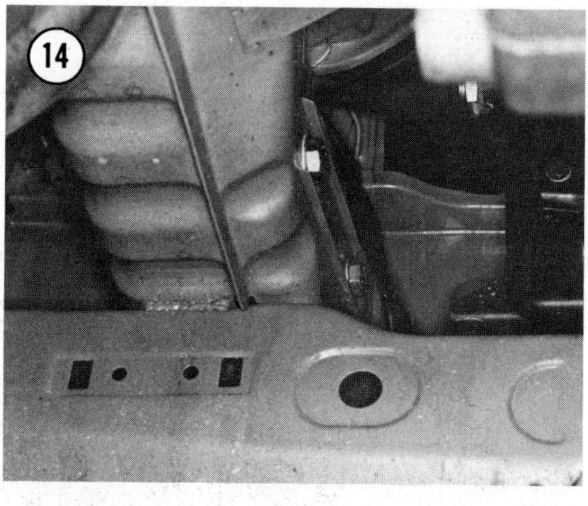

3. Pull bumper assembly with energy absorbers out of the body.
4. Remove nuts securing energy absorbers to bumpers.
5. Installation is the reverse of these steps.

FRONT GRILLE

1. Open hood.
2. Remove screws shown in **Figure 16**.
3. Remove grille.
4. Installation is the reverse of these steps.

15

16
CALIFORNIA
691 MKM

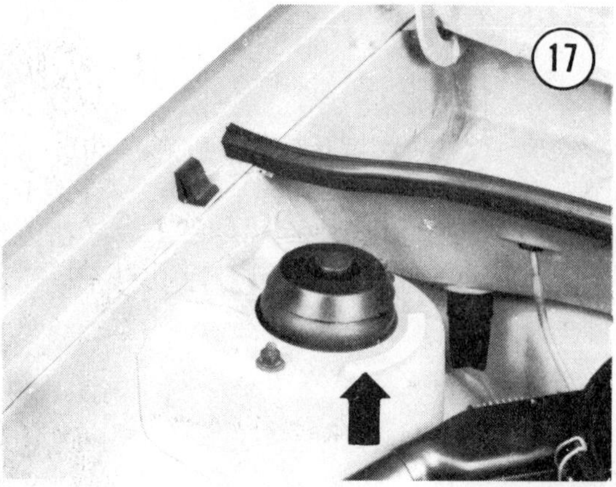

VEHICLE IDENTIFICATION

Several identification numbers are important when ordering spare parts or identifying the automobile for registration purposes. Refer to **Figure 17**. The chassis number is stamped in the engine compartment on the right suspension strut mounting and on the left windshield pillar. The identification plate showing manufacturer's name, place of origin, model, weights, and chassis serial number is located on the upper front crossmember in the engine compartment. The transmission number is stamped at the front of the transmission where it joins the engine.

TOWING

There are four towing eyes on the Rabbit/ Scirocco: two at the front and two at the rear. See **Figures 18 and 19**. Do not use bumpers or any other point for towing. Be sure that you observe all state and municipal ordinances governing towing.

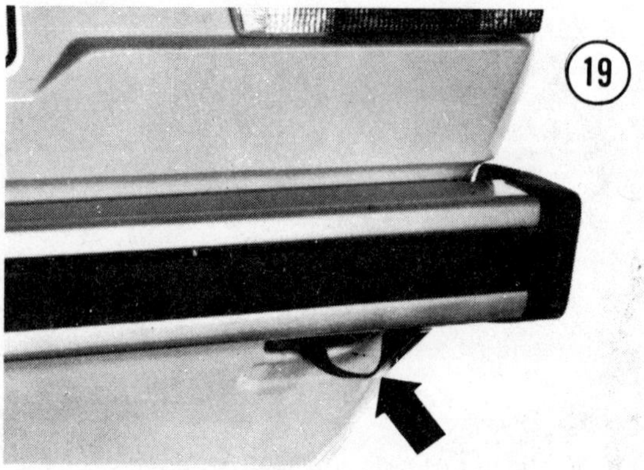

Vehicles With Automatic Transmission

The transmission oil pump does not operate unless the engine is running. Therefore, follow these directions *exactly* to prevent costly damage.

1. Move selector lever to NEUTRAL.
2. Do not tow faster than 30 mph, and no farther than 30 miles.
3. If you must tow farther than 30 miles, the front wheels must be lifted clear of the road.
4. Do not attempt to start engine by towing or pushing vehicle.

WARNING

More brake pedal force is required to stop a vehicle equipped with brake booster when the engine is not running.

JACKING

To prevent damage to the underside, lift the car only at the points indicated in this section.

At the front on Rabbit and Scirocco models, use lifting socket under hinge pillar. See **Figures 20 and 21**.

CAUTION

When jacking up the car, do not damage the fuel line.

At the rear, lift under the welded flange of the side member at the triangular mark. See **Figures 22 and 23**.

The same points are used whether using a hoist or a garage type floor jack. **Figure 24** shows the Rabbit lifted correctly on a hoist.

WARNING

If components such as the rear axle, fuel tank, spare tire, etc., are removed while the car is supported on a hoist, be sure to add compensating weight to the rear of the car. Otherwise, the weight or the engine, transmission, and front axle could tip the car from the hoist, causing damage to the car and possible injury or death to personnel.

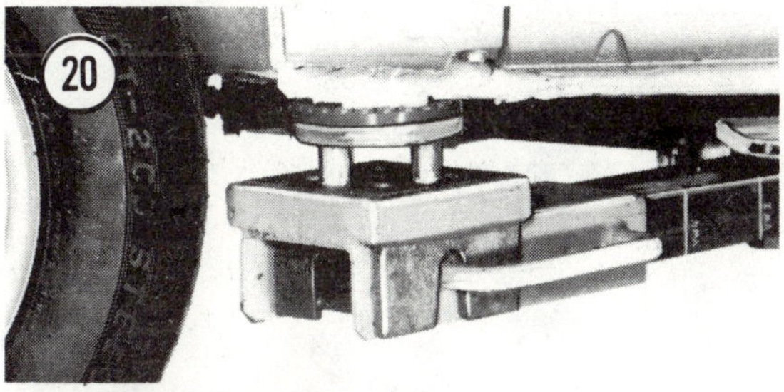

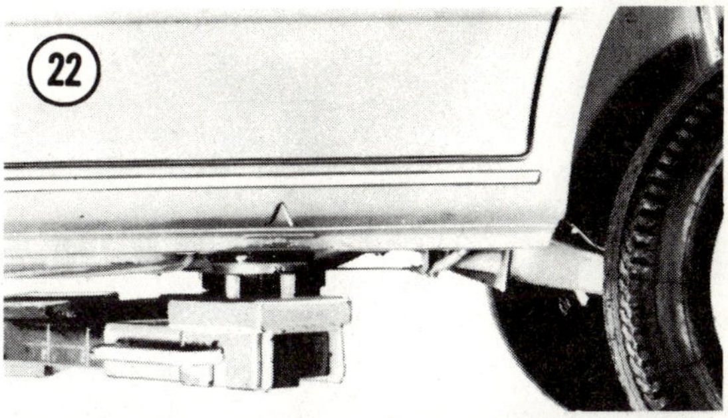

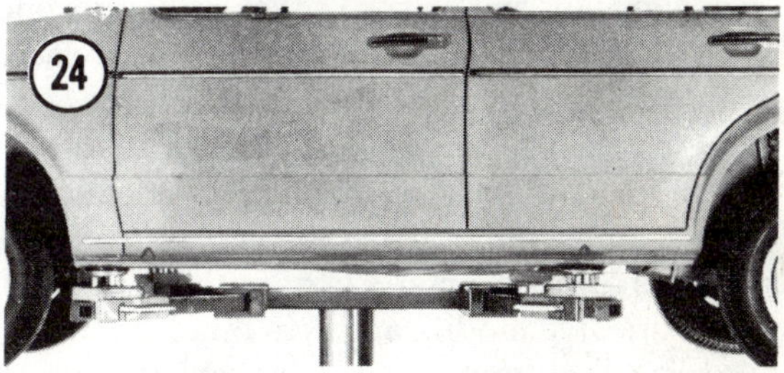

CHAPTER THIRTEEN

PERFORMANCE IMPROVEMENT

This chapter talks about performance — what it consists of, and how to improve it. It explains what various high-performance parts will and won't do, and discusses the ways parts and systems affect each other. For the inexperienced or unwary, it points out common mistakes.

While there is a wide variety of high-performance equipment available, few of you will ever actually enter your car in competition. Therefore, this chapter has been prepared with street-oriented modifications in mind.

Most of the accessories in this chapter are of the "bolt-on" variety. Bolt-on equipment materials and designs change frequently. We cannot control how the equipment will be installed, or how the car will be used. Good judgment and common sense will help you avoid disappointment. "Bolt-on," as used here, means accessories which you can add to your car with ordinary hand tools and a reasonable degree of mechanical expertise. Generally speaking, if you can carry out the service procedures outlined in this manual, you can also install the bolt-on, high-performance accessories illustrated in this chapter.

It is impossible for us to show you how to install all of the items discussed in this chapter — it would take an entire book — but we will show you what is available, and we'll supply you with the addresses and other vital information to get you going.

CAUTION
Clymer Publications cannot guarantee or be responsible for performance, possible damage to the car, or personal injury resulting from the performance modification procedures given in this manual.

WHAT DO YOU WANT?

You may be able to answer the question better after reading this chapter, but at some point, it's going to need serious thought. Every modification has its tradeoffs. Quicker cornering may come at the expense of a rougher ride. Increased horsepower can mean reduced gas mileage and shorter engine life. And of course, performance can be expensive, in both money and time. The best way to guarantee getting what you want is to modify the car one step at a time, in a logical order.

Chassis Modifications

Without question, the chassis should be modified first. It is foolish (and dangerous) to modify an engine for more horsepower than the chassis is capable of handling.

Chassis modifications are generally less expensive (and easier to make) than engine modifications, and you can add various bits and pieces (heavy-duty shocks, stiffer sway bars, etc.) as you get the money. Therefore, if for no other reason than economy, the chassis-first approach makes sense.

Quite possibly, in view of today's 55 mph speed limit, you may decide to modify the chassis only, and leave the stock engine alone. Chassis improvements will allow you to travel from one point on the map to another in less time, and with less dramatics (body lean, wheel hop, etc.), even without an increase in horsepower.

Engine Modifications

As mentioned previously, you should not even consider modifying the engine until you have modified the chassis. Of course, this does not apply to the addition of such items as an electronic ignition system, or a more efficient exhaust system. These will improve performance and gas mileage without adding too much horsepower for the suspension and brakes to cope with.

NOTE: *The stock engine should always be checked for soundness, then tuned perfectly before attempting any modifications. Raising the horsepower is a sure way to destroy a tired engine.*

It is possible to modify your engine to almost any horsepower stage that you wish. Conventional engine modification components are available (high-lift cams, lightweight pistons, exhaust systems, etc.), as well as turbocharger kits, so you are free to pick and choose, using your own mechanical (and financial) capabilities as a guide.

Body Modifications

Body modifications are the last step in the modification process. When your chassis has been properly set up (stiffer springs, heavier sway bars, modified shock absorbers, etc.) and your engine has been modified and tuned to the proper degree, the only area of modification left to explore is the body.

Air-flow devices, such as spoilers and air dams (which provide more downforce on the chassis at high speed), are more effective at high speed than when used at the legal speed limit, although they are worthwhile even then. At high speed they add tremendously to the overall stability of the car.

Fender flares, which are attached to the body by bolts or rivets, can be used to cover extra-wide wheels and tires. The flares can be molded in and painted to match the car, or left as is for a serious, functional appearance.

Replacing heavy stock body panels (fenders, hood, doors, trunk lid, etc.) with lightweight fiberglass components makes a great deal of sense, as reducing overall weight is more effective than adding horsepower. With less weight, your car will accelerate faster without additional horsepower; it will corner better, as there is less inertia that forces it to continue in a straight line when the front wheels are turned to negotiate a curve; and it will stop faster, since there is less momentum to force it to continue going forward when the power is cut off and the brakes are applied.

Fiberglass body components are also an ideal replacement for damaged or rusted steel body panels.

ACCESSORY SOURCES

Table 1 at the end of this chapter lists manufacturers and/or suppliers who offer a complete range of accessories (everything from the smallest add-on part to complete engines).

THE BASICS

These are the details that need attention before you get to the fun stuff. The main rule is start with a healthy car. Performance modification usually means brisk driving. A brief technical inspection will ensure that the car is up to it.

All bolts in the front and rear suspensions should be checked for looseness. This includes wheel lug nuts.

Front wheel bearings should be adjusted. If the maintenance schedule says it's near time to repack them, go ahead and do it.

Unless the car is nearly new, the front suspension should be checked for wear.

Brakes should be carefully inspected. Check pad and lining wear, and look for damaged discs or drums. Make sure the brake pedal is

Table 2 CHASSIS HANDLING GUIDE*

Adjustment	To Increase Understeer	To Increase Oversteer
Front tire pressure	Lower	Higher
Rear tire pressure	Higher	Lower
Front tire section	Smaller	Larger
Rear tire section	Larger	Smaller
Front wheel camber	More positive	More negative
Rear wheel camber	More negative	More positive
Front springs	Stiffer	Softer
Rear springs	Softer	Stiffer
Front anti-sway bar	Thicker (stiffer)	Thinner (weaker)
Rear anti-sway bar	Thinner (weaker)	Thicker (stiffer)
Weight distribution	More forward	More rearward

*Courtesy Quickor Engineering, Beaverton, Ore.

firm. If in doubt, bleed the brakes or repair the hydraulic system.

CHASSIS MODIFICATIONS

The following chassis modifications will result in a noticeable improvement in handling. For the most part, items such as heavy-duty shock absorbers, sway bars, etc., are installed the same way as their stock counterparts (refer to the appropriate chapters in the main body of this manual for procedures).

Refer to **Table 2** for a chassis handling guide.

Wheels and Tires

This should be the first area you look at. Tires affect cornering, braking, rolling resistance, ride quality, and noise level. The right selection can make solid improvements in all these areas, at reasonable cost and with little effort. Inadequate tires will neutralize any improvement to suspension or brakes.

First, size up what you have. A set of good quality 70-series radials on 6 in. wheels (maximum unless flared fenders are installed) is fine for most street applications. You can modify the suspension, then come back to the tires later if necessary.

If you decide to shop for tires, you'll need to know what the letters and numbers mean. On a tire designated "185/70SR-13," for example, the 185 is the width of the tire (cross section, not tread width) in millimeters. The 70 means the tire is a 70-series (the tire's height is 70 per cent of the width). The proportion of height to width is the "aspect ratio."

The S indicates the tire's ability to sustain a given high speed. No letter is lowest, H is higher, S is higher still, and V is highest. The R stands for radial. The 13 is the wheel diameter in inches.

Two of the most important characteristics of a tire are its coefficient of friction and slip angles. Coefficient of friction describes the ability of a tire to resist sliding when subjected to a force. The maximum force that a tire can sustain without sliding may be described as the "limit of adhesion" for that tire.

In order for a tire to be steered, i.e., maintain a desired course, it must be *rolling,* not sliding. A sliding tire has absolutely no directional discretion. It will slide sideways just as willingly as forward.

Friction is only important at the "limit of adhesion." Obviously, at that point it assumes overwhelming importance as the tire "breaks loose." But tire friction does not explain any of the handling characteristics of an automobile *below* the limit of adhesion of the tires.

To explain handling behavior such as understeer and oversteer, you must understand another important tire characteristic — slip angle.

1

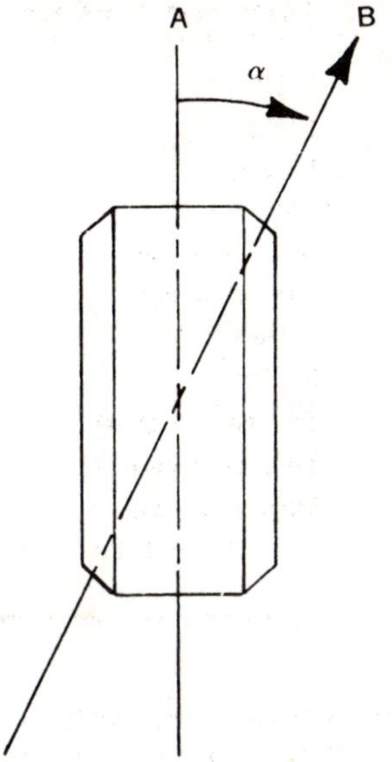

a = Slip angle
A = Tire centerline
B = Actual path traveled

A rolling tire normally follows a path in line with the direction of the tread. But if the tire is subjected to a side force, e.g., during cornering, the tire deflects and its patch diverges from the path in line with the tread. The tire actually travels in a direction at an angle to the direction that the tire points. This angle is called a "slip angle." See **Figure 1**.

Slip angle is one of those unfortunate, misleading terms that we are stuck with. It does not mean that the tire is sliding. The tire does not have to be anywhere near its limit of adhesion to operate at a slip angle. Slip angle causes the familiar effects of understeer, oversteer, and neutral steering.

Oversteer occurs when the slip angle at the rear tires changes more than at the front tires. This steers the car into a smaller circle than intended and increases centrifugal force. Increased centrifugal force in turn causes the tires to operate at even higher slip angles, making the car steer into an even smaller circle, and so on. It is truly a "vicious circle," which if allowed to continue will result in a spin-out, even in the hands of a skilled driver.

Understeer occurs when the slip angle at the front tires changes more than at the rear. The car steers into a larger circle than intended, reducing centrifugal force. This decreases the tire slip angle and further increases the circle, thereby decreasing centrifugal force, and so on. The car automatically seeks a turning circle which balances tire forces with no correction from the driver.

Understeer may seem more desirable than oversteer, but if the equilibrium turning circle is larger than the curvature of the road, the driver may helplessly watch his car head for the bushes.

Neutral steer means that slip angles change at the front and rear at the same rate. The vehicle path tends to follow the curvature of the road without a tendency to increase or decrease the turning circle.

Slip angle is not fixed for any tire. Factors that change it are centrifugal force, wind gusts, road plane (level, banked), wheel plane (camber, toe, deflection), and vertical forces (acceleration, braking, lateral weight transfers).

Since the slip angle at which a tire operates is constantly changing, there is no such thing as a "state of understeer," for example. A car which understeers under one set of circumstances may oversteer under another set. Neutral steer is simply the transition between oversteer and understeer; it is not a condition which can be set up and maintained by chassis tuning.

Several manufacturers produce excellent radial tires: Semperit, Veith, Michelin, Goodyear, Pirelli, and Goodrich. All offer good road holding (some better in the wet than others), reasonable ride comfort, and long tread life (a characteristic of all radial tires).

NOTE: *Racing tires shouldn't be used on the street. They have very thin, easily damaged sidewalls. Racing tires meant for dry pavement are dangerously slippery on wet pavement. Those meant for wet pavement use super-soft rubber compounds which wear very quickly, and may overheat on dry pavement.*

With wider tires, you'll need wider wheels. Widened steel wheels are available, or you can have your own steel wheels widened by a

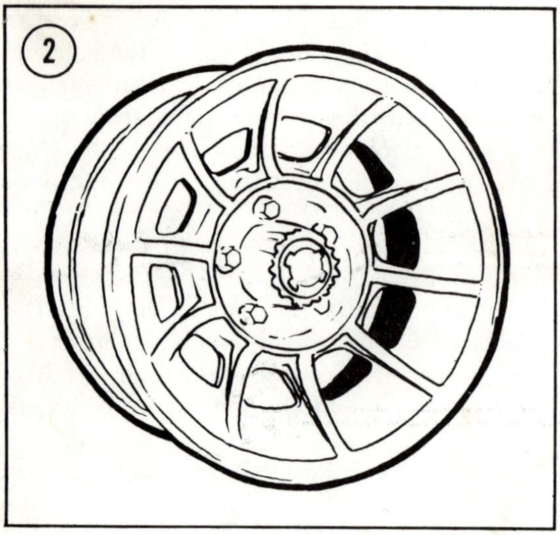

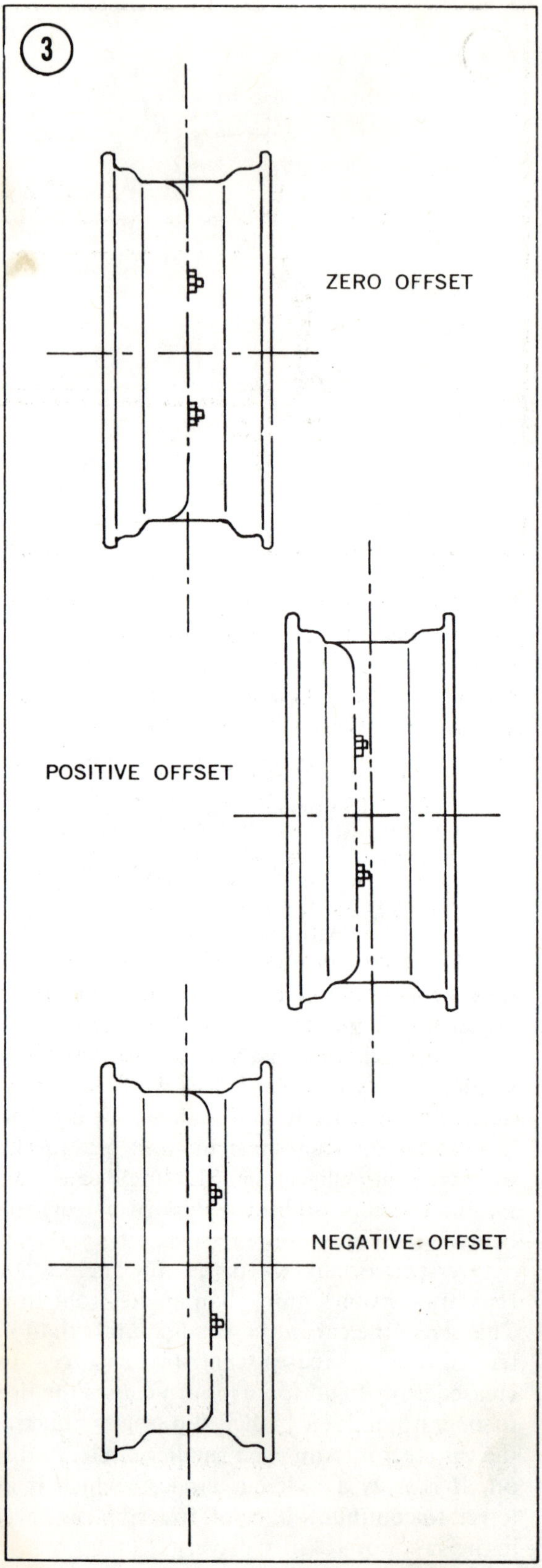

specialty shop. The most popular accessory wheels are cast aluminum or magnesium "mags." Those shown in **Figure 2** are typical.

Three things must be considered when buying wheels: compatibility with tubeless tires, wheel width, and wheel offset.

Some "mag" wheels require tube-type tires. If you're going to use tube-type tires anyway, this doesn't matter. Check before buying, though, to make sure your tires and wheels are compatible.

Wheel width should be proportional to the tire. As a rule of thumb, the wheel should be approximately two inches narrower than the tire's cross-section width. Once you've selected a specific brand of tire, the tire dealer can give you exact size recommendations.

Wheel offset (**Figure 3**) is the relationship of the wheel center to the wheel rim. Positive offset moves the wheel rim outward (the car's track is wider). Negative offset moves the wheel rim inward (the car's track is narrower). Too much negative offset can cause clearance problems between the tires and wheel wells. In front, the wheels may rub on the brake calipers or tie rod ends. Too much positive offset may cause the tires to rub on the fenders. Also, positive offset increases the strain on wheel bearings and hubs. If you use wheels with much positive offset, the wheel bearings should be checked frequently for wear.

The number of wheel manufacturers makes it impossible for us to list them all here, so you

4

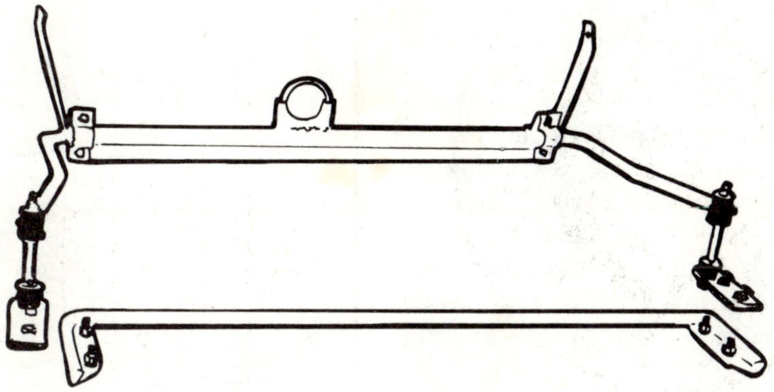

will have to do some of the detective work yourself and check through automotive magazines such as *Road & Track, Car & Driver, Autoweek,* etc., and send for some of the catalogs from these wheel manufacturers.

> NOTE: *In addition to obtaining the catalogs offered by the various wheel manufacturers, you will find a wealth of information concerning tires and wheels in Auto World's Motorsports Catalog (refer to* **Table 1** *for their address).*

Once you've picked out a combination of wheels and tires, have a pair of them mounted and installed, one on the front and one on the rear. Check clearance with the suspension bottomed out, and with the front wheels at full left and full right lock.

If the tire dealer doesn't want to let you try a set before buying (and you don't feel like looking for another tire dealer), offer to pay the mounting charge if the tires don't fit. When you're spending hundreds of dollars to last thousands of miles, it's worth $10 or so to avoid a bad purchase.

CAUTION

Alloy wheels can easily be chipped or gouged during tire mounting, and some are more difficult to balance than steel wheels. Have mounting and balancing done by a shop experienced with alloy wheels.

Sway (Anti-roll) Bars

These bars reduce body roll during hard cornerning, resulting in a flatter cornering attitude and better control and tire adhesion. Refer to **Figure 4**.

It is necessary to "balance" the car by carefully coordinating the diameter of the rear sway bar with that of the front one. A rear sway bar should definitely not be installed without using a front sway bar which has a larger than stock diameter.

Installation of sway bars is a simple nuts-and-bolts operation requiring a couple of hours of work. Kits generally come with installation instructions.

Front and Rear Springs

Heavy-duty springs are available for street, autocross, or race conditions (refer to **Figure 5**), and installation is straightforward. Refer to the procedures outlined in the proper chapter of the main body of this manual.

The addition of stiffer springs reduces "body wallow" in corners and generally keeps the car more stable on winding or undulating roads.

> NOTE: *Heavy-duty shocks must be used in conjunction with stiffer springs, as conventional shock absorbers cannot control the movements set up by stiffer springs.*

The installation of some high-performance coil springs will reduce the height of your car by an inch or more, so take this into consideration when buying wheels and tires.

Shock Absorbers

The installation of high-performance shock absorbers is an absolute necessity if you choose to install heavy-duty springs. Even if you keep the stock springs, it is a good idea to install high-performance shock absorbers, which control the road wheels much better than stock shock absorbers, due to their special valving and construction.

There are a number of popular high-performance shock absorbers available for the Rabbit and Scirocco: Koni, Mulholland, Bilstein, KYB, Boge, and Carrera seem to be the front-runners. All are excellent; the choice is simply a personal one which you must make. Refer to **Figure 6**.

Unlike stock MacPherson strut shocks, which have to be filled with oil, performance shocks usually come as sealed cartridges. Therefore, all the old oil must be removed from the strut before installing the new shock absorber.

If you have never driven a car equipped with high-performance shock absorbers of this quality, you will immediately appreciate the difference in handling.

Suspension Bushings

Stock suspension bushings are fairly soft, to give a smooth, quiet ride. However, their softness allows the suspension to flex, making control less precise. Harder bushings increase control, but may also roughen the ride and increase road noise.

Wheel Spacers

Wheel track can easily be widened by adding wheel spacers. Installation is easy: simply remove the wheels, slip the spacers over the wheel studs, and install the wheels again. Refer to **Figure 7**. Increasing the track makes the car more stable in corners, as it widens the car's stance.

5

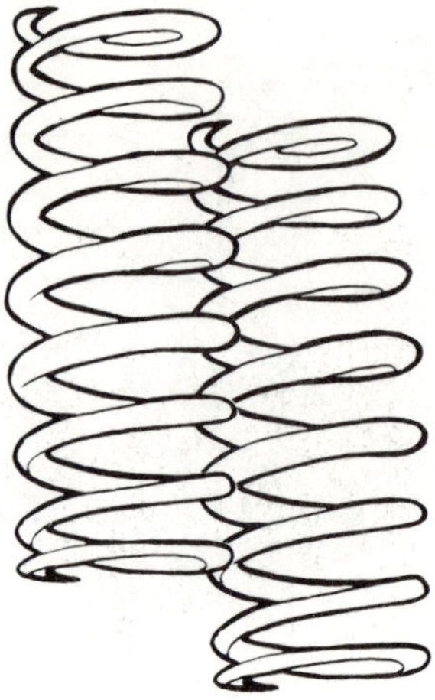

6

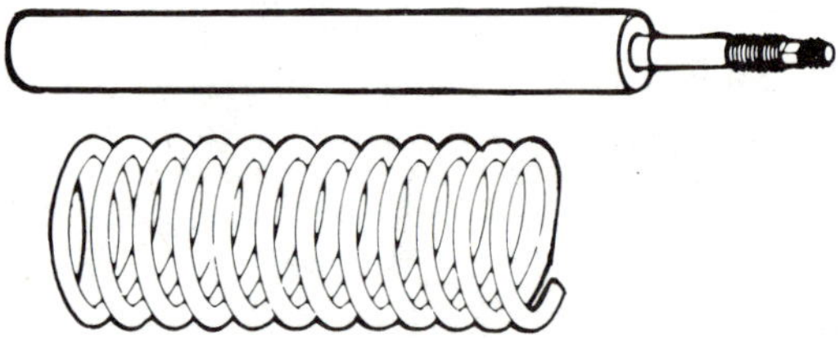

7

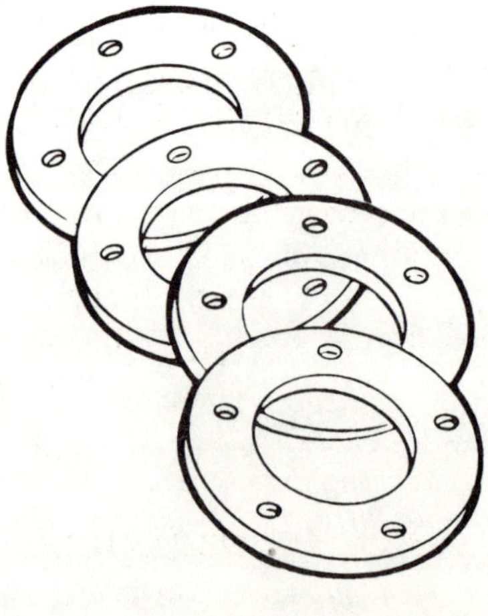

8

Another use for wheel spacers is to gain additional brake caliper clearance when installing special alloy wheels.

CAUTION
Spacers may keep the wheel nuts from threading all the way onto the studs. In this case, longer studs must be installed.

Brake Linings

Several manufacturers offer excellent high-performance brake pads which can be installed in place of the stock brake pads. Repco pads seem to be the most popular, and they are widely available in auto parts stores. These pads offer more consistent control and less fading during heavy braking, less brake dust, and they do not squeal.

Brake Discs

You can have your brake discs drilled for additional cooling and reducing unsprung weight. This service is performed by German Motors and Parts (refer to **Table 1**).

ENGINE MODIFICATIONS

Engine modifications should be carried out in logical sequence in order to extract the most benefit from each component. The recommended modifications are given in stages, starting with components which will increase efficiency and performance, as well as laying the groundwork for more extensive modifications.

STAGE I

Many stock engines suffer from a mediocre ignition system, restricted exhaust system, and a fuel system which "breathes" through a less-than-ideal air filtering system. The simple addition of an efficient header/exhaust system, a high-performance ignition coil, an electronic ignition system, and a more efficient air filter will bring a surprising increase in horsepower and make the engine start more easily, deliver better gas mileage, and (in the case of the ignition) need less maintenance than its stock counterpart.

Ignition Coil

Many manufacturers offer "hotter" ignition coils which are supposed to provide more voltage to your distributor (and therefore to your spark plugs). Some do, and some don't. Most of the reputable manufacturers (Accel, Mallory, Bosch, etc.) offer high-quality ignition coils that meet their claims. They are a simple nuts-and-bolts replacement item for your stock coil. Refer to **Figure 8**.

Electronic Ignition

There are also many manufacturers who offer electronic ignition systems such as Mallory, Permatune, Allison, Jacobs, Tiger, Piranha, etc. These units are easy to install and reasonably priced. High-performance coils are mandatory or recommended with some; others replace the coil altogether.

There are two basic types of electronic ignition. One type retains the points, but uses them only to carry a low-voltage trigger signal. This prolongs point life. The other type replaces the points with a photo-optical or magnetic trigger. These highly accurate triggering systems provide stable ignition timing, and eliminate point bounce at high rpm.

13

All of the systems provide a longer lasting, higher voltage spark. This allows easier starting and may increase horsepower and gas mileage. It also ensures that the spark plugs will fire at high rpm. See **Figure 9**.

Spark Plugs and Spark Plug Wires

A modified engine usually requires plugs just slightly colder than stock.

Spark plugs are designed to work within a specific heat range. Below 1,000°F (550°C), carbon deposits do not burn off the tip and may form a conducting track which short circuits the plug. Above 1,550°F (850°C), the plug tip gets so hot it can pre-ignite the mixture like a glow plug. The spark plug operates best when center electrode is 1,300-1,400°F (700-750°C).

Modified engines usually run hotter and require a "cold" plug that can dissipate heat rapidly. This prevents the center electrode from running hotter than desired. The center electrode and insulating core are made short so that there is a short heat conduction path to the metal body and the comparatively cool cylinder head. Refer to **Figure 10**.

A cold-running engine requires a hot plug that does not quickly dissipate the heat. Thus, the central electrode stays hotter. Otherwise, the central electrode temperature would drop below the desired range. The central electrode is made long so that the heat conduction path is long. Refer to **Figure 11**.

Most plug manufacturers use a number to indicate heat range. Champion uses higher numbers to indicate a higher heat range. For example, an N9 plug is hotter than an N5. Bosch and NGK use lower numbers for higher heat ranges. For example, a Bosch W95T2 plug is hotter than a W125T2. An NGK BP6ES is hotter than a BP7ES.

It is a good idea to replace your stock spark plug wires with high-energy capacity, high-performance spark plug wires such as the Thundervolt "Fire Wire" offered by Auto World (see **Table 1**). This metallic wire is made up of 19 strands of silver-plated copper (finished size is 16 ga., 7mm in diameter), and covered with special silicone rubber that is immune to ozone, corona, moisture, corrosion, cracking, and hardening. The rubber is self-extinguishing and resists extreme heat and cold (+600°F to −100°F) with a temperature rating of 550°F.

NOTE: *Metallic plug wires create radio interference, so you may have to use noise suppressors with them.*

Exhaust System

Replacing the stock exhaust system with an efficient header and complete free-flow exhaust system can improve the performance of a stock engine, and is necessary for a highly modified engine.

"Back pressure" (the accumulation of exhaust gas in the exhaust system which has not found its way out of the engine from the

9

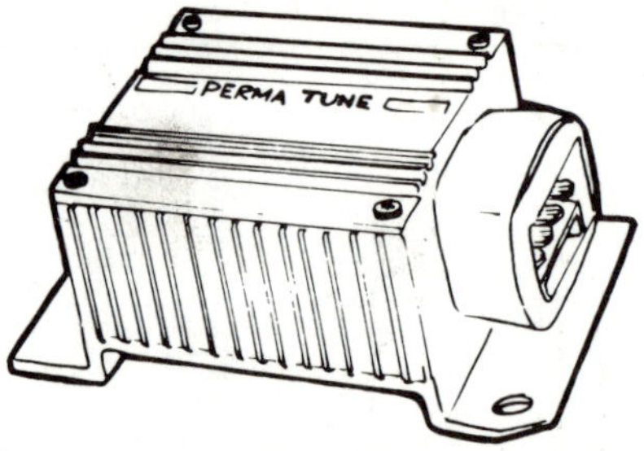

10

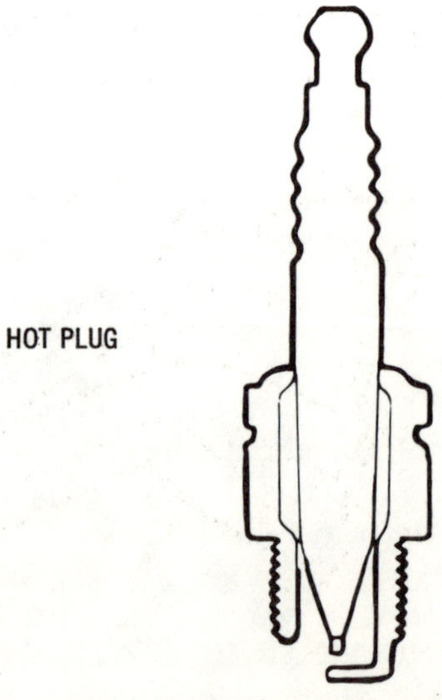

previous exhaust stroke at the time that the intake stroke takes place) can rob an engine of 15-20% of its horsepower. By simply providing a smooth, uninterrupted path for this exhaust gas to be expelled from the engine, the maximum fresh charge of air and fuel can be drawn into the cylinders, providing all of the horsepower that your engine was designed for.

NOTE: *The addition of a more efficient exhaust system is occasionally against the law, due to Federal smog regulations. Check the laws in your state to see if they apply.*

An example of a truly efficient header is shown in **Figure 12**, and a free-flow exhaust system is shown in **Figure 13**. Installation can be done by anyone with average mechanical ability and a moderate tool collection.

Header quality can vary widely from one manufacturer to another. Before buying, note whether the mounting surface is flat and smooth. If not, it must be surface ground to prevent exhaust leaks. Make sure welds are strong, even, and gas-tight. Poor fit is a common problem, so some drilling and filing may be necessary.

Air Cleaners

Replacing the standard air cleaner with a more efficient unit is a simple operation. It improves the appearance of the engine compartment, and permits the engine to breathe better. Approximately 2-3 horsepower can be gained from the installation of this simple accessory, and it is virtually "free" horsepower, as it is obtained without adding any strain to your engine.

STAGE II

Stage II modifications include all Stage I modifications, plus the addition of an oil

(11)

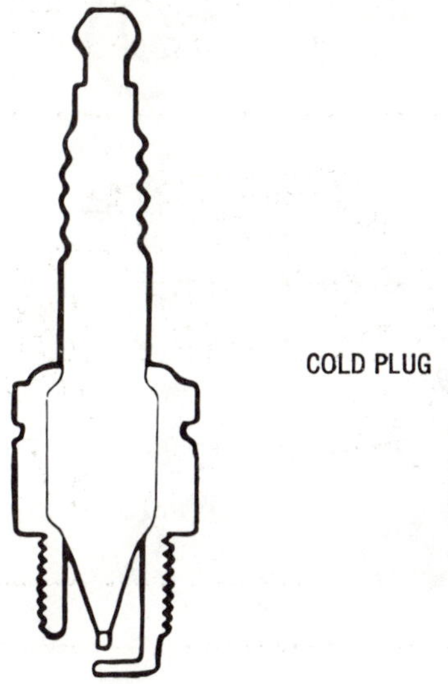

(12)

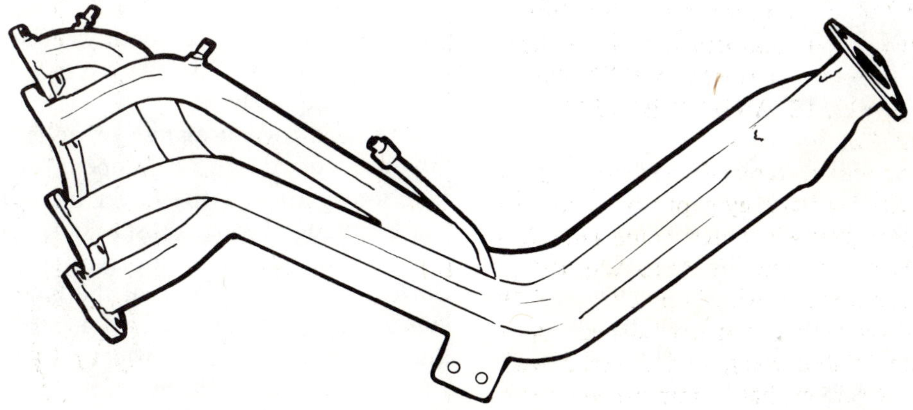

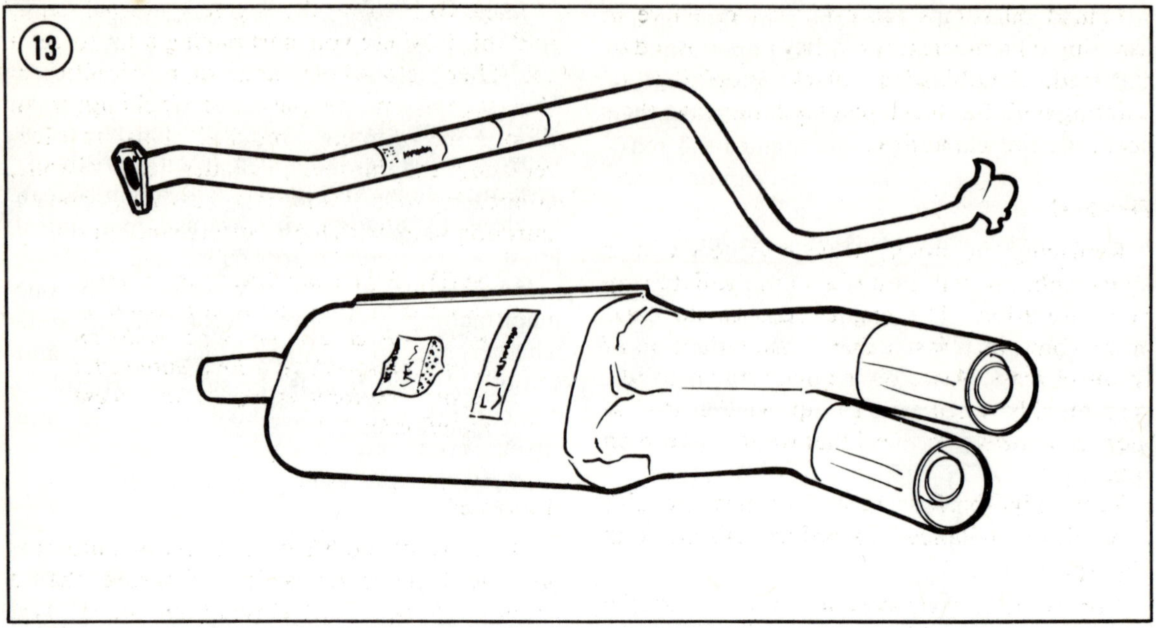

cooler; baffled, high-capacity oil sump; lightweight flywheel; and heavy-duty clutch.

Oil Cooler

In the interests of making your engine live as long as possible while putting out all of the horsepower you require, it is a good idea to install an engine oil cooler.

Accessory oil coolers built especially for your car are available from some of the manufacturers listed in **Table 1**, or you can install one of the universal accessory oil coolers, as illustrated in **Figure 14**. These bolt-on, multi-finned alloy coolers keep the oil from reaching extreme temperatures which can eventually destroy an engine. There are many sizes and configurations to choose from.

Oil Sump

The installation of a baffled, high-capacity oil sump only takes a few minutes (it is installed the same way as a stock one), and it is a worthwhile addition to your engine because of the extra margin of safety it provides. The baffles and extra oil capacity prevent oil starvation during hard cornering or acceleration. (Oil starvation can occur even when negotiating a freeway onramp; it is a result of oil sloshing to one side of the oil sump, away from the oil pump pickup.)

This extra safety is vital for any car driven ''enthusiastically'' as oil starvation can destroy an engine very quickly.

Contrary to what many say, added oil capacity will not reduce oil temperatures. It may take longer to heat the larger quantity of oil, but eventually it will get just as hot.

Finned oil sumps do not significantly reduce oil temperatures. The oil at the bottom of the sump is cooled, but this increases its viscosity and it remains there instead of circulating through the engine. In addition, the cooler oil in the bottom insulates the oil above it so that no further cooling occurs.

Finned oil sumps are even less effective in lowering oil temperatures if they are polished or chromed. Sandblasting, black anodizing, or painting with flat black paint will improve their heat radiating capability.

Flywheel

Replacing the stock, heavy flywheel with a lightweight one will result in an immediate gain in acceleration. The engine reaches its maximum rpm much faster due to the reduction of flywheel mass. Also, the engine returns to idle very quickly when you let up on the gas, as there is no heavy flywheel that wants to keep on rotating.

These high-performance flywheels are also dynamically balanced to reduce vibration at high speed.

Competition flywheels are not suited for street use. In addition to smoothing out the engine's power pulses, a flywheel's weight provides momentum to keep the engine turning when the clutch is engaged. With a super-light racing flywheel, very high engine speeds are necessary to move away from a stop. In many cases, it is necessary to rev the engine to several thousand rpm and pop the clutch.

Clutch

Most stock clutches are not capable of handling increased horsepower without slipping. Before you really dig into the engine's internal parts (as in Stage III), it is wise to replace the stock clutch with a heavy-duty, balanced one. If you have also installed an aftermarket flywheel, make sure the flywheel and clutch are compatible.

STAGE III

The modifications which you have performed in Stages I and II provide a healthy, quicker-than-stock engine which is still very much understressed. Quite likely you can stop at this point, unless you really have a need for additional horsepower, since an engine modified to Stage II specifications, used with the suspension modifications outlined earlier, will get your car over the road with admirable quickness and ease.

Stage III involves the engine's internal parts, and this is where you start paying a lot to get a lot. There is a whole range of possibilities in this stage, from a simple camshaft change to an all-out performance rebuild. This involves replacing the camshaft, cylinder head, pistons, connecting rods, crankshaft, bearings, and carburetion setup with high-performance parts.

> NOTE: *Engine modifications, as mentioned earlier, are sometimes in conflict with Federal and/or State emission laws. Check with your local authorities before performing any of these modifications.*

Camshafts

A camshaft modified for street or autocross use opens the valves earlier and farther than a stock camshaft, and closes them later. This allows more fuel and air to enter the cylinder, and allows more exhaust gas to clear the cylinder.

Mild-performance camshafts improve power and throttle response over a broad rpm range. As the grind becomes more radical, the power band narrows and the idle becomes rough.

With a mild grind, heavy valve springs are usually the only modification required. With more radical grinds, improved carburetion and increased compression may be necessary to get the most out of the camshaft.

Steel camshafts offer the greatest resistance to wear. If you buy a cast iron camshaft, make sure it has been hardened.

Carburetion

Weber carburetors are the overwhelming choice of most engine modifiers. These Webers are usually mounted on the individual manufacturer's polished and ported alloy intake manifold and come complete with all linkage and instructions. Refer to **Figure 15**.

The purpose of installing one or more larger carburetors on an efficient intake manifold is to let the engine "breathe" deeper (take in a denser fuel/air mixture) than the stock carburetion system allows.

With their removable jets and venturis, Webers can be set up for any engine, from stock to full race. Each manufacturer or supplier of these carburetion systems has his own pet camshaft/carburetion combinations for street or autocross use. Follow their recommendations (racing setups seldom work satisfactorily on the street).

Cylinder Head

Special cylinder heads increase horsepower due to their larger intake and exhaust valves, polished and ported intake and exhaust ports, and "cc'ed" and polished combustion chambers. They may also be milled for higher compression.

> NOTE: *"Cc'ed" means that the combustion chambers have been contoured so that each one has exactly the same capacity. This is done so that the shape of each combustion chamber is as close to identical as possible, which will result in increased horsepower.*
>
> *"Porting and polishing" means that the intake and exhaust ports have been carefully enlarged, followed by careful matching and polishing of the junction points where the intake and exhaust manifolds meet the cylinder head. This is done so that there are as few restrictions to the incoming fuel charge and outgoing exhaust gas as possible. This operation should be done by a professional.*
>
> *"Milling the head" means metal has been ground from the head's block mating surface. This makes the combustion chambers smaller and increases compression. It also brings the valves closer to the block and pistons, so these parts may have to be notched to keep the valves from hitting them.*

You can buy heads already modified, or have your own head reworked by a specialty shop.

Valves tend to "float" off their seats at high engine rpm, because stock valve springs are not strong enough to snap the valves back down onto their valve seats completely before the rotating camshaft lobes start to push them back up to open them again on the next cycle. This steals horsepower, as the cylinder is not completely sealed during its power stroke. Replace

15

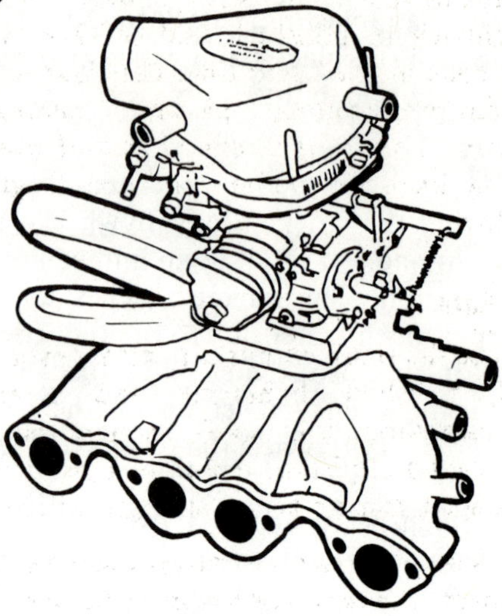

the stock valve springs with heavy-duty valve springs. These stiffer springs seat the valves immediately, even at high rpm.

The use of oversize valves in any cylinder head (even a stock one reworked to accept these valves), will result in more horsepower.

Pistons

Replace the stock pistons with lightweight, balanced, forged aluminum pistons to reduce rotating weight. This will increase engine rpm and result in more horsepower. In addition, these pistons are stronger than stock ones.

Performance pistons often raise the compression ratio. This is a good way to gain horsepower, but it shouldn't be carried to extremes. With a ratio higher than about 10:1, it may be difficult to find gas with a high enough octane rating to prevent detonation (pinging). Detonation creates extreme heat that can burn valves and melt holes right through piston crowns.

Oversize pistons must be used when the cylinders are bored to a larger diameter than stock. This is done when the cylinders are worn to a point where engine performance is affected. It is also done to increase the cubic displacement of the engine to produce more horsepower.

Connecting Rods

It helps to replace the stock connecting rods with lightweight, polished, and balanced connecting rods at the same time that you install the high-performance pistons mentioned previously. The weight reduction and precise balancing increase engine rpm and lengthen engine life.

Crankshaft

Replace the stock crankshaft with a precision ground, polished, lightened, and balanced high-performance crankshaft. As with the connecting rods and pistons mentioned previously, higher engine rpm and extra strength will result.

NOTE: *The stock crankshaft assembly (crank, bearings, connecting rods, and pistons) can be polished, shot peened (for additional strength), and balanced if you cannot afford to purchase the more expensive high-performance components mentioned earlier. Check the Yellow Pages of your telephone directory for a shop near you which specializes in engine balancing. Be sure to inspect and measure all dimensions with a micrometer and make any repairs necessary prior to balancing.*

Bearings

Heavy-duty main and connecting rod bearings should be used whenever the engine is modified for more performance. Vandervell bearings are widely used in high-performance engines, and are available in most auto parts stores, or from the mail order outlets listed in **Table 1**.

TURBOCHARGING

The easiest way to obtain a significant increase in horsepower is by turbocharging your engine. Turbocharging can be used as an alternative to Stage III, as outlined in the previous section, or in conjunction with Stage III modifications, providing that the compression ratio is kept down to that recommended by the individual turbocharger manufacturers for their kits. (High-compression ratios are not compatible with turbocharging for street use.)

NOTE: *It is advisable to discuss any engine modifications which you have already made (or would like to make) with the turbocharger manufacturer prior to purchasing and installing the turbocharger kit.*

Turbocharging Theory

Special high-lift cams, multiple carburetors such as the big Webers outlined in Stage III, high-compression heads, and tuned exhaust systems can't compare to simply forcing more air/fuel mixture into the cylinders with a properly designed turbocharger system. Furthermore, if properly maintained, a turbocharged engine seems to live approximately as long as a normally aspirated one.

Anyone reading this chapter is probably familiar with the basic operation of a naturally-aspirated, 4-cycle, spark-ignition engine. On the intake stroke, the descending piston draws an air/fuel charge through the intake valve. Theoretically, the volume of the incoming air/fuel charge should equal the volume of the cylinder at full throttle. In fact, this is impossible to achieve. The incoming charge volume is less than the cylinder volume. The reasons are:

a. Small, but unavoidable pressure drop through the fuel induction system
b. Restrictions in intake manifold ports and valves
c. Incomplete exhaust of burned gases from previous cycle
d. Exhaust valve and exhaust manifold port restrictions

The ratio between induced air/fuel volume (at 60° F and 14.7 psi) and calculated cylinder volume (piston area x stroke) is usually expressed as a percentage and is called "volumetric efficiency." If the induced charge equals the cylinder volume, the volumetric efficiency is 100%; most engines have a volumetric efficiency of about 80%.

In order to increase power from an engine, all we have to do is get more air/fuel charge into the cylinder. One method is to design very low restriction intake and exhaust systems. This explains how some exotic racing engines with

16

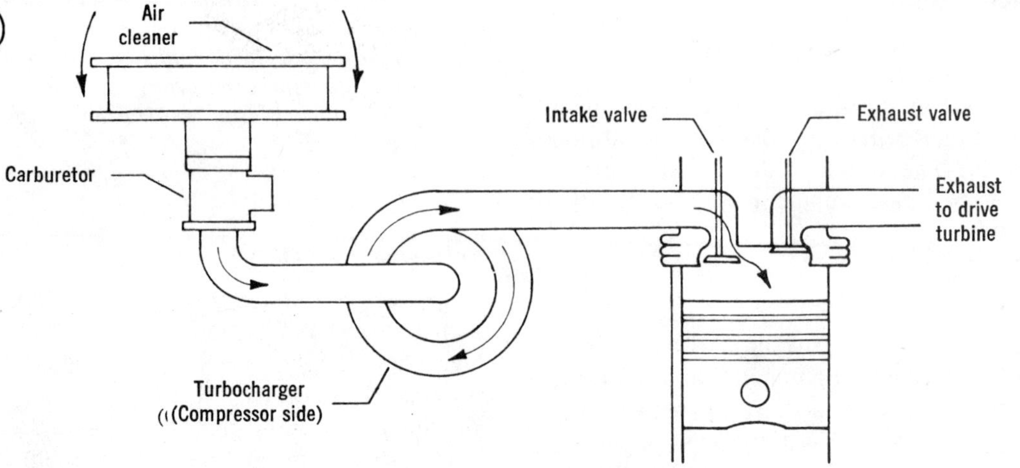

tuned intake and exhaust systems achieve nearly 100% volumetric efficiency over a very narrow speed range. However, they are not nearly flexible enough for everyday street driving.

Another method is to force the air/fuel charge into the combustion chamber under pressure, using a compressor. This will force more charge into an engine than is possible with low restriction and tuned intake/exhaust systems, and it will do it over a much broader speed range. This is how a turbocharger works. See **Figure 16**.

A turbocharger consists of a turbine wheel and a compressor wheel. See **Figure 17**. Exhaust gases from the engine drive the turbine wheel at speeds of up to 120,000 rpm. The compressor wheel, in turn, pumps a tremendous volume of air to the engine, under pressure. The turbocharger sucks through the standard fuel intake system, although some turbocharger kit manufacturers offer a Weber carburetor as an option, which increases the efficiency still more. The compressor is sealed to ensure that the oil is not drawn into the intake system from the turbocharger lubrication system.

Turbocharger Installation

Most turbocharger kits come with complete instructions. Installation time depends upon your own mechanical skill, but an average time is approximately 12 hours, depending on your working conditions and tool collection (although no special tools are required other than normal mechanic's tools).

Turbocharger Maintenance

The main maintenance item consists simply of changing the oil every 3,000 miles, in order to provide the turbocharger with a clean supply of lubricant.

Fuels Recommended For Turbocharger Operation

Catalytic converter-equipped cars must use unleaded gasoline; non-catalytic converter-equipped cars must use premium fuel.

NOTE: *Always use the highest octane fuel that you can buy.*

Turbocharger Performance

At low rpm, the turbocharger is hardly a factor in engine performance — this is one of the main advantages of this efficient, power- producing unit; when you don't need it, it literally "loafs"; when you do need it, stand on the throttle and watch what happens. The turbo boost comes on at medium rpm and steadily increases to its maximum boost. The power is delivered smoothly, since the turbo just starts pumping air in increased volume as the exhaust gases flow faster. The "turbo-lag" that you hear so much about has been reduced to a minimum and presents very little problem.

17

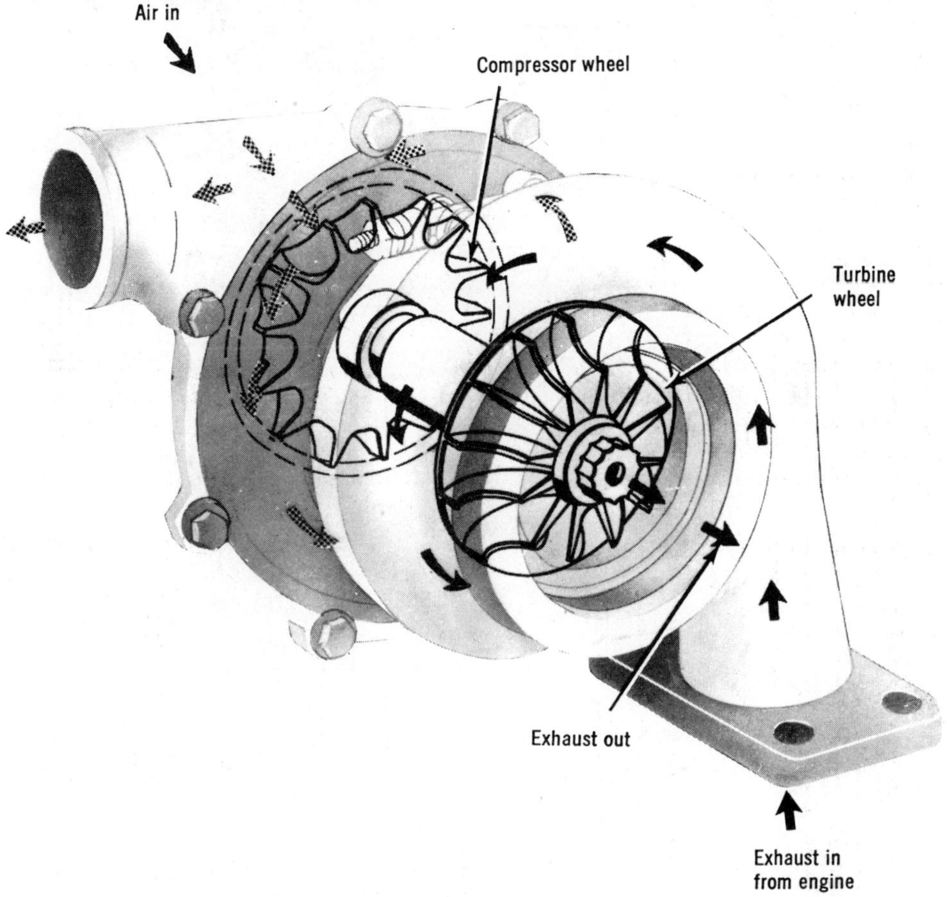

DRIVE TRAIN

With the suspension system firmed up and the engine putting out an abundance of horsepower, the object now is to deliver all of this horsepower to the ground in an efficient manner.

Transmission

Careful matching of transmission gears and final drive ratio with your engine's power curve will result in a car that is smooth and powerful. Refer to **Table 1** for availability, and check with supplier for their gear ratio recommendations.

Ring and Pinion Gears

The final drive ratio determines the top speed and acceleration times. A lower gear ratio (higher numerically) provides faster acceleration and a lower top speed (and also results in the engine turning more rpm's at any given road speed than a higher final drive gear ratio). A higher gear ratio (lower numerically) provides a bit less acceleration, but higher top speed, and at 55 mph, for instance, the engine will be turning over several hundred rpm less than a car equipped with a lower final drive gear ratio.

Limited Slip Differential

A limited slip differential allows both drive wheels to apply power to the ground evenly under all conditions. When one drive wheel spins on wet pavement on a car not equipped with a limited slip differential, the remaining drive wheel receives no torque from the engine at all, as all power is diverted to the wheel that is spinning uselessly.

18

A limited slip differential is an absolute necessity, especially when the driven wheels have the job of trying to transfer to the ground the considerable power that your modified engine is transmitting to them.

BODY MODIFICATIONS

The final step in modifying your car is the replacement of the standard, heavy body panels with lightweight fiberglass units; and the addition of aerodynamic devices called spoilers and air dams.

Body Panel Replacement

Several manufacturers offer fiberglass front fenders and rocker panels, fender flares, and hoods (with or without air scoops). Refer to **Figure 18**. These units bolt on just like their normal, stock counterparts, for the most part. They are lighter and stronger than stock panels, and they will not rust or dent.

Spoilers

The prime objective of a front spoiler is to keep air from flowing under the car, which has a tendency to lift the car at high speeds. The spoiler directs the air up over the hood, creating a high pressure area at that point which actually creates downforce on the front wheels. This device works very well at higher speeds; at low speeds the effect is somewhat lessened, but still worthwhile. Some spoilers are equipped with ducts that route cooling air to the front brakes.

An air dam's purpose is also to keep air from flowing under the car, thus creating a low pressure area beneath the car, which in turn increases greater downforce on the car due to the normal air pressure on top of the car. The air dam is more effective than a conventional spoiler at low speeds, because its effectiveness is not dependent on its ability to push air up and over the hood to create a downforce (which only occurs at fairly high speeds).

Strangely enough, even though the air dam adds to the car's frontal area, the overall drag is actually reduced due to the fact that the car's irregularly-shaped chassis no longer catches the wind as it did prior to installing the air dam. Therefore, air drag under the chassis is greatly reduced (refer to **Figure 18**).

A rear spoiler's job is to smooth out the turbulent air which follows in the wake of the car. This improves the air flow and lessens drag.

IN CONCLUSION

The components illustrated in this chapter, if properly selected and installed, will result in a far safer, more enjoyable, better handling, and far quicker car than the one you purchased in stock form.

As indicated previously, due to the very large variety of components available, it has been impossible to list, in detail, all of the variations and specifications for each item. Rather, we have tried to show you generally what is available, what the accessory is designed to do, and when it should be used.

Table 1 ACCESSORY SOURCES

Firm	Remarks
Addco Industries 701 Watertower Rd. Lake Park, Fl. 33403 (305) 844-2531	Sway bar kits (Catalog, free)
Anderson Racing Center 3634 Elm St. Pittsburgh, Pa. 15234 (412) 563-6999	Full range of accessories (Catalog, $1.00)
Ansa Mufflers Corp. P.O. Box 1288 Fitzgerald, Ga. 31750 (912) 423-9302	Ansa exhaust system (Catalog, free)
Auto World, Inc. 701 N. Keyser Ave. Scranton, Pa. 18508	Full range of accessories (Turbocharger catalog, $1.00; Motorsports catalog, $1.00)
BAE 3032 Kashiwa St. Torrance, Ca. 90505 (213) 530-4743	Turbocharger kits (Catalog, $2.00)
Bilstein Corp. of America 11760 Sorrento Valley Rd. San Diego, Ca. 92121	Bilstein shock absorbers (Catalog, $2.00)
The Book 3400 E. 42nd St. Minneapolis, Mn. 55406 (612) 729-7779	Full range of accessories (Catalog, $2.00)
Cannon Induction Systems 2741 Toledo St. Torrance, Ca. 90503 (213) 328-3060	Weber carburetion systems (Catalog, $1.00)
Carrera Racing Shocks 203 Marray Dr. Atlanta, Ga. 30341 (404) 451-8811	Carrera racing shock absorbers (Information, free)
CCL Enterprises 24 Ledin Dr. Avon, Mass. 02322	Supersprint exhaust systems (Catalog, free)
Crown Mfg. Co., Inc. 858 Production Pl. Newport Beach, Ca. 92663	Turbocharger kits (Catalog, $1.00)
Earl's Supply Co. P.O. Box 265 Lawndale, Ca. 90260 (213) 679-1438	High-performance hardware and fittings (Catalog, $2.00)
German Motors & Parts 1830 Tamworth Dr. Charlotte, NC 28210 (704) 525-0941	Full range of accessories (Catalog, free)
Paul Hacker Racing 45 Point View Dr. East Greenbush, NY 12061 (518) 477-5603	Suspension components

(continued)

Table 1 ACCESSORY SOURCES

Firm	Remarks
KAMEI U.S.A., Inc. 5213 W. Broadway Minneapolis, Mn. 55429 (612) 535-5600	Spoilers, air dams, etc. (Catalog, free)
Kensington Products Corp. 150 Green St. Hackensack, NJ 07601	Koni shock absorbers (Information, free)
KYB Corporation of America 207 Eisenhower Lane South Lombard, Ill. 60148	KYB shock absorbers (Information, free)
PAECO 213 S. 21st St. Birmingham, Ala. 35233	Full range of accessories (Catalog, free)
Parts & Polish 12952 W. Washington Pl. Los Angeles, Ca. 90066 (213) 391-8206	Full range of accessories (Catalog, $1.00)
Quickor Engineering 6710 S.W. 111th Beaverton, Ore. 97005 (503) 646-9696	Sway bars and springs (Catalog, free)
Race Quip 4760 Hayden Run Rd. Amlin, Oh. 43002 (614) 889-9527	Full range of accessories (Catalog, $1.00)
Stebro 10 Leach St. Massena, NY 13662	Stebro exhaust systems (Information, free)
Time Machines, Inc. 13 Neptune Ave. Brooklyn, NY 11235 (212) 743-8874	Full range of accessories (Catalog, free)
Turbo Systems 23669 Park Capri #52 Calabasas, Ca. 91302 (213) 884-5912	Turbocharger kits (Catalog, $1.00)
Turbo Systems 12954 Washington Bl. Los Angeles, Ca. 90066 (213) 391-8701	Turbocharger kits (Catalog, $1.00)
WREP Industries, Ltd. 2965 Landwehr Rd. Northbrook, Ill. 60062 (312) 498-0670	Full range of accessories (Information, free)

INDEX

F

G

H

I

T

V

W

Z

NOTES

NOTES

MAINTENANCE LOG

DATE	TYPE OF SERVICE	COST	REMARKS

WIRING DIAGRAMS

The following wiring diagrams are included in the back of this book:

1975 Rabbit

1975 Scirocco

1976 Rabbit

1976 Scirocco

1977 Basic and Custom Rabbit

1977 DeLuxe Rabbit

1977 Scirocco

1978 Custom Diesel Rabbit

1978 Custom and DeLuxe Rabbit

1978 Scirocco

1979 Westmoreland Rabbit

1979 Custom Diesel Rabbit

NOTE: Wiring diagrams for the 1979 Custom and DeLuxe Rabbit and the 1979 Scirocco are not available at this time.

WIRING DIAGRAM SYMBOLS

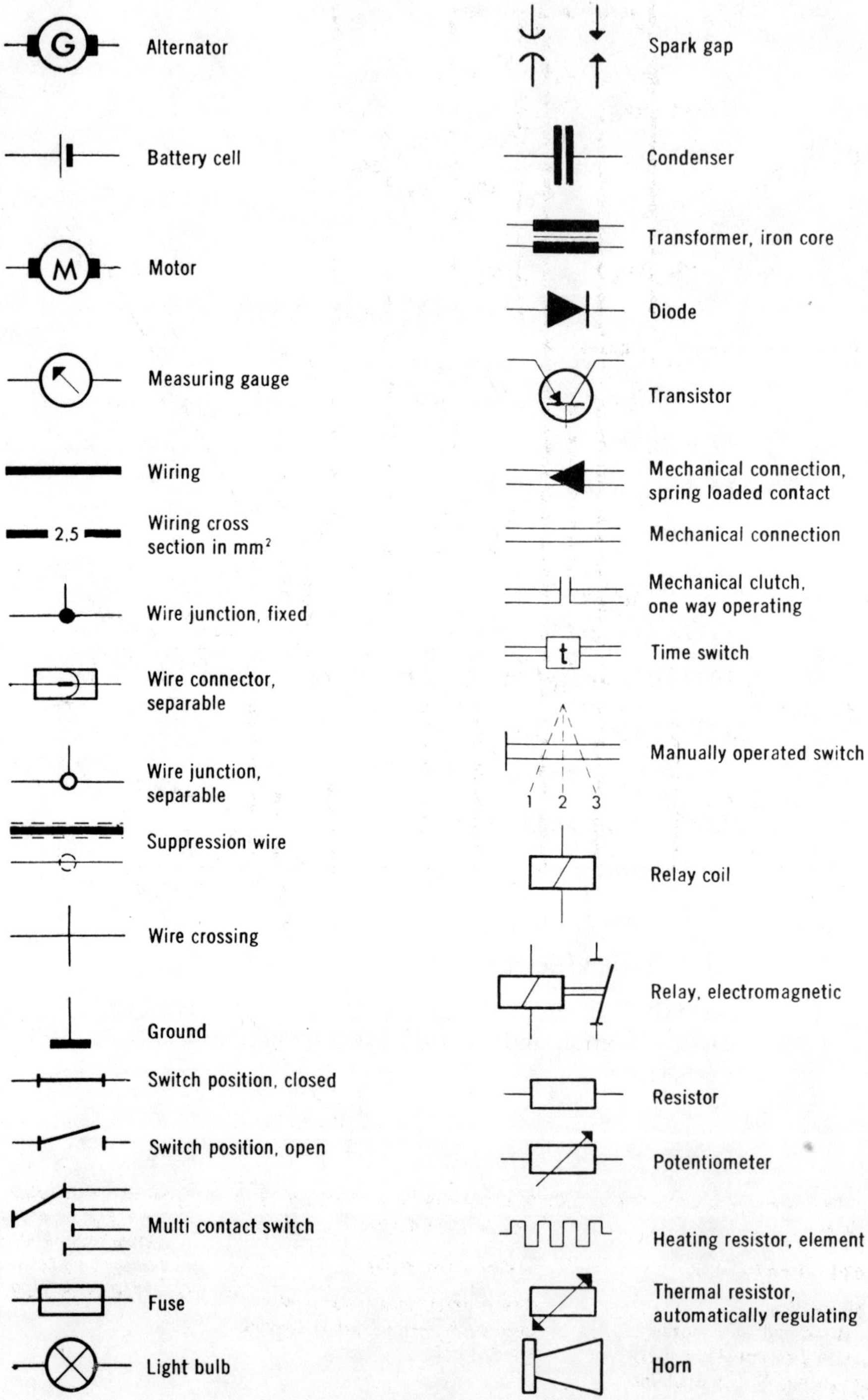

HOW TO READ CURRENT FLOW DIAGRAMS

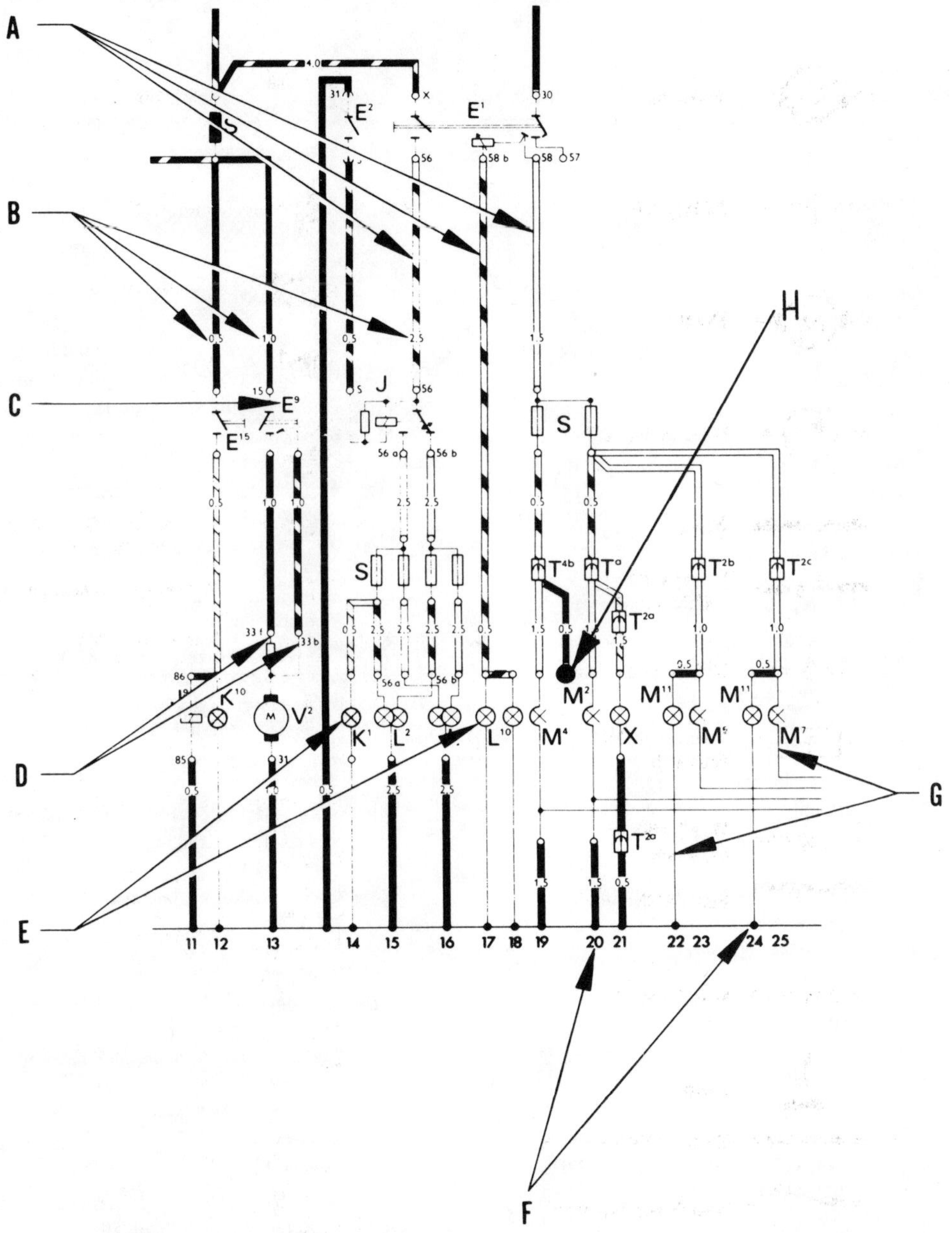

A. **Wire color** (corresponds with color in vehicle)

B. **Wire cross section** in mm²

C. **Part designation**
Helps you to find, in the legend, the part which the symbol in the diagram belongs to, e.g. E⁹ = Switch for fan motor.

D. **Terminal** with the designation which is on the actual part.

E. **Symbol** (here: Bulb)

F. **Current tracks** with track numbers to facilitate finding of part in diagram (see legend).

G. **Internal connections** (thin lines). These are not actual wires but ground connections which go through parts such as bulb holders, for example.

H. **Analysis socket terminals** (Dealer only)

KEY TO

WIRING DIAGRAM — 1975 RABBIT (Part I)

Page 1 of 8

Description		Current track
A	- Battery	3
B	- Starter	4, 5, 6
C	- Alternator	1, 2
C1	- Regulator	2
D	- Ignition/starter switch	17, 18, 19, 20
E9	- Fresh air fan	8, 9
E24	- Safety belt lock with contact, left	18
E25	- Safety belt lock with contact, right	18
F	- Brake light switch	36, 37
F1	- Oil pressure switch	46
F2	- Door contact and buzzer alarm switch, left	16, 17
F3	- Door contact switch, right	15
F4	- Backup light switch	40
F9	- Parking brake control switch	28
F24	- Switch in catalytic operating time recorder converter (on speedometer)	32
F27	- Switch in EGR operating time recorder (on speedometer)	29
G	- Fuel gauge sending unit	48
G1	- Fuel gauge	21
G2	- Coolant temperature sending unit	47
G3	- Coolant temperature gauge	22
G7	- TDC marker unit	24
G20	- Temperature sensor for catalytic converter	33
H	- Horn button	39
H1	- Horn	38
J34	- Safety belt warning system relay	16, 17, 18, 19, 20 20, 21
J42	- Relay for catalytic converter (behind dashboard)	32, 33
K2	- Alternator charging warning light	25
K3	- Oil pressure warning light	24
K5	- Turn signal warning light	26
K7	- Dual circuit brake, warning, parking brake warning and safety belt warning light	27, 28, 29
K21	- Catalytic converter warning light	31
K22	- EGR warning light	30
L15	- Ashtray illumination	11
L28	- Cigarette lighter illumination	12
M9	- Brake light, left	44
M10	- Brake light, right	45
M16	- Backup light, left	42
M17	- Backup light, right	43
N	- Ignition coil	34

Description		Current track
N6	- Series resistance	34
O	- Ignition distributor	34, 35
P	- Spark plug connectors	35, 36
Q	- Spark plugs	42, 43
S7 S9 S11	- Fuses in fuse box	9, 13, 41
T	- Wire connector, behind dashboard	
T1a	- Wire connector, single behind dashboard	
T1b	- Wire connector, single, behind dashboard	
T1c	- Wire connector, single, in engine compartment	
T1d	- Wire connector, single, in engine compartment, front left	
T1e	- Wire connector, single, in engine compartment, front right	
T1f	- Wire connector, single, in luggage compartment	
T1g	- Wire connector, single, in luggage compartment, right rear	
T1h	- Wire connector, single, in luggage compartment, left rear	
T2a	- Wire connector, double, in engine compartment	
T2b	- Wire connector, double, behind dashboard	
T2c	- Wire connector, double, behind dashboard	
T2d	- Wire connector, double, behind dashboard	
T3a	- Wire connector, 3 point, in engine compartment, left front	
T3b	- Wire connector, 3 point, in engine compartment, right front	
T12	- Wire connector, 12 point, on dashboard cluster	
T20	- Test network, test socket	21
U1	- Cigarette lighter	13
V2	- Fresh air fan	9
W	- Interior light	14
W6	- Glove compartment illumination	10
(1)	- Ground strap, battery/body	
(2)	- Ground strap, alternator/engine	
(10)	- Ground connector, dashboard cluster	
(11)	- Ground connector, body	
(15)	- Ground connector, engine compartment, front left	
(16)	- Ground connector, engine compartment, front right	

1975 RABBIT (Part I)

Page 2 of 8

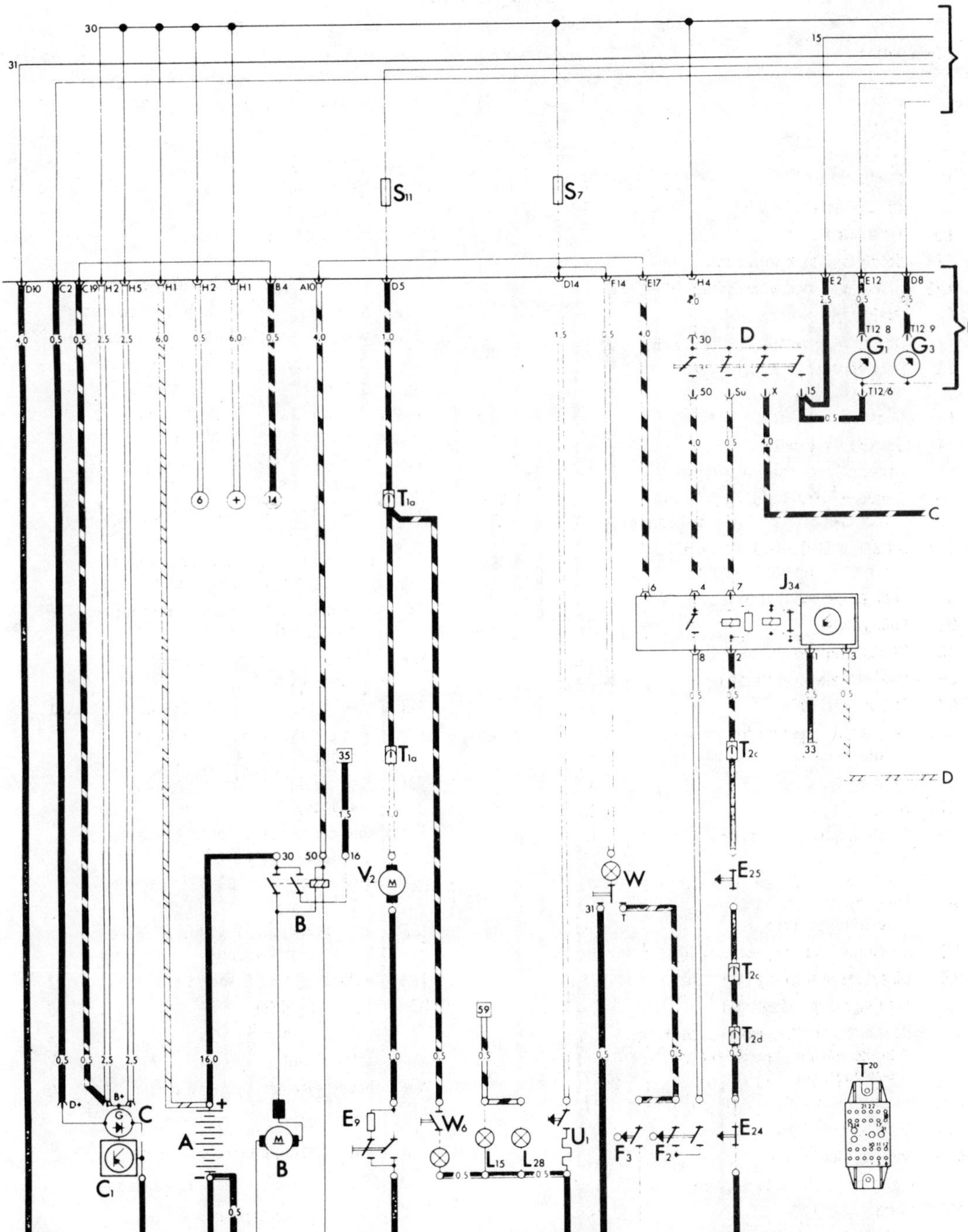

1975 RABBIT (Part I)

Page 3 of 8

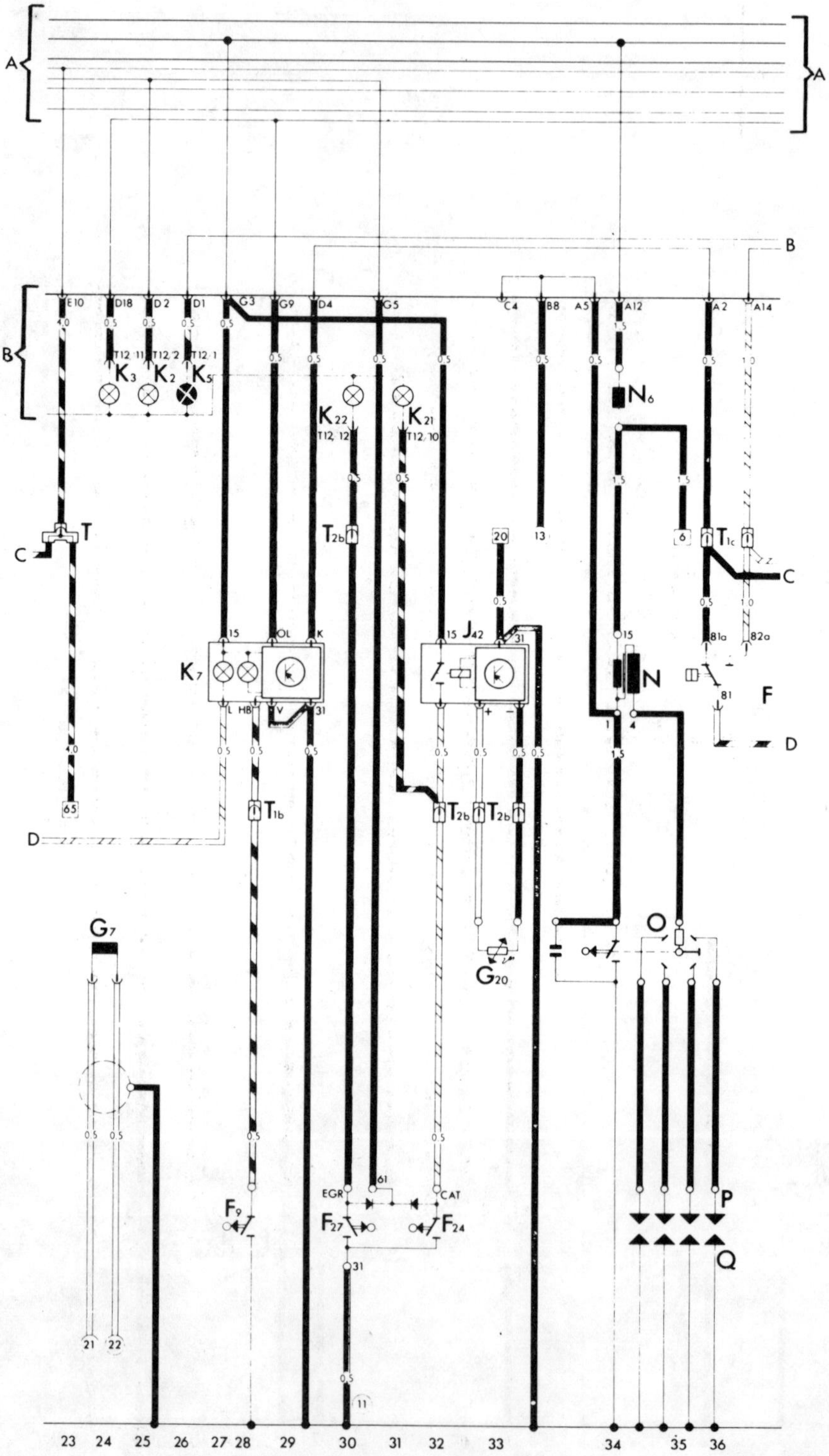

1975 RABBIT (Part I)

Page 4 of 8

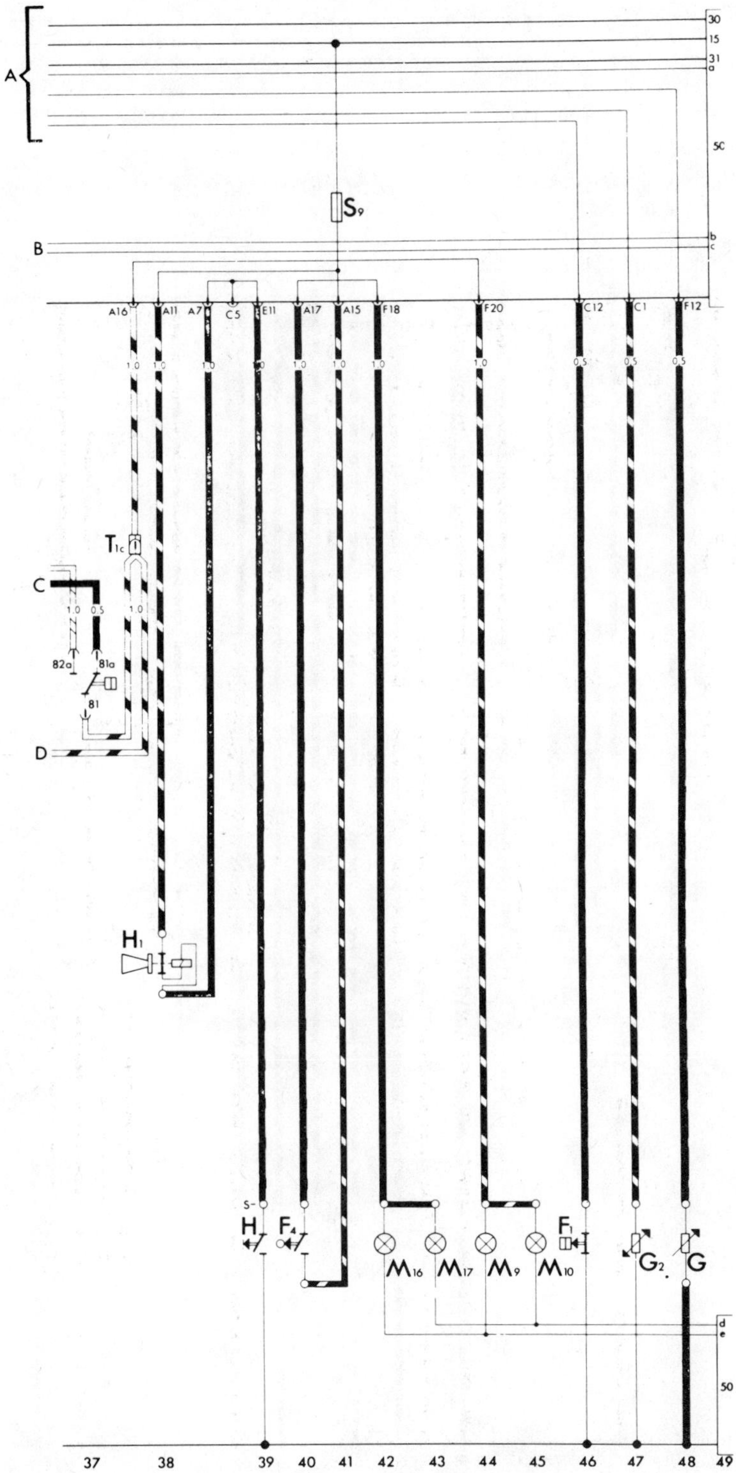

1975 RABBIT (Part II)

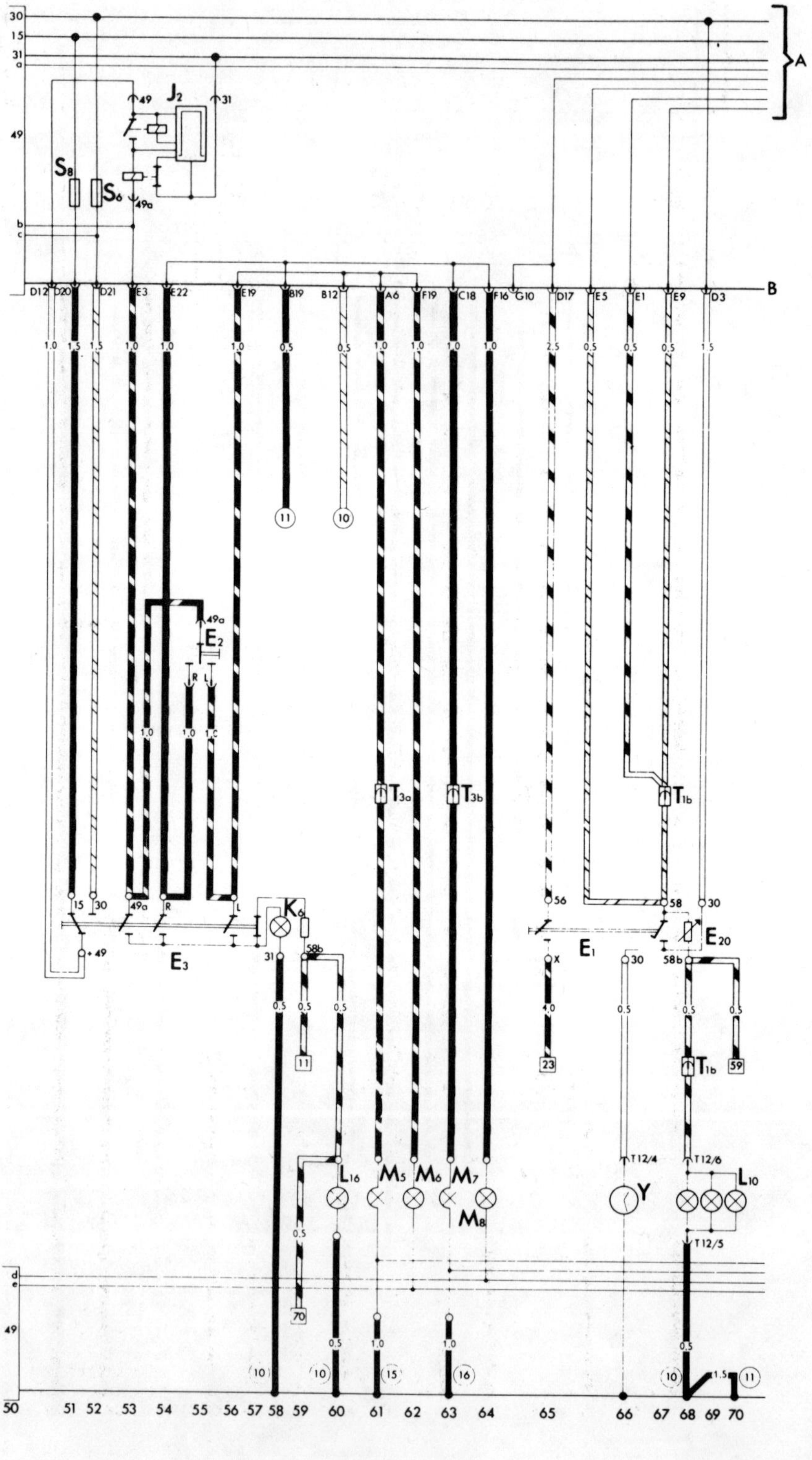

1975 RABBIT (Part II)

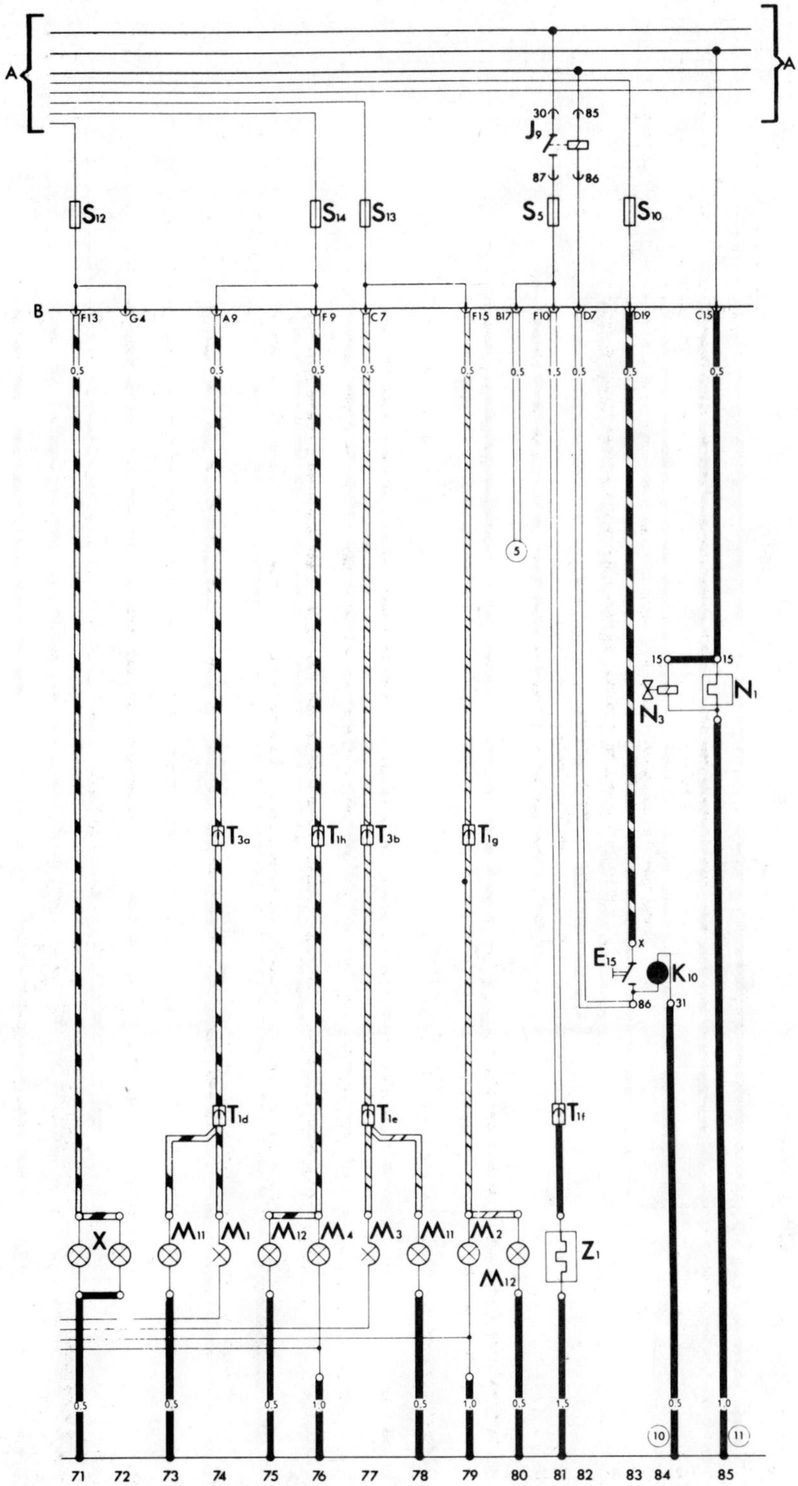

1975 RABBIT (Part II)

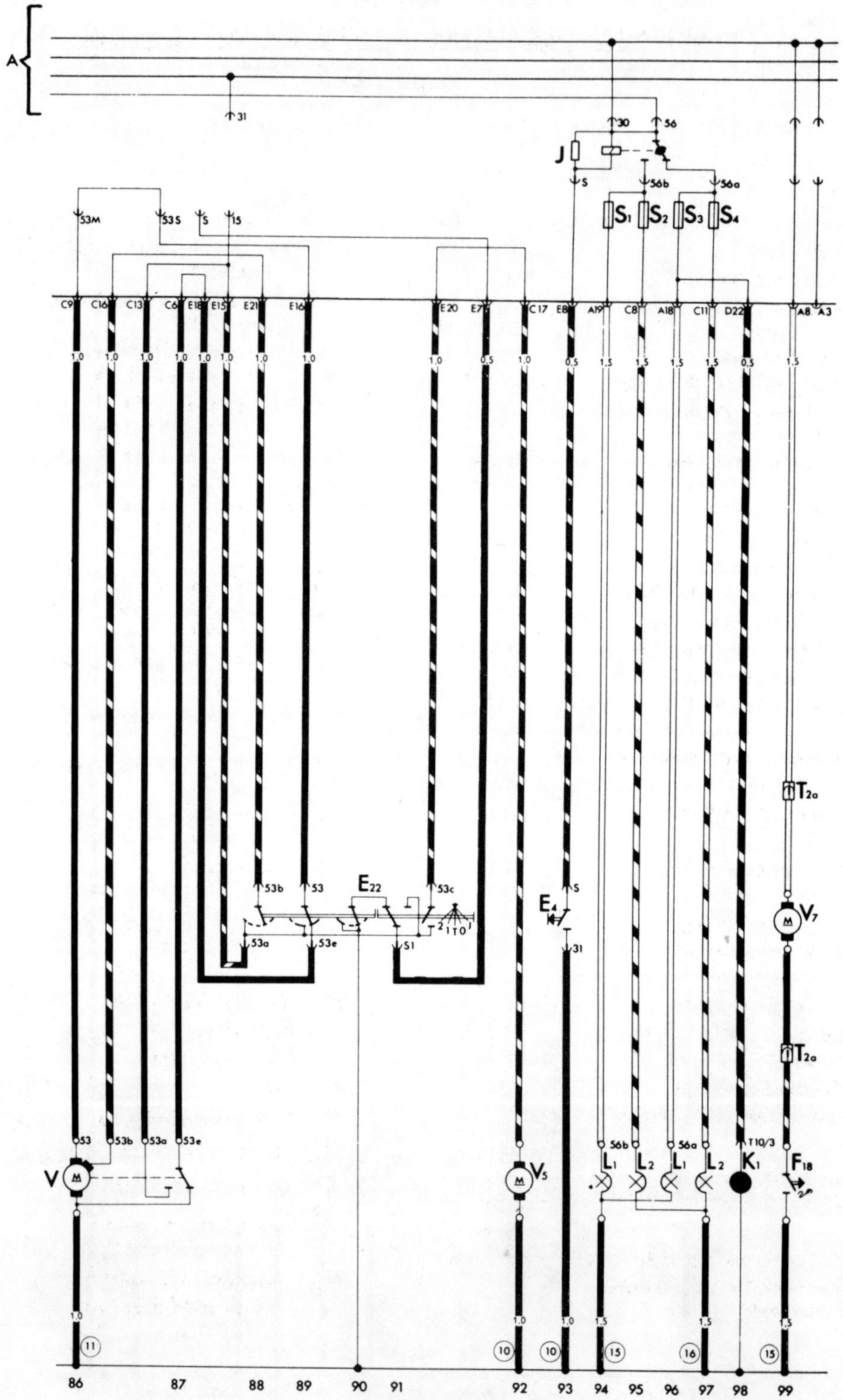

KEY TO
WIRING DIAGRAM — 1975 RABBIT (Part II)
Page 8 of 8

Description	Current track
E1 - Light switch	65, 66, 67
E2 - Turn signal switch	55
E3 - Emergency flasher switch	51, 52, 53, 54 56, 57, 59
E4 - Headlight dimmer switch	93
E15 - Rear window defogger switch	83
E20 - Instrument panel lighting control switch	68
E22 - Windshield wiper intermittent switch	88, 89, 90, 91
F18 - Radiator fan thermo switch	99
J - Headlight dimmer relay	93, 94, 95
J2 - Emergency flasher relay	53, 54, 55
J9 - Rear window defogger relay	81, 82
K1 - Headlight high beam warning light	98
K6 - Emergency flasher warning light	58
K10 - Rear window defogger warning light	84
L1 - Sealed beam unit, left headlight	94, 96
L2 - Sealed beam unit, right headlight	95, 97
L10 - Instrument panel illumination	68, 69, 70
L16 - Heater operation lever illumination	60
M1 - Parking light, left front	74
M2 - Taillight, right	79
M3 - Parking light, right front	77
M4 - Taillight, left	76
M5 - Turn signal, left front	61
M6 - Turn signal, left rear	62
M7 - Turn signal, right front	63
M8 - Turn signal, right rear	64
M11 - Sidemarker, front	73, 78
M12 - Sidemarker, rear	75, 80
N1 - Automatic choke	85
N3 - Electromagnetic cut-off valve	84
S1, S2, S3, S4, S5, S6, S8, S10, S12, S13, S14 } Fuses in fuse box	51, 52, 71, 76 77, 81, 83, 94, 95, 96, 97
T - Wire connector, behind dashboard	
T1a - Wire connector, single, behind dashboard	

Description	Current track
T1b - Wire connector, single, behind dashboard	
T1c - Wire connector, single, in engine compartment	
T1d - Wire connector, single, in engine compartment, front left	
T1e - Wire connector, single, in engine compartment, front right	
T1f - Wire connector, single, in luggage compartment	
T1g - Wire connector, single, in luggage compartment, right rear	
T1h - Wire connector, single, in luggage compartment, left rear	
T2a - Wire connector, double, in engine compartment	
T2b - Wire connector, double, behind dashboard	
T2c - Wire connector, double, behind dashboard	
T2d - Wire connector, double, behind dashboard	
T3a - Wire connector, 3 point, in engine compartment, left front	
T3b - Wire connector, 3 point, in engine compartment, right front	
T12 - Wire connector, 12 point, on dashboard cluster	
V - Windshield wiper motor	86, 87
V5 - Windshield washer pump	92
V7 - Radiator fan	99
X - License plate light	71, 72
Y - Clock	66
Z1 - Rear window defogger heating element	81
(10) - Ground connector, dashboard cluster	
(11) - Ground connector, body	
(15) - Ground connector, engine compartment, front left	
(16) - Ground connector, engine compartment, front right	

KEY TO

WIRING DIAGRAM — 1975 SCIROCCO (Part I)

Page 1 of 8

Description		Current track
A	- Battery	2
B	- Starter	3, 4, 5
C	- Alternator	1
C1	- Regulator	1
D	- Ignition/starter switch	15, 16, 17, 18
E9	- Fresh air fan switch	6
E24	- Safety belt lock with contact, left	21
E25	- Safety belt lock with contact, right	19
E31	- Contact strip in driver's seat	21
E32	- Contact strip in passenger seat	19
F	- Brake light switch	43, 44
F2	- Door contact and buzzer alarm switch, left	13, 14
F3	- Door contact switch, right	12
F4	- Backup light switch	39
F9	- Parking brake control switch	24
F24	- Switch in catalytic converter operating time recorder (on speedometer)	32
F27	- Switch in EGR operating time recorder	31
G1	- Fuel gauge	19
G3	- Coolant temperature gauge	20
G5	- Tachometer	27
G7	- TDC marker unit	44
G14	- Voltmeter	8
G20	- Temperature sensor for catalytic converter	34, 35
H	- Horn button	37
H1	- Dual horn	33, 36
J4	- Dual horn relay	34, 35, 36
J34	- Safety belt warning system relay	14, 15, 16, 17 19, 21, 22
J42	- Relay for catalytic converter (behind dashboard)	32, 33, 34, 35
K2	- Alternator charging warning light	23
K3	- Oil pressure warning light	22
K5	- Turn signal warning light	24
K7	- Dual circuit brake warning, parking brake warning and safety belt warning light	28, 29, 30
K21	- Catalytic converter warning light	26
K22	- EGR warning light	25
L15	- Ashtray illumination	11
L28	- Cigarette lighter illumination	10
M9	- Brake light, left	46
M10	- Brake light, right	45
M16	- Backup light, left	38
M17	- Backup light, right	39
N	- Ignition coil	41
N6	- Series resistance	41
O	- Ignition distributor	41, 42
P	- Spark plug connectors	42, 43
Q	- Spark plugs	42, 43

Description		Current track
7, S9, 11	- Fuses in fuse box	6, 9, 40
T	- Wire connector behind dashboard	
T1a	- Wire connector, single, behind dashboard	
T1b	- Wire connector, single, behind dashboard	
T1c	- Wire connector, single, in engine compartment	
T1d	- Wire connector, single, in engine compartment, front left	
T1e	- Wire connector, single, in engine compartment, front right	
T1f	- Wire connector, single, in luggage compartment	
T1g	- Wire connector, single, in luggage compartment, rear left	
T1h	- Wire connector, single, in luggage compartment, rear right	
T1i	- Wire connector, single, in luggage compartment	
T2a	- Wire connector, double, in engine compartment	
T2b	- Wire connector, double,in engine compartment	
T2c	- Wire connector, double, behind dashboard	
T2d	- Wire connector, double, on frame, right	
T2e	- Wire connector, double, under passenger seat	
T2f	- Wire connector, double, under driver's seat	
T2g	- Wire connector, double, on frame, left	
T6	- Wire connector, 6 point, behind dashboard	
T20	- Test network, test socket	29
U1	- Cigarette lighter	9
U2	- Fresh air fan	6
W	- Interior light	12
W6	- Glove compartment light	7
(1)	- Ground strap, battery/body	
(2)	- Ground strap, alternator/engine	
(10)	- Ground connector, dashboard cluster	
(11)	- Ground connector, body	
(15)	- Ground connector, engine compartment, front left	
(16)	- Ground connector, engine compartment, front right	

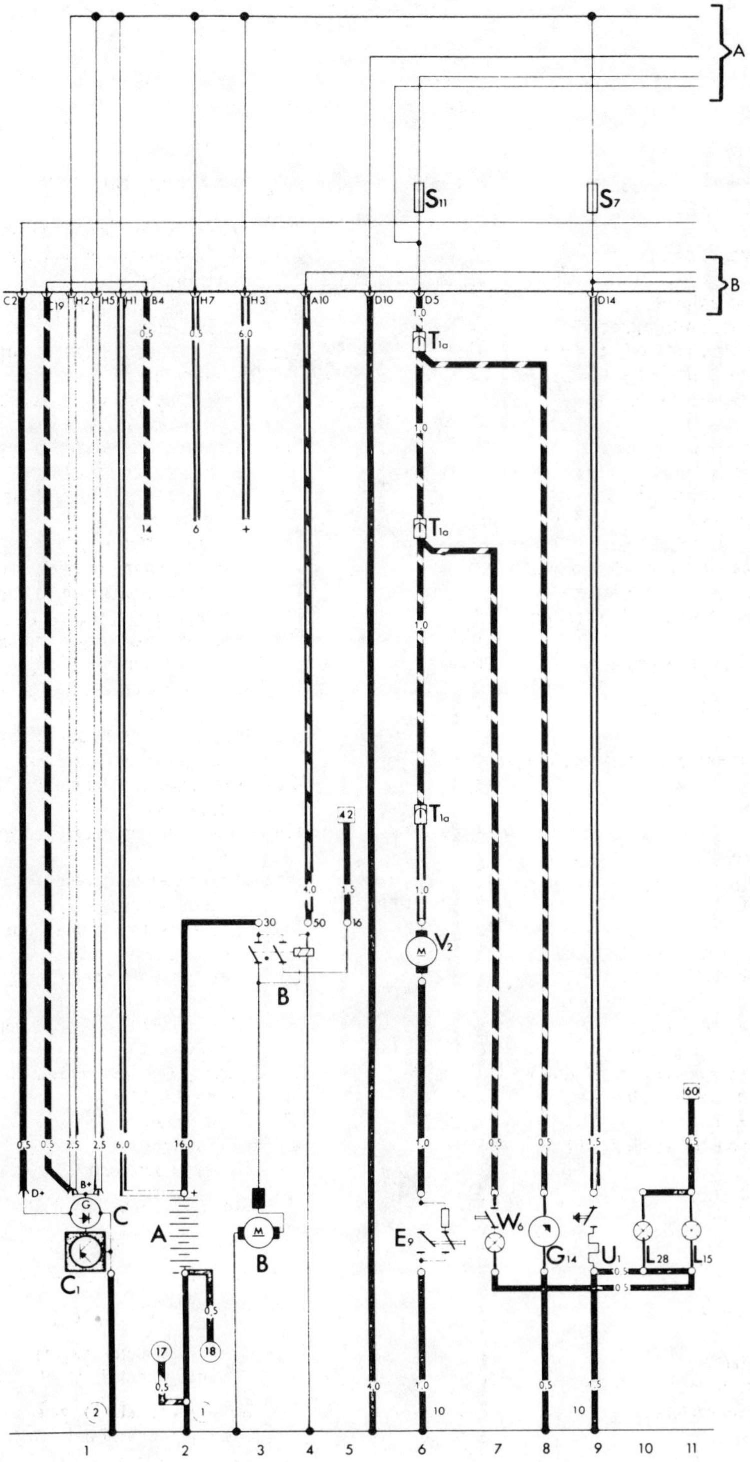
A
B
S11
S7
C2
C19
H2
H5
H1
B4
H7
H3
A10
D10
D5
D14
T1a
V2
E9
W6
G14
U1
L28
L15
C
C1
A
B
B
30
50
16
42
60
D+
B+
1
2
3
4
5
6
7
8
9
10
11

1975 SCIROCCO (Part I)

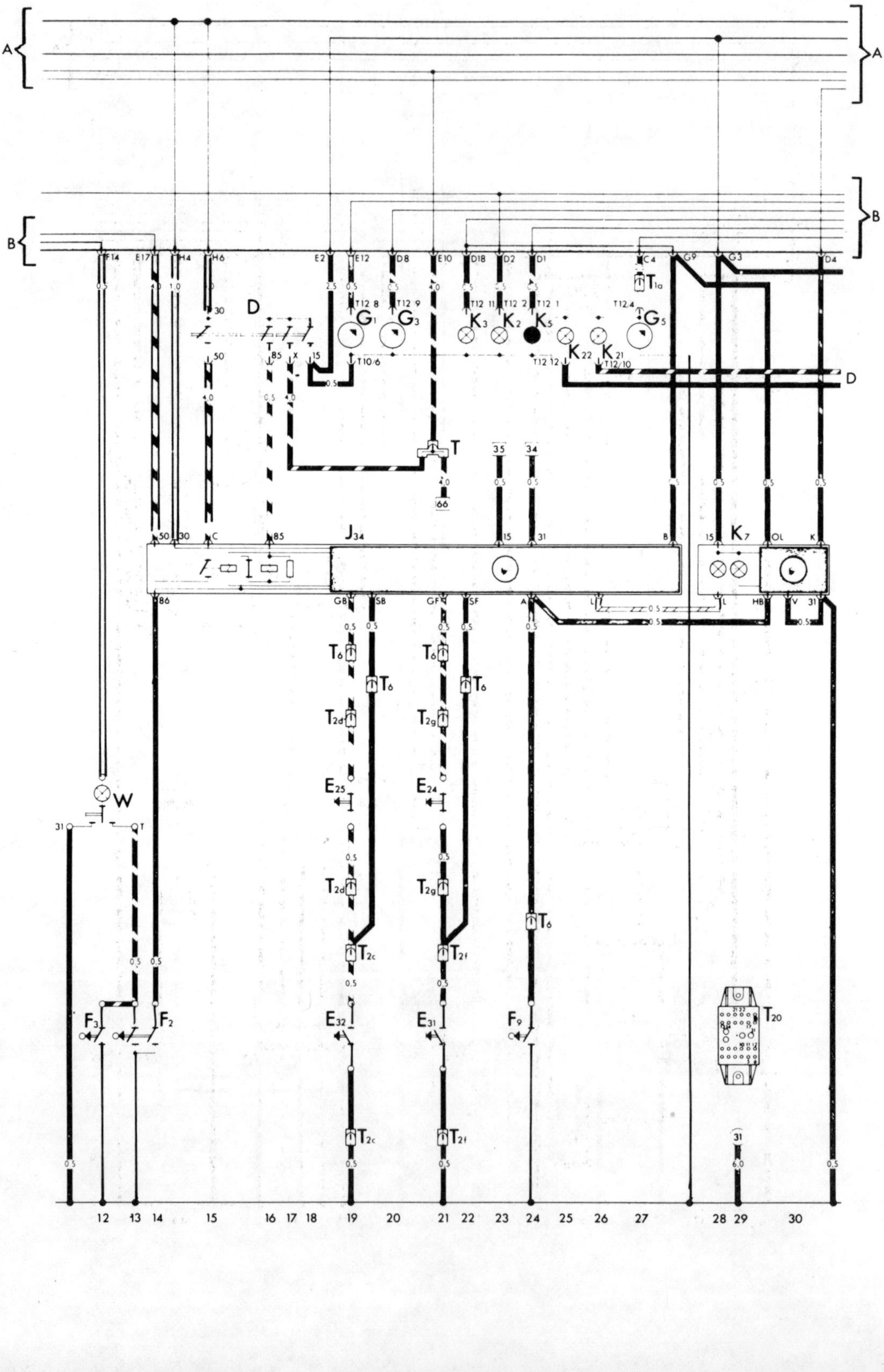

1975 SCIROCCO (Part I)

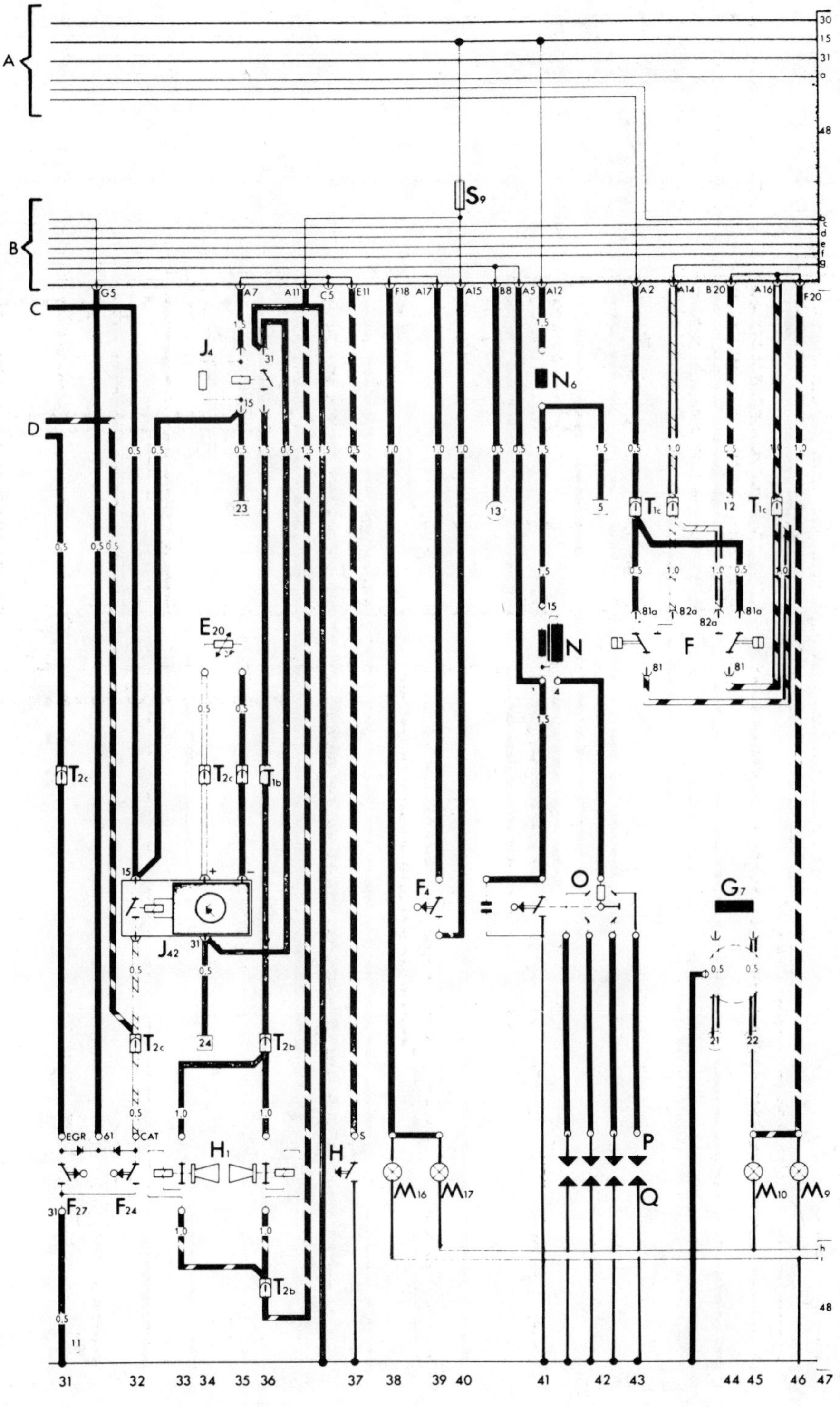

1975 SCIROCCO (Part II)

Page 5 of 8

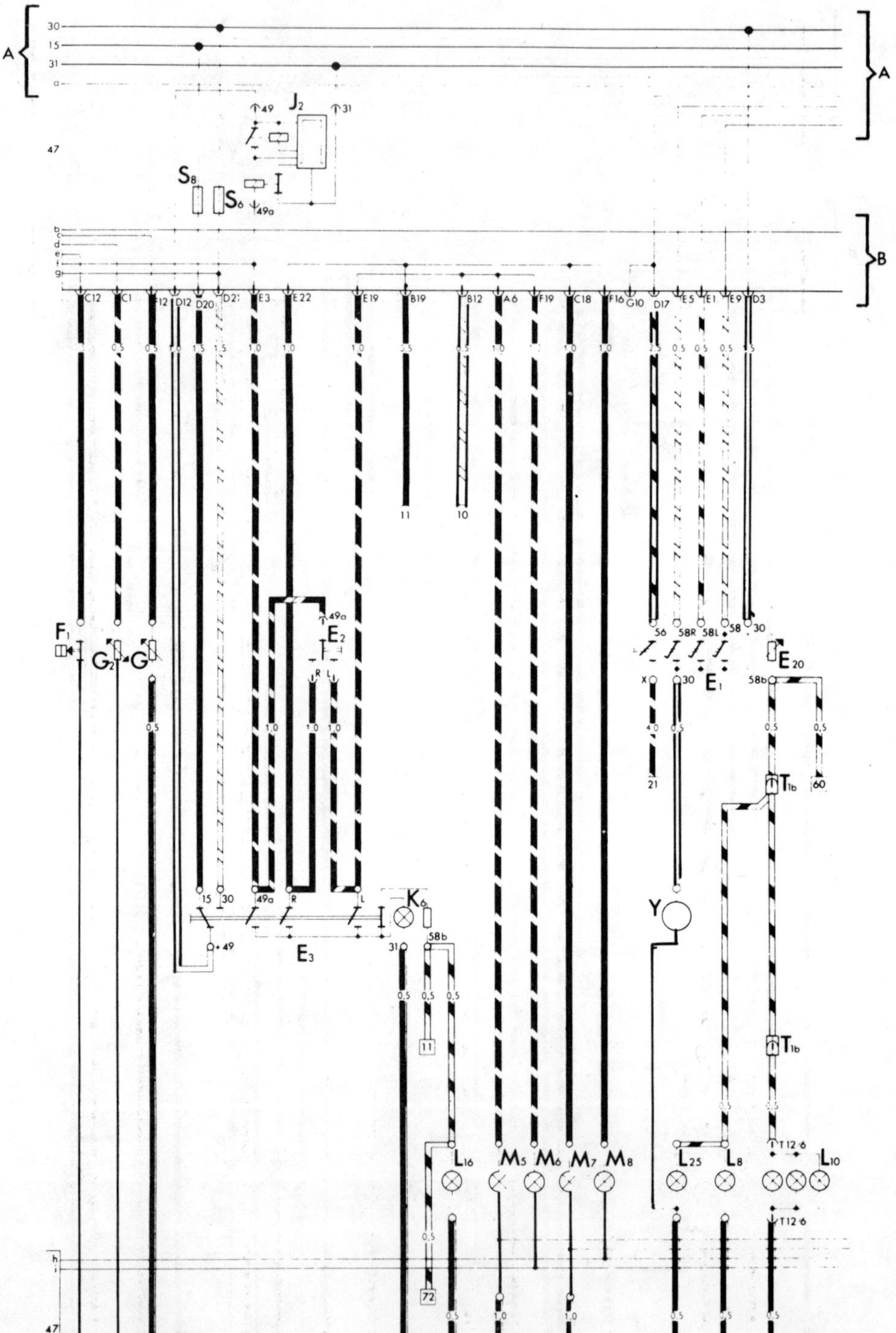

1975 SCIROCCO (Part II)

Page 6 of 8

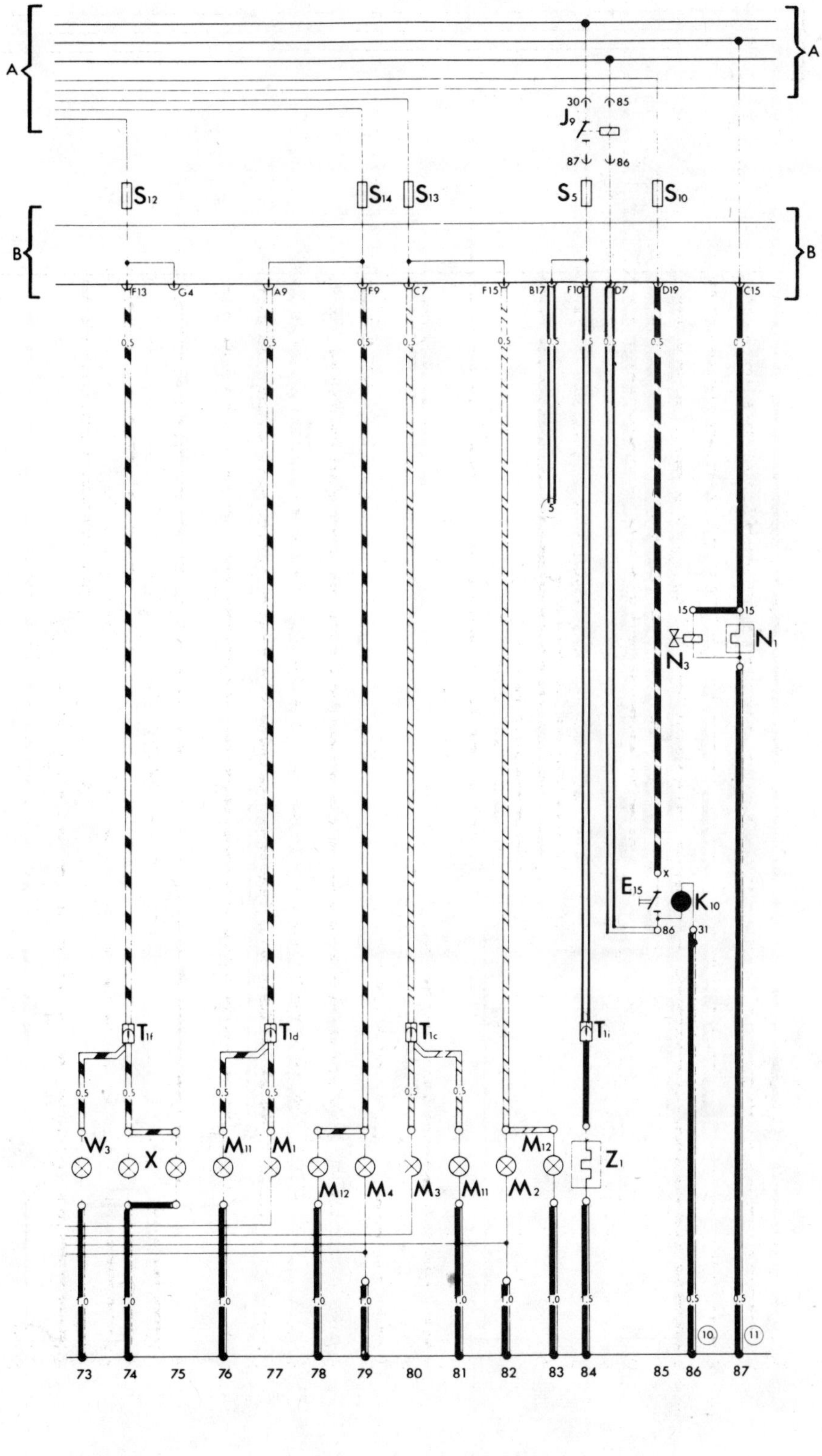

1975 SCIROCCO (Part II)

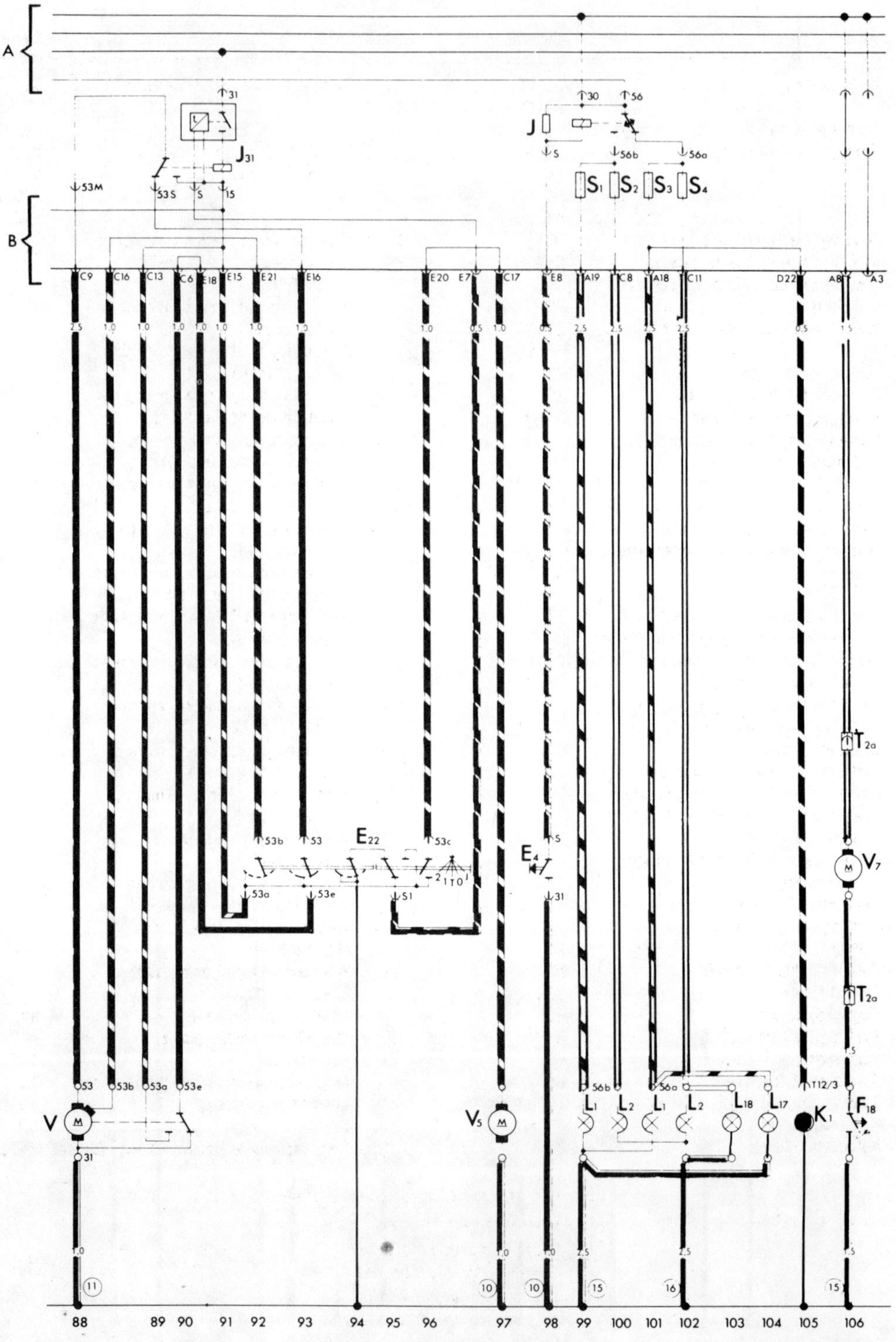

KEY TO

WIRING DIAGRAM — 1975 SCIROCCO (Part II)

Page 8 of 8

Description		Current track
E	- Light switch	66, 67, 68, 69
E2	- Turn signal switch	56
E3	- Emergency flasher switch	52, 53, 54, 55, 56, 57, 58, 60
E4	- Headlight dimmer switch	98
E15	- Rear window defogger switch	85
E20	- Instrument panel lighting control switch	70
E22	- Windshield wiper intermittent switch	92, 93, 94, 95, 96
F1	- Oil pressure switch	49
F18	- Radiator fan thermo switch	106
G	- Fuel gauge sending unit	51
G2	- Coolant temperature gauge sending unit	50
J	- Headlight dimmer relay	98, 99, 100
J2	- Emergency flasher relay	54, 55, 56
J9	- Rear window defogger relay	84
J31	- Windshield wash/wiper intermittent relay	89, 90, 91
K1	- Headlight high beam warning light	105
K6	- Emergency flasher warning light	59
K10	- Rear window defogger warning light	85
L1	- Sealed beam unit, left headlight, high and low beam	99, 101
L2	- Sealed beam unit, right headlight, high and low beam	100, 102
L8	- Clock illumination	69
L10	- Instrument panel illumination	70, 71, 72
L16	- Heater operation lever illumination	61
L17	- Sealed beam unit, left headlight, high beam	104
L18	- Sealed beam unit, right headlight, high beam	103
L25	- Voltmeter illumination	67
M1	- Parking light, front left	77
M2	- Taillight, right	82
M3	- Parking light, front left	80
M4	- Taillight, left	79
M5	- Turn signal, left front	62
M6	- Turn signal, left rear	63
M7	- Turn signal, right front	64
M8	- Turn signal, right rear	65
M11	- Sidemarker, front	76, 81
M12	- Sidemarker, rear	78, 83
N1	- Automatic choke	87

Description		Current track
N3	- Electric magnetic cut-off valve	86
S1, S2, S3, S4, S5, S6, S8, S10, S12, S13, S14	fuses in fuse box	52, 53, 54, 79, 80, 84, 85, 99, 100, 101, 102
T	- Wire connector behind dashboard	
T1a	- Wire connector, single, behind dashboard	
T1b	- Wire connector, single, behind dashboard	
T1c	- Wire connector, single, in engine compartment	
T1d	- Wire connector, single, in engine compartment, front left	
T1e	- Wire connector, single, in engine compartment, front right	
T1f	- Wire connector, single, in luggage compartment	
T1g	- Wire connector, single, in luggage compartment, rear left	
T1h	- Wire connector, single, in luggage compartment, rear right	
T1i	- Wire connector, single, in luggage compartment	
T2a	- Wire connector, double, in engine compartment	
T2b	- Wire connector, double, on body bottom, right	
T2c	- Wire connector, double, behind dashboard	
T2d	- Wire connector, double, on body bottom, right	
T2e	- Wire connector, double, under passenger seat	
T2f	- Wire connector, double, under driver's seat	
T2g	- Wire connector, double, on body bottom, left	
T6	- Wire connector, 6 point, behind dashboard	
V	- Windshield wiper motor	88, 89, 90
V5	- Windshield washer pump	97
V7	- Radiator fan	106
W3	- Luggage compartment illumination	73
X	- License plate light	74, 75
Y	- Clock	67
Z1	- Rear window defogger heating element	84

⑩ - Ground connector, dashboard cluster

⑪ - Ground connector, body

⑮ - Ground connector, engine compartment, front left

⑯ - Ground connector, engine compartment, front right

1976 RABBIT

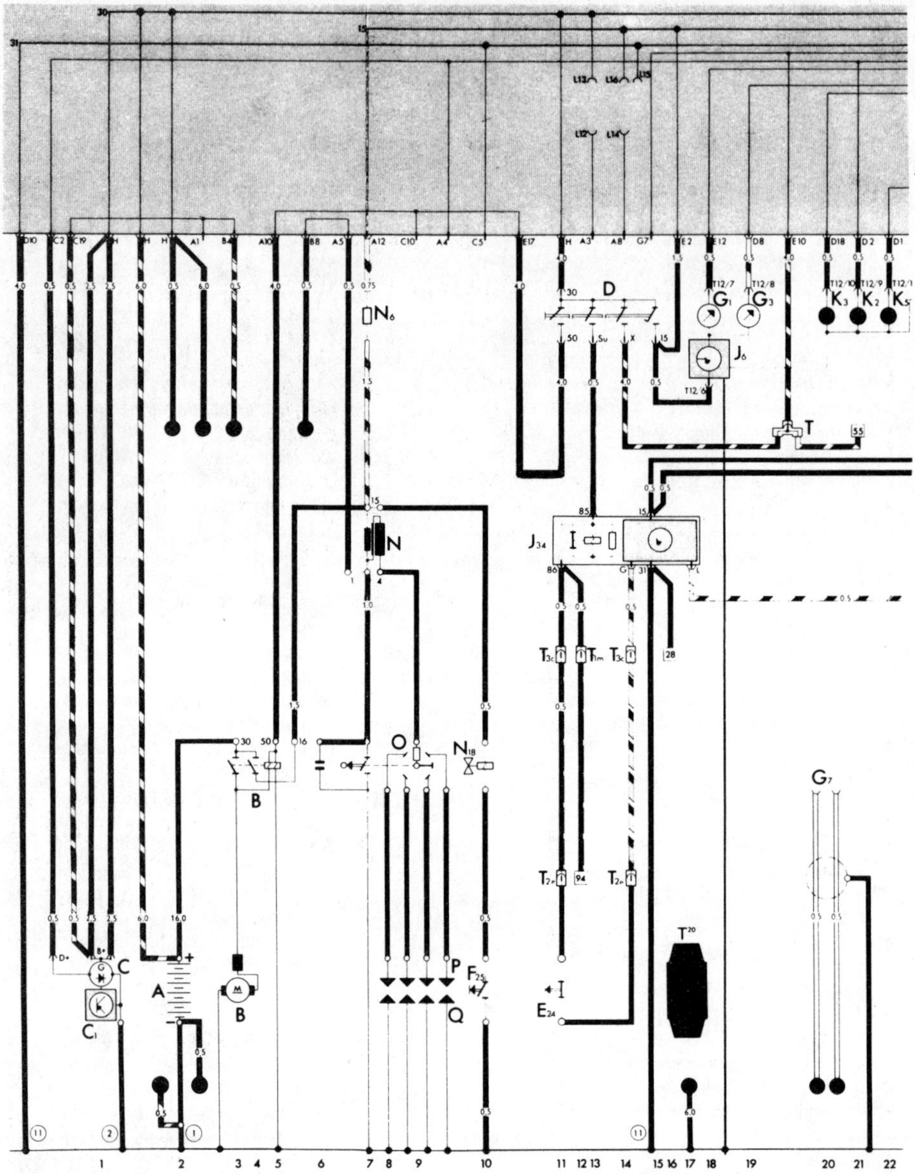

A	– Battery	2
B	– Starter	2, 3, 5
C	– Alternator	1
C 1	– Regulator	1
D	– Ignition/starter switch	11, 12, 13, 14
E 24	– Safety belt lock, left, with contact	11
F	– Brake light switch	36, 37
F 1	– Engine oil pressure switch	40
F 4	– Back-up light switch	32
F 9	– Parking brake warning light switch	24
F 24	– CAT converter elapsed mileage odometer	27
F 25	– Throttle valve micro switch	10
F 26	– Thermo-time switch for cold start device	31
F 27	– EGR elapsed mileage odometer	25
F 37	– Thermo-time switch for second stage (pull-down)	32
G	– Fuel gauge sending unit	42
G 1	– Fuel gauge	18
G 2	– Coolant temperature sending unit	41
G 3	– Coolant temperature gauge	19
G 7	– TDC indicator sensor	20
G 20	– Temperature sensor for CAT converter	28
H	– Horn button	35
H 1	– Horn	34
J 6	– Voltage stabilizer	18
J 34	– Safety belt warning system relay	11, 12, 13, 14
J 42	– CAT converter relay	27, 28, 29
K 2	– Alternator charging warning light	21
K 3	– Engine oil pressure warning light	20
K 5	– Turn signal warning light	22
K 7	– Dual circuit brake, parking brake and safety belt warning light	23, 24

(1) – Ground strap, battery/body

(2) – Ground strap, alternator/engine

(10) – Ground strap, dashboard

(11) – Ground strap, body

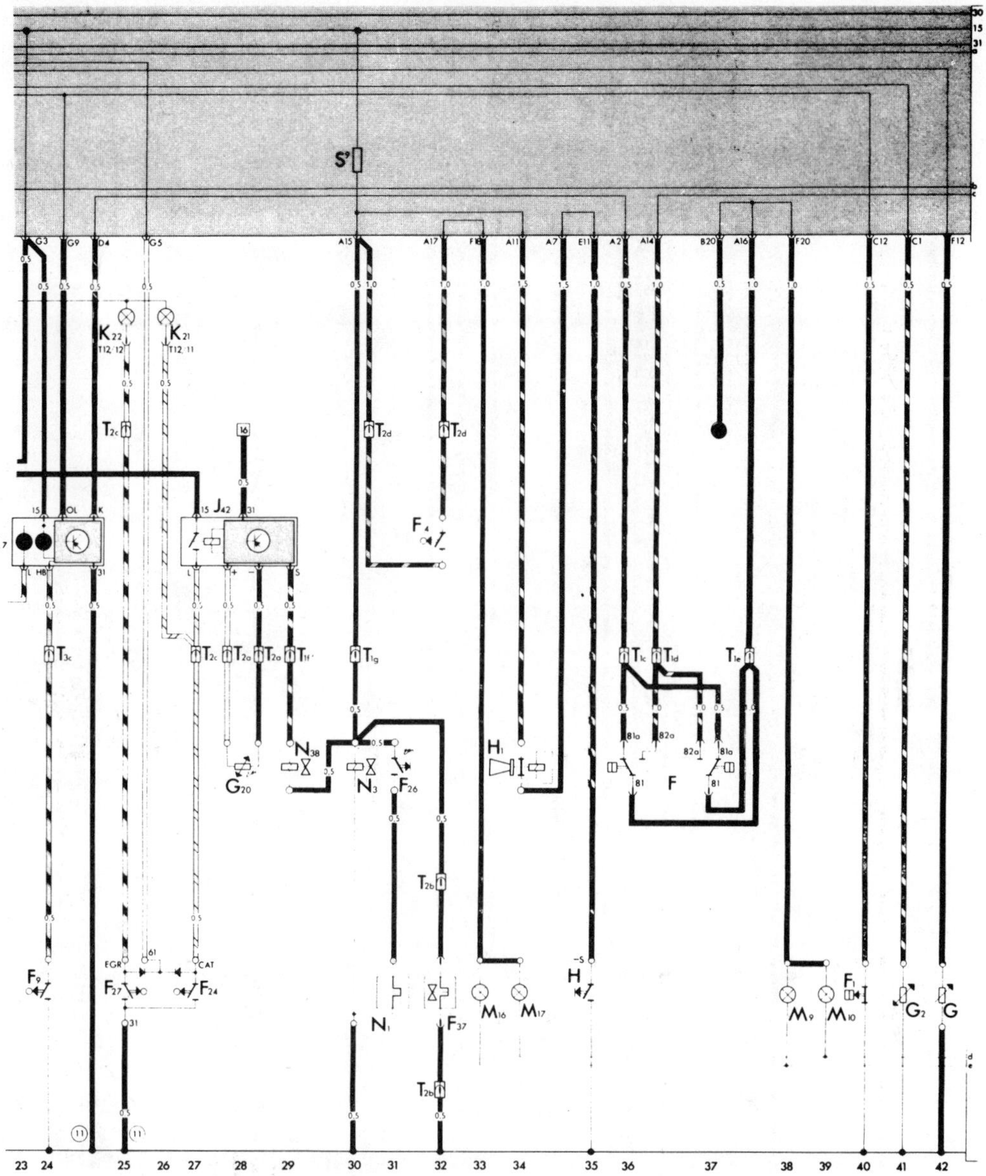

K 21 – CAT converter warning light 26
K 22 – EGR warning light 25
M 9 – Brake light, left 38
M 10 – Brake light, right 39
M 16 – Back-up light, left 33
M 17 – Back-up light, right 34
N – Ignition coil 7
N 1 – Automatic choke 31
N 3 – Electromagnetic cutoff valve 30
N 6 – Ballast resistor 7
N 18 – EGR valve 10
N 38 – Diverter valve for air injection 29
O – Ignition distributor 7, 9
P – Spark plug connectors 8, 9
Q – Spark plugs 8, 9
S 9 – Fuse in fuse box
T – Wire connector, behind dashboard
T 1c – Wire connector, single; next to brake master cylinder
T 1d – Wire connector, single; next to brake master cylinder
T 1e – Wire connector, single; next to brake master cylinder
T 1f – Wire connector, single; behind dashboard
T 1g – Wire connector, single; behind dashboard
T 1m – Wire connector, single; behind dashboard
T 2a – Wire connector, double; behind dashboard
T 2b – Wire connector, double; in engine compartment
T 2c – Wire connector, double; behind dashboard
T 2d – Wire connector, double; in engine compartment
T 2e – Wire connector, double; under driver's seat
T 3c – Wire connector, 3-point; behind dashboard
T 20 – Diagnosis system, diagnosis socket 17

1976 RABBIT

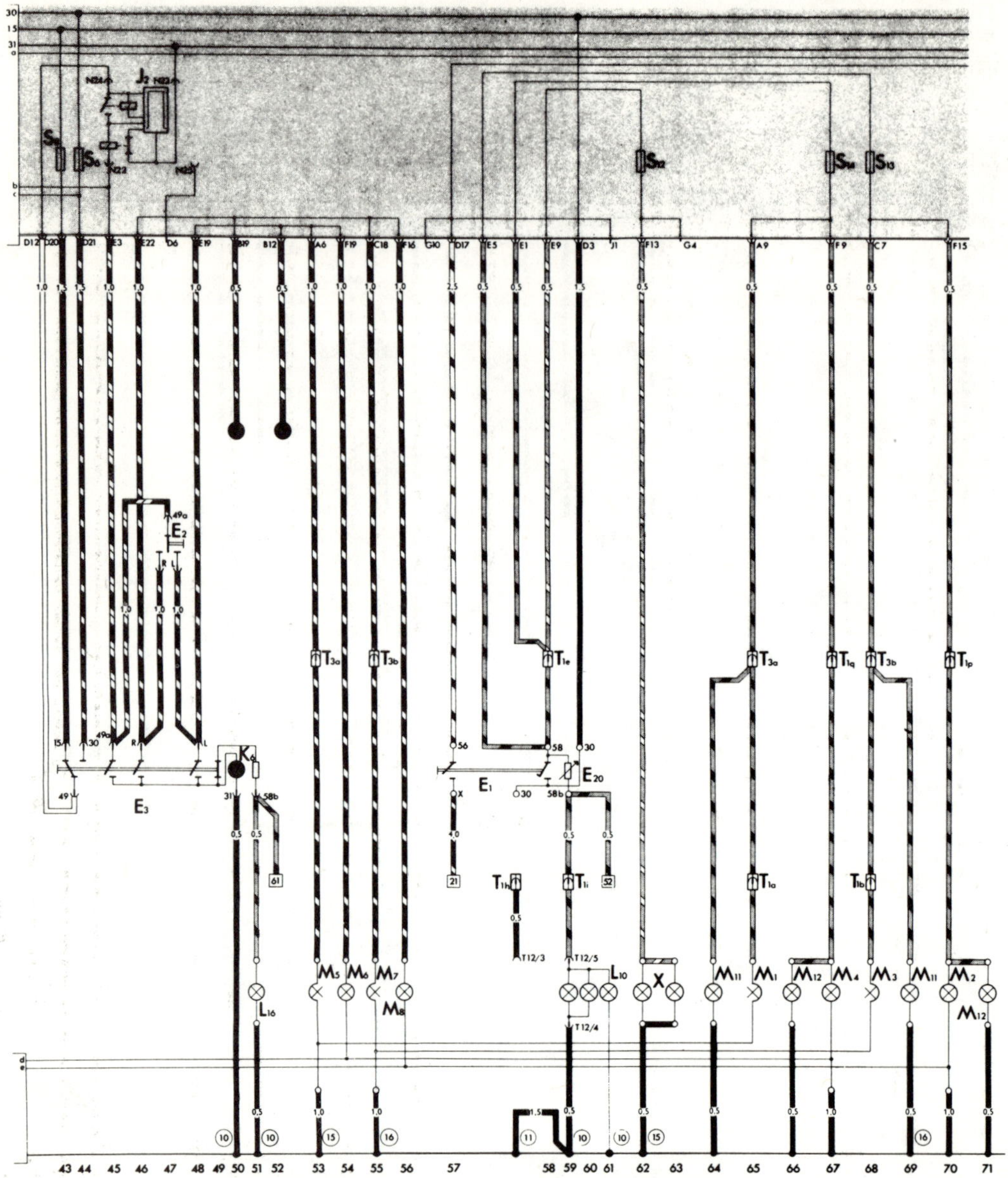

E 1	Light switch	57, 58, 59, 60
E 2	Turn signal switch	47
E 3	Emergency flasher switch	43, 44, 45, 46 48, 49
E 4	Headlight dimmer switch	84
E 9	Fresh air fan switch	75
E 15	Rear window defogger switch	73, 74
E 20	Instrument panel lighting switch	59
E 22	Windshield wash/wipe intermittent switch	78, 79, 80, 81, 82
F 2	Door contact switch for buzzer, front left	93, 94
F 18	Radiator cooling fan thermo switch	90
J	Headlight dimmer relay	84, 85, 86
J 2	Emergency flasher relay	45, 46
J 9	Rear window defogger relay	72
J 31	Windshield wash/wipe intermittent relay (not installed)	77, 78
K 1	Headlight high beam warning light	89
K 6	Emergency flasher warning light	50
K 10	Rear window defogger warning light	74
L 1	Sealed beam unit, left	85, 87
L 2	Sealed beam unit, right	86, 88
L 10	Instrument panel light	59, 60, 61
L 16	Fresh air operation lever light	51
M 1	Parking light, left	65
M 2	Taillight, right	70
M 3	Parking light, right	68
M 4	Taillight, left	67
M 5	Turn signal, front left	53
M 6	Turn signal, rear left	54
M 7	Turn signal, front right	55
M 8	Turn signal, rear right	56

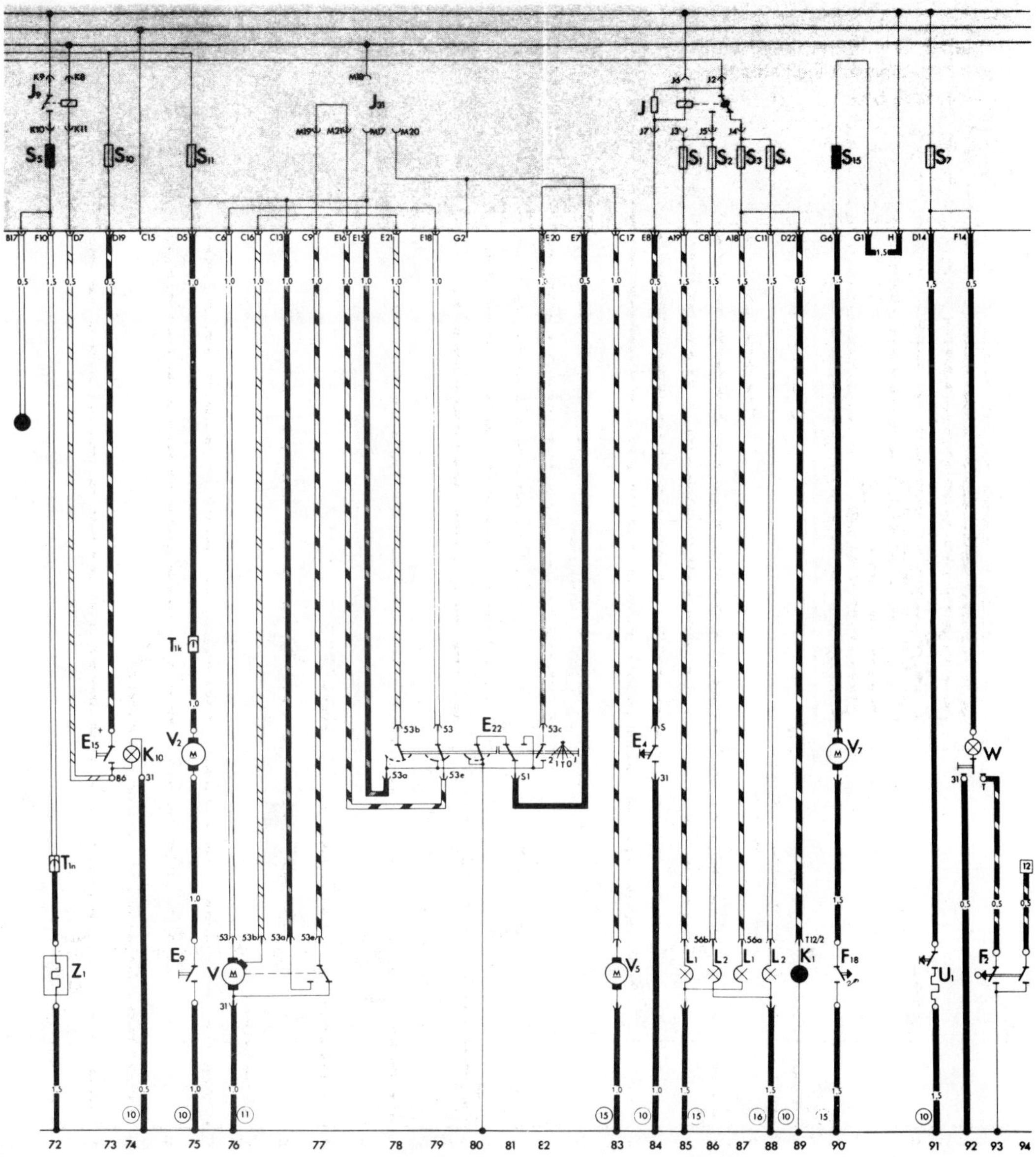

M 11 – Side marker lights, front 64, 69
M 12 – Side marker lights, rear 66, 71
– Fuses S 1, S 2, S 4, S 5, S 6, S 7, S 8, S 10, S 11, S 12, S 13, S 14, S 15 in fuse box
T 1a – Wire connector, single; in engine compartment front left
T 1b – Wire connector, single; in engine compartment front right
T 1h – Wire connector, single; behind dashboard
T 1i – Wire connector single; behind dashboard
T 1k – Wire connector, single; behind dashboard
T 1l – Wire connector, single; behind dashboard
T 1n – Wire connector, single; in luggage compartment left
T 1p – Wire connector, single; in luggage compartment rear right
T 1q – Wire connector, single; in luggage compartment rear left
T 3a – Wire connector, 3-point; in engine compartment front left
T 3b – Wire connector, 3-point; in engine compartment front right
T 12 – Wire connector, 12-point; on instrument panel cluster
U 1 – Cigarette lighter 91
V – Windshield wiper motor 76, 77
V 2 – Fresh air fan 75
V 5 – Windshield washer pump 83
V 7 – Radiator cooling fan 90
W – Interior light 92
X – License plate light 62, 63
Z 1 – Rear window defogger element 72
⑩ – Ground strap, dashboard
⑪ – Ground strap, body
⑮ – Ground strap, engine compartment; left
⑯ – Ground strap, engine compartment; right

1976 SCIROCCO

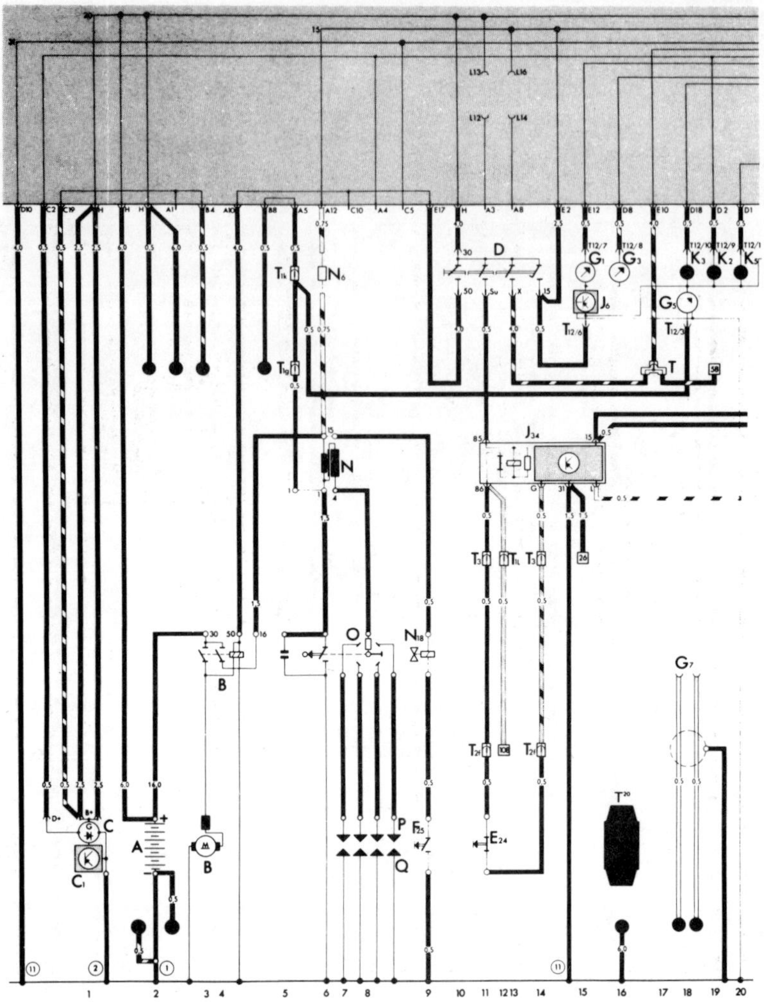

A	– Battery	2
B	– Starter	3, 4
C	– Alternator	1
C 1	– Regulator	1
D	– Ignition/starter switch	10, 11, 13, 14
E 24	– Safety belt lock, left	11
F	– Brake light switch	36, 37
F 1	– Engine oil pressure switch	39
F 4	– Back-up light switch	31
F 9	– Parking brake control light switch	22
F 24	– CAT converter elapsed mileage odometer (on speedometer)	25
F 25	– Throttle valve micro switch	9
F 26	– Thermo-time switch for cold starting device	30
F 27	– EGR elapsed mileage odometer	23
F 37	– Thermo-time switch for second stage (pull-down)	31
G	– Fuel gauge sending unit	41
G 1	– Fuel gauge	15
G 2	– Coolant temperature sending unit	40
G 3	– Coolant temperature gauge	16
G 5	– Tachometer	18
G 7	– To TDC indicator sensor	18
G 20	– Temperature sensor for CAT converter	26
H	– Horn button	36
H 1	– Dual horn	33, 34
J 4	– Relay for dual horn	35, 36
J 6	– Voltage stabilizer	15
J 34	– Safety belt warning system relay	11, 14, 15
J 42	– Relay for CAT converter	25, 26, 27, 28
K 2	– Alternator charging warning light	19

1976 SCIROCCO

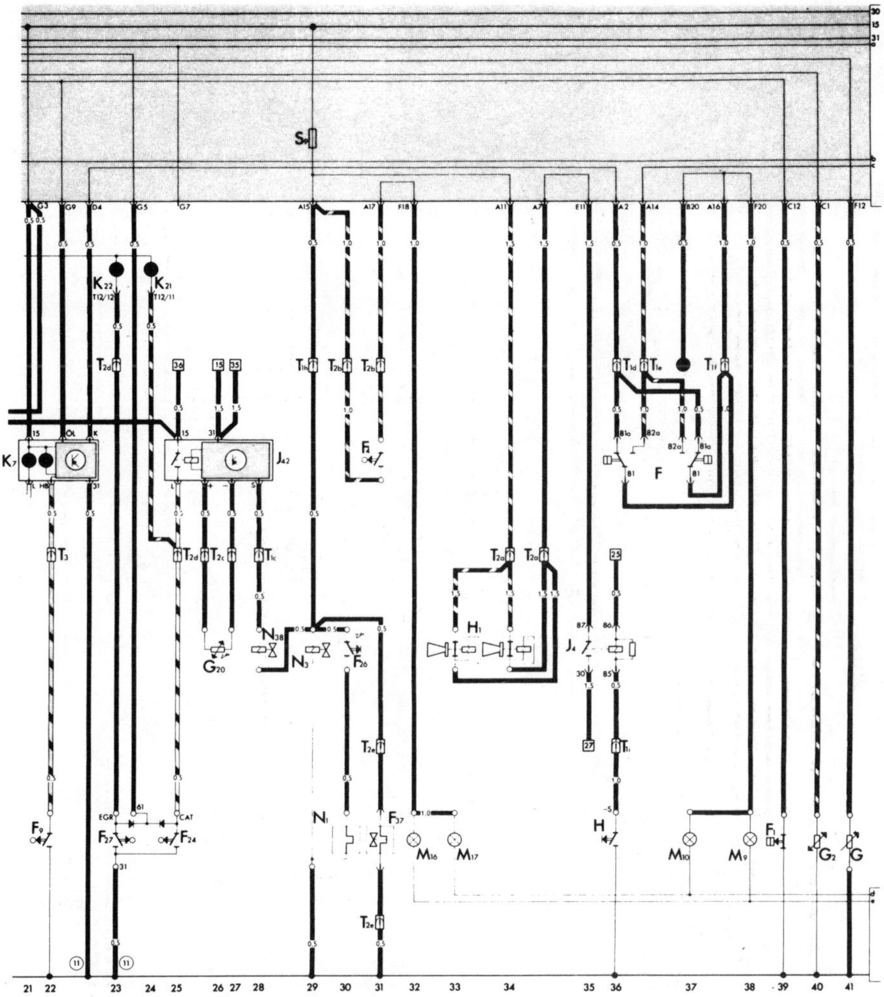

K 3	– Engine oil pressure warning light	18
K 5	– Turn signal warning light	20
K 7	– Dual circuit brake, parking brake, and safety belt warning light	21, 22
K 21	– CAT converter warning light	24
K 22	– EGR warning light	23
M 9	– Brake light, left	38
M 10	– Brake light, right	37
M 16	– Back-up light, left	32
M 17	– Back-up light, right	33
N	– Ignition coil	6
N 1	– Automatic choke	30
N 3	– Electromagnetic cutoff valve	29
N 6	– Ballast resistor	6
N 18	– EGR valve	9
N 38	– Diverter valve for air injection	28
O	– Ignition distributor	6, 8
P	– Spark plug connector	8
Q	– Spark plugs	8
S 9	– Fuse in fuse box	
T 1c	– Wire connector, single; behind dashboard	
T 1d	– Wire connector, single; in engine compartment	
T 1e	– Wire connector, single; in engine compartment	
T 1f	– Wire connector, single; behind dashboard	
T 1g	– Wire connector, single; behind dashboard	
T 1h	– Wire connector, single; behind dashboard	
T 1i	– Wire connector, single; behind dashboard	
T 1k	– Wire connector, single; behind dashboard	
T 1l	– Wire connector, single; behind dashboard	
T 2a	– Wire connector, double; in engine compartment, front	
T 2b	– Wire connector, double; in engine compartment on fire wall	

1976 SCIROCCO

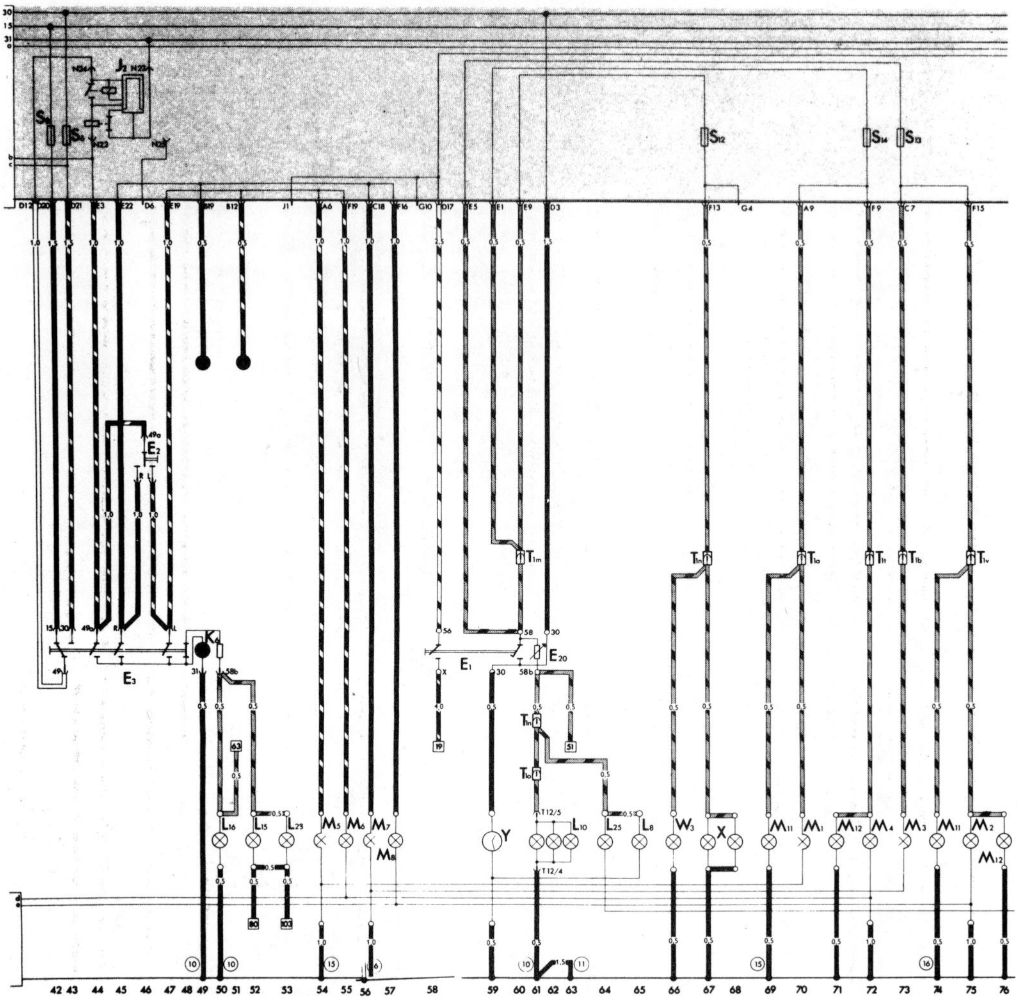

E 1	– Light switch	58, 60
E 2	– Turn signal switch	46
E 3	– Emergency flasher switch	42, 43, 44, 45, 47, 48
E 4	– Headlight dimmer switch	93
E 9	– Fresh air fan switch	78, 79
E 15	– Rear window defogger switch	91
E 20	– Instrument panel lighting control switch	61
E 22	– Windshield wash/wipe intermittent switch	84, 85, 86, 87, 88
F 2	– Door contact switch for buzzer alarm, front left	107, 108
F 3	– Door contact switch for buzzer alarm, front right	106
F 18	– Radiator cooling fan thermo switch	102
G 14	– Voltmeter	77
J	– Headlight dimmer switch	93, 94, 95
J 2	– Emergency flasher relay	44, 45, 46
J 9	– Rear window defogger relay	90
J 31	– Windshield wash/wipe intermittent relay	82, 83, 84
K 1	– Headlight high beam warning light	101
K 6	– Emergency flasher warning light	49
K 10	– Rear window defogger warning light	92
L 1	– Sealed beam unit, left	94, 96
L 2	– Sealed beam unit, right	95, 100
L 8	– Clock light	65
L 10	– Instrument panel light	61, 62, 63
L 15	– Ashtray light	52
L 16	– Fresh air operation lever light	50
L 17	– Sealed beam unit headlight, left	98
L 18	– Sealed beam unit headlight, right	99
L 25	– Voltmeter light	64
L 28	– Cigarette lighter light	53
M 1	– Parking light, left	70.
M 2	– Taillight, right	75
M 3	– Parking light, right	73
M 4	– Taillight, left	72
M 5	– Turn signal, front left	54

1976 SCIROCCO

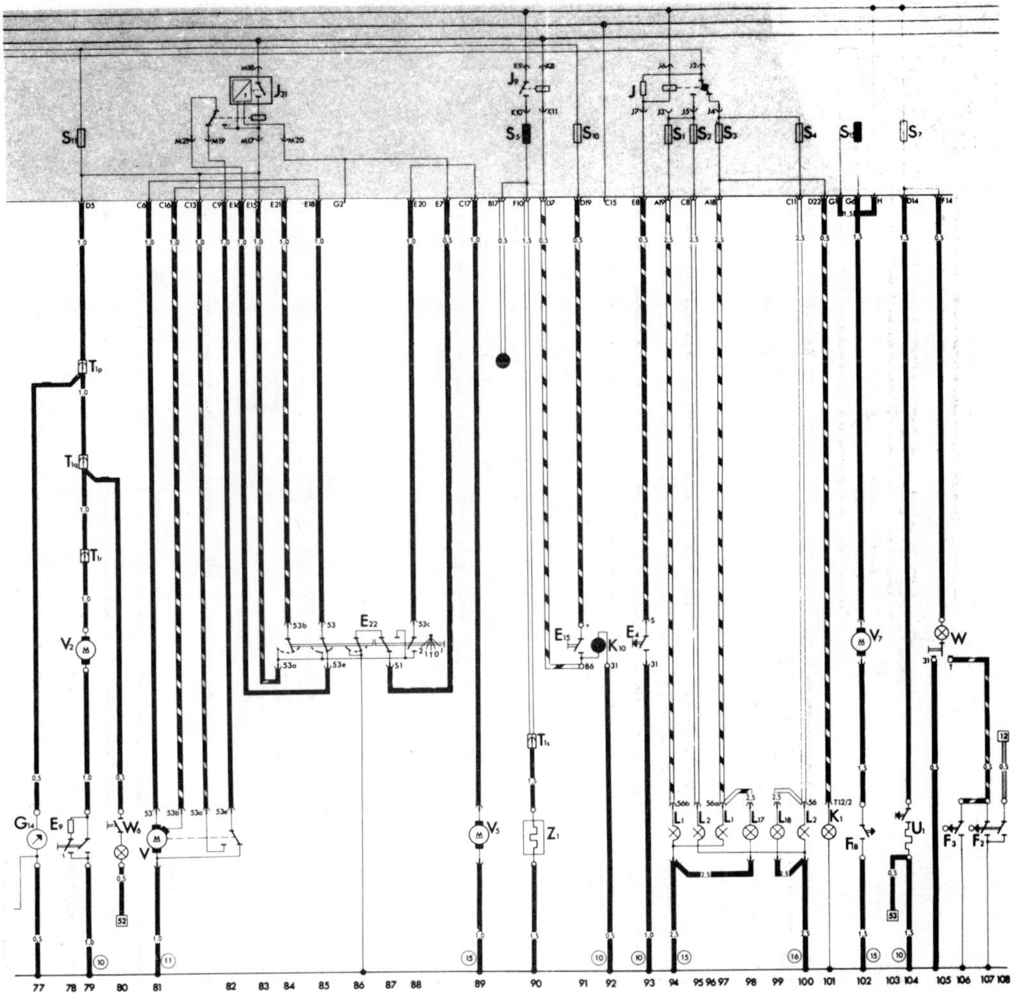

M 6 – Turn signal, rear left 55
M 7 – Turn signal. front right 56
M 8 – Turn signal, rear right 57
M 11 – Side marker light, front 69, 74
M 12 – Side marker light, rear 71, 76
– Fuses S 1, S 2, S 3, S 4, S 5, S 6, S 7, S 8, S 10, S 11, S 12, S 13, S 14, S 15 in fuse box
T 1a – Wire connector, single; in engine compartment front left
T 1b – Wire connector, single; in engine compartment front right
T 1m – Wire connector, single; behind dashboard
T 1n – Wire connector, single; in luggage compartment
T 1o – Wire connector, single; behind dashboard
T 1p – Wire connector, single; behind dashboard
T 1q – Wire connector, single; behind dashboard
T 1r – Wire connector, single; behind dashboard
T 1s – Wire connector, single; in luggage compartment
T 1t – Wire connector, single; in luggage compartment, left
T 1v – Wire connector, single; in luggage compartment, right
T 12 – Wire connector, 12-point; on dashboard cluster
U 1 – Cigarette lighter 104
V – Windshield wiper motor 81, 82
V 2 – Fresh air fan 79
V 5 – Windshield wiper pump 89
V 7 – Radiator cooling fan 102
W – Interior light 105
W 3 – Luggage compartment light 66
W 6 – Glove compartment light 80
X – License plate light 67, 68
Y – Clock 59
Z 1 – Rear window defogger light 90
⑩ – Ground strap, dashboard cluster
⑪ – Ground strap, dashboard
⑮ – Ground strap, engine compartment, front left
⑯ – Ground strap, engine compartment, front right

1977 RABBIT — Basic and Custom Models

Page 1 of 4

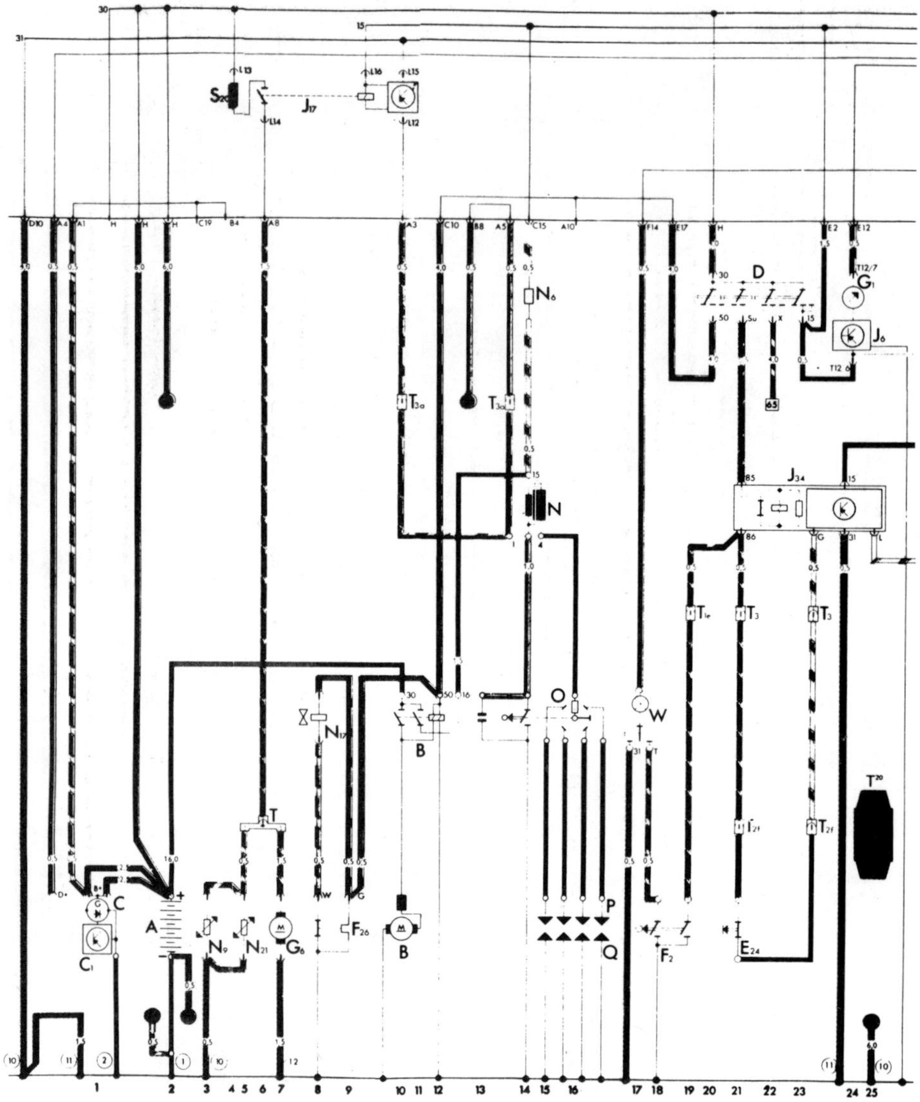

A	–	Battery	2
B	–	Starter	10–12
C	–	Alternator	1
C 1	–	Regulator	1
D	–	Ignition/starter switch	20–23
E 24	–	Safety belt lock, left, with contact	21
F	–	Brake light switch	41,42
F 1	–	Engine oil pressure switch	33
F 2	–	Door contact switch, left	18
F 4	–	Back-up light switch	37
F 9	–	Parking brake warning light switch	31
F 14	–	Coolant temperature warning light switch	34
F 26	–	Thermo-time switch for cold-start device	8, 9
F 27	–	Elapsed EGR mileage switch	32
G	–	Fuel gauge sending unit	35
G 1	–	Fuel gauge	24
G 6	–	Electrical fuel pump	7
H	–	Horn button	40
H 1	–	Horn	39
J 6	–	Voltage stabilizer	24
J 17	–	Electrical fuel pump relay	6, 10
J 34	–	Safety belt warning system relay	21–25
K 2	–	Alternator charging warning light	28
K 3	–	Engine oil pressure warning light	27
K 5	–	Turn signal warning light	29
K 7	–	Dual circuit brake, parking brake, and safety belt warning light	30, 31
K 22	–	EGR warning light	32
K 28	–	Coolant temperature warning light	26

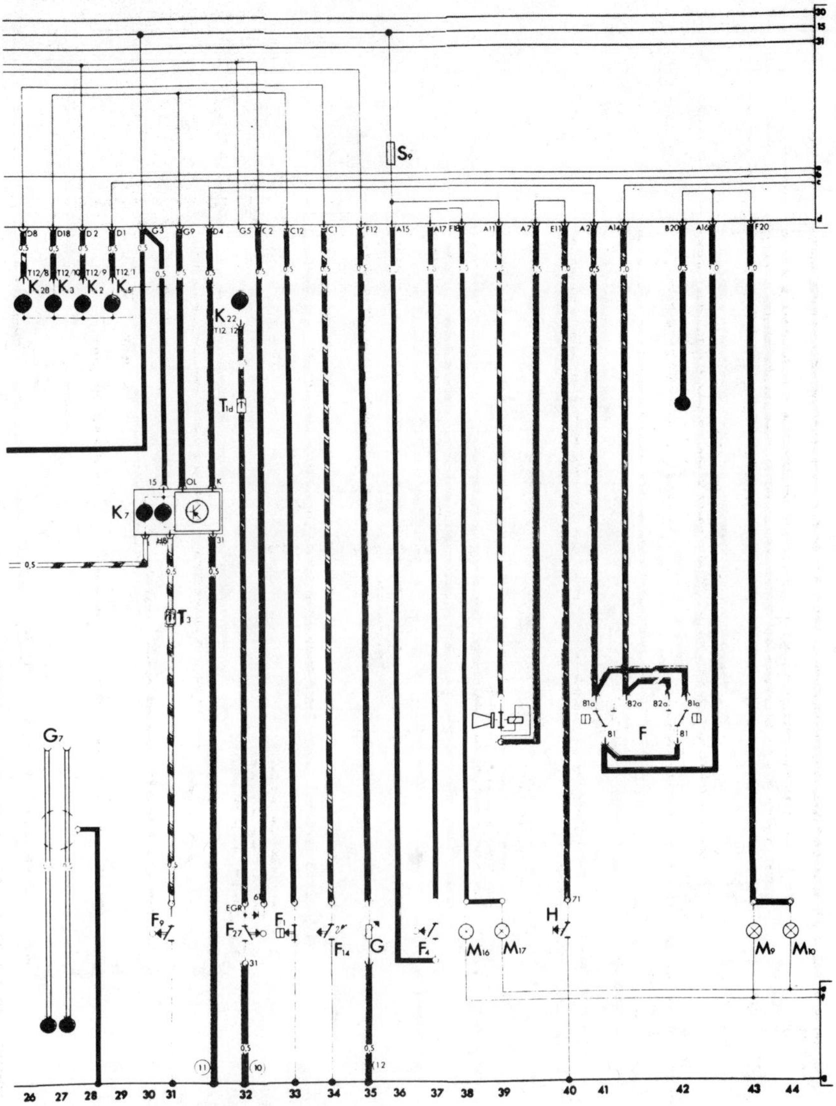

M 9	– Brake light, left	43
M 10	– Brake light, right	44
M 16	– Back-up light, left	38
M 17	– Back-up light, right	39
N	– Ignition coil	14
N 6	– Ballast resistor wire	14
N 9	– Control pressure regulator	3
N 17	– Cold start valve	8
N 21	– Auxiliary air regulator	5
O	– Ignition distributor	15, 16
P	– Spark plug connectors	15, 16
Q	– Spark plugs	15, 16
S 9	– Fuse in fuse box	
S 20	– Fuse for electrical fuel pump (16-amp) on relay J 17	
T	– Wire connector, single; in engine compartment	
T 1d	– Wire connector, single; behind dashboard	
T 1e	– Wire connector, single; next to relay board	
T 2f	– Wire connector, double; on frame, left	
T 3	– Wire connector, 3-point; behind dashboard	
T 3a	– Wire connector, 3-point; behind dashboard	
T 12	– Wire connector, 12-point (Canada 10-point) on dashboard cluster	
T 20	– Analysis system, analysis socket	25
W	– Interior light	17,18

① – Ground strap, battery/body/engine

② – Ground strap, generator/engine

⑩ – Ground strap, steering column support

⑪ – Ground strap, next to instrument panel cluster

1977 RABBIT — Basic and Custom Models

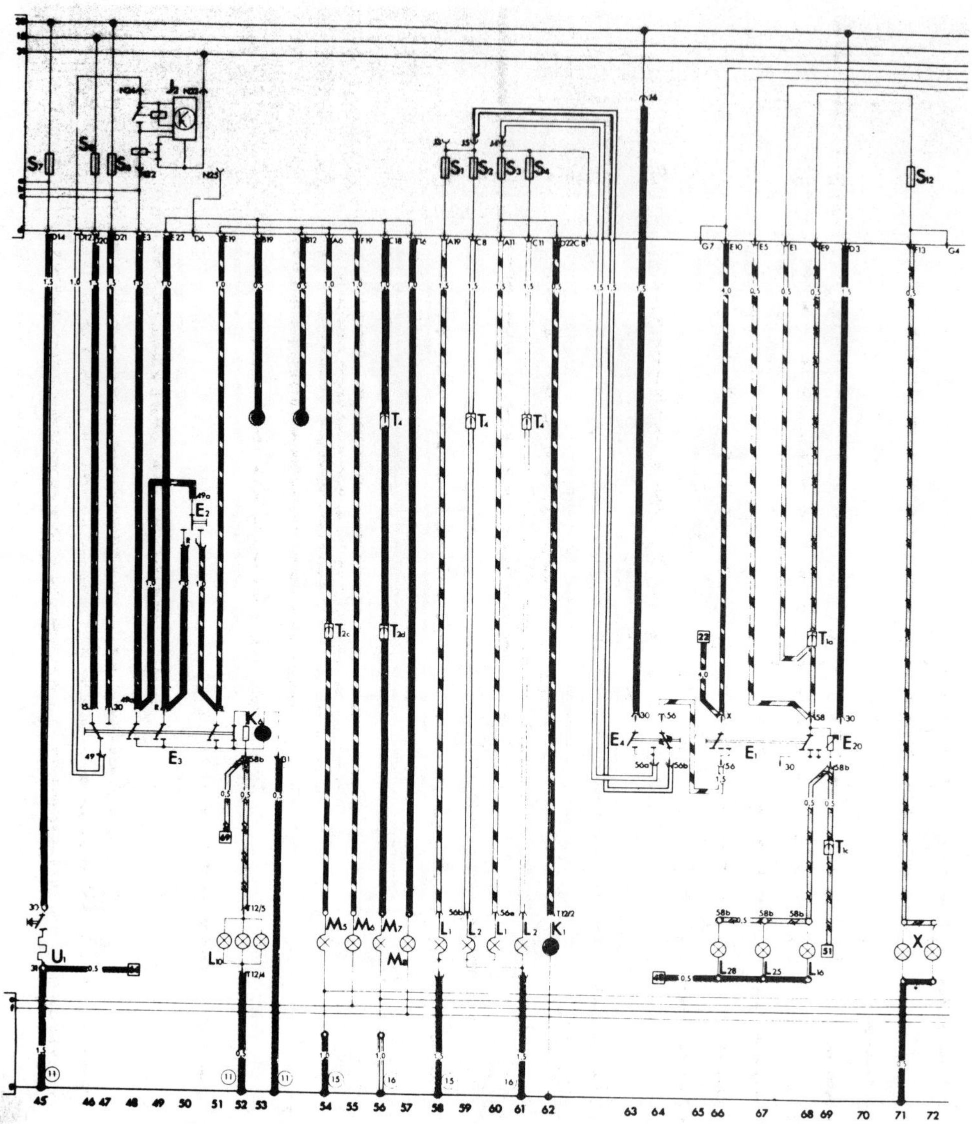

E 1	Light switch	66–69
E 2	Turn signal switch	50
E 3	Emergency flasher switch	46–53
E 4	Headlight dimmer switch	63, 64
E 9	Fresh air fan switch	81, 82
E 15	Rear window defogger switch	84, 85
E 20	Instrument panel lighting switch	69
E 22	Windshield wash/wipe intermittent switch	88–92
F 18	Radiator cooling fan thermo switch	94
J 2	Emergency flasher relay	48–50
J 9	Rear window defogger relay	83
K 1	Headlight high beam warning light	62
K 6	Emergency flasher warning light	52, 53
K 10	Rear window defogger warning light	85
L 1	Sealed beam unit, left	58, 60
L 2	Sealed beam unit, right	59, 61
L 10	Instrument panel light	52
L 16	Fresh air operation lever light	68
L 25	Ashtray light (custom model only)	67
L 28	Cigarette lighter light (custom model only)	66
M 1	Parking light, left	74
M 2	Taillight, right	79
M 3	Parking light, right	77
M 4	Taillight, left	76
M 5	Turn signal, front left	54
M 6	Turn signal, rear left	55
M 7	Turn signal, front right	56
M 8	Turn signal, rear right	57
M 11	Side marker lights, front	73, 78
M 12	Side marker lights, rear	75, 80
N 23	Ballast resistor for fresh air blower	81

1977 RABBIT — Basic and Custom Models

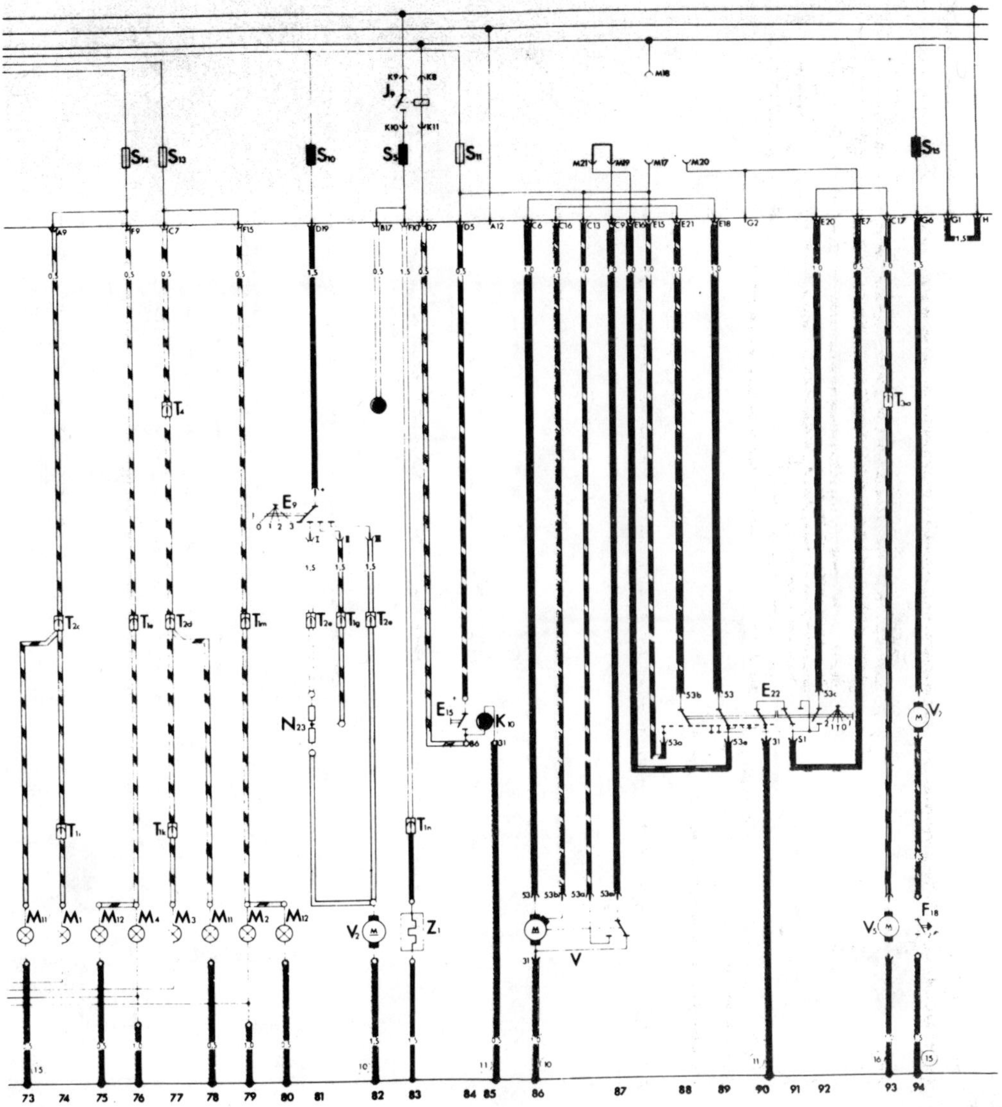

S 1, S 2, S 3, S 4, S 5, S 6, S 7, S 8,
S 10, S 11, S 12, S 13, S 14, S 15 } Fuses in fuse box

T 1a – Wire connector, single; behind dashboard
T 1c – Wire connector, single; behind dashboard
T 1e – Wire connector, single; in luggage compartment, left
T 1g – Wire connector, single; behind dashboard
T 1i – Wire connector, single; in engine compartment, left
T 1k – Wire connector, single; in engine compartment, right
T 1m – Wire connector, single; in luggage compartment, right
T 1n – Wire connector, single; in luggage compartment, left
T 2c – Wire connector, double; in engine compartment, left
T 2d – Wire connector, double; behind dashboard
T 2e – Wire connector, double; behind dashboard
T 3a – Wire connector, 3-point; behind dashboard
T 4 – Wire connector, 4-point; behind dashboard
T 12 – Wire connector, 12-point (Canada 10-point); on instrument panel cluster
U 1 – Cigarette lighter 45
V – Windshield wiper motor 86
V 2 – Fresh air fan 82
V 5 – Windshield washer pump 93
V 7 – Radiator cooling fan 94
X – License plate light 71, 72
Z 1 – Rear window defogger element 83

⑩ – Ground strap, dashboard
⑪ – Ground strap, next to instrument panel cluster
⑮ – Ground strap, engine compartment; left
⑯ – Ground strap, engine compartment; right

1977 RABBIT — DeLuxe Models

Page 1 of 4

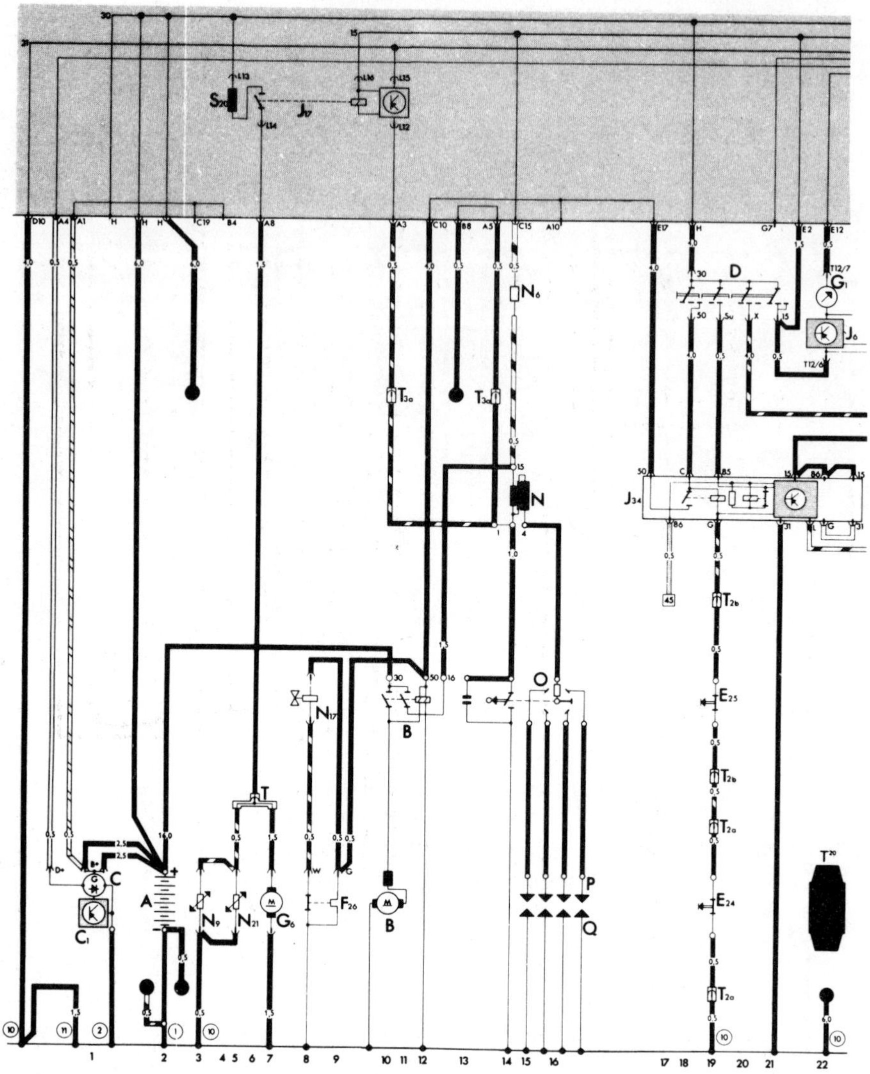

A	–	Battery	2
B	–	Starter	10–12
C	–	Alternator	1
C 1	–	Regulator	1
D	–	Ignition/starter switch	18–21
E 24	–	Safety belt switch, left	19
E 25	–	Safety belt switch, right	19
F	–	Brake light switch	38, 39
F 1	–	Engine oil pressure switch	30
F 4	–	Back-up light switch	34
F 9	–	Parking brake warning light switch	28
F 26	–	Thermo-time switch for cold starting valve	8, 9
F 27	–	Elapsed EGR mileage switch	29
G	–	Fuel gauge sending unit	32
G 1	–	Fuel gauge	22
G 2	–	Coolant temperature sending unit	31
G 3	–	Coolant temperature gauge	23
G 6	–	Electric fuel pump	7
G 7	–	Connections for TDC indicator sensor	24
H	–	Horn button	37
H 1	–	Horn	36
J 6	–	Voltage stabilizer	22
J 17	–	Electric fuel pump relay	6–10
J 34	–	Safety belt warning system relay	17–21
K 2	–	Alternator charging warning light	25
K 3	–	Engine oil pressure warning light	24
K 5	–	Turn signal warning light	26
K 7	–	Dual circuit brake, parking brake, and safety belt warning light	27, 28
K 22	–	EGR warning light	29

1977 RABBIT — DeLuxe Models

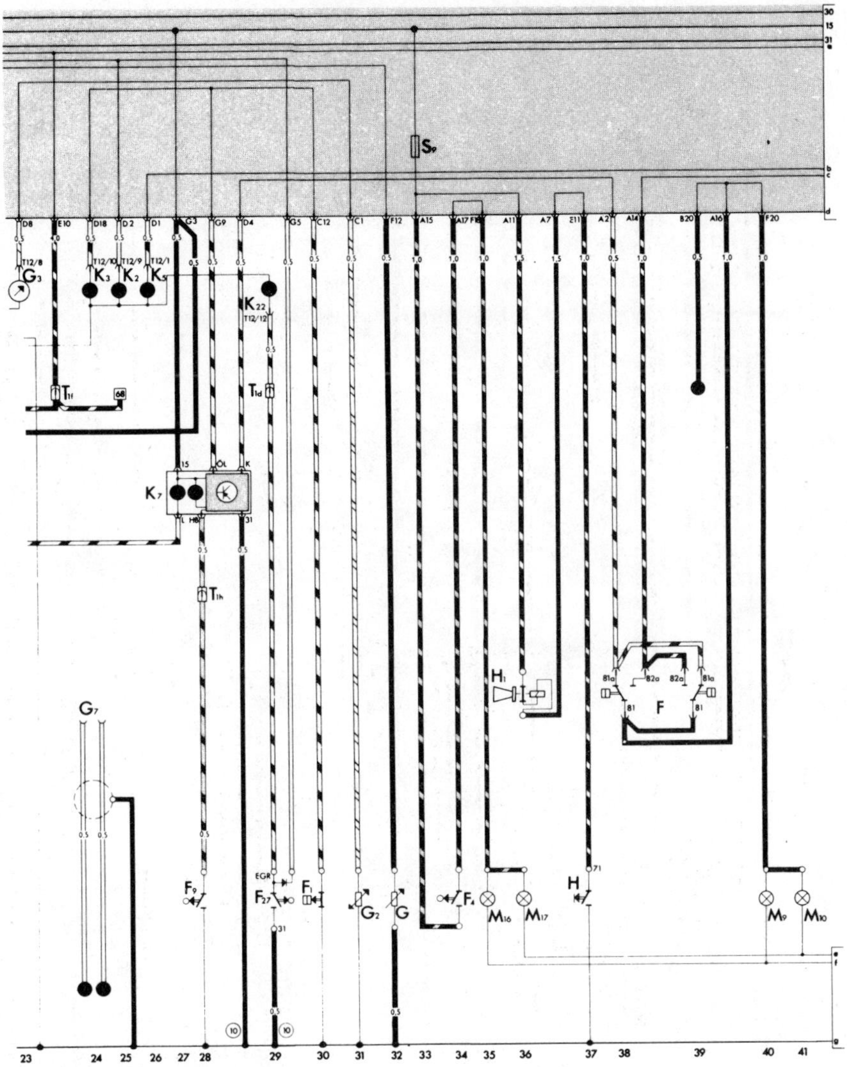

M 9	– Brake light, left	40
M 10	– Brake light, right	41
M 16	– Back-up light, left	35
M 17	– Back-up light, right	36
N	– Ignition coil	14
N 6	– Ballast resistor	14
N 9	– Control pressure regulator	3
N 17	– Cold-start valve	8
N 21	– Auxiliary air regulator	5
O	– Ignition distributor	14, 15
P	– Spark plug connector	15, 16
Q	– Spark plugs	15, 16
S 9	– Fuse in fuse box	
S 20	– Fuse (16 amp) for electric fuel pump on relay J 17	4
T	– Wire connector; in engine compartment	5–7
T 1d	– Wire connector, single; behind dashboard	29
T 1f	– Wire connector, single; behind dashboard	23–24
T 1h	– Wire connector, single; behind dashboard	28
T 2a	– Wire connector, double; behind dashboard	19
T 2b	– Wire connector, double; behind dashboard	19
T 3a	– Wire connector, 3-point; behind dashboard	10, 13–14
T 12	– Wire connector, 12-point; on dashboard cluster	22–29
T 20	– Analysis system, analysis socket	22
(1)	– Ground strap, battery to body and engine	
(2)	– Ground strap, alternator to engine	
(10)	– Ground connectors, dashboard cluster	
(11)	– Ground connector, steering column support	

1977 RABBIT — DeLuxe Models

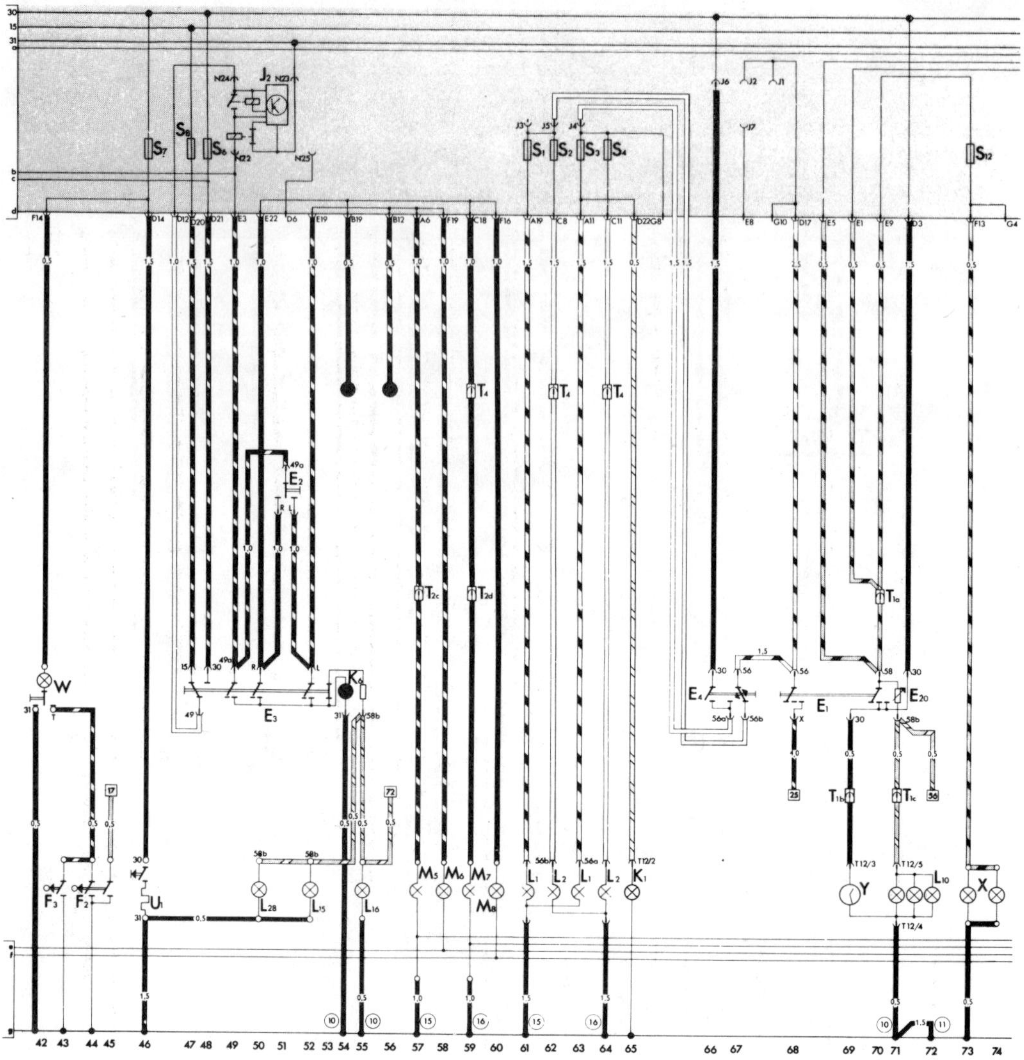

E 1	Light switch	68–70
E 2	Turn signal switch	51
E 3	Emergency flasher switch	47–50, 52, 53, 55
E 4	Headlight dimmer and headlight flasher switch	66, 67
E 9	Fresh air fan switch	83
E 15	Rear window defogger switch	86
E 20	Instrument panel lighting control switch	71
E 22	Windshield wash/wipe intermittent switch	91–94
F 2	Door contact switch, for buzzer alarm, front left	45
F 3	Door contact switch, front right	43
F 18	Radiator cooling fan thermo switch	96
J 2	Emergency flasher relay	49, 50
J 9	Rear window defogger relay	85
J 31	Windshield wash/wipe intermittent relay	89, 90
K 1	Headlight high beam warning light	65
K 6	Emergency flasher warning light	54
K 10	Rear window defogger warning light	86
L 1	Sealed beam unit, left	61, 63
L 2	Sealed beam unit, right	62, 64
L 10	Instrument panel light	71, 72
L 15	Ashtray light	52
L 16	Heater lever light	55
L 28	Cigarette lighter illumination	50
M 1	Parking light, left	76
M 2	Taillight, right	81
M 3	Parking light, right	79
M 4	Taillight, left	78
M 5	Turn signal, front left	57
M 6	Turn signal, rear left	58
M 7	Turn signal, front right	59
M 8	Turn signal, rear right	60
M 11	Side marker light, front	75, 80
M 12	Side marker light, rear	77, 82

1977 RABBIT — DeLuxe Models

Page 4 of 4

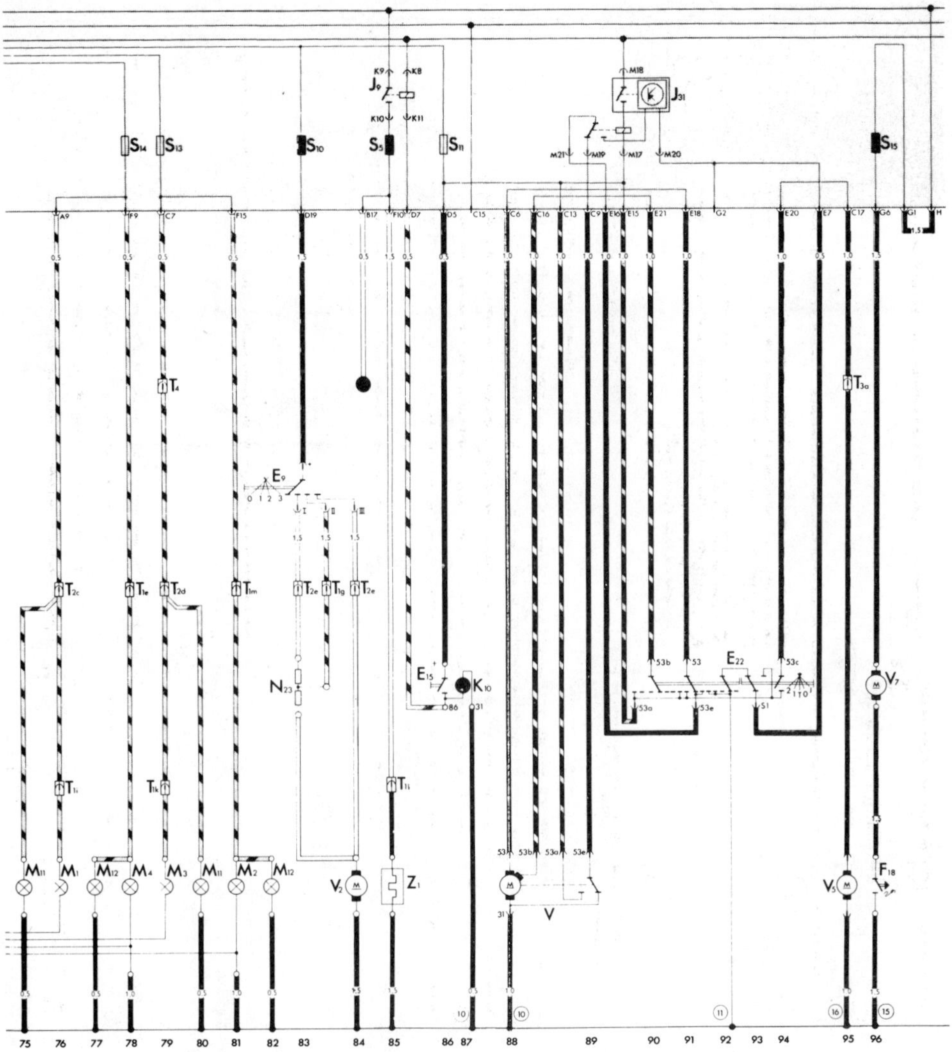

N 23 – Speed control resistors for fresh air fan 83
– Fuses S1, S2, S3, S4, S5, S6, S7, S8, S10, S11, S12, S13, S14, S15 in fuse box
T 1a – Wire connector, single; behind dashboard 70
T 1b – Wire connector, single; behind dashboard 69
T 1c – Wire connector, single; behind dashboard 71
T 1e – Wire connector, single; in luggage compartment, rear left 78
T 1g – Wire connector, single; behind dashboard 83, 84
T 1i – Wire connector, single; in engine compartment, front left 76
T 1k – Wire connector, single; in engine compartment, front right 79
T 1l – Wire connector, single; in luggage compartment, rear left 85
T 1m – Wire connector, single; in luggage compartment, rear right 81
T 2c – Wire connector, double; in engine compartment, front left 57, 76
T 2d – Wire connector, double; in engine compartment, front right 59, 79
T 2e – Wire connector, double; behind dashboard 83, 84
T 3a – Wire connector, 3-point; behind dashboard 95
T 4 – Wire connector, 4-point; behind dashboard 59, 62, 64, 79
T 12 – Wire connector, 12-point; on dashboard cluster 71
U 1 – Cigarette lighter 46
V – Windshield wiper motor 88, 89
V 2 – Fresh air fan 84
V 5 – Windshield washer pump 95
V 7 – Radiator cooling fan 96
W – Interior light 42
X – License plate light 73, 74
Y – Clock 69
Z 1 – Rear window defogger element 85
(10) – Ground connectors, dashboard cluster
(11) – Ground connectors, steering column support
(15) – Ground connectors, engine compartment front left
(16) – Ground connectors, engine compartment front right

1977 SCIROCCO

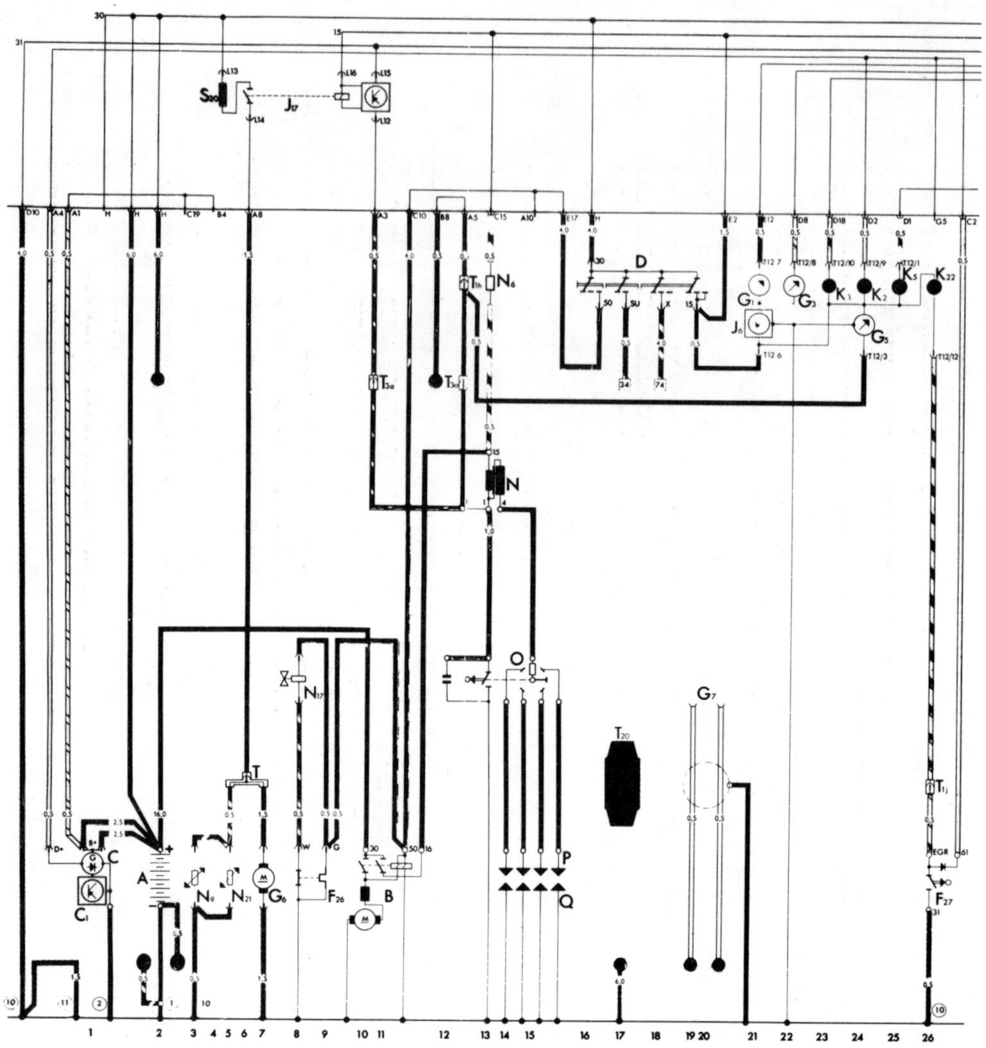

A	– Battery	2
B	– Starter	10, 11
C	– Alternator	1
C 1	– Regulator	1
D	– Ignition/starter switch	16–19
E 24	– Safety belt lock switch, left	34
F	– Brake light switch	48, 49
F 1	– Engine oil pressure switch	27
F 2	– Door contact switch for buzzer alarm, left	32
F 3	– Door contact switch, right	31
F 4	– Back-up light switch	45
F 9	– Parking brake control light switch	39
F 26	– Thermo-time switch for cold-start device	8
F 27	– Elapsed EGR mileage switch (not for CANADA)	26
G	– Fuel gauge sending unit	29
G 1	– Fuel gauge	21
G 2	– Coolant temperature sending unit	28
G 3	– Coolant temperature gauge	22
G 5	– Tachometer	24
G 6	– Electric fuel pump	7
G 7	– to TDC sensor	19–21
G 10	– Oil pressure switch	36
G 11	– Oil pressure gauge	36
H	– Horn button	43
H 1	– Dual horn	40, 41
J 4	– Relay for dual horn	42, 43
J 6	– Voltage stabilizer	21
J 7	– Electric fuel pump relay	6, 11
J 34	– Safety belt warning relay	34, 35
K 2	– Alternator charging warning light	24
K 3	– Engine oil pressure warning light	23
K 5	– Turn signal warning light	25

① – Ground strap, battery to body

② – Ground strap, alternator to engine

⑩ – Ground connector on steering column

⑪ – Ground connector next to instrument cluster

1977 SCIROCCO

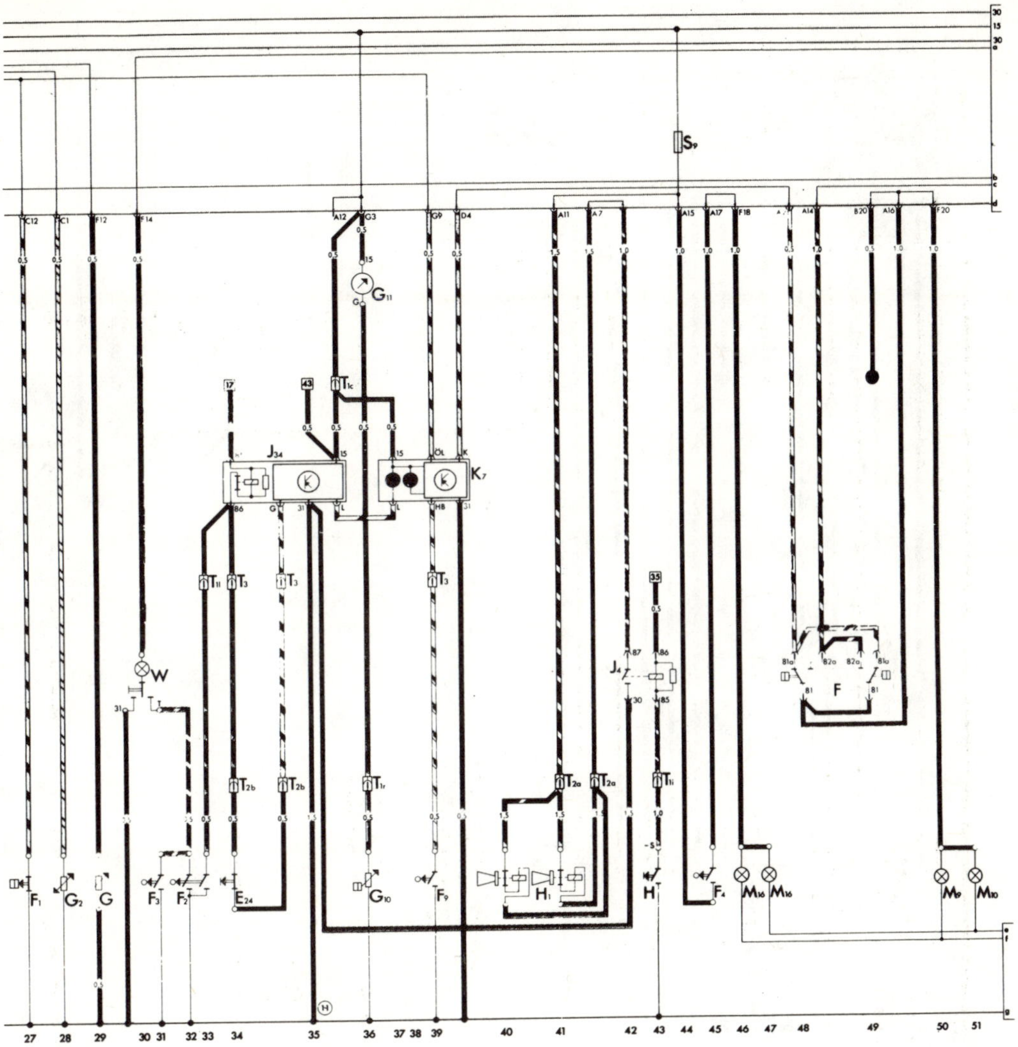

K 7	–	Dual circuit brake, parking brake, and safety belt warning light	37–39
K 22	–	EGR warning light	26
M 9	–	Brake light, left	50
M 10	–	Brake light, right	51
M 16	–	Back-up light, left	46
M 17	–	Back-up light, right	47
N	–	Ignition coil	13, 14
N 6	–	Ballast resistor	13
N 9	–	Warm-up regulator	3
N 17	–	Cold-start regulator	8
N 21	–	Auxiliary air regulator	5
O	–	Ignition distributor	14, 15
P	–	Spark plug connector	14, 15
Q	–	Spark plugs	14, 15
S 9	–	Fuse on fuse/relay panel	S
S 20	–	Fuse for electric fuel pump (16-amp) from relay J 17	
T	–	Wire connector; in engine compartment	
T 1c	–	Wire connector, single; behind dashboard	
T 1h	–	Wire connector, single; behind dashboard	
T 1i	–	Wire connector, single; behind dashboard	
T 1j	–	Wire connector, single; behind dashboard	
T 1l	–	Wire connector, single; behind dashboard	
T 1r	–	Wire connector, single; behind dashboard	
T 2a	–	Wire connector, double; in engine compartment, front	
T 2b	–	Wire connector, double; on frame, left	
T 3	–	Wire connector, 3-point; behind dashboard	
T 3a	–	Wire connector, 3-point; behind dashboard	
T 12	–	Wire connector, 12-point; dashboard cluster	
T 20	–	Analysis socket	
W	–	Interior light	30

1977 SCIROCCO

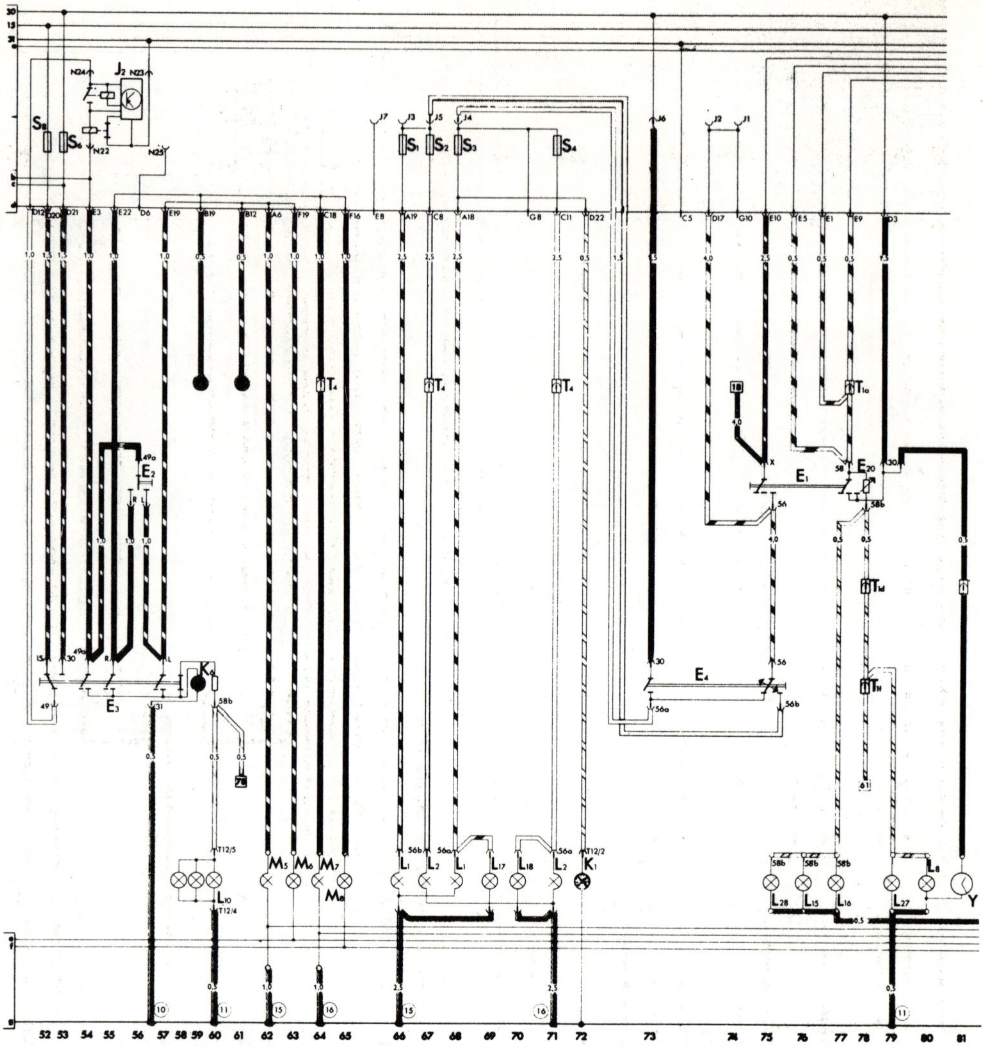

E 1	Light switch	75–79
E 9	Turn signal switch	56
E 3	Emergency flasher switch	52-60
E 4	Headlight dimmer switch and flasher	73–75
E 9	Fresh air fan switch	94
E 15	Rear window defogger switch	97, 98
E 20	Instrument panel lighting switch	78
E 22	Windshield wiper intermittent switch	102–106
F 18	Radiator cooling fan thermo switch	108
J 2	Emergency flasher relay	54-56
J 9	Rear window defogger relay	96
J 31	Windshield wiper intermittent relay	100-103
K 1	Headlight high beam warning light	72
K 6	Emergency flasher warning light	59
K 10	Rear window defogger warning light	98
L 1	Left headlight, high/low beam	66, 68
L 2	Right headlight, high/low beam	67, 71
L 8	Clock light	80
L 10	Instrument panel light	60
L 15	Ashtray light	76
L 16	Fresh air lever light	77
L 17	Left headlight, high beam	69
L 18	Right headlight, high beam	70
L 27	Oil pressure gauge light	79
L 28	Cigarette lighter light	75
M 1	Parking light, front left	87
M 2	Taillight, right	92
M 3	Parking light, front right	90
M 4	Taillight, left	89
M 5	Turn signal, front left	62
M 6	Turn signal, rear left	63
M 7	Turn signal, front right	64
M 8	Turn signal, rear right	65

1977 SCIROCCO

Page 4 of 4

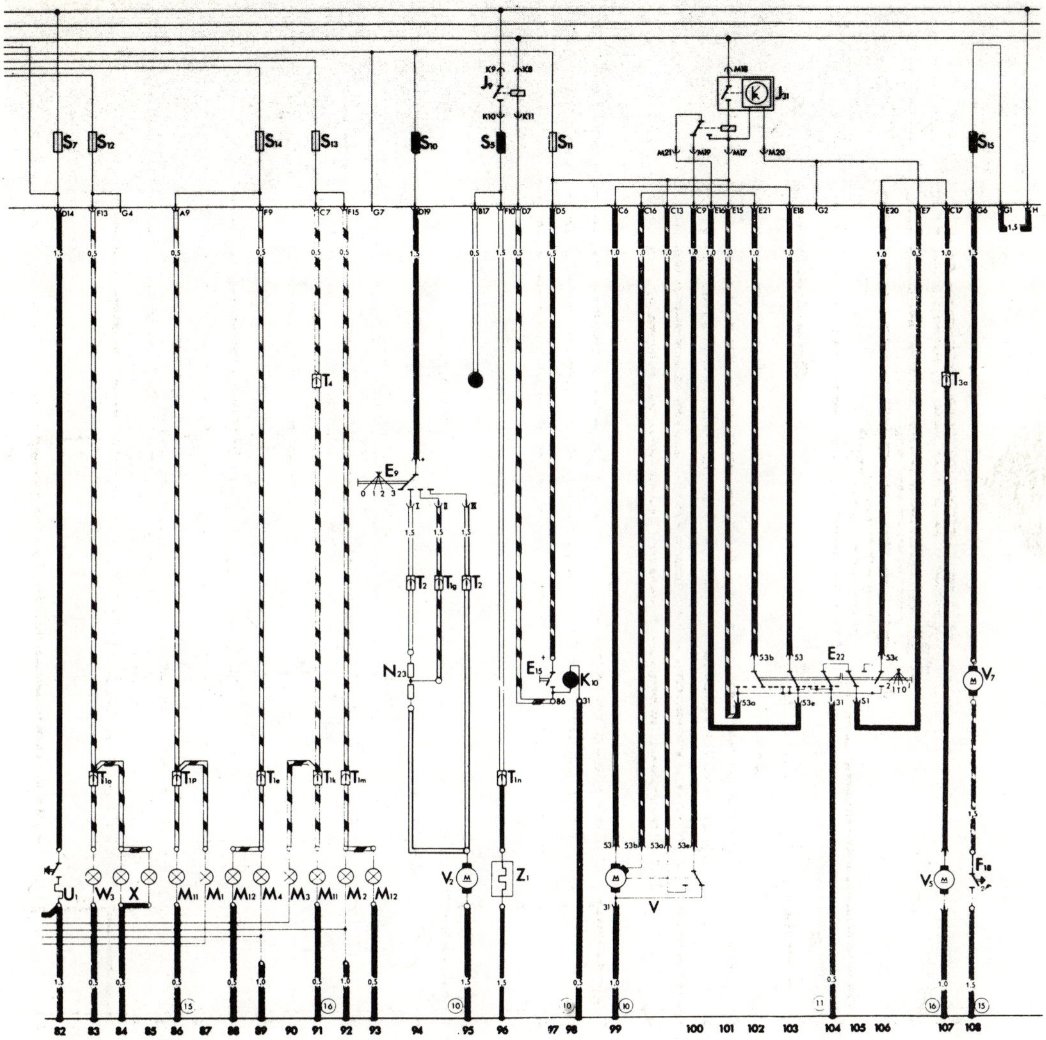

M 11 – Side marker light, front — 86, 91
M 12 – Side marker light, rear — 88, 93
N 23 – Ballast resistor for fresh air fan — 94

S 1, S 2, S 3, S 4, S 5, S 6, S 7, S 8, S 10, S 11, S 12, S 13, S 14, S 15 } Fuses on fuse/relay panel

T 1a – Wire connector, single; behind dashboard
T 1b – Wire connector, single; behind dashboard
T 1d – Wire connector, single; behind dashboard
T 1e – Wire connector, single; in luggage compartment
T 1f – Wire connector, single; behind dashboard
T 1g – Wire connector, single; behind dashboard
T 1k – Wire connector, single; in engine compartment, right
T 1m – Wire connector, single; in luggage compartment, right
T 1n – Wire connector, single; in luggage compartment, left
T 1o – Wire connector, single; in luggage compartment, center
T 1p – Wire connector, single; in engine compartment, left
T 2 – Wire connector, double; behind dashboard
T 3a – Wire connector, 3-point; behind dashboard
T 4 – Wire connector, 4-point; behind dashboard
T 12 – Wire connector, 12-point; on instrument cluster
U 1 – Cigarette lighter — 82
V – Windshield wiper motor — 99
V 2 – Fresh air fan — 95
V 5 – Windshield washer pump — 107
W3 – Luggage compartment light — 83
X – License plate light — 84
Y – Clock — 84
Z 1 – Rear window defogger light — 96

⑩ – Ground connector on steering column
⑪ – Ground connector next to instrument cluster
⑮ – Ground connector in engine compartment, left
⑯ – Ground connector in engine compartment, right

1978 RABBIT — Custom Diesel

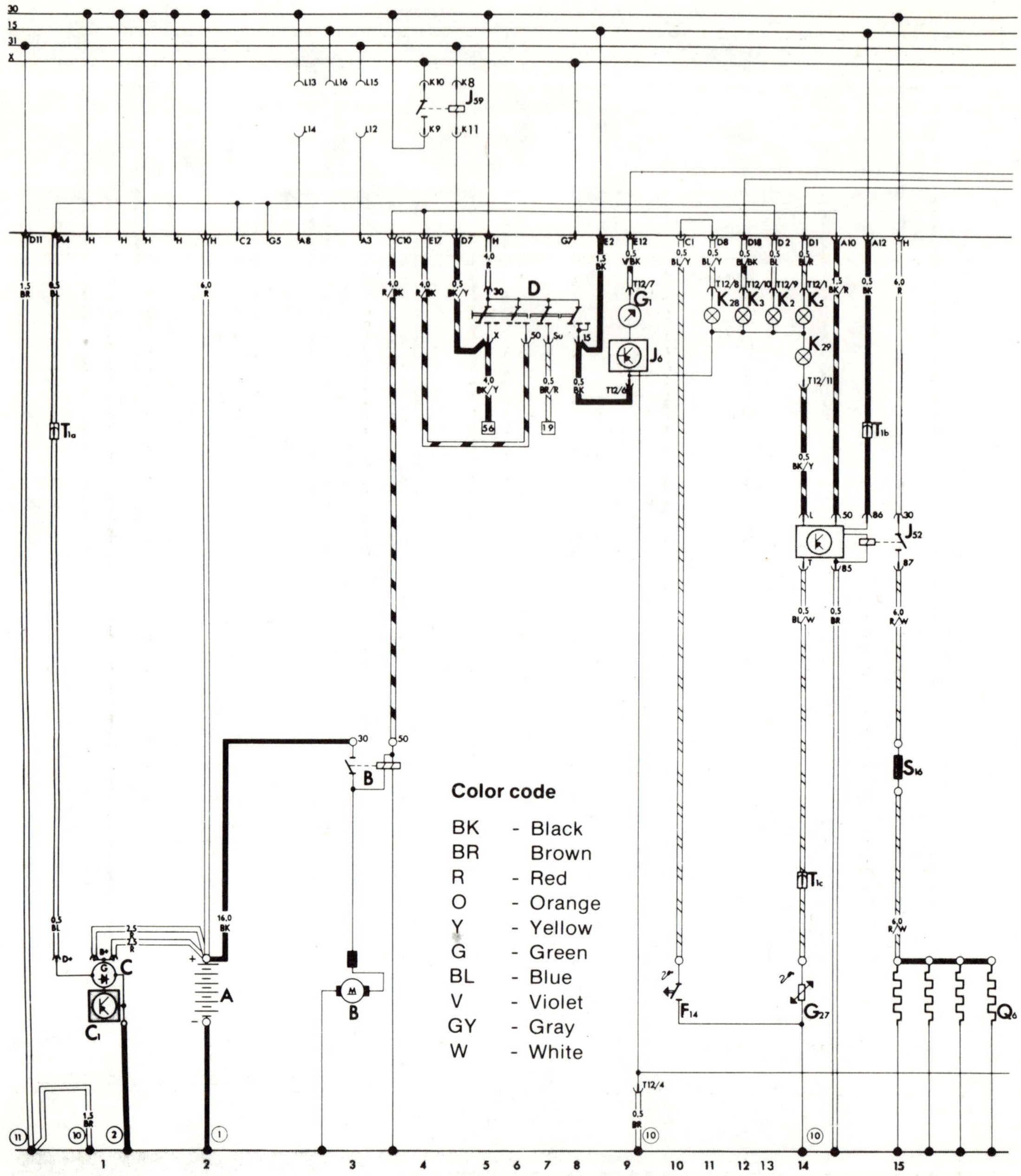

A	- Battery	2
B	- Starter	3
C	- Alternator	1
C 1	- Regulator	1
D	- Glow/starter switch	5-8
E 24	- Safety belt switch, left	19
F	- Brake light switch	30, 31
F 1	- Engine oil pressure switch	23
F 2	- Door/buzzer switch, front left	17, 18
F 4	- Back-up light switch	26
F 9	- Parking brake warning light switch	21
F 14	- Coolant temperature control switch	10

G	- Fuel gauge sending unit	24
G 1	- Fuel gauge	9
G 27	- Engine temperature sending unit	14
H	- Horn button	29
H 1	- Horn	28
J 6	- Voltage stabilizer	9
J 34	- Safety belt warning relay	19
J 52	- Glow plugs relay	14,15
J 59	- Load reduction relay for X terminal	4-5
K 2	- Alternator charging warning light	13
K 3	- Engine oil pressure warning light	12
K 5	- Turn signal warning light	14
K 7	- Dual brake system/parking brake warning light	21

1978 RABBIT — Custom Diesel

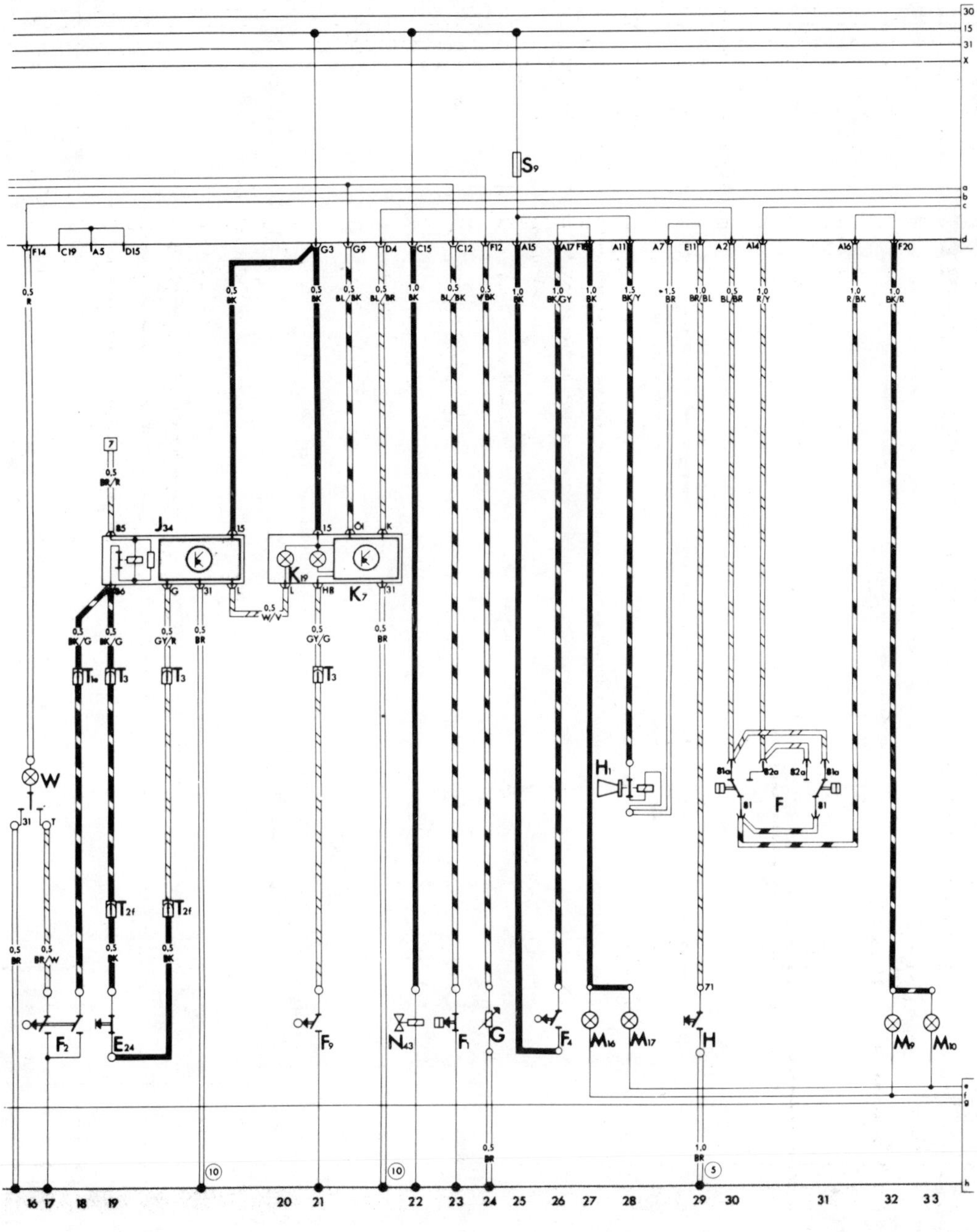

K 19 - Safety belt warning light 20
K 28 - Coolant temperature warning light 11
K 29 - Pre-glow warning light 14
M 9 - Stop light, left 32
M 10 - Stop light, right 33
M 16 - Back-up light, left 27
M 17 - Back-up light, right 28
N 43 - Electromagnetic cutoff switch 22
Q 6 - Glow plugs 15
S 9 - Fuse in fuse box
S 16 - Fuse for glow plugs (50 amps) 15
T 1a - Wire connector, single; in engine compartment
T 1b - Wire connector, single; behind dashboard
T 1c - Wire connector, single; behind dashboard
T 1e - Wire connector, single; behind dashboard
T 2f - Wire connector, double; behind dashboard
T 3 - Wire connector, 3-point; behind dashboard
T 12 - Wire connector, 12-point, behind dashboard
W - Interior light 16

① - Ground connector, battery/body/engine
② - Ground connector, alternator/engine
⑤ - Ground connector, steering gear
⑩ - Ground connector, instrument cluster
⑪ - Ground connector, steering column bracket

1978 RABBIT — Custom Diesel

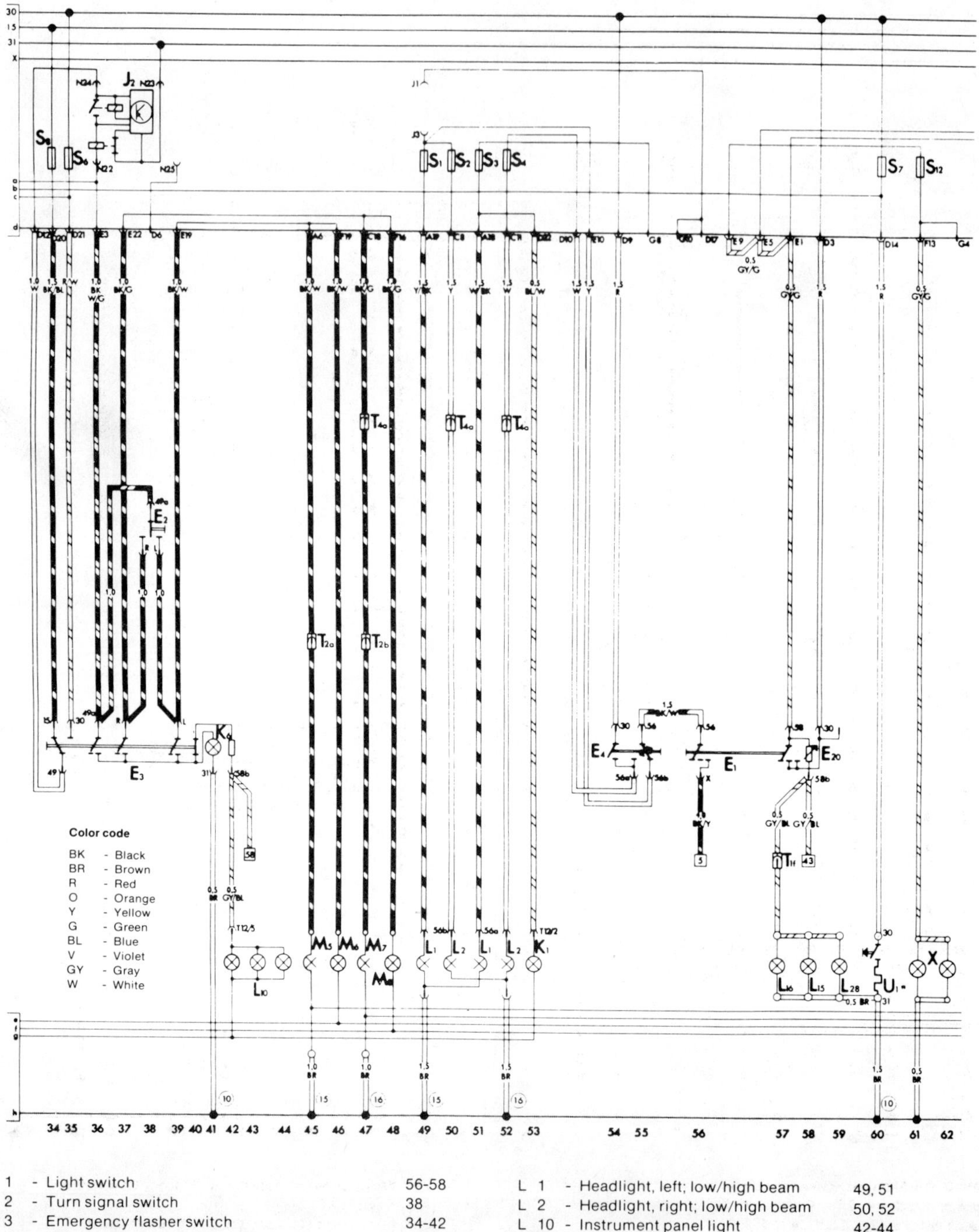

- E 1 - Light switch 56-58
- E 2 - Turn signal switch 38
- E 3 - Emergency flasher switch 34-42
- E 4 - Headlight dimmer/flasher switch 54, 55
- E 9 - Fresh air fan switch 71, 72
- E 15 - Rear window defogger switch 74, 75
- E 20 - Instrument panel light switch 58
- E 22 - Windshield washer/wiper intermittent switch 78-81
- F 18 - Radiator cooling fan thermo switch 83
- J 2 - Emergency flasher relay 36-38
- K 1 - Headlight high beam warning light 53
- K 6 - Emergency flasher warning light 42
- K 10 - Rear window defogger warning light 75
- L 1 - Headlight, left; low/high beam 49, 51
- L 2 - Headlight, right; low/high beam 50, 52
- L 10 - Instrument panel light 42-44
- L 15 - Ashtray light 58
- L 16 - Heater lever light 57
- L 28 - Cigarette lighter light 59
- M 1 - Parking light, left 64
- M 2 - Taillight, right 69
- M 3 - Parking light, right 67
- M 4 - Taillight, left 66
- M 5 - Turn signal, front left 45
- M 6 - Turn signal, rear left 46
- M 7 - Turn signal, front right 47
- M 8 - Turn signal, rear right 48
- M 11 - Side markers, front 63, 68
- M 12 - Side markers, rear 65, 70

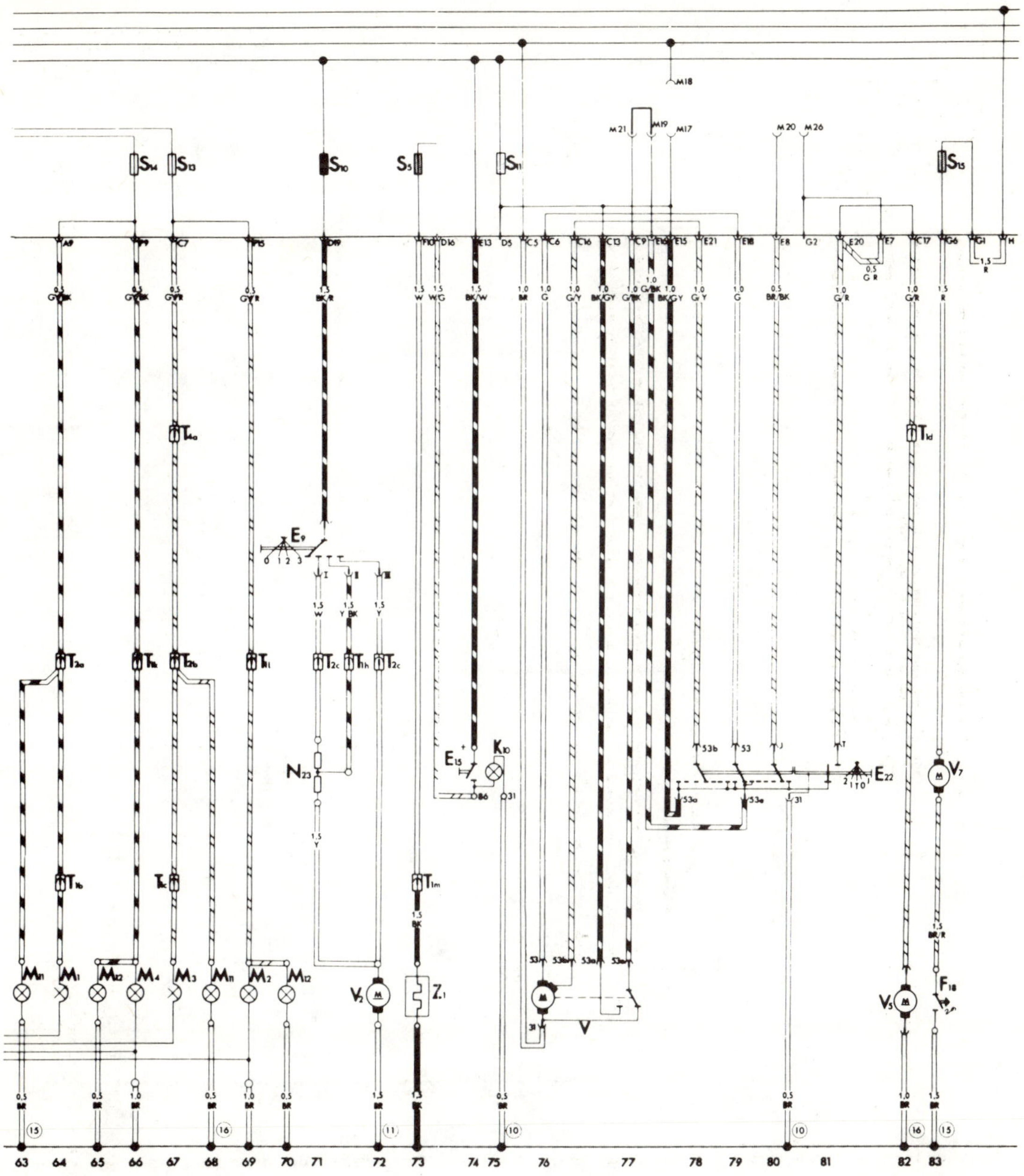

N 23 - Ballast resistor for fresh air fan 71
S 1, S 2, S 3, S 4, S 5, S 6, S 7, S 8, S 10, S 11, S 12, S 13, S 14, S 15 Fuse box
T 1b - Wire connector, single; in engine compartment left
T 1c - Wire connector, single; in engine compartment, right
T 1d - Wire connector, single; behind dashboard
T 1f - Wire connector, single; behind dashboard
T 1h - Wire connector, single; behind dashboard
T 1k - Wire connector, single; in trunk, left
T 1l - Wire connector, single, in trunk, right
T 1m - Wire connector, single; in trunk, left
T 2a - Wire connector, double; in engine compartment, front left
T 2b - Wire connector, double; in engine compartment, front right
T 2c - Wire connector, double; behind dashboard
T 4a - Wire connector, 4-point behind dashboard
T 12 - Wire connector, 12-point, on instrument cluster
U 1 - Cigarette lighter 60
V - Windshield wiper motor 76, 77
V 2 - Fresh air fan 72
V 5 - Windshield washer pump 82
V 7 - Radiator cooling fan 83
X - License plate light 61, 62
Z 1 - Rear window defogger element 73

⑩ - Ground connector next to instrument cluster
⑪ - Ground connector on steering column
⑮ - Ground connector, engine compartment, front left

1978 RABBIT — Custom and DeLuxe Models

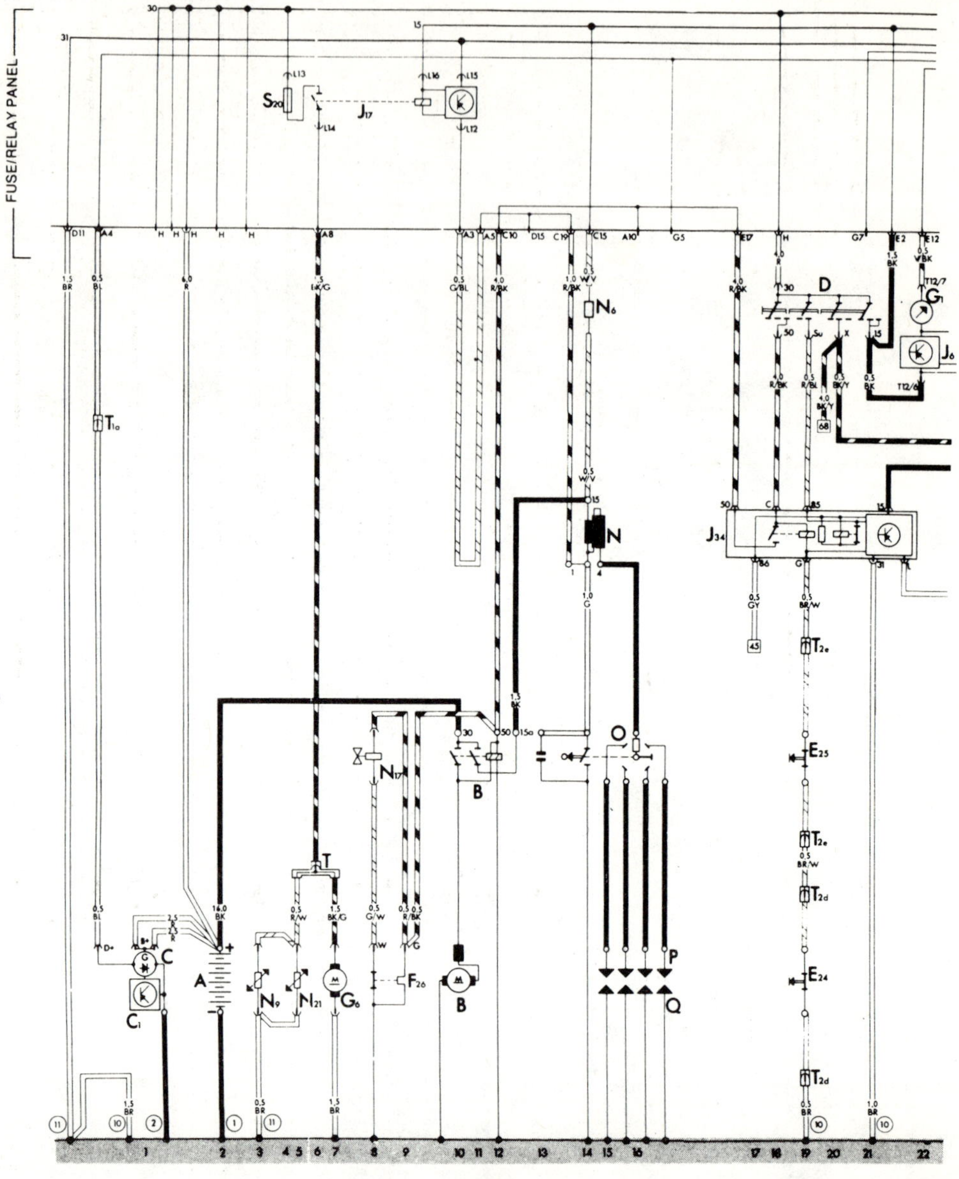

Color code

BK	- Black
BR	Brown
R	- Red
O	- Orange
Y	- Yellow
G	- Green
BL	- Blue
V	- Violet
GY	- Gray
W	- White

A	- Battery	2
B	- Starter	10-12
C	- Alternator	1
C 1	- Regulator	1
D	- Ignition/starter switch	18-21
E 24	- Safety belt switch, left	19
*E 25	- Safety belt switch, right	19
F	- Brake light switch	38,39
F 1	- Oil pressure switch	30
F 4	- Back-up light switch	34
F 9	- Park, brake warning light switch	28
F 26	- Thermo-time switch for start. valve	8, 9
F 27	- Elapsed EGR mileage switch	29
G	- Fuel gauge sending unit	32

G 1	- Fuel gauge	22
*G 2	- Coolant temperature sending unit	31
*G 3	- Coolant temperature gauge	23
G 6	- Electrical fuel pump	7
H	- Horn button	37
H 1	- Horn	36
J 6	- Voltage stabilizer	22
J 17	- Electrical fuel pump relay	6-10
J 34	- Safety belt warning relay	17-21
J 59	- Load reduction relay (on fuse/relay panel)	23
K 2	- Alternator charging warning light	25
K 3	- Oil pressure warning light	24
K 5	- Turn signal warning light	26
K 7	- Dual circuit brake/safety belt warning light	27, 28

*** DeLuxe Models only**

1978 RABBIT — Custom and DeLuxe Models

Page 2 of 4

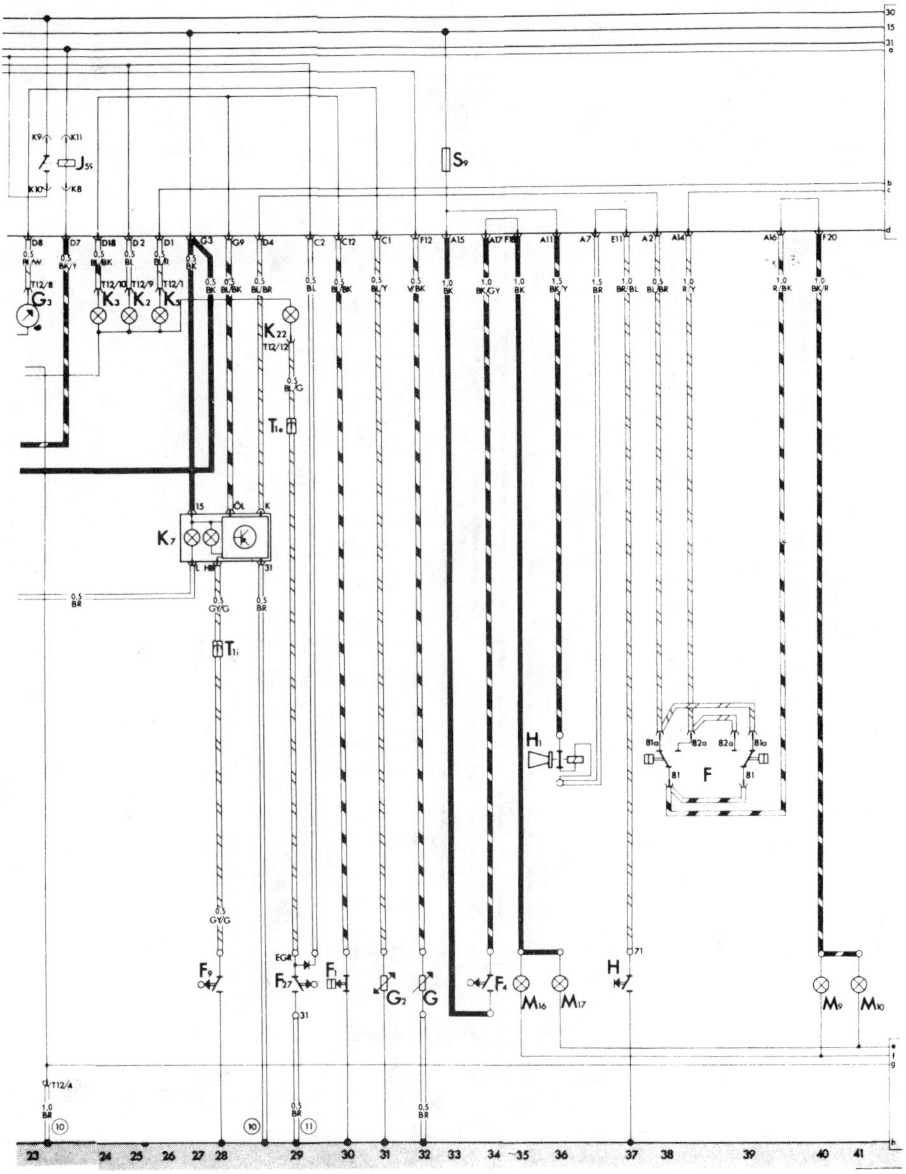

K 22	- EGR warning light	29	T	- Wire connector; in engine compartment	5-7
M 9	- Brake light, left	40	T 1a	- Wire connector, single; in engine compartment	1
M 10	- Brake light, right	41	T 1e	- Wire connector, single; behind dashboard	29
M 16	- Back-up light, left	35	T 1i	- Wire connector, single; behind dashboard	28
M 17	- Back-up light, right	36	T 2d	- Wire connector, double; behind dashboard	19
N	- Ignition coil	14, 15	T 2e	- Wire connector, double, behind dashboard	19
N 6	- Ballast resistor wire	14	T 12	- Wire connector, 12-point; on dashboard cluster	22-26, 29
N 9	- Control pressure regulator	3			
N 17	- Cold-start valve	8			
N 21	- Auxiliary air regulator	5	①	- Ground strap, battery/body/engine	2
O	- Ignition distributor	14-16	②	- Ground strap, alternator/engine	1
P	- Spark plug connectors	15, 16	⑩	- Ground connectors, instrument cluster	1, 19, 21, 23, 28
Q	- Spark plugs	15, 16			
S 9	- In-line fuse	33	⑪	- Ground connector, steering	1, 3, 29
S 20	- Fuse (16A) on fuse/relay panel (on relay J17)	4			

1978 RABBIT — Custom and DeLuxe Models

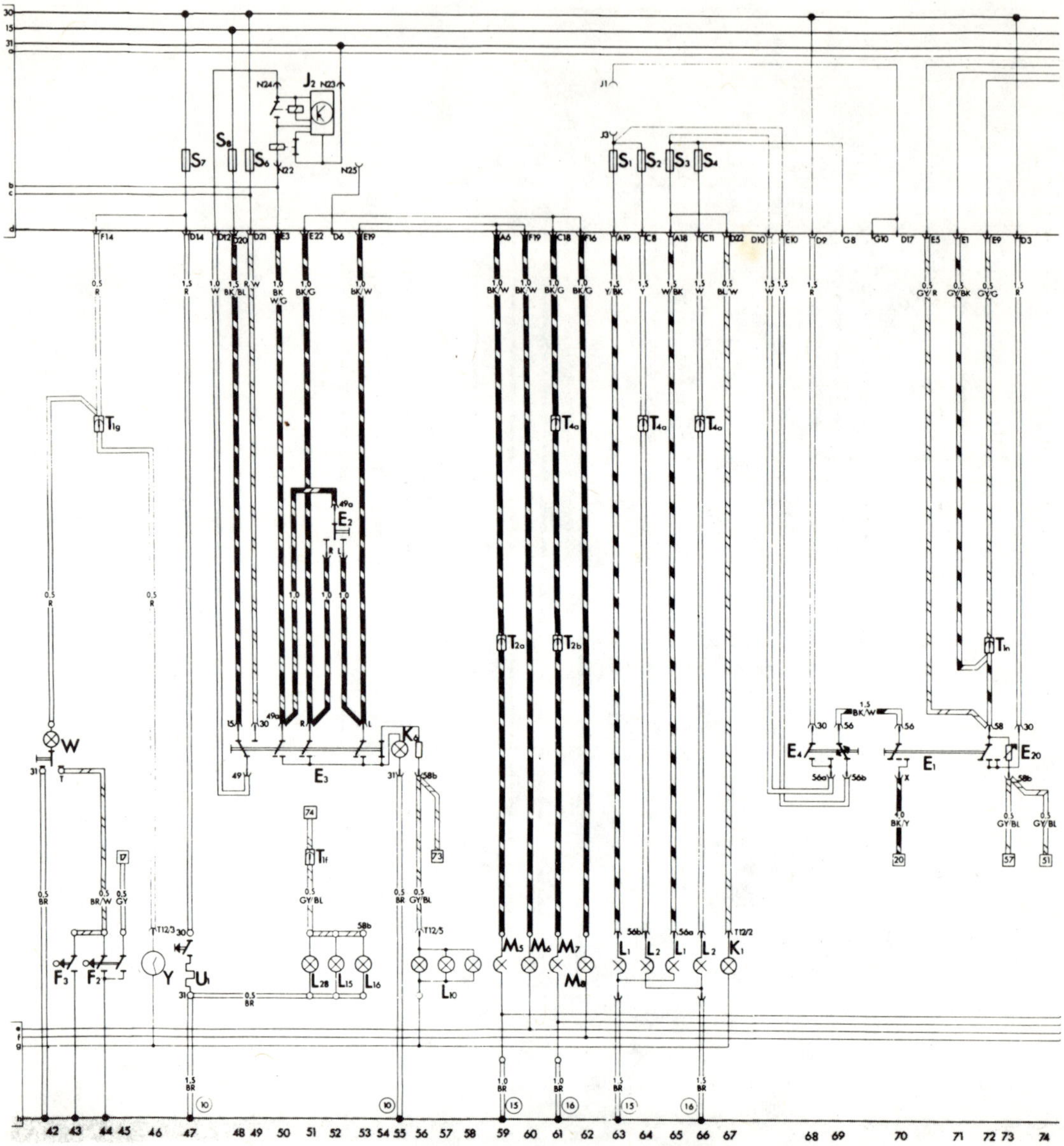

E 1	- Light Switch	70-72	L 10	- Instrument panel light	56-58
E 2	- Turn signal switch	52	L 15	- Ashtray light	52
E 3	- Emergency flasher switch	48-54	L 16	- Heater lever light	53
E 4	- Headlight dimmer/flasher switch	68, 69	L 28	- Cigarette lighter light	51
E 9	- Fresh air fan switch	84,85	M 1	- Parking light, front left	78
E 15	- Rear window defogger switch	88	M 2	- Taillight, right	83
E 20	- Instrument panel lights switch	73	M 3	- Parking light, front right	81
E 22	- Washer/wiper intermittent switch	92-96	M 4	- Taillight, left	80
F 2	- Door switch/buzzer, front left	44,45	M 5	- Turn signal, front left	59
* F 3	- Door switch/buzzer, front right	43	M 6	- Turn signal, rear left	60
F 18	- Radiator fan thermo switch	98	M 7	- Turn signal, front right	61
J 2	- Emergency flasher relay	50-52	M 8	- Turn signal, rear right	62
K 1	- Headlight high beam warning light	67	M 11	- Side marker lights, front	77, 82
K 6	- Emergency flasher warning light	55	M 12	- Side marker lights, rear	79, 84
K 10	- Rear window defogger warning light	89	N 23	- Speed control resistors for fresh air fan	85
L 1	- Left headlight, high/low beam	63, 65		Fuses on fuse/relay panel S1, S2, S3, S4,	
L 2	- Right headlight, high/low beam	64, 66		S5, S6, S7, S8, S10, S11, S12, S14, S15	

*** DeLuxe Models only**

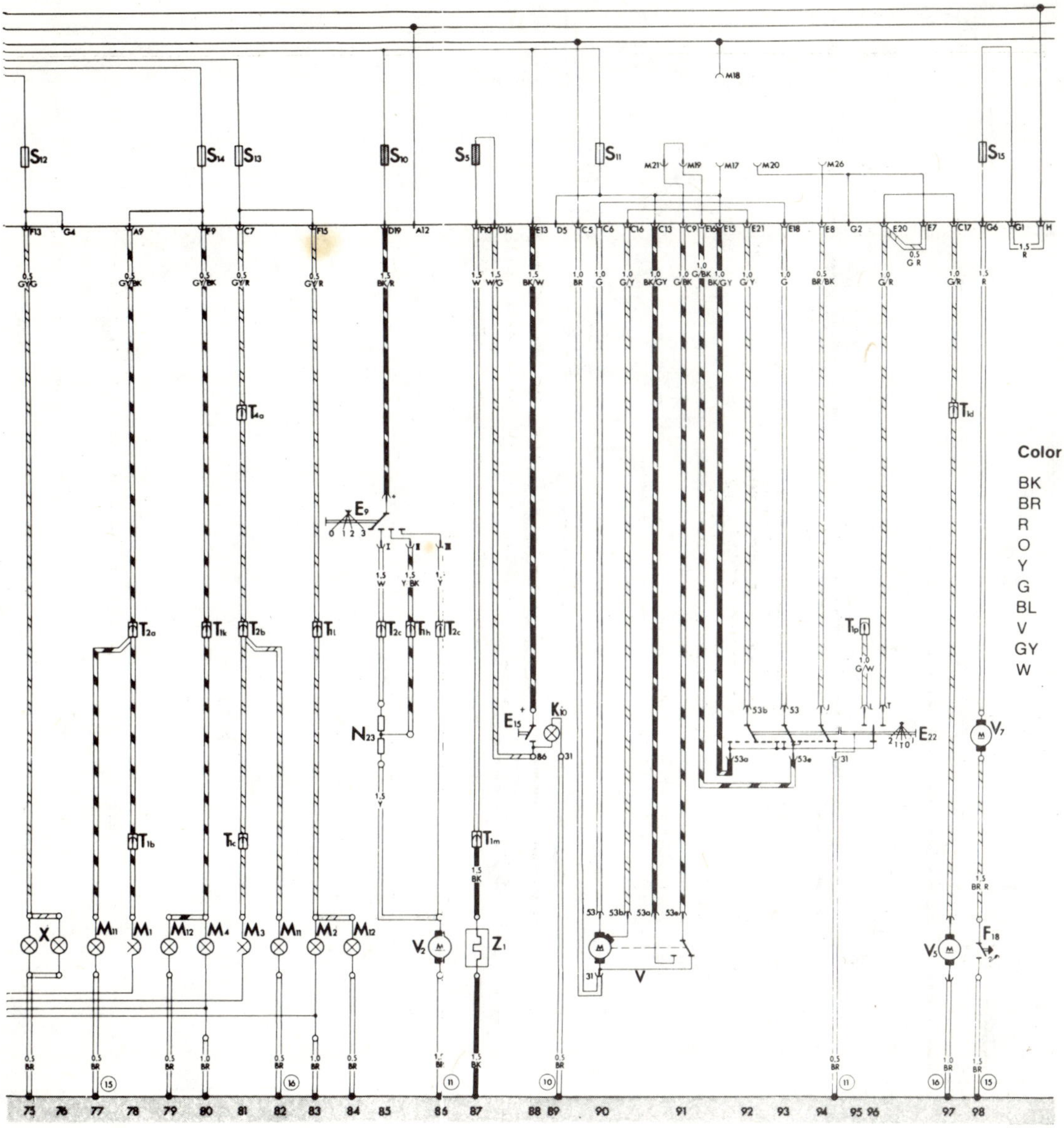

Color code

BK	-	Black
BR		Brown
R	-	Red
O	-	Orange
Y	-	Yellow
G	-	Green
BL	-	Blue
V	-	Violet
GY	-	Gray
W	-	White

T 1b	-	Wire connector, single; in engine compartment, front left	78
T 1c	-	Wire connector, single; in engine compartment, front right	81
T 1d	-	Wire connector, single; behind dashboard	97
T 1f	-	Wire connector, single; behind dashboard	51
T 1g	-	Wire connector, single; behind dashboard	44
T 1h	-	Wire connector, single; behind dashboard	85
T 1k	-	Wire connector, single; in trunk, rear left	80
T 1l	-	Wire connector, single; in trunk, rear right	83
T 1m	-	Wire connector, single; in trunk, rear left	87
T 1n	-	Wire connector, single; behind dashboard	72
T 1p	-	Wire connector, single; behind dashboard (connection for rear window wash/wipe)	95
T 2a	-	Wire connector, double; in engine compartment, front left	59, 78
T 2b	-	Wire connector, double; in engine compartment, front right	61, 81
T 2c	-	Wire connector, double; behind dashboard	85, 86
T 4a	-	Wire connector, 4-point; behind dashboard	61, 64, 66, 81
U 1	-	Cigarette lighter	47
V	-	Windshield wiper motor	90, 91
V 2	-	Fresh air fan	86
V 5	-	Windshield washer pump	97
V 7	-	Radiator cooling fan	98
W	-	Interior light	42
X	-	License plate light	75, 76
Y	-	Clock	46
Z 1	-	Rear window defogger element	87
⑩	-	Ground connectors, instrument cluster	47, 55, 89
⑪	-	Ground connectors, steering column support	86, 94
⑮	-	Ground connectors, engine compartment, front left	59, 63, 77, 98
⑯	-	Ground connectors, engine compartment, front right	61, 66, 82, 97

1978 SCIROCCO

Page 1 of 4

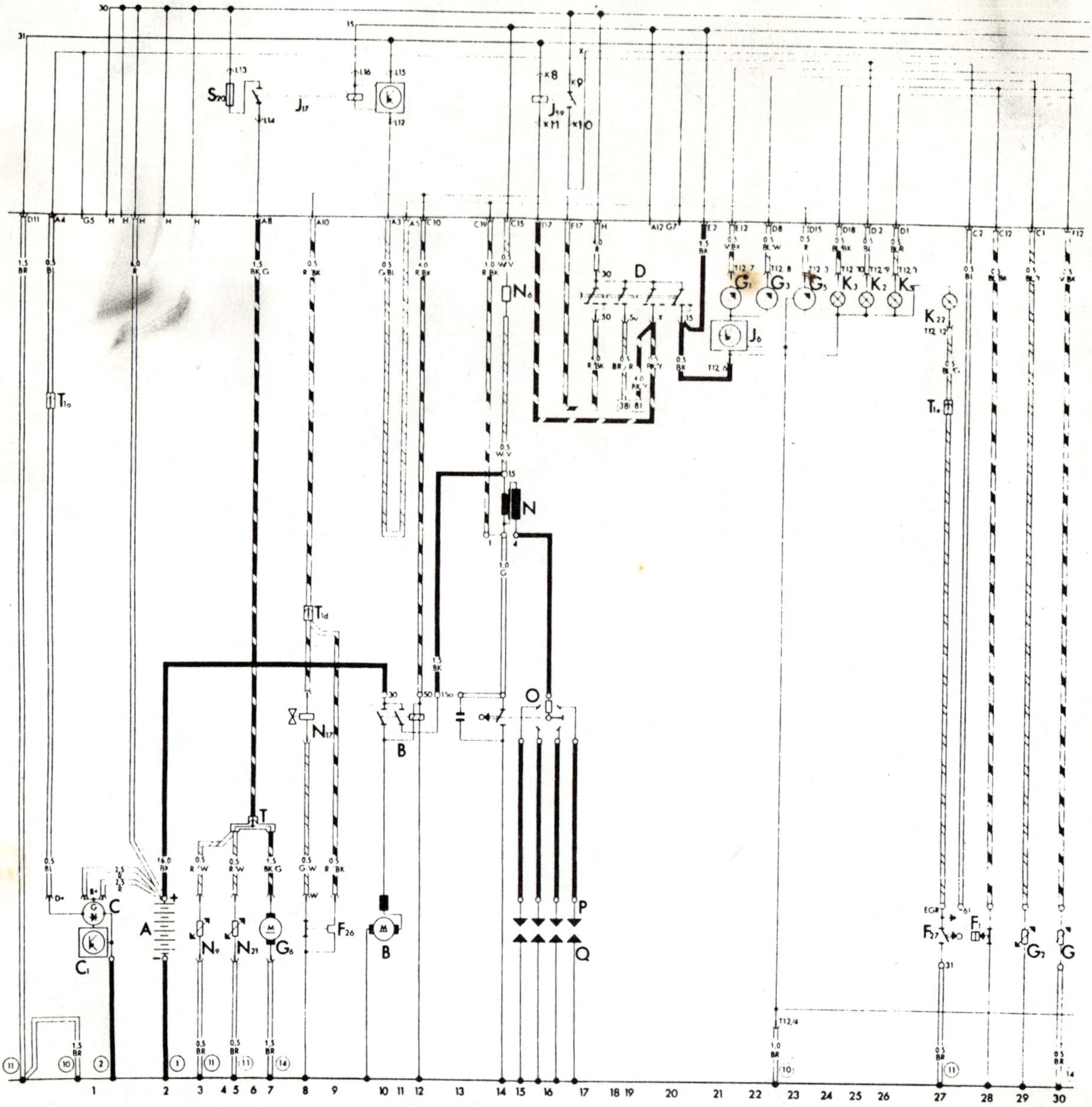

Description	Current track
A - battery	2
B - starter	10 - 12
C - alternator	1
C1 - regulator	1
D - ignition/starter switch	17 - 20
E24 - safety belt switch,left	38
F - brake light switch	43,44
F1 - engine oil pressure switch	28
F4 - backup light switch	32
F9 - parking brake warning light switch	42
F26 - thermo-switch/cold start valve	8
F29 - elapsed mileage switch/EGR light (not for Canada)	27
G - fuel gauge sending unit	30
G1 - fuel gauge	21
G2 - coolant temperature sending unit	29
G3 - coolant temperature gauge	22

Description	Current track
G5 - Tachometer	23
G6 - electrical fuel pump	7
G8 - engine oil temperature sending unit	37
G9 - engine oil temperature gauge	37
H - horn button	36
H1 - dual horn	34,35
J4 - dual horn relay	35,36
J6 - voltage stabilizer	21
J17 - electric fuel pump relay	4 - 10
J34 - safety belt warning relay	38,39
J59 - load reducing relay -Xterminal	15,16
K2 - alternator charging warning light	25
K3 - engine oil pressure warning light	24
K5 - turn signal warning light	26
K7 - dual circuit brake/parking brake warning light	41
K19 - safety belt warning light	40
K22 - EGR-warning light (not for Canada)	27

1978 SCIROCCO

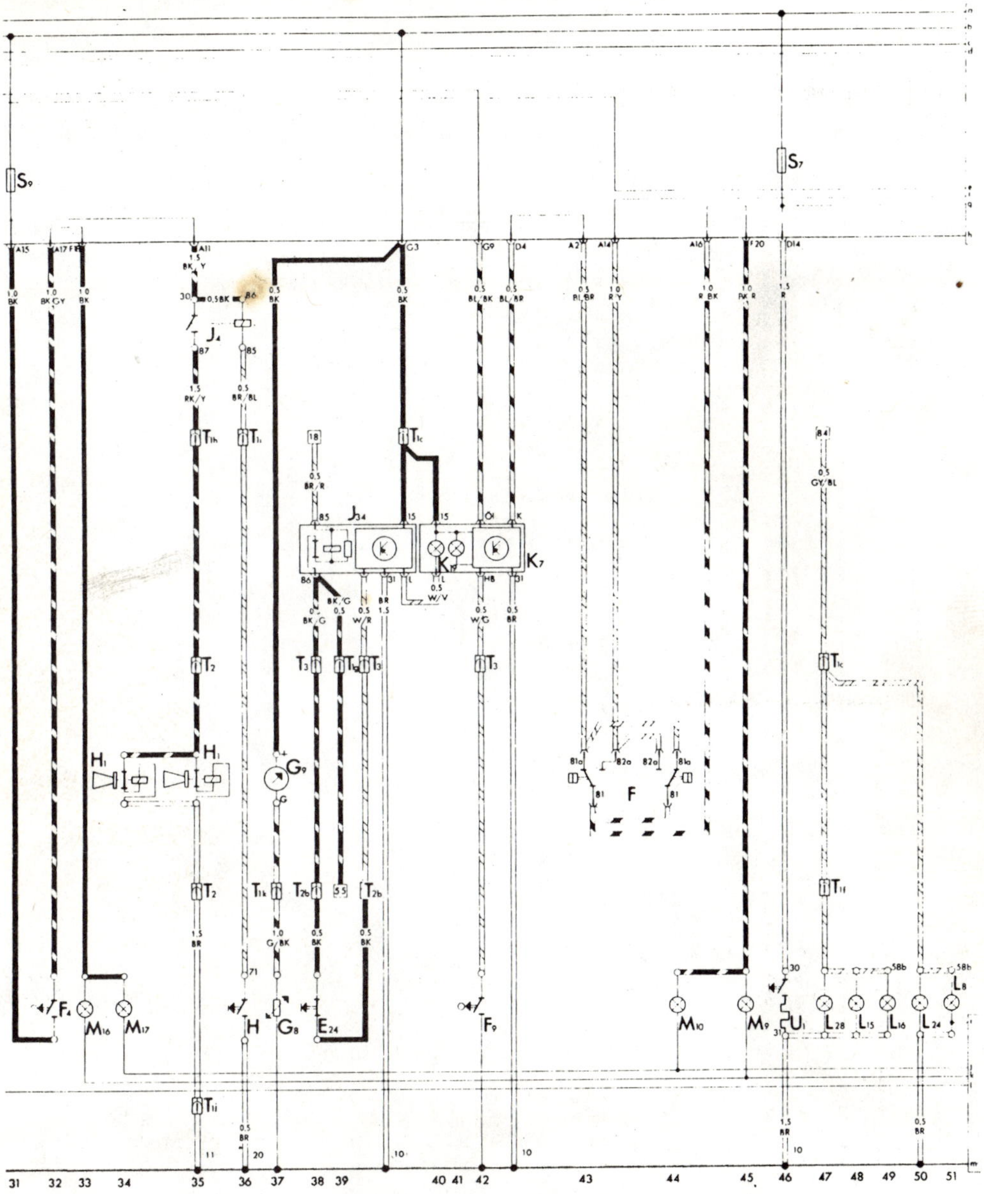

Description	Current track
L8 - clock light	51
L15 - ashtray light	48
L16 - fresh air operating lever light	49
L24 - engine oil temperature gauge light	50
L28 - cigarette lighter light	47
M9 - brake light, left	45
M10 - brake light, right	44
M16 - backup light, left	33
M17 - backup light, right	34
N - ignition coil	14,15
N6 - ballast resistor wire	14
N9 - control pressure regulator	3
N17 - cold start valve	8
N21 - auxiliary air regulator	5
O - ignition distributor	16
P - spark plug connectors	16
Q - spark plugs	16

S7, S9 - fuses in fuse box

S20 - fuse for electrical fuel pump (on J17)

Ground connectors

① — Battery/body/engine
② — Alternator/engine
⑩ — Instrument cluster
⑪ — Steering column bracket
⑭ — Footwell, right
⑳ — Steering gear

Color code

BK	- Black
BR	Brown
R	- Red
O	- Orange
Y	- Yellow
G	- Green
BL	- Blue
V	- Violet
GY	- Gray
W	- White

1978 SCIROCCO

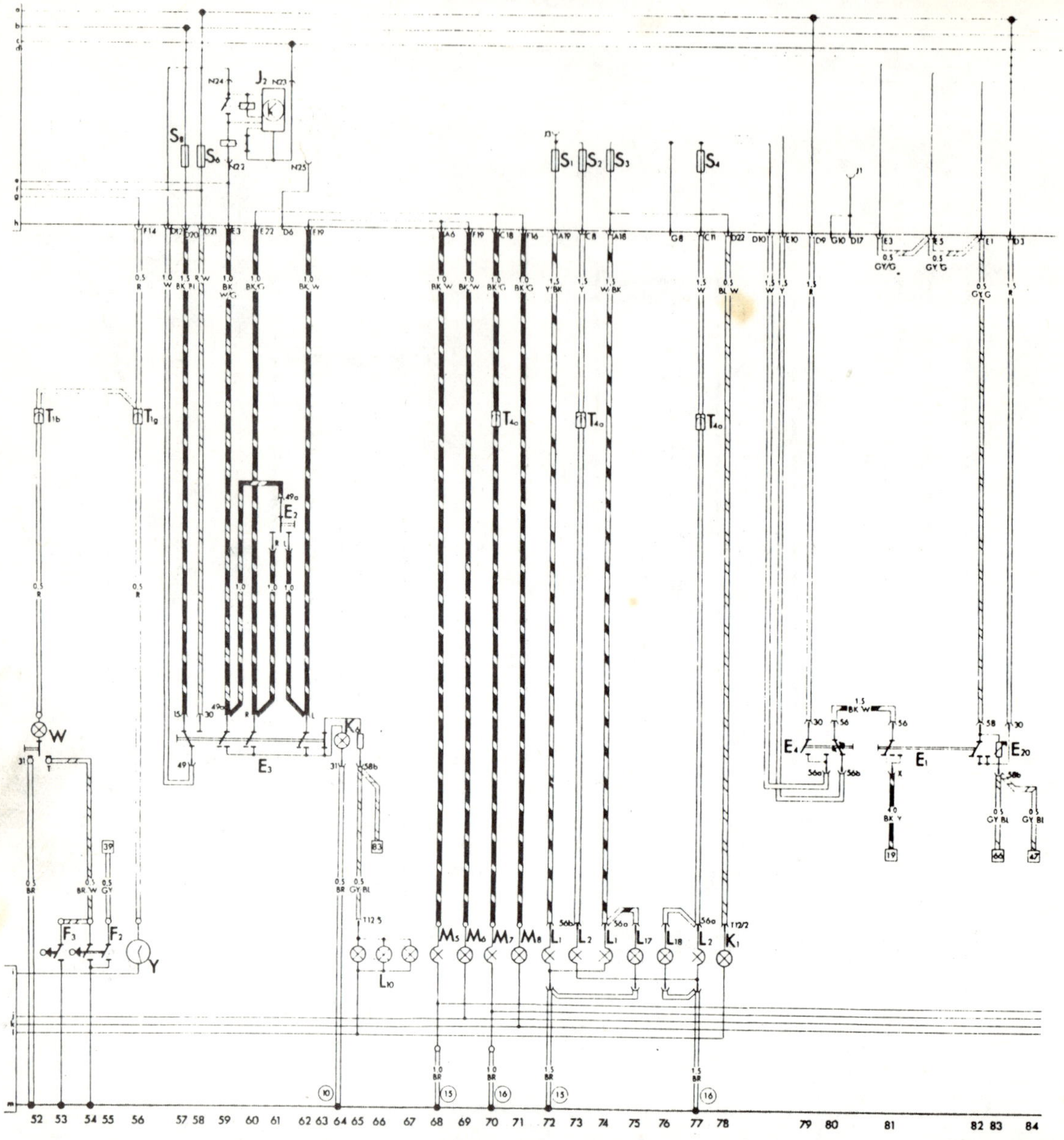

Description	Current track
E1 - light switch	81-84
E2 - turn signal switch	61
E3 - emergency flasher switch	57-65
E4 - head light dimmer/flasher switch	79,80
E5 - fresh air fan switch	94,95
E15 - rear window defogger switch	97,98
E20 - instrument panel lights switch	83
E22 - windshield washer/wiper intermitt. switch	101 -105
F2 - door switch/buzzer,front left	54,55
F3 - door switch,front right	53
F18 - radiator fan thermo switch	107
J2 - emergency flasher relay	59-61
J31 - windshield washer/wiper intermitt. relay	100-103
K1 - headlight high beam warning light	78
K6 - emergency flasher warning light	64
K10 - rear window defogger warning light	98
L1 - left head light,low/high beam	72,74
L2 - right head light,low/high beam	73,77

Description	Current track
L10 -instrument panel light	65-67
L17 - left head light,high beam	75
L18 - right head light,high beam	76
M1 - left front parking light	88
M2 - right tail light	92
M3 - right front parking light	91
M4 - left tail light	90
M5 - left front turn signal	68
M6 - left rear turn signal	69
M7 - right front turn signal	70
M8 - right rear turn signal	71
M12 - rear side marker lights	89,93
N23 - fresh air fan ballast resistor	94
S1- S6,S8 S10- S14 - fuses in fuse/relay panel	

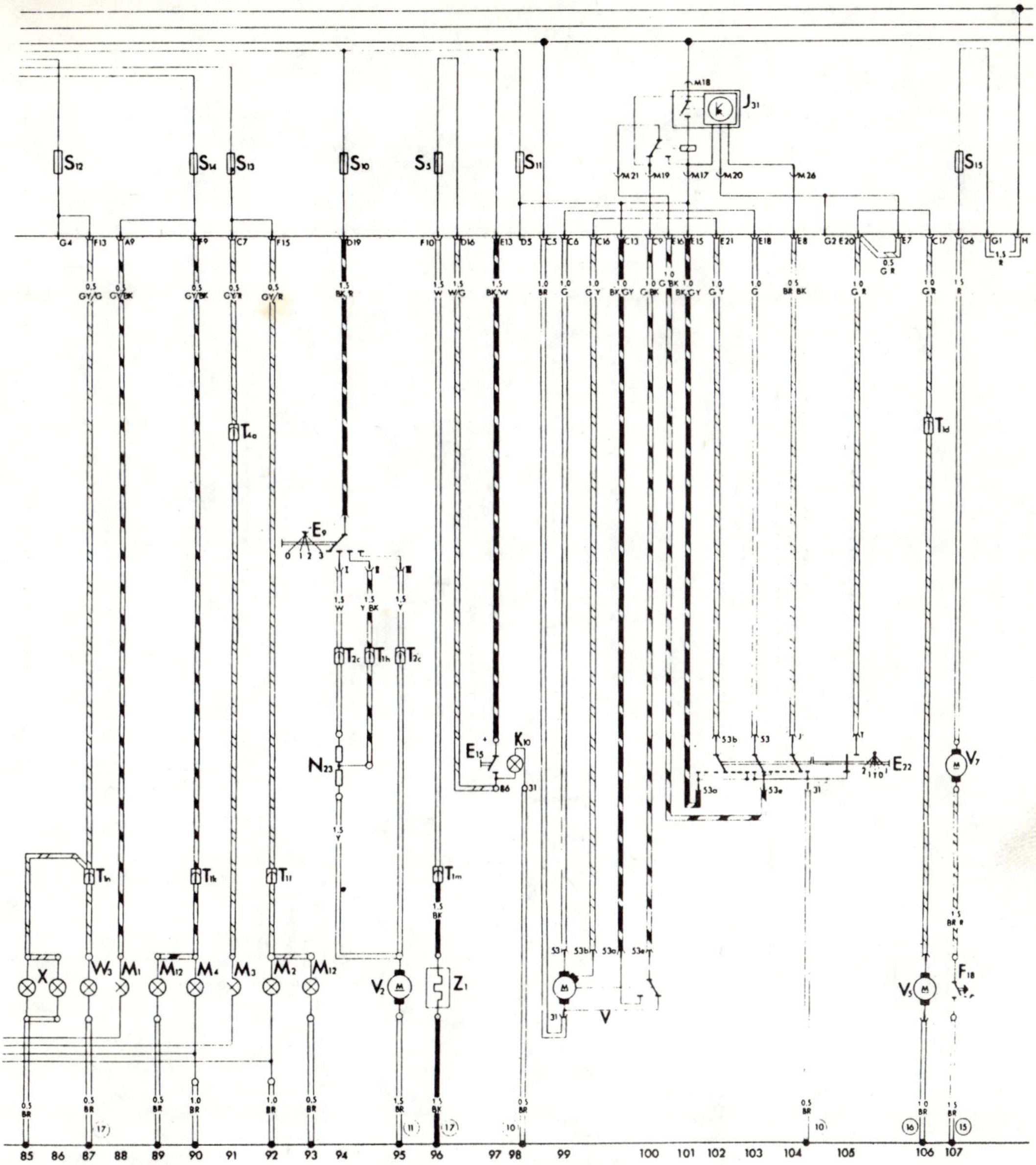

Description	Current track
V - windshield wiper motor	99,100
V2 - fresh air fan	95
V5 - windshield washer pump	106
V7 - radiator cooling fan	107
W - interior light	52,53
W3 - trunk light	87
X - license plate light	85,86
Y - clock	56
Z - rear window defogger element	96

ground connectors

(10) -- instrument cluster

(11) - steering column bracket

(15) - engine compartment front left

(16) - engine compartment front right

(17) - trunk

Color code

BK - Black
BR - Brown
R - Red
O - Orange
Y - Yellow
G - Green
BL - Blue
V - Violet
GY - Gray
W - White

1979 WESTMORELAND RABBIT

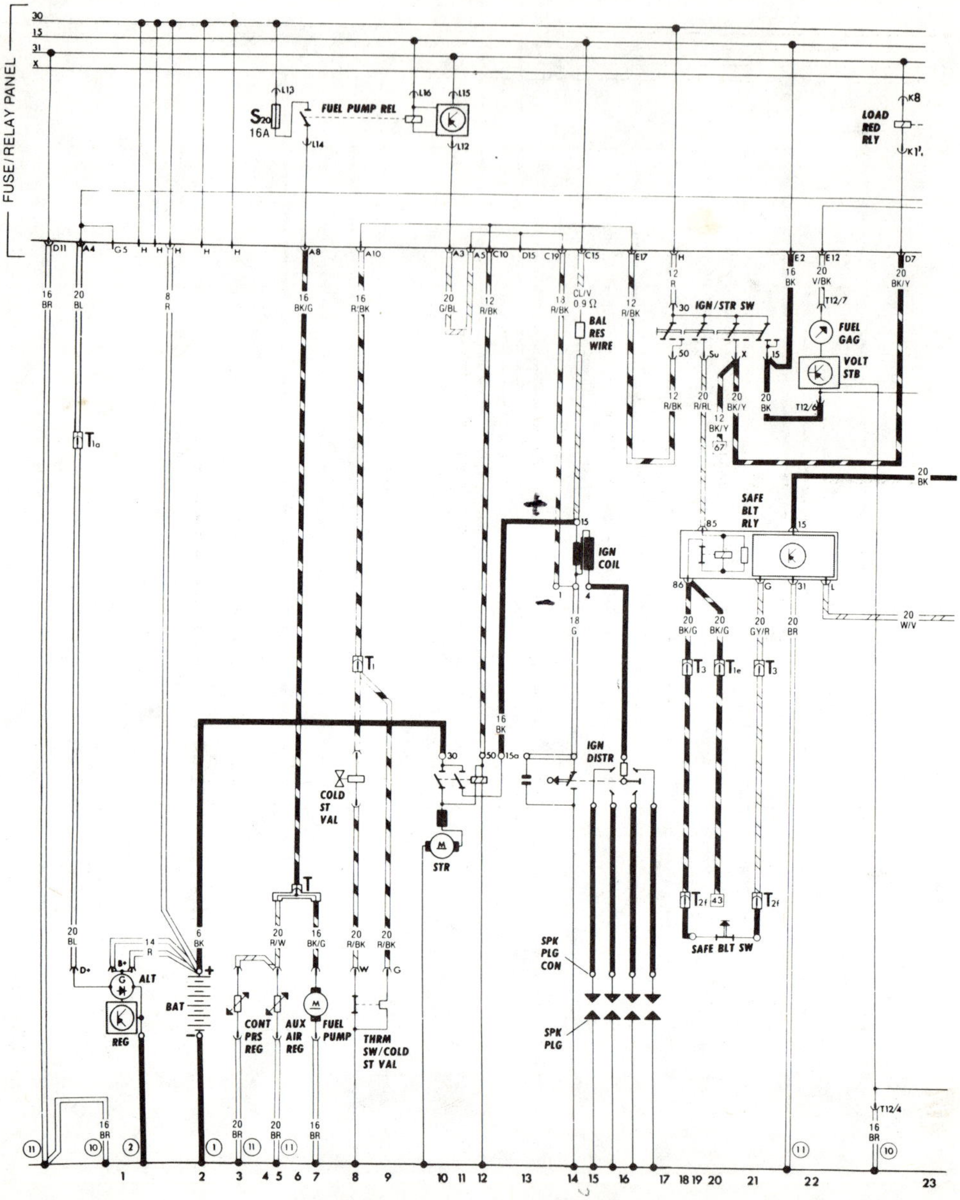

Description	Current track
Alternator	1
Alternator warning light	24
Auxiliary air regulator	5
Back-up light	34, 35
Back-up light switch	33
Ballast resistor wire	14
Battery	2
Brake light	39, 40
Brake light switch	37, 38
Brake warning light	27
Cigarette lighter	44
Cold-start valve	8
Control pressure regulator	3
Coolant temperature switch	30
Coolant temperature warning light	28
Directional light warning light	25
Door switch/buzzer	42, 43
EGR warning light	28
Elapsed mileage switch — EGR light	28
Fuel gauge	22
Fuel gauge sending unit	31
Fuel pump	7
Fuel pump relay	4–10
Horn	35
Horn button/ring	36

1979 WESTMORELAND RABBIT

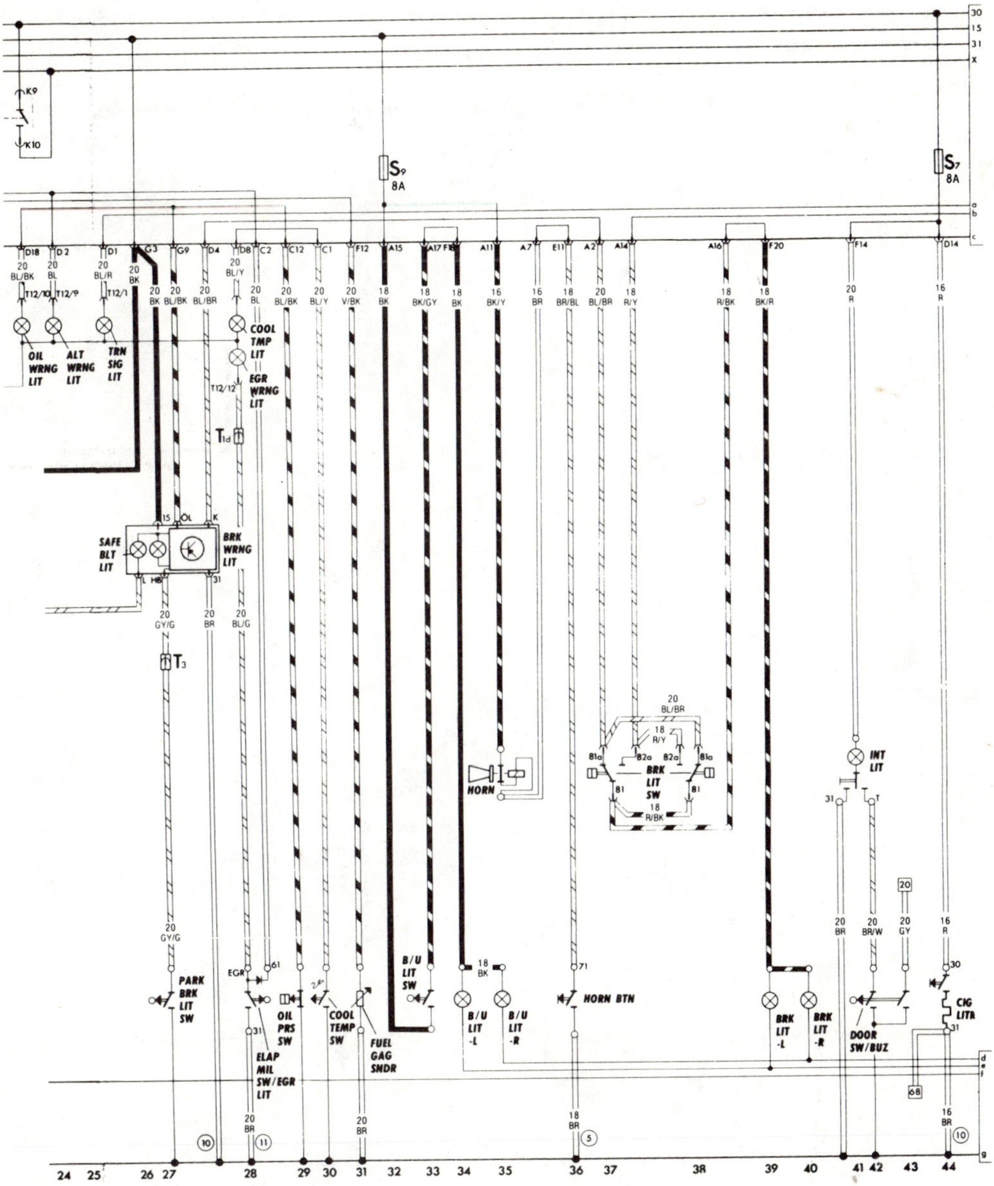

- Ignition coil 14, 15
- Ignition distributor 16
- Ignition/starter switch 17–21
- Interior light 41
- Load reducing relay 23
- Oil pressure switch 29
- Oil pressure warning light 23
- Parking brake warning light switch 27
- Regulator 1
- Safety belt switch 18
- Safety belt warning light 26
- Safety belt warning relay 18–22
- Spark plugs 16
- Starter 10–12

- Thermo switch/cold-start valve 8, 9
- Voltage stabilizer 22
- T – Wire connector, next to fuse/relay panel
- T 1 – Wire connector, single; behind dashboard
- T 1a – Wire connector, single; in engine compartment
- T 1e – Wire connector, single; behind dashboard
- T 2f – Wire connector, double; behind dashboard
- T 12 – Wire connector, 12-point; on instrument cluster
- ① – Ground connector, battery/body/engine
- ② – Ground connector, alternator/engine
- ⑤ – Ground connector, on steering gear
- ⑩ – Ground connector, on instrument cluster
- ⑪ – Ground connector, on steering column bracket

VW Rabbit, Westmoreland Model (rectangular hea

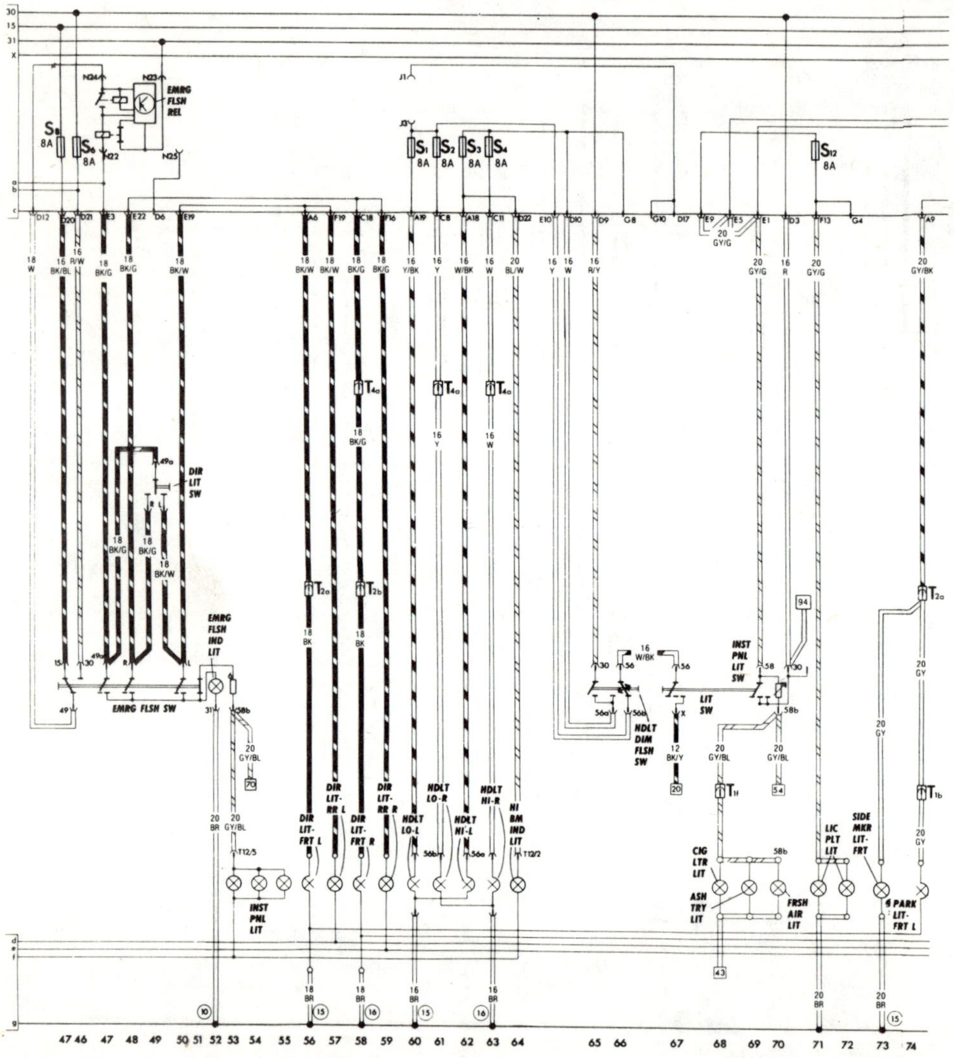

Color code

BK	–	Black
BR	–	Brown
CL	–	Clear
R	–	Red
Y	–	Yellow
G	–	Green
BL	–	Blue
V	–	Violet
GY	–	Gray
W	–	White

Description	Current track
Ashtray light	69
Cigarette lighter light	68
Coolant fan	93
Coolant fan thermo switch	93
Directional light	56–59
Directional light switch	49
Emergency flasher relay	47–50
Emergency flasher switch	46–53
Emergency flasher warning light	52
Fresh air ballast resistor	81
Fresh air fan	82
Fresh air fan switch	81, 82
Fresh air control light	70
Headlights	60–63
Headlight dimmer/flasher switch	65, 66
High beam indicator light	64
Instrument panel lights	53–55
Instrument panel light switch	70
License plate light	71, 72
Light switch	67–70
Parking light — front	74, 77
Radio	94
Rear window defogger	83

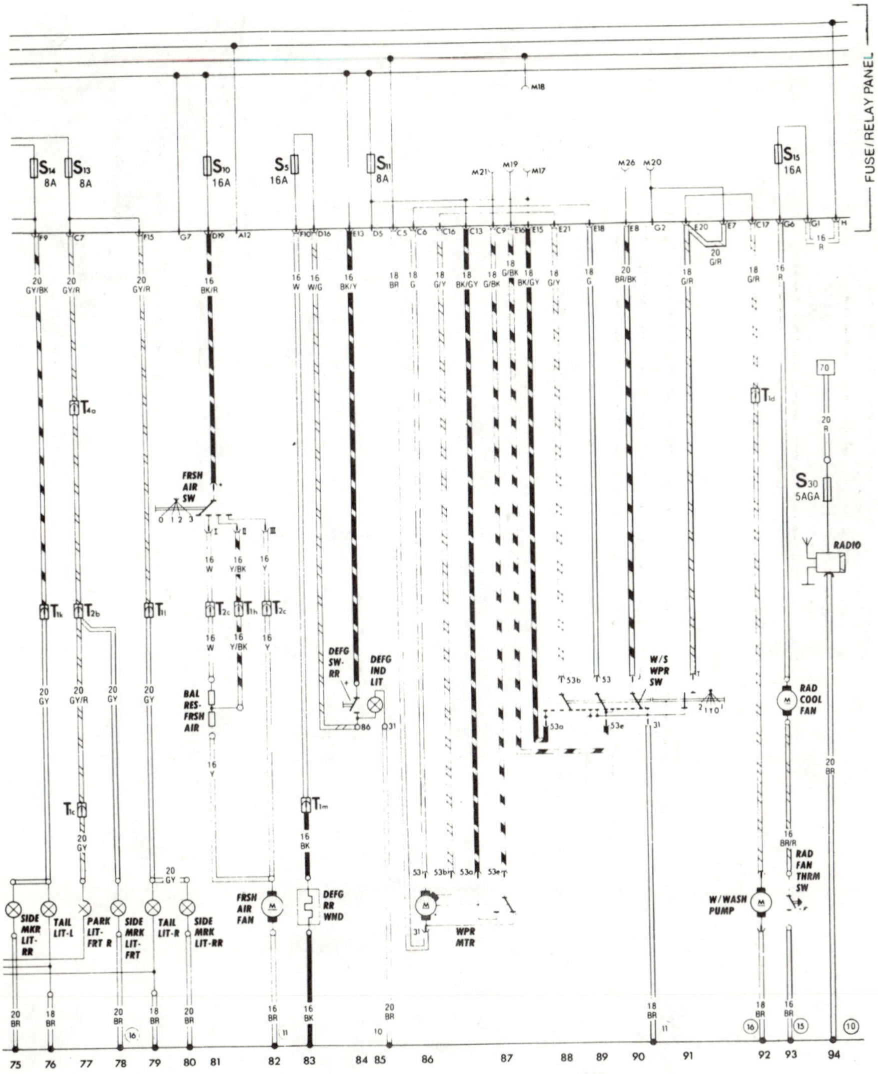

Rear window defogger switch 84, 85
Rear window defogger warning light 85
Side marker light 73, 75, 78, 80
Taillight 76, 79
Windshield washer pump 92
Windshield wiper motor 86, 87
Windshield wiper switch 88, 91

T 1b – Wire connector, single; in left engine compartment
T 1c – Wire connector, single; in right engine compartment
T 1d – Wire connector, single; behind dashboard
T 1f – Wire connector, single; behind dashboard
T 1h – Wire connector, single; behind dashboard
T 1k – Wire connector, single; in trunk, left
T 1l – Wire connector, single; in trunk, right
T 1m – Wire connector, single; in trunk, left
T 2a – Wire connector, double; in engine compartment, left
T 2b – Wire connector, double; in engine compartment, right
T 2c – Wire connector, double; in engine compartment, right
T 4a – Wire connector, 4-point; behind dashboard
⑩ – Ground connector, on instrument cluster
⑪ – Ground connector, on steering column bracket
⑮ – Ground connector, engine compartment, front left
⑯ – Ground connector, engine compartment, front right

1979 CUSTOM DIESEL RABBIT

Page 1 of 5

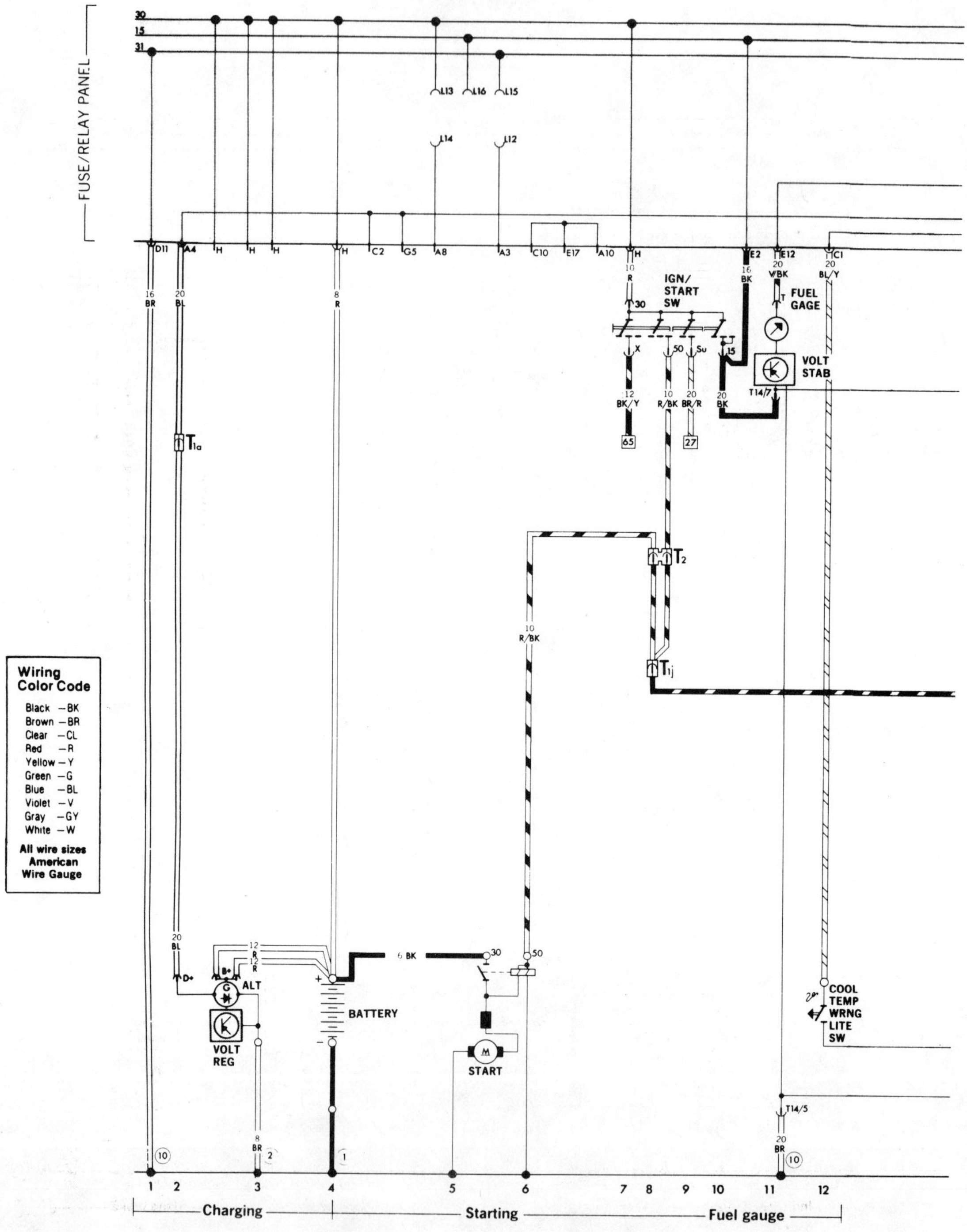

Description	Current Track
Alternator	3
Alternator warning light	15
Ash tray light	67
Back-up lights	35-36
Back-up light switch	34
Battery	4
Cigarette lighter	70
Cigarette lighter light	68

Description	Current Track
Coolant temperature warning light	13
Coolant temperature warning light switch	12
Door buzzer switch, front left	25-26
Door switch, front right	24
Emergency flasher relay	44-47
Emergency flasher switch	42-49
Emergency flasher warning light	48
Fresh air fan	82

Description	Current Track
Fresh air fan speed control resistors	81
Fresh air fan switch	81-82
Fuel gauge	11
Fuel gauge sensor	22
Fuel shutoff solenoid	20
Fuse, S16, glow plug (50 A), in engine compartment	18
Fuses, S1 - S15, on fuse/relay panel under dash	
Glow plug preheat light	16

1979 CUSTOM DIESEL RABBIT

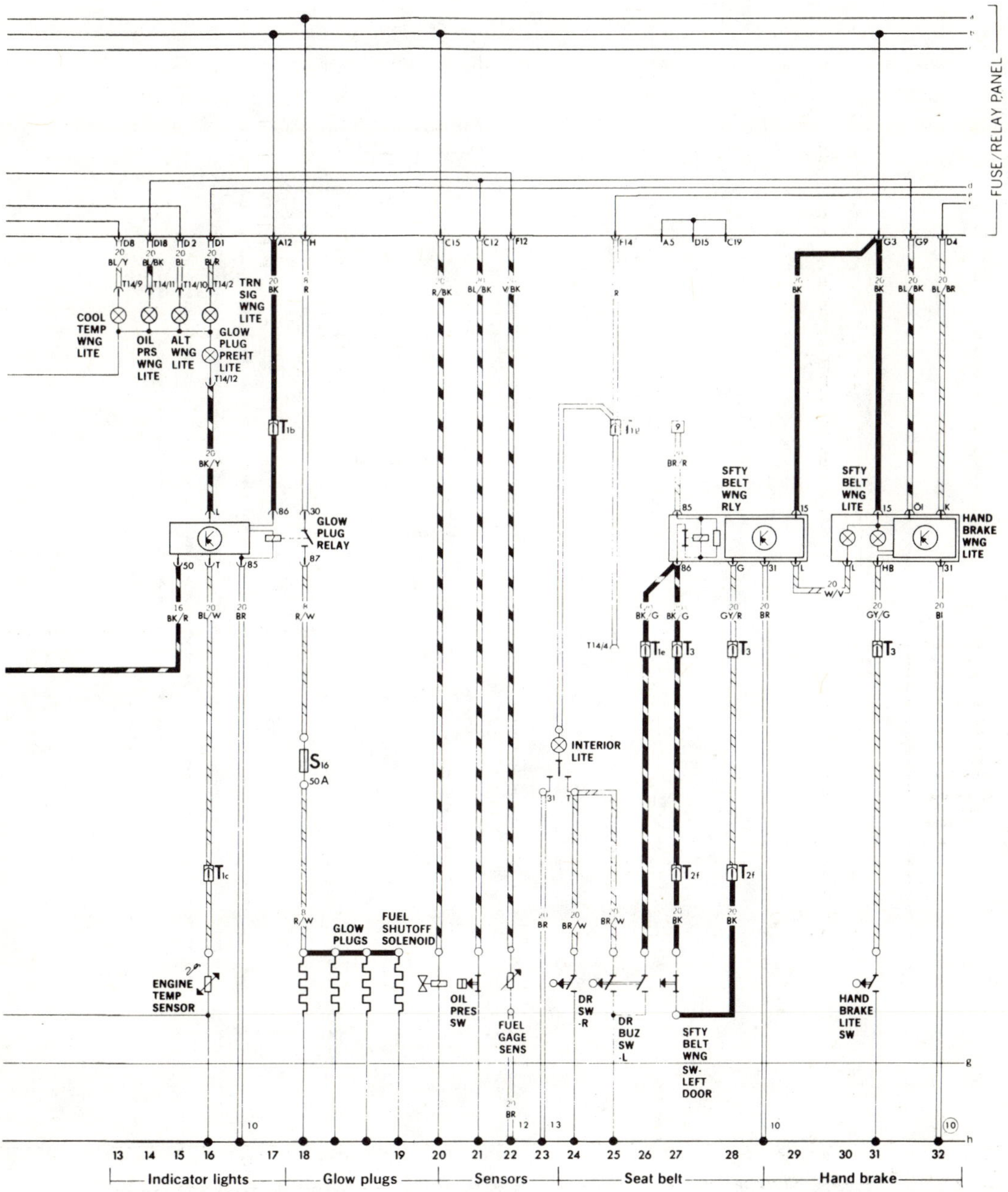

Description	Current Track	Description	Current Track	Description	Current Track
Glow plug relay	15-18	Horn button	37	Oil pressure switch	21
Glow plugs	18-19	Ignition/starter switch	7-10	Oil pressure warning light	14
Handbrake warning light switch	31	Instrument panel dimmer control	67	Parking light, left	74
Handbrake warning light	31-32	Instrument panel lights	49-51	Parking light, right	77
Headlight, left	56, 58	Interior light	23-24	Radiator fan	97
Headlight, right	57, 59	License plate lights	71-72	Radiator fan thermal switch	97
Headlight dimmer/flasher switch	61-62	Light switch	63-67	Radio connectors, back of instrument panel	68-69
Headlight high beam indicator light	60	Load reduction relay	63-64		
Heater lever light	66				
Horn	36				

1979 CUSTOM DIESEL RABBIT

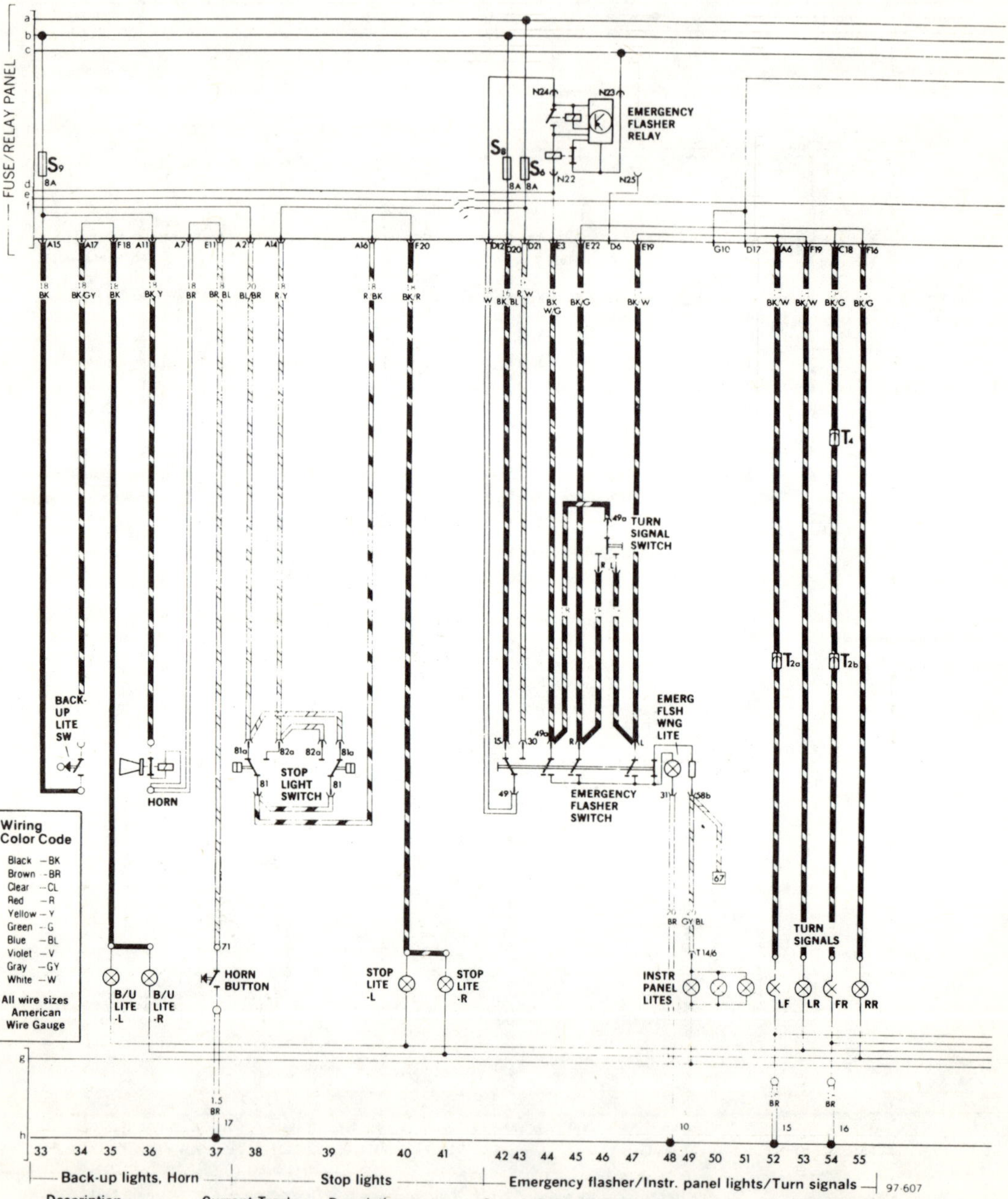

Description	Current Track	Description	Current Track	Description	Current Track
Rear window defogger	83	Stop light, left	40	Turn signal, rear left	53
Rear window defogger light	85	Stop light, right	41	Turn signal, rear right	55
Rear window defogger switch	84-85	Stop light switch	38-39	Turn signal switch	46
Safety belt warning light	30	Tail light, left	76	Voltage regulator	3
Safety belt warning relay	27-29	Tail light, right	79	Voltage stabilizer	11
Safety belt warning switch, left front door	27	Turn signal, front left	52	Windshield washer pump	96
Side marker lights, front	73, 78	Turn signal, front right	54	Windshield wiper motor	86-89
Side marker lights, rear	75, 80	Turn signal indicator light	16	Windshield wiper switch	91-95
Starter	5-6				

1979 CUSTOM DIESEL RABBIT

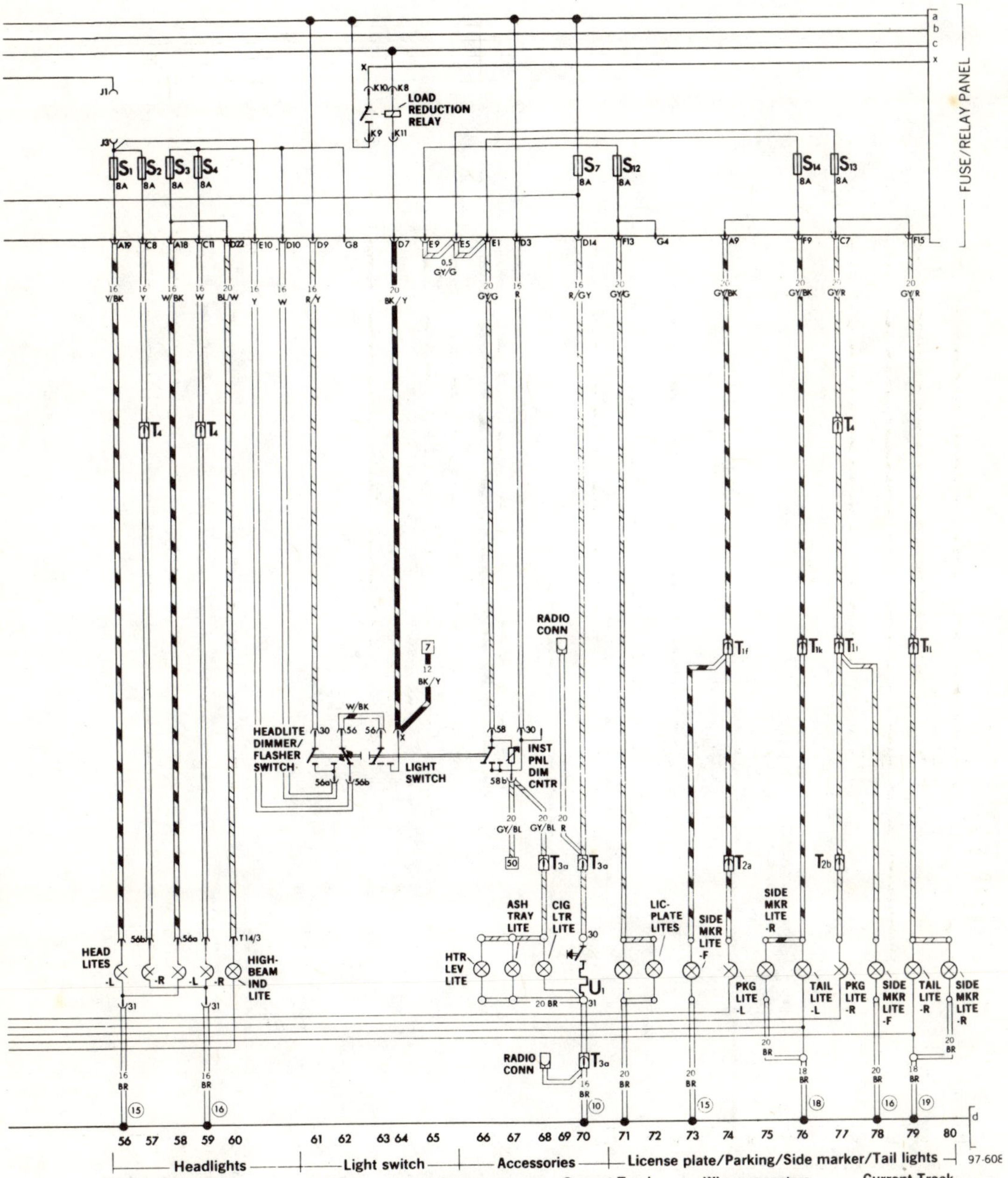

Wire connectors	Current Track
T1a - engine compartment	2
T1b - behind instr. panel	17
T1c - behind instr. panel	16
T1d - behind instr. panel	96
T1e - alongside fuse/relay panel	26
T1f - engine compartment, front left	74
T1g - behind instr. panel	25
T1h - behind instr. panel	81
T1i - engine compartment, front right	77

Wire connectors	Current Track
T1j - behind instr. panel	8
T1k - luggage compart., left rear	76
T1l - luggage compart., right rear	79
T1m - luggage compart., left rear	83
T1n - engine compart., front left	74
T1o - engine compart., front right	77
T1p - behind instr. panel	94
T2 - behind instr. panel	8-9
T2a - engine compart., front left	52, 74

Wire connectors	Current Track
T2b - engine compart., front right	54, 77
T2c - behind instr. panel	81, 82
T2f - behind instr. panel	27, 28
T3 - behind instr. panel	27, 28, 31
T3a - behind instr. panel (to right of steering column)	68, 70
T4 - behind instr. panel	54, 57, 59, 77
T14 - on rear of instr. panel	13, 14, 15, 16, 60

1979 CUSTOM DIESEL RABBIT

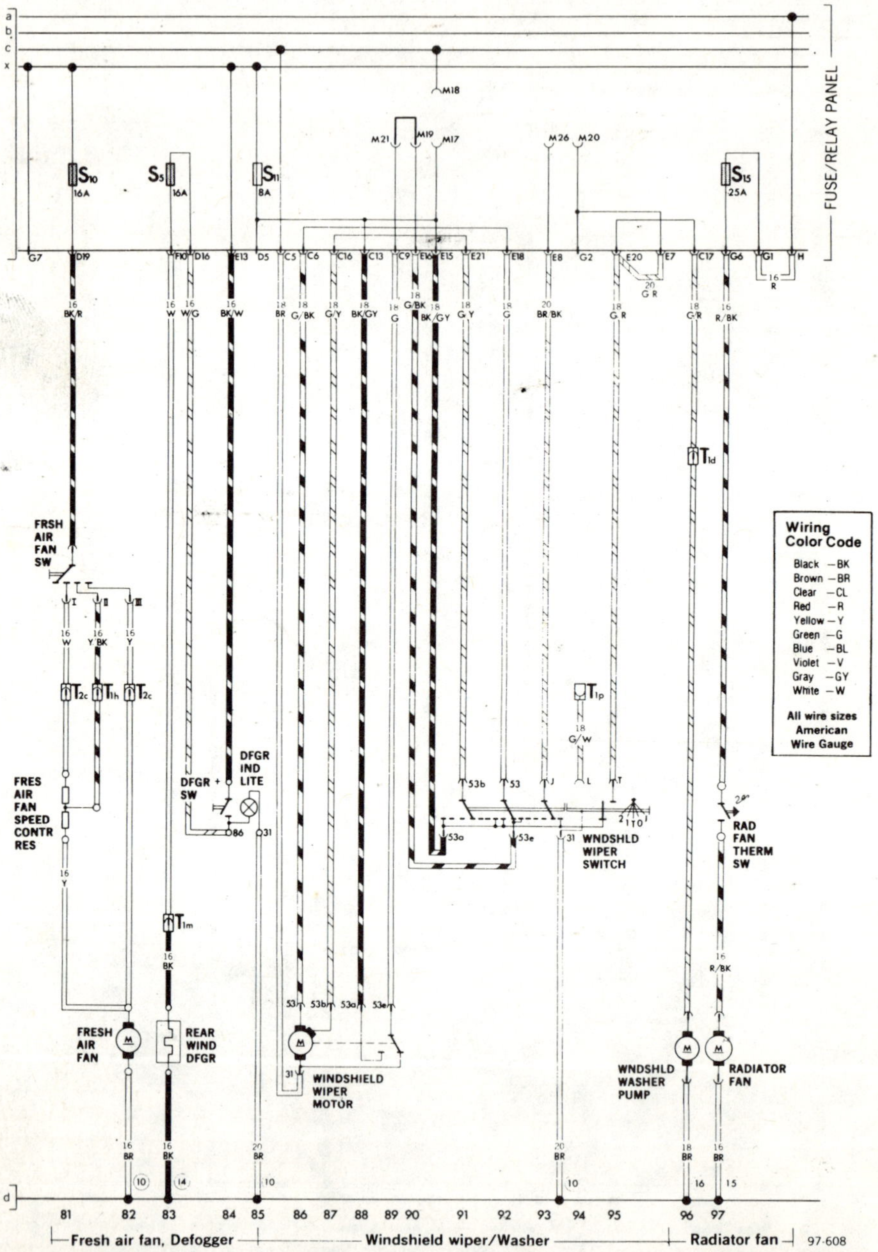

Ground connectors

(1) -battery to transmission

(2) -alternator to engine block

(10) -on steering column support

(12) -luggage compartment floor

Ground connectors

(13) -interior lighting

(14) -rear middle roof crossmember

(15) -front left side of engine compartment

(16) -front right side of engine compartment

Ground connectors

(17) -on steering assembly

(18) -on left rear light cover

(19) -on right rear light cover